THE BRITISH INVASION
FROM THE FIRST WAVE TO THE NEW WAVE

Nicholas Schaffner

McGraw-Hill Book Company

New York   St. Louis   San Francisco   Auckland   Bogotá
Guatemala   Hamburg   Johannesburg   Lisbon   London   Madrid
Mexico   Montreal   New Delhi   Panama   Paris   San Juan
São Paulo   Singapore   Sydney   Tokyo   Toronto

Patrick Dillon is a freelance writer and editor. . . . **Scott Isler** is the editor of *Trouser Press*. . . . **David Keeps** writes for the *New York Rocker*. . . . **Bill King** writes for the *Atlanta Constitution* and is the publisher of *Beatlefan*. . . . **Henry McNulty** is the Life/Style editor of the *Hartford Courant*. . . . **Steve Mirkin** is a freelance writer. . . . **Wally Podrazik** is the co-author of *All Together Now, The Beatles Again,* and *Watching TV*. . . . **Parke Puterbaugh** writes for *Rolling Stone*. . . . **Karen Rose** is co-founder of *Trouser Press*. . . . **Elizabeth Schaffner** is co-author of *505 Rock and Roll Questions*. . . . **Timothy Schaffner** plays drums in New York bands. . . . **Sue Weiner** is co-author of *The Beatles A–Z*.

First McGraw-Hill Edition, 1982.

1 2 3 4 5 6 7 8 9 D O D O 8 7 6 5 4 3 2

ISBN 0-07-055089-1

LIBRARY OF CONGRESS CATALOGING IN PUBLICATION DATA

Schaffner, Nicholas
  The British invasion.

  Bibliography: p.
  Includes index.
  1. Rock music—Great Britain—History and criticism. I. Title.
ML3534.S32   784.5′4′00941   82-174
ISBN 0-07-055089-1 (pbk.)   AACR2

Book design by Jerry Wilke

Contents

Thank-You's

**PHOTOGRAPHS
OF RECORDS AND MEMORABILIA
BY JOHN JACOBSON**

Special thanks to the "Hot Hundred All-Stars"—especially my wonderful sister, Elizabeth Schaffner, Henry McNulty, and Sue Weiner, all of whom helped beyond any conceivable "call of duty"—as did Patrick Dillon and Parke Puterbaugh (who reduced a potential twelve-volume epic to its present compact size) and David Keeps (who provided invaluable insights into "the Next Wave") . . .

. . . And to Natalie McDonald and John Steele, editors of the mid-Seventies fanzines *Electric Warrior* and *Terrapin*, for their sterling insights into (respectively) Marc Bolan and Syd Barrett; and to Olivia Kelly Datene (a.k.a. Sandi Stewart), for her penetrating interviews with "Beatle people." And to Clive Epstein and his family for showing me Liverpool. And to Linda Patrick (for a thousand and one editorial suggestions), Tom Lentakis, Louise Rush, Markku Piri, Nancy Moorthy, Francis and Christine Pratt, and Philip Powers; also Steve Kolanjian, Ron Furmanek, James Kalmbach, Steven Blau, and David Jeffrey Fletcher . . .

. . . And to the British Invasion fanzine *Aware!* (c/o Kolanjian, Box 242, Gravesend Station, Brooklyn, N.Y. 11223) and Record Runner (5 Cornelia Street, New York, N.Y. 10014) for providing many of the record sleeves and memorabilia . . .

. . . and last and most, to PJ Haduch
—to whom I dedicate this book.

Introduction

THIS BOOK IS AN AMERican fan's history of British rock music. Unlike most histories, however, *The British Invasion* is not a single cohesive narrative. It is a collection: of over one hundred separate prose pieces and of several hundred rare and historical photographs, many of which represent the records and memorabilia that have themselves become collector's items. Rather than attempt one sweeping overview, complete with the usual bewildering parade of perfunctorily sketched characters, I have chosen instead to focus on the careers of certain leading players: the Beatles, the Rolling Stones, the Kinks, The Who, Pink Floyd, T. Rex, and David Bowie. Though any of the seven longer sections on these artists or groups may be read as a self-contained "book," it is my hope that together they will also serve as one interlocking chronicle; each of them presents a different facet of the overall picture. For instance, I have used the Beatles as the springboard for forays into such subjects as Bob Dylan's impact on British pop in general and the emerging phenomenon of "progressive" rock. The rise and fall of British R&B is treated as part of the Rolling Stones' story; the Mods are invoked along with The Who; and so on.

If asked to defend my selection of *The British Invasion*'s seven featured acts, I might note that each represented a unique phenomenon; all boasted charismatic personalities and a fanatic cult following; and all registered a profound influence on their contemporaries and successors and (with the possible exceptions of the Kinks and T. Rex) on the popular culture of these United States.

Still, I can't deny that the choice of my Magnificent Seven was highly subjective and personal. One might make an equally valid case for a British rock tome spotlighting, say, Cream, Led Zeppelin, Rod Stewart, Fleetwood Mac, Yes, Elton John, and Queen. Only I wouldn't be the person to write it.

But those interested in the above-mentioned titans need not despair; all are to be found within the covers of this very book. The reader may discover that there's a lot more to *The British Invasion* than Beatles, Stones, Kinks, Who, Floyd, Rex, and Bowie. One hundred additional artists or groups (or extended "families" of same) are covered in a section called "The British Hot Hundred." For this encyclopedic task I solicited a little help from some friends—all of them young American Anglo-rock fanatics who also happen to be talented up-and-coming writers in the field. Each has contributed succinct and evocative histories of his or her favorite British artistes.

When I originally dreamed up the Hot Hundred idea, I actually wondered whether we would find a hundred British rock stars worth writing (or reading) about. But I realized soon enough that over the past two decades the United Kingdom has spawned enough notable talent—not to mention commercially successful product—to warrant a British Hot Thousand. Considerations of space, however, have obliged me to stick with my original number. I (and my "Hot Hundred All-Stars") have tried to give everyone who was anyone at least a mention, if not a picture, most likely in the two general sections—the one devoted to the original mid-Sixties British Invasion, the other to the New Wave(s) of the late Seventies and early Eighties—that bracket the chronicles of our Magnificent Seven. We've also had to draw a somewhat arbitrary line between citizens of the U.K. and sundry Americans, Australians, and the like who have been associated with the London pop scene; this accounts for the absence of entries on Jimi Hendrix, the Bee Gees, the Easybeats, or Sparks. (We have, however, included Irish bands like Them and the Boomtown Rats.) Please check the index for references to people not specifically included in the Hot Hundred. If anyone indispensable has been left out altogether, we can only extend—to aficionados and to the artists themselves—our humblest apologies.

The very idea of "rock history" may seem something of a self-contradiction. One of the music's greatest attributes has always been its up-to-the-minute immediacy. For most rock & roll addicts, music provides the very pulse of life; and life, by definition, means *now!* Yet rock has also been around longer than I have—longer than half the countries in the U.N. have—long enough to have accumulated a great deal of history.

That history, however, encompasses more than the stories of its major performers. We the fans, for whose lives their music has always provided a soundtrack, are also a part of that history. And that history is a part of us. To play back the old records is to release powerful associations, permanently stored in those words and notes back when then was *now!*, when the songs insinuated themselves into our subconscious whenever we were within range of a jukebox or a transistor or car radio (not to mention the device that was once fondly known as a "hi-fi"). To play back those records is to play back the stories of our own lives.

As I mentioned at the start, *The British Invasion* is a fan's history. Reviewing another effort in this peculiar subgenre (one on the Fifties), *Publisher's Weekly* noted that the author "writes with an awareness that rock & roll, for many, is almost a music of epiphanies, inextricably bound to vivid and deep memories." I (and my Hot Hundred colleagues) have attempted to write with the same awareness.

Back in 1968, a twenty-two-year-old Nik Cohn wrote of rock & roll, "It has surrounded me always, cut me off, and it has given me heroes, it has given me my myths. Almost, it has done my living for me. Six hours of trash every day, and it's meant more to me than anything else." Everyone involved with this project would echo those sentiments, taking possible exception (as children of the Sixties and Seventies rather than Mr. Cohn's less artsy and relevant Fifties) only to his choice of the word "trash."

Since *The British Invasion* has its roots in "fandom," I wouldn't be insulted were someone to describe it as a great big fanzine. The sections on the Beatles, Stones, Kinks, Who, Pink Floyd, T. Rex, and Bowie are (like everything else in this book) totally unauthorized by the principals concerned. Except as a star-struck teenager, I haven't even met most of the people I'm writing about here. Nor would I particularly wish to; I'd rather keep my fantasies, and my enthusiasm, intact. (It's often bad enough listening to records, and witnessing performances, wherein certain of these aging "survivors" look and sound increasingly like counterfeits or parodies of their own legendary selves.) But I do believe that the fantasies should be presented within a framework of historical accuracy. And I have spoken with certain associates whom I chanced to encounter in my researches and travels (in the Beatles' case, people like Clive Epstein, Sid Bernstein, and Walter Shenson). But on the whole I was content to hobnob with my fellow cultists, and to rummage through flea markets, fans' attics, and old scrapbooks—and, most of all, through endless musty back issues of *Melody Maker* and *New Musical Express, Rolling Stone, Billboard,* and *16 Magazine.*

This was the approach I used in compiling my first book, *The Beatles Forever.* To the extent that *The British Invasion* is a sequel of sorts, I was presented with a small dilemma. Much as I have tried to find different quotes and perspectives, *The British Invasion*'s requisite Beatles section inevitably covers ground I have already explored in finer detail. (It also retells a story with which some readers may already feel sufficiently familiar.) By way of compensation, I have gone to some lengths to obtain a choice collection of unpublished Beatles photographs for this book. Pictorially, at least, I was determined to avoid any overlap between the two books.

Apart from all this, writing about the Beatles (or even the Rolling Stones) requires a slightly different approach than writing about less celebrated figures. I'm assuming that every reader will know who John, Paul, George, and Ringo are, and will most likely have heard nearly all of the two-hundred-odd songs in their discography. But I expect many readers will be less familiar with the "songs, pictures, and stories of the fabulous Kinks," or with the names Syd, Roger, Rick, and Nick.

I should also note that the time frame of this book—particularly as set forth in the British Rock Diary, as well as the discographies and tables of chart positions—ends in the neighborhood of December 1980. As I had to select for my cutoff point some date in the recent past, I felt that, symbolically at least, the end of the era that began with the original British Invasion was finally sealed with the terrible death of the man most responsible for launching it in the first place.

Until John Lennon and his merry companions exploded onto the scene, rock & roll had never been anything more (or less) than unselfconscious junk, a disposable product for the consumers of Coca-Cola and pimple cream, brought to them courtesy of (in Joe Jackson's phrase) "the man who gave you the yo-yo." That it took a British Invasion to transform, for better or worse, this heretofore all-American greasy kid stuff into something more nearly approximating Art is attributable only in part to the Britons' Old World sophistication. It also had a lot to do with distance—the physical, cultural, and emotional distance separating Britain from the United States. English groups such as the Rolling Stones and The Who had never even been to this country when they recorded songs like "Route 66" and "Heatwave." (In Britain there was no such word as "highway," and—at least by the standards of my hometown of New York—no such thing as a heatwave.) Even at the beginning, the sounds of the British Invasion were steeped in artifice, if not yet in what highbrows would recognize as Art.

From the start, then, British rock was a "double fantasy"—a British fantasy vision of the American fantasy world conjured by Fifties rock & roll. Such groups as the Beatles, the Kinks, Pink Floyd, and T. Rex went on to refine their music into fantasies that were distinctly British. And so those old tables were turned, as millions of American fans (such as myself) came to view Britain in the light of a rock & roll fantasy world. That is the world I have attempted to explore in this book.

Since the Fifties, much of the distance separating America and Britain has been bridged. The States have blessed the U.K. with the likes of decimal currency, Kentucky Fried Chicken, commercial TV, and the ice cube. In return, Old Blighty gave America the British Invasion.

THE BRITISH INVASION

I N BRITAIN, THE LAST COUNTRY to resist "decimalization," they still divided their unit of currency, the pound (£), into twenty shillings (s.). These were subdivided into twelve pence (d.), with each penny worth, in turn, four farthings. Britain's fittingly dubbed "LSD" monetary system was further complicated by prices reckoned in guineas (21s.), crowns (5s.), and florins (2s.).

To the uninitiated, the British class system seemed no less baffling and Byzantine, and very nearly a caste system; a man's background—and telltale accent—appeared to mark him for life. Yet Britain's long democratic tradition had culminated in the rule, during much of the postwar era, of working-class Socialists hell-bent on soaking the rich and the well-born.

By the standards of young America, Britain was a primitive backwater. The nation had only one radio and TV network (the BBC), government-owned and commercial-free—and only one fast-food chain, appropriately called Wimpy's. There was little or no life after hours. In every pub (bar) a patron was obliged to down his last pint of lukewarm beer by 11:00 P.M., and the buses and the Underground, or "tube" (subway), came to a standstill around midnight. Most shops remained closed from Saturday noon through Monday morning.

In Britain, all roads led to the capital, which remained not only the world's most populous city, but also one of its most relaxed and sedate. London was still a well-scrubbed landscape of white town houses, red telephone booths and double-decker buses, black taxicabs, and spacious green parks. On rare summery days, these last would invariably be strewn with sun-starved natives, absorbing those precious rays through their dark three-piece suits.

An American visiting the U.K. in the early Sixties might have concluded that there was no other race on earth so bound by decorum, so lily white or so unfailingly polite. Nor, it seemed, was there any place more cozy and "civilized." The average Briton said "sorry" at least a dozen times a day, addressed strangers of the opposite sex as "love" or "dear," and, as the saying went, it only took two of them to form an orderly queue. The bobbies (policemen) never carried anything more lethal than a nightstick, and racial "minorities" (not to mention race riots) were still virtually unheard of, except as news items from southern Africa or the equally distant States.

If the British national character appeared to outsiders some-

Ringo, George, Ed Sullivan, John, and Paul, two days after D-Day (*Popperfoto*)

what repressed and more than a bit eccentric, so too, it seemed, were many individual Britons. Despite the Victorian trappings, in Britain one might, within the proscribed limits, cultivate one's own individuality more freely than in any other country on earth.

From this small island kingdom so steeped in the glories of its millennium-old history, rock & roll music—that most contemporary, American, and black-derived of all popular art forms—was to receive its second lease on life. . . .

On February 25, 1963, on a British package tour headlined by child star Helen Shapiro, the youngest member of the fourth-billed act celebrated his twentieth birthday. In Chicago, some six thousand miles away, his group's first American single was released by Vee-Jay Records. The importance that the small independent company attached to this event might be gauged by the spelling of the name on the record label: THE BEATTLES.

"Please Please Me" was already a runaway hit in the U.K., but the Beatles' British distributor's own U.S. subsidiary, Capitol Records, had waived its option to issue the group's product. After all, the worldly tastemakers of the music indus-

3

try could scarcely envisage British rock & roll (or "beat music," as they dubbed it in the land of cricket and shepherd's pie) making any impression on the nation that had created the genre—especially since teen America appeared to be kicking the rock habit, or, at any rate, to be taking its pop sweetened up and watered down with the schmaltz and the slop of Las Vegas and Tin Pan Alley.

Vee-Jay's interest in the Beatles, such as it was, had been stirred by its most successful pop act, the Four Seasons, and their producer Bob Crewe. "We heard a lot of Beatle music when we were in Europe, and loved it," Crewe was to recall. Crewe and the Four Seasons even toyed with giving "Please Please Me" their own inimitable castrato treatment, but after settling on another song they "told Vee-Jay about the record and said: 'This is a smash if it's ever released here.' "

Brian Epstein, the Beatles' manager, had, in turn, been impressed by Vee-Jay's extraordinary achievement a few months earlier with Frank Ifield's "I Remember You," which made the U.S. Top Five. Mr. Ifield, though certainly no rock & roller, was more or less an Englishman.*

Even so, the Rhythm & Blues–oriented label went nowhere with "Please Please Me," or with the Liverpudlians' first U.S. album, *Introducing the Beatles,* issued in July. The next single, "From Me to You," did slightly better, giving the Beatles their first toehold on the American charts. On August 10 "From Me to You" hit its peak in *Billboard*—at number 116.

That wasn't high enough to suit either Epstein or Vee-Jay, so the Beatles' subsequent 45 was entrusted to a tiny Philadelphia label called Swan. "She Loves You" even garnered a few spins on New York's WINS by the celebrated Murray the K, and placed third in a field of five on his listeners' poll. The phenomenon known as Beatlemania was now sweeping Britain, and "She Loves You" was already well on its way to becoming the island kingdom's all-time biggest seller. Stateside, however, it failed to duplicate even the token success of "From Me to You."

As the Beatles' American platters rolled into oblivion on third-string labels, Epic Records (a division of powerful CBS) attempted to launch Britain's veteran teen idol Cliff Richard among U.S. teenagers with what it called "one of the greatest introductory campaigns in history." Often backed by Britain's popular instrumental combo the Shadows, Richard had already perpetrated over twenty Top Ten hits in the mother country. But despite the hype, Richard's strongest U.S. showing (with "It's All in the Game" in late 1963) was a lackadaisical number 25—which was nonetheless far better than such peers as Billy Fury and Tommy Steele ever managed.

Back in 1956, Lonnie Donegan—a pioneer of England's skiffle craze—had cracked the American Top Ten with "Rock Island Line." But every British hit that subsequently duplicated this feat could have been collected on a seven-inch British EP with room to spare—bringing to mind that old adage about selling coals to Newcastle. Visiting his transplanted sister in St. Louis in mid-1963, the youngest Beatle was astounded to see Cliff Richard's latest film, a box-office smash back home, relegated to the bottom of a drive-in double feature.

* "I Remember You" was a Beatles concert staple at the time, and the Ifield record's prominent harmonica had inspired the copying of this gimmick on the group's own debut British single, "Love Me Do." Today the Australian-born song-and-dance man's claim to fame among Beatle people rests with the rare Vee-Jay LP Jolly What! The Beatles and Frank Ifield on Stage, slapped together after both acts had graduated to Capitol, and now worth a fortune to collectors. The LP's liner notes included the revealing statement: "It is with a good deal of pride and pleasure that this copulation [sic] has been presented."

That was the sort of ignominy the Beatles, at least, did not intend to subject themselves to. Soon after their original Vee-Jay signing, *Melody Maker* had announced the group's plans to fly to the U.S. on May 18, 1963, to join a package tour. But the boys from Liverpool had some second thoughts. According to Paul McCartney, "We were cheeky enough to say: 'We won't go to the States, ever, until we have a Number One record.' " But that prospect seemed thoroughly unlikely, unless the U.S. entertainment industry was somehow jolted out of its self-satisfied ethnocentricity. Which, indeed, it soon was, thanks to an otherwise dismal twist of fate.

On November 22, 1963, the Beatles' second British album, *With the Beatles,* was released to precedent-shattering advance orders. In Dallas, some seven thousand miles away, a dynamic young President John F. Kennedy was felled by an assassin's bullet. Suddenly, though neither yet knew it, America did, after all, need the Beatles.

The case has often been made that the loss of Kennedy left young Americans with a subconscious need for a charismatic new hero, and that they seized upon the Beatles to fill this vacuum. Be that as it may, there can be little doubt that the media (after a decent interval) were on the lookout for a story—any story—that might provide comic relief from the funereal atmosphere that had enveloped America. *Life, Newsweek,* and the TV networks suddenly took note that the staid old mother country seemed to have gone merrily off its rocker over a group of four boys from Liverpool with a creepy-crawly name, who apparently specialized in what Associated Press called "a weird new kind of music that makes rock & roll seem tame by comparison" (or, as *16 Magazine* elaborated in its first Beatles mention, "a socking combination of Liverpool folk heritage tunes and what is called a 'Mersey Beat' "). Most singularly of all, these Beatles came equipped with hairstyles (if indeed they weren't wigs) that nonchalantly flouted America's cardinal definition of maleness, yet evidently caused English girls to swoon with admiration and shower their unlikely heartthrobs with "jelly babies." Such outlandish buffoonery, it was figured, should be good for at least a laugh in Britain's dispirited former colonies.

Those shots in Dallas, then, may well have made possible the Beatles' arrival on these shores in the guise of an "overnight sensation" (though few of those early accounts of Britain's Beatlemania carried any suggestion that America might itself succumb to the epidemic). But even prior to November 22, the groundwork had been laid for some sort of American breakthrough.

Early in 1963, a young promoter from The Bronx was studying Civilization under Max Lerner at Manhattan's New School for Social Research. "One of Professor Lerner's assignments," recalls Sid Bernstein, "was simply to read the English newspapers. So I started reading about the Beatles. Around March, when they began to move from the entertainment page to the news pages, I said, 'I've *got* to bring them over here.' I knew they would go over well in America because they had already built up such incredible momentum. It was like tanks—there was no stopping them.

"I finally got hold of Brian Epstein's home phone number, and called to tell him I wanted to bring the Beatles to New York. 'They don't mean anything there,' he said. 'Are you crazy?'

" 'How about six, twelve, months from now?'

" 'Where would you put them on?' he asked me.

"When I suggested Carnegie Hall, his tone changed completely. Brian was very impressed by the idea of his boys, as he called them, playing at this famous hall. He was also impressed by my offer of $6,500 for two shows, which was even more than the Beatles were getting in England at the time.''

One remaining hurdle was Carnegie Hall's policy prohibiting rock & roll concerts. But as chance would have it, "the lady who did the booking had a heavy Rumanian accent and was hard of hearing. When I described the Beatles as a 'quartet' and a 'phenomenon,' she must have thought I meant 'a phenomenal string quartet.' She still had an opening for February 12—Lincoln's birthday—so I grabbed it.''

On November 5 Brian Epstein arrived in New York, with his handsome young protégé Billy J. Kramer, to make arrangements for the Beatles' upcoming visit. While in town, Epstein met with television's legendary Ed Sullivan, who had personally witnessed Beatlemania during a recent trip to England. Though he proved amenable to the idea of presenting the Beatles on his show, Sullivan was flabbergasted by Epstein's insistence that the British group receive top billing. Sullivan finally capitulated when the Beatles' manager agreed to accept the minimum fee for their services.

Brian Epstein's other major New York appointment was with Capitol Records. Convinced that "if the Beatles were to make a record that would sell in America, then 'I Want to Hold Your Hand' was that record,'' Epstein lobbied hard with the label to issue his clients' newest single. With Beatlemania now rampant on the continent of Europe as well as in Britain, Capitol finally took the bait; the signing was officially confirmed in *New Musical Express* on December 13, with the single slated for U.S. release just a month later.

Meanwhile, American coverage of the Beatles phenomenon grew ever more extensive—particularly in the trade publications of the music and entertainment industries. *Variety,* for instance, accorded the "clicko English group" three consecutive page-one headlines in the weeks following the Kennedy assassination.

Around the middle of December Capitol suddenly divined that its new British acquisition just might, given the right push, break all precedent and capture the American market in a big way. "I Want to Hold Your Hand" 's release date was moved up nearly three weeks, to the day after Christmas (with an album, *Meet the Beatles,* slated to follow on January 20), and the company decided to lavish fifty thousand dollars (still an unheard-of sum in the annals of show-biz hype) on a "crash publicity campaign" intended to turn John Lennon, Paul McCartney, George Harrison, and Ringo Starr into American household names by the time they arrived in New York. In a secret memo circulated among the company brass on December 23, Capitol outlined its strategy:

On Monday, December 30, a two-page spread will appear in *Billboard.* . . . We have also ordered easel-backed reprints of this ad in large quantity. . . . Put it where consumers will see it, where they'll be impelled to buy both the Beatle single and LP.

Shortly after the first of the year, you'll have bulk quantities of a unique see-through plastic pin-on button. Inserted in each button is a shot of the Beatles, with each boy identified. What to do with the buttons? First, have all your sales staff wear one. Second, offer them to clerks and jocks. Third, arrange for radio station give-aways of the buttons. . . .

Again shortly after the First, you'll have bulk quantities of a Beatle hair-do wig. As soon as they arrive—and until further notice—you and each of your sales and promotion staff are to wear the wig during the business day! Next, see how many of the retail clerks in your area have a sense of humor. . . . Then, offer some to jocks and stores for promotions and you'll find you're

helping to start the Beatle Hair-Do craze that should be sweeping the country soon.

As soon as possible after the First, you'll have fantastic quantities of "THE BEATLES ARE COMING" teaser stickers. . . . Put them up anywhere and everywhere . . . it may sound funny but we literally want your salesmen to be plastering these stickers on any friendly surface as they walk down the street. . . . Make arrangements with local high school students to spread the stickers around town. Involve your friends and relatives . . . it's going to be "BEATLES ARE COMING" stickers everywhere you look. . . .

The memo also offered advice on the development of its elaborate Beatles window displays and over one million copies of *National Record News—Beatle Issue.* A few weeks later, Capitol was to add to its arsenal the most ingenious device of all: a promotional record of open-ended interviews, with which even the most obscure cow-town disc jockey might "converse" with the Beatles at his leisure—simply by reading questions from the accompanying script, then playing back the appropriate prerecorded responses.

Coming as it did on the heels of a spontaneous eruption of American press coverage, Capitol's Beatles campaign worked like a charm. "I Want to Hold Your Hand" proved to be the fastest-selling record in Capitol history, passing the million mark before its progress had even been translated into a *Billboard* Hot Hundred showing.

Yet even industry insiders and show-biz commentators evinced little comprehension of the monster they were helping to unleash on an equally unsuspecting public. *Billboard's* reviewer, for instance, characterized "I Want to Hold Your Hand" as "surf on the Thames." When *The Jack Paar Show* gave America its first glimpse of the Beatles in action on January 3, Jack Gould of *The New York Times* deemed it possible that the Beatles' music might "find favor with indigenous teenagers," but contended that it was not "quite so likely that the accompanying fever known as Beatlemania will also be successfully exported."

A week after "I Want to Hold Your Hand" began its rapid ascent up *Billboard's* Hot Hundred, the number just heard on *The Jack Paar Show*—Swan Records' "She Loves You"—made its own belated debut. Next issue, Vee-Jay's "Please Please Me" joined in the fray, while MGM Records ran ads proclaiming THE HIT! OF THE WEEK—THE BEATLES SING "MY BONNIE." This was a three-year-old track on which the Beatles had merely provided instrumental accompaniment for an Irish Presley-soundalike named Tony Sheridan. But despite the fact that the Beatles didn't even "sing" on "My Bonnie," it, too, was an instant hit.

Two ways to wring a buck out of unsuspecting Beatlemaniacs

LP, U.S.A., 1964 (Vee-Jay)

LP, U.S.A., 1964 (Coronet)

5

There was a sudden surfeit of Beatles albums as well. As Capitol, with appropriate fanfare, issued *Meet the Beatles,* Vee-Jay reserviced *Introducing the Beatles.* Upon discovering that it controlled the publishing rights to two of its competitor's songs, Capitol withdrew permission thereto, forcing a reshuffling of the Vee-Jay album's contents. MGM, meanwhile, conjured a Beatles LP of its own by padding its four prehistoric Beatles numbers (discreetly labeled "with Tony Sheridan") with contributions by some uninvited nonentity "guests."*

The free-market free-for-all was inevitably accompanied by suits and countersuits among Capitol, Vee-Jay, and Swan. Billboard reported that even distributors and retailers had "received telegrams from one or more of the parties, noting that appropriate legal action would be taken if they persisted in selling the others' product."**

There remained, of course, dozens of U.S. record labels large and small, lacking even a Tony Sheridan outtake with which to claim a slice of the action. A few outfits actually stooped to manufacturing lookalike-soundalike groups with names like Beetles, Buggs, and Beatlemania, calculated to deceive the unwary and add to the crossfire of litigation.

Later Atco did the same thing with four more Hamburg-era unearthings; several racketeers concocted unauthorized interview albums; and Vee-Jay served up Jolly What! The Beatles and Frank Ifield on Stage (all studio tracks, of course). Most of these ripoffs would subsequently be repackaged with new covers and titles, go mercifully out of print, and eventually command huge premiums on the collector's market.

** *The issue was ultimately settled out of court, with Vee-Jay accepting a license from Capitol to sell off its existing Beatles product—which it afterward continued to repackage in various deceptive guises.*

Less disreputable companies banked on the theory that more gold must surely be found in the general area where that desirable commodity had first been unearthed; they reversed overnight their long-standing disinterest and began to scour the British pop scene for local hot properties. At least seven were snapped up in the weeks preceding the Beatles' arrival in New York: the Dave Clark Five (Epic), the Searchers (Kapp), the Fourmost (Atco), Gerry and the Pacemakers (Laurie), Billy J. Kramer and the Dakotas (Liberty), the Swinging Blue Jeans (Imperial), and Manfred Mann (Prestige). It was no coincidence that all but two of these bands came from Liverpool, and even the suburban London origins of the Dave Clark Five did not deter Epic from advertising their "Glad All Over" in *Billboard* as "The Mersey sound with the Liverpool beat." Such companies did their utmost to shift the association of hits like "I Want to Hold Your Hand" and "She Loves You" from the Beatles themselves to a generic Liverpool or English "sound."

Because most of those newly "inked" groups already had a backlog of British chart toppers, many were to duplicate what *Billboard* called "the retroactive Beatles effect": "Records that originally bombed by these artists will become hits once the artists are established here." By the time the Beatles landed in the flesh, the preponderance of British pop music in the American teen marketplace was virtually a fait accompli. As the *Variety* headline proclaimed: BRITANNIA RULES AIRWAVES.

If the British Invasion can be said to have had a D-Day, that date would doubtless be February 7, 1964. At the time, New York disc jockeys and most of their listeners referred to it sim-

ply as "Beatle Day." For several weeks, Murray the K of WINS, the "Good Guys" of WMCA, and Cousin Brucie of "W-A-Beatle-C" had been whipping up a fervor of anticipation. Now, on the cold, misty morning of the seventh ("six thirty Beatle time . . . the temperature is thirty Beatle degrees"), deejays were counting down the very hours to the Beatles' landing. Already, "I Want to Hold Your Hand," "She Loves You," and "Please Please Me" occupied the top three slots on local playlists. And wherever one flicked the transistor dial that day, there was no escaping those trans-Atlantic accents, sometimes wailing insouciantly off-key, backed by the biggest beat to be drummed into the American hit parade since Elvis traded rock & roll for a GI's uniform and Buddy Holly's four-seat Bonanza crashed in a blizzard. Despite the best efforts of Phil Spector, the Beach Boys, and Motown Records, the U.S. music scene had remained, for the most part, a teenage wasteland. When the Beatles suddenly materialized on the scene, it was as the saviors of (if nothing else) the spirit of rock & roll.

Accordingly, several thousand young New Yorkers saw fit to cut school and greet the Beatles at Kennedy Airport. To keep the mob under control, the city sent along 110 men in blue. Surveying the packed observation deck, an airport official declared: "We've never seen anything like this before—not even for presidents or kings." When the Beatles finally emerged from a Pan-Am jet at 1:35 P.M., they were welcomed by the largest crowd they had yet seen—and by the unmistakable noise of Beatlemania, amplified to decibel levels rivaling those of the jets lifting off the neighboring runways.

At the obligatory airport press conference, the Beatles quickly demonstrated that they had more going for them than just hype, hysteria, and noise. Even skeptical reporters were impressed by the wit and intelligence with which their condescending questions were parried. The opening salvo—"Will you sing for us?"—brought the instant John Lennon rejoinder: "We need money first." As the *Times* reported: "The Beatle wit became contagious. Everyone guffawed. The show was on—and the Beatle boys loved it."

"What is your message for American teenagers?" "Our message," Paul McCartney shot back, "is buy some more Beatle records." "How do you account for your success?" "We have a press agent." "Don't you guys ever get a haircut?" "I just had one yesterday," said George Harrison. Added Ringo Starr: "You should have seen him the day before."

Already it was apparent that the Beatles were a new breed of teen idol. Silly, yet never stupid; bright, but not (yet) the least bit serious—these, plainly, were no prepackaged puppets dangling from the strings of some calculating middle-aged businessman. In that they looked so unreal yet acted so normal, the Beatles reversed the long-standing formula that had given the U.S. pop music scene one too many mindless all-American phonies. Their "ridiculous haircuts" (as *The Daily News* called them) and their very Britishness made the Beatles refreshingly novel compared to their predecessors—but so too did the fact that they were intelligent and honest human beings who spoke their own minds to an unheard-of degree; they even smoked and drank in public.

Not that this cut very much ice with the majority of American adults, many of whom were offended by the loud music, bemused by the Beatlemania, and vaguely threatened by the hair. A few hours after the Beatles' arrival, Chet Huntley announced to viewers of NBC's evening news: "Like a good little news organization, we sent three cameramen out to Kennedy Airport today to cover the arrival of a group from England known as the

(*Freelance Photo Guild*)

Beatles. However, after surveying the film our men returned with, and the subject of that film, I feel there is absolutely no need to show any of that film."

Few sensibilities were more affronted than those at the exclusive Plaza Hotel. When the Beatles' suites had been reserved a month earlier, the management, as unfamiliar as most Americans with the names Lennon, McCartney, Harrison, and Starr, had anticipated nothing more unorthodox than a quartet of tweedy British businessmen. Despite vain attempts to place their controversial guests elsewhere, the Plaza (like every other hotel the Beatles were subsequently to patronize) was obliged to withstand the intrusion of reporters, cameramen, disc jockeys, and—most demeaningly of all—hundreds of giddy fans, who kept a round-the-clock vigil behind heavily policed barricades, brandishing "Beatles 4-Ever" banners from trees and atop fountains, and chanting choruses of "She Loves You" or the new novelty hit "We Love You Beatles" that dribbled into hysterics wherever a face—any face—materialized in one of the Plaza's eagerly scanned twelfth-storey windows.

On February 9, some 73 million curious Americans—a record audience for a TV entertainment program—were moved to tune in to *The Ed Sullivan Show*. The morning-after account of Beatlemania in *The Daily News* mirrored the perspective of most adult viewers: ". . . a wild screaming as if Dracula had just appeared on stage. The screams reached a pitch dangerous to the eardrums at times when the Beatles shook their shaggy locks." Evangelist Billy Graham, who broke the Sabbath expressly to see what the fuss was about, pronounced the Beatles "symptoms of the uncertainty of the times" and "a passing phase." But millions of younger viewers were irrevocably hooked by what they saw and heard. By the time Sullivan's "shew" was over, Beatlemania had swept into the remotest crannies of the North American continent.

Two days later the Beatles flew to the nation's capital to make their American concert debut at the Washington Coliseum and serve as guests of honor at a British Embassy charity ball. There John Lennon distinguished himself by stalking out after one too many scissor-wielding socialites attempted to claim samples of the Beatles' famous hair as souvenirs.

The next day the Beatles returned to New York for their Carnegie Hall dates, taking the train after a snowstorm had grounded their flight. Thousands of fans turned out to greet them at both Penn Station and the Plaza. "In the shrieking pandemonium," reported *The Daily News,* "one girl was knocked down and trampled, another fainted, and a police sergeant was kicked by a horse. . . . Beatle-lovers broke through barricades in wild assaults in the station and the hotel." According to *The New York Times,* the celebrated Carnegie concerts lasted precisely thirty-four minutes, at the end of which "all four Beatles fled amid a hail of jelly beans. During this time the Beatles appeared to be singing and playing twelve songs," all of them made inaudible by enthusiasts "who paid from $3 to $5.50 for the privilege of outshrieking their idols."

"We'd had to turn away about a hundred thousand ticket applicants," says Sid Bernstein. "When the Beatles were rehearsing for the Sullivan show, I told Brian Epstein that we should try to accommodate those kids. I got him to take a walk with me to the old Madison Square Garden on Fiftieth Street. I'd already learned that we could get the twenty thousand tickets printed overnight, and asked him to do just one show. Well, Brian looked the place over, then turned to me and said: 'Sid, let's pass for now. Next time.' "

On February 13 the Beatles flew to Miami for what Epstein had originally envisaged as a quiet week in the sun. There they performed their second and third Sullivan spots before returning to England to begin work on the film *A Hard Day's Night.*

Only a fortnight after Beatle Day, the blitzkrieg was over. Yet the group's conquest of the American music world could hardly have been more unequivocal, and the repercussions of their brief visitation would only continue to multiply during the ensuing months.

Until the backlog was finally exhausted in April, hardly a week passed without a "new" Beatles record surfacing on one of several labels. (To these last was added Tollie Records, a new Vee-Jay subsidiary that was launched with the Beatles single "Twist and Shout.") When Capitol announced its March 16 release date for the truly new "Can't Buy Me Love," an unprecedented two million advance orders poured in. And Capitol's patchwork *Beatles Second Album* (which mingled old singles with cover versions of familiar R&B and rock & roll hits that had been left off *Meet the Beatles*) was to become the first LP ever to hit Number One in *Billboard* within two weeks of its release. But the most impressive record of all—and one that will probably never be broken—was set on April 4, when the top five entries in *Billboard*'s Hot Hundred looked like this:

1. Can't Buy Me Love. The Beatles (Capitol).
2. Twist and Shout. The Beatles (Tollie).
3. She Loves You. The Beatles (Swan).
4. I Want to Hold Your Hand. The Beatles (Capitol).
5. Please Please Me. The Beatles (Vee-Jay).

That same week the Beatles also boasted the top two positions on the LP chart and seven additional entries in the singles chart. (The latter also featured seven showings by such "redcoats" as the Dave Clark Five, the Searchers, and the Swinging Blue Jeans.)

But as far as the new Beatles industry was concerned, record sales weren't even the half of it. *The Wall Street Journal* estimated that Beatles merchandise alone would generate $50 million by the year's end. There were Beatle brands of junk food (e.g., "long-eating licorice records," Beatle Nut Crunch Popsicles), jewelry (beetle and guitar-shaped brooches), musical instruments (shocking pink plastic Beatle guitars, banjos, and ukeleles), and every imaginable kind of knickknack, stationery, clothing, and toy. Even the tackiest of these trinkets have come to command huge premiums on the collector's market—much to the anguish of countless first-generation fans who allowed their mothers to toss out their Beatle "junk" in the course of spring cleaning.

Among all these novelties, the best-seller was easily the Beatle wig—which, at the time, was deemed as important a manifestation of the Beatles craze as the records themselves. Even adults who found the music unendurable were likely to purchase a wig as a party gag. By posing for photographers in their Beatle wigs, celebrities such as billionaire J. Paul Getty could demonstrate that they were still young at heart; those less game—like President Johnson and former vice-president Nixon—were subjected to countless Beatle-browed renditions by retouch artists and cartoonists. Among older Americans, many were willing to concede that the Beatles' hair, at least, was a very good joke. The rest, of course, felt that it was a rather bad joke, or even (in light of perceived "homosexual" connotations) a downright sick one. But superannuated citizens seemed unanimously agreed that the young Britons' appearance was indeed a joke. That the feeling might be mutual never occurred to that blandly self-satisfied culture whose elected representatives were so busily hatching their "great adventure" in Vietnam.

Indeed, one reason for the group's instant appeal among American girls was that the Beatles' style of hair and dress offered a highly refreshing alternative to the traditional look of the U.S. male, whose notions of "masculinity" dictated a dreary regimentation in all matters of personal appearance. In that more blatantly sexist period of American social history, appearance was one of many areas in which the male citizen's freedom of expression was severely proscribed.

American boys lost little time in growing their hair as long as parents and teachers would allow (which by the standards of the next decade usually wasn't terribly long). They did so partly in emulation of the Beatles, partly as a means of individual self-expression—or simply because boys with "long hair" seemed to attract more girls than those who kept the stubble on the top of their heads cropped to the bone. And it was precisely because grown-ups were so extraordinarily uptight about this development (one millionaire would even litter America's highways with billboards reading KEEP AMERICA BEAUTIFUL: GET A HAIRCUT!) that hair was to become such an important symbol, the litmus test to distinguish "us" from "them" when the so-called generation gap widened into a chasm dividing the adult Establishment from a bona fide youth counterculture. Taunts of "sissy," "faggot," or "miss" were apt to follow long-haired youths down certain streets until the early Seventies, at which time long hair, like everything else, was finally co-opted by the American mainstream, and began sprouting from the heads of Republican congressmen and truck drivers.

As we have already seen, the very first convention to fall to the Beatles' onslaught was the notion that rock & roll was by definition American. But apart from an abundance of hair, youthful enthusiasm, and English accents, the British Invasion offered little initial promise of adding anything new to the genre.

LP, U.S.A., 1964
(Interphon)

LP, U.S.A., 1965
(World Artists)

LP, U.S.A., 1965 (London)

LP, U.S.A., 1965 (Fontana)

Even the Beatles had yet to reveal the scope of their talents, though they at least were originals insofar as they wrote most of their own material, and had managed to synthesize their various American influences into a sound uniquely their own. But of the groups that immediately followed the Beatles across the Atlantic, few dispensed anything more than pallid imitations—either of the Beatles themselves, of American Fifties rock or early-Sixties schlock, or some combination thereof.

A case in point was the first U.S. Number One hit sung by a British act other than the Beatles: Peter and Gordon's "A World

The Undertakers (*with Jackie Lomax at center*) (*Keystone Press Agency*)

Without Love," which many listeners initially mistook for a Beatles record. It was, in fact, an unused Beatles song that Paul McCartney had bequeathed to the fledgling duo after he began dating Peter's sister, Jane Asher. Many other groups without such fortuitous connections also patterned their vocal harmonies and overall sound after the Beatles'.

Beatles outtakes also helped to launch the recording careers of such Brian Epstein protégés as Billy J. Kramer, Cilla Black, and Gerry Marsden (of Gerry and the Pacemakers). Despite the mystique engendered by their Liverpool origins and Beatles associations, all these singers were at heart "mainstream" entertainers, destined to become fixtures of the British cabaret circuit once the original Invasion had run its course.

Some of the more rock & roll–oriented groups were equally derivative, cranking out virtual photostats of decade-old American hits. A classic example was offered by the heavily hyped Hullaballoos, whose sole hit, "I'm Gonna Love You Too," proved nearly indistinguishable from the Buddy Holly original, right down to the last hiccup. Such notoriety as the Hullaballoos achieved was almost entirely thanks to their uniformly bleach-blond hair.

The Hullaballoos were not the only British Invasion group to exploit some outlandish gimmick; almost every successful artist boasted at least one. And when talent, originality, or Beatles associations were in short supply, gimmickry often sufficed to lift an act out of the rank and file. Freddie Garrity (of Freddie and the Dreamers) reeled to prominence with a dance craze—"the Freddie"—that basically consisted of kicking one's feet and waving both arms in the air like a lobotomized spastic. Liverpool's the Undertakers (whose lead singer, Jackie Lomax, is best remembered as a late-Sixties George Harrison protégé) turned up at gigs in a hearse and performed in black frock coats and top hats. The main attention grabber for the Honeycombs (also known for their infectiously Hollyesque "Have I the Right?") was their female drummer.

Nonetheless, gimmick mongers such as these were in distinguished company. Even the early Kinks had their crimson Edwardian riding outfits, and The Who their instrument-smashing routines and "pop art" schtick. The Rolling Stones' very persona—the foul-mouthed scruffiness, the aura of anarchy and menace—was to a large extent a calculated gimmick. John, Paul, George, and Ringo arrived in America a veritable showcase of pop-star gimmickry, from their identically styled hair and collarless jackets right down to the Cuban heels of their "Beatle boots."

There was, however, one British group that attained vast Stateside success without benefit of outsize talent, originality, or even gimmickry—unless this last term might be applied to the concept of a band led by and named after its drummer. The Dave Clark Five also made it without any direct assistance from the Beatles, yet their fame was almost entirely thanks to the linking of the two group's names, made possible by a fortuitous twist of fate.

When the Dave Clark Five released "Glad All Over," they had already perpetrated five British flop singles, the first of which had preceded the Beatles' own debut effort by two months. But when "I Want to Hold Your Hand" finally relinquished its long grip on Britain's Number One slot, the record that took its place happened to be the DC5's "Glad All Over." To those unfamiliar with the workings of weekly record sales charts, the impression that Dave Clark and his "Tottenham Sound" had "crushed" the Beatles and Mersey Beat was readily fostered.

The Hullaballoos: Britain's first all-blond group, fifteen years before the Police (Keystone Press Agency)

This angle provided the Dave Clark Five with an invaluable selling point—particularly in America, where Epic Records stopped hawking its group as "the Liverpool beat" and instead issued blurbs predicting that "the Tottenham Sound of the Dave Clark Five is on its way towards overthrowing the reign of the Beatles in this country as well."

To his credit, the enterprising young Clark (who managed and produced his own act) grabbed the momentum, touring the States tirelessly and cranking out a staggering amount of product, until by mid-1964 his press agents' hype had been turned into something of a self-fulfilling prophecy. In the space of a year, Epic would issue ten smash DC5 singles and five DC5 albums, all dominated by the band's relatively unusual organ/sax combination and Clark's own drums. These he played with the finesse of a metronome, but mixed prominently enough to inject into ditties like "Bits and Pieces" the biggest beat of the entire British Invasion.

And so the Dave Clark Five were briefly enshrined as the Beatles' challengers, giving rise to endless Beatles vs. the DC5 radio polls and magazine articles. The recipients of all this attention were five innocuously "cute" boys who wore their "long hair" a trifle shorter than the Beatles', who were as immaculately groomed as showroom dummies, and who never said anything the least bit controversial or even witty. Ultimately, the Dave Clark Five proved utterly disposable and forgettable. They also summed up as well as anyone the original spirit of the British Invasion.

They came, they saw, they conquered! And in turn the swingingest, handsomest group to hit these shores in ages—the Dave Clark Five—*got* conquered by our enthusiastic American teenage girls!

It all began when the boys stepped off their plane at Kennedy Airport. . . . There they were greeted (and almost over-run) by 2900 screaming, happy fans. Dave, Mike, Lenny, Dennis, and Rick were each stashed into a separate limousine. . . .

When the boys arrived at the hotel, the scene was the same as the airport! Police had put wooden barricades all along the block and were standing arm-in-arm, holding back the crowds. . . . But the girls were not outsmarted. With a flying wedge that would have been the envy of the New York Giants football team, a cordon of teeners broke through the police lines and gleefully snatched buttons from Dave's coat, the tie from Mike's neck, a sleeve from Lenny's jacket, a handkerchief from Dennis' trouser pocket, and a lock of Rick's hair! . . .

The Dave Clark Five were flipped with happiness at what American girls had done for them!

Like *16 Magazine*'s prose, most of the music from the first onslaught of the British Invasion was effervescently mindless trash: here today and gone tomorrow, but wasn't it fun while it lasted. Which, after all, was all rock & roll had ever promised—until the Beatles themselves (with the assistance of certain British groups that surfaced later in 1964) began to rid us of that small convention, too.

Unadulterated silliness continued to dominate the British Invasion until well into 1965, the year Freddie and the Dreamers and Herman's Hermits scored their U.S. Number Ones. Nonetheless, the second half of 1964 was highlighted by the Animals' "House of the Rising Sun," a Number One hit, together with the Kinks' "You Really Got Me" and the Rolling Stones' "Time Is on My Side," which came close. These groups—and others such as Manfred Mann, the Yardbirds, the Zombies, Them, and finally The Who—took the more radical implications of the Beatles' achievement and amplified them to the fullest. As Keith Richards of the Stones has conceded: "The Beatles were perfect for opening doors. . . . When they went to America they made it wide open for us. We could never have gone there without them. . . ."

Groups like the Stones wore their hair even longer than the Beatles; they were yet more outspoken, and dressed and acted still more outrageously; and their music was generally far blacker, more raucous, and explicitly sexual. If pop was to become a revolutionary art form, these groups were to supply in equal measure both the revolution and the art. They would also provide real competition for the Beatles, who were hardly averse to the challenge. In consequence, the British Invasion of 1964 was to turn into a virtually permanent occupation of the American music scene.

The original breed of British pop stars, however, conspicuously failed to make the Atlantic crossing. Cliff Richard and the Shadows, Tommy Steele, Adam Faith, and the rest all lacked a quality that was evident in even the wimpiest British Invasion group. Those earlier singers had been born too soon to have rock & roll in their blood; they had simply been cloned by British music moguls in the image of Elvis, and even discerning local fans found them unconvincing. People like John Lennon and Keith Richards had been playing, breathing, and living rock & roll since they were young teenagers.

But rock & roll was only a part (albeit an important one) of a larger phenomenon that had profoundly affected many young Britons and other Western Europeans born since the outbreak of World War II. Lennon's was the first generation to grow up under the shadow of America, whose real and fancied trappings—gangster films, Coca-Cola, big fast cars, blue jeans, and above all rock & roll—exuded an irresistible mystique. It was this obsession with America that caused the future legions of the British Invasion to plug in their guitars in the first place, and to reinvent America as a rock & roll fantasy world, unconsciously adding a modicum of Old World style and class in the process.

The end result was that Britain, in turn, was transformed—in the imaginations of the next generation of young Americans—into a rock & roll wonderland. Place names like "Merseyside," or "Carnaby Street" and "King's Road" (London's two fashion meccas), acquired the same magical ring that "Memphis, Tennessee" or "Route 66" had evoked for the standard bearers of the British Invasion. Tutored by *Teen Screen* and *16 Magazine,* young Americans cultivated a vocabulary of British slang expressions such as "fab" and "gear" (both synonymous with "terrific"); the Beatles themselves were popularly dubbed "the Fab Four." No longer caricatured as stuffy and square, Britain found itself in the unwonted position of setting American trends instead of merely following them, especially in the interrelated fields of fashion and pop music.

American popular music was hardly immune to the British Invasion either. The Beach Boys, one of the few early-Sixties U.S. groups who didn't carry on as if the Invasion had never occurred, were also among the few to survive it. As Al Jardine was to recall in a 1966 *Melody Maker* interview: "The English groups cleaned up. Even our records didn't sell as well as usual—though I must admit they weren't as good as they should have been. The thing is, the coming of the English Invasion gave us a chance to look at ourselves and reflect. . . . Sometimes I'm still amazed we ever survived it."

The British Invasion directly inspired the formation of new American groups, some of whose members might otherwise never have picked up the electric guitar. In 1965 Chris Hillman of the Byrds told *Melody Maker:* "We acknowledge a tremendous debt to the English pop scene . . . because it was really *A Hard Day's Night* and the creativity of the Beatles which swung David Crosby and [Roger] McGuinn away from folk and took me from bluegrass and mandolin playing."

In this atmosphere of trans-Atlantic cross-pollination, such efforts as the Beach Boys' *Pet Sounds* and the Byrds' "Eight Miles High" were, for their part, to register a potent influence on the English groups. Nobody, however, was more affected by the British Invasion than that brilliant and ambitious young "folk singer" named Bob Dylan—who would, in his turn, provide the greatest influence of all.

During the mid-Sixties, the British pop music industry differed markedly from its American counterpart. For one thing, the British released fewer—and better—records. Their average LP contained fourteen selections; U.S. album buyers were lucky to get twelve. British LPs also seldom included material previously issued on singles. To the Americans, however, no album was complete without at least one familiar "hit"—and hits by definition were singles.

American consumers were generally more affluent than their British counterparts; there were also more of them. Many could afford to deem singles beneath their dignity and purchase only albums. The British were more likely to consider an LP a major investment; when they did shell out their twenty-nine shillings and eleven pence, they expected all-new material.

Should a British LP track arouse great popular demand, it might *then* be released on a single—or, more likely, an EP. Though flirting with extinction in America, the Extended Player was still viable enough overseas to warrant a weekly U.K. hit parade of its own in many trade publications. For British fans, the EP containing a popular album's four "greatest hits" offered a sort of poor man's alternative to the original. Many British groups—including the Beatles, the Rolling Stones, the Kinks, and The Who—also issued EPs of all-new material.

These nuances insured that there were to be few common denominators among the mid-Sixties American and British discographies of each of the above-mentioned groups. The Beatles, for instance, released 102 songs between 1962 and 1966. In Britain these appeared on eight LPs (including one compilation), twelve EPs, and thirteen singles. The same 102 selections were repackaged for U.S. consumption on eleven albums, three EPs, and twenty singles. With the exception of a handful of the singles, no two records in the two sets featured the same contents!

In dealing with the output of their new British money-makers, all American record companies applied more or less the same magic formula: Take an album, split it in half, add a sprinkling of old 45s, and abracadabra . . . the cigar smoke clears to reveal two albums where there had been but one. The Rolling Stones' first six British LPs yielded ten in America; two Kinks albums worked out to four, and so on. (And in those days there were no bins of British imports to be found in large American record emporiums; aficionados without friends or relatives in the U.K. were obliged to take whatever the local butchers served up.)

By the turn of the decade, however, Britain's quaint traditions with regard to the relative functions of the LP, EP, and single (and much else besides) were to be superseded by the Great American Way. The Yanks, for their part, would shelve their meatcleavers upon belated recognition of the likes of *Sgt. Pepper's Lonely Hearts Club Band, Their Satanic Majesties Request, Face to Face,* and *The Who Sell Out* as organic entities not to be tampered with.

Some of the differences in the ways the British and the Americans marketed their product may be traced to the virtual absence in the U.K. of commercial Top Forty radio until April 1964—when the "pirates" commenced fire from ships stationed just outside British territorial waters. The disc jockeys on Radios Caroline and London affected American-style personality cults and were in turn coddled with luxurious cabins, duty-free liquor and cigarettes, and extended leaves to shore. Unlike the prim and proper BBC, the pirates often treated listeners to LP tracks and records by obscure and relatively "way out" artists, and in so doing helped steer British pop in a more progressive direction. Nonetheless, payola often proved the speediest route to a pirate playlist; for £100, Radio Caroline would guarantee a song thirty airings from each of its two ships. (Though the British government charged that the pirates were interfering with emergency radio signals, it did not take decisive action until August 15, 1967, when a new law made it illegal for any British citizen to work for the pirates, advertise with them, provide goods and services for them, or publicize their programs. This effectively torpedoed the outlaw stations, though the BBC was to co-opt most of the top pirate deejays for its own new "progressive" Radio One.)

Even after the advent of alternative radio, television played a far more important role in the British pop scene than was ever the case in America. The U.K. had long boasted several weekly music programs, including *Top of the Pops, Juke Box Jury,* and *Thank Your Lucky Stars.* In August 1963 these were joined by *Ready Steady Go,* whose influence on British music in the mid-Sixties rivaled that of the pirates. The Who's Peter Townshend remembered *Ready Steady Go* as "rock television at its best . . . insanity and abandon." According to pop commentator George Melly: "In the McLuhanesque sense *RSG* was an important breakthrough. It plugged in direct to the center of the scene and only a week later transmitted information as to clothes, dances, gestures, even slang to the whole British teenage Isles. . . . It made pop work on a truly national scale."

Like the other shows, *RSG* enforced until 1966 a regulation requiring all acts to mime to their own records, but Townshend claimed he preferred it that way: "No worry about throats or atmosphere, or getting in tune, just about what color pants to wear." (In the wake of the British Invasion, American networks would briefly attempt to duplicate the English pop TV formula with *Shindig* and *Hullabaloo*.)

But the most important of all the British pop media was the press, particularly the national music weeklies. These included *Melody Maker, New Musical Express* (usually known as *NME*—or "en-em-y," as Paul McCartney once dubbed it), *Disc,* and *Record Mirror*. (Britain also boasted glossy monthlies such as *Fabulous* and *Rave,* and publications exclusively devoted to the Beatles, Gerry and the Pacemakers, and the Rolling Stones.) The pop weeklies offered comprehensive coverage of the music scene with exclusive interviews, up-to-the-minute news, and almost obsessively detailed charts and readers' polls. All Britain's top stars (including members of the Beatles, Stones, Kinks, and Who) regularly answered queries from readers, and participated in such features as *Melody Maker*'s "Blind Date" record review column or its "Think In" page, wherein guests delivered themselves of stream-of-consciousness reactions to a list of provocative words or phrases such as "cars," "marriage," "pirate radio," "Vietnam," and "Dylan."

In some respects these papers were still fairly staid and conservative, at least in comparison with, say, the *NME* of the early Eighties. The record reviews were cursory, and often accompanied by a photograph of the short-haired, middle-aged, horn-rimmed reviewer. Certain four-letter words, along with explicit allusions to sex or drugs, were still taboo—though such foul-mouths as Mick Jagger or John Lennon might be quoted as calling the Dave Clark Five or Herman's Hermits "a load of ----." By 1966, however, the weeklies began to take on younger, hipper, and more distinctive writers such as *NME*'s Keith Altham and *Melody Maker*'s Chris Welch.

In any case, America at the time offered nothing remotely comparable. There were the dry "trades" such as *Billboard*—available only to subscribers within the music industry—and there were the teen fan magazines as exemplified by *16, Teen Screen,* and *Hit Parader* (one of the few to attract readers of both genders); and never the twain would meet until the advent of *Crawdaddy* and *Rolling Stone*. By mid-1964 the pulp fan magazines were devoting nearly all their "fax" and "pix" to the stars of the British Invasion; a sample cover of *16 Magazine* from this period blares such headlines as GEORGE & RINGO: "I CONFESS . . ." . . . STONES ANSWER QUESTIONS YOU DON'T DARE ASK! . . . PETER & GORDON FLIP OUT WITH CHAD & JEREMY . . . DC5 KING-SIZE KARESSABLE KOLOR. Editor Gloria Stavers even hired George Harrison's new girl friend, Pattie Boyd, to supply a monthly "Letter from London":

> Yes, I do get freckles, but only if I go into the sun. Jane Asher has little golden ones. She is a natural redhead. . . .
> "Chips" . . . are the same as your French Fries, but only just a little longer. In every city here you find a fish 'n' chips shop . . . they give you a bit of hot fish . . . and a handful of chips, all wrapped up in a piece of newspaper . . . it's absolutely *fab!*
> The Stones recently returned from Australia and Mick . . . looked sensaysh! All tanned, healthy, and handsome. . . .

Such was the extent and the caliber of the popular music press in America until around 1967. But U.S. newspapers, news weeklies, and "family" magazines continued to give the Beatles ample coverage, which occasionally extended to other leading British groups and trends. In this vein, perhaps the clearest confirmation of Britain's grip on the American imagination would come on April 15, 1966, with *Time* magazine's cover story "London: the Swinging City." For millions of American readers, *Time*'s article anointed London *the* city of the Sixties, no less than Paris had been the city for the Twenties, or Rome for the Fifties: "It swings; it is the scene. This spring, as never before in modern times, London is switched on. Ancient elegance and new opulence are all tangled up in a dazzling blur of op and pop. The city is alive with birds (girls) and beatles. . . . The guards now change at Buckingham Palace to a Lennon and McCartney tune, and Prince Charles is firmly in the longhair set."

Time's cover story proved, if nothing else, the infectiousness of Anglomania. Like the Beatlemania that had engendered it, America's Anglomania had spread from the still young to the would-be young; it had become respectable. By the spring of 1966, however, the original British Invasion had just about run its course. The Dave Clarks, the Freddies, the Gerrys and the Billy J.'s, were falling by the wayside, as pop music began to undergo a metamorphosis that would have been unimaginable three years earlier. Yet throughout the cultural upheavals to follow, it was Britain that continued to call the tune and provide much of the soundtrack—and that, too, would have seemed utterly inconceivable three years earlier, when a moribund Chicago record company quietly placed on sale a 45 rpm record by "the Beattles."

THE BRITISH INVASION

The Beatles

John Lennon and Stu Sutcliffe on stage in Hamburg (Jurgen Vollmer)

THAT IT SHOULD ALL BE-gin in Liverpool might seem, at first, peculiar.

Throughout the previous century, the port city had played a major role in the unfolding saga of Queen Victoria's Empire—a good part of whose spoils were unloaded at the teeming Mersey-side docks. Liverpool was, for instance, selected as the launching site for the world's first passenger train and ocean liner. The city's fame and glory, furthered by an imposing array of Victorian monuments, was crowned in 1880 by the emergence of Britain's largest cathedral.

Over the first half of the twentieth century, however, a uni-form soot-gray cast gradually accrued to the grand skyline, and construction within the city itself was generally limited to end-less rows of shabby lookalike tenements. Following the devasta-tion of World War II and the dismemberment of the British Empire, the seedy port of Liverpool was obliged to adjust to its new status—a provincial outpost quite devoid of wealth, conse-quence, or glamour.

But the Liverpudlians are a warm and hardy people, sus-tained through difficult times, like other downtrodden peoples, by such natural resources as music and humor. Liverpool tradi-tionally provided Britain with most of its comedians—which might be why the nation's funnybone was to be subconsciously tickled by the mere sound of the Beatles' Scouse accents. The town's strong musical bent may conceivably have had some-thing to do with the fact that so many Liverpudlians—including Mr. Freddie Lennon and Mr. and Mrs. Jim McCartney—were the offspring of Irish immigrants.

Come the mid-Fifties, the rock & roll of Bill Haley and Elvis Presley struck an especially responsive chord among Liver-pool's tough, underemployed, and restless working-class youth, who almost instinctively began banding together to create music themselves. Initially, most of these teenage amateurs, including John Lennon's first group, the Quarrymen, were inspired by that peculiarly British phenomenon known as skiffle. Originally imported from the backstreets of Chicago, skiffle made use of such homemade instruments as the washboard and the tub bass—a cinch to play, and within the financial means of the most destitute street urchin.

In most of Britain, as in America, the rock & roll explosion quickly burned out, leaving the hit parade in the hands of the pop crooners. But such was not the case in Liverpool, where the local groups continued to proliferate, fueled by the R&B and rockabilly 45s that, unavailable elsewhere in Britain, were con-stantly being brought in from America by sailors. In England, where there was no commercial radio (other than what could be heard of Radio Luxembourg through the static), musical tastes were dictated by the airwaves far less than in the United States; in Liverpool, the kids kept rock & roll alive almost as an oral tradition.

"It was a working-class sort of musical revolution," original Beatles manager Allan Williams would recall in *Melody Maker*. "The music curbed the violence completely. The energy they put into kicking someone around the streets was put into beating a drum or thumping a guitar. It was the Golden Age of beat music." In early 1963, *Melody Maker* estimated that there were

13

between two hundred and three hundred groups on the burgeoning Liverpool scene.

When John Lennon made that scene he was in a sense slumming; seedy, subterranean dives such as the Cavern Club were a world removed from his Aunt Mimi's semidetached suburban home across the road from one of England's most exquisitely landscaped municipal parks. John, Paul, George, and Ringo came, in that descending order, each from a different rung on the socio-economic ladder. Mr. McCartney was a cotton salesman and Mr. Harrison a bus driver; their families' circumstances each represented a distinct gradation within the spectrum of Liverpool's vast working class. The eldest of the future Beatles was also the one to suffer the most deprived childhood; when he wasn't in the hospital, the sickly Richard Starkey (born July 7, 1940) grew up in a notorious slum called Dingle.

The extraordinary "chemistry" that would sustain and strengthen the Beatles may be traced, in part, to the marked differences in their early home environments. John Lennon, the only child of a broken middle-class home, became the group's fiercely independent guiding spirit. The youngest of four siblings, George Harrison naturally assumed something of a "kid brother" role within the band. And by his own account, Paul McCartney, a great team player, "came from a very close family, like Italian families. I'm from that kind of very loving, close-knit family, and John isn't, so that's one big difference in our personalities right there."

Shortly after John Winston Lennon's birth on October 9, 1940, his parents drifted apart. His merchant seaman father ranged as far as New Zealand and did not set eyes on his son again until the Beatles materialized on his TV screen some twenty years later. Neither was John's mother, Julia, anyone's model of a responsible parent. She readily agreed to let her sister, Mimi Smith, take over the boy's custody, and though she remained and remarried in Liverpool, John did not see much of his mother until he reached his teens.

Despite his conventional middle-class upbringing by his brisk, protective, and practical Aunt Mimi, John showed every sign of taking after his delinquent parents. Art was the only subject in which he consistently managed a passing grade; his report cards branded him "hopeless," "a clown in class," and "just wasting other students' time."

Though he shirked his assignments, John was always a compulsive reader (Lewis Carroll was a favorite author). He began at an early age to write and illustrate whimsical stories of his own. His talent just sufficed to gain him admittance to that haven for young British misfits known as art college.

The emergence of rock & roll in the mid-Fifties provided John with an even greater passion. Now he had two modest ambitions: "To write an *Alice in Wonderland* and be bigger than Elvis." Despite Aunt Mimi's daily admonishment (which he would one day return to her engraved on a plaque)—"The guitar's all right, but you'll never make a living with it"—John formed the Quarrymen with the active encouragement of his irrepressible banjo-strumming mother.

A few months later, Julia Lennon was mowed down by the car of an off-duty policeman just outside her sister and son's home. More than a decade afterward, John would finally bare his deeply tender feelings for his mother in the Beatles' "Julia." At the time, however, the seventeen-year-old youth only appeared to nurture what he would describe in another Beatles song as "a chip on my shoulder that's bigger than my feet." To all but a handful of cronies, John seemed to grow ever more callous, hard, and altogether disagreeable.

His circle of friends now included a recent addition to the Quarrymen named James Paul McCartney (born June 18, 1942). Paul's mother had also died recently, leaving his devoted dad to singlehandedly provide a good home for a pair of rambunctious teenagers (the younger of whom, Mike, was also destined to make an impression on the mid-Sixties British pop scene with the satirical group the Scaffold, using the pseudonym "McGear").

Despite Mr. McCartney's background as a semiprofessional ragtime pianist, his elder son evinced little musical interest until the advent of Elvis, at which time Paul cashed in his trumpet (a birthday present from his father) for a guitar. Though the left-handed McCartney made scant progress until it occurred to him to switch the strings around, he already knew more chords than Lennon when their paths finally crossed—know-how that provided Paul's entree into the Quarrymen. As an added bonus, the fact that Paul held his instrument to the left rather than the right was to give the group a visual symmetry that no entirely right-handed band could approximate.

In his very last interview, on December 8, 1980, John Lennon recalled: "Paul met me the first day I did 'Be-Bop-a-Lula' live onstage. . . . We met and talked after the show, and I saw he had talent; he was playing guitar backstage, doing 'Twenty Flight Rock' by Eddie Cochran. I turned to him right then and said: 'Do you want to join the group?' "

Paul McCartney was an eager youth who found—then, as later in life—that his exceptional allotment of brains, charm, and good looks enabled him to fulfill most of his goals and obligations with a minimum of effort. When he did fall short of the mark, he could generally fudge his way through any difficult situation; when even that failed, he was invariably forgiven.

Heretofore, Paul had been a reasonably conscientious student, with attitudes and aspirations considerably more conventional than those of his iconoclastic new partner. Over the next fifteen years, John's ample imagination, along with his low tolerance of the facile, the false, and the merely ordinary, would continually prod Paul into channeling his own superior musical abilities in directions he might otherwise have never dreamed of. McCartney, for his part, would bring to the partnership a semblance of discipline and a flair for showmanship, along with a keen sense of public relations and a notably pretty face.

Almost from their first meeting, the two inspired one another to write material of their own, at a time when (and in a place where) songwriting was thought to be well beyond the scope of rock & roll musicians: John's "One After 909" and "I Call Your Name" and Paul's "A World Without Love" and "Love Me Do" were all proudly labeled, as a sign of their mutual loyalty, "Lennon-McCartney" originals.

Paul soon encouraged an even younger schoolmate to tag along with the Quarrymen. Though George Harrison (born February 25, 1943) was easily the best guitarist John had encountered, his tender years and slowness on the uptake were initial strikes against him. But George's intense dedication to guitar practice ultimately carried the day.

After the other Quarrymen faded from the picture, the three guitarists experienced difficulty roping in a compatible bassist and drummer. Lennon eventually persuaded his best friend from art college—a highly talented painter named Stuart Sutcliffe, who had no musical aptitude whatsoever—to squander on a bass guitar the £65 he had recently earned from the sale of an award-winning painting.

The inclusion of the brilliant and sensitive Sutcliffe is said to have cost the group a number of gigs, but the fiercely loyal

Lennon, McCartney, and Harrison already had their "us against the world" stance down pat and adamantly rejected any promoter's suggestion that they secure a more accomplished bassist. The young painter's main contribution to the group was a sense of visual style. Stu himself, with his pink shirts, skin-tight jeans, ever-present shades, and deceptive aura of remote moodiness, came across as Liverpool's answer to James Dean.

Acquiring a permanent drummer proved even more difficult, according to Lennon. "We had all sorts of different drummers all the time, because people who owned drum kits were few and far between; it was an expensive item. They were usually idiots." Their penultimate choice was Pete Best, a somnolent second James Dean figure whose plusses included his mother's ownership of a club called the Casbah. As the group's local following grew, they picked up increasing numbers of gigs at the larger Cavern Club and at dance halls across Liverpool bearing such evocative nicknames as "the Blood Baths," where the band often provided the soundtrack for clashes among the Merseyside's demented teenage gangs.

Somewhere along the line, the act had begun billing itself as the Beatles. "Why Beatles? Ugh, Beatles, how did the name arrive? So we will tell you," John Lennon wrote soon afterward.* "It came in a vision—a man appeared on a flaming pie and said unto them, 'From this day you are Beatles with an *a*.' " (In a more prosaic explanation four years later, John would tell the American reporter Jim Steck that his group's name, like much of their music, had been inspired by Buddy Holly and the Crickets. "I was looking for a name like the Crickets that meant two things. From Cricket I went to Beatles . . . when you said it, people thought of crawly things; when you read it, it was beat music.")

Lennon's original account continued: "And then a man with a beard cut off said—will you go to Germany (Hamburg) and play mighty rock for the peasants for money? And we said we would play mighty anything for money." The aforementioned hustler was Allan Williams, a colorful Liverpool character who drove the boys to the Continent in an old van, and who reports in his memoirs that Lennon risked deportation almost the instant he first set foot on foreign soil—by shoplifting the harmonica he promptly adopted as his second instrument.

Liverpool and Hamburg had much in common; both were Northern industrial port cities (largely reduced to moonscapes during the war) with a lively underworld and a healthy predilection for American rock & roll. But the German version was far larger and rougher, and Liverpool certainly boasted no equivalent of the Reeperbahn—a vast seedy strip of clubs and emporiums catering to every vice ever known to man or beast.

Until the Beatles got to Hamburg, nobody else had shared their own belief in the group's future. But as Paul McCartney said in a 1976 radio interview: "You can't do what people want you to do. My dad wanted me to get a job, and if I did I would never have become a Beatle. . . . Half the thing was just thinking positively. . . . If you want a thing badly enough, you're going to do the things to get there. All along, we thought it would happen."

And Hamburg was where it began to happen. The experience

certainly entailed some heavy dues paying: a grimy dressing room behind a flickering cinema screen (complete with soundtrack) served as the Beatles' communal living quarters when they weren't putting in incredibly grueling hours at the adjacent Indra Club, or partaking of the Reeperbahn's manifold carnal and chemical stimulations. Yet Hamburg very quickly transformed them from just another Liverpool group with a handful of chestnuts and a few crummy originals up their leather-jacketed sleeves into something out of the ordinary. "We used to play eight hours a night," said McCartney, "and as you didn't like to repeat tunes, you had to [come up with] eight hours of material."

The Beatles soon learned other ruses with which to hold their audiences' attention; encouraged to "*mach' Schau*" at all costs, they mugged and writhed and stomped, punctuating their expanded repertoire with obscene and insulting remarks, tossing food and beverages at one another and at their spectators. "We had to work our asses off to try and get people in . . . to sell beer for the manager," McCartney recalled twenty years later in *Musician*. "We'd rock out and get three of them in. . . . Then we started to know it was going to be big. We got a Saturday night audience, then sold the whole week out."

The Reeperbahn's fluctuating population of hookers, hustlers, drag queens, gangsters, and marauding sailors was transfixed by the almost savage intensity of the Beatles' sound and appearance. The band moved from the Indra to the larger Kaiser-keller Club, and the antics grew ever wilder. Lennon, for instance, was apt to appear onstage clad only in his shorts and a toilet seat, or to taunt the drunken Germans with his impersonations of their late Führer.

To those who weren't the butts of his scathing wit and cruel gags, Lennon was almost invariably funny; but from the start "fun" was one thing he wasn't. Wielding the group's driving rhythm guitar, John was already using rock & roll to exorcise his demons, channeling a lifetime's accumulation of anger, hurt, and pain through his distinctive rasping voice, many years before it occurred to him to develop this theme explicitly in his own songs. Though many of his early-Sixties vocal showcases may originally have been intended to invoke funtime on the dance floor—e.g., "Twist and Shout" and "Do You Wanna Dance?"—John (unlike Paul or George) took up his own invitation almost as rarely as the Beach Boys' Brian Wilson took to a surfboard.

Lest the going get too heavy, however, the Beatles' unbeatable chemistry came once again into play, with the intensity and crudeness of Lennon's music and personality counterbalanced by McCartney's more ingratiating brand of showmanship and Harrison's relatively accomplished musicianship.

Recently surfaced recordings from a later Beatles stint in Hamburg confirm that the magic was more a matter of energy, enthusiasm, and sheer volume than of musical expertise. Bum notes fly like beer bottles (or is it the other way around?) with each salvo the band pumps out from its vast arsenal of three-chord classics. The image of these young rock & rollers in perspiration-drenched leather hardly seems so far removed, in style or spirit, from that of such latter-day capital-P Punks as the Ramones (who reportedly derived their name from McCartney's 1960 pseudonym, Paul Ramon). The major difference is that in the case of Lennon, McCartney, Harrison & Co. this was no calculating comic-book pose, but the unselfconscious beginnings of the Beatles' self-creation—which marked the start of that entire era of rock history the stylists of a later generation were to draw from, build upon, and react against.

---

* Lennon's piece "Being a Short Diversion on the History of the Beatles" appeared in the debut issue of **Merseybeat**, the newspaper his friend Bill Harry launched in July 1960 to cover the burgeoning Liverpool music scene. Over the next three years John would contribute poetry and short stories under the pseudonymous byline "Beatcomber," and occasionally intersperse his own offbeat messages among the prosaic classifieds: e.g., "Hot Lips, missed you Friday, Red Nose."

This evolutionary process was accelerated when the Reeperbahn regulars were joined by a more sophisticated, artsy college crowd. The first of these bohemian "exis" (the Beatles' shorthand term for "existentialists") was Klaus Voorman, a well-bred youth whose ambition was to design rock & roll record sleeves. After stumbling into the Kaiserkeller's irresistible din, Klaus dragged his reluctant girl friend, Astrid Kirschherr, and their friend Jurgen Vollmer—both aspiring photographers—to his unlikely new watering hole.

The Beatles and the exis became fast friends, each profoundly influencing the other. For the first time, the Liverpudlians' intellectual horizons were stretched beyond their heretofore provincial and unsophisticated outlook. Klaus, for his part, was to become a successful rock bassist; and he realized his original ambition with the cover of the Beatles' 1966 LP *Revolver*. In the Beatles Astrid and Jurgen found willing subjects for their lenses, creating the brilliant pictures wherein these unusually photogenic rock & rollers first developed a distinct visual image. Astrid, with little discouragement from Klaus, became Stuart Sutcliffe's fiancée.

The Kaiserkeller stint came to an untimely end soon after George Harrison was deported for being underage. The police may have made this belated discovery thanks to a tipoff from the club's manager, Bruno Korschmider, who was irked because the Beatles had jammed at the rival Top Ten Club with their compatriot, singer Tony Sheridan. Around this time, the Beatles also destroyed the Kaiserkeller's rickety stage with a little help from their fellow Liverpudlians, Rory Storm and the Hurricanes, whose drummer, Ringo Starr, had become a close friend.

The police received the final call from Korschmider when the Beatles set his club's curtains aflame. McCartney and Best were extended the hospitality of a Hamburg jail and furnished with one-way plane tickets to England the next morning. The two remaining Beatles were obliged to find their way home under their own steam, with Lennon unceremoniously turning up at Mimi's door, his amp on his back, and chucking stones at the window to awaken his tart-tongued aunt.

When the demoralized musicians finally regrouped, they found that having successfully weathered their Hamburg experiences made almost anything else seem easy by comparison. "We always thought we had this ace up our sleeve of having this hard background in Hamburg," McCartney commented twenty years later, reflecting back on the intervening madness and all its attendant pressures. To spark the electricity of their Kaiserkeller performances among their fellow Liverpudlians at the Cavern Club, the Beatles discovered, was well within their heightened powers.

Once Allan Williams succeeded in pulling some well-placed German strings (and George Harrison turned eighteen), the Beatles were able to embark on a series of return visits to Hamburg, playing at the Top Ten Club and later the Star Club (where their Liverpool colleague King Size Taylor would capture one of their less inspired 1962 performances for posterity on his home tape recorder). The second visit was highlighted by the Beatles' first professional recording sessions, for which they were hired by producer Bert Kaempfert as backup musicians on Tony Sheridan's German-release single "My Bonnie." Along with five other numbers featuring Sheridan, the Beatles also taped John's own version of the evergreen "Ain't She Sweet" and the Lennon-Harrison instrumental Shadows impersonation, "The Beatle Bop" (whose title was changed to "Cry for a Shadow").

Also on this trip, Astrid persuaded Stuart Sutcliffe to forgo his greaser hairstyle for the floppy bangs favored by Voorman and his exi friends. By the time the Beatles returned to Liverpool in July 1961, all but Pete Best had, at least temporarily, followed suit. The group member who had initiated the "Beatle cut," however, elected to remain in Hamburg with Astrid to devote his talents to his painting, allowing Paul McCartney to inherit his bass guitar. Widely regarded as the Beatle most likely to leave his mark on the world, Stuart Sutcliffe was fated to die of a brain hemorrhage the following April 10, at the age of twenty-one.

Complete with their new trademark hairdos and a four-man lineup, the Beatles' impact in their hometown began to approach that of an underground phenomenon—which Bob Wooler, who served as disc jockey at the Cavern Club and other local venues, analyzed in a remarkably prophetic piece published in the August 31, 1961 issue of *Merseybeat*:

> The Beatles are the biggest thing to have hit the Liverpool rock & roll set-up in years. . . . They hit the scene when it had been emasculated by figures like Cliff Richard [who lacked] the drive that inflamed the emotions. . . .
>
> Here again, in the Beatles, was the stuff that screams are made of. Here was the excitement—both physical and aural—that symbolized the rebellion of youth in the ennuied mid-1950s. This was the real thing. Here they were, first five and then four human dynamos generating a beat which was irresistible. . . . Here they were, unmindful of uniformity of dress. Unkempt like long hair. Rugged yet romantic, appealing to both sexes. With calculated naivete and an ingenious throw-away approach to their music. Affecting indifference to audience response and yet always saying "Thank-you." Revising interest in, and commanding enthusiasm for, numbers which descended the Charts way back. . . . A remarkable variety of talented voices . . . rhythmic revolutionaries. An act which from beginning to end is a succession of climaxes. A personality cult. Seemingly unambitious, yet fluctuating between the self-assured and the vulnerable. Truly a phenomenon—and also a predicament to promoters! Such are the fantastic Beatles. I don't think anything like them will happen again.

Sharing the page with Wooler's article was a new column, "Record Releases, by Brian Epstein of NEMS." NEMS was an electrical appliance and music store owned by Harry and Queenie Epstein, whose twenty-seven-year-old son, after attaining scant success in such pursuits as acting and dress design, had reluctantly agreed to manage the record department of his family's business. With his characteristic flair for organization and presentation, Brian transformed it into one of Liverpool's most popular and reputable record shops.

Brian's early association with a newspaper so dominated by coverage of the Beatles suggests a touch of poetic license in his own account (generally accepted as gospel) that he first heard of the group on October 28, 1961, when a leather-jacketed youth asked him for a copy of "My Bonnie." Be that as it may, subsequent requests for Tony Sheridan's Beatle-backed German release prodded the conscientious record dealer to import copies of the single, which quickly proved one of NEMS's hottest items. Twelve days later, Brian's curiosity had been sufficiently piqued for the dapper yet shy young salesman to venture personally into the alien netherworld of the Cavern—just around the corner, as it turned out, from NEMS.

"In that dark, dank, stuffy atmosphere," he recalled in *Melody Maker* two years afterward, "at the end of the place stood four ill-presented youths with untidy hair. Sitting right here today, I can't think why I didn't walk out right then."

Again, Brian was being somewhat disingenuous. Hamburg's exis had already proven that superior breeding offered no guarantee of immunity to the Beatles' primitive spell; Epstein,

Brian Epstein with the first album by his "boys" (RDR Productions)

too, succumbed. He had a strong hunch that the scruffy street kids in the audience were onto something that might, with proper packaging, register an equal impact on the flagging national pop scene. Even more to the point, Brian was sexually aroused by what he saw and heard at the Cavern. Refined almost to the point of prissiness himself, Epstein found the rough, animal energy of the Beatles (particularly John) and their following irresistibly attractive. At the same time, he could perceive and empathize with the group's innate talent and sensitivity.

Brian kept coming back, compulsively, for more, establishing himself on friendly speaking terms with the four young scruffs. Soon his yearning to (in Oscar Wilde's phrase) "tame the panther" got the better of him completely. Less than a month after his first exposure to the Beatles, he surprised the group and his own parents with a proposal that inflated the hopes of John, Paul, George, and Pete almost as much as it deflated those of Harry and Queenie: He would become the Beatles' manager.

Certain elements of this story were far from unusual at the time. In his irreverent 1969 survey *Rock [Pop] from the Beginning*, Nik Cohn summed up "British pop in the Fifties" as a homosexual farce: "Nobody could sing and nobody could write, and nobody gave a damn. All anyone ever had to do get himself a hit was bend over in the right place at the right time." But the Beatles' inexperienced manager was hardly a cynical predator; in fact, his clients were a lot tougher than he was. If anyone was being "used" at first, it was probably Brian Epstein. Sure, the Beatles had signed over to him a quarter of their future income; but at the time that promised little more than 25 percent of nothing.

Still, because he was what he was, Brian was better qualified than most to gauge, and empathize with, the fantasies of the young females who constituted most of the record-buying pub-

lic. Knowing that the Beatles' image was too rough—both too tough and too unpolished—to ingratiate them with a wider audience, he had them clean up their act. To Epstein's neatly typed notes detailing upcoming gigs, postscripts were added: "On ALL the above engagements, during the performances, smoking, eating, chewing, and drinking is STRICTLY PROHIBITED." The leather gear was permanently retired to the closet.

Clive Epstein, Brian's brother and assistant, says that back then "the vision for the Beatles was completely Brian and John. John seemed so intelligent, and aware of everything that was going on around him. The others didn't give the same impression, but often people learn and grow after they become successful, and Paul and George certainly developed into thinking people as well." But while Brian and John jointly plotted the Beatles' future, this odd couple differed, frequently and sharply, over the strategy they should follow.

"In the beginning," Lennon was to recall in *Melody Maker*, "it was a constant fight between Brian and Paul on one side, and me and George on the other. Brian put us in neat suits and shirts, and Paul was right behind him. I used to try to get George to rebel with me. I'd say to him: 'Look, we don't need these fucking suits. Let's chuck them out the window.' My little rebellion was to have my tie loose, with the top button of my shirt undone, but Paul would always come up to me and put it straight." Yet John was subsequently to rate the Epstein "flair" a key ingredient in the Beatles' success.

Epstein may have been an unlikely hustler, but his unrequited passion for the Beatles proved stronger than his inhibitions. When Brian's crusade to fulfill his own preposterous prophecy that "one day these boys will be bigger than Elvis" at last gathered momentum, he asserted his influence more and more. The four Beatles' "pudding bowl" hairdos were styled almost identically; then came the gray collarless suits, courtesy of Pierre Cardin, which John hated most of all.

The first object of that one-man crusade was obviously a recording contract. After a friendly contact from Decca had made politely encouraging noises upon attending one of their performances at the Cavern in December 1961, the Beatles' battered van took to the motorway, bound for the record company's London studios. On New Year's Day, 1962, the Beatles cut their legendary Decca audition demo—fifteen numbers ranging from Lennon-McCartney's own "Hello Little Girl" and "Like Dreamers Do" to such perennial Beatles standbys as "Money," "Please Mr. Postman," and "Till There Was You." The sound was derivative and the performance barely professional; and the tape was shortly rejected by Decca (and then by all the other London heavies) with those immortal words: "Rock & roll groups are on the way out, Mr. Epstein. You have a good record business in Liverpool. Stick to that."

Part of the problem was London snobbery. "We were looked down upon as animals by the southerners, the Londoners," Lennon remembered. "We were hicksville." Dick James, future publisher of the Lennon-McCartney songbook, was to furnish that other classic line: "Liverpool? You're joking! So what's from Liverpool?"

But Brian—who could count on a withering reception from Lennon whenever he came home empty-handed—finally chanced upon the sympathetic ear of an employee of London's HMV record shop, where Epstein had brought the Beatles' tape for transferral to acetate discs. This gentleman directed him to Syd Coleman, manager of a music publisher on the floor above. Coleman, in turn, arranged an appointment with the producer and A&R man for Parlophone Records—George Martin.

Though a subsidiary of EMI, Britain's largest and most successful record conglomerate (which had already twice rejected the Beatles), Parlophone itself had fallen on lean times. Despite earlier triumphs with comedy records by the likes of Peter Sellers and Spike Milligan, Martin was desperate for new talent, preferably a Cliff Richard and the Shadows of his own. He gave the Beatles demo a close listen and concluded that there might just be something there. Following yet another stint in Hamburg, John, Paul, George, and Pete returned to London for their June 6 Parlophone audition.

"They were *awful*," recalled Martin's engineer, Norman "Hurricane" Smith, in a 1971 *New Musical Express* interview. "I was even patching up their amplifiers, they were that bad. They recorded for us for about twenty minutes . . . then came up to the control room.

"I remember we ended up just sitting there talking to these four blokes. We just kept talking and talking, because, frankly, they were fascinating." Even Lennon, an avid fan of the Sellers and Milligan recordings, was impressed with Martin—who in turn was disarmed by the Beatles' own offbeat sense of humor. He decided to give them a contract—albeit one whose royalty scale would entitle them to but one penny per record sold.

"Let's be honest," said Smith. "They were signed without anyone realizing their musical potential. It was just that they had so much personality and so much magic that they had to do *something*."

Throughout that first encounter, the group's surviving James Dean character said not a word. If Martin had mixed feelings about the musical talents of Lennon, McCartney, and Harrison, he was unequivocal in his low opinion of Pete Best's drumming. That seems to have cast Pete's die as far as the other Beatles were concerned; as a personality, he had always been the odd man out. Paul and George are also said to have resented Pete's good looks and popularity.

If ever Brian Epstein was used like an old condom, it was when the three original Beatles had him inform Best that Ringo Starr would henceforth fill their drummer's seat. "Eppy" was appalled at the assignment; not only did it violate his innate sense of decency, but he must have been as aware as anyone of Pete's animal magnetism. Ringo offered no such obvious attraction; and, anyway, why break up what finally promised to be a winning team? Nonetheless, Brian dutifully wielded the axe that the three Beatles had handed him, then issued his statement that "Pete left the group by mutual agreement. There were no arguments or difficulties, and this has been an entirely amicable decision."*

Pete's large Liverpool following proved less agreeable about the affair. During Ringo's August 18 baptism as a Beatle, George Harrison (Starr's main advocate within the group) received a black eye entering the Cavern Club. To protect himself from the angry gangs, Brian Epstein hired a bodyguard. "Overnight," he wrote, "I became the most disliked man on the seething beat scene." After lending his name to such Merseyside

George Martin supervises the Beatles' second recording session (**RDR Productions**)

footnotes as Lee Curtis and the All Stars, Pete would be exploited on a flop LP misleadingly titled *Best of the Beatles* and wind up slicing bread for fifty dollars a week. Meanwhile, John, Paul, George, and Ringo went to town to cut their first Parlophone single.

The otherwise uncataclysmic "Love Me Do"/"P.S. I Love You" set two important precedents. Even though a relatively democratic *group* had never before been promoted successfully, Martin had been persuaded to forget the idea of spotlighting John or Paul as the Beatles' Cliff Richard figure and relegating the rest to the shadows. Also, his skepticism about Lennon-McCartney's songwriting prowess notwithstanding, Martin allowed them to tape two of their original numbers. Despite the conventional wisdom that pop singers were incompetent to write their own records, Martin didn't have any suitable material at hand. He settled for "Love Me Do" because John's harmonica gave it an unusual appeal. At Martin's insistence, however, the tempo was quickened, lending the erstwhile ballad a more infectious sound. (The take used for the Beatles' first British release was one of the few on which Ringo had actually played drums, though session man Andy White is heard on the LP and subsequent singles editions.) "Love Me Do" promptly hit Number One on *Merseybeat*'s "Merseyside Tops," and the heavy Liverpool sales propelled it as high as number seventeen nationwide.

Heartened by this response, Martin found just the tune to make the Beatles famous—"How Do You Do It?" by Mitch Murray, twenty-four-year-old author of the book *How to Write a Hit Song*. But all the debonair producer got for his pains were disparaging remarks from Lennon and the others. Though their cocky attitude had been a major factor in Martin's attraction to the musically illiterate Liverpudlians, he felt they were pushing their luck, and made them record "How Do You Do It?" anyway. The Beatles' lackluster rendition still languishes in the EMI vaults, though the ditty soon became a Number One hit for Epstein's second batch of Merseyside marvels, Gerry and the Pacemakers.

Instead, Lennon and McCartney put forward a rocked-up version of a song they had written a year earlier as a Roy Orbison–style crooner, and even Martin was knocked out. So were Britain's teenagers, following the revamped "Please

---

* *If you can swallow that, try this account, from the early 1964 "Beatles Diary" bubblegum card series:*

Dear Diary,
   Pete Best, our drummer, surprised us today. He told the boys that he was going to quit the group. With Pete leaving, we'll have to find a new drummer quickly. We've been friendly with Ringo Starr, a fellow who has been playing the drums for several other Liverpool groups. He is a sock man with the sticks and we'll ask him to come join us.
                                                                                                    Paul

Please Me'''s release on January 12, 1963. All the basic Beatle ingredients were now churning in the mix: the bouncy melodies, ''Beatle-esque'' harmonies, and Ringo's triumphant drum fills, with everyday adolescent phrases such as ''oh yeah, like I please you'' replacing the stilted moons and Junes of Tin Pan Alley tradition. ''Please Please Me'' was, as the reviewer for *NME* noted, ''a really enjoyable platter, full of beat, vigor, and vitality—and what's more, it's different.'' ''We did this one strictly for the hit parade,'' John told *Merseybeat.* ''Now we're keeping our fingers crossed.''

(RDR Productions)

Within eight weeks of issue, the Beatles' second single had hit Number One on *Melody Maker*'s national chart. By that time, John and Paul had already knocked off a catchy follow-up in the back of their van between gigs. Like its two predecessors, ''From Me to You'' showcased John's harmonica. ''Then we dropped it,'' Lennon remembered. ''It got embarrassing.''

The Beatles cut their debut LP in a single day—February 11, 1963—with half the group suffering bad colds. ''We did their first album in one take,'' recalled their engineer, ''and John's voice was shot. I still remember the big can of Hacks standing there on the desk. They kept him going.''

George Martin had considered recording the LP live at the Cavern Club, and *Please Please Me*'s selections closely reflected a typical Beatles set from that era. Six were covers of American hits, and, as would be the case on future albums, each Beatle sang lead at least once. The best of the covers was taped almost as an afterthought, when Martin announced they had

''Like a heart that's oh so true . . .'' (*Globe Photos*)

enough time to do one more—the Isley Brothers' ''Twist and Shout,'' with John shredding his hoarse throat to a raw pulp.

There were also more Lennon-McCartney songs: ''Misery,'' ''There's a Place,'' ''I Saw Her Standing There,'' and ''Do You Want to Know a Secret?,'' the last of which was promptly covered by yet another of Epstein's Liverpool protégés. By the time Billy J. Kramer's single replaced ''From Me to You'' at the top of the charts, the notion that the Beatles would need slick professionals to write their hits had been dispelled by a growing awareness that John and Paul were among the most commercially potent tunesmiths in Britain. According to *Merseybeat*, they had already turned out one hundred songs.

Most of *Please Please Me* (retitled *Introducing the Beatles* and then *The Early Beatles* for the U.S. market) remained unpolished and derivative, but it represented a remarkable stride from that demo of just a year earlier. The album soon hit Number One—where it stayed for seven months, until another Beatles LP arrived to take its place.

Meanwhile, back in Liverpool, as Allan Williams recalled in *Melody Maker* a decade later, ''you'd have all sorts of wheeler dealers coming in. One lot, maybe Decca, would be in one corner doing a little deal with a group, and EMI in another. . . .

(*Globe Photos*)

(*Photo Trends*)

They'd just sign up everyone in sight hoping they'd get somebody good out of it.'' While the record companies cleared the city of talent, headlines such as IS LIVERPOOL BRITAIN'S NASHVILLE? and BEAT CRAZY—THAT'S BRITAIN* were splashed across *Melody Maker*'s front page.

The Beatles themselves crisscrossed Britain virtually nonstop, upstaging the long-since-forgotten acts they opened for, then headlining over top American names such as Roy Orbison. Ticket queues grew longer and longer, until fans hoping to get seats were obliged to bring sleeping bags, umbrellas, and a forty-eight-hour supply of sandwiches. To avoid getting torn to pieces, the Beatles had to arrive at their venues in disguise, or with a heavy police escort. Once onstage, they faced a steady hail of stuffed animals and ''jelly babies''—George's favorite candy, but not for long. The adolescent squeals elicited by Paul's winks and patter and by John's sardonic gestures and quips turned into a deafening roar that obliterated the Beatles' every word and note, and hit a crescendo whenever Paul and George shook their gleaming locks in unison while sharing a mike for those falsetto ''oooooh''s that highlighted so many of their songs.

And so it went, all good clean fun—Brian Epstein saw to that. The official *Beatles Monthly Book* launched the first of its seventy-seven issues in April 1963, and every hamlet in the land sprouted its own chapter of the Beatles Fan Club. New recruits were kept as much in the dark as possible about the days of amphetamines and leather—and also about John's August 23, 1962 wedding to a pregnant blonde named Cynthia Powell, whom he had dated since their meeting at art college. Not even Ringo had been in on the secret; but by the time Julian Lennon was born the following April 8, word of the marriage was out.

The ''married Beatles' '' first anniversary coincided with the release of ''She Loves You,'' with its trademark ''yeah, yeah, yeah'' chorus. It went on to become the best-selling record ever issued in Britain (until Paul McCartney and Wings' ''Mull of Kintyre'' finally outsold it in 1977). Yet—despite the boys having just scored a whopping 55 percent of all votes cast in the

''British group'' category of *Melody Maker*'s readers' poll—the Beatles phenomenon generally went unnoticed outside the world of pop music until the group's televised October 13 performance at the London Palladium. The hysteria in the theater and on the streets outside were beamed into the living rooms of millions of Britons, and by next morning the word ''Beatlemania'' had exploded onto the front pages of the national dailies.

Overnight, the whole of the United Kingdom seemed to lose its collective marbles over the long-haired lads from Liverpool. Everyone analyzed and argued, commended or condemned. Psychiatrists and editorialists, preachers and politicians, all added their tuppence worth about the phenomenon. Each issue of every newspaper and magazine carried a new story, if not on the boys themselves, then on their families—or on such and such manufacturer's plan to put out this much Beatle wallpaper or that much Beatle candy or so many collarless Beatle jackets—or on some headmaster's decision to forbid Beatle haircuts. The ''mop tops'' even got a boost from the old guard of ''longhairs'' when William Mann, classical music critic for the august London *Times,* anointed Lennon and McCartney ''the outstanding English composers of 1963'' and praised their remarkable facility with ''pandiatonic clusters'' and ''Aeolian cadences.''

The Beatles were the first rock & rollers ever to break the age and class barriers. Many parents and younger siblings were nearly as enthusiastic as the teenagers, and the group proved

---

* Melody Maker *perceived ''beat'' as somehow different from ''rock,'' which it called ''a craze over seven years ago.''*

equally popular among factory girls and debutantes. The Beatles were even chosen to perform on the November 4 Royal Variety Show. Before doing "Twist and Shout," John Lennon peered vaguely in the direction of the Queen Mother and Princess Margaret (he could hardly see an inch without the glasses he was too self-conscious to wear in public) and announced: "For the last number I'd like to ask your help. Would the people in the cheaper seats clap your hands? And the rest of you—if you'd just rattle your jewelry. . . . " Exclaimed the Queen Mother: "They are so fresh and vital. I simply adore them!"

With the Beatles represented another giant stride musically, as would every Beatles album through at least 1967. Instead of merely imitating each of their favorite American artists in turn, the Beatles were developing a synthesis that was more English and uniquely their own. Robert Freeman's high-contrast black-and-white LP jacket (tinted green on the American edition *Meet the Beatles*) was a pop classic unto itself: just those four famous faces peering out of the darkness, lit from one side like a quartet of half-moons.

Destined to become Britain's first-ever million-selling album, *With the Beatles* offered fourteen brand-new recordings, nearly all of them top-notch. This was almost revolutionary in a day when rock & roll LPs invariably consisted of one or two "hit" singles plus nine or ten throwaways. The Beatles deliberately changed all that. They also brought an unheard-of respectability to single B-sides. Many of their 45s would become double-headed hits because both songs were so good. In fact, all four Beatles considered "This Boy," the B-side of their new seven-incher, the best song they had ever recorded.

That single, "I Want to Hold Your Hand," racked up nearly a million orders even before its release a week after the album. With its inventive rhythmic stumbles, dissonances, and thrilling octave leap to the word "hand," this, of course, was the electrifying record that caused the first cracks in America's stone wall of resistance to British pop. And with each Stateside airing of "I Want to Hold Your Hand" the cracks spread, until the wall came crashing down once and for all.

Mr. and Mrs. Harrison accepting their son's fan mail (Photo Trends)

LP, France, 1963 (Odeon)   *LP, U.K., 1963 (Parlophone)*

EP, France, 1963 (Odeon)   *EP, France, 1964 (Odeon)*

And so four rock & rollers from—of all places—Liverpool, England, were catapulted to center stage on the world scene. Beneath the identical oddball hairdos, each proved to be an individual character and star in his own right. This was rock & roll's first group of equals, and fans had their pick of four distinct heroes.

Like the animals on George Orwell's farm, however, some Beatles were slightly more equal than others. Their names automatically rolled off everyone's lips John, Paul, George, and Ringo, in that order.

John, the group's guiding spirit, pulled the fewest squeals in those days. This was partly due to the presence (albeit well in the background) of a Mrs. Cynthia P. Lennon, but also because of a certain brutishness that no amount of Epstein grooming could ever quite swab away. John spoke his mind and suffered fools not at all; the wit came sharp and fast as a stiletto, and some young girls found the cynicism disconcerting. But to other fans Lennon personified the word "cool"; for those with an "intellectual" or "rebellious" streak, he was clearly *the* Beatle.

Paul had all the "star quality," in the traditional sense; he was the best showman, possessed the prettiest face and voice of all the Beatles, and was their built-in PR man. "I was always the one who would kind of sit the press down and say, 'Hello, how are you? Do you want a drink?'" He was also the nicest to fans; George has described him as "the one with a smile, a wave, and an autograph. We'd always be sitting in the car waiting for him—'C'mon Paul!'—and he'd be signing away."

George, not yet twenty-one when Beatlemania struck, was the last to really emerge as a personality. The best and most serious musician of the four, he tended to gravitate toward the background both onstage and off. Still, he was also handsome and attracted hordes of female admirers.

The solid and unassuming Ringo had doubtless got his job with the understanding that he was to take a backseat to his more creative colleagues. And so he generally would throughout the group's career; yet when the Beatles landed in America, the last to join proved the first to get individual recognition. Ringo may not have been much to look at, but he boasted the

LP, U.S.A., 1964 (*Liberty*)   LP, U.S.A., 1965 (*Elektra*)

most distinctive name and face of all the Beatles; and his characteristic hangdog expression brought out the mothering instinct in millions of doting girls. Though he lacked the scathing Lennon wit or the easy McCartney charm, Ringo's quips—classic one-liners deadpanned out of nowhere—often stole the show at the Beatles' press conferences.

Like the four elements of medieval alchemy—fire, air, water, earth—John, Paul, George, and Ringo complemented and reinforced one another; the sum was always greater than the parts. If John had the innovative ideas, then Paul came through with the teen appeal and the commercial sense to put them across to the multitudes. If Paul at times seemed almost too good to be true, John came on tough and off-the-wall. And if John threatened, Paul reassured. If John and Ringo weren't exactly virtuoso instrumentalists, George could be counted on for some well-crafted licks. And later, when the whole enterprise veered off into the ether, the down-to-earth Ringo would often put matters in perspective—as when he left the Maharishi's Indian retreat after but a week with the line "The food was too spicy." And so on, round and round and round in their hermetically sealed circle; the combination couldn't be beat.

The Beatles spent much of 1964 consolidating their grip on the "free world" with over 125 concerts and TV appearances in ten different countries. Nonetheless, they found the time for some groundbreaking projects that were greatly to enhance the group's stature.

March brought a slim volume of John Lennon's stories, verse, and doodles, titled (at Paul's suggestion) *In His Own Write*. The notion of a rock & roll singer writing a book promised little more than a clever PR stunt; "the married Beatle" could now add

(*Photo Trends*)

"the literary Beatle" to his string of titles. But John's brutal and bawdy vignettes turned out to be surprisingly clever, albeit well over the heads of many adolescent Beatlemaniacs. Some dated back to the early issues of *Merseybeat*, when Lennon had been but a struggling local artist with an oversized chip on his shoulder. Filled with zany puns and gruesome endings, they offered the world's first substantial glimpse into the unique (if deranged) intelligence at work beneath the mop top of the Beatles' de facto leader.

The rave reviews compared John's work with that of his beloved Carroll and Thurber—and even with Joyce's *Finnegan's Wake*, of which Lennon had never heard. *In His Own Write* ousted Ian Fleming's latest James Bond from the top of the best-seller list, and its author was honored with a prestigious Foyles Literary Lunch on Shakespeare's four-hundredth birthday. The assembled literati clamored for a speech, but John wasn't about to give them one. "Thank you very much, you've got a lucky face," he reportedly mumbled, resuming his seat amidst a chorus of jeers. Brian Epstein stepped in to repair the damage with some pleasantries of his own.

John began puttering away at a sequel, 1965's *A Spaniard in the Works*. "I put things down on sheets of paper and stuff them in my pockets. When I have enough, I have a book."

And then the Beatles made a movie. This in itself was no novelty: Frankie Avalon and Cliff Richard and the rest had all gone the "jukebox musical" route, with invariably dire results. As director Richard Lester admits: "The idea was to make it as quickly as possible and get it out before their popularity faded."

Because United Artists conceived this brainwave when Beatlemania was still confined to the British Isles, only some half-million dollars were earmarked for the black-and-white film. But the Beatles were never ones to lend their name to shoddy product. As evinced by John's Foyles "speech," these headstrong lads weren't about to try something if they suspected they might fall on their faces in the process. Nonetheless, one of their great qualities was a continual eagerness to embark on unexpected ventures that almost always *did* succeed as brilliantly as the Beatles doubtless knew they would.

"It was precisely because of what we were, and realistic, we didn't want to make a fuckin' shitty pop movie," Lennon remembered. "We insisted on having a real writer to write it." This turned out to be a fellow Liverpudlian named Alun Owen, who, like Lester, was chosen because the Beatles had admired his work for television. To take notes for the screenplay, Owen joined them on a tour of Ireland. According to John, "he stayed with us for two days and wrote the whole thing based on our characters then: me, witty; Ringo, dumb and cute; George, this; Paul, that." For some scenes, such as the Beatles' press conference, just about all Owen had to do was jot down what he heard: Q: Are you a mod or a rocker? A: A mocker. Q: What do you call your hairstyle? A: Arthur [in the process christening the Sixties' most chichi New York discotheque].

Filmed between March 2 and April 24, the Beatles' first movie was lumbered with such titles as *Let's Go, Moving On*, and *Beatlemania* before Ringo came to the eleventh-hour rescue with his throwaway phrase *A Hard Day's Night*.

Few anecdotes illustrate the Beatles' talent better than one related by their film producer, Walter Shenson: "I [then] told John that it would be great to have a song called 'A Hard Day's Night' to play over the title and credits . . . he just said he'd think about it. That night we were driving back into town together, and he asked the driver to let him off first because he had some work to do. The next morning at about eight thirty John asked me to step aside into this little room. Paul was in there, and they began playing their guitars, singing words John had written out on a matchbook. The song was 'A Hard Day's Night.'"

The film itself was a fictional documentary on "a day in the life" of the Beatles. But subtle exaggeration throughout turned it into a witty satire of Beatlemania as well. John has said that the group wanted it to be even more realistic, yet conceded: "It was a good projection of us on tour, in a hotel, having to perform before people. We were like that."

The plot follows the Beatles dodging hordes of Beatlemaniacs at every turn. They give interviews, pose for photographs, cut a record. Finally, they perform the concert that brings the film (and the nubile fans in the audience) to a resounding climax—thus resolving the movie's sole element of "suspense": Will they make it to the show on time?

For to the Beatles of *A Hard Day's Night*, those glamorous activities are merely the everyday routine, to be shirked at every opportunity. Rather than face their responsibilities, the Fab Four, like their teenage fans, prefer to romp in the fields or flirt with the opposite sex (in this case Pattie Boyd, who would become the real-life Mrs. George Harrison on January 21, 1966). Adult intruders like the pompous businessman on the train to whom Lennon turns the other cheek, lisping "give us a kiss"—or the patronizing entrepreneur seeking a Beatle's endorsement of his trendy "fab" shirts (George calls them "grotty," in the process adding a new word to the English language)—are dispatched with good-humored impertinence.

Even older moviegoers found themselves rooting for the Beatles in such confrontations with stuffed shirts, slick con men, and figures of authority. For these lovable mop tops were hardly the same Beatles who used to interpolate obscenities into their versions of the Fifties classics ("Shitty, Shitty," etc.), who one sunny day surprised a flock of nuns with a rain of golden showers from a Hamburg window. Thanks to Brian Epstein, the Fab Four had been purged of unpleasantness; "the idiotic hairdo" notwithstanding, JFK speechwriter Arthur Schlesinger, Jr. could hail *A Hard Day's Night* as "the astonishment of the month," and the Beatles themselves as "the timeless essence of the adolescent effort to deal with the absurdities of an adult world."

Reviewers praised Lester's inventive techniques, some borrowed from the French New Wave—helicopter shots, hand-held cameras, and frantic cutting, which was often synchronized to the beat of the Beatles' soundtrack music. But all this would have been wasted had the four principals not proved to be as photogenic in motion pictures as on record covers, and fully able to project their engaging personalities before the movie cameras. Their slapstick routines even earned widespread comparisons with the Marx Brothers.

A Hard Day's Night's July 6 premiere at the London Pavilion was a scene of glittering bedlam (to be re-enacted in 1965 for *Help!* and in 1968 for *Yellow Submarine*). Except for the parade of limousines disgorging such celebrities as Princess Margaret and the Beatles themselves, traffic was barred from the area. The heavily policed and barricaded Piccadilly Circus overflowed with thousands of screeching Beatlemaniacs. Starting the next day, the hoi polloi flocked to the cinemas in such numbers that more prints of *A Hard Day's Night*—fifteen thousand, all told—were run off than of any other film ever released.

The *Hard Day's Night* album benefited greatly from the Beatles' increased musical expertise and ability to draw on the resources of the recording studio. Gone for good were the flat

voices and fluffed licks that had marred such earlier efforts as "Hold Me Tight" and "I Call Your Name." In addition, every song sounded unmistakably like the Beatles and no one else. *A Hard Day's Night* was the first album to consist entirely of Lennon and McCartney numbers. At least one of Paul's contributions positively oozed Universal Appeal; "And I Love Her," the first of many McCartney tunes to become an easy-listening "standard," was instantly devoured by dozens of recording artists of every description.

Following completion of film and album, the Beatles embarked on whirlwind blitzes of Denmark, Holland, Hong Kong, Australia, and New Zealand. Despite Ringo's collapse at a photograph session just prior to departure, the show had to go on; and substitute drummer Jimmy Nicol (from Georgie Fame and the Blue Flames) had his fifteen minutes of fame. When Ringo rejoined the others in Melbourne, the Australian Fan Club made good on its February 11 congratulatory telegram to the Beatles in New York, promising an even greater reception Down Under. A quarter million people lined the streets of Melbourne in the largest gathering of Beatlemaniacs—or Australians—ever.

On August 19, a San Francisco ticker-tape reception launched the Beatles' first full-scale cross-country American tour. In the aftermath of the Goldwater and Johnson nominations, Beatlemaniacs held a mock convention of their own, and autumn issues of *Teen Screen* included "Ringo for President" stickers and other campaign paraphernalia. Two employees of Chicago's radio WBKB shelled out $1,150 for the sheets the

(*Photo Trends*)

Ringo and Maureen (Transworld Feature Syndicate/Henry Grossman)

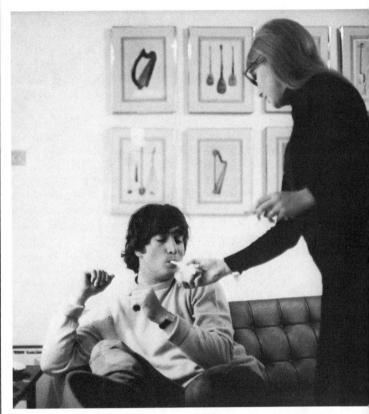

John and Cynthia (Transworld Feature Syndicate/Henry Grossman)

pattern: another volume of best-selling Lennonisms, another movie and soundtrack LP, another late-summer American tour. But the New Year would also be highlighted by a wedding, a controversial award, and the inescapable influence of one Mr. Robert Zimmerman—and with it, the first stirrings of a musical revolution.

boys had slept on in Detroit and Kansas City; these were cut into 150,000 pieces and mounted on parchment labeled "suitable for framing." *"Now . . . You Can Own The Actual Sheets, Towels, and Pillow Cases Used By The Beatles!"* blared the ad in *Teen Pin-Ups* magazine. "Own a big two-inch square of the actual pillow case Paul placed his dreamy head upon. . . ."

Then it was back to the U.K. to crank out another single and album in time for Christmas and yet another run of shows. December's *Beatles for Sale* (delivered to Americans in two installments, *Beatles '65* and *Beatles VI*) offered the first signs of the group's penchant for "coloring" their songs with unusual instruments: timpani, Arabian drums, an increasing reliance on keyboards, which were now often played by Paul or John rather than their producer. With 900,000 copies snapped up in one week, *Beatles for Sale* was the fastest-selling LP ever released in Britain.

The 45, "I Feel Fine," opened to the electric whine of an "accident" produced by John's guitar feedback—a sound destined to become an "Acid Rock" staple over the next few years. On other songs—"I'm a Loser," "I Don't Want to Spoil the Party"—these erstwhile purveyors of teen-dream puppy love offered lyrics of unaccustomed realism (and grimness). Yet this progression became apparent only in retrospect; at the time it was all just more terrific noise.

As evinced by the Beatles' nineteen "Christmas Shows" at London's Hammersmith Odeon (co-starring the Yardbirds and Freddie and the Dreamers), the group had yet to steer British pop clear out of traditional show-biz territory. The Beatles' performances opened with a scene in which they were "delivered" as gifts from a Christmas tree. This was followed by a skit in which they were captured by abominable snowmen, and another in which the boys played the parts of waxworks dummies (having recently been enshrined at Madame Tussaud's).

Beatles '65 would in large measure follow the previous year's

The February 11 wedding of Maureen Cox (an eighteen-year-old Liverpool hairdresser) and Ringo Starr ("the most popular Beatle," according to *The New York Times*) received enormous coverage, partly because marriage, for an established teen heartthrob, was then thought to be a suicidal career move. In those relatively innocent times, the sexual fantasies of the teenage girls who still constituted the main audience for "pop groups" were assumed to be predicated on the holy institution of marriage. Beatle "birds" had learned to keep an extremely low profile; even so, George's girl friend, Pattie Boyd, had been assaulted by jealous Beatlemaniacs during one of the recent Christmas shows. "I had to be careful because of the fans," said the new Mrs. Starkey. "I might easily have been killed otherwise. Not being married was all part of their image, and none of them were supposed to have steadies."

Most Beatlemaniacs, however, survived the trauma with their loyalties intact; and less than a year later George and Pattie were to marry as well. That left only Paul, who was in fact living with the accomplished young actress Jane Asher and her cultured, artistic family. Jane's influence was soon to become apparent in the taste in clothes, books, theater, and music adopted by the Beatles' most compulsive self-improver.

But if Paul was raising his social standing somewhat, he and the other Beatles were met far more than halfway by the highest echelons of their rigidly class-conscious society on June 12, when Queen Elizabeth included them in her birthday honors list as Members of the British Empire. The MBEatles (as *Hullabaloo* magazine began calling them) received their medals on October 26 during a solemn ceremony in the Great Throne Room, while shrieking Beatlemaniacs besieged the gates outside Buckingham Palace.

Following the Queen's announcement, several distinguished former recipients had sent their MBEs back—"it had become debased," said the Royal Air Force squadron leader; so as not to be seen "on the same level as vulgar nincompoops," said the Canadian MP. John Lennon observed that the Beatles were really being honored by the Socialist government for bringing so much foreign exchange into the country: "If someone had got an award for exporting millions of dollars' worth of machine tools, everyone would have applauded." Still, their MBEs were an apt symbol of the inexorable demise of Britain's rigid class divisions—whose barriers the four young lower-to-middle-class Liverpudlians had proved unprecedentedly successful in penetrating since at least the time of 1963's Royal Variety Show.

Paul and Jane (Photo Trends)

George and Pattie (Popperfoto)

While the British Establishment tried to come to terms with pop music and some of the forces it represented, pop in turn was about to broaden its horizons at a dizzying speed, to become something far more important, both artistically and sociologically—and, ironically, far more threatening to the Establishment. The main catalyst for all this was a twenty-five-year-old Minnesotan who, also ironically, was still associated in only the most tenuous way with the world of pop stars and rock & roll.

In early 1965, Bob Dylan (née Zimmerman) was known as a "folk singer." The little chart action he had stirred was via interpretations of his songs by sweeter-voiced peers such as Joan Baez and Peter, Paul and Mary. The heir apparent to Woody Guthrie as troubadour of the downtrodden and disaffected, Dylan relied only on his own acoustic guitar and trademark harmonica to drive home his harshly delivered message. His concert audiences—college students mostly, and very seri-

ous indeed—hung in awe onto their spokesman's every word. It was a scene far removed from what most folk purists viewed as the cheap, mindless noise of the Beatles and their fans; the folkie's taste in mob scenes was more likely to run to civil rights demonstrations and Ban the Bomb rallies, for which "The Times They Are a-Changing" and "Blowin' in the Wind" provided the perfect soundtrack.

Yet the figurehead of "protest" proved to be a lot more complicated than many of his slogan-happy admirers; as early as 1962, the dark, rhymeless visions of "A Hard Rain's a-Gonna Fall" clearly harked more to Allen Ginsberg's "Howl" than to the earnest, literal-minded commentary of a Woody Guthrie.

By late 1964, Dylan had become something of a cult figure among the hippest young adults in Britain, including members of the Animals, the Rolling Stones, Manfred Mann, and, most notably, all four Beatles. The Animals had already scored a Number One with their reading of Dylan's arrangement of the traditional folk song "House of the Rising Sun." Dylan, in turn, had grown up with the same rock & roll heroes as had the Beatles; and, sneers from his entourage notwithstanding, he cranked up the volume of "I Want to Hold Your Hand" when it first came over his car radio. Where the Beatles wailed "I can't hide," he thought they were saying "I get high," so he showed up at their hotel during the 1964 American tour to turn them on. It was the Beatles' first bout with marijuana.

All four Beatles were enraptured—Lennon even affected a Dylan cap—and tirelessly proselytized in Bob's behalf back home, turning up in the front row when he toured Britain in the spring of 1965. Some bemused Britons viewed Dylan almost as a creation of the Fab Four. "Are the Beatles laughing at the pop-buying public?" one wrote *NME*. "I and several of my friends think they chose Dylan as a guinea pig to see how susceptible we are. Look at the results—his records are selling without any singing ability on his part whatsoever. If the Beatles

The Beatles with road manager Mal Evans (Photo Trends)

were to withdraw their support, Dylan would fade back into obscurity where he belongs.''

Many folkies, of course, held an even dimmer view of the Beatles; but if they supposed the two styles would remain, musically at least, worlds apart, they were soon in for a shock. Dylan, who by now had completely renounced topical platitudes for a more personal style of verbiage, cut a rock & roll single called ''Subterranean Homesick Blues'' and drew howls of outrage when he desecrated the stage of the Newport Folk Festival with his new band of electric warriors.

Meanwhile, John Lennon adopted a Dylanesque sound in ''I'm a Loser'' and ''You've Got to Hide Your Love Away.'' And it dawned on the author of *In His Own Write* and *A Spaniard in the Works* that he could instill his own unique poetic voice into his songs. ''I'd have a separate songwriting John Lennon, and I didn't consider the lyrics to have any depth at all. That got embarrassing, and I began writing about what happened to *me.*'' (Not coincidentally, John never wrote another book.)

The record that definitively bridged the two worlds of folk and pop was ''Mr. Tambourine Man,'' a Number One hit by ''America's first long-haired group''—the Byrds. All certified folkies a year earlier, the five Californians had been electrified by *A Hard Day's Night,* and subsequently hit upon the inspired notion of recording one of Dylan's most poetic acoustic songs—with an arrangement dominated by Beatle-esque harmonies and a twelve-string electric guitar just like the one George Harrison had recently adopted. The Beatles themselves were among the first to extend their seal of approval.

Dylan promptly weighed in with his own Number One recording, ''Like a Rolling Stone.'' By summer's end, the ''Folk Rock'' boom, as the trade publications labeled it, had swept the pop music scene, and the Beatles' erstwhile cult hero was its undisputed king. That August alone saw the release of fifty different cover versions of Dylan songs. Many more recording artists cranked out self-composed imitation Dylan numbers. (''The songs are getting a bit silly, aren't they?'' McCartney commented in *Melody Maker.* ''Sonny [Bono]'s even on about protests on the length of his hair!'') But creative groups such as

the Beatles were inspired, more by Bob's example than by his specific style, to find a poetic voice all their own.

The emergence of Bob Dylan effectively ended the first wave of the British Invasion by sifting out the men, so to speak, from the boys. Those who could grow with the times—the Beatles, the Rolling Stones, the Kinks, The Who—would still be going strong many years later; but those unable to evolve—the Dave Clark Five, Gerry and the Pacemakers, Freddie and the Dreamers, Herman's Hermits—were destined for the junk heap.

Not that all this was instantly apparent to either the audience or the industry. The 1964-model bandwagon had yet to run out of gas, and outside the recording studio the Beatles still allowed themselves to be used as props in what they increasingly viewed as a charade. Their 1965 American tour, for instance, had little to do with art, or music, or even showmanship; rather, it offered nothing more or less than mass hysteria, inflated and amplified, for fun and profit, to a scale and a pitch previously unheard of in the world of mere entertainment.

Though the Beatles played only ten cities that August—less than half as many as on 1964's tour—they were actually ''seen'' by more American fans than during their last visit. Their 1964 experiments with large outdoor concerts having proved so profitable, the Beatles were now booked only into the most enormous coliseums available—few of which had previously been exposed to any strains of music other than of the National Anthem. As the sound systems used for live rock & roll were still crude and primitive in the best of circumstances, the acoustics at these Beatles concerts were a total fiasco.

Not that anyone came to listen; as one Beatlemaniac shrieked into a microphone: ''We didn't pay $5.75 for nothing.'' Captured on a TV special aired a year later, the August 15 show at New York's Shea Stadium was the most notorious of all, with the fifty-six thousand ticketholders constituting the largest audience not only of that or any Beatles tour, but indeed for any musical event ever staged until that time. The hysterics at Shea were well out of proportion even to the record numbers, which seemed to inspire each individual Beatlemaniac present to record levels of delirium, as if the amount of hysteria could be computed by squaring the size of the audience. Long before the Beatles themselves had even arrived from Manhattan—by helicopter and armored car—a sound akin to a jet taking off could be heard a mile away, drowning out even the opening acts (one of which, Sounds Incorporated, was accompanied by the go-go dancers still deemed indispensable to a rockin' good time) and the rantings of such would-be Fifth Beatles as Murray the K. The noise hit its most deafening crescendo as Ed Sullivan announced the Beatles' arrival, and the four boys in matching beige suits bounded for their second-base stage to the fireworks of ten thousand Instamatic flashbulbs. Any distinction between ''Twist and Shout'' and ''She's a Woman,'' or ''I Feel Fine'' and ''Dizzy Miss Lizzie,'' was all but obliterated; the most one could ever catch of the Beatles' music was the indefinite rumble of guitar chords. Not that it much mattered; the fans were the whole show.

This was particularly true because, while it had long been accepted that no one was likely to *hear* the Beatles in concert, the choice of such venues as Shea Stadium now insured that nobody could really *see* them either; even those in the best seats needed powerful binoculars for the Beatles to appear much larger than four insects. To keep zealous fans from getting any closer, the parameters of the playing field were heavily fortified by police barricades, guarded by hundreds of New York's Finest. Even so, just about every song was highlighted by the spectacle of at least one enthusiast managing to beat the obstacle course and hurtle into the baseball diamond, only to be tackled and dragged out of the arena by a team of beefy cops. Also failing to last the entire show were literally hundreds of Beatlemaniacs who fainted from a combination of overexcitement and New York's lethal midsummer humidity.

After a mere half-hour, the Beatles took their bows and rolled off in their armored car $160,000 richer. That works out to $100 for every second they stood on stage, virtually unseen and unheard by the self-deafened throng, for whom the Beatles' mere presence as specks in the spotlight occasioned the unshackling of 56,000 human beings from all restraints of everyday rational behavior, and their virtual transformation into a single ecstatic organism. Attending the somewhat smaller-scale San Francisco rites, Ken Kesey saw (according to Tom Wolfe's *The Electric Kool-Aid Acid Test*) an "animal with a thousand waving pink tentacles—vibrating poison madness and filling the universe with the teeny agony torn out of them." Kesey, of course, was on a bad acid trip at the time; for most of the celebrants at these events, the atmosphere was hardly poisonous, but few would have argued with his use of the word "madness."

Another highlight of this American trip was the Beatles' pilgrimage to Elvis Presley's Beverly Hills mansion. The five stars reportedly passed the time playing billiards and jamming on such selections as the Beatles' "I Feel Fine," for which Presley attempted the bass guitar part. "Coming along, quite promising on bass, Elvis," coaxed Paul. John told the aging "King" he should get back to singing rock & roll; Presley replied that he was too busy conquering Hollywood.

Speaking of which, the Beatles' 1965 U.S. tour coincided with the release of *Help!* on both vinyl and celluloid. According to the fan magazines of the day, Ringo's original title—*Eight Arms to Hold You*—was scrapped during the filming of one of the final scenes, which featured a live tiger, at the sight of which the Beatles all reportedly fell over shouting "Help!" "If you want to believe that, you can," producer Walter Shenson told me fifteen years later. The prosaic fact of the matter, he says, is that "we were already using the song 'Help,' and suddenly realized it would make a great title for the film."

In any event, the film was made under far more favorable circumstances than *A Hard Day's Night,* whose enormous success prodded United Artists to budget ten times as much money for a Technicolor sequel. Characterized by George Harrison as "a fast-moving comic strip," Richard Lester's satirical comedy benefited from enough explosive gadgetry and gimmickry to make mincemeat of James Bond, and from such relatively exotic locations as the Austrian Alps and the Bahamas (where the Beatles received some rare bad press for serenading an eminent hostess with the chorus "She's a fat old bag"). On the strength of *Help!,* Brian Epstein confidently predicted that films would prove the medium of the Beatles' future, and the key to their lasting success.

Nonetheless, the Beatles in *Help!* once again appeared, to some extent, to be playing along while outsiders manipulated the monster the boys had created; John Lennon later likened the Beatles' status in Lester's film to that of "clams in a movie about frogs." But the group had already done a "fictional documentary"; as actors, they weren't really equipped to take on straight dramatic roles; and as creative artists they had yet to develop the sort of pretensions that would result in 1967's *Magical Mystery Tour*. So they let themselves be co-opted into playing John, Paul, George, and Ringo getting chased around the world by a bloodthirsty Eastern cult intent on retrieving a sac-

rificial ring that, predictably enough, turns out to be stuck to Ringo's finger.

Fast-paced, surrealistic, and witty in a highly topical and uniquely British way, the movie *was* good fun; and so were the performances of its four stars—especially, again, Ringo. (The response to the *Melody Maker* pollster's query "Which Beatle wins the honors in the film *Help!*?" netted 70 percent for Ringo, 20 percent for John, 8 percent for Paul—and 1 percent for George.) Lester still considers *Help!* one of *his* best pictures, better even than *A Hard Day's Night*. According to John Lennon, however, "he forgot about who and what we were. And that's why the film didn't work."

Unlike the music in *A Hard Day's Night,* little on the *Help!* LP had been written specifically for the movie. "Help" itself proved to be Lennon's most personal song yet, one of the first on which he lets down his abrasive guard to bare a notably troubled soul. If anyone was really listening, "I feel so insecure" and "Help me get my feet back on the ground" must have seemed odd lines, coming from the epitome of cool; but, as the song goes, "Those days are gone . . . [I've] opened up the doors." Years later John was to rate "Help" among the finest and most honest of all his Beatles numbers and declare: "I'm not a tough guy. I always had a facade of being tough to protect myself, but I'm really a sensitive, weak guy."

LP, U.S.A., 1965
(United Artists)

EP, Spain, 1965
(Odeon)

In his very last interview (for RKO Radio Network), Lennon recalled having deliberately begun to shed his invulnerable rock & roll image: "I don't want to go through life pretending to be James Dean or Marlon Brando." He also noted: "In that sort of pop business . . . it was most uncomfortable when I didn't feel I was being myself, when I would have to smile when I didn't wanna smile; it became like being a politician."

Murray the K remembered Lennon (in *The Soho News*) for "this sense of truth that I got from nobody else in the business. . . . It was one thing that set him apart from George or Paul or Ringo . . . he could at one hand be the most cynical and most biting, and at the same time be the most sympathetic. . . . I saw him take the abuse and still say what he believed in; [he] saw the thing through and turned out to be right."

Paul's standout contribution to the mid-'65 batch of Fab product was "Yesterday," an instant easy-listening classic that silenced once and for all those older folks who had deemed the new generation incapable of producing melodies up to the standards of their own yesterdays. Since the release of the original, some two thousand other artists have recorded versions of "Yesterday," making it not only the most widely interpreted

Beatles song ever, but also one of the most frequently recorded tunes ever written.

"Yesterday" is a landmark in Beatles recording history as well; the original rendition, though credited to the group, is in fact a solo performance by Paul McCartney, accompanied by a string quartet. That came about, Paul told *NME,* because he felt many of his ballads "got crummier and crummier as we added the rest of our sounds, [so] we decided to leave this one as it was. Then George Martin said: 'What about an orchestra?' and I said: 'Well, okay—but just a little one then,' and ended up with a quartet.''

Though strings were hardly foreign to pop ballads, rarely had they been used in so tasteful a manner. Thanks, perhaps, to the success of "Yesterday," the day was not far when many of the Beatles' songs would feature but one or two members of the group, relying heavily on the strings, horns, and woodwinds (not to mention instruments previously unknown to the general public) of outside musicians.

"Act Naturally" also rates a mention, for its status as Ringo's signature tune (along with 1967's "With a Little Help from My Friends," the other Beatle song he would revive on his 1978 *Ringo* TV special). This account of a melancholy yokel making a big splash on the silver screen by merely playing himself— delivered in a voice as disarmingly plain as its owner—sounds as if it had been specially tailored for the undisputed star of *A Hard Day's Night* and *Help!.* In fact, it had originally been recorded by country-and-western singer Buck Owens. Like most of Starr's cameos on later Beatles LPs, "Act Naturally" revealed his long-standing roots as a country music and cowboy fanatic; as a youth, Richard Starkey had even applied unsuccessfully for a job in Houston, Texas.

"Yesterday" and "Act Naturally" appeared in the U.S. not on *Help!* but as the Beatles' eighth million-selling single. The choicest morsel from each British album—"Eight Days a Week," "Yesterday," etc.—was sure to be held off the U.S. version and served up later as a hot "new" 45; finally, it would appear as a prime cut on a subsequent Capitol album.

The American *Help!* LP contained only half the songs from the British version—the seven actually featured in the film— filled out with "exclusive instrumental music from the picture's soundtrack." Yet even this dreary Ken Thorne Muzak was to play an important (if indirect) role in Beatle history. To lend some "Eastern" atmosphere to the shenanigans of Leo McKern's "Eastern" cult, Thorne made use of a sitar—an obscure twenty-one-string North Indian instrument that promptly caught the fancy of George Harrison, who had already accumulated a large collection of unusual guitars (and professed ambitions to design one himself).

George's new toy very quickly turned into an obsession, leading him to the feet of India's classical sitar master Ravi Shankar. "When I listen to this music," he told *Hullabaloo,* "I dream of what it must be like to be inside Ravi's sitar." Harrison's deepening involvement inevitably exposed him to the religious beliefs and practices with which Indian classical music is so closely interwoven. Thus the youngest Beatle finally found an identity and outside interest of his own. And by gradually introducing elements of Indian music and mysticism into the Beatles' work, George was to set an important trend in the British pop world and help invent that curious mid-to-late-Sixties subgenre known as Raga Rock.

This was but one of several departures signaled on the Beatles' next album. For the first time, Lennon and McCartney's lyrics were almost on a par with the music—which, for the most part, was characterized by a mellower, predominately acoustic, Folk Rock sound. *Rubber Soul* owes much of its inspiration to a pair of influences that the Beatles had by now digested fully— Bob Dylan, and that subtropical weed he had initiated them into a year earlier.

Should you harbor the opinion that rock & roll must by definition remain mindless junk, *Rubber Soul* will be the album on which the Beatles first began to go soft, lose their animal vitality, and wax pretentious. But the more prevalent wisdom celebrates it as the record wherein the Beatles claimed full artistic control of their product, redefined the role of the pop star—and came up with a masterpiece.

Without question, the Beatles now viewed themselves as Artists with a capital *A.* Lennon began to mutter (in *NME*) that "only about a hundred people in the world really understand what our music is all about." And later he remembered *Rubber Soul* as the album with which the Beatles "finally took over the studio."

The jacket of *Rubber Soul* was extraordinary at a time when the packaging of rock & roll records still evinced about as much imagination and taste as the cardboard containers of such other kiddie products as candy or cereal. It shows the Beatles' faces subtly distorted, as if reflected in a pool—or stretched like rubber. The letters of the title (a McCartney pun on "rubber sole" and the "soul music" with which London's In Crowders were becoming increasingly enamored) are similarly rubberized into a shoe-shaped logo; the word "Beatles" is conspicuous in its absence—a liberty no American label had previously allowed a recording artist. Thanks to the Beatles and *Rubber Soul,* the art of record packaging was about to evolve as dramatically as the music itself.

Though *Rubber Soul* was recorded at a relatively leisurely pace, Lennon and McCartney found themselves having to crank out half the material in the last week before entering the studio.

They managed to maintain an amazingly high standard, especially considering the care they took with their lyrics. John's ranged from sardonic ("Girl") to poignant ("In My Life"). "Social commentary" reared its head on "Nowhere Man," the first Beatles lyric to make no conceivable reference to "romance." In another song the Beatles began promoting "The Word"—Love—as a universal principle rather than merely a fab mop top's endearment to his teen-dream queen. "It sort of dawned on me that love is the answer," John recalled in his last interview. "It seemed that the underlying theme to the universe, of everything that was worthwhile, was love, love, love."

Best of all was the cryptic "Norwegian Wood," which, with its mysteriously evocative language, proved meaningful to many listeners even when it didn't yield literal "sense." After all, pop songs weren't generally something one *listened* to carefully from start to finish. Rather, they insinuated themselves piecemeal in the subconscious over the course of repeated *hearings*—which made them, in the hands of true artists like a Lennon or a Dylan, perfect vehicles for the "Norwegian Wood"–style dream logic that would inform most of John's work over the next two years.

Lennon, without question, was one of rock's born poets; even many of his early lyrics, trivial though they may have been, restated the clichés of teen romance in tough, colloquial language. Paul, on the other hand, could be pretty dreadful when writing on his own ("She gives me everything/and tender-*lee*"); as his solo and Wings efforts would emphasize, the music always came far more easily to McCartney than the words. But once John's example prodded him into trying harder, his Beatles lyrics could be very good indeed ("For No One," "Penny Lane")—even if he seldom achieved John's idiosyncratic brilliance. Though Lennon-McCartney, despite the joint credit, seldom wrote together after *Rubber Soul,* they remained an unbeatable combination until the day their wavelengths finally diverged completely.

Rubber Soul also featured a nice pair from the recently activated pen of George Harrison. "If I Needed Someone" was even covered as a single by the Hollies, who ranked among Britain's most consistent hitmakers. Far from being honored, Harrison—as much a master of diplomacy and tact as Lennon—dismissed their rendition as "roobbish" in the pages of *NME.*

The Beatles' version wasn't released in America at the time; like "Drive My Car," Ringo's rockabilly "What Goes On," and "Nowhere Man" (the next "new" U.S. single), it was held off *Rubber Soul* in favor of two leftovers from *Help!* Still, *Rubber Soul* was the first American Beatles album to contain no previously issued singles (and to duplicate exactly the artwork of the British version), which was something of a breakthrough in itself.

Some truly dramatic breakthroughs—as well as controversies—were in store for Beatles '66, the year in which the erstwhile Fab Four released (in the astute words of *Melody Maker*'s record reviewer) "a brilliant album which underlines once and for all that the Beatles have definitely broken the bounds of what we used to call pop."

Over the spring of 1966, John, Paul, George, and Ringo, having cleared their schedules of such petty distractions as filming and touring, returned to the recording studio, their fertile imaginations seething with new ideas. While Paul had been taking classical music lessons from Mrs. Asher, and generally going on a culture binge, George was sitting cross-legged on the floor of his Esher bungalow for hours every day, balancing his giraffe-necked new toy on his left foot to practice scales in his incense-filled study till his fingers bled—just as he had long ago mastered the guitar that he now disdained to touch outside the recording studio. He and John were voraciously reading books on Eastern religion. Both Beatles had also recently had LSD slipped into their coffee by George's dentist; and both, electrified by the revelations they felt they had experienced from their first trip, had begun eating acid almost daily. John began turning his visions into extraordinary songs, the likes of which nobody had ever before written.

The pop stars and other artists who formed the elite of what would soon be known as London's Underground were all going through similar "changes." The rival groups frequently hobnobbed at such fashionable discotheques as the Ad-Lib to swap brain waves through the night, fueled by "mind expanding" substances still unknown to the general public or even to the legislators who would soon make them illegal. But though the Rolling Stones, The Who, Donovan, the Yardbirds, and the rest were also donning paisleys and rose-tinted granny glasses, to rethink the pop song and the state of the cosmos, it was the Beatles who were the undisputed kings of this magic mountain. As The Who's Roger Daltrey told *Melody Maker:* "They are always one jump ahead on everything. They really amaze me."

The material the Beatles began recording in all-night sessions that March drew from their own experiences and imaginations, eschewing the formula "love songs" that had predominated even on *Rubber Soul.* The group's customary lineup of two guitars, bass, and drums was largely abandoned in favor of a smorgasbord of jazz, classical, and Indian instruments; and for the first time they ventured into the areas of sound effects, tape loops, backwards recordings, and other forms of electronic sorcery (all of which, of course, precluded live performances of their new work). Nineteen sixty-six inaugurated what would come to be known as the Beatles' "psychedelic" period—and witnessed the full flowering of a genius for words and music unsuspected by even the most rabid Beatlemaniac of two years earlier.

Back in 1964—which would soon seem another era entirely—the Beatles had made their impact simply as a wacky teenage fad. It was not in the nature of such things—or of rock & roll itself—to endure. The Elvis Presleys graduated to Las Vegas and Hollywood; lesser lights took to managing or producing a new generation of disposable heartthrobs; many wound up on Skid Row. Because the Beatles were smarter and more talented than their predecessors and contemporaries, one might have expected Paul to carve himself a niche in, say, "legitimate" musical theater, and John, perhaps, to publish many more slim volumes of literary nonsense. George would design his guitar, and Ringo launch his chain of beauty parlors, as Beatlemania faded to a pleasant memory, leaving little residue save longer hairstyles and a handful of melodies pretty enough to be piped into elevators and airports by Muzak, Inc.

But the Beatles, as was their wont, broke all the patterns and precedents. They neither grew out of rock & roll (as Presley had), nor kept up the same old din until the kids outgrew it. Instead, and on their own terms, the Beatles grew with the times (or was it the other way around?) and in growing made no compromises with the traditional "adult" world of show biz; instead of abandoning rock & roll, they transformed it; and the fans grew up with—rather than outgrew—the Beatles.

In making their bold experiments with the pop form, the Beatles were, of course, fortunate to have the platform afforded by their original success; as McCartney put it: "We're so well established that we can bring our fans with us and stretch the limits of pop." Though some might lament the passing of "the Beatles we used to know before they went stark, raving mad" (to quote one dissatisfied *Beatles Monthly* customer), the group's experiments were guaranteed at least a fair hearing.

The Beatles were also in the enviable position of being able to hire ace musicians—even symphony orchestras—as their guinea pigs. Most of all, they were lucky to have in George Martin a brilliant and sympathetic editor who could translate their musical whims into notes and squiggles for the session men and technical recording jargon for the engineers. Martin, in turn, feels that the Beatles' lack of formal training—coupled with their natural genius—actually gave them free rein to dream up ideas that would never have occurred to a more conventionally accomplished musician like himself; but the Beatles, for their part, needed a George Martin to give tangible shape to their brainstorms.

As experiments by definition are a process of trial and error, it seems almost uncanny how few errors the Beatles made, how nearly all their experiments would achieve enduring success. As pioneers in uncharted territory, they appeared to know exactly where they were going. If some of Harrison's Raga Rock seems dated and heavy-handed—and "Revolution 9" remains every bit the "pretentious piece of old codswallop" *NME*'s Alan Smith deemed it at the time—nearly everything else the Beatles recorded between 1966 and 1968 sounds as good now as it did then, perhaps because underlying the exotic instrumentation and lyrics one could always find a damn good tune. Indeed, three-minute *songs* remained the Beatles' specialty; their impact was seldom dissipated by lengthy instrumental ego trips. ("I've never done a solo because it bores me," said Ringo.) But the sound and the sense of the songs changed almost beyond recognition, and the transformation was as sudden and dramatic as that moment in the old movie when Dorothy finds herself in the Land of Oz, and the film abruptly switches from black-and-white to glorious color.

The Beatles themselves, however, were obliged to return briefly to Kansas before resuming their trip to the Emerald City. The nubile masses of Germany, Japan, and America, unaware that they were about to be swept off on a Magical Mystery Tour, were eagerly awaiting the next opportunity to shout down their idols and, where seating arrangements permitted, to pelt them with stuffed animals and underwear. (For the Japanese, who filled 220,000 applications for 27,000 tickets to Tokyo's Budokan judo arena, it would be their first and only chance.) Emerging from their Abbey Road cloister, the Beatles were duly fitted with matching pink and green suits and hit the road with a bag of old chestnuts dating back to the days of *Help!* and *Beatles for Sale*.

Lennon, according to *NME*, "could barely croak a note." He also had difficulty remembering the words to his old hits, which, he admitted, "sound like big drags to me now. I turn the radio off if they're ever on." Only McCartney maintained a semblance of professionalism, belting out his Little Richard impersonations with his usual flair. In all other respects, the Beatles' performances were lackluster at best—not that anyone on either side of the barricades cared.

Following the German and Japanese shows, the Beatles made a brief stopover in the Philippines to break their own Shea Stadium record by playing to nearly a hundred thousand at Manila's Aranita Coliseum. But any sense of triumph was dissipated the next afternoon when the Beatles woke up and turned on the TV. The big news story showed dignitaries at the presidential palace impatiently awaiting the Beatles' arrival at a dinner first lady Imelda Marcos was giving in their honor. The entire country felt it had been wantonly insulted, despite Epstein's insistence that the group had never received an invitation; and the Beatles were instant pariahs.

In what George has called the worst nightmare of their career, the Beatles were obliged to flee for the next plane out of the country, with only the most token protection from mobs of enraged patriots. They escaped almost intact to New Delhi, where John and Paul joined George in a shopping spree for Indian instruments.

While the boys recuperated in London, further controversies preceded them to America. The first centered on an LP jacket. Capitol Records, deeming it time to wring some dividends from its backlog of recent Beatles singles and deleted LP cuts, had sent to England for three new songs and a cover photo to complete the package. The Beatles responded with their now notorious butcher impersonation, masterminded by photographer Robert Whittaker, who, Lennon would tell WNEW-FM's Dennis Elsas in 1974, "was a bit of a surrealist and brought along all these coats and babies. I really got into it because that's how I felt. I wanted it for the album, to break the wholesome image."

There may have been another reason why the Beatles selected a photograph of themselves in butcher smocks, flaunting slabs of meat and chopped-up baby dolls, for a compilation of leftovers chopped from their original brainchildren. "We'd put a lot of work into sequencing the albums to have it the way we wanted it to sound," said John. "Then we'd come over to America. . . . It would drive us crackers!"

In any event, advance recipients of the album—christened *Yesterday and Today*—were mortified by what *Time* magazine was to term the Beatles' "first serious lapse in taste." Capitol, deluged with protests from disc jockeys and distributors, decided to take the unprecedented step of destroying 750,000 "butcher covers" and an unspecified quantity of streamers and other promotional material. In some cases the substitute picture of the Beatles gathered around a trunk was merely pasted over the butcher covers, and Beatlemaniacs have been peeling away at their copies of the album ever since in the hopes of—almost literally—striking gold; a decade after it wasn't released, the butcher cover would command three figures on the collectors' market. The whole episode cost Capitol a quarter million dollars. Apparently the label thought it would be worth it in the long run, to salvage that wholesome image Lennon seemed so intent on sabotaging.

Any gains on that score were promptly wiped out by the circulation of a months-old quote from—who else?—John Lennon: "Christianity will go. It will vanish and shrink. I needn't argue about that; I'm right and will be proved right. We're more popular than Jesus now. I don't know which will go first, rock & roll or Christianity. Jesus was all right, but his disciples were thick and ordinary. It's them twisting it that ruins it for me."

John had made those remarks in the course of an earnest discussion about religion with the London *Evening Standard*'s Maureen Cleave, one of the few journalists he felt close to. Neither realized how inflammatory (literally!) Lennon's words would prove upon their belated airing in an American teen magazine called *Datebook*. "I can't express myself very well," John told *NME*. "That's my trouble. I was just saying in my illiterate way what I'd gleaned from a book I'd been reading— *The Passover Plot* by Hugh J. Schonfeld."

With their faggy hair, black-derived music, and general disregard for authority and convention, the Beatles had never exactly endeared themselves to the self-appointed moral guardians of the Bible Belt. The "Christian Crusade" had already published a booklet, *Communism, Hypnotism, and the Beatles* by a Reverend David A. Noebel, revealing that the Fab Four were "a systematic plan geared to making a generation of American youth mentally ill and emotionally unstable . . . to hypnotize [them] and prepare them for future submission to subversive control."*

"We're more popular than Jesus" gave these paragons of decency the perfect opportunity to reassert the finer Christian virtues. In Alabama one disc jockey denounced the phrase as "an outright sacrilegious affront to Almighty God"; another station lined the street with garbage pails bearing the legend "Place Beatle Trash Here"; and a third invested in a tree-grinding machine to pulverize donations by reformed Beatlemaniacs. Across the Old Confederacy and parts of the Midwest, thousands of Beatles collections—and even effigies of the offending foursome—went up in the flames of massive bonfire rallies.

The rage spread as far as Franco's Spain, and South Africa, where Beatles music would remain banned from the airwaves until 1971. From the Vatican, *L'Osservatore Romano* warned: "Some subjects must not be dealt with profanely, not even in the world of beatniks." In London, the price of a share in the Beatles' Northern Songs Ltd. dropped thirty-eight cents. Meanwhile, back in Longview, Texas, the Beatle-burning KLUE was struck by lightning and knocked off the air for the night; undeterred by any thought that somebody up there might not like them after all, the deejays resumed their crusade the following morning.

Roused from his sickbed, Brian Epstein caught a trans-Atlantic flight two weeks earlier than planned. In America, he gave a press conference to explain that Lennon had merely expressed his "deep concern" at the decline of interest in religion. Epstein also offered to cancel his contracts with any or all of the promoters of the upcoming Beatles concerts. He found no takers.

When the Beatles themselves arrived in Chicago on August 12, an enervated Lennon delivered his qualified apology: "If I had said television was more popular than Jesus, I would have gotten away with it. . . . I was not saying we were greater or better." The tour proceeded without undue incident. Nonetheless, the hostility and tension the Christian crusaders had generated only exacerbated the Beatles' distaste for the whole charade of touring. Off the record, John told *Melody Maker*'s Ray Coleman: "I just stand there and make mouth movements. Nobody knows. I reckon we could send our four waxworks dummies of ourselves and that would satisfy the crowds. Beatles concerts are nothing to do with music anymore. They're just bloody tribal rites."

Though no dramatic announcement was given to the media, the concert at San Francisco's Candlestick Park on August 29, 1966, was to be the Beatles' last. The first rock & roll heroes to have won total freedom—artistically, financially, and personally—John, Paul, George, and Ringo could now proceed entirely on their own terms.

A few months later Paul confirmed to *NME* the widespread

suspicion that a 1966 Beatles Christmas show was no longer in the cards:

> One reason we don't want to tour anymore is that when we're on stage nobody can hear us or listen to us. Another is that our stage act hasn't improved one bit since we started touring four years ago.
> Many of our tracks nowadays have big backings. We couldn't produce the sound onstage without an orchestra. . . . We feel that only through recordings do people listen to us, so that's our most important form of communication.
> We've never been frightened to develop and change. I think this has been the reason for our continued success. We could have brought out "Son of Please Please Me." . . .
> Before, we had a set time in the recording studio, and if it wasn't exactly as we wanted that was too bad.
> Now we can take time because we haven't any pressing engagements like tours to limit us. All we want is to make one track better than the last. We make all "A" sides and never go into the studio thinking: "This will be our next single."

On that last tour, the Beatles, significantly, hadn't attempted to perform even one tune from the new album they were theoretically promoting, though they did manage a version of the single that had preceded it. Unlike the earlier "I Feel Fine" and "Day Tripper," which had been built around a lead guitar riff ("nicked" in both instances from Bobby Parker's "Watch Your Step," said Lennon), "Paperback Writer" revolves on a Power Pop chord sequence highly reminiscent of The Who's recent "Substitute." The Beatles borrowed almost as freely from their leading contemporaries as vice versa; Dylan and The Who, McCartney told *Melody Maker,* were their "two great influences for 1966."

One department in which the Beatles were far in advance of groups like the Stones and The Who was reasserted with "Paperback Writer"'s intricate four-part harmonies, which build to a climax that is effectively swept away on a wave of reverberation. (While three Beatles spent a full day devising and overdubbing harmonies, Ringo—as would increasingly be his fate—was left to play cards with roadies Mal Evans and Neil Aspinall.) And the words were no less ingenious, taking the form of a "Dear Sir or Madam" letter to a publisher from a struggling hack writer. This was an unusual subject for a pop single at the time, but McCartney wrote from experience: in pre-Epstein days, it had been Paul's job to write such letters to promoters on behalf of the struggling Beatles. ("Paul was a real hustler," says Mick Jagger. "Still is.")

The subject matter of the Lennon-composed B-side concerned a favorite pastime of England's older generation: complaining about the weather. That John Lennon had graduated to more cosmic concerns is emphasized by "Rain"'s distorted guitar effects, which helped define the term "psychedelic." The crowning touch is in the coda—onto which Lennon's vocal track is reprised *backwards*. As John would tell *Rolling Stone*'s Jonathan Cott, "I got home about five in the morning, stoned out of me head. I staggered up to me tape recorder and put it on, and I was in a trance in the earphones, what *is* it, what *is* it? Too *much*. . . . I just happened to have the tape the wrong way round . . . so we tagged it onto the end."

Such lucky accidents and strokes of intuitive genius abound on the subsequent *Revolver*—the album that many still rate as the Beatles' finest. (The U.K. pressing, that is; the U.S. edition is marred by the absence of the three Lennon concoctions that Capitol purloined for *Yesterday and Today.* Henceforth all British Beatles LPs would cross the Atlantic more or less intact.)

---

* Pravda, *ironically, had also labeled the Beatles a conspiracy: "a plot by the ruling classes to distract . . . youngsters from politics and bitter pondering over disgraced and shattered hopes."*

George Harrison's enhanced stature is emphasized by the inclusion of three of his songs, the best of which opens the program. Brian Epstein called George "the business Beatle"; "he is curious about money, and wants to know how much is coming in and what is best to do with it and make it work." The British "Taxman"—who literally claimed up to nineteen (out of twenty) shillings from every pound earned in the Beatles' income bracket—offered a natural target for Harrison's first stab at "social commentary." But George's obsession with money was fast losing ground to the more transcendental demands of Indian music and religion. "Love You To" represented Harrison's first attempt to write and perform an Indian-style tune on the sitar, an instrument that was already de rigueur in Britain's "progressive" pop circles.

Ringo took his obligatory turn at the helm on "Yellow Submarine," unquestionably *the* novelty record of 1966. George Martin's experience producing Peter Sellers's comedy recordings doubtless came in handy as the boys tossed into the mix the most ludicrous sound effects they could think of. Ringo made "waves" splashing rags in a bucket; George, deprived of his guitar solos, blew bubbles through a straw. Everyone in the vicinity—engineers, roadies, and Donovan (who later claimed he wrote some of the lyrics)—was dragged before the microphone to chant the almost infuriatingly catchy chorus. Only a year earlier, the image of the Fab Four taking a merry voyage on a yellow submarine might have strained credulity; soon the yellow sub would seem the most congenial of vehicles as thousands of Beatle people made arrangements for similar trips of their own.

"I knew it would get connotations," Paul was to say. "But it really was a children's song. I just loved the idea of kids singing it." Nonetheless, the yellow submarine proved to be an apt metaphor for the fantastic cocoon into which the Beatles retreated following their retirement as a flesh-and-blood entity.

If "Yellow Submarine" offered the ultimate in Beatles comedy, the song selected as its 45 rpm companion piece was the closest they came to writing tragedy. The only thing "Eleanor Rigby" had in common with "Submarine" was that neither sounded anything like the Beatles. (Then again, the music was becoming so eclectic—and so largely the work of individual members—that the group was fast losing any semblance of a collective "sound.") Doubling "Yesterday"'s string component, "Rigby" incorporates four violins, two violas, and two cellos. None of the Beatles plays a note.

The banality of the tune actually contributes to the impact of the words. Eleanor Rigby waits by her window for visitors who never arrive, Father McKenzie writes sermons no one will hear. The two lonely old people's paths finally cross when Father McKenzie officiates at Eleanor Rigby's funeral, which nobody attends; "No one was saved."

The lyric itself was saved by its haunting ambiguities—which proved a gold mine for sociologists who specialized in "explaining" the Beatles and, through them, the entire generation that the Beatles were thought to represent. Did the forgotten preacher symbolize "vanishing, shrinking" Christianity? Was Eleanor Rigby's "face in a jar by the door" a touch of makeup—or a touch of Magritte? (McCartney had just bought one of the surrealist master's paintings.) The answer (as with all true art) was probably all the above—but none in particular.

Paul McCartney, who was primarily responsible for "Eleanor Rigby," shines elsewhere on *Revolver* with relatively straightforward romantic ballads such as "Here There and Everywhere"—which, it is worth noting, was directly inspired

by the Beach Boys' *Pet Sounds,* a profound influence on all the mid-Sixties British "progressives." In his *Musician* interview fifteen years later, Paul recalled his initial response to it: "This is *the* album of all time. What are *we* going to do?"

Both romance and social observation are conspicuously absent from Lennon's contributions, which conjure the picture of a Beatle who prefers to lie in bed all day, staring vacantly at the ceiling ("I'm Only Sleeping," he demurs)—unless sufficiently roused by the pick-me-ups of one "Dr. Robert" to take part in arcane philosophical exchanges. "She Said She Said" describes an actual encounter between an LSD-doused Lennon and the equally high-flying Peter Fonda (the "she" in the song), who had repeatedly announced: "I know what it's like to be dead." John's response, at least for the record: "You're making me feel like I've never been born." And so the psychedelic repartee continues, to a musical setting calculated to make the listener's head spin all the more.

Far from being the work of a chemically sustained vegetable, however, these songs present a musical innovator at the height of his powers, painting his somewhat deceptive self-portraits with subtle and surprising strokes. In the lyrically impenetrable "And Your Bird Can Sing," for instance, John twice in a row sings the phrase "I'll be 'round"—but substitutes a completely different set of chords when he repeats himself vocally note for note.

The most startling departure of all was the track Lennon originally called "The Void," but wound up naming "Tomorrow Never Knows" at the suggestion of the group's built-in dispenser of titles, Ringo Starr. Lennon had also wanted a few hundred chanting Tibetan monks on backup vocals—his lyrics had been adapted from LSD advocates Richard Alpert (a.k.a. Baba Ram Dass) and Timothy Leary's translation of *The Tibetan Book of the Dead*—but for once George Martin couldn't fill the order. Instead, he gave all four Beatles the "homework" assignment of creating tape loops on their home tape recorders; these were fed into the mix forwards, backwards, and at every conceivable speed, sometimes sounding incongruously like the cries of stampeding elephants as the distorted voice of John Lennon, accompanied by a droning Indian tambura, recites an account of the soul's journey into the afterlife. Martin later told *Melody Maker* that "Tomorrow Never Knows" reflected the Beatles' recent infatuation with Stockhausen, and added: "We'd put John's voice through a Leslie speaker because he said to me: 'I want my voice to sound as if it's coming from a hilltop in Tibet.'" Delivered without recourse to rhymes or chords, the message "Turn off your mind, relax, and float downstream" may have initially confounded listeners weaned on "I Want to Hold Your Hand" and "I'm Happy Just to Dance with You"—but not for very long.

In the meantime, Paul McCartney offered *NME* this straightforward explanation: "We did it because I, for one, am sick of doing sounds that people can claim to have heard before. Anyway, we played it to the Stones and The Who, and they visibly sat up and were interested." Jonathan ("Everyone's Gone to the Moon") King, on the other hand, denounced "Tomorrow Never Knows" as "pseudointellectual rubbish" in the pages of *Disc.* Like the fans, London's pop music community was sharply divided over the metamorphosis taking place within its ranks.

One of the more enthusiastic mouthpieces for pop's Brave New World was Donovan, the former Dylan clone whose current hit, "Sunshine Superman," had originally been announced as "Song for John and Paul." "I think of pop songs as being like books," he told *NME*. "Today we have Lennon and McCartney writing a novel called 'Eleanor Rigby' that takes only two and a half minutes to digest. And we enjoy romantic stories and adventure yarns from the pens of Ray Davies and Bob Dylan. . . . We have a very good cream of ideas, writers, and thinkers."

A more sour view was advanced in the same forum by Ron Richards, formerly George Martin's assistant and now the Hollies' producer: "Many of the groups are getting above the heads of their public. The Beatles, the Stones, and The Who . . . go along to the latest 'in' discotheque and pat each other on the back and say: 'We've just made a disc backwards hanging from a chandelier on the ceiling.'"

Some groups were themselves split down the middle over the question of "progress"—among them Mr. Richards's own Hollies. A *NME* microphone captured Graham Nash and Tony Hicks in heated debate:

NASH: It's time for the Hollies to grow up. I want to make records which say something.

HICKS: I think "Carrie Anne" [the latest Hollies single] does say something. It says something very simple—a boy-girl relationship, which anyone can understand. I'm frightened of going over the heads of the kids.

NASH: All I want is for people to listen. . . . Did you see Donovan at the Saville?

HICKS: I thought Donovan at the Saville was rubbish!

NASH: All I'm saying is that after five years of screamagers I'm getting a little tired. . . . I want to move forward—do something different. Maybe put on an illusionist—a poet—a film—something different on the show.

HICKS: I don't want to see a bullshit poet.

A third Holly, Allan Clarke, put in his tuppence worth a few weeks later: "We're as psychedelic as a pint of beer with the lads. . . . Graham talks a lot about the inner mind and psychedelic things, but to tell you the truth I don't understand half of what he's on about. It's just too weird." Manifestly outgunned, Nash would finally turn in his notice in 1968, and team up with a pair of dope-smoking Yanks to form Crosby, Stills, and. . . . (Clarke's parting shot: "All of Graham's songs are very slow and very boring. He wants to go all soppy, artistic, and beautiful. But we just want to stay the Hollies.")

The British pop revolution was gathering steam; but even with such influential recruits as the Rolling Stones, The Who, Donovan, and Graham Nash, it remained a minority movement, and perhaps always would—a point that once and future Beatles aide Derek Taylor, writing in *Melody Maker*, was among the few to make:

> The illusion of increasing standards is caused simply because the Beatles forced their mighty wanton wedge of flair into a tiny crack in the vast mass of compressed garbage, and hammered it home with a relentless maturing force leaving just enough room for a handful of creative contemporaries to clamber in and make music.
> But for the most part, the charts are still littered with lousy records made by inadequate, shambling puppets manipulated by the same awful people who've been haunting and contaminating show business for nearly half a century.

Upon completion of their first all-studio masterpiece and their last concert tour, John, Paul, and George each seized his first real opportunity to pursue an independent existence outside the group. Lennon, cast as Private Gripweed in Richard Lester's antiwar black comedy *How I Won the War*, cut off his Beatle hair and departed for Germany and Spain—with Ringo tagging along to keep him company off-camera. To complete his transformation, John started wearing glasses—granny glasses with round frames. Once back in England, he continued deliberately to annihilate his ego with ever more immoderate doses of LSD. "Don't forget," he said in *NME*, "that under this frilly shirt is a hundred-year-old man who's seen and done so much—but at the same time knowing so little."

McCartney, too, lent his token presence to turn an obscure British comedy film into a permanent historical footnote. After concocting incidental music for *The Family Way*, Paul took time off from his music lessons and gallery openings, and the decoration of his new townhouse in St. John's Wood, to go on an African safari with Mal Evans.

Able at last to make an extended pilgrimage through the landscapes of his heart's desire, George Harrison cropped his hair as short as John's, and even sprouted a mustache, to avoid detection by reporters and fans. This vain hope collapsed soon after George and Pattie registered at Bombay's Taj Mahal Hotel under a false name; as Ravi Shankar, there to give George a crash course in the sitar, was to recall in his memoirs: "One young Christian page boy happened to recognize them and within twenty-four hours almost all Bombay came to know that George Harrison was there." The party was obliged to flee to the remote tranquility of Kashmir for the balance of George's visit.

Thanks to India, the Beatle who had once seemed merely the most colorless now became quite the most mysterious. Somber George, no longer dismissed as the least animated and witty of the Fab Four, was suddenly the "deepest" of the lot. "It was really after acid," he would recall, once the word could be mentioned in *Melody Maker*, "because acid . . . pushes home to you that you're only little, really, and there's all that infinity out there. . . . Then the Indian music just seemed to have something very spiritual for me, and it became a stepping stone [to] a whole lot of other things."

As always, where one Beatle ventured, the other three followed—and then the multitudes. For those unable to find solace in the antiseptic state of organized Judeo-Christian worship, the Bhagavad Gita–quoting Beatle appeared to show the light, and to symbolize, as much as any figure in the popular culture of those times, an irresistible alternative.

The first to emulate Harrison were his former drinking buddies at the Speakeasy and the Ad-Lib. The Rolling Stones, Donovan, the Animals, the Moody Blues, and the Hollies (still subject to the "progressive" whims of Graham Nash) all incorporated into their music the sitar's timeless resonance—often together with fifth-hand nuggets of "Eastern philosophy." When teenage R&B prodigy Stevie Winwood resigned from the Spencer Davis Group to form Traffic, the latter's first singles—"Paper Sun" and "Hole in My Shoe"—effervesced with multi-tracked sitars. Thousands of Beatle people purchased a copy of "Lord Sitar"'s Raga Rock readings of current hits under the mistaken impression—which Capitol Records did little to redress—that the pseudonymous twangler was none other than Beatle George.

The sitar was occasionally put to imaginative use, by artists such as the Incredible String Band, to lend some "Eastern" atmosphere to a piece of whimsical fantasy. Usually, however, the instrument was exploited in a superficial fashion, simply to "color" a piece with a few subservient notes (e.g., "Lucy in the

Sky with Diamonds"). Yet this was generally preferable to quixotic attempts (such as George's) to create "Indian style" music, set, almost invariably, to heavy-handed regurgitations of Hindu holy writ.

Raga Rock per se was soon to be revealed, and discarded, as just another fad. Nonetheless, Indian music, with its "bent" notes and extended improvisations, did register a lasting influence on the rock scene. The attendant mysticism, of course, would linger and proliferate.

In the autumn of 1966, meanwhile, the other three Beatles responded to George's arrival back at the Abbey Road studios by growing mustaches of their own.

As 1966 faded into 1967, while the rest of the British pop scene flourished to the reverberations of *Revolver,* still nothing more had been heard from the Beatles themselves. In America, where fans were accustomed to a constant glut of new Beatles product, rumors of the group's breakup gathered momentum.

In February, however, the eerie silence was broken at last with the release of "Penny Lane" and "Strawberry Fields Forever," which arrived in a picture sleeve coupling the Beatles' newly mustachioed image with childhood snapshots from their family scrapbooks. In much the same way, themes of both songs nostalgically reflected the Liverpool of the Beatles' youth even as the music itself plunged forward into the unknown.

From the "Strawberry Fields Forever" promotional film (Photo Trends)

As early as 1965, Paul had confided to *NME:* "We have always wanted to write a number about the places in Liverpool where we were born. Places like Penny Lane and Docker's Umbrella have a nice musical sound, but when we strung them all together in a composition [an early version of 'In My Life'] they sounded so contrived we gave up." But by late 1966, the newly confident lyricists were prepared to tackle an entire proposed album loosely based around their Liverpool childhoods (a concept aborted with the premature release of "Penny Lane" and "Strawberry Fields").

These two recordings—surely the ultimate in "double A-sided" singles—presented the two most creative Beatles at the height of their respective powers. Paul's "Penny Lane"— "part fact, part nostalgia . . . blue suburban skies as we re-

member it"—is populated with a gallery of superbly drawn characters, by turns touching, droll, and bawdy (though "finger pie in summer" eluded even the censors of the BBC). The music, at once good-timey and lilting, is enhanced by trumpet obbligatos inspired by Bach's Brandenburg Concerti; McCartney originally hummed these into the ear of George Martin, who instantly committed them to sheet music.

In stark contrast with Paul's tidy imagery, John's visionary trip through "Strawberry Fields" (the name of a gloomy Victorian orphanage around the corner from his childhood home) yields few rhymes and less reason—only clusters of contradictions, and insoluble riddles. The only possible exit from this labyrinth seems to be by way of the Strawberry Fields of childhood memory, where "nothing is real . . . nothing to get hung about." "I wrote it about me," John said later, "and I was having a hard time."

"Strawberry Fields Forever"—unlike, say, "Tomorrow Never Knows"—boasts an achingly poignant melody, and this time round the exotic instruments and weird electronics—the backward tapes and the odd, mumbling voices—add up to something more than a gimmick. Paul's Mellotron, George's Indian table harp, and a hired cello create languid, dreamlike textures, which, in keeping with the lyrics, are abruptly preempted by nightmarishly discordant horns. The music finally fades away—then comes crashing back in the first of the Beatles' false endings. But with a yawn of "Cranberry sauce" the song that engineer Geoff Emerick called "the most exciting track" he'd ever worked on is indeed over.

The finished product represented, among other things, a triumph of sheer chance. The Beatles and George Martin had originally recorded two versions of "Strawberry Fields"—a fast and a slow one, each in a different key. Though satisfied with neither, they discovered that the tape of the fast version, when slowed down to the speed of the other one, fell into precisely the same key—complete with an eerily lethargic vocal that perfectly matched the dazed, stream-of-consciousness lyrics. "Bang," said Paul, "you have the jigsaw puzzle!"

Indeed, "chance music" was to become a hallmark of the Beatles' ongoing recording sessions. "A Day in the Life"— perhaps the most brilliant song in their discography—was patched together from independently written fragments. McCartney's relatively prosaic account of a typical daily routine proved a startlingly apt foil for Lennon's wildly surreal reading of "the news." The two Beatles' contributions were linked by a symphony orchestra, whose forty-one members were instructed, for the first time in their careers, to play whatever their fancy dictated. ("Being for the Benefit of Mr. Kite" was also assembled "like a huge jigsaw," Martin told Tony Palmer.)

"Contemplative, secretive, and exclusive" (in the words of a contemporary British newspaper headline), the 1967-model Beatles hawked "Penny Lane" and "Strawberry Fields" by remote control, appearing on *Top of the Pops* and *Hollywood Palace* in a pair of promotional films as arty and mysterious (if not baffling) as the music to which they were set. One showed the Beatles ambling down Penny Lane, shrouded in dark capes, then riding off on horseback to a banquet in an open field. The other depicted them pouring paint over a broken piano before disappearing into the night. With these tantalizing glimpses (and reports of unprecedentedly complicated and protracted recording sessions running up an unprecedented tab), the world at large was left to await The Word.

Suddenly, in May, via the tiny transistors that had yet to be replaced by stereo FM tuners, the "exclusive previews" came crackling over the airwaves: the noises and phrases so utterly unlike anything previously heard on Top Forty that listeners' mere likes and dislikes were suspended in sheer disbelief.

For the past three years, the imminent arrival of a new Beatles LP had always provoked, among the impatient faithful, daily pilgrimages to the nearest record store. But by May 1967 a schism had developed among those who besieged their local dealers with premature demands for what must surely rank as the most eagerly awaited LP of all time.

There were those—still in the minority—who, after growing their hair in emulation of the Fab Four and in defiance of parents, teachers, and jeering contemporaries, had recently followed (or even preceded) the Pied Pipers from Liverpool into other areas still remote from the consciousness of the nine-to-five workaday world; who, too, had jettisoned suits and ties (and bras and dresses) for bright, unisex fashions or comfortable old rags; who had responded to the mystic strains of "Tomorrow Never Knows" and "Norwegian Wood" and themselves aspired to "turn off the mind, relax, and float downstream"; who had lit a fire, inhaled deeply, and found it good. From Dylan's original impassioned exhortations against war and in favor of universal brotherhood, they had followed the Tambourine Man "through the smokerings of the mind" and "down the foggy ruins of time" as their own revulsion against an absurd, hopeless, and genocidal war—and the U.S. government's conscription of young men to fight and die in it—metamorphosed into a wholesale rejection of everything "straight" society deemed moral, purposeful, or sensible.

In pop (or rock, as it was again beginning to be called) they sensed a language and a medium unique to the under-thirty generation, an art form that defied, confounded, and transcended the drab and stifling institutions of their elders. Like their considerably more remote ancestors before the advent of the printing press, they received their poetry and song, and tidings of the wide world, from bards and troubadours; only now (thanks to the sundry marvels of electronic communications) the spellbinding incantations, and the charismatic personalities behind them, could insinuate themselves instantly into the hearts and minds of millions of listeners, and into the subconsciouses of millions more who weren't as yet specifically listening.

These were the children of the privileged classes, who, around 1967, seemed so suddenly to have coalesced, in opposition to their "materialistic" parent culture, into a distinct counterculture, complete with its own music, fashions, politics, intoxicants, religions, and sexual (im)morality—all summed up in the slogans of an endless parade of placards and buttons: "Make Love, Not War"; "Do Your Own Thing"; Jerry Rubin's "Never Trust Anyone Over Thirty"; and Dr. Leary's "Turn On, Tune In, Drop Out."

But among Beatle people, those who did not yet realize that all was now different still constituted the majority (albeit a rapidly shrinking one). Their sentiments were voiced in the May 1967 issue of *The Beatles Monthly Book,* by a girl awarded a free subscription for the best letter of the month: "I'm very proud [because] we've *never* heard of any of the Beatles being mixed up in all this drugs business. . . . If Paul took drugs, I'd be worried sick for him, but I know he's too sensible."

That very month Paul confided to a reporter from *Life* (who promptly passed the word on to the magazine's millions of readers) not only that he had sampled LSD, but that "it opened my eyes . . . it would mean a whole new world if the politicians would take LSD. There wouldn't be any more war or poverty or

famine." McCartney then revealed to another journalist that LSD had transformed him into "a better, more honest, more tolerant member of society . . . brought closer to God."

Ironically, Paul had been the last Beatle to succumb to LSD. John and George, he later recalled, "said you're never the same after it, that it changes you. And that was the big thing with me—I wasn't sure if I wanted to be changed."

For his *Life* revelations, McCartney incurred the wrath of countless editorial writers, politicians, and the Reverend Billy Graham, who advised Beatlemaniacs that LSD must be "shunned like the plague." *Melody Maker*'s diligent pollster found that 57 percent of Paul's fans thought he was wrong to admit taking LSD; only 2 percent felt inclined to follow his example.

To demonstrate solidarity, veteran acid eaters Lennon and Harrison came out of the closet; Paul's experience also moved George to pen a ditty called "See Yourself" ("It's easier to tell a lie than it is to tell the truth"), which was to go unrecorded for twelve years. But even they were agog when their staid manager chimed in with a similar public confession. Brian Epstein later told *Melody Maker:* "I believe that an awful lot of good has come from hallucinatory drugs, [but] neither Paul nor I advocate the use of LSD by all and sundry."

Epstein soon joined the four Beatles and other public figures in signing a full-page *Times* of London ad headlined: "The law against marijuana is immoral in principle and unworkable in practice." By the time of its July 24 appearance, however, the Beatles had already issued the most powerful advertisement imaginable for mind-expanding drugs—and just about every other facet of the emerging counterculture. All that, of course, comprised but one almost incidental feature of the album whose release marked the first (and probably the last) occasion on which the marketing of a twelve-inch vinyl disc could truly be called a major historical event. For millions of Americans who grew up in the Sixties, the unveiling of "the new Beatles" on June 2, 1967 (a day later than in Britain), remains a moment frozen in memory, comparable only to the first flickering images of JFK's assassination, or of a man on the moon, or perhaps of a midwinter night's dream way back in 1964, of four grinning lads in fluffy bangs and dark suits, striking a simple chord: "Close your eyes and I'll kiss you. . . ."

Three and a half years later, those guitar-toting mop tops had effected an astonishing metamorphosis, re-emerging from the soundproof cocoon of their four-track yellow submarine, transformed, as surely as the caterpillar, into their elaborately contrived alter egos: Sgt. Pepper's Lonely Hearts Club Band.

There they were, resplendent in the most Day-Glo-antiquarian uniforms that the West End's leading costumers could conjure, posing in a garden of unearthly delights specially built for the photograph: John, Ringo, Paul, and George, the four letters of the word L-O-V-E. (If you don't believe me, just check out the back cover, and the configurations of those sly Liverpool fingers, starting, far left, with George's L.)

Over what suspiciously resembles a grave, complete with floral arrangements spelling out the word B-E-A-T-L-E-S, Sgt. Pepper's Lonely Hearts Club Band stand among the artifacts, the bric-a-brac, and the phantoms of their (and our) past lives: Madame Tussaud's Fab Four dummies, marijuana plants, various trophies picked up along the way.

A crowd of people stand and stare: Lewis Carroll and Edgar Allan Poe; Stuart Sutcliffe and Bob Dylan; W. C. Fields and Marilyn Monroe; Karl Marx and Lawrence of Arabia and five of George's favorite gurus. ("We just thought we'd like to put together a lot of people we like and admire," Ringo told *NME*.)

That particular whim had necessitated finding photos of the sixty-odd personalities, securing clearances from those still alive, and enlarging the pictures into life-size cutouts. A harried Brian Epstein, suffering premonitions of his own death, scribbled his last wish: "Brown bags for Sergeant Pepper." But he lived long enough to arrange for EMI's indemnification—to the tune of some $50 million—should Mae West or William S. Burroughs elect to sue.

Once again, the Beatles set new precedents in the business of album packaging. Against the protests of their music publisher (who feared for its song folios' sales), the boys insisted that all their lyrics be printed on the back cover. After *Sgt. Pepper,* this became de rigueur for every artist with "something to say" (except Dylan and the Stones); similarly, "progressive" albums came to be routinely stuffed with souvenir cutouts, posters, and other extraneous goodies, just like *Sgt. Pepper.*

But the most momentous legacy of the Beatles' "magic presentation" (as McCartney called it), beyond even the revolutionary qualities of the individual songs, was the "concept album." *Sgt. Pepper* set the stage for such extended narratives as *Tommy, Arthur,* and *Ziggy Stardust* (to name but three), albums in which individual songs were merely as chapters to a novel. The Beatles' album boasted no such cohesiveness, musically or thematically; indeed, it was the most eclectic collection of sounds any group had yet assembled, a crazy quilt of rock & roll, folk, vaudeville, Indian, classical, and electronic influences (masterfully blended by George Martin on a mere four tracks). The illusion of unity was achieved with one simple stroke of genius: "We're Sgt. Pepper's Lonely Hearts Club Band, we hope you will enjoy the show." "We're figments of our own imagination," they said in effect, "and so are you; welcome to the cabaret."*

The boys compounded the trick by doing away with the bands of silence separating one tune from the next—another unheard-of breach of convention, which the Beatles had wanted to try on *Revolver,* though EMI "wouldn't wear it." Cohesive in form, kaleidoscopic in content, *Sgt. Pepper* simulated the perfect trip: One minute you're "in a boat on a river, with tangerine trees and marmalade skies"; a moment later you're likely to be in a ring at the circus, or in India, or at a geriatric revue. (Even within individual selections, time signatures and musical settings were apt to undergo startling transformations. In the title song, for instance, rhythms of drill-sergeant brittleness suddenly give way to racy syncopation, and blaring rock & roll to a baroque trumpet obbligato. The verses of "Lucy in the Sky with Diamonds" drift languidly in waltz time, then perk up to a 4/4 chorus. "Within You Without You" 's instrumental interlude abandons the 4/4 signature for a truly exotic 5/8.)

Overall, *Sgt. Pepper*'s stature was somehow far more monumental than the sum of its incongruous parts, a few of which ("Fixing a Hole," "Good Morning, Good Morning") were actually somewhat weak by the Beatles' own recent standards. Still more weak links have been exposed only with the passing years; nowadays the blend of Indian soundtrack music and George's Liverpool adenoids may not automatically trigger a state of cosmic bliss, and Paul's attempt at Social Significance, "She's Leaving Home," sounds, for all its lovely counterpoint, increasingly like a maudlin soap opera for spoiled brats.

During 1967's Summer of Love, of course, "Fun is the one thing that money can't buy" struck a million middle-class runaways as poignant and timely. In almost every tune on *Pepper,* one or another facet of the emerging counterculture appeared to crystallize: the mysticism in "Within You Without You," the "generation gap" in "She's Leaving Home," the fantasy in "Lucy in the Sky with Diamonds." And reflected in song after song, or so it seemed, were those ubiquitous Drugs.

Now that drugs (and the Beatles' apparent endorsement of them) had become fodder for exposés in *Life* and *Time,* said substances began to serve as all-purpose objects of conservative paranoia, in much the same way that "the Communists" had been the scapegoats of the McCarthy decade. In the late Sixties, the righteously untainted were wont to attribute every unconventional mannerism or opinion, every paisley or poetic turn of phrase, to such subversive agents as marijuana and LSD. The confirmed "heads" were often equally single-minded, and ignored the possibility that, however much chemicals may have expanded the artistic horizons of groups like the Beatles, the words and music that resulted might still have little direct connection with drugs.

Admirers and detractors alike were guilty of a lack of imagination. Two of John Lennon's most "psychedelic" works, "Lucy in the Sky with Diamonds" and "I Am the Walrus," were largely inspired by his childhood love for the fantasy of Lewis Carroll. Many of the odd juxtapositions and non sequiturs either followed a subconscious "dream logic" common to much great poetry and fantastic literature (including Carroll's) or were simply manifestations of the Beatles' penchant for the ridiculous; they had always been admirers of Peter Sellers and *The Goon Show,* but had only gradually come to channel their absurd sense of humor into their songs. As Paul was to comment about John's yawn of "cranberry sauce" at the end of "Strawberry Fields Forever": "If you don't realize that John's apt to say 'cranberry sauce' when he feels like it, then you hear a funny word there and you think 'Aha!' "

Many people, however, insisted that every incongruous sound, every poetic image, had to "mean" something. Archibald MacLeish's adage "A poem should not mean/but be" not withstanding, the songs of the Beatles were subjected to endless explication, much of it banal beyond belief. Among the many phenomena inaugurated by *Sgt. Pepper* was the ongoing treasure hunt for hidden meanings and "clues" in the Beatles' music. It was only a matter of time before the A. J. Webermans* and Charles Mansons of the world—not to mention the "Paul Is Dead" freaks—began linking all the clues into an overall pattern of surpassing idiocy.

But for the less obsessive, drugs sufficed as a blanket explanation for all the Beatles' post-*Rubber Soul* peculiarities. Though John Lennon (who was usually forthright about such matters) insisted to his dying day that the title "Lucy in the Sky with Diamonds" had been conjured by his son, Julian, for one of the five-year-old's paintings, the acrostic for LSD enabled both Timothy Leary and a rampaging Vice-President Agnew to pigeonhole Lennon's imaginative fantasy as a drug anthem.

Sgt. Pepper's unquestioned masterpiece, "A Day in the Life," was similarly trivialized by the BBC, and provided the first instance in which a Beatles song was banned from the British airwaves. ("I Am the Walrus," with its "obscene" reference to "knickers," would supply the second.) All the surreal

---

Credit is due the Beatles' late road manager, Mal Evans, for coming up with the name "Sgt. Pepper's Lonely Hearts Club Band," and for contributing lyrics both to the title song and to "Fixing a Hole." Though the two songs were credited only to the traditional "Lennon-McCartney," the "gentle giant" was awarded a percentage of the royalties.

Weberman was the self-styled "Dylanologist" who claimed to have cracked the elaborate "code" behind Dylan's imagery.

fragments, the impressionistic evocations of alienation, confusion, and ecstasy, were reduced in the closed minds of the censors to a piece of pro-drug propaganda. ''Blew his mind'' was seized out of context from John's vignette about a car crash, and ''had a smoke'' and ''went into a dream'' from Paul's recollection of smoking cigarettes on the upper deck of a Liverpool bus on his way to school. Robbed of its multiple implications, the line ''I'd love to turn you on'' branded the Beatles as corrupters of youth; even John's gibberish about ''holes in Blackburn, Lancashire'' (originally inspired by a newspaper reference to potholes on the roads in Blackburn) was taken as an allusion to needle marks. The orchestral crescendos, of course, were said to represent the ''rush'' conveyed by certain drugs.

Timothy Leary also pictured *Sgt. Pepper*'s audience as ''millions of kids turned on pharmacologically, listening to stoned-out electronic music designed specifically for the suggestible, psychedelicized nervous system by stoned-out, long-haired minstrels.'' Leary, however, meant that as a supreme compliment, and hailed the Beatles as ''prototypes of a new race of laughing freemen: evolutionary agents sent by God, endowed with a mysterious power to create a new human species.'' He dubbed their new music ''the most powerful brainwashing device our planet has ever known.''

Sgt. Pepper's detractors included stick-in-the-mud Beatlemaniacs who did not wish to turn on and tune in, so they simply tuned out. One of them wrote *NME:* ''For years I have absolutely loved the songs of Lennon and McCartney, but I am sorry to say I find their new LP very disappointing. It is impossible to compare songs like 'And I Love Her' and 'Yesterday' with the way-out rubbish on the *Sgt. Pepper* disc. These songs will be remembered long after *Sgt. Pepper* has been forgotten.''

In at least one respect, *Sgt. Pepper* did fail to measure up to its predecessors. Instead of the usual stampede of cover versions, only Ringo's happy-go-lucky signature tune, ''With a Little Help from My Friends,'' turned up on the A-side of other people's singles. Four years earlier, the Beatles had set a new standard within the record industry by filling their LPs with potential 45s. *Sgt. Pepper,* however, completed the evolution of the rock album into a valid medium quite distinct from the single. Before long, all ''progressive'' artists would think in terms of albums, thus obliging progressive American radio stations to do the same. (Hence the rise of AOR, trade jargon for Album-Oriented Radio.)

In any case, the critical acclaim accorded *Sgt. Pepper* was close to unanimous. (For years, Richard Goldstein's greatest claim to fame was having panned *Sgt. Pepper* in *The New York Times*.) Hundreds of reviews echoed Tom Philips's statement in *The Village Voice* that *Sgt. Pepper* was ''the most ambitious and most successful record album ever issued.'' While such esteemed colleagues as Leonard Bernstein, John Cage, and Aaron Copland extended *Sgt. Pepper* their seal of approval, composer Ned Rorem wrote in the ultra-highbrow *New York Review of Books* that ''She's Leaving Home'' ''is a mazurka equal in melancholy and melodic distinction to any of Chopin's,'' and that ''the Beatles exemplify . . . a new and golden renaissance of song.''

Because *Sgt. Pepper* was the first rock album to be taken so seriously as a work of Art, one of its by-products was the proliferation of serious writing about rock music. Britain, of course, had long boasted the likes of *Melody Maker, Disc,* and *NME;* but until the advent of *Sgt. Pepper* their record reviews had seldom consisted of more than the cursory paragraph. In the United States, the youth-culture explosion that the Beatles'

album both reflected and incited spawned a rash of sophisticated rock journals such as *Rolling Stone*.

Rock fans turned intellectual; intellectuals turned into fans. In some ways this proved a mixed blessing, as Beatles imitators old and new, ranging from Eric Burdon to Vanilla Fudge, waxed insufferably pretentious. Furthermore, most of the established music critics and ''serious'' artists who attempted to illuminate the Beatles' brilliance did so by invoking the ghosts of Schubert or T. S. Eliot, never Buddy Holly; the stamp of legitimacy was given *despite,* rather than because of, the Beatles' own rock & roll heritage—a legacy that even the youthful scribes of the alternative press sometimes tended to belittle or forget. Mazurkas and surrealism were all well and good, but at the root of it all remained a solid rock whose existence owed little to Chopin or even to Magritte.

Be that as it may, the ''underground'' writers at least invested the new music with powers that were literally cosmic. During the Summer of Love, a transplanted Englishman named Charles Royal proclaimed in the newspaper *Countdown:*

> Music is more than an art form today—it . . . is the most powerful single emotional force that man can produce because it begets Love and it stimulates Love. Universal Love. Therefore music is a power for good, stronger than hate, a power that can, if allowed, unite people—people of all colors, tribes, languages, former ideologies, factions, circumstances, and from all physical locations on the earth. . . .
> If the world leaders could be turned on . . . this music—from which springs peace and love—would flow over and heal the nations. . . .
> Music is definitely where it's at today . . . music can and will penetrate the ''establishment barriers'' of fear, materialism, and hate . . . music power stimulates peace.

Around the time that was written, the Beatles were selected to represent Britain on *Our World,* TV's first-ever live-by-satellite worldwide broadcast—a golden opportunity, if ever there was one, to ''unite people of all colors, tribes, languages . . . and from all physical locations on the earth.'' Millions now looked to the Beatles for The Answer—which is exactly what they resolved to provide an audience estimated in the hundreds of millions. ''We had one message for the world—LOVE,'' Paul told *NME.* ''We need more love in the world. It's a period of history that needs *love.*''

Outfitted in Nehru jackets and love beads, the Beatles were shown recording the vocals to ''All You Need Is Love,'' accompanied by strings and horns and multicolored balloons. For the benefit of the non-English-speaking majority, John limited his words to two syllables, readily translatable on multilingual placards. Despite its sly lapses into 7/8 time, the Beatles' ''message'' came across as a stunningly simple one.

Vintage Beatles flippancy was certainly much in evidence, in their gentle mockery of both their current role of counterculture prophets and their earlier music; ''All You Need Is Love,'' framed by orchestral strains of the French National Anthem and the four-hundred-year-old English tune ''Greensleeves,'' incorporated an equally irreverent quote from ''She Loves You.'' Brian Epstein, in his last *Melody Maker* interview, called it ''the best thing they've ever done,'' truly ''an inspired song because they wrote it for a worldwide program and they really wanted to give the world a message. It could hardly have been a better message.''

The single's B-side, ''Baby You're a Rich Man''—another Lennon confection, whose lyrics took the form of a cryptic self-interview—also received a live performance of sorts, when

"Just a smile would lighten everything. . . ." (*Transworld Features Syndicate/Henry Grossman*)

George Harrison turned up at the hippie mecca of San Francisco's Haight-Ashbury. Strumming a guitar, followed past the head shops and free clinics by an adoring train of flower children, panhandlers, and acid casualties (not to mention reporters), the Pied Piper from Liverpool surveyed the scene through his purple heart-shaped sunglasses and found it wanting. "A hippie," George subsequently declared, "is supposed to be someone who becomes aware; you're hip if you know what's going on. But if you're really hip you don't get involved with LSD and things like that. It can help you to go from A to B, but when you get to B, you see C. And you see that to get really high, you have to go at it straight. There are special ways of getting high without drugs—with yoga, meditation, and all those things."

George had long searched for a charismatic guru who might reveal and personify India's mystic secrets in much the same way Ravi Shankar had embodied that country's music. One candidate had kept the Beatle up all night, climbing a hill in Cornwall, waiting for the revelations that never quite came. Through his wife Pattie, Harrison was introduced to the Maharishi Mahesh Yogi, whose Spiritual Regeneration Movement had previously attracted most of its recruits via ads in the London Underground—the subway, that is.

The tiny, giggling monk actually held a physics degree from an Indian university; early on, young Mahesh had sensed that his life's mission was to give a "scientific" grounding to Indian mysticism, and to package "transcendental" meditation (TM) in a manner palatable to Westerners. After studying the Sanskrit scriptures with the late Guru Dev (who was to be invoked in Lennon's "Across the Universe"), he adopted the title Maharishi (meaning saint or seer) and in 1959 set up shop in the U.K.

"He didn't know what the Beatles were," reported Ringo. "He was one of the few people in the world." But the Beatles were charmed by the Maharishi and his commonsensical parables, and above all by his remarkably effortless nonsectarian technique for spiritual advancement. As Harrison was to explain it on *The David Frost Show,* "each person's life pulsates in a certain rhythm, so they give you a word or sound known as a mantra, which pulsates with that rhythm." Repeated silently, "the mantra becomes more subtle and more subtle, until finally you've lost even the mantra, and then you find yourself at that level of pure consciousness."

To reap the transcendental benefits, one needed only enact this twenty-minute procedure twice daily. The Maharishi didn't request his adherents to forgo alcohol, tobacco, or fornication, or to commit themselves to any other forms of asceticism or spiritual dogma. On the contrary, they were advised that TM would *further* their material success, by enabling everyone— musicians, businessmen, soldiers, Christians—to apply a heightened sensibility to their chosen pursuits. Drugs, to be sure, were discouraged, on the practical grounds that they interfered with the clarity of mind that meditation required; but who needed drugs anyway when high on life?

"Instant Karma" indeed—back in the Fifties, the Maharishi could hardly have dreamed how well his product would fill the demand among affluent young Westerners for an "Eastern" panacea. Such illustrious meditators as Donovan, the Beach Boys, and members of the Rolling Stones and the Doors were to be joined in good time by the likes of General Franklin Davis, Apollo 11 astronaut Michael Collins, and conservative Los Angeles Mayor Sam Yorty. These last were probably less interested in a painless route to spiritual enlightenment than in TM's much-touted relief from alcoholism, high blood pressure, and stress. But, as Maharishi biographer Martin Ebon was to note in discussing TM's infiltration into the mainstream of Western life, the Beatles connection "was extremely important, for it permanently established the Maharishi in the public eye."

Only days after their first encounter, the scraggly-bearded guru was enshrined in the media as the latest (and least likely) in a long line of Fifth Beatles. The Maharishi's new disciples agreed to attend a TM conference in Bangor, Wales, over August's Bank Holiday weekend. Typically, the expedition was turned into a media carnival, with mobs of reporters, cameramen, and fans (and policemen to keep them in line) showing up to see the Beatles and Mick Jagger off at Euston Station.

It was in Bangor, on August 27, that the Beatles were jolted out of their transcendental haze by word that Brian Epstein, the most pre-eminent of all Fifth Beatles, had been found dead in his London townhouse. Dazed and confused, they turned to the Maharishi for words of reassurance, which George duly echoed to reporters: "There is no such thing as death. It is a comfort to us all to know he is okay." John, however, later recalled: "I was scared. I thought, we've had it."

In some respects, the Beatles had outgrown their thirty-one-year-old manager, whose major functions had been to package their original image and to arrange their concert tours. The imminent expiration of their contract gnawed at Epstein almost as much as his tormented personal life, which had driven him to increasing dependence on drink and the pills that ultimately killed him. But had Epstein lived to continue as their manager, the Beatles might well have been steered away from the series of looming mantraps that were to hasten the group's demise.

They didn't, initially, attempt to find a new manager. "No one could possibly replace Brian," said McCartney, who took it upon himself to hold the band together, keep an eye on their finances, and guide their career. Paul, Lennon remembered, "made an attempt to carry on as if Brian hadn't died by saying, 'Now, now, boys, we're going to make a record.' And that's when we made *Magical Mystery Tour*."

To fans and Beatles alike (not to mention Brian Epstein and Walter Shenson), Beatles Movie Number Three had long been well overdue. Shortly after the 1965 release of *Help!*, plans for a Western called *A Talent for Loving* had been announced, then canceled when the Beatles grew uncomfortable with the prospect of straight dramatic roles. In 1966, the British music press trumpeted the Beatles' choice of a script by Owen Halder (famous for *A Funny Thing Happened on the Way to the Forum*). According to *NME*, *Shades of a Personality* would "focus on one member of the group (yet to be chosen) who will supposedly have a split personality with four different sides to his character. Beside his real self he will imagine himself in turn as three other people—the three other Beatles!"

In January 1967, Joe Orton (whose play *Loot* was much admired by Paul) was commissioned to write a new screenplay along these lines. But the young playwright took little heed of Shenson's recommendation that the Beatles "shouldn't be made to do anything in the film that would reflect badly on them, [as] the kids will all imitate whatever the boys do." In *Up Against It*, Orton cast the Beatles as revolutionary anarchists who, in his own words, "have been caught *in flagrante*, become involved in dubious political activity, dressed as women, committed murder, been put in prison, and committed adultery." The Beatles' capers were even to include the assassination of Britain's first woman Prime Minister. In one of the screenplay's few concessions to the original "shades of a personality" concept, *Up Against It* climaxed with the consummation of the heroine's marriage to all four Beatles: "The young men kiss her. There is a struggle. Miss Drumgoogle squeals with delight and disappears under the coverlet with her husbands. The End." (De-

spite Epstein's rejection of his script, Joe Orton remained a Beatles fan to the end; "A Day in the Life" was selected as his funeral music after he was bludgeoned to death by his boyfriend, some two weeks before Epstein's own demise.)

By this time, however, *NME* had passed word that shooting for *Shades of a Personality* was to commence shortly in Spain, with Michelangelo Antonioni directing, and that Lennon was to be cast as "the man himself, while the three other Beatles will portray each of the faces of his split personality." But the Beatles ultimately left the quadrophenic field to Pete Townshend and The Who, and *Disc*'s speculation that John, Paul, George, and Ringo were to take the parts of (respectively) Gollum, Frodo, Gandalf, and Sam in a film based on Tolkien's *The Lord of the Rings*, also proved premature.

With Epstein out of the picture, the Beatles chose instead to pursue the whim of writing and directing their own hour-long TV film, whose "plot" was summed up thus in a Beatles press release: "Away in the sky, beyond the clouds, live four or five musicians. By casting Wonderful Spells they turn the Most Ordinary Coach Trip into a Magical Mystery Tour. . . ."

Largely inspired by the 1965 adventures of Ken Kesey's roving Merry Pranksters, the Mystery Tour was primarily Paul's trip. "In England," he later told *Rolling Stone*, "they have these things called Mystery tours . . . you pay so much and you don't know where you're going. So the idea was to have this little thing advertised in the shop windows somewhere called Magical Mystery Tours. Someone goes in and buys a ticket and rather than just being the kind of normal publicity hype . . . it was actually a real magical trip. I did a few little sketches myself and [John and George] thought up a couple of little things. . . . Then we hired a coach and picked actors out of an actor's directory and just got them all along with the coach, and said, 'Okay, act.' An off-the-cuff kind of thing." And so the Beatles went careening through the English countryside with their busload of oddballs, filming whatever happened to happen.

The intent was to create a 1967-style substitute for concert tours, what Lennon tagged "a film vehicle to go with the new music," duplicating on celluloid all the fantasy and weirdness of *Sgt. Pepper's Lonely Hearts Club Band*. The actual result was a colorful home movie full of elementary gimmicks such as slow and fast motion, double exposures, and dizzy rooms in and out of close-up. As Paul readily admitted, "we didn't know anything about making films." But this time the Beatles' innocence proved to be less than a virtue.

After two months of arduous editing ("We've been working regularly, just like people!" McCartney marveled in *NME*. "We start at eleven every morning . . . finish about seven") the Beatles and fifteen million other Britons switched on their tellies the night after Christmas, waiting for the latest Fab brainwave to work its magic. The reaction of both the critics and the general public was as brutal as it was unexpected. Almost every review was liberally spiked with such words as "chaotic," "appalling," and "blatant rubbish." "It's colossal, the conceit of the Beatles," wrote the *Daily Mail* critic. "The whole boring saga confirmed a suspicion of mine that the Beatles are four rather pleasant young men who have made so much money they can afford to be contemptuous of the public." For the first time, it seemed, the Beatles had made fools of themselves.

The accompanying music proved, unsurprisingly, far more magical and mysterious than the film itself, with John's "Walrus" and Paul's "Fool on the Hill" ranking with the Beatles' most powerful creations. By and large, the *Mystery Tour* recordings represented the last of the group's psychedelic concoc-

Neighborhood businesses are scandalized when Apple brings a splash of cosmic color to the drab Baker Street landscape. (Photo Trends)

tions, wherein the Beatles and Mr. Martin threw into the mix everything save the proverbial kitchen sink.

The *Magical Mystery Tour* score appeared in Britain on an innovative double EP; in America the six tracks (and the accompanying picture book) were blown up to album size with the addition of the Beatles' 1967 singles on side two.* The film itself was never widely shown in the U.S. until the following decade, when it became a popular midnight screening and a fan convention staple.

The Beatles were to perpetrate one more psychedelic fiasco before the magic year 1967 had run its course: their short-lived Apple Boutique. But the name Apple, inspired by a Magritte painting in Paul's living room, was soon to reattach itself to another Beatles enterprise—the most visionary, and disastrous, of them all.

In February 1968 the Beatles departed for the Himalayas, where they planned to spend the next three months quietly studying with the Maharishi at his Rishikesh retreat. They left behind four new songs, two of which were to be issued as a single in their absence. John's "Across the Universe," originally eyed for the A-side, was a lyrical evocation of TM. But the Beatles' rendition failed, in Lennon's view, to do justice to the exquisite lyrics; so the original version was virtually thrown away, onto a British charity LP aiding the World Wildlife Fund.**

The honors then went to Paul's "Lady Madonna," the first Beatles track in years to explore their American rock & roll roots. "It sounds like Elvis, doesn't it?" said Ringo. "No, it doesn't sound like Elvis—it *is* Elvis."

For the first time in the Beatles' career, nostalgia seemed to carry the day; they took their collarless jackets out of mothballs for the promotional pictures, and the ads read:

anewrockandrollcombo
directfromhamburgwith
themerseybeatnow
onemiladymadonna.

---

* *Technically, this was an "electronically rechanelled" disaster area, thanks to Capitol's negligence in tracking down original stereo masters.*
** *It remained unissued in the U.S. until the 1980 release of the* Rarities *album.*

This snappy tune was loosely based on a number ("Bad Penny Blues") by an early George Martin client named Humphrey Littleton. The words, however, were as cryptic as ever. Many Beatleologists explained the riddle of how Lady Madonna managed "to make ends meet" by invoking the world's oldest profession; her "johns," they insisted, were identified by the days of their appointments (e.g., "Friday night arrives without a suitcase").

Far removed from Elvis or "the Mersey beat," the Harrisong on the B-side concerned itself with the more transcendental preoccupations of Beatles '68. "The Inner Light" 's instrumentals had been prerecorded on location in Bombay; Paul, however, advised fans to "forget the Indian music and listen to the melody . . . it's really lovely." So were the words—though these, it transpired, had been "borrowed" (without credit) from a poem by Tao, the Chinese philosopher. (Tao at least wasn't about to sue; but thirteen years later Holy George's peccadillos would set him back $587,000—for the alleged plagiarism from the Chiffons' "He's So Fine" in his first, and biggest, solo hit, "My Sweet Lord.")

None of the Beatles lasted the full course with the Maharishi, though John and George came close. When the two stalwarts did leave, the official explanation was that they had elected to avoid the cameras of an American documentary film crew. In fact, Beatles court jester "Magic Alex" Mardas, sensing Lennon was growing bored, had decided to liven things up with rumors about the Maharishi's designs on fellow meditator Mia Farrow. John, infuriated by the alleged hypocrisy of the supposedly celibate monk, announced his departure, subsequently compounding his revenge by writing a song called "Maharishi" ("You made a fool of everyone . . ."). (Following a name and sex change, the guru was to be immortalized as "Sexy Sadie.")

TM, stripped of His Holiness's "scientific" graphs and grandiose World Plans, was actually a good product, a simple and effective means of relaxation and self-awareness. But John, as he admitted, "always expected too much" (especially from his "substitute daddies"), only to feel later that he'd been taken for a ride. Lennon was henceforth to dismiss TM as "colored water" and restlessly continue to shop around in the

---

The Harrisons and John and Yoko at "Magic" Alex Mardas's wedding (Photo Trends/Stefan Tyszko)

consciousness-raising marketplace. Harrison, by contrast, saw the Maharishi episode as merely the prelude to an involvement with more exacting forms of Indian mysticism (notably the Radha Krishna Temple). The trip to Rishikesh proved, both literally and figuratively, to be the last that the four Beatles ever took together.

Meanwhile, back in London, McCartney (who was to outgrow all interest in mystical mumbo jumbo or hurdy gurdy men of any description) had got a new Apple rolling. Readers of *NME* received their first inkling of the latest Beatles brainwave from a series of cryptic ads on the back page, in which the single word "Apple" was attached to photos of such subjects as a wild-eyed gentleman in antique military regalia, or a naked baby sprawled on the grass, surrounded by apples. "Paul picks them all out at the Keystone picture agency," said Ringo. "He just went down there and browsed through the old photos they had."

Following Lennon's return, he and McCartney flew to New York to shed further light on their new Apple Corps ("That's a

George blisses out with the Radha Krishna Temple (Photo Trends/ *Guru Das*)

pun," said Paul helpfully) at a mid-river press conference on a Chinese junk. Having long boasted the wealth and influence of kings, the Beatles now intended to channel this immense power into a multimillion-dollar, multimedia corporate Pepperland, to be run according to the principles of what McCartney called "Western Communism," free from those interfering "men in suits." The Beatles' own music was henceforth to appear on Apple Records, by arrangement with EMI and Capitol, who were to handle the distribution. The Beatles also envisaged a network of six satellite companies: Apple Electronics, Apple Publishing, Apple Films, Apple Tailoring, Apple Merchandising, and an Apple Foundation for the Arts.

"*We* always had to go to the big man on our knees," said McCartney, "touch our forelocks, and say: 'Please, can we do so and so?' And most of those companies are so big, and so out of touch with people like us who just want to sing and make films, that everybody has a bad time. We're just trying to set up a good organization, not some great fat institution that doesn't care. If you come to me and say, 'I've had such-and-such a

dream,' I will say: 'Here's so much money. Go away and do it.' "

For good measure, Paul even placed a full-page want ad in the British pop weeklies. Printed below a photo of a young musician were the words: "THIS MAN HAS TALENT. One day he sang his songs to a tape recorder, and, remembering to enclose a picture of himself, sent the tape to Apple Music, 94 Baker St., London W.1. If you were thinking of doing the same thing yourself, do it now! This man now owns a Bentley!"

To the surprise of nobody—except, it seems, the Beatles—the new company was hit by an avalanche of tapes, manuscripts, and outlandish proposals, many delivered in person. "All the lepers in Britain and America came to see us," said Lennon. "Our lives were getting insane!"

As active talent scouts and producers, however, Paul and George acquitted themselves admirably. "It's ridiculous," Paul told *NME,* "that people with talent like Dave Mason and Denny Laine have to struggle to get their work accepted. What we want to do is to try and provide a complete service, so eventually they won't have to go round knocking on doors. . . . We'll have some of the best writers and musicians under one roof." Long after the business side of Apple turned sour, McCartney would defend the records in *Rolling Stone:* "Apple was together in a lot of ways. . . . It was right for James Taylor to make his first record there. . . . Billy Preston, Badfinger, Mary Hopkin, all the people we did take on, had very good records. George, even with the Radha Krishna Temple, I think that's great stuff. I don't think you can fault any of the artistic decisions."

Meanwhile, the Hellenic ingenuity of Magic Alex was given the run of Apple Electronics—and a fortune to squander on such inventions as an apple-shaped transistor radio and (John's favorite) a "nothing box" guaranteed to do absolutely nothing for five years.

Indeed—despite those mounds of unsolicited novels, films, and demos left to gather dust—Apple Corps generally lived up to the Spirit of '67 until the chill winter of '69. Few business decisions were made without consulting the *I Ching* or the astrologer on Apple's payroll. Everyone's favorite intoxicants were made freely available throughout business hours; assorted bands of hippies, Hell's Angels, and nudists gravitated toward the Apple headquarters on swanky Savile Row and quite literally made themselves at home. Nobody—least of all a Beatle—was about to be such a stick-in-the-mud as to ask them to leave.

Yet to all outward appearances Apple Records could scarcely have got off to a more brilliant start. The label (featuring a whole green apple on the A-side, a sliced apple on the B) was launched in August 1968 with four singles: The Beatles' "Hey Jude"/ "Revolution"; former Undertaker Jackie Lomax's "Sour Milk Sea," written and produced by George; the Van Dyke Mills brass band's "Thingumybob," composed and produced by Paul; and McCartney discovery Mary Hopkin singing "Those Were the Days," a song Paul had picked as a hit back in 1964. And he was right: the seventeen-year-old Miss Hopkin's rendition was to top the charts on both sides of the Atlantic—once "Hey Jude" had finally relinquished its grip on the Number One slot.

Apart from being Apple's debut release, "Hey Jude" was something of an historical landmark in other respects. To the dismay of time-conscious AM radio jocks, the song clocked in at an unprecedented 7:11. But the number proved to be lucky indeed; "Hey Jude" was so good that stations had no choice but to air it extensively. The single was to set two records: as the longest Number One song up to that time, and, five million copies later, as the Beatles' biggest-selling American hit.

The song starts off a miracle of simplicity, just Paul at the piano. The chords remain utterly basic throughout, but scores of other instruments—including a forty-piece symphony orchestra—are gradually added by the time the record explodes into its seemingly endless chanted fadeout.

The tune began life as "Hey Jules," Paul's consolation prize for five-year-old Julian Lennon, whose parents' marriage (as the world was soon to note) was on the rocks. "He's a nice kid, Julian. And I was going out there in me car just vaguely singing this song, and it was like, 'Hey Jules . . . don't make it bad/ take a sad song . . . .' And then I just thought a better name was Jude."

Paul's relationship with Jane Asher had disintegrated as well, and "Hey Jude," unlike most McCartney songs, was infused with highly charged and personal emotions. This magnificent anthem represented both a catharsis for all the pain being suffered within the Beatles' entourage and a hopeful invocation of a new and better beginning.

The sliced-apple side of the record was also noteworthy, both as a hit in its own right and as the first in a long series of Lennon broadsides, explicitly reflecting events in his own life and in the world around him. Rather than create artifacts for the ages, John was increasingly determined to write of, and for, the moment.

To the likes of the radical *Berkeley Barb,* the apparent moderation of John's "Revolution" sounded "like the hawk plank adopted this week in the Chicago convention of the Democratic Death Party." According to Lennon, "the idea was don't aggravate the pig by waving the red flag in his face. You know, I really thought that love would save us all. There were two versions of that song, but the underground left only picked up on the one that said, 'Count me out.' The version on the LP says 'Count me in' too; I put both in because I wasn't sure. On the single I said: 'When you talk about destruction, you can count me out.' I didn't want to get killed."

The other major Beatles event that summer of 1968 was the July 17 London premiere of the feature-length, animated *Yellow Submarine.* King Features' desire to build upon the previous year's successful Beatles kiddie cartoon TV series neatly dovetailed with the group's contractual obligations to United Artists with regard to Beatles Movie Number Three. *Yellow Submarine* is a classic example of an existing myth generating new episodes, even in the absence of any input from the gods themselves. Apart from a perfunctory appearance at the film's end, and the contribution of four *Magical Mystery Tour*–era rejects to the musical score, the flesh-and-blood Beatles had little part in the making of their third celluloid hit; even their voices were impersonated by actors.

The brilliantly imaginative psychedelic cartoon nonetheless captured the spirit of the Beatles' recent musical fantasies far more successfully than *Mystery Tour* had. In its odd way, *Yellow Submarine* also caught the spirit of the Beatles' post-*Pepper* public image in much the same manner that *A Hard Day's Night* had mirrored and built upon people's fantasies of the 1964-model Fab Four. In *Yellow Submarine* John and Ringo were still cast as the tart-tongued "intellectual" and the lovable schlemiel; Paul and George, however, had acquired new identities as, respectively, flower-twirling dandy and spaced-out mystic.

Producer Al Brodax (whose visions of an animated *Lord of the Rings* had been dashed by a horrified J. R. R. Tolkien)

claimed that the genesis of his Beatles film had been the 3:00 A.M. phone query from John Lennon: "Wouldn't it be great if Ringo was followed down the street by a yellow submarine?" This led to a short story by New York psychotherapist Lee Minoff, later turned into a screenplay with a little help from Yale classics professor and future *Love Story* author Erich Segal. "We derived a lot from the *Sgt. Pepper* album," said Brodax. "We took the word 'pepper,' which is positive and spicy, and created a place called Pepperland which is full of color and music. But in the hills around live Blue Meanies. . . ."

Yellow Submarine's visual feast was assembled from five *million* separate sketches supervised by the German poster artist Heinz Edelmann. These ran the gamut, as *The Leader* noted, of "Art Nouveau and psychedelic, op and pop, Dada and surrealist, Hieronymus Bosch and just plain bosh." *Yellow Submarine* became a cult favorite among acid heads, yet proved equally popular with young children and established film critics. Like Walt Disney's classic *Fantasia,* it worked its most potent magic when set to music; indeed, *Yellow Submarine*'s only major flaw is the heavy-handed triteness of the screenplay itself. The twelve Beatles numbers alone would make a superb album-length video disc.

Yellow Submarine is also fondly remembered by latter-day Beatles collectors for spawning the second tidal wave of Beatles merchandise. Twenty-two companies were licensed to produce over seventy-five novelties ranging from stationery, lunch boxes, and key chains to calendars, inflatable swim toys, masquerade costumes, and, best of all, a yellow submarine Corgi Toy from which tiny Beatles emerge at the flick of a button. These items updated the original trinkets' Fab Four mop top and beetle motifs with trendy late-Sixties psychedelia, as exemplified by the film itself. Perhaps things hadn't changed so much after all; as film critic Pauline Kael drily noted: "Attacks on the consumer society become products to be consumed."

But the main thrust of Beatles news reports that July 17 concerned neither the actual film being premiered at the London Pavilion nor the crowd of Beatlemaniacs jamming Piccadilly Circus for the very last time. Coupled with the absence of Jane Asher (or anyone else) on Paul McCartney's arm, the presence of Yoko Ono on John Lennon's made for far more riveting copy.

For several weeks now, British newspapers had hinted that John's "yen these days is far more Eastern than India." John and Yoko had actually met in late 1966, at the Indica Art Gallery, run by Marianne Faithfull's ex-husband, John Dunbar. To the BBC, on December 6, 1980, Lennon recalled:

[Dunbar] sent me this pamphlet . . . about this Japanese girl from New York who was going to be in a bag, doing this Event or Happening. I thought, Hmm—you know, sex. So I went. . . .

There was, like, a few nails on a stand, and an apple . . . Found Objects that had been painted white, with little messages on them. . . . A hundred pounds for a bag of nails? Are you kidding? . . . Dunbar's trying to hustle a bit, because he thinks the Millionaire Beatle's coming to buy. So he introduces me to this strange-looking Japanese woman. . . .

I said, "Where's the sort of happening, the event?" She gives me a little card. And it just says "Breathe" on it. So I said [*breathes heavily*] "You mean, like that?" She says, "Yeah, that's it." So I'm looking for action, and see this thing called Hammer and Nail, and it's a board with a chain and a hammer hanging on it, and a bunch of nails at the bottom. I said, "Well, can I hammer a nail in?" She says . . . "You can hammer one in for five shillings." I said . . . "I'll give you an imaginary five shillings and hammer an imaginary nail in." . . .

That's when we fell . . . but it was eighteen months to two years before we really got together . . . we were both very shy.

Nonetheless, Dunbar and Ono realized their original goal; the millionaire Beatle readily agreed to finance further exhibits by the intriguing conceptual artist. "Then I went to India with the Maharoonie and we were corresponding. The letters were still formal, but they had a little side to them," Lennon remembered in *Rolling Stone*.

"When I got home from India we were talking to each other on the phone. I called her over, it was the middle of the night and Cyn was away, and I thought, well now's the time if I'm ever going to get to know her any more." John was to describe their first evening together in his very last interview (for RKO Radio Network):

I used to have a place . . . where I made kind of freaky music at home. . . . I didn't know what to do with her so I said, 'You wanna go upstairs and play with the tapes?' . . .

I was running around pushing buttons and playing the Mellotron, and she started into her Yoko Ono stuff, which you now hear on B-52's and Lene Lovich. . . . We made a tape all night and in the morning we made love as the sun came up.

"Being artists, when we get into something, we get into it!"—John Lennon (Photo Trends/Tom Blau)

Overnight, everything in John Lennon's world had changed.

Though he may not have consciously realized it, John's two key relationships—his marriage to Cynthia and his artistic partnership with Paul—had long grown stale, contributing to the very sense of boredom and passivity that had kept him from breaking loose from his rut. In the Japanese banker's daughter, seven years his senior, John finally found someone else on his own peculiar wavelength; "Yoko," he declared, "is me in drag!"

This discovery was to doom more than the Lennons' marriage; as McCartney would recall, with his usual diplomatic understatement: "He wanted a very strong, intimate life with her; at the same time, we'd always reserved the intimacy for the group." As Yoko noted in *Melody Maker*, "We're always together, like twenty-four hours a day." To *NME* John would reveal his only "regret": "That Yoko wasn't my child. I don't like the idea of her being born in someone else's womb. That's one of my great jealousies."

The couple lost little time in launching their artistic collabora-

tion with a series of "happenings." There was a "living art sculpture" consisting of two acorns planted "for peace" outside Coventry Cathedral. (After these were dug up by souvenir hunters, a substitute pair of acorns had to be accorded round-the-clock protection by security guards.) There was a ritual immolation of a hundred plastic dolls, burned on the Kings Road after John and Yoko were told of the effects of American napalm in Vietnam. There was a Yoko film, featuring ninety straight minutes of John's smile, and there was John's own Yoko-influenced exhibit of White Art at the Indica Gallery, whose highlights included hundreds of white balloons released into the London skies as the artist, dressed all in white, intoned the words: "I declare these balloons high."

Most notorious of all, there was the album—*Two Virgins: Unfinished Music No. 1*—that the couple had made during their first intimate evening together. The actual contents (consisting mostly of random squawks both from the inimitable Yoko and from the awakening birds outside John's window) had been "composed" and recorded in the amount of time required for one listen (not that very many fans managed to sit through the whole LP). The cover, however, left nothing to the imagination—at a time when mere nudity was still likely to arouse the heavy hand of British and American antivice laws. In *NME* John reported that "Paul gave me long lectures and said, 'Is there really any need for this?' "

By the time it was finally distributed in brown paper wrappers by the independent Track (U.K.) and Tetragrammaton (U.S.) labels, the album had generated countless lurid headlines and a novelty single, "John You Went Too Far This Time," by a new artist called "Rainbo" (later to become famous as Sissy Spacek). In one of several such incidents, thirty thousand copies were seized by New Jersey police. And, hardly coincidentally, on October 18 Lennon's London digs received an unexpected visit from one Detective Sergeant Pilcher, armed with a search warrant, six police officers, and a cannabis-sniffing dog.

As would be the case in a subsequent raid on the Harrisons' psychedelic bungalow, Pilcher found what he was looking for; indeed, both John and George were to claim he brought it with him. But to spare his newly pregnant lover the anguish of a protracted court battle, Lennon agreed to plead guilty and pay the £171 fine. The major effects of his conviction, however, were a radical tilt in Lennon's views of "Revolution" and the subsequent harassment of American immigration authorities anxious for a pretext to deny him the right to settle in New York. And five weeks after the arrest, Yoko lost her baby anyway.

Many in the Beatles' circle felt that John's recent escapades with his "Japanese mistress" had cost the Beatles their immunity from an Establishment backlash. Nonetheless, the "nude picture" provided an apt symbol for John's "awakening." Following his avowed abandonment of LSD and the role of "the dreamweaver," Lennon's work turned explicitly autobiographical, a direct and conscious outlet for his own long-suppressed feelings. Quite unlike anyone else in his lofty position, either before or since, John Lennon resolved to rip away all the masks of his celebrity, and use his powers as a media hero to expose to countless rapt voyeurs both the man and the machinery behind the glittering facade of his stardom. In tandem with his interviews and media adventures, John's new songs were to mirror his soul like a one-way glass, giving the world an unprecedentedly intimate and revealing picture of one of its foremost stars.

Sometimes this only fostered laziness and sheer self-indulgence, and even John's diehard admirers would often feel embarrassed by the stupidity, naivete, and arrogance of some of his pronouncements and "happenings." Many fans were uncomfortable with the brutal honesty by which John strove to dismantle their fondest illusions; but millions more admired him for it, and considered him more of a hero than ever.

Paul McCartney, meanwhile, had replaced Jane Asher with a New York go-getter of his own, the lovely Linda Eastman, who, like Yoko before her, had attended Sarah Lawrence College. Her father, born Lee Epstein, was a prominent music-business lawyer and art collector; Linda, however, had temporarily abandoned her Park Avenue and Scarsdale roots to become a backstage habitué at the Fillmore East. Her career as a photographer furthered her intimate familiarity with numerous rock icons (if not the other way around). Following her selection as one of only fourteen photographers invited to the Beatles' *Sgt. Pepper* unveiling, Linda caught Paul's roving eye during a Georgie Fame show at the Bag of Nails Club. The acquaintance was renewed during Lennon and McCartney's Apple-raising visit to New York, and Paul invited Linda and her daughter, Heather, to stay with him in England. "And then, I suppose because Yoko was doing it with John, when I met up with Linda I was doing it too."

Like John-and-Yoko, Paul-and-Linda now aspired to a "strong, intimate life" outside the Beatles. But if Yoko, as John claimed, "brought the bananas part of me out of the closet," Linda's influence was to reinforce Paul's growing affinity for the time-tested values of the bourgeoisie.

Small wonder, then, that the making of *The Beatles*—the group's first double album—was blighted by conflicting loyalties and personality clashes. "That was *the* big tension album," Paul said long afterward. "Never before had we recorded with, like, beds in the studio."

Stretched over six months, the recording sessions were turned into an endurance test by Lennon and McCartney's insistence on recording virtually all of the thirty songs they had written during and after their stay in India. (One reason was their eagerness to fulfill contractual obligations as quickly as possible, so they might strike a better deal with EMI.) But their disinclination to record more than a handful of Harrison's fifteen offerings aroused considerable disgruntlement in the third quarter of the group. It was Ringo, however, who actually walked out at one point, despite the inclusion of his first self-composition, "Don't Pass Me By."

But to an outside world still blissfully ignorant of these tensions, the Beatles' new music seemed to signify retrenchment and consolidation rather than disintegration. Few traces remained of the electronic experimentation, or of the trumpet flourishes, string octets, and Eastern instruments (all usually played by outside musicians) that had dominated the last few Beatles albums. The emphasis was back on the Beatles' own voices, guitars, and drums. The Beatles, John insisted in *Rolling Stone,* were "coming out of a shell in a new way, kind of saying: remember what it was like to play." "I'm back to being a rocker now—for a bit, at least!" George told *NME.*

In this respect the Beatles were hardly operating in a vacuum. Early in 1968, Bob Dylan had emerged from his long convalescence to confound the competition; instead of challenging Sgt. Pepper's Band and Their Satanic Majesties at their own game, Dylan's *John Wesley Harding* cleared the air with straightforward balladry and an all-acoustic sound. In the meantime, the formerly discredited rock & roll of the 1950s had been resurrected as nostalgia; and with the advent of the British Blues

Boom, blues guitar virtuosos had grown as ubiquitous as last year's magic mushrooms.

The Beatles' album cover could hardly have been more stark and simple. Doubtless inspired by John's own conceptual White Art, the sheer dazzling whiteness was broken only by the embossed words "The Beatles" and by the numbers, separately stamped after each copy came off the press, that qualified the so-called "White Album" as the most *un*limited numbered edition in history.

The contents, however, were "simple" only by comparison with *Revolver* or *Sgt. Pepper*. The variety of styles represented in this encyclopedic compilation moved *Rolling Stone* boss Jann Wenner to proclaim: "*The Beatles* is the history and synthesis of Western music."

It certainly wasn't a step back to the sound of *Help!* or *A Hard Day's Night,* let alone the Cavern Club. Words, music, performance, and production all evinced a sophistication unheard of in pre–*Rubber Soul* days. But perhaps the main difference between then and now was that *The Beatles,* its title notwithstanding, was scarcely a group effort. Lennon remembered it as "just me and a backing group, Paul and a backing group. . . ." (In many instances a single Beatle—usually Paul—simply overdubbed all the instruments himself.) Though few remarked it at the time, the White Album boasted great Lennon songs, McCartney songs, and Harrisongs—but no Beatles songs.

If John and Paul had grown up and apart, the mere presence of the other continued to bring out the best in each. Meanwhile, George Harrison's songwriting talents had blossomed impressively to produce such mainstream rock classics as "While My Guitar Gently Weeps" (featuring guest guitarist Eric Clapton).

In the absence of real Beatle music, *The Beatles* was dominated by affectionate (McCartney) pastiches and scathing (Lennon) satires of virtually every other major genre and artist in popular music. Paul's cheekier concoctions ranged from a miniature cowboy melodrama ("Rocky Raccoon") and a West Indian singalong ("Obladi-Oblada") to a scratchy old 78 ("Honey Pie"). "My dad," he told *NME,* "always played fruity old songs like this. . . . I would like to have been a 1920s songwriter because I like that top-hat-and-tails thing." Best of all was "Back in the U.S.S.R." (originally conceived as "I'm Backing the U.K."), which gave a wickedly subversive twist to the patriotic Americana of Chuck Berry's "Back in the U.S.A." and a whole slew of Beach Boys hits with the letters "U.S.A." in the title. (The Christian Crusade, needless to say, took "Back in the U.S.S.R." as proof positive that the Beatles were a Soviet plot.)

Even Paul's sillier love songs on the White Album—such as his ode to his English sheepdog, "Martha My Dear"—were neatly constructed and polished, both musically and lyrically. McCartney, after all, still extolled Dylan (in *NME*) as his model lyricist, against whom the rhymers of Tin Pan Alley rated poorly: "I used to like them, but now I think they're a lot of *merde.*" When Paul chose to infuse his balladry with inspired lyrics—as in "Blackbird," widely interpreted as a sympathetic nod to Black Power—he could be heartrending indeed.

Despite the unjustified stereotyping of McCartney's music as "soft" and Lennon's as "hard," the White Album's heaviest bone-cruncher was Paul's. "Helter Skelter," he told *Musician* in 1980, was inspired by a *Melody Maker* piece about The Who, "talking about a track they made . . . 'the loudest, most raucous rock 'n' roll, dirtiest thing we've ever done.' . . . I totally got off on that one little sentence in the paper, and I said, 'We gotta do the loudest, most raucous. . . .' That was 'Helter Skelter.' '' The phrase itself—which, along with others on the White Album, was to trigger a Beatle-obsessed Charles Manson's murderous rampage—was hardly intended to signify the Apocalypse. A helter skelter, as every English child knows, is a playground slide.

John, for his part, took exception to the notion that Paul had cornered the market with regard to tender Beatle ballads. In his soul-baring period, Lennon's soft touch proved especially poignant. "Like a little child," he radiated wide-eyed wonder in "Dear Prudence" (which featured a delicate tapestry of multiple overdubbed guitars) and "Cry Baby Cry" (wherein Alice tripped gently through Lennonland for the last time). The words "ocean child," used to invoke his mother in "Julia," took on added significance with the revelation that they were the English translation of the Japanese "Yoko." (In time, John was to address Yoko as "Mother.")

Elsewhere on the White Album, John takes savage aim at the British Blues Boom ("Yer Blues") and—bitterly ironic as it now must seem—at the National Rifle Association. "Happiness Is a Warm Gun," which also satirizes doo-wop and Motown, was originally inspired by a perusal of an American gun magazine shortly after Robert Kennedy's assassination.

Beatle people—those who passed the time combing the group's records for hidden meanings and "clues"—were the target of "Glass Onion." "Here's another clue for you all," Lennon taunted, informing sleuths that "the Walrus was Paul," the Fool on the Hill was "living there still," and so on. No doubt they promptly added these clues to their files—notwithstanding John's own admission in the chorus that all he was *really* up to was "trying to roll a dove-tail joint."

Too bad that particular message never penetrated the likes of Charles Manson. Nonetheless, there *were* secret messages and clues waiting to be discovered between the lines of *The Beatles*—all to the effect that John, Paul, George, and Ringo were now individual artists with little left in common. "I enjoyed it," Lennon was to remember, "but we broke up then."

On the second morning of 1969, the four Beatles filed into Twickenham Film Studios, with cameramen on hand to capture every note or gesture as the group began creating a new album from scratch. The intended spirit of the LP was summed up by its proposed title: *Get Back.* Other than Billy Preston's occasional keyboards, there were to be no contributions from outside musicians, no overdubbing or electronic gimmickry whatsoever. "If there's a mistake," Lennon advised George Martin, "that's hard luck. It's going to be honest."

As Michael Lindsay-Hogg's documentary film crew recorded the making of a Beatles album, the record itself was supposed to take on something of a documentary quality. Finished tracks were to be interspersed with the sounds of the Beatles chatting, tuning their guitars, and launching into some of the oldies with which they customarily "warmed up."

Though the concept was McCartney's, Lennon at first seemed equally enthusiastic, telling *NME:* "All these characters complain about us and Dylan not being progressive, but *we're* the ones that turned them on to the other stuff—so let 'em take our word for it: This is *music,* baby. . . . And remember: There can be as much complexity in one note as in any symphony or *Sgt. Pepper.* Not that I'm interested in classical music; I think it's history . . . I'm interested in *now.*"

And he might have added: in *then. Get Back* was to include one of his earliest efforts, "One After 909"; a remake of "Love Me Do" was also under consideration. For the album's cover, the Beatles—complete with beards and shoulder-length hair—would pose on the same housing-project balcony where, in early 1963, they had been photographed for their first British LP sporting matching brown suits, cherubic grins, and what now seemed like military-regulation hairstyles. John was later to announce the album as *Get Back, Don't Let Me Down, and 12 Other Titles;* over a decade before Elvis Costello, the Beatles were the first to propose resurrecting, as camp nostalgia, the most hopelessly unhip motifs of the pre-Beatles record industry.

In the film studio, however, the vibes seemed all wrong. "We couldn't get into it," John was to recall. "It was just a dreadful, dreadful feeling in Twickenham Studio. . . . You couldn't make music at eight in the morning . . . in a strange place with people filming you, and colored lights." Ringo would complain that "Lindsay-Hogg liked Paul more than the rest of us . . . so I got about two shots." But to McCartney, the problem was that "everyone was annoyed that John's new chick was in the film."

The tensions came to a boil over McCartney's plans for a live Beatles concert to provide the film with a spectacular climax. Fans had already swamped *Beatles Monthly* with entries for its contest to win tickets, and Derek Taylor, now Apple's press officer, had affirmed: "There will be a show—and that's a promise."

But George Harrison's initial reservations only hardened as Paul's choice of a photogenic concert site progressed from London's Roundhouse (which the Beatles had actually booked for a week) to an ancient Tunisian coliseum, or even an ocean liner—a notion that George found "very expensive and insane. . . . I don't think you're going to get the perfect acoustic place by the water out of doors." Nor did he appreciate Paul's unsolicited advice with respect to his guitar work. As the argument gathered steam, Lennon quipped: "I'm warming to the idea of an asylum."

George registered his protest by walking out of the studio; upon his return, a compromise was worked out. For the climax of their film, the Beatles would simply accompany their equipment to the roof of Apple; the *Beatles Monthly* contest winners would have to settle for free LPs. On January 30, in just about the only magical episode of the *Get Back* saga, four windswept Beatles briefly previewed their new material as crowds gathered on nearby rooftops and among the snarled traffic below—until the police, summoned by a local bank, put a stop to the disturbance.

Though Paul's sizzling title track was issued as a single in April 1969, to ads proclaiming "The Beatles as Nature Intended," the rest of *Get Back* was a sorry mess. After hearing it, Elton John declared: "They're going to kill themselves. . . . Oh, God, was it bad." According to Lennon, however, "We were going to let it out with a really shitty condition . . . [to] show people . . . what we're like with our trousers off." Advance copies of *Get Back** were actually sent out to various media heavies—and promptly circulated as one of rock's first bootlegs—before the Beatles changed their minds, to let it rot on the shelf along with the film. In lieu of *Get Back* consumers were treated to John and Yoko's *Unfinished Music No. 2* and George Harrison's equally unlistenable *Electronic Sound.* Both

---

* *The album included "Get Back," "Don't Let Me Down," and twelve other titles: "One After 909," "Save the Last Dance," "Dig a Pony," "I've Got a Feeling," "For You Blue," "Teddy Boy," "Two of Us," "Maggie May," the uncut "Dig It," "Let It Be," "The Long and Winding Road," and a reprise of "Get Back."*

appeared on Apple's short-lived subsidiary label, *Zapple,* a cut-price disposable "paperback records concept."

Meanwhile, John revealed—in a January *Disc* interview—that much was rotten in the state of Apple. The millionaire Beatle's disclosure that "if it carries on like this we'll be broke in six months" was promptly reprinted on the world's front pages. To *Melody Maker,* Ringo later elaborated: "We had a ninety-quid booze bill a week . . . [and] like a thousand people that weren't needed . . . getting paid for sitting around. We had a guy there just to read the Tarot. . . . Suddenly we realized the craziness, that it's not a business, that nothing's getting done."

Upon reading the news, a tubby New York wheeler-dealer named Allen Klein invested in an air ticket to London. Among the first American businessmen to make his fortune from the British Invasion, Klein had decorated his Times Square offices with gold records by Herman's Hermits, the Animals, Donovan, the Dave Clark Five, and the Rolling Stones. But the grand prize appeared beyond even Klein's clutches, at least until (as he was to tell *Playboy*) "the moment . . . I heard on the radio that Epstein had died, and I said to myself: 'I got 'em.' "

Even Klein was surprised by the eagerness with which Lennon accepted his offer of a meeting. John, in turn, was bowled over by the accountant's encyclopedic grasp of Beatles history. "He not only knew my work, and the lyrics . . . he also understood them," Lennon remembered in *Rolling Stone.* "He told me what was happening with my relationship with . . . Paul and George and Ringo. He knew everything about us. He's a fuckin' sharp man." The working-class hero sensed a common bond with the kosher butcher's son; both had been orphaned at an early age.

McCartney, having hit upon the obvious idea of putting Lee Eastman in charge of the Beatles' affairs, conspicuously failed to share Lennon's enthusiasm. A compromise was worked out, with Eastman appointed Apple's general counsel and Klein its business manager. But the arrangement was doomed: Eastman and Klein frankly despised one another, and the latter's brashness and uncouth manners, so admired by Lennon, were precisely the qualities McCartney deemed "uncool." By the same token, John thought Eastman's social pretensions and patronizing aura were uncool. Because the other two Beatles tended to side with Lennon in this increasingly bitter feud, Klein was to get the upper hand—ultimately, however, finding himself manager not of the Fab Four, but of three ex-Beatles.

It is beyond the scope of this book to chronicle all the Byzantine intrigues that were to preoccupy the Beatles for much of 1969, concerning their record royalties and merchandising and publishing rights—and the very roles Klein and Eastman were to play during the delicate business negotiations. Suffice to say, Klein's dictatorship quickly transformed Apple Corps from a freak's paradise to a prosaic, profit-oriented business. Superfluous spinoffs such as the Zapple budget label were terminated with the words "If it's good we'll charge"; the likes of Magic Alex and the house astrologer—anyone, in fact, who wasn't, as one employee put it, "indispensable or harmless"—were summarily struck from the Apple payroll.

No matter; there was to be no further nonsense in the Apple kingdom—except, of course, for Beatle nonsense, which remained in abundant supply. Indeed, for projecting an image of sheer dottiness, none of the group's previous incarnations could rival Beatles '69. It was John who appeared to dominate the picture—"Crazy John," as Tom Paxton dubbed him in a novelty song—with his Bed-Ins and Bagism and the nonexistent Plastic Ono Band. Bearded and pale ("These days I'm completely macrobiotic"), Lennon took to alternating all-white and all-black outfits; when supplemented with a top hat, the latter gave him the aura of a Hasidic rabbi. Then there was Hare Krishna George, with his chanting, shaven-headed entourage; and Ringo, ever the bit-part player, launching a solo film career in *Candy* and Peter Sellers's *The Magic Christian.* Even he seemed to get his picture in the paper more often than Paul McCartney after March 12, when the music world's most eligible bachelor broke a million hearts to tie the knot with the former Miss Eastman, only to disappear into unwonted seclusion at his recently acquired Scottish farm by the Mull of Kintyre.

John and Yoko, interpreting the McCartneys' wedding as a "dry run" for their own (Cynthia Lennon had been granted her divorce the previous November 8), interrupted a Paris vacation on March 20 to take their vows on the rock of Gibraltar. "Intellectually, of course, we didn't believe in marriage," said John; but the potential for "a fantastic happening" had proved irresistible. Added Yoko: "You'll know soon enough what it is."

Paul with bride and new stepdaughter, March 12, 1969 (Transworld Features Syndicate)

Upon checking into the Amsterdam Hilton, the newlyweds summoned fifty reporters to their bedside to witness the happening. Even in Europe's most permissive city, police warned of prompt measures should anything untoward occur. But the journalists, rather to their disappointment, found John and Yoko languishing in pajamas, each brandishing a Dutch tulip. Apologizing for the letdown—"We wouldn't make love in public; that's an emotionally personal thing"—John announced that he and Yoko planned to spend a week in bed, growing their hair for peace: "This is our protest against all the suffering and violence in the world." The newspeople themselves, he might have added, were to be cast as stooges in the Lennons' theater of the absurd.

Though some columnists might rail that "the Lennon peace circus debases the coinage of protest," while others insisted that John and Yoko had replaced Richard Burton and Elizabeth Taylor as the world's most boring couple, the media seemed incapable of simply ignoring the Lennons' escapades.

At the week's end, the Lennons roused themselves for a

lightning trip to Vienna, to see their film *Rape* premiered on Austrian TV. Reporters were invited to witness yet another "happening" at the grand Sacher Hotel, only this time John and Yoko were concealed inside a bag on top of a table. Proclaiming "bagism" the key to world peace, Lennon noted that no man would be prejudged by his looks if everyone were hidden in bags. "People were saying 'C'mon, get out of the bag.' And we wouldn't let them see us. It was just great." According to the UPI dispatch, "Hummed strains from the 'Blue Danube' waltz floated out from inside the bag," as Lennon, by his own account, strove to repress a fit of the giggles. "Our policy," he later declared, "is not to be taken seriously. All the serious people like Martin Luther King and Kennedy got shot. We're willing to be the world's clowns."

The next morning—April Fools' Day—John and Yoko caught the early plane back to London, with fifty acorns tied in a sack—each destined for a different world leader, to be planted in the name of peace. "We're exhausted," John quipped upon his return. "In fact, we're going to bed for a week to recover."

Lennon promptly wrote up his adventures in the musical broadside "The Ballad of John and Yoko." With Harrison and Starr unavailable at such short notice, Paul was corraled into doubling as bassist and drummer while John overdubbed guitar parts and jangled the ivories. Though "Get Back" had been released only ten days earlier, Lennon insisted "The Ballad of John and Yoko" be issued immediately as a Beatles single (he also changed his middle name from Winston to Ono the day it was recorded). With its rough-hewn instrumentation enhanced by gobs of echo, "The Ballad of John and Yoko" "got back" even more convincingly than its predecessor, sounding almost like an early yellow Sun record from Nashville. Nonetheless, few Top Forty stations in Bible Belt towns like Nashville proved amenable to playing a song with the chorus "Christ you know it ain't easy." Though more adventurous programmers merely blipped out the profanity, the lack of airplay limited the single's American chart showing to number eight. John protested that he was "Christ's biggest fan." But he was quick to add: "Yes, I still think it. Kids are more influenced by us than by Jesus."

The Lennons' honeymoon was also to be commemorated with a third volume of "unfinished music." *The Wedding Album* proved to be an overpriced boxed set, complete with facsimiles of the couple's marriage certificate and wedding cake. On one side, John and Yoko could be heard ordering breakfast from the Amsterdam Hilton's room service, bantering with reporters, and jamming off-key. For side two, they warbled, squawked, and cooed one another's names for twenty-two minutes. As with all John-and-Yoko happenings, however, the main point of interest was not the event or artifact itself, but people's reactions. After reviewers were sent advance test pressings on two separate LPs, with each side of *The Wedding Album* backed by a set of blank grooves, *Melody Maker*'s Richard Williams heaped special praise on sides three and four. Though these seemed to "consist entirely of single tones maintained throughout," he discovered that "in fact . . . the pitch of the tones alters frequently, but only by microtones. . . . This oscillation produces an almost subliminal uneven 'beat' which maintains interest." Lennon shot back a telegram: DEAR RICHARD THANK YOU FOR YOUR FANTASTIC REVIEW ON OUR WEDDING ALBUM INCLUDING C & D SIDES STOP WE ARE CONSIDERING IT FOR OUR NEXT RELEASE STOP LOVE AND PEACE STOP JOHN AND YOKO LENNON.

Though the Lennons intended to stage their next Bed-In in the United States to protest the Vietnam War, John's assertion that "these days I don't take drugs, alcohol, meat, or sugar" cut little ice with American immigration authorities. John and Yoko had to settle for Montreal's Queen Elizabeth Hotel, where for ten days they held court in a horizontal position to legions of American reporters and disc jockeys and such luminaries as Timothy Leary, Murray the K, Tommy Smothers, Dick Gregory, and the local chapter of the Radha Krishna Temple—all of whom could be heard on the single John wrote and recorded in his Montreal bed. "'All we are saying is give peace a chance' literally came out of my mouth as a spoken word to a reporter, after being asked millions and millions of times: 'What *are* you doing?'"

"Give Peace a Chance," the first Beatle solo record of any substance, was credited to the Plastic Ono Band. To underscore the conceptual nature of this "group," ads for the single featured the image of a microphone and tape recorder encased in clear plastic, superimposed over a random page of the London telephone book, and the legend "YOU are the Plastic Ono Band." Apple described "Give Peace a Chance" as "a fantastic song that will change the world around." Indeed, this repetitive chant was probably John's most effective exercise in musical sloganeering, and was promptly adopted by antiwar demonstrators everywhere. But the commercial success of a second Lennon band—however imaginary—hardly augured well for John's wavering commitment to the Beatles.

Nonetheless, he was willing enough to play along when Paul emerged from seclusion to rally the Beatles to excel themselves one last time. Like seasoned professionals, the four men managed to transcend their differences and polish off a new LP in a matter of weeks. A strong candidate for the title of the Beatles' best album, *Abbey Road* reveals each of the group's songwriters and musicians at the height of his distinctive powers. Yet for the first time in years, all four Beatles could be heard playing on nearly every track, and *Abbey Road* boasts more three-part harmonies than any other Beatles LP.

Apart from his incomparably melodic bass playing—"I was always a frustrated guitar player"—Paul's talents are shown to best advantage in the ambitious medley that dominates side two. This, George Martin was to tell *Rolling Stone*, "was Paul and I getting together. I was trying to make a symphony out of pop music, trying to get Paul to write stuff that referred back to something else. Bring some form to the thing." According to Martin, "Paul really dug what I was trying to do," and wanted to weave the entire LP into a "pop symphony." John, however, "hated that—he liked good old rock & roll. So *Abbey Road* was a compromise, too. Side one was a collection of individual songs."

"I liked the A-side," Lennon agreed, "but I never liked that sort of pop opera on the other side. I think it's junk because it was just bits of songs thrown together [including his own 'Sun King,' 'Mean Mr. Mustard,' and 'Polythene Pam']. 'Come Together' is all right, that's all I remember. That was *my* song." Chuck Berry's music publisher, however, thought it sounded like one of *their* songs—"You Can't Catch Me"—and lodged a suit for plagiarism. (The dispute was eventually resolved when John agreed to record "You Can't Catch Me" and another Berry tune on his *Rock 'n' Roll* solo LP.)

"Come Together"'s lyric, at least, was highly original; though the song first took shape as the campaign theme for Timothy Leary's proposed race against Ronald Reagan for the governorship of California, the long-haired Walrus from Bag Productions was clearly a self-portrait. Like other Lennon contributions on *Abbey Road*, "Come Together" reaffirmed John's love of words and his sense of fun—two qualities often missing from the direct and passionate material he was now writing. "Whatever I'm singing I really mean; I don't mess about."

Surprisingly enough, it was George Harrison's two contributions that garnered the most cover versions and airplay. Frank Sinatra, who recorded "Something," called it "the greatest love song of the past fifty years." Released as the Beatles' new single, it became the group's fourth all-time U.S. best-seller. But George betrayed his bitterness when he noted to David Wigg of *The Daily Express:* "They blessed me with a couple of B-sides in the past, but this is the first time I've had an A-side. Big deal, eh?"

Equally popular was "Here Comes the Sun," which, Harrison told Wigg, "was from the same period as Paul's song 'You Never Give Me Your Money.' We'd had meetings and meetings on bankers and lawyers and contracts and shares, and it was really awful because it's not the sort of thing we enjoy. One day I didn't come into the office, it was like slagging off school, and I went to [Eric Clapton's] house in the country. It was a really nice day and I picked up the guitar for the first time in a couple of weeks. The first thing that came out was that song."

The success of his new material only increased George's resentment at being allotted a mere two songs per Beatles LP. As he told *NME:* "I've got about forty tunes which I haven't recorded and some of them I think are quite good. I wrote one called 'The Art of Dying' three years ago." The group's inability to contain such burgeoning creativity would rank high on the list of reasons for the Beatles' breakup. Even John felt he was squandering his talents on McCartney's "nice little folk songs for the grannies" (e.g., "Maxwell's Silver Hammer"). "None of us want to be background musicians most of the time," he told *NME.* And yet the sublimation of the individual Beatles' "megalomania" (John's word) in favor of genuine teamwork was what made *Abbey Road* such a great record.

Abbey Road sold more copies than any previous American Beatles album—five million within a year. That, however, was not entirely on account of its musical qualities, for *Abbey Road* had already earned the more dubious distinction of having inspired the most pervasive hoax in rock history.

At their very first U.S. press conference, the Beatles had been asked: "What about the movement in Detroit to stamp out the Beatles?" It was Paul McCartney who had shot back: "We're starting a movement to stamp out Detroit." On October 12, 1969 (eleven days after the release of *Abbey Road*), the Motor City finally settled scores—with a movement to stamp out Paul McCartney.

The rumor was first aired on the local progressive station WKNR-FM, after deejay Russ Gibb took a call from an agitated listener, advising him of the weird pattern formed by many of the heretofore mysterious sound effects and mutterings in the Beatles' records—some of which had to be played backward for the "clues" to emerge. Gibb was startled to discover, upon spinning the White Album counterclockwise, that all those neatly clipped "number nine"'s on John's impressionistic "drawing of revolution" did indeed reveal themselves as "turn me on, dead man," and that the gibberish following "I'm So Tired" announced: "Paul is dead man, miss him, miss him." And what was that again, at the end of John's "Strawberry Fields Forever"? "I bury Paul," of course.

Two days later, *The Michigan Daily* chimed in with an *Abbey Road* review that took the form of an obituary, accompanied by an eye-catching likeness of Paul's severed head. The LP cover, noted reviewer Fred LaBour, shows the Beatles leaving a cemetery, dressed as a minister (John), an undertaker (Ringo),

and a gravedigger (George). Paul, out of step with the others, holds a cigarette in his right hand—proof positive that this is in fact an imposter for the left-handed McCartney. He is also barefoot; according to LaBour, English corpses are often buried without their shoes. The clincher was the license plate number of that deceptively innocuous-looking Volkswagen parked on Abbey Road—28IF. Twenty-eight *if* he had lived: Paul McCartney R.I.P.

LaBour also dragged in "evidence" from earlier LP covers: the grave on *Sgt. Pepper,* adorned with flowers in the shape of Paul's guitar; the hand extended over McCartney's head, an omen of death. And in the *Magical Mystery Tour* picture book, Paul sits in front of a sign reading "I was"; in another photograph he sports a black carnation while the other Beatles wear red ones.

Russ Gibb, meanwhile, could talk of little else during his shifts on WKNR; like a chain reaction, "underground" stations and newspapers across the country picked up on the sensational revelations. When Alex Bennett of New York's WMCA-AM began discoursing at length on McCartney's demise, rival Top Forty station WABC got into the act as well. WMCA then sent Bennett to the U.K. to investigate personally the status of James Paul McCartney.

The Paul-Is-Dead controversy proved a godsend for countless amateur Beatleologists anxious to put their expertise to practical use—and also for Capitol Records. As sleuths wore out their Beatles records playing them backwards and at various speeds, the demand for fresh copies of the evidence sent *Sgt. Pepper* and *Magical Mystery Tour* back into the chart's upper reaches, and a Capitol vice-president proclaimed "the biggest month in history in terms of Beatle sales." No wonder Capitol and Apple took their own sweet time confirming McCartney's continuing existence. Paul himself privately called the affair "probably the best publicity we've ever had, and I won't have to do a thing except stay alive."

The rumors, meanwhile, grew ever more elaborate, with each Beatles song yielding its own plethora of clues. Perhaps because Paul-Is-Dead was largely a campus phenomenon, some of the references were quite erudite. "I Am the Walrus," for instance, included not only the telling phrase "O untimely death" (from its "found" Shakespeare reading), but also "goo goo goo joob," which, in James Joyce's *Finnegan's Wake,* are Humpty Dumpty's last words before he has his great fall and cracks his head open. (And hadn't John already revealed, in "Glass Onion," that "the Walrus was Paul"?) Furthermore, "walrus" was said to mean "corpse" in Greek. And even sleuths who weren't literature majors could see that the Walrus figure in the *Mystery Tour* booklet wore black.

So what exactly was supposed to have happened to the hapless McCartney? As always, there were as many variations as there were rumormongers, but certain specifics were generally agreed upon. Paul, the tale went, had angrily driven away from the Abbey Road studios on November 9, 1966—a "stupid bloody Tuesday"—following a fight with the other Beatles. Such was his state that he didn't even "notice that the lights had changed," and, needless to add, "he blew his mind out in a car." (Sound effects from the accident were said to have been recreated in "Revolution 9"). The Beatle's head was severed from his body, and Paul was Officially Pronounced Dead (he wears an OPD armpatch on the inside of the *Sgt. Pepper* cover) on "Wednesday morning at five o'clock" (the phrase that George's superimposed likeness fingers on the *Pepper* libretto).

But how could Paul pose for such pictures if he had been

Officially Pronounced Dead? And whose dulcet voice is to be heard on such uncannily McCartneyesque ballads as "Hey Jude" and "Fool on the Hill"? It seems that the surviving Beatles took on the services of a Paul McCartney lookalike/soundalike contest winner, who then underwent plastic surgery to complete the deception. And why? John, George, and Ringo supposedly thought it would be good for a laugh to "cover up" the tragedy, then reveal it piecemeal to the public by planting "clues" in each subsequent Beatles release.

Paul-Is-Dead, according to psychologists Ralph Rosnow and Gary Fine's study *Rumor and Gossip: The Social Psychology of Hearsay*, "had the markings of a budding legend or literary invention, rather than the news item it supposedly was. . . . The clearest function of this rumor . . . was its entertainment value. It was 'fun' hunting for clues and talking about the mystery with friends."

The whole episode has continued to fascinate sociologists and second-generation Beatlemaniacs. Many fans will always be convinced that the clues were all planted deliberately. But as John was to testify in *Rolling Stone:* "The whole thing was made up. We wouldn't do anything like that. . . . People have nothing better to do than study Bibles and make myths about it, and study rocks and make stories about how people used to live and all that."

Paul-Is-Dead, then, wasn't even a hoax; it was a self-hoax. But therein lies the very reason for its ongoing fascination. Paul-Is-Dead was a powerful demonstration of the Beatles cult's capacity for generating its own elaborate mythology without any input from the principals; as such, it is a genuine folk tale of the age of mass communications.

One reason the story circulated in the first place was simply that the world hadn't seen very much of Paul lately. John, by contrast, was making himself inescapable. On September 13, he even gave the first concert performance by a Beatle in over three years. *Live Peace in Toronto 1969* (as the resultant live LP was to be titled) was the consequence of a typically Lennon-esque whim; two days earlier, when the producer of the open-air rock & roll revival called to invite John to attend the show, Lennon accepted—on condition that he and Yoko appear onstage rather than in the audience. This, of course, necessitated a more tangible Plastic Ono Band lineup, for which John recruited Eric Clapton, Hamburg exi-turned-bassist Klaus Voorman, and future Yes drummer Alan White. But Lennon himself developed severe qualms about his spur-of-the moment commitment, and barely made the last possible flight. The closest approximation of a Plastic Ono Band rehearsal had to be held on the plane.

Come showtime, John was so frazzled that he threw up before lurching onstage to mumble into the microphone: "We're just gonna do numbers that we know, y'know, 'cause we've never played together before, and . . . " At the mere sound of that familiar Scouse, ten thousand fans erupted ecstatically. Buoyed by the ovation, John later recalled, "we got it together like we'd been playing for years." Well, almost: the performance was certainly raw, and Lennon's occasional leads were hardly a match for Clapton's quicksilver runs. Yet few rock concerts have ever been so charged with the electricity of history in the making. After the old rock chestnuts and—"this is what we came for really"—"Give Peace a Chance," Yoko emerged from a large white bag for a session of her inimitable caterwauling—toward the end of which the musicians themselves exited the stage, leaving their somewhat bemused audience with several minutes' worth of searing amp feedback.

The only new song John performed at Toronto was "Cold Turkey." Written from experience, this account of a junkie's withdrawal symptoms was Lennon's most wrenching and minimalistic composition so far. By his account John approached the other Beatles with the words: "Hey lads, I think I've written a new single." Upon hearing the song, however, Paul instantly vetoed the idea. So John (backed by Clapton, Voorman, and Ringo Starr) recorded "Cold Turkey" for release as the second Plastic Ono Band single—and effectively ended the nominal Lennon-McCartney songwriting partnership by omitting Paul's name from the credits.

In a sense, however, McCartney's instincts were right: Lennon's howl of pain did not constitute a hit single. As "Cold Turkey" flailed around the lower reaches of the charts, John decided to perpetrate another antiwar happening. Snatching his MBE off the top of his aunt's TV set, he returned it to Queen Elizabeth as a protest against British support of the Nigerian government in Biafra and the Americans in Vietnam—and "Cold Turkey"'s poor chart showing. This caused even more offense than when the Beatles won the award in the first place; even Aunt Mimi told reporters: "I cannot agree that this is any way to register a protest. If I'd known what he wanted to do with it, I would not have let him have his MBE."

John's other activities during the Sixties' final weeks included airing his slogan "War Is Over! If You Want It" on billboards and full-page newspaper ads in the major cities of the non-Communist world; discussing his plans for an abortive Toronto Peace Festival with Prime Minister Pierre Trudeau; and replacing the Gregorian calendar. "Everyone who's into peace," John announced, "will regard the New Year [1970 A.D.] as Year One A.P., for After Peace. All our letters and calendars from now on will use this method."

Augmented by such luminaries as George Harrison and Keith Moon, the Plastic Ono Band also gave a Christmas concert in London benefiting UNICEF. The program consisted of just two songs: greatly extended versions of "Cold Turkey" and Yoko's B-side, "Don't Worry Kyoko, Mummy's Only Looking for a Hand in the Snow." "Without wishing to be offensive," wrote *NME*'s Alan Smith, "it gave me the biggest headache since I-don't-know-when."

George had also renewed his acquaintance with the concert stage, joining Eric Clapton as one of Delaney and Bonnie's anonymously billed "Friends." But both he and John proved unreceptive to Paul McCartney's notion that the four Beatles should make a live comeback by turning up unannounced at small clubs. At one point during their acrimonious discussions, John stunned his partner with the words: "I want a divorce." For once, McCartney joined forces with Allen Klein, to persuade Lennon not to say anything publicly. "There was a lot to do businesswise," John later conceded. "It would not have been suitable at the time. Paul and Allen said they were glad I wasn't going to announce it. Paul said: 'Oh well, that means nothing really happened if you're not going to say anything.'"

All the Beatles, however, did go along with John's suggestion that Phil Spector be hired to turn the *Get Back* tapes into a marketable album. (By way of an audition, Spector had produced the third Plastic Ono Band single, "Instant Karma"—which, unlike its predecessor, soon qualified for a gold record.) But only Ringo volunteered to help with the editing, and even he belittled the album as "the soundtrack from the film we completed last year. It shouldn't be regarded as the official next Beatles LP." By this time, the title of both album and film had been changed to *Let It Be*.

Nobody seems to have taken less interest than Paul McCartney, who would later charge in court that while his back was turned, the others had deliberately ruined his "Long and Winding Road" with cloying strings and (God forbid!) "female voices." Be that as it may, *Let It Be* is surely the most unsatisfactory of all Beatles albums. The real problem had less to do with the relatively second-rate material, or even with the Beatles' low morale at the time they recorded it, than with Spector's indecisiveness. He should either have remained faithful to the casual and intimate atmosphere that the original *Get Back* concept had called for, or else gone whole hog with his trademark walls of sound. But he tried to do both, dubbing his kitsch orchestrations and heavenly choirs over a program of "back-to-the-roots" music that retained the Beatles' tunings-up and between-song chatter. The combination sounded ridiculous.

While Spector administered his surgery, even outsiders began to sense McCartney's growing alienation from the others. In February 1970 *NME* ran an ominous report by Alan Smith under the headline THE BIG BEATLES QUERY: WHY IS PAUL THE HERMIT OF ST. JOHN'S WOOD?: "It would have been a personal pleasure to report an imminent 'Come Together' between the worlds of old Fair Isle McCartney and Plastic Lennon fantastic. Sadly—no such luck. . . . Paul's firm-minded wife seems to have taken over as a kind of barrier between him and the rest of the world. Callers to their St. John's Wood house either meet Linda or a member of the staff, and Paul is 'not available' or 'out' or 'busy.'"

(*Photo Trends/Stephen Goldblatt*)

For the course he was about to take, perhaps Paul McCartney deserves more empathy than he is often accorded. After all, it was he who had almost singlehandedly kept the Beatles going since Brian Epstein's death, only to see all his pet projects sabotaged or wrested away from him; Apple, now firmly under the dominion of a man he detested, was only the most striking example. Worst of all, John, George, and Ringo, while sharing little of Paul's enthusiasm for the band itself, seemed to have banded together for the sole purpose of thwarting McCartney's own cherished plans.

The crunch appears to have come after Paul completed work on his first solo LP, which had been recorded in secret mostly at his home studio in Scotland. The other Beatles voted to delay its release, on the grounds that it would drain sales from the forthcoming *Let It Be*. Ringo was dispatched to St. John's Wood to explain the decision, only to get thrown out of the house by McCartney with the parting words: "I'll finish you all." "While I thought he had behaved like a spoiled child," Ringo was later to testify, "I could see that the release date of his record had a gigantic emotional significance for him, and felt we should let him have his way."

But when advance copies of *McCartney* were circulated on April 9, they arrived with a special bonus—the self-interview in which Paul announced his "break with the Beatles" on account of "personal differences, musical differences, business differences, but most of all because I have a better time with my family." And his famous last words: "My plan is to grow up."

Few Beatlemaniacs took the next day's headlines literally. Apple even issued a guarded denial that the Beatles had actually split. But after Paul did his utmost to make it clear that "the party's over," the Klein regime proclaimed that "any individual Beatle cannot offer his services, appear alone or with any other person in any branch of the entertainment industry . . . without the consent of Apple." It was this sort of blackmail that caused Paul to initiate court proceedings officially to dissolve the Beatles partnership. His lawsuit, though ultimately successful, sealed McCartney's undeserved reputation as "the one who broke up the Beatles."

John, for all his bitterness, was the first to admit that wasn't so. "The cartoon is this," he cracked in *Rolling Stone*. "Four guys on stage with a spotlight on them. Second picture, three guys breezing out of the spotlight. Third picture, one guy standing there shouting 'I'm leaving.'"

So John, Paul, George, and Ringo went their separate ways, leaving the world with one final revelation: the extent to which, as Beatles, they had always managed to inhibit or cancel out one another's weaknesses. Lennon alternated between sheer brilliance and dismaying banality. He embraced a string of new causes and consciousness-raising panaceas, but his seal of approval had lost the power to do for the Primal Scream or the Yippies what it had once done for Bob Dylan, transcendental meditation, and LSD. He split up with Yoko, was reconciled, and after winning his agonizing four-year struggle with U.S. immigration authorities, disappeared from view to build a new family-oriented life within the Gothic confines of the turreted Dakota, overlooking that part of New York's Central Park now known as Strawberry Fields.

Upon forming a new band in late 1971, Paul told *NME:* "I feel a lot more free and easy. I certainly prefer it to that last bit with the Beatles, with . . . people saying, 'He's bossing them all.' I just felt that was my role—when everybody gets stoned it needs somebody to pull it together. I felt the pressure of that. . . . Wings don't mind me telling them what to do." Some old-timers shared Marianne Faithfull's assessment of Wings: "A travesty of everything we once held sacred." But once Paul got his new act together, his collection of gold and platinum records came to exceed the combined holdings of his three former colleagues.

For George, the breakup amounted to the rupturing of a dam that had long kept his creativity in check. His first solo album was an outpouring of inspired devotional music that filled three LPs and briefly swept him well ahead of the other ex-Beatles in the public's esteem. His 1971 all-star Concerts for Bangla Desh were perhaps the last great manifestation of the ideals of the rock counterculture; but most everything after that smacked, inevitably, of anticlimax.

Even Ringo, ever the "bit-part player," had his hits, though these, too, were eventually outnumbered by the misses. Yet it was Ringo who best summed up the ex-Beatles' careers with the quip: "Paul has the teenagers, John has the intellectuals, George has the mystics, and I have the mums."

But if the solo ex-Beatles failed to produce even one Great Song on the order of "Hey Jude" or "Strawberry Fields Forever," or to set a single trend in or beyond the music scene, well—what does it matter? After sustaining one disappointment after another (interspersed with such occasional shots-in-the-arm as *All Things Must Pass, Imagine,* and *Band on the Run*), Beatlemaniacs finally came to realize that the Beatles had been a unique and magical amalgam with a life all its own, and that Lennon, McCartney, Harrison, and Starr were now entitled to live theirs. Having transformed the world of popular music—and the hairstyles, choice of intoxicants, and political and religious views of an entire generation—what could they possibly do for an encore? Because the Beatles, unlike certain of their British Invasion colleagues, went out at the end of the Sixties with perfect timing (if less than perfect grace), their magic could never be debased, and it lives on forever, on record and in the memories of all who shared it.

In an *NME* interview shortly after the breakup, John Lennon related a parable that may stand as the Beatles' epitaph: "There was this Japanese monk, and it happened in the last twenty years. He was in love with this big Golden Temple, y'know, he really dug it like—and y'know he burned it down so it would never deteriorate.

"That's what I did with the Beatles. I never wanted them to be has-beens. . . . I wanted to kill it while it was still on top."

On December 8, 1980, John Lennon—back at last from his five-year "retirement"—told an interviewer: "I consider my work won't be finished until I'm dead and buried, and I hope that's a long, long time."

Everyone knows what happened only a few hours later. All whose lives were touched by John Lennon will always remember the worldwide outpouring of shock and grief, and the sense that an important part of their own lives had been sundered from them, once and for all. To first-generation Beatles fans, those terrible days were eerily reminiscent of a time barely seventeen years earlier, a time of futile vigils enacted before the TV screen, to see and hear, again and again and again, the same "instant replays," old film clips, and tear-stained faces, the same reactions and tributes and dismal details. There was also an awful symmetry in the notion that the era the Beatles personified, which in a sense had been triggered with a hail of bullets in Dallas, had finally ended in New York, in very much the same manner. Only John Lennon meant more in the lives of his public than any President possibly could.

If that weren't so, John would still be alive today. This is perhaps the most bitter irony of all: John and the Beatles affected countless people in such an intense and personal way, and one of those individuals was sufficiently twisted and psychotic to use real bullets against the real man, merely to exorcise the John Lennon of his own dreary fantasies.

But it should in no way diminish the importance of John Lennon, or the horror of his assassination, to point out that his passing was less the actual end of an era than an extremely painful reminder—or confirmation—that the times he had personified were already, irretrievably, behind us. John Lennon had already made his contribution. And the words of Yoko Ono still apply: "The Golden Temple exists in perfect form forever."

(Photo Trends/Alex Agor)

(followed by their highest chart positions, as listed in *Billboard*)

THE BEATLES' HITS

U.S. Singles

1964 I Want to Hold Your Hand/ I Saw Her Standing There (**1/14**); She Loves You (**1**); Please Please Me/ From Me to You (**3/41**); My Bonnie (with Tony Sheridan) (**36**); Twist and Shout/ There's a Place (**2/74**); Can't Buy Me Love/ You Can't Do That (**1/48**); Do You Want to Know a Secret/ Thank You Girl (**2/36**); Love Me Do/ P.S. I Love You (**1/10**); Why (with Tony Sheridan) (**88**); EP: Roll Over Beethoven/ Please Mr. Postman/ All My Loving/ This Boy (**92**); Sie Liebt Dich (**97**); A Hard Day's Night/ I Should Have Known Better (**1/53**); Ain't She Sweet (**19**); And I Love Her/ If I Fell (**12/53**); I'll Cry Instead/ I'm Happy Just to Dance with You (**25/95**); Matchbox/ Slow Down (**17/25**); I Feel Fine/ She's a Woman (**1/4**)

1965 Eight Days a Week/ I Don't Want to Spoil the Party (**1/39**); EP: Honey Don't/ Mr. Moonlight/ I'm a Loser/ Everybody's Trying to Be My Baby (**68**);

Ticket to Ride/ Yes It Is (**1/46**); Help (**1**); Yesterday/ Act Naturally (**1/47**); We Can Work It Out/ Day Tripper (**1/5**)

1966 Nowhere Man/ What Goes On (**3/81**); Paperback Writer/ Rain (**1/23**); Yellow Submarine/ Eleanor Rigby (**2/11**)

1967 Penny Lane/ Strawberry Fields Forever (**1/8**); All You Need Is Love/ Baby You're a Rich Man (**1/34**); Hello Goodbye/ I Am the Walrus (**1/56**)

1968 Lady Madonna/ The Inner Light (**4/96**); Hey Jude/ Revolution (**1/12**)

1969 Get Back/ Don't Let Me Down (**1/35**); Ballad of John and Yoko (**8**); Something/ Come Together (**1/1**)

1970 Let It Be (**1**); The Long and Winding Road (**1**)

1976 Got to Get You into My Life (**7**); Obladi-Oblada (**49**)

1978 Sgt. Pepper's Lonely Hearts Club Band—With a Little Help from My Friends (**71**)

(BY JOHN LENNON AND/OR THE PLASTIC ONO BAND)

1969 Give Peace a Chance (**14**); Cold Turkey (**30**)
1970 Instant Karma (**3**); Mother (**43**)
1971 Power to the People (**11**); Imagine (**3**)
1972 Woman Is the Nigger of the World (**57**)
1973 Mind Games (**18**)
1974 Whatever Gets You Thru the Night (**1**); #9 Dream (**9**)
1975 Stand by Me (**20**)
1980 Starting Over (**1**)

(BY PAUL McCARTNEY AND/OR WINGS)

1971 Another Day (**5**); Uncle Albert (**1**)
1972 Give Ireland Back to the Irish (**21**); Mary Had a Little Lamb (**28**); Hi Hi Hi (**10**)
1973 My Love (**1**); Live and Let Die (**2**); Helen Wheels (**10**)
1974 Jet (**7**); Band on the Run (**1**); Junior's Farm/ Sally G (**3/39**)
1975 Listen to What the Man Said (**1**); Letting Go (**39**); Venus and Mars—Rock Show (**12**)
1976 Silly Love Songs (**1**); Let 'Em In (**3**)
1977 Maybe I'm Amazed (**10**); Seaside Woman (as Suzy and the Red Stripes) (**59**)
1978 Mull of Kintyre/ Girls' School (**33**); With a Little Luck (**1**); I've Had Enough (**25**); London Town (**39**)
1979 Goodnight Tonight (**5**); Getting Closer (**20**); Arrow Through Me (**29**)
1980 Coming Up (**1**)

(BY GEORGE HARRISON)

1970 My Sweet Lord/ Isn't It a Pity (**1/46**)
1971 What Is Life (**10**); Bangla Desh/ Deep Blue (**23/95**)
1973 Give Me Love (**1**)
1974 Dark Horse (**9**); Ding Dong (**36**)
1975 You (**20**)
1976 This Song (**25**)
1977 Crackerbox Palace (**17**)
1979 Blow Away (**16**)

(BY RINGO STARR)

1971 It Don't Come Easy (**4**)
1972 Back Off Boogaloo (**9**)
1973 Photograph (**1**); You're 16 (**1**)
1974 Oh My My (**5**); Only You (**6**)

1975 No No Song/ Snookeroo (**3/90**); Goodnight Vienna/ Oo-Wee (**31/95**)
1976 A Dose of Rock 'n' Roll (**26**)
1977 Hey Baby (**74**)

U.S. LPs

1964 Meet the Beatles (**1**); Introducing the Beatles (**2**); The Beatles with Tony Sheridan and their Guests [sic] (**68**); Jolly What! The Beatles and Frank Ifield on Stage [sic] (**103**); The Beatles' Second Album (**1**); The Beatles' American Tour with Ed Rudy (**20**); A Hard Day's Night (**1**); Something New (**2**); Beatles vs. Four Seasons: Battle of the Century [sic] (**142**); Songs Pictures and Stories of the Fabulous Beatles (**68**); The Beatles' Story (**7**); Beatles '65 (**1**)

1965 The Early Beatles (**43**); Beatles VI (**1**); Help! (**1**); Rubber Soul (**1**)

1966 Yesterday and Today (**1**); Revolver (**1**)

1967 Sgt. Pepper's Lonely Hearts Club Band (**1**); Magical Mystery Tour (**1**)

1968 The Beatles (**1**)

1969 Yellow Submarine (**2**); Abbey Road (**1**)

1970 Hey Jude (**2**); Let It Be (**1**)

1973 The Beatles/1962–1966 (**3**); The Beatles/1967–1970 (**1**)

1976 Rock 'n' Roll Music (**2**)

1977 The Beatles at the Hollywood Bowl (**2**); Live at the Star Club in Hamburg, Germany 1962 (**111**); Love Songs (**24**)

1980 Rarities (**21**)

(BY JOHN LENNON AND/OR YOKO ONO AND/OR THE PLASTIC ONO BAND)

1969 Two Virgins (**124**); Life with the Lions (**174**); Wedding Album (**178**)

1970 Live Peace in Toronto 1969 (**10**); John Lennon/Plastic Ono Band (**6**)

1971 Imagine (**1**)
1972 Some Time in New York City (**48**)
1973 Mind Games (**9**)
1974 Walls and Bridges (**1**)
1975 Rock 'n' Roll (**6**); Shaved Fish (**12**)
1980 Double Fantasy (**1**)

(BY PAUL McCARTNEY AND/OR WINGS)

1970 McCartney (**1**)
1971 Ram (**2**); Wild Life (**10**)
1973 Red Rose Speedway (**1**); Band on the Run (**1**)
1975 Venus and Mars (**1**)
1976 Wings at the Speed of Sound (**1**); Wings Over America (**1**)
1978 London Town (**2**); Wings' Greatest (**29**)
1979 Back to the Egg (**8**)
1980 McCartney II (**3**)

(BY GEORGE HARRISON)

1969 Wonderwall (**49**); Electronic Sound (**191**)
1970 All Things Must Pass (**1**)
1972 Concert for Bangla Desh (**2**)
1973 Living in the Material World (**1**)
1974 Dark Horse (**4**)
1975 Extra Texture (**8**)
1976 Thirty-three and a Third (**11**)
1979 George Harrison (**14**)

(BY RINGO STARR)

1970 Sentimental Journey (**22**); Beaucoups of

Blues (65)
1973 Ringo (2)
1974 Goodnight Vienna (8)
1975 Blast from Your Past (30)
1976 Ringo's Rotogravure (28)
1977 Ringo the Fourth (162)
1978 Bad Boy (129)

U.K. Singles

1962 Love Me Do (17)
1963 Please Please Me (2); From Me to You (1);
My Bonnie (with Tony Sheridan) (48); Twist
and Shout EP (2); She Loves You (1); Beatles
Hits EP (14); Beatles No. 1 EP (19); I Want to
Hold Your Hand (1)
1964 All My Loving EP (12); Can't Buy Me Love
(1); Ain't She Sweet (29); Long Tall Sally EP
(14); A Hard Day's Night (1); A Hard Day's
Night EP (34); I Feel Fine (1)
1965 Ticket to Ride (1); Help (1); Day Tripper/ We
Can Work It Out (1)
1966 Paperback Writer (1); Yellow Submarine/
Eleanor Rigby (1)
1967 Penny Lane/ Strawberry Fields Forever (2);
All You Need Is Love (1); Hello Goodbye (1);
Magical Mystery Tour EP (2)
1968 Lady Madonna (1); Hey Jude (1)
1969 Get Back (1); Ballad of John and Yoko (1);
Something (4)
1970 Let It Be (2)
1976 Yesterday (8); Back in the USSR (19)

(BY JOHN LENNON AND/OR THE PLASTIC ONO BAND)

1969 Give Peace a Chance (2); Cold Turkey (14)
1970 Instant Karma (5)
1971 Power to the People (7)

1972 Happy Xmas (War Is Over) (2)
1973 Mind Games (26)
1974 Whatever Gets You Thru the Night (36)
1975 #9 Dream (23); Stand By Me (30); Imagine
(1)
1980 Starting Over (1); Woman (3)

(BY PAUL McCARTNEY AND/OR WINGS)

1971 Another Day (2); Back Seat of My Car (39)
1972 Give Ireland Back to the Irish (16); Mary Had
a Little Lamb (9); Hi Hi Hi (5)
1973 My Love (9); Live and Let Die (9); Helen
Wheels (12)
1974 Jet (7); Band on the Run (3); Junior's Farm
(16)
1975 Listen to What the Man Said (6); Letting Go
(41)
1976 Silly Love Songs (2); Let 'Em In (2)
1977 Maybe I'm Amazed (28); Mull of Kintyre (1)
1978 With a Little Luck (5); I've Had Enough (42)
1979 Goodnight Tonight (5); Old Siam Sir (35);
Wonderful Christmastime (6)
1980 Coming Up (2); Waterfalls (9)

(BY GEORGE HARRISON)

1971 My Sweet Lord (1); Bangla Desh (10)
1973 Give Me Love (8)
1974 Ding Dong (38)
1975 You (38)

(BY RINGO STARR)

1971 It Don't Come Easy (4)
1972 Back Off Boogaloo (2)
1973 Photograph (8)
1974 You're 16 (4); Only You (28)

THE BRITISH INVASION

The Rolling Stones

IN THE SPRING OF 1964, AS THE British Invasion hit full gear, scarcely a week passed without another jet landing at Kennedy Airport bearing reinforcements: the Dave Clark Five . . . Peter and Gordon . . . Gerry and the Pacemakers . . . the Rolling Stones.

These last, odd as it may now seem, were the only major contingent to encounter tough and prolonged resistance from an American music scene that otherwise appeared to have succumbed totally to the invading aliens.

Though five hundred young New Yorkers turned out at Kennedy to cheer the Stones' June 2 arrival, across the rest of the country the quintet would often have difficulty attracting as many people to their actual concerts. Almost everywhere they went, the reaction of the natives ranged from sheer indifference to outright hostility.

One of the Stones' first U.S. engagements was on TV's *Hollywood Palace,* where they were obliged to share the bill with a stand-up comedian and a troupe of dancing elephants. After the Stones manfully stormed through ''I Just Wanna Make Love to You'' and ''Not Fade Away,'' host Dean Martin returned with a smirk. ''Aren't they great?'' he deadpanned, rolling his eyes upward to draw uproarious guffaws from the middle-aged studio audience. ''They're off to England to have a hair-pulling contest with the Beatles. [*laughter*] . . . Their hair is not that long—it's just smaller foreheads and higher eyebrows.'' Following the routine of a trampolinist, Mr. Martin brought the house down: ''That's the father of the Rolling Stones. He's been trying to kill himself ever since.''

''He was just a symbol of the whole tour for us,'' Brian Jones told a *Melody Maker* reporter toward the end of the trip. Added Mick Jagger: ''What I'd really like to say you couldn't print.'' The British music weekly divided its front page between two contrasting pictures, each emblazoned with a one-word, two-inch headline: on one side, the Dave Clark Five and HIT!; on the other, the Rolling Stones and MISS!

And so it went: At an all-star show in San Antonio, a trained monkey was called back for an encore—but not the Rolling Stones. ''We all wanted to pack up and come home,'' Bill Wyman later admitted.

There were a few hopeful signs. In Cleveland—the birthplace of rock & roll, ever receptive to tasty new sounds—the Stones were trapped in a TV studio by rioting fans following an appearance on *The Mike Douglas Show*. ''In the Douglas melee,'' *Vari-*

(*From 1.*): *Mick Jagger, Charlie Watts, Brian Jones, Keith Richards, Bill Wyman, early 1964 (RDR Productions)*

ety reported, ''teenagers snuck into station as early as three hours before showtime and hid out in ladies' room, men's room, under stairways, etc. Only when police were called did order prevail and could the singers get out.''

The same positive spirit was present during the group's New York debut two days later, though *Variety*'s reviewer complained that the Stones turned Carnegie Hall into a ''teenage kooksville.'' ''The key to success for these British groups is apparently provided not by their musical arrangers, but by their barbers. If the Beatles have coifs that come down below their ears, the Rolling Stones have hairdos that fall to their shoulderblades, and in an assortment of colors from brunet to blonde.'' The article went on to note that the Stones tapped a ''Freudian vein of savagery and malignancy in music, appearance, and performance.''

Even such praise as the Stones *did* garner within the entertainment industry tended to have a dubious ring. *Billboard,* for instance, reviewed their third U.S. single—the relatively tame ''Tell Me''—as ''Neanderthal music at its best.'' But if the Stones weren't quite musical gorillas, they would soon enough demonstrate their remarkable capacity as musical *guerrillas,* hastening toward obsolescence that very world of show-biz schmaltz epitomized by the smug Mr. Martin.

I first heard of the Rolling Stones in May 1964, at my very first rock concert—a scene of mindless, harmless hysteria for those most mindless and harmless of all the original Invaders, the Dave Clark Five. On each seat was a handbill plugging the Stones' upcoming show in the same (Carnegie) hall, for which an embarrassing percentage of the tickets remained unsold. I mention this because, though I was among the youngest of all the Dave Clark buffs present, all the nubile lasses near me seemed to have the same reaction (which in many cases would doubtless undergo similar modifications). One was initially repelled by the photograph; the Stones looked dour and dangerous, and their hair obviously took a good thing too far. But then, as one heard these vague sentiments voiced far more authoritatively by assorted fuddy-duddies at the front of the classroom, in the news media, and at the dinner table, the Stones began to acquire the fascination of forbidden fruit. In those days, becoming a Rolling Stones fan was often akin to acquiring a secret vice.

Though their records had yet to be aired on the local Top Forty, I furtively invested in a copy of the Stones' British Number One hit, "It's All Over Now." From the frontal assault of Jones's ominous opening chords and Jagger's lasciviously drawled entrance ("Welll, baby used to stay *OUT*, all night *LONG*"), the single hammered home in no uncertain terms the message that these guys—quite unlike their neatly turned out, grinning colleagues—meant business.

For many young Yanks, this revelation would be occasioned a bit later, by "Time Is on My Side" or "The Last Time" or, most likely, "(I Can't Get No) Satisfaction"; yet slowly but inexorably the Rolling Stones emerged in America (as they had done in Britain) as the Beatles' only serious competition. That very refusal to compromise, which at first seemed to inspire mainly derision, also engendered a fanatic loyalty among the growing ranks of converts. The Stones and their young manager, Andrew Loog Oldham, deliberately fed this equation, and then exploited it for all it was worth.

It wasn't as if the Stones got as far as they did without a great deal of hype. London Records, lifting its cues from the Capitol/Beatles blueprint, launched the Rolling Stones with the biggest promotional campaign in the label's history. Full-page ads appeared in all the trades, proclaiming: "They're great! They're outrageous! They're rebels! They sell! They're England's *hottest*! . . . but *hottest* group!" The record company even helped organize fan clubs, supplying petitions demanding airplay for the Stones' music with which card-carrying members might barrage radio stations. A huge billboard presently rose to dominate Times Square with the glowering image of the Rolling Stones, proclaiming them "the sound, face, and mind of today . . . five reflections of today's children."

The most effective Stones hype, however, was rather more innovative and subtle. The idea was to grab the media's attention at every opportunity—even if that meant sacrificing oneself to a hatchet job—on the astute assumption that negative coverage in the adult world would eventually translate into kudos from the kids.

So the Stones proceeded to break all the rules that had ever been laid down for stars of show biz. They shunned uniforms and stage makeup (only to reappear with makeup *off* stage); they got photographed for record covers in all their pimply glory. "The general rule was *be yourself*," says Oldham—part of whose job was to make certain the Stones were "themselves" with a vengeance.

This still being 1964, some venerable institutions—such as the "fax sheet"—could not yet be dispensed with altogether; but even these were used to best diabolical advantage. They noted, for instance, that "blond Brian smokes sixty cigarettes a day," and that the favorite color of nearly all the Stones was black. Adding a touch of the absurd, they invariably listed Bill Wyman's passions in life as "astronomy, cashew nuts."

They also made the Stones out to be taller, more emaciated, and considerably younger than they really were. The *stance* was indeed uncompromising, though it was a rather tenuous line that separated the group's "realism" from outright cynicism and contempt for their audience.

All this superciliousness might not have succeeded had the Beatles not led the way, with their own less brazen assault on American preconceptions regarding, say, long-haired boys and pop stars with minds of their own. But in taking everything a few steps farther, the Stones played a part in hastening the

LP, U.S.A., 1965 (*Radio Pulsebeat*)

LP, U.K., 1964 (*Decca*)

LP, U.S.A., 1965 (*London*)

Single, Italy, 1966 (*Decca*)

revolution in youthful attitudes and appearance that was soon to sweep all the Western World. From one standpoint, the Rolling Stones were perhaps the greatest corrupters of the young in recent memory. Viewed from this side of the trenches, however, they simply cut through more crap than anyone else around; as that Times Square billboard insinuated, the Stones merely reflected aspects of "today's children" that had been there all along, but that adult authority figures often preferred to suppress or ignore. In any case, they certainly established themselves as the "radical" alternative to the Beatles.

John Lennon was never too pleased about this sort of thing and was wont to point out that (a) the Beatles came up with all the revolutionary innovations (true enough) and (b) Mick Jagger was no more unbourgeois than *he* was (very likely, Jagger was at heart far *more* bourgeois than Lennon). No doubt the Stones were not *really* the gangrenous vagabonds of some of their detractors' (and admirers') alleyway gang-bang fantasies—any more than the flesh-and-blood Beatles were those cherubic mop tops so dear to the hearts of the subscribers of *16 Magazine*. A case might be made that back in those obscure Hamburg dives the Beatles had been as tough and sleazy as the Stones would ever be.

But—with all due respect to John—so what? In rock (or pop, as they used to call it in swinging London), it's the image that counts; and in the mythology of those times the Stones were to the Beatles like darkness to sunshine, black against white.

In 1964 the four Beatles had a great many common attributes, ranging from accents and shared mannerisms to the color of their identically styled hair. Even the differences in their personalities seemed to complement one another; the "chemistry" was perfect. The Rolling Stones, by contrast, were a distinctly motley crew; each member's presence appeared to clash with the others'. In the chemistry department, the Stones seemed highly combustible. There was also an unmistakable hierarchy within the band, though Mick Jagger was by no means the automatic focus of attention he later became.

Despite their differences, the Rolling Stones' stage lineup was every bit as classic as the Beatles'. Drummer Charlie Watts sat way in the back with his mouth ajar; bassist Bill Wyman stood off at left wing, almost in the shadows. These were the two great stone faces of the Rolling Stones, impassive gargoyles grinding each number to a raw pulp. Wyman would hold his instrument (custom-made for his abnormally small fingers) in a near-vertical position, and the only parts of his anatomy that ever seemed to move were his hands and his jaw (and those only very slowly); he was constantly chewing gum.

Nearer center stage, and considerably more mobile, were the two guitarists. Keith Richards shuffled in and out of the spotlight, a dark and intense figure who held the music together and seldom indulged in a flashy move just for the sake of it. Brian Jones, on the other hand, flitted and fluttered shamelessly. Something of a musical butterfly as well, he was apt to switch his instrument between selections, to diddle on a slide guitar or a harmonica (or, in later years, a dulcimer or a sitar). The only Stone who could be called pretty, Jones was also the only one who ever threatened to upstage the man in the middle, that "short thin boy with a sweat shirt on, the neck of the sweat shirt almost falling over his shoulders . . . with the hair puffing down over the forehead and ears, this boy has exceptional lips. They hang off his face like giblets . . . spreading into the most languid, most confidential, the wettest, most labial, most concupiscent grin imaginable."*

Jagger played a lot of harmonica when he wasn't singing or rattling his maracas or a tambourine. But he never stopped moving, which in itself made the Stones unique at that time; as he himself put it, "everybody else just stood up there like a bunch of assholes, with their suits and their ties." Jumpin' Jack Flash could move faster than the darting eyes of his mesmerized audience; even Rudolf Nureyev was to be impressed. "That's very kind of him, because he's a *great* dancer," Jagger would say in a 1978 *Rolling Stone* interview. "I can't dance a waltz or a quickstep. I can't dance steps. I just leap about, and sometimes it's very ungainly. It's hard dancing while you're singing."

There was, it should be noted, an element of flippancy in the style of this androgynous rabble-rouser, which tended later to slip into self-parody and sheer camp. And however much the Stones seemed to represent the antithesis of show biz, Mick was always a consummate showman. From the start Jagger was, to quote one of his songs, "very complicated."

---

* *Tom Wolfe,* The Kandy Kolored Tangerine Flake Streamline Baby *(1964)*

In any event, the response Mick's antics triggered during mid-Sixties Stones performances caused one reporter to observe that the group didn't play concerts, they played riots. "I am sure that it must be a highly sexual thing," Jagger told *New Musical Express* in 1967. "And things that are sexual are violent. . . . There is a rapport, a tremendous, basic affection. But on top of this affection is violence. On top of that is sex."

And at the bottom of everything, of course, was something we've scarcely mentioned yet: the music.

> The essential difference between ourselves and the British groups that are well known in the United States at the moment is that we're the first to have a really strong Negro rhythm & blues influence. We haven't adapted our music from a watered-down music like white American rock 'n' roll. We've adapted our music from the early blues forms. . . .
> We've come along with the right thing at the right time. Things were getting rather sloppy and sentimental. A new sort of vital urge seemed to be growing up among the young people, and we provided the music.
>
> Brian Jones to Ed Rudy, 1964

One can hardly separate the vital urges and the music when speaking of the early Rolling Stones. Compared with any previous *white* music, their sound was devastatingly earthy, physical, *urgent*. While the Beatles and their imitators were still merely wanting to hold your hand, "happy just to dance with you," Jagger came right out with it: "Welll, I'm a king bee, buzzin' round yo' hive . . . let me come inside."

Of course, like nearly all the early Stones material, "King Bee" originated not with Jagger and Richards, but with a relatively obscure black American blues man—in this case Slim Harpo. Such artists often openly celebrated sexual pleasure, and as an end in itself, unadulterated by sentiment or romance. But for a long time this music had been effectively quarantined in the ghetto by the dominant white culture—whose snobbery, prudishness, and racial prejudice nonetheless only enlarged the legend (so threatening, *so* irresistible) of the black male's sexual prowess.

Into the breach came rock & roll—as personified by Elvis Presley, who hollered and swaggered like the archetypal black stud, but was as white as the proverbial boy next door. Not only did the likes of Elvis unleash an electrifying current of sexuality among their young Caucasian audiences; they also enhanced the status of the male—the traditional pursuer—as an object of sexual desire in his own right. When Elvis the Pelvis triggered overt erotic fantasies among the opposite sex, he also made it plain that should the dream come true, *he* would be doing *her* the favor.

As Mick Jagger put it in *Rolling Stone:* "Music is one of the things that change society. That old idea of not letting white children listen to black music is *true,* 'cause if you want white children to remain what they are, they musn't."

At lilac evening I walked with every muscle aching amongst the lights of 27th and Welton in the Denver colored section wishing I were a Negro, feeling that the best the white world has offered me was not enough ecstasy for me, not enough life, joy, kicks, darkness, music, not enough night.

Jack Kerouac, *On the Road*

Yet even if it hadn't been discouraged, "race music" (as it was labeled in the Fifties) might still have found only a limited white audience. The performers were too alien from the experience of most white kids for the latter to relate easily to them as either heroes or sex objects. As Jagger wrote *Melody Maker* months before the Stones had even set foot in America: "Girl fans, particularly, would rather have a copy by a British group than the original [black] version—mainly, I suppose, because they like the British blokes' faces, and they feel nearer to them." More bluntly, Richards subsequently listed the R&B artists' liabilities among white teenagers: "One, they're old; two, they're black; three, they're ugly."

The Stones took the role of "white niggers" considerably farther than Elvis had; despite his demeanor and the orgasmic grunts with which he punctuated his songs, Presley's words and music were still relatively diluted. The Rolling Stones drew full proof from the original still.

In those days the Stones were quick to emphasize that they played *rhythm & blues,* not pop, or beat music, or even rock & roll. The distinction may seem academic now, but at the time the band, their numerous imitators, and many of their followers were deadly serious about it. The British R&B movement that the Stones spearheaded viewed itself almost in the light of a crusade.

Unlike the British beat boom, this movement was born not in the provinces, but in the sophisticated big city. Its original strongholds were the art colleges and universities of Greater London. Many of the young musicians who first took up R&B were upper-middle-class intellectuals, apt to possess horn-rimmed glasses or Oxford degrees. It was almost as if they were attempting to compensate for their genteel family and academic backgrounds with the most primitive and physical music available.

Be that as it may, it took the Rolling Stones to match the implications of the music with a *visual* persona—and to turn British R&B into a national phenomenon. The groups that re-

placed them in such London dives as the Crawdaddy and the Marquee—the Yardbirds, Manfred Mann, and the rest—were in turn catapulted into prominence. And once the Stones finally conquered America, the British Invasion's ranks were swollen with scores of pale, weedy English boys wielding mouth harps, maracas, and endless choruses of "Smokestack Lightning," "Got My Mojo Workin'," and "I'm a Man."

Meanwhile, back in the U.K., the pedantic intellectual within the R&B monster reasserted itself in the letters columns of *Melody Maker* and *NME*, which were dominated for months by contentious arguments over who and what did or didn't qualify as "authentic" R&B—or whether mere pop groups such as the Beatles could be taken as seriously as dedicated purists like the Rolling Stones. Yet already the more commercial strains of black R&B were being superseded in the country of its origin by soul music. Though this, too, attracted an enormous following among London's pop elite and Mods everywhere, few British groups ever convincingly advanced the concept of "blue-eyed soul." (Though the Stones did go on to cover a few songs that might be deemed "soul," they stuck to their basic R&B/rock & roll lineup of guitars, bass, and drums.)

In other words, British R&B as such very quickly became a dead end—and excruciatingly passé. Nonetheless, it did set the stage for the more musically ambitious scions of the British Blues Boom—the likes of Cream and Fleetwood Mac—and for Led Zeppelin, progenitors in turn of that still more recent genre known and loved as "heavy metal." All this might be said to have evolved out of the original accomplishments of Mick, Keith, Brian, Bill, and Charlie. Yet when British R&B went under, the Stones were already far away, having abandoned the sinking ship with their usual impeccable timing—only to ride higher than ever by activating their most potent resource: the previously unrealized songwriting talents of Jagger and Richards.

The implications inherent in white boys mouthing the sentiments and accents of a suppressed black subculture were enormous to begin with. The Stones retained the accents, but went on to create a sound of their own with a series of blockbuster hits whose lyrics (when audible) made explicit all that had merely been implied in the original Rolling Stones fantasy. The heroes of this fantasy were rebels whose only cause was to demolish every obstacle that stood in the way of their living their lives solely for kicks—and to collect a million dollars in the process.

The female protagonists in this distinctly male fantasy were mostly moronic and neurotic sluts, who very occasionally got the better of our heroes ("Off the Hook"), but were more often put in their places: "Under My Thumb" ("a squirming dog who's just had her day") or "Out of Time" ("you're obsolete, my baby"). Such ditties as "Yesterday's Papers" celebrated the use and disposal of women like so many pieces of Kleenex.

Boys will be boys, of course, and take to that sort of thing in a big way; but so, evidently, did the young ladies. Years later the Stones would be severely taken to task by a number of prominent feminists; but, as Jagger recalled in that 1978 interview: "At the time there was no feminist criticism because there was no such thing, and one just wrote what one felt. . . . My talent seems to lie in that direction. . . . I choose what I do best, that's all."

Stuck in the outer reaches of London's suburban sprawl, the town of Dartford is distinguished solely for having spawned one of rock & roll's most dynamic and enduring partnerships.

Michael Philip Jagger was born there on July 26, 1943, and Keith Richards the following December 18. "I met [Keith] when I was six," Jagger would recall in *Rolling Stone* twenty-nine years after the event. "We lived on the same block for a while . . . went to the same school at one point, and we walked home together. . . . We're very close, and we always have been. He was born my brother by accident by different parents."

"Then I moved into a tough neighborhood," said Richards.* "What they'd call in the States a housing project. Just been built. Thousands and thousands of homes, everyone wondering what the fuck was going on. Everyone was displaced. They were still building it and there were gangs everywhere. I didn't see Mick for a long time. I once met him selling ice creams outside the public library."

Jagger, by contrast, was by his own admission "brought up in a very protected environment. It was a middle-class home." "I was just an ordinary rebellious studious hard-working kid," he said in a 1974 *NME* interview. "I really did used to work very hard at school." Mike (as his family called him) was eventually admitted to the London School of Economics, where he became infatuated with left-wing politics. His ultimate ambition was to become a politician himself.

Richards, meanwhile, had been expelled for truancy from the Dartford Technical School. Like John Lennon, Ray Davies, Eric Clapton, and Pete Townshend, he wound up "hanging out" at art college. "It's somewhere they put you if they can't put you anywhere else—if you can't saw wood or file metal. It's where they put me to learn graphic design."

Keith grew up something of a loner, fascinated, like so many postwar British teenagers, by all things American. His mother, Doris, always a kindred spirit, has said that he knew far more about the United States than about his own country. When Keith started to discover contemporary American music through an Elvis Presley album, she indulged him with his first guitar.

"I was rockin' away, avoiding the bicycle chains and razors in those dance halls. I went straight into this art school, and I heard these cats playing [Big Bill] Broonzy songs. And I suddenly realized it goes back a lot further than just the two years I'd been listenin'. Then I started to discover Robert Johnson and those cats. You could never get their records though.

"I get on this train one morning and there's Jagger—and under his arm he has four or five albums. I haven't seen him since the time I bought an ice cream off him . . . and under his arm, he's got Chuck Berry, Little Walter, Muddy Waters." Mick, it turned out, had not only made the same series of musical discoveries Keith had—from Buddy Holly and Little Richard through Waters and Broonzy—he had even corresponded with Chess Records in Chicago and sent away for their priceless recordings. "So I invited him up to my place for a cup of tea. He found that I could play a little and that he could sing a bit."

With a mutual friend named Dick Taylor (later of the Pretty Things), the Glimmer Twins formed their first embryonic band to "lay down some of this Chuck Berry and Little Walter stuff. No drummer or anything, just two guitars and a little amplifier. And suddenly in '62, just when we were getting together, we read this thing about a Rhythm and Blues Club starting in Ealing."

The founders of this establishment turned out to be the British blues pioneer Alexis Korner and the late harmonica player Cyril Davies, who also formed the nucleus of a band called Blues Incorporated; their drummer at the time was one Charles Robert Watts. The Ealing club soon became a magnet for young R&B fanatics from across Britain, including future members of not only the Rolling Stones, but also the Animals, the Kinks, John Mayall's Blues Breakers, Cream, and countless other celebrated combos. All found in the thirty-five-year-old Korner a close friend and mentor, who often encouraged them to jam with his own band. Though some of Blues Incorporated's jazz-weaned musicians were less than enamored with Keith Richards's predilection for Chuck Berry licks, Mick Jagger was soon accepted as a permanent fixture, alternating on vocals with Long John Baldry and future Manfred Mann singer Paul Jones (née Pond).

Among Korner's most ardent disciples was Lewis Brian Hopkin-Jones, who had latched on to the "grandfather of British rock" when Blues Incorporated performed at his native Cheltenham. Richards described Cheltenham as "a very genteel town full of old ladies, where it used to be fashionable to go down and take the baths once a year at Cheltenham Spa." Born on February 28, 1942, Brian Jones had already earned a certain notoriety in his hometown for having abandoned his impeccable upbringing and promising academic career to bum around the Continent with his guitar—and for having gotten two local teenagers simultaneously pregnant.

The soft- and well-spoken Jones was extremely serious about his music, advertising for musicians in *Jazz News,* to which he also wrote a long, earnest letter on the relative merits of jazz, R&B, and rock & roll. Though initially disparaging toward the latter, Brian was turned on to Chuck Berry by Keith as the two guitarists began trading licks and songs. When Paul Jones decided to pursue his studies in Oxford rather than sing in Brian's band, Jagger gradually emerged as the logical choice for vocalist. Brian also introduced a squat, square-jawed pianist in leather shorts named Ian Stewart.

According to Richards, some of the older and more traditional musicians in Korner's circle took exception to Brian's new sidekicks. "'What are ya hangin' with them rock & rollers for?' they'd ask. Brian turned around and said: 'Fuck off, you bastards, you're a load of shit and I'm going to get it together with these cats.' So we decided we got to live in London to get it together. Time to break loose."

During the autumn of 1962, Jagger, Richards, and Jones set up house in a grimy flat near the unfashionable end of the King's Road. Apart from Jagger's studies, there was little to distract the slumming trio from playing and listening to their chosen forms of music virtually all their waking hours. Brian christened the fledgling band "Rollin' Stones," after the Muddy Waters tune. Like the "Silver Beatles" before them, they briefly tarted up the billing to "Silver Rollin' Stones."

The Beatles were making their first national impact, and their progress was followed closely by certain Stones; though ostensibly R&B purists, Brian and (to a lesser extent) Mick began to have visions of attracting similar adulation themselves. Despite his physical fragility, Jones was driven by a consuming ambition. Jagger, though scarcely less ambitious, still kept open the option of a glorious future in economics or politics. Richards, on the other hand, was primarily interested in playing music.

The band's debut performance had already taken place at Soho's Marquee Club on July 12, 1962. This was a Thursday night, which the Marquee normally reserved for Blues Incorpo-

---

* *This and many subsequent Richards quotes are excerpted from Robert Greenfield's 1971* Rolling Stone *interview.*

rated; Korner, however, had accepted a booking on the BBC's Jazz Club radio show. Though Jagger was still involved with Korner's band, the budget provided for only six musicians, and Mick was deemed dispensable for the occasion. Instead of feeling rejected, Jagger engineered the Marquee's substitution of his *other* band for Blues Incorporated that Thursday evening. At this and subsequent gigs the Stones began to offer an exciting alternative to the professional British blues players, who tended to be stronger on pedantry than on charisma. Jagger, Richards, Jones, and Co. were raw, spirited, and—above all—young; and they started to build a fanatic teenage following of their own.

For a drummer, the Stones were still obliged to alternate among such stand-ins as Carlo Little (a Cyril Davies sidekick), Mick Avory (later of the Kinks), and Tony Chapman. Their first choice was always Charlie Watts; but Charlie, despite the occasional gig with the Stones and his personal affinity for them, was playing hard to get. He had even left his post with Blues Incorporated, who still appeared to offer far more in the way of prospects and prestige than did the Stones—and Charlie, after all, was a jazz fanatic who professed to loathe rock & roll. His top priority at the moment was his new job as a commercial artist at a reputable advertising agency. Born on June 2, 1941, Watts was a Harrow Art School graduate who had already combined his two main interests to produce a charming picture book about the late jazz innovator Charlie "Yardbird" Parker. (*Ode to a High Flying Bird* would be marketed in 1964 as the Stones' answer to *In His Own Write*.)

The Stones also found themselves short of a bassist when Dick Taylor decided to study art full-time. For a replacement, they finally settled on a friend of Tony Chapman's named Bill Wyman (née Perks)—despite the fact that Bill (born on October 24, 1936) was seven years older than Jagger and Richards, and his attitudes and life-style considerably more conventional. A self-confessed "straight working-class type," Wyman had served in the Royal Air Force before settling down with a steady job (clerical engineer), wife (Diane), and baby (Stephen). (Pressures created by Bill's career would cause the marriage to break up in 1967.) All parties agree that it was primarily Wyman's impressive amplifier that induced the Stones, who lacked a proper amp of their own, to overlook his aberrations. Shortly afterward, in January 1963, the Rolling Stones' lineup (which still included Ian Stewart on piano) was completed when Charlie Watts finally agreed to be their permanent drummer.

Brian Jones, meanwhile, was relentlessly hustling on behalf of what he continued to view as *his* band. He approached Giorgio Gomelsky, a former experimental filmmaker who ran a new club called the Crawdaddy in Richmond's Station Hotel. After a few gigs there the Stones were given a residency when the Dave Hunt Rhythm and Blues Band (featuring Ray Davies on guitar) failed to turn up for a date. Despite the name of their predecessor's band, Jagger has claimed that the Stones were "playing rhythm & blues because that's what we liked, we were playing it well, and nobody else seemed to be doing it." In this 1974 *NME* interview, Mick added that they began to sprinkle their three-hour sets with such recent material as Barrett Strong's "Money," "which was a really big R&B hit in America but didn't happen when it came out in England. . . . We saw that those things were, like, popular."

In April 1963 the band received its first major write-up, under the five-column *Record Mirror* headline THE ROLLING STONES—GENUINE R AND B:

As the trad [jazz] scene gradually subsides, promoters of all kinds of teen-beat entertainments heave a long sigh of relief that they have found something to take its place. It's rhythm 'n' blues . . . [and] at the Station Hotel, Kew Road, the hip kids throw themselves around to the new "jungle music" like they never did in the more restrained days of trad.

And the combo they writhe and twist to is called the Rolling Stones. Maybe you've never heard of them . . . but by gad you will! The Stones are destined to be the biggest group in the R&B scene—if that scene continues to flourish. Three months ago only fifty people turned up to see the group. Now promoter Gomelsky has to close the doors at an early hour—with over 400 fans crowding the hall. . . .

Unlike all the other R&B groups worthy of the name, the Rolling Stones have a definite visual appeal. They aren't like the jazzmen who were doing trad a few months ago and converted their act to keep up with the times. They are genuine R&B fanatics themselves and they sing and play in a way that one would have expected more from a colour U.S. group than a bunch of wild, exciting white boys who have the fans screaming. . . .

The boys do not use original material—only the American stuff. "After all," they say, "can you imagine a British-composed R&B number—it just wouldn't make it."

"Six is too many for them to remember the faces in the picture." (*RDR Productions*)

In the wake of such coverage, hordes of new visitors flocked to the Crawdaddy. Among the first were various Beatles—and their manager's fast-talking nineteen-year-old press officer, Andrew Loog Oldham. "I was about forty-eight hours ahead of the rest of the business in getting there," said Oldham. "But that's the way God planned it."

In a 1972 *NME* interview, Oldham recalled having been transfixed in equal measure by the music, "the sex," and "the fact that in just a few months the country would need an opposite to what the Beatles were doing. I remember seeing the Beatles when they were about eighth on the bill to Helen Shapiro and Tommy Roe. I sat there with a lump in my throat. In one night you knew they were going to be very big. It was just an instinctive thing.

"From that night on it registered subconsciously that when they made it, another section of the public was gonna want an opposite." The moment Oldham first laid eyes on the Rolling Stones, he was convinced that "the Stones were gonna be that opposite."

When he introduced himself to the group, they hit it off immediately. "We just had the same basic desire to do something—a hustling instinct. . . . I wasn't coming on with a cigar and a silk suit going 'listen, kids.' I was the same age as them. We talked the same language." Within twenty-four hours, Oldham had graduated from writing Billy J. Kramer's press releases to co-managing the Rolling Stones. His somewhat ill-matched partner was Eric Easton, who dated back to the silent-film era, when he had been a cinema organist, and who would address the Stones as "gentlemen of the orchestra." Described by Richards as "a bumbly old Northern agent," Easton nonetheless had money at his disposal and "could get you gigs in ballrooms [across] England."

Another visitor to the Crawdaddy around this time was Decca Records' Dick Rowe. While judging a Liverpool talent show with George Harrison, Rowe, notorious throughout the industry for having turned down the Beatles a year earlier, had listened intently as Harrison raved about his favorite new group. Within hours, the A&R man, not wishing to make the same mistake twice, could be found behind the wheel of his car, racing toward Richmond. Impressed both by the Stones and by their new manager's references to other A&R men purportedly on their trail, Rowe snapped up the group for Decca on terms unprecedented for a new act. Once the contract was signed, Jagger finally withdrew from the London School of Economics.

Approximately one week later the Stones were in Olympic Sound cutting their first single under the direction of Oldham, a self-styled "producer" who had never before seen the inside of a recording studio. When it came time to balance the tracks, Andrew didn't even know what the engineer meant by "mixing," and cut short the discussion with the words "You do that." Dick Rowe, unsurprisingly, pronounced the result "dreadful" and made the Stones rerecord it. The single, "Come On," was unleashed on June 7, 1963.

Eleven years later Jagger said that they selected this obscure Chuck Berry opus because "nobody knew it and to the best of our knowledge nobody had done it"; the idea was to pick a relatively commercial number unlikely to be duplicated by any of the countless groups getting signed up in the wake of the Beatles. One of the first printed responses to "Come On" appeared courtesy of pop singer Craig Douglas, *Melody Maker*'s "Blind Date" reviewer for the week: "Very, very ordinary. Can't hear a word they're saying and I don't know what this is all about."

Two weeks later, however, "Come On" claimed the bottom rung of *Melody Maker*'s Top Fifty—boosted by the Stones' devoted following and a valuable plug on the *Thank Your Lucky Stars* TV program the night of its release. But the Stones' debut single was indeed ordinary, even wooden, and Jagger himself said they "disliked it so much we didn't used to do it on any of our gigs. And that used to cause arguments with Andrew."

Another bone of contention was the uniform Oldham insisted they don for *Thank Your Lucky Stars*—matching checked jackets with dark trousers and ties. "The TV people were used to dealing with groups like the Searchers and the Swinging Blue Jeans," Oldham explained. "Someone even said we would have

"Rock & roll's no way a virtuoso thing. It's what three or four or five guys can do together . . . simple as that."—Keith Richards (RDR Productions)

to get rid of the lead singer because he would never pass the BBC audition. If the Stones had dressed the way they wanted, they wouldn't even have been allowed inside the building. So they all wore those checked jackets. But we got rid of them as soon as we could." Richards, however, claims Oldham made them retain their uniform throughout their first national tour that autumn (supporting the Everly Brothers and Bo Diddley) and only relented after various Stones made a practice of "spilling whisky all over it, or chocolate pudding."

In this particular, Oldham may have briefly borrowed a page from his former boss's success story with the Beatles; but he very quickly wised up, and, indeed, made his whole pitch on the premise that "you could invite the Beatles in for tea, but you couldn't invite the Rolling Stones." No matching hairstyles, collarless jackets, or Royal Variety Shows for this lot.

Andrew Loog Oldham and Brian Epstein did have a number of things in common: both were relative outsiders to the music business, brilliant innovators, and deeply committed to their artists on a personal level—all of which made them radically different from the usual breed of pop music manager. For all his fine qualities, however, Brian Epstein was never exactly, well, hip. Before those four boys in leather caught his eye, he had much preferred Sibelius to Elvis.

Andrew, on the other hand, was himself a flashy, street-smart rock & roll kid. He was possessed by outrageous fantasies, for which he found, in the Rolling Stones, a perfect conduit. All he had to do was draw out the arrogance and the anarchy and the sex that were already implied in their music and their style. To market his explosive contraband, Oldham proceeded to bring to bear what Richards has called "a genius for getting messages through the media without people knowing—before people really knew what the media was."

One of Oldham's first moves was to downgrade the status of the Rolling Stones' piano player Ian Stewart to road manager and behind-the-scenes accompanist. "Well, he just doesn't look the part," Richards recalls Oldham saying, "and six is too many for them to remember the faces in the picture." Oldham also chopped the *s* off Keith's surname. (It would reappear in the credits on virtually every second Stone release; for the sake of continuity I have retained it here.) Then, armed with the first of his bold slogans—"The Rolling Stones are more than just another group; they're a way of life"—he put his game plan into action.

It was the most brazen assault show business had ever witnessed—or been subjected to. Presley, for instance, may have come on like a horny delinquent in performance; but when the show was over he addressed strangers as "sir," regularly attended church, and even joined the Army when Uncle Sam beckoned. The Rolling Stones, however, were encouraged to be outspokenly iconoclastic, even downright rude, at all times; to sprout hair twice as long as the Beatles'; and to make the news whenever possible by getting thrown out of fancy restaurants for not wearing a tie.

The idea, of course, was for the Stones to be everything every rebellious adolescent would if he but could, were he not thwarted by such authority figures as parents, teachers, and police officers—who would, in turn, be duly scandalized by the Stones, causing the teenagers to identify all the more. (To further this identifying process, the Stones' ages were revised downward. Jagger, Richards, and Jones each lost a year or two to become nineteen again; and a full five years were subtracted from Wyman's age, now officially twenty-two.)

The whole scam worked like a charm. The major dailies began titillating readers with Stones photographs and exploits, beneath such headlines as WOULD YOU LET YOUR DAUGHTER GO OUT WITH A ROLLING STONE? The sensationalistic *News of the World* would subsequently anoint the group as "symbols of a rebellion . . . against the boss, the clock, and the clean-shirt-a-day routine" and describe the Stones themselves as "five indolent morons [who] give one the feeling that they really enjoy wallowing in a swill-tub of their own repulsiveness." Back in 1963 and early '64, even *Melody Maker* and *NME* made routine references to "the ugliest pop group in Britain" and "the caveman-like quintet."

The Stones mostly played right along; as early as June 1963, *Melody Maker* quoted Watts saying of the Beatles: "They can't like our faces, they must like our music." Only Jones would seem sensitive to the criticism, telling American radio personality Ed Rudy: "I resent it very much, being called dirty . . . we're not dirty, we're not scruffy, and we're not thick." But Keith would tell Rudy: "I don't care *what* they write about us, just so long as they *write* about us." The gathering controversy only encouraged the Stones' ticket and record sales; "Come On" may have been a lousy record, but it was still in the charts when the second single appeared in November.

Though Decca had originally scheduled another pair of softcore American R&B carbons ("Poison Ivy" and "Fortune Teller"), Oldham and the Stones chose instead to contrive a major publicity coup out of the occasion—by tapping the goodwill of their archetypal opposites for a brand-new Lennon-McCartney original. The caveman quintet's primeval treatment of "I Wanna Be Your Man" bludgeoned right into the Top Ten.

Around this time, in Richards's words, "you can tell by the way the gigs are going there's something enormous coming. You can feel this energy building up as you go around the country. You find it winding tighter and tighter, until one day you get out

there halfway through the first number and the whole place is full of chicks screaming. We'd walk into some of these places and it was like they had the Battle of Crimea going on—people gasping, tits hanging out, chicks choking, nurses running around."

When they weren't traveling the length and breadth of Britain in Ian Stewart's beat-up van, Mick and Keith were now sharing a London flat with Oldham. The latter had just adopted as his bible *A Clockwork Orange,* Anthony Burgess's futuristic novel of gratuitous violence, which Oldham hoped to turn into the Rolling Stones' answer to *A Hard Day's Night.* In the meantime, Oldham imitated the protagonists' Russian-sounding teenage slang in his infamous Stones blurbs and liner notes, and the three roommates consciously modeled themselves after Alex and his "droogs."

Mick, Keith, and Andrew began setting policy without consulting Charlie, Bill, and Brian—much to the displeasure of the

Andrew Loog Oldham and Mick Jagger (RDR Productions)

latter, who reminded all who would listen that *he* was the founder, *and* the leader, of the Rolling Stones. Long afterward Keith told *NME* that "Mick getting all the attention . . . caused Brian some upset which he never really quite got over. It brought about some other forms of paranoia later."

Brian's sense of exclusion only deepened when at Oldham's urging Mick and Keith began to write songs together; heretofore the occasional Stones original had always been a group endeavor, credited to the pseudonymous "Nanker Phelge." Until 1965, however, little Jagger-Richards material was actually used by the Stones; as Mick (who generally provided the words for Keith's music) explained to Ed Rudy: "We find that the American songs are better for ourselves. The songs that Keith and I write . . . we give to other people. They're mostly ballads."

The pair's first effort, "It Should Be You," was recorded on Decca by George Bean in the last weeks of 1963. This was shortly followed by "That Girl Belongs to Yesterday," which the American recording star Gene Pitney decided to use after meeting the Stones during a joint appearance on *Thank Your Lucky Stars.* Even many Stones afficionados may be unaware of the fact that Pitney's Jagger-Richards single entered *Billboard*'s American Hot Hundred on the same day—January 18, 1964—as the Beatles' and Lennon-McCartney's first U.S. hit, "I Want to Hold Your Hand," and months before any of the Stones' own recordings were issued on these shores.

Oldham, however, contended in his 1972 *NME* interview that the Stones' next single, Buddy Holly's "Not Fade Away," was really "the first song Mick and Keith 'wrote' . . . in that they picked the concept of applying that Bo Diddley [rhythm] to it. The way they arranged it was the beginning of the shaping of them as songwriters." By lending so thoroughly *black* a sound to a tune by Holly—perhaps the least black-influenced of the great Fifties rock & roll stars—the Stones dramatically reversed the tradition whereby singers like Pat Boone would turn a Little Richard song antiseptically *white*.

The sessions that produced "Not Fade Away" were buoyed by the inebriated presence of Phil Spector, who joined in on maracas and co-wrote the B-side, "Little by Little," with the mysterious Mr. Phelge. (The Stones had just concluded their first headlining tour, supported by the Ronettes. The two groups promptly disobeyed the legendary producer's command that they keep their hands off each other in his absence.) Oldham's infatuation with Spector shortly manifested itself in a lasting predilection for forty-piece pop orchestras and round-the-clock sunglasses. "Andrew was so openly influenced by him," says Jagger, "that it was disgraceful."

In any event, "Not Fade Away" fully realized, for the first time, the sound of the Rolling Stones—and British R&B generally—in all its explosive urgency. *NME* pronounced the disc "sensational," and it got to number three. The next single, "It's All Over Now," would be the clincher.

"Not Fade Away" was followed by what some have called the finest debut album in rock history. The LP—issued in April 1964—offered a well-rounded sampler of the Stones' black American influences, from Chuck Berry ("Carol") and Marvin Gaye ("Can I Get a Witness") to Slim Harpo ("King Bee") and Jimmy Reed ("Honest I Do"). Though the Stones' arrangements often differed radically from the originals, some observers accused them of ripping off black music. Jagger defended the band's position with a long letter published in the March 21 issue of *Melody Maker:*

> To the critics then, who think we're a beat group who came up overnight, knowing nothing about it, we invite them to examine our record collection. It contains things by Jimmy Reed, Elmore James, Hooker, and a stack of private tapes by Little Walter . . . these legendary characters wouldn't mean a light commercially today if groups were not going round Britain doing their numbers. It's made them all popular again, particularly Berry and Diddley.

One admirable trait the Stones shared with the Beatles from the start was a determination "to make each [LP] track good—work almost as hard on it as you would work on a single," as Richards put it in his *Rolling Stone* interview. "Both us and the Beatles had been through buying albums that were filled with ten tracks of rubbish . . . so maybe we changed that concept." Unlike previous managers and producers, Oldham allowed his clients the major say in what was recorded and released.

The Rolling Stones was actually cut in mono at a demo studio, partly to simplify matters for the band's young Dr. Frankenstein. Andrew was still unfamiliar with more sophisticated recording equipment, but unwilling to let any outside producer meddle with the monster he was raising. Even so, the Stones' first album hardly sounds worse than anything else they recorded through 1967; indeed, it would be inaccurate to suggest that the group's original classics were, purely in terms of the production, anything but a shambles. Harmonies and guitars were wont to disappear into the mix, and the drums to sound, as The Who's Pete Townshend once observed, "like a cardboard box." "It did have an awful lot to do with the fact that Andrew Oldham had never listened to an R&B record in his life," Richards told *NME*'s Nick Kent.

Not that the Stones themselves were above singing and playing out of tune during their final takes. Yet perhaps all this actually contributed to the anarchic atmosphere so successfully conveyed by the Stones' records. The spirit at least was always there; and somehow the whole mess seemed to gel with a logic of its own. (Fifteen years later, the off-key din of a Stones trailblazer would be subjected to scientific scrutiny by a seasoned producer hoping to recreate the ancient magic formula.)

Perhaps the clearest demonstration of the Stones' and Oldham's chutzpah was the absence of any name or title on the front cover of that debut album—just a photo of five glowering Stones, with the Decca logo off to one corner. So brazen a tactic had never been attempted by anyone, let alone a group releasing its very first LP. In America, however, London Records would emblazon across the top the words "England's Newest Hitmakers The Rolling Stones"—blithely ignoring the fact that the Stones had yet to score a U.S. hit.

To rectify America's intransigence, the Rolling Stones undertook that first, somewhat ill-starred voyage through the landscapes of their song lyrics and lifelong fantasies. (Covering a later U.S. tour for *Ramparts,* Michael Lydon reported that the Stones "think the cars, papers, TV, freeways, clothes, slang, and even airport shops filled with the products of a thousand 'fad merchandisers' are all far-out and fascinating. Dallas,

Alabama, Chicago—they get a buzz from just being in such exotic, storied places, and it all comes out in the music.'')

If the infatuation was not yet entirely mutual in mid-1964, the Stones were nonetheless able to realize some cherished ambitions—most notably some recording sessions at Chicago's Chess studio at 2120 South Michigan Avenue, where the boys had a chance to hobnob with their favorite Chess artists. "Chuck Berry wandered in while we were recording 'Down the Road Apiece,'" Wyman recalled in *NME* eight years later, "and he said to us: 'Wow, you guys are really getting it on.' Muddy Waters was also there.''

Unsurprisingly, the Stones found the ambience and facilities far more conducive to the sound they were striving for than anything available back home. "The engineers in England just couldn't get it together," said Wyman. "We'd play a number in the studio and it would be just great, but when we listened to the playback it sounded like Herman's Hermits.'' The fruits of the Chicago sessions* were to appear on the British EP *5 × 5* and the American LP *12 × 5* (the title originally announced for the first album).

Most important, the first American visit laid the groundwork for a far more successful return trip in the autumn, by which time the Stones would finally crack the U.S. Top Ten with the prophetically titled "Time Is on My Side." Their October appearance on *The Ed Sullivan Show* wreaked such havoc that the redoubtable impresario declared: "I promise you they'll never be back on our shew. Frankly, I didn't see the group until the day before the broadcast. They were recommended by my scouts in England. I was shocked when I saw them. It took me seventeen years to build this shew; I'm not going to have it destroyed in a matter of weeks. Now the Dave Clark Five were nice fellows—they are gentlemen and they performed well.'' (When the Stones juggernaut gathered further momentum, Mr. Sullivan would retract his promise; the Stones, for their part, gave precedence to his "shew" over all others as late as 1969—because, said Keith, it was "so funky.")

Around this time a calculated gamble paid off handsomely when the Stones scored their second British Number One with an uncompromisingly hard-core blues interpretation of Willie Dixon's "Little Red Rooster." This featured some stunning slide guitar from Brian Jones, who always reckoned it his favorite Stones track. But "Rooster" was never issued as a single in the States, where Sam Cooke's more obviously commercial treatment had been a hit a year earlier. Instead, the Stones followed "Time Is on My Side" with a similarly soul-tinged ballad. "Heart of Stone" was not only almost as successful and effective as its prototype but, significantly, a Jagger-Richards composition.

"Little Red Rooster" and "Heart of Stone" formed the nucleus of the American LP *The Rolling Stones, Now!*, the blackest and moodiest—and most magnificent—of all the early Stones albums. (Not that any of the pre-*Aftermath* LPs—save the very first—were anything other than random collections of tracks recorded at various times and places.) Perhaps the quintessential selection on both *Now!* and its British counterpart, *Rolling Stones No. 2,* was "Down Home Girl." Originally written by white American boys Leiber and Butler as an affectionate

New York's Allen Klein takes Keith and Mick for a ride (Popperfoto)

parody of R&B, this number—with all its ludicrous references to the cotton fields, muddy rivers, and turnip-scented perfumes of Dixieland—is rendered absolutely deadpan by the Stones. After all, viewed from the perspective of Dartford and Cheltenham, it was *all* sheer fantasy.

Both the British and the American albums ran into trouble with Oldham's ersatz *Clockwork Orange* liner notes, in which prospective purchasers were advised: "Cast deep in your pockets for loot to buy this disc of groovies and fancy words. If you don't have bread, see that blind man—knock him on the head, steal his wallet, and low and behold you have the loot, if you put in the boot, good, another one sold!" A new back cover omitting the offending passage was pasted over the originals, à la the Beatles' *Yesterday and Today;* Oldham's exhortation was dropped altogether from subsequent printings.

Oldham, with the connivance of the Stones, was about to execute a purge of business manager Eric Easton, replacing him with the more formidable Allen Klein. Meanwhile, Oldham was expanding his interests into a business empire of his own, which included a highly successful new record company. His Immediate label's roster soon boasted the Small Faces; Chris Farlowe (who would translate the Jagger-Richards songbook into a string of British chart toppers—all produced by Jagger); and Keith Richards's Aranbee Pop Symphony Orchestra (whose 1966 LP *Today's Pop Symphony* may be considered the first Rolling Stones solo release).

But it was back in 1964 that Oldham made his most remarkable discovery (after the Stones)—a strikingly beautiful seventeen-year-old straight out of a Reading convent school. In Marianne Faithfull, Andrew discerned the essence of vulnerability and wide-eyed innocence, as surely as he had earlier recognized the Rolling Stones as the embodiment of some rather less savory characteristics. "I've always seemed to be in this cap-in-hand position," Marianne recalled in *NME* a decade later. "I've gone through life saying: 'Look at me, aren't I pretty, please buy me.' Which is what I did as a pop singer, and I've done it with every man since.''

Andrew—who neither knew nor cared whether Marianne could carry a tune—asked his in-house tunesmiths to write her a

---

* Melody Maker *revealed the following list of made-in-Chicago titles as the contents of a projected British LP:* "It's All Over Now," "Confessin' the Blues," "I Can't Be Satisfied," "If You Need Me," "Look What You've Done," "Down the Road Apiece," "2120 S. Michigan Ave.," "High Heel Sneakers," "Reelin' and Rockin'," *and* "Stewed."

single; Mick and Keith obliged with "As Tears Go By." "We never dreamed of doing that ourselves when we wrote it," says Jagger; even Marianne described it as "wet" and "drippy" in her first big *Melody Maker* interview.

Miss Faithfull's delicate sensibilities were offended by her initial exposure to the Stones, whom she found "horrible people—dirty, smelly, spotty." The recording itself, she told *NME,* was "all done in half an hour . . . it was very strange because they wouldn't speak to me. There was Andrew and Mick and Keith and friends and I just went in and did it. I was quite staggered that they wouldn't even give me a lift to the station."

And yet Marianne soon found these very louts irresistibly attractive. Ever possessed by an imp of the perverse, she was also highly ambitious. "My first move was to get a Rolling Stone as a boyfriend. I slept with three and then decided the lead singer was the best bet. . . . In the beginning I was really in love with Keith. . . . He's the epitome of the Romantic Hero, and if you're a middle-class girl and you've read your Byron, that's Keith Richards—even now. He's turned into Count Dracula, but he's still an injured, tortured, damned youth— which is really such fun, isn't it?"

Marianne duplicated the success of "As Tears Go By" with several similarly pastoral ballads, yet her flirtation with pop stardom seemed oddly reluctant; she really wanted to be an actress. In that first *Melody Maker* feature she not only disparaged the song that had made her famous, but called herself "a bad singer" and rambled on about how much she loathed her new career. In any event, she later insisted, her pursuits in both music and theater were doomed, along with her recent mar-

Marianne Faithfull at the ballet with Mick and Chris Jagger (Popperfoto)

riage, by her growing obsession with Jagger. For his part, Mick broke off his celebrated liaison with Chrissie Shrimpton (model Jean's sister) to set up house with Marianne.

"I fell in love with him, and that was that. From that moment I couldn't calculate. . . . It really was difficult pursuing my own work when I was so involved with Mick . . . to do movies you have to go away for three months. . . . The effort of restraining myself and not working was terrible, and I ended up on drugs."

Outspokenly scorning the institution of marriage, Mick and Marianne remained one of the London pop scene's most celebrated couples through the Sixties, though the relationship was evidently somewhat vampiric on both sides. While she drained him emotionally, he used her as raw material for his lyrics. "All my traumas and all my unhappiness he changed into brilliant songs, and it made me sick to see him, like a really good writer or artist, turning the traumas in his own home into work . . . to see these things which were destroying me making him greater and greater. . . .

"It's like having a butterfly on a pin, it's beautiful and fascinating. I was, and I am, so complex and get so disturbed, and he couldn't let me go. He had me on a pin and he was watching me flail and writhe, but it was something that fascinated him as an artist."

During the relationship's final year or two, Marianne would suffer a miscarriage, a suicidal and near-fatal overdose, and an unsuccessful attempt at a pop comeback with another custom-made Jagger-Richards single (to which she contributed some lyrics)—this one titled "Sister Morphine."* From "hear the children sing" to "watch the sheets stain red," the ghostly siren from St. Joseph's Convent had indeed come a long way. Hooked on heroin, separated by the state from the child of her original marriage, Marianne was reduced to spilling some rather incredible beans for Anthony Scaduto's sensationalistic hatchet job, *Mick Jagger: Everybody's Lucifer.*

Years later, however, Marianne would confound all observers with a bona fide comeback album, the disco-tinged *Broken English*—whose impact was, if anything, intensified by the fact that her voice was irrevocably shot. Many critics would rate this distillation of fifteen years' pent-up bitterness and self-hatred among the best albums of 1979—if not rock's most powerful female performance since Janis Joplin.

Marianne Faithfull was among the first in a long line of refined and well-bred ladies, many of them rich and titled, to insinuate themselves on the irresistibly rancid Stones. (The list would eventually include Princess Lee Radziwill and erstwhile Canadian first lady Margaret Trudeau). Some of these encounters furnished raw material for songs in which the Stones rubbed the noses of their blue-blooded groupies in the degradation to which they had voluntarily brought themselves. "Don't play with me, 'cause you're playing with fire," Jagger warned (or titillated) the chauffeur-driven heiress out slumming for the sort of "kicks" upper-class Knightsbridge could never offer. (A few months later he would maliciously portray the spoiled deb in the throes of her "19th Nervous Breakdown," suffered after the singer failed to "rearrange" her psyche during a "trip"—an early LSD reference that was to sail over the heads of the Top Forty jocks.)

The deceptively sweet-sounding "Play with Fire"—recorded

---

* *When the Stones released their own version of "Sister Morphine" on* Sticky Fingers, *the name Faithfull was stricken from the composer credits.*

at seven in the morning by Mick and Keith with Phil Spector and Jack Nitzsche on second guitar and harpsichord, after Andrew and the boys had gone to bed—originally appeared in early 1965 on the B-side of "The Last Time." The first of the great Jagger-Richards hits, "The Last Time," like most of its successors, revolves around an insistent guitar riff that succeeds, with almost nonstop repetition, in sounding hypnotic rather than merely monotonous. This insidious pre–Raga Rock drone is enhanced by some typically sloppy (yet oddly haunting) Stones vocal harmonies. The whole production is characterized by an anarchic dissonance, while the murky rumble in the lower registers conveys the impression of overloaded circuits just about to short. The only ingredient lacking is a lyric with a message to match the immediacy of the Stones' music.

Any talk here of "messages" does not, of course, refer to the sort of articulate protest or arty poetasting that was just coming into vogue in the wake of Bob Dylan. With the songs of the Rolling Stones, the sense, like the sound itself, was nihilistic and crude in both execution and content—and yet by no means artless.

> The first impression you get of our records is an exciting sound . . . it's a case of hunt the words.
>
> Keith Richards, *NME*

> We're not Bob Dylan. It's not supposed to mean anything. It's just about a neurotic bird, that's all. I thought of the title first. It just sounded good.
>
> Mick Jagger, *NME*

Keith and Mick were each discussing a specific new Stones single (respectively, "Get Off of My Cloud" and "19th Nervous Breakdown"), but their remarks apply equally to any of the classic hits that followed "The Last Time." As the "point" of those records was to convey a mood—which was almost always mean and magnificent—it didn't even matter that Mick's slurred delivery rendered many lyrics indecipherable. ("I read an article by Fats Domino which has really influenced me," Jagger would tell *Rolling Stone*'s Jonathan Cott. "He said: 'You should never sing the lyrics out very clearly.'")

The Stones single that really brought together their medium and their message was "(I Can't Get No) Satisfaction"— Jagger-Richards's first rock classic and probably the most unconsciously brilliant song they ever wrote. They were, in fact, so unconscious of its brilliance that they originally regarded "Satisfaction" as a throwaway—"a B-side, maybe an LP track," said Keith.

"He didn't think it would do very well . . . just felt it was a silly kind of riff," Jagger later told Cott. At the time he said in *Melody Maker:* "We like it, but didn't think of it as a single. Then London [Records] said they had to have a single immediately because 'The Last Time' was long gone and we had a *Shindig* TV date and had to have something to play. So they just released 'Satisfaction.'"

In Britain, the decision to use "Satisfaction" on an EP— reversed only after it became the Stones' first runaway U.S. hit—led to a two-month delay in the single's release. "We already had the EP all pressed, the covers done, and the plugs lined up," said Mick. Then the Beatles issued a new single, and the charts-conscious Stones were unwilling to settle for second place to their rivals' inevitable Number One. "If 'Help' hadn't come out then, we would have brought ours out a month ago," said Jagger, responding to complaints from British fans that the Stones had abandoned them for America.

One can only surmise that "Satisfaction" was so simple and effortless, so (in a sense) pure and quintessentially *them*, that the Rolling Stones at first had no idea of what they had perpetrated. Again built around an insistent and repetitive riff—in this case filtered through Keith's new fuzz box—"Satisfaction" was (to paraphrase Oldham) more than just a record; it was a slice of life. "Satisfaction" was an *attitude:* three minutes and forty-five seconds of noise that perfectly captured a stance—epitomized by the Stones themselves and shared by their rebellious adolescent fans—of inarticulate cynicism, frustration, and boredom with the consumer society that had spawned them, and from which there was no escape.

According to the record, Jagger is bombarded with "useless information" coming over the airwaves, and by transparently inane and fraudulent commercials for useless products; but it would never occur to him to turn off his radio or TV. The females he encounters are similarly vapid and manipulative; but he goes after them anyway, well aware that in the end all he'll have gained from the experience will be . . . "no satisfaction." With all the subtlety of a sledgehammer, the music advances a state of numbness comparable to that described by the lyrics— yet Jagger's vocal is so seductive, steeped with a lust so unfocused, unadulterated, and pure, one is hard put to resist his contemptuous invitation to nowhere.

Though few lines were sufficiently explicit to give censors grounds for an outright ban of "Satisfaction," a number of established publications seized upon its sexual implications to fascinate and horrify adult readers. An August 1965 article in *Newsweek* described the Stones as a "leering quintet" best known for their pornographic lyrics. It not only "exposed" "Satisfaction," but "revealed" that the American B-side, "The Under Assistant West Coast Promotion Man," was filthier still. But the man in the seersucker suit celebrated therein was in fact hardly a pimp, but quite simply the under assistant promotion man for London Records, George Sherlock, who had accompanied the Stones on their first American tour.

To little avail did the moralists flail: "Satisfaction" was an almost overnight Number One in the United States, where the Rolling Stones had heretofore been unable to crack the Top Five, and where they now dislodged the Dave Clark Five (or was it Herman's Hermits?) as the country's second most popular group.

"Satisfaction" and "The Last Time" provided the cornerstones for the American *Out of Our Heads,* whose release was heralded with a typical effusion from Oldham's fertile pen:

> faces of today: sounds of tomorrow
> spots, not gauze, and peepers of truth
> an audience in a sea of fear
> for big daddy doesn't relate any more
> this does: so float into tomorrow.

Out of Our Heads became the Stones' first American Number One LP—and Gold Album—within weeks of its release. I can remember rows of empty seats at a Stones concert in New York's Academy of Music (now the Palladium) the week "Satisfaction" was released in May 1965; the band's return engagement that November was sold out well in advance.

Meanwhile, "Satisfaction" was reportedly Top of the Pops in no less than thirty-eight other countries, including Turkey, Greece, Finland, South Africa, Argentina, the Philippines, Lebanon, Israel, and Bermuda. Though other groups enjoyed Number One records, the "Satisfaction" breakthrough, in tandem with a uniquely potent image, firmly established the Rolling Stones as an international legend second to none but the Beatles.

"The Rolling Stones don't play concerts—they play riots."

Top Photo   (Keystone Press Agency)   (Photo Trends)

Throughout 1965 the Stones shored up both their popularity and their image with grueling tours of Ireland, Australia, New Zealand, Scandinavia, Germany, Britain, and North America—and with some notorious incidents along the way. In Berlin, Oldham recalled in his 1972 *NME* interview:

Someone said to Mick that it would be hysterical if he did the goosestep during the instrumental break of "Satisfaction." Well, Jagger being Jagger not only does that, he goes on stage and does the whole Hitler routine. The audience were going crazy anyway and that just drove them berserk. There were too many fuzz and dogs in the theater for them to do anything then, but when they got outside they overturned 130 cars, and every train leaving the city for the suburbs was wrecked completely. Well, at the time I thought: That was a buzz, that was a good show.

This German tour was also noteworthy for adding a permanent fixture to the Stones' entourage in the form of yet another beautiful blond actress. Unlike Marianne Faithfull, however, Anita Pallenberg carried not even the aura of innocence; an Italian national and scion of the international jet set, her willful character and "decadent" appetites would soon become legendary. Having previously met Brian Jones in Paris, Anita now accompanied him back to London.

The Rolling Stones scored their most lurid 1965 headlines on July 22, when three of their number were fined £5 apiece for "insulting behavior" perpetrated after a show in Romford, England, the previous March 18. The attendant of an all-night service station in East London testified that a "shaggy-haired monster" in shades—Bill Wyman—had confronted him with an obscenely phrased request to use the toilet. When the man refused permission, Jagger, Jones, and unidentified friends piled out of a car, locked arms with Wyman to chant "We can piss anywhere, man"—and did just that.

Despite Wyman's sworn testimony that the Stones had not been "in the mood to be aggressive; our mood was more gay and amusing," the chairman of the bench lectured the trio (who had got their suits and ties out of mothballs for the occasion): "You have been found guilty of behavior not becoming young gentlemen. Just because you have reached exalted heights in your profession does not give you the right to behave in this manner. On the contrary, you should set a standard of behavior. You should be a moral pattern for your many supporters."

"None of those things the Stones got up to were done as stunts," insists Oldham. "It was just, like, 'I want a piss, I'll take it in the nearest alley.' "

Yet deliberately or not, the Stones seemed to flirt with further controversy and notoriety almost every time they opened their mouths (if not their flies). Even before his day in court, Jagger had addressed—in a January 1965 *Melody Maker* story—a question about the Stones' moral "obligation to teenagers" with characteristic bluntness: "Everybody has their own moral code. I conduct myself as I see fit, and what I do is my own affair. In the same way I feel this should be the right of every teenager today.

"If *they* want to smoke, drink, swallow purple hearts and pills, then the decision is theirs. Stars and celebrities should not try to set any level in morals. . . . I would never appear on television and suggest teenagers *should* have sex before marriage. It's up to them to decide. Let teenagers live as they please."

The Stones, in other words, felt that their job was to reflect reality as *they* perceived it; let the kids do with that information what they would. No "star" had ever spoken like this before, or stated, as Keith did in the same article, "We're atheists and we're not ashamed to admit it." The Stones only grew bolder, and within a year or so Brian would tell *Melody Maker* that marriage was "an anachronism," while Mick would be quoted in the sensationalistic *News of the World:* "As soon as a daughter of mine reached the age of puberty I'd tell her to start taking the pill."

Back in 1965, however, even a Rolling Stone would not admit publicly to taking drugs or having sex with strangers. Radical as the Stones were in comparison with their contemporaries, much was still left unsaid, or suggested only through implication. It was even possible for younger and more innocent fans, unable to read between the buttons, to suppose that—"wild" music and looks notwithstanding—all the Rolling Stones were up to was good clean fun.

Anita Pallenberg and Brian Jones (Popperfoto)

This, at any rate, was the picture promulgated by *The Rolling Stones Monthly Book*, launched by Beat Publications of London in the format of its earlier *The Beatles Monthly Book*. Unlike the Fab Four, the Stones were even credited with editing—each in turn—every issue of their magazine, the tone of which may be gauged from a typical pair of "editorials" by, respectively, Charlie Watts and Mick Jagger:

Here we are again, back in the "Old Country" after spending what seemed like months away . . . it's great to be back.

Bill and I returned home two weeks before Christmas while the others were either still in the States or elsewhere relaxing. But there was no rest for us, we had to be back early to get our new homes into shape.

I'm near enough settled in now in my 16th Century home in Sussex, although I'll be adding little items of furniture all the time . . . plus, of course, my ever-growing collection of swords and relics from the American Civil War.

Bill's OK as well, I think. . . .

What have I been doing while I have been home? Well, I've spent a lot of time with my parents in Dartford . . . also made a point of dropping into the fan club and had a terrific surprise! There was a surfing shirt waiting for me sent in by an American fan. . . .

Oh another thing I must tell you—I've bought a dog! It's a Yorkshire terrier and is a bitch. I'll leave it at home while I'm travelling, and I can rest assured they will really look after it because my mum has a dog of her own.

Just before I go, I must mention that despite all this cold weather we've been having it's not getting through to me. I brought a big cuddly fur coat back from the States and I couldn't have timed it better. It's something like that sealskin one I had, remember?

Bye for now. . . .

Apart from concert and court appearances and the acquisition of new houses, dogs, and girl friends, the top priority on the Stones' agenda was a follow-up to "Satisfaction." "We knew it wouldn't be as good," Jagger told Cott, "but so what." Actually, they managed the difficult feat of coming up with a record that was both very similar and very nearly as good.

Though "Get Off of My Cloud" was based not on a solo guitar riff but a rapid-fire chord sequence—"just the old 'Twist and Shout' progression with an extra chord thrown in on the chorus," said Keith—the lyrics and general mood echoed "Satisfaction." Jagger, according to the song, is sitting alone in his high-rise, oblivious to the world, records blasting. But his reverie is continually disturbed, by a door-to-door salesman and

by neighbors complaining of the noise. Finally he takes a drive downtown and dozes off in his car, only to awaken to the sight of parking tickets plastered across his wind screen. To all those who hassle him, Jagger has one simple message: "Hey! You! Get off of my cloud!"

This recording, however, never ranked among the Stones' own favorites; and perhaps because the words, while more elaborate and surrealistic than those of "Satisfaction," were also more self-conscious, Jagger later dismissed them as "crap." In his 1971 *Rolling Stone* interview, Richards called the record a "rushed" job. "Actually, what I wanted was to do it slow like a Lee Dorsey thing. We rocked it up. I thought it was one of Andrew's worst productions." "Get Off of My Cloud" was a worldwide Number One anyway; and at the end of 1965 *NME* declared the Rolling Stones Britain's top singles act of the year.

In the United States, the Stones now found themselves in the Beatles-like position of having their record company eager to pump out "new" product faster than the band could get it down on tape. "Get Off of My Cloud" was used as the centerpiece for the American LP *December's Children*—a mélange of British EP tracks (including "You Better Move On," one of the Stones' first recordings) and leftovers from the U.K. *Out of Our Heads*.

Of the few truly new selections on *December's Children*, Jagger and Richards's own rendition of their Marianne Faithfull hit, "As Tears Go By," proved so popular that it was turned into an American hit single (and subsequently earned the distinction, when crooned in Italian as "Con Le Mie Lacrime," of being the only song the Stones ever re-recorded in a foreign language). Apart from being so out of character, the arrangement—solo voice, acoustic guitar, and string quartet—was inescapably reminiscent of Paul McCartney's recent "Yesterday." For the first time (though hardly the last) the Rolling Stones were taking their musical cues from the Beatles.

Not that the Stones had ever troubled to conceal the fact that they were opportunists; this, paradoxically, had always been a facet of their "uncompromising honesty" and "realism." They had, furthermore, grown tired of covering black American numbers, so around the end of 1965 they made the abrupt transition to relying almost exclusively on their own material. Aside from the occasional blockbuster single, however, Mick and Keith had yet to master the trick of consistently writing in a distinct Rolling Stones style. So they, like everyone else at the time, tended to copy the Beatles—despite the fact that nobody, not even Jagger-Richards, could match the songwriting genius of Lennon-McCartney.

Jagger and Richards's newly acquired musical self-sufficiency also served to make their domination of the band complete. Wyman and Watts (who was now happily married) didn't seem to care; from the start, says Bill, musical policy "was all pretty much down to Mick, Keith, and Brian . . . Charlie and I just slotted in." Jones, however, turned increasingly bitter and paranoid, notwithstanding his admission (in *Melody Maker*) that "without Mick the Stones would have been nothing."

Some say Brian had little ear for songwriting in any case (though he would eventually compose the score for *A Degree of Murder*, Germany's entry at 1967's Cannes Film Festival, with Anita Pallenberg in a starring role). At any rate, unable for whatever reason to contribute on a par with Mick and Keith, Brian channeled his restlessness into the mastery of an almost endless assortment of increasingly exotic instruments.

According to Richards, Jones had "dropped the guitar" as far back as 1963. "The harp became his thing. . . . He was a cat who could play any instrument. It was like, 'There it is, music comes out of it, if I work at it for a bit I can do it.' It's him on the marimbas on 'Under My Thumb' . . . the strings on '2,000 Light Years from Home,' [the] mellotron and the brass on 'We Love You.'''

On the other hand, as Keith told *NME* in 1974, "he just wouldn't touch the guitar, so it would be down to me to lay down all the tracks while he would be leaping around on the dulcimer or the marimba." Nonetheless, Brian's virtuosity added a range of colors and textures that the Stones' musical palette conspicuously lacked after his departure.

Brian asserted himself in other ways. From a distance, at least, he was the group's most charming and articulate spokesman. Perhaps the most elegantly flamboyant Beau Brummell ever conjured by rock & roll, Jones was also a crucial part of the Stones' visual image—right down to the ringed and puffy eyes with which he peers from the later LP covers. Somebody once wrote that Brian actually lived all the things Mick merely sang about.

Out of the public eye, Brian distinguished himself with his early and prodigious drug experimentation, and by knocking off as many as sixty-four groupies over the course of a single month. "Brian would go out and meet a lot of people, before we did," Keith told *Rolling Stone,* "because Mick and I spent most of our time writing. He'd go out and get high somewhere, get smashed. We'd say: 'Look, we got a session tomorrow, man, got to keep it together.' He'd come, completely out of his head, and zonk out on the floor . . . which was a drag 'cause it meant the whole band wasn't playing."

"Brian was a leader," added Anita. "With the Stones, he was the first one that had a car. He was the first into flash clothes. And smoke. And acid. It was back when it seemed anything was possible."

When Keith, too, began taking LSD, he and Brian enjoyed a brief rapprochement—shutting out their still-uninitiated lead singer. Said Keith:

There was always something between Brian, Mick, and myself that didn't make it somewhere. . . . He was either completely into Mick at the expense of me . . . or he'd be completely in with me tryin' to work something against Mick. . . . He wouldn't be able to make it with two other guys at one time. . . .

As he went along, he got more and more fragile and delicate. His personality, and physically. . . . People were always laying stuff on him because he was a Stone. And he'd try it. He'd take anything. Any sort of trip, too, head trips. He never had time to work it out 'cause we were on the road all the time, always on the plane the next day. Eventually, it caught up. . . .

When the record-breaking million-pound deal that Allen Klein had engineered for the Stones was announced on New Year's Day, 1966, its most newsworthy stipulation was the group's agreement to make five movies, all to be financed by Decca. Over the next few months no less than three different Stones flicks were said to be imminent: first *Back Behind and in Front,* with a script by Andrew Loog Oldham; then *A Clockwork Orange* (to which the group would prove unable to acquire the rights); and finally *Only Lovers Left Alive.* This last was described in a May 1966 Stones press release as "a novel by Dave Willis dealing, in essence, with an imaginary conquest of England by its violent and rebellious youth."

But none of these films ever materialized, even though at the time it seemed inevitable that the Rolling Stones saga would generate its own equivalent of *A Hard Day's Night* and *Help!* The only actual Stones celluloid to come out of the endless

From the Aftermath *photo sessions (London Records/Peter Kanze Collection)*

speculation and announcements was *Charlie Is My Darling,* Oldham's hour-long documentary of the Stones touring Ireland.

On the musical front, the group followed "As Tears Go By" with the more archetypal Stones single "19th Nervous Breakdown." This was originally one of the titles announced for inclusion on an LP called *Could* You *Walk on the Water?,* whose release was subsequently delayed and ultimately canceled. Decca, according to one of its spokesmen, "would not issue it with that title at any price."*

The album's cover photo (of the group alongside a reservoir) and ten-page picture book were used, along with "19th Nervous Breakdown" itself, for the first Stones "greatest hits" compilation, the coyly titled *Big Hits (High Tide and Green Grass).* Much of the rest of *Could* You *Walk on the Water?* surfaced in the spring on *Aftermath,* an album that stands as a landmark in the Stones' career for several reasons—not least of which is that it remains perhaps the finest, certainly the most creative, of all the LPs in the first five years of their discography.

At fifty-two minutes and twenty-three seconds, the British version of *Aftermath* also broke all records as the longest-running single pop LP to date (the Stones' previous U.K. album had clocked in at 29:02). Likewise, *Aftermath*'s "Goin' Home" beat out Dylan's "Desolation Row" in the category of longest individual song. (The 11:35 "Goin' Home" was furthermore the first extended improvisation released by a major rock group—though by no means the last.) Finally, *Aftermath* was the first Stones album to consist entirely of Jagger-Richards

* *The full track listing for* Could *You* Walk on the Water? *was: "19th Nervous Breakdown," "Sad Day," "Take It or Leave It," "Think," "Mother's Little Helper," "Goin' Home," "Sittin' on the Fence," "Doncha Bother Me," "Ride on Baby," and "Lookin' Tired" (described by Keith as "Nashville Blues").*

originals; and the extent to which these were covered by other groups—including such flagging British Invasion veterans as the Searchers—soon approached Beatle-esque proportions.

Musically, *Aftermath* was so pop-oriented that the Stones might have been accused of heresy had some of the material appeared eighteen months earlier; but by 1966, of course, British R&B had become a dead issue. Brian's budding eclecticism further distances much of *Aftermath* from the Stones' original black American sources. On several cuts the most prominent instrument is a baroque-sounding harpsichord; and "Lady Jane," with Jones on dulcimer, is Elizabethan to the core. "What to Do" (left off the U.S. edition) even mimics that most WASP-ish of all American bands, the Beach Boys.

Lyrically, *Aftermath* explored the related themes of sex, drugs, and rock & roll. Fifteen years later this may sound unremarkable, but the Stones were the first to tackle simultaneously all three topics with both a measure of intelligence and a corresponding lack of sentimentality or even romanticism. The brutal thrust of such ditties as "Stupid Girl," "Under My Thumb," and "Out of Time" has since, of course, induced paroxysms of rage among feminists. Rock & roll—specifically, Life on the Road—is given an equally unvarnished portrayal in songs like the aforementioned "What to Do" ("Nothing to do, nowhere to go, talking to people that you don't know"). So much for the glamour and the glitter of stardom!

But Jagger reserved his cruelest irony for *Aftermath*'s most overt "drug song," "Mother's Little Helper" (held off the LP in America, where it was issued as a single). At a time when the adult media were beginning to rant about *teenage* drug abuse, the Stones retaliated by zeroing in on all those harried middle-aged housewives incapable of getting through the day, or getting to sleep at night, without the help of their legally prescribed "little yellow pills."

Perhaps the most interesting piece from this juncture is the single "Paint It, Black." Though the lyrics retained the sur-

(Popperfoto)

realism and nihilism of, say, "Get Off of My Cloud," the music represented quite a departure from the Rolling Stones' hit formula. Because the lead instrument was Brian's sitar, the Stones were once again accused of imitating the Beatles. But George Harrison never explored the sitar's possibilities as a *rock* instrument with this much imagination. The sitar had become—for at least a few weeks—Brian's first love. "It has completely different principles from the guitar and opens up new fields for a group, in harmonics and everything," he told *Melody Maker*.

That paper's singles reviewer rated "Paint It, Black" "a glorious Indian raga-rock riot that will send the Stones back to #1 and probably give pop the biggest punch up the Punjab since Peter Sellers met Sophia Loren. . . . Charlie creates a galloping beat suggesting high-speed elephants, and Mick's accent gets progressively more curried. Oh yes, very pleasing, very pleasing indeed!" Keith would later tell *Rolling Stone* that "Paint It, Black" (unlike Harrison's solemn forays into Raga Rock) was actually conceived as "a comedy track. Bill was playing an organ, doing a take-off of our first manager who started his career as an organist in a cinema pit. . . . Brian playing the sitar makes it a whole other thing.

"There were some weird letters, racial letters. 'Was there a comma in the title? Was it an order to the world?'"

Over the summer of 1966, the Stones promoted *Aftermath* with what would prove to be the original lineup's last American tour. The shrieking bedlam of a '66-vintage Stones concert was captured for the American album *Got Live If You Want It!* Ironically—as it was not issued in Britain—the LP was recorded (on September 23, 1966) at London's Royal Albert Hall. Strictly as a piece of recorded music, the record is a travesty, what with the primitive state of in-concert rock & roll recording techniques and the fact that the Stones couldn't hear themselves for all the screaming. Acute imbalance renders some of their instruments inaudible, and Jagger's off-key whimpering on "Time Is on My Side" is enough to make the most fanatic archivist cringe.

Even the documentary value of *Got Live If You Want It!* is somewhat negated by the fact that some tracks aren't really "live." Perhaps because numbers like the "Paint It, Black" curtain raiser had been interrupted by full-blown riots in the Albert Hall (whose management responded with a ban on further pop concerts there), Oldham elected to pad the album with ancient studio outtakes such as "I've Been Loving You Too Long" and "Fortune Teller." Onto these he overdubbed screaming "fans" in what must rank among his—if not the Stones'—most cynical and contemptuous ploys.

The album's title was originally announced as *Have You Seen Your Mother, Live,* due to its inclusion of a version of "Have You Seen Your Mother, Baby, Standing in the Shadow?" This was the Stones' new single, described by Keith as "our most progressive yet!" A year later Mick called it "the ultimate freakout . . . What more could we say?" For the trade advertisements and the American picture sleeve, the boys donned an assortment of ladies' wigs and stockings, makeup, skirts, and high heels. While Flossie Jones (as Brian was rechristened for the occasion) impersonated a relatively enticing airline stewardess, Molly Richards, Sarah Jagger, and Millicent Watts took on the personae of cadaverous crones. A severely uniformed—and truly mortifying—Penelope Wyman settled into the role of a disabled citizen. ("I think Bill must get the king of the queens award for his portrayal of the bird in the wheelchair," Molly later told *NME*.) After Jerry Schatzberg snapped the picture, Flossie wheeled Penelope into a nearby bar, where their three fellow witches joined them for a round of beers, attracting little notice from the regular clientele.

The picture itself, however, inspired a great deal of comment, ranging from the predictably censorious to this from a Swedish *NME* subscriber: "The most fantastic, great, fabulous, superb, exciting thing I've ever seen in my whole life."* But the Stones' music, if not their image, was turning rather too peculiar for many fans. "Have You Seen Your Mother" was a barrage of electronic noise, whose sinister imagery transcended mere adolescent angst to anticipate the direction the Stones' songs were to take in the next year or two. "We live in the shadow . . . glimpse through the shadow . . . hate in the shadow." Eight years later Richards would still defend the Stones' original vision of the song as "a monster" to *NME*'s Nick Kent: "We did this *unbelievable* backing track. Somehow it got completely lost by the time it was transformed into vinyl, probably [because] Andrew Oldham has never been able to record a brass sound properly. . . . And then we had to deal with Andrew's little delusions of grandeur which made him want us to turn out like the Ronettes or the Righteous Brothers. [Both groups were essentially putty in the hands of Andrew's idol, Phil Spector.] He used to think anything was possible if you put enough echo on it!"

The single snapped the Stones' chain of Number Ones in Britain, where it attained only the fifth position; in the U.S. it climbed no higher than number nine. But this did not discourage the Stones from veering off into the outer limits when the magic year 1967 came to pass.

"The revolution is at hand!" Brian Jones proclaimed in *NME*. "Censorship is still with us in a number of ugly forms, but the days when men like comedian Lenny Bruce and artist Jim Dine are persecuted is coming to an end. Young people are measuring opinion with new yardsticks and it must mean great freedom of expression. Pop music will have its part to play in all this."

The Rolling Stones actually kicked off 1967 with a single that was somewhat less experimental than its predecessor—though scarcely less controversial. The title alone—"Let's Spend the Night Together"—sufficed to keep the designated A-side off most American Top Forty playlists. "If people have warped, twisted, dirty minds," Jagger commented in *Melody Maker*, "I suppose it could have sexual overtones." Ed Sullivan, for his part, demanded that Mick change the words "the night" to "some time" when the Stones plugged the record on his program. Quoth Uncle Ed: "I have hundreds of thousands of kids watching my shew and I won't stand for anything like that."

The charge that the Stones had "sold out" for the occasion evidently rankled. "I never said 'time,' I really didn't," Jagger insisted to *Rolling Stone*'s Jonathan Cott the following year. "I said mumble 'Let's spend some *mmmm* together, let's spend some *mmmm* together.' They would have cut it off if I had said 'night.' "

The most ironic aspect of the "Let's Spend the Night Together" controversy was that U.S. radio stations elected instead to play the flip side of the single—which soon proved to be the Stones' biggest hit since "Satisfaction." A lilting ballad turned all the more pastoral by Brian's recorder, "Ruby Tuesday" was said to have been named after a famous groupie.

Yet despite this unexpected (and well-deserved) success, few aficionados have rated the album that followed as highly as, say, *Aftermath*. Only two years later Jagger would vote *Between the Buttons* his least favorite Stones LP, telling *NME*: "I must have had a mental aberration. I can't even remember doing it."

Though not without its charms, *Buttons* does seem rather a limp noodle in the context of such aural gang bangs as "Satisfaction." The sound of the Stones had not only turned soft, but gone downright vaudevillian. And Jagger (no Paul McCartney, let alone a Ray Davies) could be insufferable indeed when he slipped into his newfound music-hall persona—though "Something Happened to Me Yesterday" at least came across as a droll evocation of the influence of "something oh so trippy" [LSD] on the virginal psyches of these preposterous song-and-dance peddlers. Elsewhere on *Between the Buttons*—"Who's Been Sleeping Here?"—Mick and the Stones merely ape Bob Dylan and his recent *Blonde on Blonde*.

Some related tidbits of trivia: On one of those rare occasions upon which Charlie Watts was actually heard to speak, he revealed (in *Melody Maker*) that the album got its title when "Andrew told me to do the drawings for the LP and he told me the title would go between the buttons [on the cover photo]. I thought he meant the title was *Between the Buttons*, so it stayed. It was all my fault."

Also, *Between the Buttons* featured the first "Jagger-Richards" songs written individually by Mick or Keith alone. Though Jagger would set a policy of keeping such details secret, Richards did let slip that he was entirely responsible for "Connection," and Jagger for "Yesterday's Papers."

Unlike all previous new Stones LPs, *Between the Buttons*, held at bay by the Monkees, failed to claim the Number One spot in Britain. It did, however, occasion the Stones' first invitation to appear on the country's most popular televised variety show, *Sunday Night at the London Palladium*. Any suspicions of sellout were dispelled when the Stones declined to join the rest of the evening's attractions for the show's traditional finale—during which everyone stepped onto a revolving stage to wave goodbye to ten million Britons sitting in front of their tellies. On this occasion they had to settle for some Rolling Stones dummies that had been constructed by Gerald Scarfe for a previous skit, and which were now taken in hand by comedians Peter Cook and Dudley Moore.

Judging from the vitriol this incident aroused among Britain's top show biz personalities, it would appear that the Stones had committed some unspeakable sacrilege. "All those people have is a nonexistent glitter which they believe surrounds them," Jagger retorted in *Melody Maker*. "It saved me those few minutes of embarrassment, not watching myself going round on that thing. I've thought it was stupid since I was a little kid. I can't bear waving—that's really the reason."

Meanwhile, the outspokenness of the Stones—particularly Brian—had gone far beyond those loutish one-liners of yore. "Our real followers have moved on with us," Jones declared in *NME*,

and are questioning some of the basic immoralities which are tolerated in present-day society—the war in Vietnam, persecution of homosexuals, illegality of abortion and drug taking. All these things are immoral. We are making our own statement—others are making more intellectual ones. . . .

I believe we are moving toward a new age in ideas and events. Astrologically we are at the end of the Pisces age—at the beginning of which people like Christ were born. We are soon to begin the age of Aquarius, in which events as important as those at the beginning of Pisces are likely to occur. There is a young revolution in thought and manner about to take place.

---

* Brian subsequently outdid himself by posing as a uniformed Nazi grinding a baby doll under his shiny black boot in what was described as an antifascist protest.

While the Stones had always antagonized the Establishment as a means of rallying support from the young and disaffected, now the stakes mounted as both camps came to take the band more seriously. In this context, even the Palladium incident was seen as a wanton assault on a venerable British institution. "We bothered them," Richards remembered in his 1971 *Rolling Stone* interview. "We bothered 'em because of the way we looked, the way we'd act. Because we never showed any reverence for them whatsoever. Whereas the Beatles had. They'd gone along with it so far, with the MBE's and shaking hands. Whenever we were asked about things like that we'd say: 'Fuck it. Don't want to know about things like that. Bollocks. Don't need it.' That riled 'em somewhere."

In 1967, insists Keith, someone "quite a way up" decided to teach the Stones a lesson. Until that time, as Jagger would tell Cott, "it was just the boring newspapers [that attacked the Stones], but when the fuzz start getting into that it can be very draggy. They have the wherewithal to do it to you if they want to. The newspapers can only scream from their drunken haunts like the Wig and Feather Club, but they can't do anything. The police can."

And did. To rehash an oft-told tale: At 7:55 P.M. on February 12, 1967, at his stately Sussex home "Redlands," Keith Richards was jolted from his LSD reverie by a series of sharp knocks. Opening the front door, he was confronted by one Chief Inspector Dinely, several men and women in police uniform, and a search warrant. The visitors made their way into a room where they noticed a "strong, sweet, unusual smell" and a party of seven young men and a young woman, who (as Detective-Constable Evelyn Fuller would testify) "was naked, apart from a fur rug wrapped round her, and in a merry mood . . . completely unconcerned about what was going on around her." The woman was Marianne Faithfull; one of the male guests was Mick Jagger.

Some of the policemen found traces of cannabis in a pipe and further small quantities of the drug in a tin and upon a table. Meanwhile, another had ransacked a bedroom to discover four pep pills in the pocket of a green jacket belonging to Jagger. Some tablets of heroin were found in the possession of one Robert Fraser, but the only really substantial quantity of cannabis turned out to be on the person of a mysterious Canadian acquaintance who was subsequently allowed to slip quietly out of the country.

The two Stones and their entourage maintained a supercilious and flippant attitude throughout the proceedings. Keith declined to turn off the stereo and reprimanded one of the policewomen for soiling a valuable Moroccan cushion with her shoe. Marianne let her rug drop to the floor at every opportunity. When the search was completed, Keith would recall in *Rolling Stone*, "as they started going out the door somebody put on [Dylan's] 'Rainy Day Women' really loud. 'Everybody must get stoned.'"

According to Richards, the whole episode was orchestrated by the scandal rag *News of the World*, whose vendetta against the Stones had, he says, been inflamed by Jagger's serving a libel writ over an article portraying him as a dope fiend. (Shades of Oscar Wilde, who after suing the Marquess of Queensberry for spreading tales of Wilde's homosexuality, himself ended up in jail when the "libel" proved to be true.) The Stones bust was kept out of the papers for a week—"held back," said Keith, "to see how much bread they could get off us. . . . Unfortunately none of us knew what to do, who to bum the bread to, and so went slightly via the wrong people and it didn't get up all the

way." It was *News of the World,* of course, that finally broke the story—complete with intimate details supplied by a mysterious witness. And so the matter rested for several months while the prosecution prepared its case.

The following month the Stones swept through nine European countries, their last series of concerts prior to an extended Beatles-like retirement from touring. The story of the Redlands raid having preceded them, all the Stones were thoroughly searched—and often stripped naked—whenever they went through customs.

The band even ventured behind the Iron Curtain on April 13 for a memorable pair of performances in Warsaw. The Official Polish News Agency noted in its brief account of "one of the famous modern music big teams, the Rolling Stones" that "the audience, consisting mainly of young people, received the performance with an enthusiasm that was too noisy." The story neglected to mention the ten thousand youths who rioted outside the Palace of Culture to protest the fact that nearly all the tickets had been distributed to the Communist Party elite. After failing to subdue the mobs with mere nightsticks and high-pressure water hoses, the police unleashed Dobermans and tear gas and made dozens of arrests.

Following the Stones' return to Britain, Brian Jones was rendered a warm official welcome home by twelve detectives who appeared at his door with a search warrant; they found what they were searching for in a matter of minutes. This just happened to be the very day—May 10—that Mick and Keith were due in court, where they learned they were to be tried on drug charges forty days thence. Somebody "quite a way up" apparently knew how to prejudice a jury against the Rolling Stones and was out to "get" them with a vengeance.

Though Brian's case was remanded with a £250 fine, the trial of Jagger and Richards (along with Robert Fraser) began on June 27. Despite testimony from Jagger's doctor that the four pep pills, legally purchased in Italy, were similar to those he had regularly prescribed for Mick, the defendant was found guilty. Along with Keith, he was hustled off to jail for the night, to await his sentence after Richards's case was tried the next day. The following morning Jagger was brought back to the court in handcuffs.

Richards's case was more complicated, and the evidence against him even slimmer; all he could be charged with was allowing "dangerous drugs" to be used in his home. The prosecution dwelt at length on the unorthodox behavior of the woman in the party, referred to as "Miss X." "Would you agree," Keith was asked, "in the ordinary course of events, you would expect a young woman to be embarrassed if she had nothing on but a rug in the presence of eight men?" "I said: 'I'm not concerned with your petty morals which are illegitimate,'" recalled Richards. "They couldn't take that one." (By this time some press reports had even insinuated that one guest had preoccupied himself throughout the raid with sucking a candy bar out of Miss X's vagina, and that George Harrison—a still-untouchable Beatle—had been quietly escorted from the scene of the crime.)

Keith, for his part, attempted to expose the role of *News of the World* (which would later admit having "passed information to the police," adding "it was our plain duty to do so"). The jury was then reminded that "you are not trying the *News of the World* and you are not trying the young lady in the rug." After the jury found the defendant guilty, Judge Leslie Block sentenced Richards to one year in prison, Fraser to six months, and Jagger to three months. "When he gave me the year sentence,"

Brian Jones goes to court to face drug charges: May 1967, November 1967, and September 1968 (Popperfoto)

remembered Keith, "he called me 'scum' and 'filth' and 'people like this shouldn't be . . . .'" The "criminals" were taken away in handcuffs.

On June 30, after three nights in jail, the two Stones were released on £7,000 ($17,000) bail apiece when their solicitors lodged appeals. In the meantime, an enormous groundswell of sympathy for the Stones had developed. The Who rush-released a hastily recorded single of "The Last Time" and "Under My Thumb" "as a protest against the savage sentences . . . the first of a series of Jagger-Richard songs to keep their work before the public until they are again free to record themselves." Though Davey Jones, in London for a concert with the Monkees, asked reporters "who needs drugs when you're getting this much fun out of life?" other members of the Prefab Four wore black armbands on stage that evening. The sentences were even protested by Members of Parliament.

But most unusual of all was the famous two thousand-word editorial in the London *Times,* headlined WHO BREAKS A BUT-

TERFLY ON A WHEEL? Though it was almost unprecedented, in Britain, for a newspaper to comment on a case until every conceivable appeal had been heard—and some people even expected the august journal's editor to be tried himself for contempt of court—the editorial noted that "the circumstances [were] sufficiently unusual to warrant such discussion." *The Times* deemed that "Mr. Jagger's is about as mild a drug case as can ever have been brought before the courts" and remonstrated that "if we are going to make any case a symbol of the conflict between the sound traditional values of Britain and the new hedonism, then we must be sure that the sound traditional values include those of tolerance and equity." On July 31 the Court of Criminal Appeal lifted the sentences; a crowd of flower children attempted to stage a Hyde Park love-in to celebrate.

Addressing a farmers' dinner some weeks later, Judge Block himself flouted the conventions of British legal procedure with his allusion to "Stones": "I refer to certain objects of no use to farmers. I may say that they are of no use to man or beast, unless they are dealt with by being ground very small. . . . We did our best, your fellow countrymen and I, and my fellow magistrates, to cut these Stones down to size. But alas, it was not to be, because the Court of Criminal Appeal let them roll free.''

The judge was apparently oblivious that he might be prejudicing the outcome of an appeal by Brian Jones, who had recently been sentenced to nine months in jail for possession of ''a total of thirty-five and a quarter grains of Indian hemp.'' Brian's defense had included the statement: ''I have taken drugs in the past to a slight extent, but have now absolutely decided to have nothing more to do with them. . . . They had only brought me trouble and disrupted my career.'' Nonetheless, he was obliged to spend twenty-four hours behind bars, until his bail was set, during which time an angry protest march down the King's Road in Chelsea resulted in the arrests of eight people, including Mick Jagger's brother Chris.

These episodes irrevocably changed not only the Stones' view of the law, but their own self-image as well. ''Up until then,'' Richards would tell *Rolling Stone*'s Greenfield, ''it had been show-biz, entertainment . . . teenyboppers. At that point you knew they considered you to be outside . . . the law. Like Dylan says, 'To live outside the law you must be honest.' ''

''It was a systematic campaign of continual harassment,'' said Jagger in a 1974 *NME* interview. ''But the thing is, they destroyed Brian in the process, which isn't very nice. . . . It finished him off, there's no doubt about that.''

Only days after his jail sentence was softened to probation, Brian would be arrested in yet a third raid—and then a fourth. Particularly in the last instance, the drugs had clearly been planted by an overzealous detective. Nonetheless, the jury could always be counted on for a guilty verdict when the case involved a Rolling Stone on a drug charge.

Meanwhile, following the Jagger-Richards bust, Brian's morale was further undermined during a trip to Morocco undertaken, in part, to cement his relationship with Keith. When Jones fell ill during the drive down and checked into a Toulon hospital (he was constantly in and out of hospitals during this period), his girl friend, Anita, continued alone with Richards. Brian eventually caught up with them in Morocco, but by the end of the trip he found himself at the far end of the triangle. He had, in effect, lost both his lover and his closest friend in the band—to each other. (His only consolation was his discovery of Moroccan trance music—an infatuation that was to manifest itself on *Their Satanic Majesties Request* and on his posthumously issued field recording *Brian Jones Presents the Pipes of Pan at Joujouka*.)

The endless traumas contributed to a dearth of new Rolling Stones product. For the American market, Oldham slapped together an album of leftovers from the British versions of *Aftermath* and *Between the Buttons* (and the unreleased *Could You Walk on the Water?*) plus some songs that *had* already appeared on the U.S. releases. Andrew christened his compendium *Flowers*. This shoddy package could hardly have been less in keeping with the ideals of ''the summer of love,'' but then again, as Richards noted, ''we didn't have a chance to go through too much flower power because of the bust. We're outlaws.'' In any case, Oldham's days with the Stones were now numbered.

He did produce one more single, the suitably psychedelic ''We Love You,'' with its apparent echoes of ''All You Need Is Love.'' Lennon and McCartney can even be heard harmonizing on ''We Love You,'' returning services rendered by Jagger

and Richards as backup singers on the Beatles song. But the Stones' record seemed rather more sardonic, especially in light of recent headlines. ''It's just a bit of fun . . . very funny I think,'' Jagger told *Melody Maker*. ''We took the warden's footsteps from an actual prison sound effects tape.'' ''We Love You'' is also highlighted by clanking chains and the noise of a cell door being slammed shut.

Melody Maker's reviewer hailed the single as ''a sinister and dramatic explosion by the mysterious circle of the world's pop empire,'' with ''a monstrous majestic climax like a soul Ravel.'' In the paper's ''Blind Date'' feature, the Kinks' Dave Davies called ''We Love You'' ''the best thing they've ever done.'' But the consumers' response was less than overwhelming.

The BBC, for its part, refused to show the promotional film the Stones had made to accompany ''We Love You'' on *Top of the Pops*. This was a pointed re-enactment of the trials of Oscar Wilde, with Keith in the role of the Marquess of Queensberry and Marianne Faithfull, complete with ''miniwig,'' as Bosie (Lord Alfred Douglas, Queensberry's son and Wilde's lover). Jagger, of course, played the part of Oscar himself.

As had been the case with the Stones' previous single, it was the originally designated B-side that wound up registering on

(Photo Trends/David Bailey)

the American charts. Though the melodic and poetic ''Dandelion'' did sound perfectly in synch with the Summer of Love, it had actually been recorded the previous autumn, during the same sessions that had produced the similar ''Ruby Tuesday.''

After the single's release, Oldham attempted to begin recording a new Rolling Stones album. But the band had come to resent his autocratic manner and his apparent unconcern during their recent ordeals. So they spewed out the most atrocious R&B they could muster—until their producer duly freaked out and left them to their own devices.

Over the following months, a series of *NME* articles (mostly by Keith Altham) offered tantalizing glimpses of the Stones at work on what promised to be their post-*Pepper* masterpiece. While Charlie mutters paeans to Gillespie and Coltrane,

Brian moves softly about the studio in painted shoes, red and black striped trousers, and a huge brown sheepskin waistcoat which makes him look like some bizarre troglodyte.

73

Keith is clad in one of those unbelievable blue creations with many other colors that billow from his arms and fall in fringes almost to the floor. . . . Jagger sits perched upon a high stool in the control room surveying the music makers with an indulgent air . . . leaning forward so that his spine sticks out through the thin purple shirt. Marianne Faithfull sits cool and detached behind him reading a copy of *A Treatise on White Magic.*

All seem convinced that the Stones' career has entered an entirely new phase; Bill Wyman even doubts they will ever play any more concerts: "It's such a drag now. It's all right leaping about the stage, but when you get to twenty-five, twenty-six, it gets a bit embarrassing." (Wyman, never much of a "leaper" anyway, was in fact already in his thirties.)

"It really began with the Beatles' *Revolver,*" says Jagger. "It was the beginning of an appeal to the intellect. Once you could tell how well a group was doing by the reaction to their sex appeal, but the days of the hysteria are fading and for that reason there will never be a new Stones or a new Beatles. We are moving after minds."

Brian Jones describes the new album as "introspective" and "a very personal thing." "Our entire lives have been affected lately by social-political influences. You have to expect those things to come out in our work. In a way songs like '2,000 Light Years from Home' are prophetic . . . things we believe to be happening and will happen."

Someone presumes to interrupt with a query about how this jibes with a pop group's role as "entertainers." "Entertainment, pah! Entertaining is boring, communication is everything." Blaming the vapidity of all pre–Rolling Stones white recording artists on the effects of the world wars, Jones goes on: "Nothing destroys culture, art, or the simple privilege of having time to think quicker than a war. And once you get the horror and terror of a war people have to escape from it. They need the escapist pop cultures that croon about moon and June and romance. I've never had to go through those times, and I thank God I have not."

(This fusillade inspired one C. More to write *NME:* "Brian Jones' adverse comments on the art of entertaining show just how far he is removed from the everyday world. When people like myself have to work from nine to five and then trudge home through the ice and snow, it's not communication we want. No! It's entertainment. Brian Jones, who lives an entirely different life from the average person, will never be able to impose his philosophy on the general public. They will merely look elsewhere for their entertainment.")

NME's Altham finally offered his own advance assessment of the album itself: "This is the trip to infinity—the journey to the dark spaces between the stars and beyond. The sounds are East and West and the lyrics both sane and insane. This is what the Beatles have been saying in part, and now the Stones have said it."

With *Their Satanic Majesties Request,** the Stones themselves seemed to think they had left the competition, even the Beatles, back in the stardust. Under the direction of *Pepper*-land mastermind Michael Cooper, they constructed their own elaborate set, complete with magic castle, strange celestial orbs, and the

Beatles' faces secreted in the foliage. "It was handicrafts day—you make Saturn and I'll make the rings," Richards recalled in *Rolling Stone.*

All this was merely the backdrop for history's first three-dimensional LP cover, photographed with special Japanese cameras that, said Keith, "take pictures at slightly different times and distances, and they're put together, and the heads move." "It's not really meant to be a very nice picture at all," Jagger told *NME.* "Look at the expressions on our faces. It's a Grimm fairy tale—one of those stories that used to frighten as a young child." As *Melody Maker* noted at the outset of its review: "The album cover is the most remarkable ever conceived. It's too good to be crushed in with its tatty cardboard brethren in record store racks."

What with all this razzle-dazzle, and the hoopla and the hype—not to mention the immense clout and mystique the Stones had accumulated among the counterculture, particularly since their martyrdom at the hands of "the pigs"—*Their Satanic Majesties* promised a resounding triumph on all levels. Well, not quite. Though many admirers did welcome the album as a cosmic masterpiece, a large minority discerned, behind the psychedelic facade, a wasteland of self-indulgence and pretension. As the spell of '67 faded, the latter view would increasingly prevail.

After complimenting *Their Satanic Majesties'* physical appearance, *Melody Maker*'s critic slipped in the knife:

> The Stones are now in the same league as the Beatles, able to indulge in musical whims at their own expense. If there is any really creative talent among them, it has a chance to emerge unrestricted by commercial considerations. This could be art for art's sake. But . . . no great melodies emerge. Nothing is particularly exciting.

In *Rolling Stone,* Jon Landau's penetrating analysis sliced through the fancy trappings to reveal a crumbling center:

> The old Stones had the unstated motto of "We play rock" . . . they knew they did their thing better than anyone else around and, in fact, they did. The new Stones have been too infused with the pretensions of their musical inferiors. Hence they have adopted as their motto "We play art." Unfortunately . . . there was far more art in the Rolling Stones who were just trying to make rock than there is in the Rolling Stones who are trying to create art. It is an identity crisis of the first order.

Crawdaddy's Paul Williams, on the other hand, viewed *Satanic Majesties* as "a great album" and "a monolith"; and in that same issue, Neil Louison revealed that the Stones had now transcended mere "terrestrial orgasms." In a five-thousand-word exegesis, *Jazz & Pop* pronounced the LP "magnificent."

Even all these years later, objective appraisals of this album don't come easy to those of us impressionable striplings who took its satanic majesty for granted, and for whom the music provided the soundtrack for an initiation into all manner of strange and wondrous things. (In my case, apart from the usual chemistry experiments, these included the science-fantasy stories of Ray Bradbury; nowadays I can't reread *The Illustrated Man* without playing "2000 Light Years from Home" in my imagination—and vice versa.) Even when the Stones were bad, they still *mattered.* Whatever they did became an inextricable part of the lives of their countless listeners (this, of course, might be said of any popular culture), all the more so when (as was the case with so much of the popular culture in the late Sixties) they were making what was supposed to be a profound and radical statement.

---

* *The original title was* **Their Satanic Majesties Request and Require,** *a corruption of the inscription in British passports: "Her Brittanic Majesty Requests and Requires." Decca, however, would not permit such an insult to the queen. (Neither would the company allow a picture of Jagger naked on the cross to be used in the collage on the interior sleeve.) Another title under consideration was* **Cosmic Christmas;** *the actual release retains a snippet of oscillation (courtesy B. Wyman) at the end of side one that when played at 45 rpm reveals itself as "We Wish You a Merry Christmas."*

Even among those who liked it, the most frequently heard indictment of *Satanic Majesties* was that it owed an exorbitant debt to *Sgt. Pepper*. No doubt the one would not have been conceived without the other, and the Beatles' masterpiece certainly had a lot going for it (Lennon-McCartney's versatile genius; George Martin) that the Stones could never approximate. The Stones' own production is, if anything, even worse than Oldham's, and while such slovenly recording techniques might be palmed off as part of the essential alchemy in "Get Off of My Cloud," they could hardly sustain "a journey to the dark spaces between the stars."

Nonetheless, the Stones did bring an entirely different set of perspectives and sensibilities to their own fantastic voyage. For example: Where George Harrison turned to India for inspiration, Brian Jones brought what he called "a touch of the Arabian Nights." Where the Beatles had dabbled in whimsy and surrealism, the Stones added science fiction and authentic references to the occult. "Citadel" is a futuristic vision of New York City that brings to mind Fritz Lang's classic 1926 film *Metropolis*; the characters "Candy [Darling] and Taffy" were actual transvestites from the stable of Andy Warhol. As for the occult references, "Gomper" (*NME* reported) got its title from "the Tibetan term for the incredible journey some Tibetan monks make while under hypnosis." Also (as David Dalton has noted) Jagger had been reading the Tao classic *The Secret of the Golden Flower,* one of whose meditation techniques—"if one closes one's eyes and, reversing the glance, directs it inward, one will see the room of the ancestors"—was transmuted into the chorus of "Sing This All Together": "If we close all our eyes together, then we will see where we all come from."

Discussing the album in *Melody Maker,* Mick said that "the thing about it which stands out to me [is] its spookiness." With the possible exception of "A Day in the Life," nothing on *Sgt. Pepper* had approximated the eerie and ominous atmosphere surrounding the Stones' dark carnival. Perhaps the essential difference between the two albums is that *Their Satanic Majesties Request* is truly decadent in a way the Beatles never were. To the Stones' old anarchic hedonism and the more recent lysergic sensibilities of the counterculture, *Satanic Majesties* introduced a peculiarly British style of decadence that harked all the way back to Oscar Wilde and the Yellow Nineties, and that had manifested itself in the occult flirtations of writers like W. B. Yeats and Arthur Machen. ("We got into a lot of those English eccentrics," said Keith.)

In America, *Satanic Majesties* spawned two singles: "She's a Rainbow" and "In Another Land." The former mines the "Ruby Tuesday" vein in perhaps the best of those rare haunting ballads wherein Jagger actually extols a lady instead of belittling her. Tasteful strings were furnished by future Led Zeppelinite John Paul Jones.

Bill Wyman's "In Another Land" marked the first and last instance of Mick and Keith allowing one of their fellows to break their songwriting monopoly on Stones albums. Bill, however, subsequently admitted it had been recorded only because Jagger, Richards, and Jones had failed to turn up in the studio that day; engineer Glyn Johns then suggested that Wyman, Watts, and pianist Nicky Hopkins use the valuable time to try out a Wyman composition. "In Another Land" proved to be as evocative a fantasy as any on the album; the electronic filters with which Bill self-consciously clouds his vocal only add to the dreamlike quality. "I was so embarrassed about putting my voice on tape that I waited until everybody had left the studio before doing it," he told *NME*. "The idea for the song is about this guy who wakes up from a dream and finds himself in another dream." The single version was released as a solo endeavor, credited only to Bill Wyman.

If *Satanic Majesties* was indeed a failure, it was certainly a fascinating one. Perhaps Mick Jagger (in *NME,* 1972) should be given the last word:

> People put it down because they were narrow-minded and insisted on comparing it with *Sgt. Pepper*. . . . It was nothing like *Pepper*. The only similarity was that both albums were made in the same year, when practically the same things were happening in the head. *Sgt. Pepper* was an album full of songs; *Satanic Majesties* contained no songs.
>
> At the time I kinda liked the album, and then I went through a period when I really hated it. Now I find it's good to listen to.

In early 1968, Bob Dylan emerged at last from his hideaway, to deflate the psychedelic balloon with a few simple, unadorned chords and the words "John Wesley Harding was a friend to the poor." Blues, down-home country, and Fifties rock & roll became fashionable again; with "Lady Madonna" even the Beatles fell back to their own roots. Following the disappointing response to *Satanic Majesties,* it was hardly surprising that the Rolling Stones should resolve to reconsolidate on their original home turf.

Reasserting himself as the band's musical leader, Keith more or less redefined the Stones' sound. "It was a case of learning everything from scratch," he recalled in *NME* six years later. Richards immersed himself in his collection of "over a thousand blues records" and began experimenting with tunings and fingerings. "It involved literally learning the guitar all over again. You had to apply yourself in almost the same way as when you started. I really enjoyed it."

Determined to re-establish themselves as "the greatest rock & roll band in the world," Keith and Mick also willed themselves to write the best songs of their career—conquering the habit of letting the words and music coalesce during the actual

LP, U.S.A., 1969 (Warner Brothers)

LP, U.S.A., 1969 (Warner Brothers)

The banned original sleeve for **Beggars Banquet**

LP, U.K., 1969 (Decca)

recording sessions. Finally, they shopped around for a good outside producer, settling on the twenty-seven-year-old American Jimmy Miller, best known for his work with British R&B prodigy Stevie Winwood's two bands, the Spencer Davis Group and Traffic.

The ensuing recording sessions proved to be the Stones' most productive in years; the only real problem was Brian Jones. When he wasn't in court, or comatose on the floor, he was wont to complain bitterly. *NME*'s Keith Altham overheard him lobbying with Miller for the inclusion of his own electronic compositions on the Stones' "back to the basics" album. "I'm very hung up on electronic music at present," said Brian. "If there's not enough room to include it on our album I would like to do something separately." Jones also announced pointedly that he had become bored with the rock music scene since "the really groovy and interesting things stopped happening."

"Jumpin' Jack Flash," unleashed at 45 rpm that May, proved to be an archetypal Stones single in the best "Satisfaction" tradition; indeed, the rhythm and even the main riff of these two classics sound virtually identical. But "Flash" and its successors were far better *recordings,* for the Stones—with Jimmy Miller's connivance—had now reduced their trademark sound to a science. Even the occasional muddiness was deliberate, achieved by recording certain parts on cassettes before incorporating them into the reel-to-reel master tape.

"Flash"'s lyrics also differed from those of its musical prototypes. Bearing little of "Satisfaction"'s angry young menace, "Jumpin' Jack Flash" was droll, upbeat, and only mildly antisocial. In the tradition of such vintage rock & roll nonsense as "Blue Suede Shoes," Jumpin' Jack Jagger portrays himself as a resilient lad who, despite having been born in a cross-fire hurricane, raised by a toothless bearded hag, and crowned with a spike through his head, now finds his circumstances entirely satisfactory.

The Stones previewed their new single in a surprise appearance at *NME*'s annual Pollwinners Concert. A few weeks later the ebullient band was moved to place a full-page ad in all the British music papers: "'Jumpin' Jack Flash' is really gassed that he made Number One. So are the Rolling Stones. Thank you. We are slaving over a hot album which is coming out next month. Until then . . . ."

The LP was originally slated to appear on July 26, Mick's twenty-fifth birthday. A lengthy advance description by *Rolling Stone*'s Jann Wenner hailed *Beggars Banquet* as a major comeback both for the band and for the state of the art in general:

> It is the best record they have yet done. In all respects it is a great album, great Rolling Stones material and performances; it is without pretense, and an achievement of significance in both lyrics and music. . . .
>
> In *Satanic Majesties,* the Stones fell hook, line, and sinker into the post–*Sgt. Pepper* trap of trying to put out a "progressive," "significant," and "different" album, as revolutionary as the Beatles. But it couldn't be done, because only the Beatles can put out an album by the Beatles.
>
> And only the Rolling Stones could put out *Beggars Banquet*. . . .

But the album was delayed indefinitely by the most acrimonious of the Stones' many clashes with Decca and London Records. This time the problem was the cover photo, depicting a somewhat unsavory gents' room. "It was so silly—who did they think they were protecting?" Jagger told *Melody Maker* a year later. "Everything written on the wall was relevant to the album. Do they really believe people don't read things on public lavatory walls when they go info them?" The Stones were convinced it was "a real funky cover," says Richards, and "dug in our heels." So did Decca.

Come September the Stones went so far as to place another full-page *Melody Maker* ad, coupling a photo of the LP cover with the words: "This is the front of our new album, which we finished two months ago. Due to religious disagreements, no release date has been set. If you would like a copy, write to Decca Records Ltd, 9 Albert Embankment, SE 1." But, says Keith, "they really wouldn't budge."

Of course it was the Stones who suffered the most from the deadlock. So the album finally appeared, four months behind schedule, in a stark white cover, with the titles and credits printed in the style of a formal invitation card. Its release was celebrated with an actual beggars' banquet at Kensington's

Beggars Banquet (*Keystone Press Agency*)

Gore Hotel, noted for its Elizabethan decor. ("Mick was very into that tattered minstrel bit then," recalls Keith.) The guests ranged from Decca executives to such pop music journalists as Chris Welch, who reported that "the Stones seemed in a suspiciously jolly mood." Dessert turned out to be custard pie—hurled into the dignitaries' faces by the gracious hosts.

The album itself proved to be everything the advance notices had promised. *Beggars Banquet* remains at once the classiest and most "literary" of the Stones' albums and also their most musical and "organic." Electronic gimmickry is conspicuous in its absence—even the guitars are mostly acoustic—and most of the forms explored throughout the LP (folk, blues, country) predate rock & roll itself. At the time, producer Jimmy Miller told *Melody Maker* that "the record is an internal advancement—not an external one. It shows progression on what you do, and trying to do it well, rather than stepping outside into something that is foreign."

Perhaps the three key songs on *Beggars Banquet* were "Stray Cat Blues," "Sympathy for the Devil," and "Street Fighting Man"; in addition to their musical merits, each made more explicit than ever an important facet of the Rolling Stones fantasy. On "Stray Cat" the boys return with a vengeance to their role of incorrigible satyrs, "corrupters of youth": "I can see that you're fifteen years old, but I don't want your I.D. . . ." (Elsewhere Jagger delivers such racy lines as "My heavy throbber's itchin' just to lay a solo rhythm down.")

In "Sympathy" Jagger has the colossal conceit to take the part of the Devil himself. This song was inspired by a banned 1930s Soviet novel, Mikhail Bulgakov's *The Master and Margarita,* wherein the Devil appears, in subtle and unlikely disguises, to wreak havoc on postrevolutionary Moscow. In Jagger's first-person dramatization, the Devil is presented as "a man of wealth and taste," suave, sophisticated, and charming—and a master of deception. In one historical scene after another—the Crucifixion, the Inquisition, the Russian Revolution, the Kennedy assassinations—this Lucifer turns up to play a discreet yet decisive role. (While the Stones were working on the song, Robert Kennedy was shot; Mick was obliged to "punch in" the plural "Kennedys" where he had previously sung "Who killed Kennedy?")

"Sympathy for the Devil" also chanced to be the ditty the Stones were working on when the acclaimed French director Jean-Luc Godard turned up to film the band developing a song from scratch, for his film *One Plus One* (later retitled *Sympathy for the Devil*). Godard's crew received yet another windfall when the recording studio mysteriously caught fire during these sessions.

On "Street Fighting Man" the Stones appeared to revel in their newfound role of revolutionary rabble-rousers. When the track was released as a U.S. single around the time of the Chicago Democratic Convention, the references to "fighting in the streets" caused it to be banned by many Top Forty program directors. They evidently missed the demurral in the chorus: "In sleepy London town there's just no place for a Street Fighting Man." "I'm pleased to hear they've banned it," Jagger commented in *Melody Maker,* "as long as it's still available in the shops. The last time they banned one of our records in America it sold a million."

One other noteworthy aspect of "Street Fighting Man"—and testimony to the all-natural flavor of *Beggars Banquet*—is that what sounds like a wash of electronic distortion on the chorus is in fact Brian Jones playing the tamboura, the instrument responsible for the drone in most Indian music. Though "Street Fighting Man" makes for unlikely Raga Rock, perhaps this only confirms the suspicion that the Stones made rather more creative use of their Eastern influences than the Beatles had.

Jagger, Richards, and Wyman have all called *Beggars Banquet* the Stones' best-ever record (as has Mick Taylor, who wasn't even around at the time), and one can hardly disagree with them. Even so, the album did not sell as astronomically as would some of its markedly inferior successors. Its November 1968 appearance was somewhat overshadowed by the Beatles' White Album, whose cover the substitute *Beggars Banquet* sleeve inadvertently resembled. Also, the Stones' popularity had suffered from the uneven quality of their previous few albums. Finally, live performances were crucial to the Stones' mystique (much more so than with the Beatles or Bob Dylan). Despite their 1967 pronouncements, most of the Stones were

The Rolling Stones' Rock 'n' Roll Circus (RDR Productions)

now anxious to return to the road, particularly in America. The only problem, again, was Brian Jones, whose physical, psychological, and legal difficulties precluded any such activity.

The Stones' temporary solution was to promote *Beggars Banquet* with a TV spectacular. Titled *The Rolling Stones Rock 'n' Roll Circus,* the film co-starred The Who, Jethro Tull, knife throwers, fire eaters, trapeze acts, clowns, and a tiger. Special guests included a one-shot "supergroup" starring John Lennon, with Richards on bass, Eric Clapton on lead guitar, and Mitch Mitchell (of the Jimi Hendrix Experience) on drums. (After warming up with "Peggy Sue," "Sweet Little Sixteen," and "Hound Dog," Lennon belted out "Yer Blues" from the White Album.)

The Stones' own set, however, was delayed until five in the morning. Many in the audience—including a full complement of children—had gone home to bed. Those who remained were somewhat bleary-eyed, including the Stones; Jagger subsequently felt he hadn't cut a sufficiently impressive figure for the occasion. So *Rock 'n' Roll Circus* was never shown (apart from the Who segment used a decade later in the film *The Kids Are Alright*).

A similar fate was nearly suffered by another film Mick was involved with around this time: Donald Cammell and Nicolas Roeg's *Performance,* which critics have variously called one of the most repulsive movies of all time and one of the Sixties' most important films. Its basic plot concerns a Cockney gangster played by James Fox, who guns down an underworld rival and then goes into hiding in a very different sort of London underworld: the home of the reclusive pop star Turner (Jagger's first straight—so to speak—dramatic role) and his "secretary," played by Anita Pallenberg.

Discomfited by the lush and chaotic decadence of his new surroundings, the gangster is revealed to be, in most respects, as conventional and "straight" as any law-abiding middle-class citizen; in his former "all mod cons" habitat, he had kept his *Playboy*s and his cufflinks meticulously arranged on the coffee table and in the bureau drawer. Only Fox's vocation enables him to give full rein to the instinctive brutality inherent (and barely suppressed) in straight society as a whole.

At first Fox is puritanically shocked by scenes of bisexuality and drug taking *chez* Turner, but Jagger gradually induces him to take part in the pop star's "kinky" life-style and, as a consequence, to re-evaluate his own assumptions and way of life. The roles of the two characters eventually overlap and become interchangeable; in one hallucinatory scene Jagger metamorphoses into a slick syndicate boss, dictating a memo in the form of his own powerful song "Memo from Turner"—as the gangsters' nude bodies are shown tangled in homosexual embrace (suggesting what their violent machismo is *really* all about). Before his pursuers finally intercept his hideaway, Fox seems poised between redemption and madness; now he murders Jagger prior to being driven off in his captors' car—at which point the doomed gangster's face is transformed into that of the pop star, their identities having merged at last.

Mick brings a distinctly Rolling Stones persona to his own performance, but those who sniffed that he was merely "playing himself" were slightly off target. In the role of Turner, Jagger managed to combine elements of the public and private personalities of *Brian* and *Keith*—abetted, no doubt, by the presence of Anita Pallenberg as one of Turner's lovers. Unlike, say, Lennon or Townshend, Ol' Rubber Lips didn't achieve greatness simply by projecting his *own* personality. Mick was, after all, a *performer*.

Dismayed by the "uncommercial" nature of this chaotic and surreal movie—not to mention its explicit scenes of violence, drug taking, and unorthodox sex—Warner Brothers was reluctant to distribute *Performance* at all; the film was riddled with heavy-handed cuts when it finally appeared a year behind schedule. In the meantime, Jagger had taken the starring role in a movie about an Australian outlaw. Filmed on location over the summer of 1969, *Ned Kelly* was released before its predecessor and unanimously dismissed as a travesty. . . .

January 1969: Three Rolling Stones on holiday in Third World countries—Brian in Ceylon, Mick and Keith in Peru—are barred from exclusive hotels for their unconventional appearance. Wearing a pink suit and a psychedelic scarf, Jones finally confronts one startled hotel manager in Kandy with an enormous wad of banknotes and the words: "I work for my living. I have money and I do not wish to be treated as a second-class citizen."

May 28: Mick Jagger and Marianne Faithfull are released on bail following their arrest for possession of cannabis during a police raid on their home.

June 8: Brian Jones announces he has quit the Rolling Stones, saying: "I no longer see eye to eye with the others over the discs we are cutting." . . .

The Rolling Stones' last photo session with Brian Jones (Popperfoto)

Brian had, in fact, been fired by Mick and Keith. At the time, however, the split was portrayed as an amicable parting. For his role in this charade, it was later revealed, Brian was promised an annual salary of £100,000.

His replacement was Mick Taylor, formerly of John Mayall's Blues Breakers, whose cherished possessions had included a guitar once owned by Keith Richards. Taylor came to the Stones a teetotaling vegetarian, telling reporters: "I want to be as naturally healthy and aware as I can." Like other young innocents drawn into the Rolling Stones vortex, the twenty-year-old Taylor would be corrupted soon enough.

At the time, Jagger announced he had "just made arrangements for the new Stones to appear at the Colosseum in Rome" on the occasion of his own twenty-sixth birthday. He later told *Melody Maker* that he "wasn't satisfied with the Rolling Stones part of the *Rock 'n' Roll Circus* film, and we wanted to do it again in the Colosseum, which was the first-ever circus." But when Roman bureaucrats added complications, Jagger negotiated another venue for the debut of the "new" Stones. A free concert in London's Hyde Park was scheduled for July 5.

Two days before the show, in the wee hours of the morning, Brian Jones was found dead—drowned in the swimming pool of his new Sussex home, the house in which A. A. Milne had once written *Winnie the Pooh.* The specific circumstances of Brian's death remain mysterious; many of those in the house at the time are said to have pulled a disappearing act, along with some valuable instruments and antiques. But the consensus seems to be that the dissipated and always asthmatic former Rolling Stone, after plunging into the pool against the advice of his live-in nurse, had been simply too stoned to come up for air.

Close friends and associates—including the other Stones—didn't seem overly surprised; Brian himself had agreed he would never make it past thirty. Informed of the news during a recording session, the band continued taping a version of Stevie Wonder's current single "I Don't Know Why." Pete Townshend's response was an unreleased song called "It Was a Normal Day for Brian, a Man Who Died Every Day." In his *Rolling Stone* eulogy, Greil Marcus admitted:

I woke up to hear that Brian Jones was dead and not more than a ripple of sorrow passed through the room. It was time for it, there was just nothing left for him to do. . . .

In a way, Jones' death shows us and maybe Mick Jagger himself that the Stones weren't kidding when they sang "Sympathy for the Devil." "I lay traps for troubadours who get killed before they reach Bombay. . . ." You can't come down from being *a Rolling Stone.* No way down, and one way out.

It happens. Traps for troubadours, and sometimes one doesn't stumble into them but goes looking for them. We grow up with death. Brian Jones, R.I.P.

For many of the rest of us, however, the news came as a profound shock. Apart from Brian Epstein, Jones was the first major British Invasion figure to die. He was also the first to pay the ultimate price for living out the fantasies inherent in much of the rock music of the Sixties—especially (it almost goes without saying) the Rolling Stones'. For his epitaph, Brian himself had selected the phrase: "Please don't judge me too harshly."

The Stones' image hardly suffered from the tragedy; as Michael Lydon put it in *Ramparts*: "The bad mean Stones are now so bad and mean that one of them is a dead man." Mick Jagger announced that the Hyde Park concert would play as scheduled. "Brian would have wanted it to go on. We will now do the concert for Brian. I hope people will understand that it is because of our love for him that we are doing it."

(Photo Trends)

The show drew a record crowd of some three hundred thousand young Britons, policed by a security force of local Hell's Angels, whom the Stones had hired in lieu of "the fuzz." Following such warm-up acts as King Crimson, Alexis Korner, and Family, ten-foot blowups of Brian Jones were mounted behind the stage, and the TV cameramen began shooting.* According to an account by Richard Neville, editor of the British underground paper *Oz*: "The murmurs from behind the stage escalated to a roar. Suddenly, it was Mick. In a white, bow-buttoned billowing frock over tight white pants, a gold-studded leather collar . . . 'we're gonna have a good time.' But first a word from Shelley. 'Cool it for a minute,' he said. 'I would really like to say something about Brian.' And he began: 'Peace, peace! he is not dead, he doth not sleep/he hath awakened from the dream of life. . . .'"

---

* *The film* The Stones in the Park *was aired by Britain's Granada TV in May 1971.*

Mick Taylor's debut with the Stones, Hyde Park, July 5, 1969 (Photo Trends)

As fans wept unashamedly, some mysterious crates alongside the stage were opened to release three thousand butterflies. The band launched into "Lemon Squeezer":

Shelley was now dancing in his grave, as Mick whipped himself into a lathering frenzy, pumping, pouting, the veins running up and down his body like cables. . . . The butterflies fluttered forth and Jagger began to disrobe.

The group seemed a musical mess—all awkward endings and misplaced cues. But it didn't matter; only Mick Taylor, Brian Jones' replacement, seemed uncomfortable, hiding behind his hair, solemn, remote, overconcentrating, with less stage presence than a road manager. Jagger removed his gold-studded antique leather belt. . . .

Taylor was understandably nervous, but even at the best of times he would remain a fairly colorless figure. In this and other respects, he could hardly have been more different from his predecessor. Where Brian had been a versatile dilettante, Taylor was simply a brilliant virtuoso guitarist. It was probably just as well for all concerned that there was so little room for comparison. "Mick Taylor just kinda slotted in very nicely," Wyman would tell *NME* three years later. "When he wasn't sure what to play, he didn't play. Neither did he try to change anything around.

"At that time Brian wasn't such a good musician as he was the year before, or the year before that. Brian just seemed to deteriorate over the last couple of years of his life. So he wasn't that much of a loss, musically, around that time. When Mick Taylor took over, he kind of gave us a little booster."

In other *NME* interviews, Wyman noted that "Mick Taylor and Charlie Watts are more into jazz than Keith and I, we tend to be more into the blues and old R&B stuff like Jerry Lee Lewis and Chuck Berry. [Jagger] is always very up to date all the time. Mick's got a very wide scope, so he sort of gets everybody together quite effectively." Taylor felt that the major divergence stemmed from Richards's predilection for classic Rolling Stones rock & roll and Jagger's eagerness to explore new styles (a view that Taylor admitted sharing).

Both sides of that musical coin were represented on the Stones' next single, "Honky Tonk Women" and "You Can't Always Get What You Want." The bawdy, bluesy A-side ranks at the top of that list of classic Stones tracks concerning which Pete Townshend once said: "I don't think they're anything more than what they are, which is incredible, delicious, and wonderful rock 'n' roll." The cinematic "You Can't Always Get What You Want" probes various decadent scenes from the declining remnants of swinging London. Like the words, the music seems poignantly ambivalent; but the mournful voices of the London Bach Choir—an inspired addition—eventually build to an ecstatic crescendo.

Yet the rest of the material the Stones put down during this difficult period included few experiments, and still fewer attempts to be "poetic" or even thoughtful (apart from the ominous and prophetic "Gimme Shelter"). Jagger was now saying (in *Melody Maker*): "Too many people are becoming obsessed with pop music. The position of rock 'n' roll in our subculture has become far too important, especially the delving for philosophical intent." It was more or less back to sex, and drugs, and rock & roll with this lot, even if these themes were no longer so fresh in the Stones' hands, or the audience so innocent, as in the days of *Aftermath*.

The Stones recorded most of *Let It Bleed* as a foursome (only two cuts feature Jones, and two Taylor), with Richards contributing numerous overdubbed guitars. Ry Cooder jammed extensively with the band during this interregnum, and subsequently charged that Keith had plagiarized all his riffs as soon as he turned his back. Another bit of "plagiarism" crops up in "Midnight Rambler," wherein Jagger intones word-for-word the rape-and-murder confession of Albert de Salvo, the Boston Strangler.

Though *Let It Bleed* is often ranked with the Stones' greats (Keith had placed it second only to *Beggars Banquet*), it is nonetheless characterized by a manipulative sensationalism that tended to overwhelm the proceedings once the musical inspiration began to taper off. Facile references to sleazy sex, sadomasochism, hard drugs, and gratuitous violence abound. The Stones were becoming, in a word, cheap.

At the time much was made of the similarity of the titles *Let It Be* and *Let It Bleed,* as if they summed up the difference between the Beatles and the Rolling Stones. People also assumed one group must have been parodying the other; in fact, the titles were dreamed up independently, at around the same time.

The release of *Let It Bleed* coincided with the most celebrated (then) and notorious (now) of all the Rolling Stones' American tours. Anyone able to salvage a ticket out of the coast-to-coast scenes of box-office pandemonium counted himself blessed by the gods (even if the seats went for an unprecedented $8.50 a throw). After all, the Stones were viewed virtually as gods within the rock counterculture, none of whose reigning triumvirate—Dylan, the Beatles, and the Stones—had performed on American soil since mid-1966. In the meantime the subculture had come into its own; now the Stones were the first of the supreme idols to return in the flesh.

This time around, it wasn't only screaming teenyboppers who threw themselves at the Stones' feet wherever the musicians ventured. Now the supplicants ranged from professional groupies and drug dealers to a Dodge representative inviting the Stones to take their free pick of the company's 1970 models— and to Abbie Hoffman vainly inviting them to assist the Chicago Seven's defense. The Stones took it all in their haughty stride; even the concert audiences were generally kept waiting for

hours before the band condescended to appear. "Every fucking gig [Jagger] made the promoter and the people bleed," charged Bill Graham after it was all over. But few others were heard to complain, at least not until the tour climaxed with the debacle of Altamont. These were, after all, *the Rolling Stones,* and they were indeed magnificent.

"I wonder what these kids are like now," Keith was overheard musing in Fort Collins, Colorado, moments before the tour's first show. "I mean, do they watch TV or turn on in the basement?" Later, in *Rolling Stone,* he would answer his own question. "Everybody had changed. Completely different kind of madness. Before, America was a real fantasy land; it was still Walt Disney and hamburger dates, and when you came back in 1969 it wasn't anymore. Kids were really into what was going on in their country."

The Stones had changed as well. For the first time they not only offered a choreographed concert *act,* but were truly making *music* instead of an off-key din, for audiences that, though wildly enthusiastic, were actually there to watch and to listen. And rock & roll arena sound systems had evolved immeasurably since the Fab Four's swan song at Candlestick Park.

But despite the newly acquired polish (courtesy, in large part, of Mick Taylor), the Stones' sound was now every bit as black as it had been back in 1964. "The poppy songs we used to do," Jagger would tell *NME,* "we couldn't get into now. We tried to

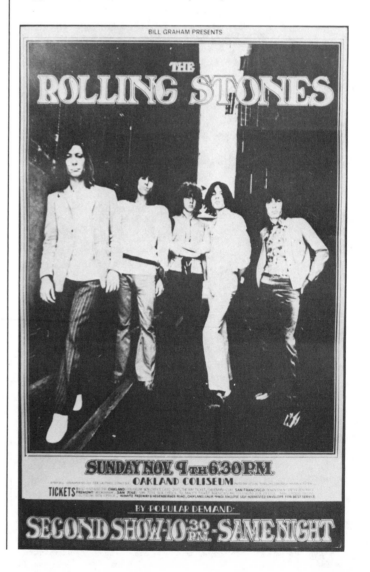

play 'Paint It, Black' . . . but we couldn't get behind it.'"*

Jagger had developed into a master showman, resplendent in Uncle Sam hat, billowing scarf, and a great studded belt that he slipped off during the shows' tour de force, "Midnight Rambler." Jagger would drop to his knees, twirling the belt over his head. "Welll, ya heard about the Boston . . ." *Slam!* The belt would lash the floor to the sound of a mammoth Rolling Stones chord, followed by a stillness broken only by ecstatic squeals from the spellbound audience—and Mick writhing in the spotlight, hissing, "Honey, it's not one of those . . ." *Slam!*

Onstage in 1969, Jagger trotted out all his diabolical personae: misogynist ("Under My Thumb"), rabble-rousing politico ("Street Fighting Man"), corrupter of youth ("Stray Cat Blues," wherein Mick changed the nymphet's age from fifteen to thirteen), the Devil himself ("Sympathy"). Not that his presentation lacked irony; indeed, his fluid movements had acquired more than a touch of "camp." (Jagger in live performance had come to resemble his screen portrayal of the androgynous Turner.) Still, many in the audience tended to lose sight of the fact that their Prince of Darkness was but a master showman putting on a performance. And Jagger, finding himself able to toy so easily with the fantasies of the stoned multitudes, seems to have let a grotesquely inflated ego get the better of his characteristically levelheaded opportunism. Which brings us to Altamont. . . .

The bright idea of an all-day free concert at a drag strip in the desert fifteen miles east of Berkeley—featuring Santana, the Jefferson Airplane, the Flying Burrito Brothers, and Crosby, Stills, Nash, and Young as well as the Rolling Stones—was a by-product of the counterculture's post-Woodstock euphoria. Those who weren't at the Woodstock Festival, and many who were, were apt to forget that Yasgur's farm had been (with good reason) declared a disaster area by the state of New York. Transformed into a vast swamp by torrential downpours, the festival site woefully lacked the provisions and sanitary and medical facilities required to sustain a crowd of some half a million people—many of whom were unable to see or even hear the musical attractions that had drawn them to Woodstock in the first place.

But instead of getting uptight about having to stand in the rain for an hour to purchase a lousy hot dog or go to the "bathroom," festival-goers magnanimously shared their granola, drugs, moral support, and sleeping bags with their neighbors. (Me, I hitched the hell out of there—and have regretted it ever since.) Because "the kids" dealt with the situation with such goodwill and good cheer, many were persuaded that the so-called Woodstock Nation, when extricated from the tentacles of "straight" society, was inherently Utopian. Apart from such "Now Generation" trappings as nudity and LSD, however, the good vibes at Woodstock weren't really all that different from those that had emerged during such crises as the Northeastern states' 1965 power blackout.

Of course, that powerful coalition of countercultural visionaries and canny promoters known as "the rock biz" attempted time and again to recapture the magic formula, cavalierly assuming that with the combination of superstar names and an ambience more appropriate to a refugee camp, everything would automatically come up flowers, peace, and love. Few of these freeze-dried Utopias came close to duplicating the elusive Woodstock recipe, though the promoters, performers, and drug dealers reaped vast profits. Unfortunately, it took the Rolling Stones' free concert at Altamont Speedway to bring about the evaporation of the Woodstock mirage.

The Stones' road show was already well underway when it occurred to Jagger that an instant West Coast Woodstock of his own would provide the tour with a splendid climax. He reckoned that some fast and fancy footwork from the Maysles brothers (who had been hired to film the tour) might even enable the Stones to beat the eagerly awaited *Woodstock* movie to the cinemas with their own documentary *Love in Vain* (later retitled *Gimme Shelter*).

Unable to wrangle a suitable venue until a mere twenty-four hours before showtime, the Stones' people ignored warnings that ranged from the cosmic (the planets were said to be in a highly unfavorable conjunction) to the prosaic (it was virtually impossible to provide facilities for a crowd of three hundred thousand on such short notice). As if the situation weren't already potentially explosive, Jagger and Co. added the metaphorical equivalent of a lighted match: for five hundred dollars' worth of beer, the Hell's Angels were hired to provide "security." It seems nobody had informed Mick that California's Angels were hardly the pussies in leather drag that their English imitators had proved to be when used as satanic props for the Stones' concert in Hyde Park.

The Altamont crowd scenes in *Gimme Shelter* afford ample evidence that every weirdo in California had crawled out of the woodwork for the occasion. ("All those nude fat people just asking for it," was Keith Richards's reaction.) Altamont was the Woodstock Nation gone totally haywire.

A lethal amount of bad acid was circulated in cups of "water" that were offered to the parched multitudes—including members of both the Maysles' film crew and the Hell's Angels. Even before the first note had been sounded from the stage, the festival atmosphere had turned to one of rampant paranoia.

"You go to something like this expecting genuinely good vibes—it just blew my mind," photographer Andy Levine told Altamont chronicler Jonathan Eisen. "This one cat was all dressed in white and got into this big hole and started dancing to calm things down . . . one Angel just hit him in the head with a pool cue. Then the cat was still dancing, he was in a daze, and they just started smashing him from Angel to Angel. You could see his teeth coming out."

During the Jefferson Airplane's set, singer Marty Balin tried to intervene when he saw a similar incident occur near the stage. The Angels abandoned their victim only long enough to knock the rock star unconscious.

Nonetheless, Mick Jagger—arrayed in red and black like some cosmic jester of revolution and anarchy—insisted on delaying his dramatic entrance until after sundown, when the spotlights might work their optimum magic. And with the Stones and with nightfall, all the demonic forces of the day came to a head. Life imitated art with a vengeance.

"I don't think [Jagger] is fully aware of how seriously the words to his songs have been taken," wrote Eisen in his *Altamont: Death of Innocence in the Woodstock Nation.* "For him they are probably merely lyrics, products of his imagination; for an audience freaked out on bad acid and mountain red . . . they were the catalyst for unloading everything in the music—all the resentment, the adulation, the phantasmagorical mosaic of bad trips, and hallucinations of the apocalypse and beyond, of real Street Fighting Men, and of people genuinely possessed by the Devil."

---

* *The superlative music was captured on the first widely circulated rock concert bootleg,* Liver Than You'll Ever Be, *causing Decca/London to retaliate with the official* Get Yer Ya-Ya's Out.

It was during "Sympathy for the Devil" that all hell finally broke loose. Angels began stomping on someone who had managed to clamber onto the stage, and the band lurched to a halt. According to spectator Andy Gordon:

> Some yelled at the stage, pissed at the interruption: "We came to see the Stones, not the Angels!" We wanted illusion and we were getting reality. Nobody understood what was happening, certainly not Jagger.
>
> After stopping the song, Jagger pleaded with the audience: "Brothers and sisters! Brothers and sisters! C'mon, just cool out a minute" and "Why are we fighting? Why are we fighting?" It was a strange schizophrenia, the celebrity stepping out of the framework of his art, songs powered by sadistic aggression, dropping the diabolic pose to become the prophet of peace. . . .

"Stray Cat Blues" and "Love in Vain" proceeded without further incident; then, during "Under My Thumb," Jagger saw the gun pointed at him by a young black man named Meredith Hunter. A group of Angels noticed as well, and within minutes Hunter was dead, stabbed in the back and head, and repeatedly kicked in the face for good measure. And without realizing exactly what was going on, one of the Maysles' cameramen captured the entire sequence on film—providing the courts with important evidence,* and *Gimme Shelter* with its horrifying climax. (The Stones' own set that night ended, as usual, with "Street Fighting Man.")

Altamont claimed the lives of three other young men, two of whom were run over at their campsite by a wayward car. The third—listed for weeks as "John Doe"—tripped stoned into a ditch and drowned. A lot of cherished illusions also died that night; indeed, many commentators declared that Altamont symbolized the end of that era loosely known as "the Sixties." (Unlike other events to be awarded that distinction, Altamont did actually take place in the decade's final weeks.)

It was certainly a textbook instance of the freaks' blind tolerance for *anyone* who wasn't "straight"—no matter how unsavory. Even *after* the events at Altamont, the staff at San Francisco's hippest radio station, KSAN, went out of their way to appease ringleader Sonny Barger when he called in to give the Angels' side of the story:

BARGER: I just went there to sit on the stage you know well you know what I'm in the way you know so maybe somebody wants to climb on stage.

KSAN: Hey, Sonny, can I ask you a question?

BARGER: Let me finish what, uh—

KSAN: Oh, I'm sorry.

BARGER: Then you can ask me anything you want.

KSAN: Beautiful.

BARGER: Anyways, finally the Stones come out . . . everything was cool. But out of all of them people in that front area . . . there was three or four people in there that come over to where the bikes were and kicked a couple of the bikes over and, uh, you know, broke a couple of mirrors off a couple of them and this and that. I don't know if you think we pay fifty dollars for them things or steal 'em . . . but most people that's got a good Harley chopper got a few grand invested in it.

KSAN: I can dig it.

* The Angel shown wielding the knife was nonetheless acquitted, and sued the Stones for violating his privacy.

BARGER: Ain't nobody gonna kick my motorcycle . . . you love that thing better than anything in the world, and you see a guy kick it, you know who he is.

KSAN: Right.

BARGER: And if you have to go through fifty people to get at him, you're gonna get him, and you know what? They got it. . . . Also in the process of it there was . . . quite a large girl that was going around topless and kept trying to climb up on stage. And, like, this Mick Jagger he used us for dupes, man, you know.

KSAN: Right.

BARGER: We were the biggest suckers for that idiot. . . .

When Barger finally finished his spiel, the KSAN announcer told him: "Thanks a lot, man. I think you've done a lot to enlighten a lot of people as to just what was going on."

"Altamont—it could only happen to the Stones, man," said Keith Richards. "Let's face it. It wouldn't happen to the Bee Gees and it wouldn't happen to Crosby, Stills, and Nash."

From this point on (in my opinion anyway), the Rolling Stones saga, like the music itself, gets progressively less interesting. They survived Brian Jones and Altamont; in fact, as measured by all the usual yardsticks of the record business, the Stones only got "bigger" than ever. The Seventies brought them their most lucrative concert tours and their all-time best-selling albums. While, for example, they had scored only one U.S. Number One LP in *Billboard* throughout the Sixties, *every* Rolling Stones studio album issued during the following decade made it all the way to the top. And yet even the most recent Stones convert would be unlikely to rate *It's Only Rock 'n' Roll* or *Black and Blue* on a par with *Beggars Banquet* and *Let It Bleed.*

More and more, something seemed lacking. It wasn't even the fault of the Stones, whose musicianship and performance abilities grew ever more accomplished. Simply, they became an institution. People came to see them not for what they were doing, but for what they had already done. From challenging the Establishment and shaking up everyone's preconceptions of "entertainment," the Stones (perhaps inevitably) turned into established entertainers themselves; all they had left to shake were the rear ends in the audience. That's fun, too, of course; but in terms of history, even rock & roll history, the Stones gradually ceased to matter.

Jagger's efforts to recapture the public's imagination with increasingly spectacular stage productions only contributed to the show-biz aura that was enveloping the Stones. For all their vaunted "decadence," they even lost the ability to shock. The lurid tales that continued to surface throughout the Seventies—of orgies at the pleasure palace of *Playboy* tycoon Hugh Hefner, of smuggled heroin and Swiss blood transfusions—came to seem more like the antics of depraved or jaded millionaires than of inspired rock & roll hoodlums.

In the spring of 1971, the Stones made a clean break with their past in two important respects. Following a "farewell tour," they left Britain to live as tax exiles in the south of France. And following the expiration of their contract, they left Decca/London to form their own Rolling Stones Records.

When Decca insisted that the fine print mandated the delivery of one more single, the band responded with a vintage Stones gesture. Jagger subsequently revealed to *NME:* "They have one cut which I gave them to terminate the old contract. It's called

'Cocksucker Blues' and they are very welcome to put that out—but somehow they've declined to do so.'' The ditty's chorus consisted of the lyric: ''Where can I get my cock sucked/ Where can I get my ass fucked. . . ?''

For their custom label (distributed by Atlantic) the Stones devised their infamous tongue logo. In *Rolling Stone*, Richards described it as ''the Kali tongue . . . that's Kali, the Hindu female goddess. Five arms, a row of heads around her, a sabre in one hand, flames coming out the other, she stands there with her tongue out. But that's gonna change; that symbol's not going to stay as it is. Sometimes it'll take up the whole label, maybe slowly it'll turn into a cock. . . .'' ('Twas not to be, but Rolling Stones Records serial numbers did utilize the prefixes COC and CUN.) To run their company, the band appointed Marshall Chess, a scion of Chicago's Chess Records family, without whom. . . .

The label's first single, ''Brown Sugar,'' duplicated the sound and stature of the Stones' classic hits—with extra spice added in the form of the horns that were to become a hallmark of the band's productions. The lyrics presented Jagger in the guise of a Colonial gentleman who affirms that his young female slave ''taste so good . . . like a black girl should.'' Racism? Sexism? Subtle parody? The debate raged among the cognoscenti. Keith, however, subsequently told *NME:* ''Brown sugar was in fact a term for Mexican smack. Mick just wrote it for a chick.''

''Brown Sugar'' also served as the opening blast for the first Rolling Stones Records album, *Sticky Fingers* (a title originally announced for the album ultimately released as *Let It Bleed*). Andy Warhol was commisioned to produce the cover's life-size crotch shot, complete with real zipper; the well-hung stud was reportedly Warhol superstar Joe Dallesandro. The Stones originally planned to have a balloon flop out when the zipper was pulled, but were persuaded that the package was elaborate enough already. (In Franco's Spain, where the album's male contours were deemed excessive for public consumption, Atlantic Records substituted as ''less offensive'' a picture of a can filled with blood and severed fingers.)

At least half of *Sticky Fingers* was in fact already two years old, including the second U.S. single, ''Wild Horses.'' This country-tinged ballad was Mick Jagger's favorite cut on the album; it had previously been bequeathed to the Flying Burrito Brothers, whose guiding spirit, the late Gram Parsons, was a close friend of Keith's. Another highlight was ''Can't You Hear Me Knocking,'' Bill Wyman's favorite and the first extended Stones improvisation in years.

But many critics agreed with *Rolling Stone*'s Jon Landau that the album's masterpiece was unquestionably ''Moonlight Mile'' (which the Stones had originally called ''The Japanese Thing''). ''The semi-oriental touch seems to heighten the song's intense expression of desire,'' Landau wrote. ''There is something deeply soulful here, something deeply felt: 'I've got silence on the radio, let the airwaves flow.' Paul Buckmaster, Elton John's arranger, does the best job with strings I can remember hearing on a rock record in a long time, while Charlie Watts only goes through the motions of loosening his style as he comes down hard on the lovely, magical line 'just about a moonlight mile.' ''

Nonetheless, Landau—who could always be counted on for one of the more insightful appraisals of each new Stones release—dismissed the rest of *Sticky Fingers* as ''middle-level Rolling Stones competence,'' then neatly summed up both the band's history and its current dilemma:

The early Stones were adolescent rockers. They were self-conscious in an obvious and unpretentious way. And they were

Andy Warhol's cover for 1971's Sticky Fingers *LP*

. . . and a special design for the Spanish market, where the original was deemed too shocking.

committed to a musical style that needed no justification because it came so naturally to them. As they grew musically the mere repetition of old rock and blues tunes became less satisfying. They . . . began to strive for a more contemporary feeling and approach. . . . After the failure of *Satanic Majesties,* they went back to rock & roll to recharge themselves, mixed it with contemporary themes and production styles. . . . [But] where the early Stones had been, if anything, too anarchic and abandoned, they now became too controlled and manipulative. . . .

If *Sticky Fingers* suffers from any one thing it is its own self-defeating calculating coldness. Its moments of openness and feeling are too few; its moments where I know I should be enjoying it but am not, too many.

Still, *Sticky Fingers* was to be the first Rolling Stones album to sell a million units in the United States alone.

In Britain, Decca attempted to claim a piece of the action by simultaneously releasing a collection of rejects and rehashes called *Stone Age*—whose jacket depicted a graffiti-covered wall in feeble but unmistakable imitation of the *Beggars Banquet* artwork that the company had so steadfastly refused to distribute three years earlier. At this point the Stones' relationship with their former label deteriorated to a state of open warfare. A full-page ad, signed by all the Stones, appeared in the pop weeklies:

BEWARE!
Message from the
ROLLING STONES
Re: STONE AGE

We didn't know this record was going to be released. It is, in our opinion, below the standard we try to keep up, both in choice of content and cover design.

But *Stone Age* was to be but the first in a long line of such abortions. Another was the deceptively titled *Gimme Shelter*, a nonsoundtrack album combining extracts from the 1966

LP, U.K., 1971 (Decca)

LP, U.S.A., 1979 (Abkco Music)

American live LP and *studio* versions of songs the Stones were shown performing onstage in the film. (The real *Gimme Shelter* soundtrack album had, of course, already been released as *Get Yer Ya-Ya's Out*.) *NME*'s front-page headline that particular week was: "JAGGER SLAMS ALBUM—But We Can't Print Comments." (In America, London would make do with a reasonably acceptable pair of "greatest hits" double albums, *Hot Rocks* and *More Hot Rocks*.)

Relations were hardly improved upon the surfacing of evidence suggesting that eight years earlier, Decca had made a secret deal with Oldham granting him the lion's share of royalties rightfully due the Stones. When it also transpired that Allen Klein had apparently swindled them out of their publishing copyrights, the Stones squared off for a series of three-cornered multimillion-dollar legal battles with Oldham and Klein. Of the latter gentleman Jagger had only this to say in *NME*: "Klein would probably sue me and your paper for libel if I told you my opinion of him. He's a person to be avoided. . . ."

Nineteen seventy-one's biggest Mick Jagger headlines, however, concerned his May 12 marriage to his Nicaraguan mirror image, Bianca Perez Moreno de Macias, whom he had met in Paris the previous autumn. Britain's rock aristocracy was flown en masse to St. Tropez for the wedding, which promised to be the media circus of the year, despite Jagger's expressed wish to the contrary. Indeed, the hordes of reporters and cameramen were greeted by a groom whose temper was such that he even threatened to cancel the entire celebration.

Mick and Bianca take their vows as Atlantic Records mogul Ahmet Ertegun (1.) looks on (Popperfoto)

The real reason for this outburst was later reported to have been Bianca's insistence that the couple take the legal option of combining their financial assets on a joint ownership basis; even on his wedding day, Mick was no sucker. Though Bianca was a lady accustomed to getting her own way, she finally backed down; the Catholic ceremony (in preparation for which Jagger had taken religious lessons with a priest) proceeded on schedule, complete with a musical selection from *Love Story*, included at the bride's request.

The liaison with Bianca seemed to complete Jagger's initiation into that glamorous jet-set world inhabited primarily by "people who are famous just for being famous." And five months after the wedding, Bianca presented him with a daughter, Jade. In return, Mrs. Mick Jagger received her entree to some choice modeling jobs, not to mention the pages of Andy Warhol's *Interview* magazine and a place of honor at New York's Studio 54. The Mick-and-Bianca soap opera—enlivened soon enough by extramarital indiscretions and catty one-liners from both central characters—was to keep the gossip columnists working overtime throughout its five-year run.

The Stones spent much of the rest of the year recording the album that would be released on the Jaggers' first anniversary at a mobile studio in Keith's new French villa—"in this disgusting basement which looked like a prison," Mick reported in *NME*. "The humidity was incredible. I couldn't stand it. As soon as I opened my mouth to sing my voice was gone. It was so humid that all the guitars were out of tune . . . by the time we got to the end of each number." "It was 120 degrees," added Keith. "Everyone sat around sweating and playing with their pants off." No wonder the album's originally announced title was *Tropical Diseases!*

Because Jagger's voice is often lost in the miasmic production, it was to be expected that many listeners would miss the unprecedented forthrightness of the lyrics. Songs like "Torn and Frayed" exposed the real effects of the dissipation and depravity that the Stones had previously glamorized—while such aural assaults as "Rocks Off" proved, upon investigation, to be confessions of impotence! (Though perhaps "I only get my rocks off when I'm dreaming" isn't, after all, such a far cry from "I can't get no satisfaction.")

Ultimately released as *Exile on Main Street*, the album was described by Jagger as "a danceable record . . . really not a thinking man's record." Producer Jimmy Miller told *NME* that the "idea was to try and get back to good old rock & roll. Looking back over the recent albums, we felt there was a need to re-establish the rock thing. . . .

"The new album became a double set even though . . . we all agreed that almost every double album we'd ever heard would have made a good single album." Even Keith—who was primarily responsible, as Mick was constantly gadding off to Paris and Bianca—would agree in retrospect that *Exile* as well dragged on too long. Still, there remains that vociferous minority of Stones aficionados who consider *Exile* to be the Grail incarnate—or at the very least "a no bones about it rock magnum opus on par with *Blonde on Blonde*," as Nick Kent wrote a year later in his *NME* exegesis:

Jagger's voice is meshed rigidly within a terse gauze of shambling razor-edged funk, power-housed throughout by the guitar work. . . . Richards' taut muscle-packed walls of rhythm chording are the perfect foil for Taylor's diamond-cutter slide work; the rest of the musicians hook themselves around the pair, packed tightly for an almost claustrophobic intensity. . . .

From pissing against a wall to that first cocaine reference, it's all been splendid fun. And then along comes *Exile* which spans the Stones' real walk to the edge, casting a doleful eye at the wreckage incurred from all the partying . . . [performances] pushed by a sense of urgency mixed with desperation as if the band are going to be suddenly swooped down on by their jaded shadow. . . .

Exile on Main Street is easily the key work from out of the whole Rolling Stones' second golden era, because it pinpoints all the pitfalls inherent in the band's graceful narcissistic self-obsessive preening . . . the last defiant lurch out of their own abyss.

Exile occasioned the next of the Stones' American tours, their first since 1969's ultimately disastrous freewheeling counterculture carnival. This one, by contrast, would not only be twice as long—spanning thirty cities over two hot and grueling months—but the operating word was to be "professionalism." Every detail was co-ordinated with a precision befitting a military campaign; indeed, the Stones Touring Party—officially dubbed ''STP''—was itself a veritable rock & roll army. Apart from tour and production managers Peter Rudge and Chip Monck, supplementary band members Nicky Hopkins, Bobby Keyes, and Jim Price, and the usual complement of roadies and sound and lighting technicians, STP included a security network (one of whose functions was to forestall the potential assassins that Jagger had so come to dread); a doctor; photographers; secretaries (whose duties included editing a daily STP newsletter); record company president Marshall Chess; ''a crazed Arkansas hillbilly boy gee-tar genius'' (Nick Kent's phrase) whose sole responsibility was to tune and care for Richards's thirty-odd guitars, including the five-string models he had custom-designed to Keith's specifications; plus recording engineers, a film crew under the direction of Robert Frank, and writer Robert Greenfield—all along to produce official chronicles of the tour for their respective media. Apart from supporting act Stevie Wonder and *his* musicians and entourage, there was also the usual fluctuating gaggle of groupies and drug suppliers, insuring for even the most lowly STP minion a constant harvest of blow jobs, orgies, gang bangs, cocaine, speed, Quaaludes, and amyl nitrite (reportedly *the* 1972 STP drug). (Greenfield's definition of STP credentials was ''the ability to get loaded and go on functioning.'')

The stage props alone necessitated the use of two enormous vans. The floor, when assembled and washed with warm 7-Up to make it ''danceable,'' was dominated by an intertwined pair of painted fire-breathing sea serpents. High above the stage was a sixteen-by-forty-foot Mylar mirror, an innovative device that enabled the spotlights to be placed *behind* the band. When beamed up and into the mirror, they in effect illuminated the Stones from both the front and the back.

Despite the elaborate precautions, there was plenty of offstage drama throughout the tour. At one point everything the Stones ingested had to be screened in advance on account of death threats from Hell's Angels, who held Jagger and Co. responsible for the tarnished reputations and exorbitant legal fees they incurred in the aftermath of Altamont. In San Francisco a ravishing lady in hot pants, having charmed her way onto the Stones' plane to get their ''autographs,'' was hurled down the stairs to the tarmac by Keith when she attempted to serve a long list of Altamont-related subpoenas. And in Warwick, Rhode Island, Mick, Keith, Robert Frank, and Marshall Chess were jailed for assaulting a paparazzo at the airport—while at the Boston Gardens fifteen thousand Rolling Stones fans were growing increasingly restless. The city's police force had more than enough on their hands, what with race riots and the ghetto in flames. Thanks to the personal intercession of Boston's Mayor Kevin White with the governor of Rhode Island, the two Stones were released from jail, and the band hit the Gardens stage five hours after showtime.

There were also such unplanned detours as Hugh Hefner's pleasure palace, of which STP was given the run for three dissipated days. And around mid-tour, much was made of the fact that the Stones' entourage had been joined by Truman Capote and Lee Radziwill. The punters' reaction was summed up in a letter to *Rolling Stone:* ''Hasn't it all become too chichi . . . ?

Lee, dearest, the next time you run into Mick darling, do give him my fondest.'' Later Keith would respond, in *NME:* ''All those jet-setters must be bored or something. . . . How they get in there, and why they get in there in the first place, I don't really know. . . . All I can say is . . . there's no way they're ever going to be in our company ever again.''

Still, following the tour's custard pie-throwing finale at New York's Madison Square Garden, there they all were at Mick Jagger's twenty-ninth birthday party at the St. Regis Hotel: Truman and Lee, Tennessee Williams and George Plimpton, Dick Cavett and Zsa Zsa Gabor, Oscar and Françoise de la Renta, and Count Vega del Ren and one Lord Hesketh, all there to mingle with the Stones and Bob Dylan and a full complement of Andy Warhol superstars, to watch a naked girl leap out of Mick's oversize birthday cake, and to drown out the performances of Muddy Waters and Count Basie with their exalted chitchat.

As noted earlier, the Rolling Stones' 1972 American tour was to have been the most thoroughly documented of all time; but only Robert Greenfield's fine book *Stones Touring Party* would actually see the light of day. Robert Frank's film, the triple-X-rated *Cocksucker Blues* (which showed various members of the Stones Touring Party in compromising positions with anonymous groupies, syringes, and other instruments of delight), was shelved in favor of the strictly in-concert *Ladies and Gentlemen the Rolling Stones*. And though Jagger vowed in October that ''there will be a live album from the tour . . . out by Christmas,'' there was to be no such thing. The covers of *Rolling Stones American Tour 1972* (a double LP incorporating performances by Stevie Wonder) were ready to go to press when Decca and Allen Klein conspired to block the album's release

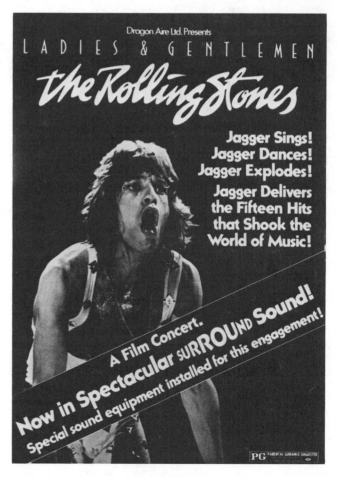

by withholding the rights to "Honky Tonk Women," "Jumpin' Jack Flash," and "Satisfaction."

"We would not be in business for very long," a spokesman for Decca Records explained in *NME*, "if we were to wash our hands of a product that is rightfully ours. We have been very easy with the Stones in the past, some of us feel too easy . . . they owed [*Sticky Fingers*] to us. But the time had come when we felt we should have a bit of fight back." Conceded a spokesman for Rolling Stones Records: "I'm afraid the album, brilliant though it is, seems doomed to die a horrible death."

The lethargic murk that seeps from the grooves of the next bona fide Rolling Stones LP, August 1973's *Goat's Head Soup*, originated for the most part in a recording studio on the hot and humid island of Jamaica. The choice of locale was largely dictated by the fact that the list of nations in which Mr. Richards was welcome seemed to be dwindling rapidly. Keith was now persona non grata even in his adopted country of France, on account of his having allegedly tainted the French blood of certain young innocents with some vile concoction. When Japanese immigration authorities got wind of the Stones' crimes, a planned series of concerts at Tokyo's Budokan judo arena had to be canceled, to the distress of fifty-five thousand ticket holders. In Australia, however, a similar ban was reversed when the minister of immigration decreed that "the Stones are an excellent example to Australian youth."

According to Mick Taylor, *Goat's Head Soup* was named after an ethnic Jamaican delicacy consisting of a goat that has been run down on the highway, scraped off the road, and served as a main course. Of the music itself, Keith said in *NME:* "I think the album marks time nicely. It's nothing I'd feel motivated to put on, but when it's on, it sounds good." If most of *Goat's Head Soup* conjures the image of dinosaurs thrashing around in a steaming swamp, at least the Stones were, in a sense, exploring new territory.

The only selection on which they seem to rouse themselves from the subtropical miasma is Mick Jagger's Chuck Berry pastiche "Starfucker," which chronicles the adventures of a supergroupie whose accomplishments include performing vaginal acrobatics with pieces of fruit and fellatio on Steve McQueen. "Starfucker" precipitated another of the Stones' legendary battles with their record company, though in this case the adversary was their handpicked distributor, Ahmet Ertegun's Atlantic Records.

After the Stones made it plain that they would not sanction the release of a "Starfucker"-less *Goat's Head Soup*, Ertegun finally agreed to market the ditty under the title "Star Star." The Stones, for their part, obtained a clearance from Mr. McQueen, but botched a feeble attempt to erase the word "pussy" from the master tape. In light of all this brouhaha, it seems surprising that Atlantic should select "Star Star" for the opening track of its *Goat's Head Soup* promotional EP.

The album went on to become one of the Stones' all-time U.S. best-sellers, thanks to the inclusion of "Angie." Rumored to have been written for David Bowie's wife, Angela, it was their most shameless tearjerker since "As Tears Go By"—and, hardly coincidentally, their first gold single in four years. . . .

September 10, 1973: "Star Star" is banned by the BBC.
September 11: The Rolling Stones—complete with mascara, rhinestones, dry ice, and glittery orbs lowered from the ceiling—begin a tour of Britain.

October 24: Keith Richards is fined £205 for possession of cannabis, heroin, Mandrax, a shotgun, a revolver, and 110 rounds of ammunition, all seized during a police raid on his Chelsea town house four months earlier. . . .

Each successive album now took the Stones upwards of a year to get together—"laughable," said Bill Wyman, "when you think the first Stones album was done in a day, the second in about three days, and the third in a week." (One reason for this was that the band was now wont to record at least two LPs worth of material before making their final selection.)

In April 1974 Wyman attempted to fill the gap with his *Monkey Grip*, the first bona fide solo LP by a Rolling Stone, and apparently the cause of a row with Keith Richards, who had recently dismissed the very idea of solo albums as "pointless." "It's something I felt I had to get out of my system once and forever," Bill told *NME*'s Roy Carr. "I haven't enjoyed myself so much [in] five years." Though many Stones aficionados were delighted to become better acquainted with the band's enigmatic bass player, *Monkey Grip* proved to be fairly undistinguished (in much the same way that the novelty of a Ringo Starr or a John Entwistle solo LP tended to wear off after a few spins). "My original aim," said Bill, "was to put together a collection of lighthearted songs with simple turnaround melodies." By those criteria *Monkey Grip* could be judged a modest success, along with its 1976 sequel, *Stone Alone* (despite Bowie/Bolan makeup wizard Pierre LaRoche's ludicrous attempts to turn Wyman into a trendy glitter queen on the latter's jacket).

The advance word on 1974's group effort, *It's Only Rock 'n' Roll*, aroused expectations of a major Rolling Stones "come-

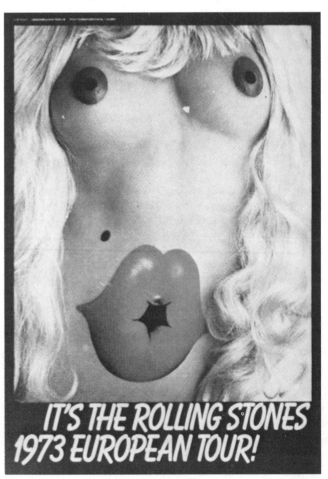

back,'' unadulterated by female singers, brass, or strings—
''not a violin in sight,'' promised Keith, who co-produced this
and all future Stones records with Jagger. The ranks of the
critics produced a few true believers, among them the redoubtable Jon Landau, whose review for *Rolling Stone* included the
following observations:

> *It's Only Rock 'n' Roll* is a decadent album because it invites us
> to dance in the face of its own despair. . . . [Jagger] sings ''Time
> Waits for No One'' with a controlled desperation that borders on
> acceptance but never quite becomes resignation. Given the rock
> star's inherent fear of aging, the song becomes an affirmation of
> Jagger's willingness to keep on trying in the face of inevitable
> doom. . . .
>
> Watts' first drumbeat on ''It's Only Rock 'n' Roll'' . . . reso-
> nates like the sound of a shotgun. That violence—transmitted
> through the singing, words, and music—makes *It's Only Rock 'n'
> Roll* one of the most intriguing and mysterious, as well as the
> darkest, of all Rolling Stones records.

 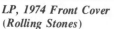 

LP, 1974 Front Cover   *Back Cover*
(*Rolling Stones*)

But the Stones' junior guitarist undiplomatically told Kent
that the LP's title song ''failed, actually. On the one hand it was
Mick and Keith maybe trying to write something in the classic
Stones style, and on the other it was a parody—and I don't think
it really worked on either level.'' (Even less diplomatically,
Taylor added that he had had a hand in composing such
''Jagger-Richards'' compositions as ''Moonlight Mile,'' ''Hide
Your Love,'' ''Till the Next Goodbye,'' ''If You Really Want to
Be My Friend,'' and ''Time Waits for No One.'')

Two months after this *NME* interview was published, Mick
Taylor abruptly quit the Rolling Stones to form a band with Jack
Bruce. ''I'd worked with them in such a way, and for so long,''
Taylor subsequently told *Rolling Stone*, ''that I didn't think I
could go much further without some different musicians. . . .
It was all for purely musical reasons. There was no personal
animosity in the split. There was no row, no quibbling or
squabbling''—over songwriting credits or anything else. The
other Stones were taken by surprise, particularly as a recording
session in Munich was imminent.

Over the next few months, guessing games concerning the
identity of Taylor's replacement ran rampant throughout the
rock biz. Prime candidates included Rory Gallagher, Robert A.
Johnson, Jeff Beck, Harvey Mandel, and Wayne Perkins—some
of whom were to be heard auditioning, as it were, on assorted
tracks slated for the *Black and Blue* album. The final choice, of
course, was Ron Wood—whom, eighteen months earlier, rumor
had touted as the replacement for the presumed-to-be moribund
Keith Richards!

Wood came to the Stones officially ''on loan'' from the Faces,
a band that neither he nor the Stones wished to be responsible
for destroying. But when Rod Stewart left the Faces at the end

of 1975, Wood felt no further qualms about ending his dual role
to take a full-time job with Messrs. Jagger, Richards, Wyman,
and Watts. He and Keith appeared to develop an almost tele-
pathic rapport, musically and otherwise. Strikingly similar in
both their physical appearance and their guitar playing, they
even took to wearing the same outfits onstage. ''Mick [Taylor]
wasn't quite so funky,'' said Wyman, ''but he led us on to other
things. Woody's a bit like Keith . . . not such a fantastic musician, perhaps, but he's more fun—got more personality.''

All in all, the Stones' new guitarist acted, played, and looked
the part flawlessly. Not that anyone, at this late date, could
really *become* a Rolling Stone.

''They weren't meant to get old. . . . If they have any sense
of neatness, they'll get themselves killed in an air crash, three
days before their thirtieth birthdays.'' That had been Nik
Cohn's famous last word on the Rolling Stones in his 1969 book
Rock from the Beginning. In 1972 Mick referred to it as ''a quote
which I didn't really like. I mean, he wouldn't like it if I said that
to him.'' Yet that same year Jagger vowed: ''When I'm thirty-
three, I quit. That's the time when a man has to do something
else. I can't say what it will definitely be . . . but it won't be in
show business. I don't want to be a rock & roll singer all my life.
I couldn't bear to end up as an Elvis Presley and sing in Las
Vegas with all those housewives and old ladies coming in with
their handbags.''

U.S. promotional EP for   *The original withdrawn*
Love You Live, *1976*   *sleeve for* **Some Girls,** *1978*

Sleeve for a promotional   *Jagger as would-be Punk on*
U.S. single of **Before They**   *Japanese reissue of ''Ruby*
Make Me Run   *Tuesday/Sympathy for the*
                           Devil,'' *1979*

The Stones, of course, *have* lasted, past their thirtieth and
thirty-third and even their thirty-sixth birthdays. Mick stayed
very much in show biz, and if crones with handbags had yet to
materialize at his increasingly cabaretlike performances, both
band and audience were nonetheless confronted with a dilemma. For second-generation fans, Jagger, Richards, Wyman,
and Watts (and whoever else they dragged along for the occa-

sion) continued to offer a superior approximation of the Rolling Stones than, say, the clones from the show *Beatlemania* could ever manage of the Fab Four. To some old-timers, however, the guys up on the stage, or on the covers of the million-selling albums, seemed almost like imposters. The balding drummer, the bass player whose *fortieth* birthday was a receding memory, the guitarist resembling "Jumpin' Jack Flash" 's "toothless hag," all fronted by a mincing twentieth-century incarnation of Dorian Gray—who *were* these people?

Stated crudely, cruelly, and all too often (but nonetheless truly): These gentlemen were *too old* to be Rolling Stones. Charlie once countered by pointing to some of his jazz heroes, still going strong into their seventies. Indeed, one could imagine the Kinks hanging in there forever, or Bob Dylan or David Bowie—but *the Rolling Stones?*

The Stones, after all, had made it so big—and had continued to "matter" so much—because, as Derek Taylor once said of the Beatles, "they became an abstraction, like Christmas." (In the case of the Stones, it was perhaps more like Halloween.) Whatever it was that they symbolized had a lot to do with being young—and everything to do with *not* being old. Carrying this kind of baggage, the Stones were denied the roles of ordinary mortals, mere songwriters, musicians, or entertainers.

*Pumping out "Starfucker," with prop (**Chuck Pulin**)*

So the Stones were trapped. What could possibly be the appeal of a bunch of defiantly disagreeable, drug-abusing, dirty old men? On the other hand, were the Rolling Stones to "age gracefully," they would by definition be selling out.

Be that as it may, the Stones elected simply to carry on—working the latest black musical idioms (reggae, street funk, disco) with more flair than most of their white contemporaries, occasionally trotting out the props to put on an exemplary show.

The whole charade was actually quite enjoyable, even if it wasn't quite the Rolling Stones.

The three-month marathon "Rolling Stones Tour of the Americas '75" (dates in Mexico, Venezuela, and Brazil were subsequently canceled) began on May 31 on New York's Fifth Avenue with a surprise performance of "Brown Sugar" from the back of a flatbed truck. Subsequent venues introduced a stage designed by Mick Jagger and Charlie Watts, shaped like a five-petaled lotus that unfolded to the strains of Aaron Copland's "Fanfare for the Common Man" to reveal five Rolling Stones (plus the ubiquitous Billy Preston) launching into the opening bars of "Honky Tonk Women." Other highlights of the show included the giant inflatable cock that Mick pummeled throughout "Starfucker" and the swing upon which he soared over the heads and grasping arms of his admirers in the front rows.

Yet even this late in the game, the Stones were able to arouse a nationally syndicated denunciation by Steve Dunleavy (the opportunistic future co-author of *Elvis: What Happened?*) headlined, IT'S TIME WE EXORCISED THIS DEMONIC INFLUENCE OVER OUR CHILDREN!: "Where have we failed that this pimple-faced disciple of dirt is a hero, a rootin', tootin' hero to our teenage kids?" he asked, calling the Stones show "a tightly packaged excess of four-letter words and tacky smut."

On tour that summer, the Stones found themselves promoting two "new" albums, each containing distinctly shopworn material. *Made in the Shade* was an uninspiring Rolling Stones Records "greatest hits" compendium. *Metamorphosis* was an out-and-out travesty, released as part of a settlement with Allen Klein and Decca. (Andrew Oldham says that his original title, *Necrophilia,* was changed on grounds of "bad taste" because it was thought "to reflect on the late guitarist.")

Though Bill Wyman had obligingly compiled an album of odds and sods (mostly old R&B numbers) which the Stones christened *The Black Box,* Klein chose instead to scrape the bottom of the barrel for original material. "Researcher" Al Steckler, however, failed to do his job properly, as Stevie Wonder's "I Don't Know Why" and Chuck Berry's "Don't Lie to Me" were both listed on early pressings of *Metamorphosis* as Jagger-Richards compositions. And many of the songs that *were* by Mick and Keith were *not* performed by the Rolling Stones! Rather, they were mid-Sixties demos that had been cut by Jagger with such session musicians as future Led Zeppers Jimmy Page and John Paul Jones, strictly for the edification of other artists interested in recording them. Klein's unsavory package (complete with Stones metamorphosing into Kafka-esque cockroaches on the cover) was filled out with early-rehearsal massacres of "Sister Morphine" (heard with its original lyrics, as "Family") and Mick's *Performance* tour de force, "Memo from Turner."

The real new Stones album, however, proved no less dismal when it finally appeared in April 1976. *Black and Blue* suffers from both a lack of cohesiveness (the lineup of musicians differs with nearly every track) and a dearth of inspired material (Keith once actually fell asleep onstage while the Stones were performing "Fool to Cry"—the selection that they had singled out as a 45). The only memorable thing about *Black and Blue,* in fact, was a Hollywood billboard contrived to promote the album and, into the bargain, reopen some old wounds. It showed a young lady bound by rope and covered with bruises, her undergarments in shreds, and the words: I'M BLACK AND BLUE FROM THE ROLLING STONES AND I LOVE IT! . . .

February 24, 1977: Customs and Royal Canadian Mounted Police narcotics agents find traces of heroin and hashish upon searching twenty-eight suitcases belonging to Anita Pallenberg when she arrives with Keith Richards at the Toronto airport.

February 27: Armed with a search warrant, Mounties and Ontario provincial police descend upon Keith Richards's rooms at the Harbour Castle Hilton, where they allegedly find one ounce of heroin.

March 4: The Rolling Stones perform for three hundred people—including Canadian first lady Margaret Trudeau—at the El Mocambo (the band's first club concert, since Bristol, England, November 13, 1964). After the show, the first lady is spied wafting down the Harbour Castle Hilton's corridors in a bathrobe.

March 8: Keith Richards appears in court and is released on $25,000 bail. Mick Jagger, Ron Wood, and Margaret Trudeau check out of the Harbour Castle Hilton and all fly to New York.

March 9: A Toronto *Sun* editorial advises the First Lady: "C'mon Maggie, either behave with distinction or stay at home."

March 14: Anita Pallenberg gets off with a $400 fine.

April 1: Having spent much of the last three weeks mixing tapes of the Stones' El Mocambo performances, Keith Richards is allowed to leave Canada for an undisclosed destination.

September 30: Rolling Stones Records issues the *Love You Live* double album, complete with Andy Warhol cover and one side of music from El Mocambo; the rest had been recorded in Paris the previous year.

June 9, 1978: *Some Girls* is released ("the best album we've done since *Let It Bleed*," says Mick). Like sleazy old sluts turning their last tricks with a vengeance, the Stones actually transform their aura of seediness and decline into a positive asset. The album yields three hit singles: the discofied million-seller "Miss You"; the poignant "Beast of Burden"; and one of the all-time-best New York rock & roll anthems, "Shattered." *Some Girls* even sparks *two* controversies: After such celebrities as Raquel Welch and Lauren Bacall allegedly take exception to their appearance on the cover alongside more Stones transvestite poses, their likenesses are stricken from the sleeve (rendering the original an instant collector's item). Meanwhile, Jesse Jackson attempts to whip up a national outcry over the title song's observation that "black girls just want to get fucked all night." One has to hand it to the Stones for their unceasing ability, even in their dotage, to provoke self-righteous diatribes from the self-appointed spokespersons for constituencies as various as the black community, women's lib, and "God, flag, and country." "If you can't take a joke," Jagger comments, "that's too fucking bad."

June 10: The Rolling Stones begin a six-week American tour, alternating between venues as large as Philadelphia's ninety thousand-seat JFK Stadium and as small as Washington, D.C.'s two thousand-seat Warner Theater. Notwithstanding the less elaborate lineup, costumes, and stage sets (the Punk influence having apparently eclipsed that of Bowie), the shows are savaged by *Rolling Stone,* causing Jagger to order the magazine's correspondent off the tour.

April 22, 1979: The New Barbarians (Ron Wood and Keith Richards's spinoff band, featuring pianist Ian McLagen, drummer Joseph Modeliste, bassist Stanley Clarke, and saxophonist Bobby Keyes) commence a North American tour by serving Richards's heroin sentence with a pair of Toronto concerts benefiting the blind that climax with a surprise appearance by the Rolling Stones.

July 20: Scott Cantrell, seventeen, dies in Keith Richards's bed in his suburban New York mansion after allegedly shooting himself with a stolen handgun in the presence of Anita Pallenberg. In a subsequent story headlined YOUTH DIED PLAYING RUSSIAN ROULETTE IN BED OF ROLLING STONE "WIFE," the *New York Post* reports that "the filth and untidyness" chez Richards were such that "an air freshener could not cover the stench."

January 1, 1980: Celebrating the New Year at his Manhattan town house, Mick Jagger tells an interviewer for *High Times* that her magazine is "disgusting. I think that you shouldn't encourage young people to take drugs anyway. I think that's just awful." He also dismisses rock & roll as "just music hall entertainment . . . rather dull, actually."

June 22: The Rolling Stones' twenty-sixth American LP, *Emotional Rescue,* sparks a running debate in *The Village Voice* over whether its contents are magnificently contrived junk or just plain

AVAILABLE ON ROLLING STONES RECORDS & TAPES

unredeemed junk. Nonetheless, the album quickly hits Number One and stays there longer than any previous Stones release.

August 21: Mick Jagger is quoted in *Rolling Stone:* "There is no future in rock & roll. It's all recycled past." Bill Wyman confirms rumors that he will quit on his twentieth anniversary with the band. "Yes, I *am* going to retire from the Rolling Stones. I really do want to do other things . . . so at the end of 1982 I'll go for something else. When I got into rock & roll, I thought it'd last two or three years, maybe five, and I was just after some extra cash. . . . Suddenly, here I am, eighteen years later . . . and I'm *still* playing rock & roll." . . .

But the Rolling Stones just wouldn't go away. Even Bill Wyman retracted his promise to quit in 1982, despite his having finally scored a solo hit with the delightfully imbecilic novelty "Si, Si, Je Suis Un Rock Star," which he croaked in "Franglais" to the backdrop of his own burbling synthesizer. And in September 1981 a full complement of Stones assembled onstage at Philadelphia's J.F.K. Stadium to commence *the* most lucrative concert tour in history. The Stones then proceeded to trot out the old "classics" for two million Americans—who constituted but a fraction of those who had coveted tickets, four million applications having been received for the New York–area concerts alone. Many of those who did get to hear Mick sing the likes of "Time Is on My Side" were young enough to

The Stones in 1980 with Ron Wood (Rolling Stones Records)

have been conceived while the Stones' first big U.S. hit was playing on their parents' clock radios.

Predictably enough, a new album was issued to coincide with the tour and its attendant hoopla. Yet *Tattoo You* bore nary a trace of the disco funk and quasi-Punk with which the Stones had previously attempted to stay abreast of trends. On one level the band seemed to be retreating into its early Sixties R&B roots, but it might also be observed that the Rolling Stones, for the first time, were retreating into *music*. Throughout their history, the Stones had always represented much more than mere music, but *Tattoo You* finally stripped away all the guises and disguises from which the Stones had derived much of their mystique. Gone were the misogynistic putdowns, drug references, and all the other paraphernalia of the Stones' vaunted "decadence"; gone, too, the self-parody and pastiche the band had resorted to on *Some Girls* and *Emotional Rescue* (for which, ironically, many of *Tattoo You*'s selections had originally been recorded and rejected). Instead, *Tattoo You* presented straightforward bluesy rockers and heartfelt soul-tinged ballads, passionately sung, magnificently played, and immaculately pro-

duced. *Tattoo You* seemed to be the Stones' acknowledgment that they could no longer bank on their own youthful legend, that the only possible key to their credibility as men in their forties playing rock & roll for the Eighties rested in their own musical chops.

Throughout their first decade, the Rolling Stones had lived up to their own original billing as "reflections of today's children," and had provided a mirror of sorts for millions who grew up with them. During the mid-Seventies, those reflections had become increasingly unrecognizable; yet by the end of the Stones' second decade, the longtime fan could almost forgive the stubborn longevity. If the reflection in the mirror now revealed wisps of gray hair and the deepening imprint of crow's feet, at least the Stones might once again be viewed as rebels with whom we might all make common cause. The rebellion was no longer against the conventions of adult authority, or the forces of sweetness and light; now it was a grown-up's defiance, still nobler and more futile, of the laws of time itself. And if you closed your eyes while these middle-aged adolescents sang "Time Is on My Side," you could almost pretend they weren't lying.

1964

1964

1964

1964

1964

1965

1965

1965

1966

1966

1966

1966

1966

1966

1967

1967

1967

1967

1968

1968

1968

1969

1978

1978

THE ROLLING STONES' HITS

U.S. Singles

1964 Not Fade Away (**48**); Tell Me (**24**); It's All Over Now (**26**); Time Is On My Side (**6**)

1965 Heart of Stone (**19**); The Last Time/Play with Fire (**9/96**); (I Can't Get No) Satisfaction (**1**); Get Off of My Cloud (**1**)

1966 As Tears Go By (**6**); 19th Nervous Breakdown (**2**); Paint It, Black (**1**); Mother's Little Helper/ Lady Jane (**8/24**); Have You Seen Your Mother, Baby, Standing in the Shadow? (**9**)

1967 Ruby Tuesday/ Let's Spend the Night Together (**1/55**); Dandelion/ We Love You (**14/50**); She's a Rainbow (**25**)

1968 Jumpin' Jack Flash (**3**); Street Fighting Man (**48**)

1969 Honky Tonk Women (**1**)

1971 Brown Sugar (**1**); Wild Horses (**28**)

1972 Tumbling Dice (**7**); Happy (**22**)

1973 Angie (**1**); You Can't Always Get What You Want (**42**)

1974 Doo Doo Doo Doo Doo (Heartbreaker) (**15**); It's Only Rock 'n' Roll (**16**); Ain't Too Proud to Beg (**17**)

1975 I Don't Know Why (**42**); Out of Time (**81**)

1976 Fool to Cry/ Hot Stuff (**10/49**)

1978 Miss You (**1**); Beast of Burden (**8**)

1979 Shattered (**31**)

1980 Emotional Rescue (**3**); She's So Cold (**26**)

(BY BILL WYMAN)

1967 In Another Land (**87**)

U.S. LPs

1964 The Rolling Stones (**11**); 12 × 5 (**3**)

1965 The Rolling Stones Now! (**5**); Out of Our Heads (**1**); December's Children (**4**)

1966 Big Hits (High Tide and Green Grass) (**3**); Aftermath (**2**); Got Live If You Want It! (**6**)

1967 Between the Buttons (**2**); Flowers (**3**); Their Satanic Majesties Request (**2**)

1968 Beggars Banquet (**5**)

1969 Through the Past Darkly (Big Hits Vol. 2) (**2**); Let It Bleed (**3**)

1970 Get Yer Ya-Ya's Out (**6**)

1971 Sticky Fingers (**1**)

1972 Hot Rocks 1964–1971 (**4**); More Hot Rocks (Big Hits and Fazed Cookies) (**9**); Exile on Main Street (**1**)

1973 Goat's Head Soup (**1**)

1974 It's Only Rock 'n' Roll (**1**)

1975 Metamorphosis (**8**); Made in the Shade (**6**)

1976 Black and Blue (**1**)

1977 Love You Live (**5**)

1978 Some Girls (**1**)

1980 Emotional Rescue (**1**)

(BY BILL WYMAN)

1974 Monkey Grip (**99**)

1976 Stone Alone (**166**)

U.K. Singles

1963 Come On (**21**); I Wanna Be Your Man (**12**)

1964 Rolling Stones EP (**20**); Not Fade Away (**3**); It's All Over Now (**1**); 5 × 5 EP (**13**); Little Red Rooster (**1**)

1965 The Last Time (**1**); Got Live If You Want It! EP (**6**); (I Can't Get No) Satisfaction (**1**); Get Off of My Cloud (**1**)

1966 19th Nervous Breakdown/ As Tears Go By (**2**); Paint It, Black (**1**); Have You Seen Your Mother, Baby, Standing in the Shadow? (**5**)

1967 Let's Spend The Night Together/Ruby Tuesday (**3**); We Love You/ Dandelion (**8**)

1968 Jumping Jack Flash (**1**)

1969 Honky Tonk Women (**1**)

1971 Brown Sugar/ Bitch/ Let It Rock (**2**); Street Fighting Man (**21**)

1972 Tumbling Dice (**5**)

1973 Angie (**5**)

1974 It's Only Rock 'n' Roll (**10**)

1975 Out of Time (**45**)

1976 Fool to Cry (**6**)

1978 Miss You/ Far Away Eyes (**3**); Respectable (**23**)

1980 Emotional Rescue (**8**); She's So Cold (**31**)

(BY MICK JAGGER)

1970 Memo from Turner (**32**)

The Kinks

The Kinks circa 1965 (from l.): Pete Quaife, Dave Davies, Mick Avory, and Ray Davies (Globe Photos)

O F ALL THE BRITISH Invasion groups, the most quintessentially British was the Kinks. The Kinks were also the most reluctant conscripts to serve in the original Invasion. Almost as an act of conscientious objection, the band—following one tour of duty in 1965—virtually disqualified itself from the American arena. Even as the Rolling Stones gathered momentum on these shores, the Kinks (whose earlier singles had charted much more strongly than the Stones') faded inexorably into an obscure cult item. And yet never has America seen a rock cult so fanatically devoted as that of the Kinks.

To some extent, it was a cult of the underdog. The better the Kinks' records got, the worse they sold—and the more the "kultists" loved them for it. (The letter *k*, by the way, loomed large in the Kink legend.) The group even sounded like underdogs, especially after they abandoned those Kink-patented "power chords" that first slammed them into prominence. The voice of Ray Davies was flat and frail, and their own American agent once confided to me that the band "couldn't play a note if their lives depended on it." Yet in the same breath he called Davies "the most brilliant artist in the business." As Nik Cohn had observed a couple of years earlier, "the whole thing is lopsided, crablike, one step from chaos, but somehow it balances out, it makes sense."

The Kinks' main claim to brilliance rested in Davies's words and music; but these, too, readily escaped wide notice for the very reason that Davies was such a master of understatement. That in itself was as peculiarly British as the people and places he wrote about, the accent with which he evoked them, or the English music-hall heritage he rediscovered in fashioning a form of British rock music that was truly indigenous. And yet, like all art worthy of the name, the songs of the Kinks struck a universal chord that left certain non-Britons deeply touched. The group's fans were often victims of hypersensitivity as well as Anglomania; like Ray Davies, they viewed themselves as "misfits" in an uncongenial world, and they were inordinately protective of their vulnerable and resolutely unfashionable heroes.

"There's some sort of real bond between Kinks-lovers the world over. I mean it's not just some rock group. It's more like a taste for fine wines from a certain valley, a devotion to a particular breed of cocker spaniel," wrote Paul Williams in his *Rolling Stone* review of 1968's *The Kinks Are the Village Green Preservation Society,* which may well be the group's greatest album. It was certainly their all-time worst seller. The album's theme song, moreover, offered some uncharacteristically explicit reasons why the Kinks were indeed so different (one of their early B-sides had been called "I'm Not Like Everybody Else")—and so special. At a time when their contemporaries were shouting the praises of fast cars, fast foods, fast highs, and fast women (which, after all, was what rock music was popularly supposed to be all about), the Kinks appointed themselves voices in the wilderness of twentieth-century mass culture, deploring the effects of modernization and Americanization on their blessed green isle: "*We are the office block persecution affinity, God save little shops, china cups, and virginity.* . . ." (Which prompted the rallying cry among kultists everywhere: "God Save the Kinks!")

Davies was the first British pop star to find songwriting fodder in the habits, quirks, and small pleasures of his fellow countrymen. But even during his R&B apprenticeship, he had tended to holler with an English accent; when his phrasing went "colored," it was by way of the West Indies rather than the Mississippi Delta (which nobody else had yet thought of either). When the Kinks made the switch to "social commentary" at the end of 1965, Davies's writing began to reveal an extraordinary eye for detail, a sardonic wit, and an unabashed romanticism tempered with a certain detachment that enabled him to empathize with both sides of every situation: "Got to stand and face it, life is *so* complicated." This ambivalence even extended to sexual role playing, culminating in 1970's saga of the transvestite "Lola"—who was to play a major part in the Kinks' eventual U.S. "comeback."

From the start, the Kinks broke all the rules, yet throughout most of their career they remained faithful to two of their own. In 1965, Davies declared in *Melody Maker:* "One of our aims is to stay amateurs. As soon as we become professionals, we'll be ruined." He also wrote from an unswervingly personal viewpoint. Personal expression was far more important to the Kinks than mere technique or such commercial considerations as "giving the people what they want."

In person, Ray Davies's most distinctive feature was his ambivalent, lopsided grin; even as one side of his face smiled, the other half remained resolutely melancholy. And when he opened his mouth to laugh or sing, one was especially struck by the vast space between his two front teeth. He had always planned to have the gap filled once he could afford it, but something made him change his mind when fame and fortune struck. And that, he would insist, "was the most important decision I ever made."

The Kinks—Ray and brother Dave Davies, Peter Quaife, and Mick Avory—all grew up in the general region of Muswell Hill, the North London working-class suburb where they would continue to reside at the height of their mid-Sixties success. In 1966 Dave Davies described it in *Melody Maker* as "a bit rough" but "a great place. . . . It's like a little village."

Raymond Douglas Davies (born June 21, 1944) and David Russel Gordon Davies (born February 3, 1947) were the youngest of eight children; their father was (in Ray's words) "an ordinary man—a gardener." According to Dave, "my mother came from a big family. . . . When we were kids and goin' to school, it was like a railway station, people in and out and the front door always open, and people drinking tea all day."

Like their six sisters before them, the Davies brothers were encouraged from an early age to play musical instruments. At nine, Ray became the proud owner of a Spanish guitar, and presently "got interested in the blues through people like Broonzy and Leadbelly," though he never outgrew "the pub-type songs I had been brought up on."

At seventeen, Ray began studying at Hornsey Art College. His most cherished ambition was to become a theatrical producer or director, and music remained only a hobby. Nonetheless, he was already on what *New Musical Express* would a decade later call "the path trodden by so many current members of the pop world. First, a flirtation with one instrument or another, then a gradual awakening to the American blues artists and, eventually, excursions into converted pub rooms and the like, all serving as instant blues clubs."

Like dozens of his contemporaries, Ray found a mentor of sorts in the British Blues pioneer Alexis Korner, who steered him in the direction of a basement dive called the Piccadilly. There Ray was enlisted as rhythm guitarist and harmonica player by the Dave Hunt Band. The rest of the lineup comprised a trombonist, a saxophonist, and Hunt himself, whom Ray de-

scribed (in a 1971 *NME* interview) as "a pianist with ginger hair" who "used to tell me off for making the wrong changes. It was a jazz band, but they could get money playing R&B"—in which capacity they were soon hired by the Crawdaddy Club in Richmond. "A fill-in group used to come along when we went out for a drink, and they were called the Rolling Stones. . . . Charlie Watts was playing in a trad band, and said: 'I might as well join the Rolling Stones.' That was a big turning point in his life." (Ray neglected to mention that Charlie's predecessor had been a drummer called Mick Avory, who, according to Keith Richards, had been fired because "he was terrible . . . couldn't find that off beat.")

"We used to do the Sunday spot [at the Crawdaddy]," said Ray, "but I was involved with exams and couldn't always do it. Our group split up and the Stones took over. . . ."

In the meantime, brother Dave had formed a group called the Ravens with his bass-playing school chum Pete Quaife. Ray,

The Kinks' first published photo, April 1964 (Popperfoto)

who took to sitting in with the Ravens, was invited to become a full-time member. "It was New Year's Day 1964 and I had to make a decision whether to leave art college and play, or forget playing and go on and finish the course. . . . My father figure [at Hornsey] was Mr. Crook, a fine old man. He suggested giving the group a try for six months, then to go back to college if it didn't work out." Dave, for his part, had already dropped out of school at fifteen with no regrets whatsoever.

Unlike the Silver Beatles and the Rollin' Stones, the Ravens were not obliged to pay their dues among the riffraff of strip clubs and subterranean dives. Thanks to the aristocratic background of their original lead singer, Robert Wace, the Ravens received an entree into the posh dance halls frequented by London's debutantes and their well-respected escorts. These audiences, however, often belied their genteel upbringing by hurling beverages at the six-foot-six vocalist. One night, over a mounting chorus of boos, Wace shouted at rhythm guitarist Ray Davies, "You'll have to sing now!"—and fled the stage, never to return. Instead, Wace elected himself the Ravens' co-manager, and financed the demo that was to score the band contracts with Pye Records and twenty-four-year-old American producer Shel Talmy.

The group's rechristening came about—according to Ray in his 1969 *Rolling Stone* interview—after he arrived at the studio "in an orange tie, and a bloke told me: 'Now you really look like a Kink.'" (Typically, Davies elaborated: "It's a good name in a way, because it's something people don't really want. I think people hate us. . . .") Others contend the name was inspired by the "Kinky boots" then in vogue; in any event, as Dave has recalled, "it created a lot of interest . . . and we'd get invited to all these gay parties." BBC announcer Brian Matthew gave the boys their first important mention by declaring on *Thank Your Lucky Stars:* "There are so many groups coming out these days, and I even heard of one the other day called the Kinks!"

The Kinks on Ready Steady Go (*RDR Productions*)

Upon installing Mick Avory as their permanent drummer, the Kinks set about recording Little Richard's "Long Tall Sally" for their Pye debut. The proceedings were so slipshod that one could detect a missing beat at the point where Talmy spliced together portions of two different takes. In his first *Melody Maker* write-up Ray conceded: "The Beatles' version was better than ours." Small wonder, then, that the Kinks' contemporaneously issued rendition went nowhere.

Nonetheless, the Kinks were invited to support the Hollies and the Dave Clark Five on a national package tour, which Dave Davies was to list (in *NME* seven years later) as one of the six career milestones "which in various ways improved the group and helped to push it a little further." "Long Tall Sally"'s follow-up was a Ray Davies original, albeit one that offered little indication of what was to come next. A lame and instantly forgettable "beat ballad," "You Still Want Me" is said to have sold precisely 127 copies. But it was at this juncture that the Kinks added to their repertoire Ray's candidate for the title of "greatest rock & roll song ever written."

"Louie Louie" had begun life as an obscure R&B single, composed and recorded in 1956 by one Richard Berry. In 1963 it was refurbished by a talentless garage band from Portland, Oregon, in whose hands it became America's last great two-minute rock & roll explosion immediately prior to the British Invasion. The Kingsmen's "Louie Louie" was leaden, repetitive, cretinously simple, and because of (rather than despite) all that, perfect. Anyone could play it, but nobody could quite understand it, for the words, either by design or ineptitude, were utterly incomprehensible—a slurred monotone through the murk of a thoroughly slapdash recording. For millions of preadolescents, one of the year's naughtier pleasures was to play the 45 at 33 rpm to determine whether the Kingsmen were indeed singing "Every night at ten I lay her again." It was impossible to be sure.

No rock & roll number has been rewritten more often than "Louie Louie," and no songwriter rewrote it more often or more successfully than Raymond Douglas Davies. Yet he got it exactly right on his very first try, which was "You Really Got Me." On this landmark record (the second of Dave's milestones) the Kinks refined the haphazard distortion of the Kingsmen's record into a conscious style (which was to remain a Kinks trademark through 1966). While they were at it, they virtually invented the heavy, slugging riffs that future rock scribes would fondly label "chunka-chunka-chunk." Entire genres such as Power Pop and heavy metal can trace their lineage back to "You Really Got Me," which, even more than "Louie Louie," has endured as a basic rock & roll classic, inspiring cover versions by artists as far removed from the original in spirit and time as Britain's Mott the Hoople and Brian Eno and America's Van Halen and George Clinton.

All this was made possible, Dave told *Melody Maker* two years after the event, because "I never was a very good guitarist . . . so I used to experiment with sounds. I had a very small amplifier which distorted badly." Turning this seeming handicap into an asset, Dave "ripped up the speakers of this little amp . . . [and] linked it up with the regular Vox amplifiers." In the process, he stumbled upon rock & roll's first "power chords," and unwittingly invented what would later be called "fuzz" (for the reproduction of which special "fuzz boxes" would soon be introduced into the marketplace and utilized on the Stones' "Satisfaction" and the Beatles' "Day Tripper").

The cumulative effect of the distortion, the repetition, and the sheer volume was at once bludgeoning and hypnotic—in which context the Kinks' own sloppy musicianship and flat, whining vocals seemed entirely appropriate. At first, however, neither Pye nor Shel Talmy saw it quite that way, and had to be dissuaded from releasing a "cleaned-up" take of "You Really Got Me."

"When that record starts," Ray told *NME* in 1971, "it's like four people doing the four-minute mile; there's a lot of emotion. It was a great experience standing next to Dave when he played [his solo] because I was shouting at him, willing him to do it, saying it was the last chance we had. There's determination, fight, and guts in that record."

(That and subsequent guitar solos, please note, were indeed the work of Dave Davies and not of a certain ubiquitous sessionman named Jimmy Page. Rumors to the contrary irked Ray Davies no end; when the name of the future Yardbird and Led Zeppelin virtuoso was fired at him during a 1965 *Melody Maker* "Think In," he shot back: "A good tambourine player. To clear up everything that's been said, Dave Davies plays every solo on

(*Photo Trends*)

monster hit with a follow-up—"All Day and All of the Night"—that sounded almost exactly the same, yet was almost exactly as good. They also recorded a fairly inauspicious debut album that, says Dave, "virtually consisted of our stage show at the time." To stock British Invasion carbons of Chuck Berry and Bo Diddley were added Talmy-penned inanities such as "Bald Headed Women" (which he was later to foist upon The Who as well). *The Kinks* (retitled *You Really Got Me* in the U.S.) was redeemed by a smattering of Ray Davies originals, some of which (e.g., "Stop Your Sobbing") were as melodic and melancholy as the group's first two hits were not. According to Dave, Pye deliberately withheld the pick of this crop "because they considered it too good for just another track on the album." Instead, the exquisitely soporific "Tired of Waiting for You" was released as the Kinks' next single, in which capacity it scored them their second British Number One.

LP, U.K., 1964 (*Pye*)

EP, U.K., 1964 (*Pye*)

LP, U.S.A., 1965 (*Reprise*)

LP, U.S.A., 1966 (*Reprise*)

every record we ever made." At most, Page fattened the sound by chiming in with an extra rhythm guitar, as he himself conceded in a 1973 *NME* interview.)

Released in August 1964, "You Really Got Me" became the first record by a native combo other than the Beatles to sell a million copies in Britain alone. The boys from Muswell Hill were instant stars, drawing far more coverage on their second tour than the top-billed Gerry and the Pacemakers. The Kinks effectively concealed their musical limitations by maximizing the volume and distortion in the manner of their Number One hit; *NME*'s Ian Dove reported that "the overpowering, over-amplified Kinks . . . roused the audience to massed rally frenzy. . . . Titles and lyrics were unintelligible." A contemporaneous *Melody Maker* front page blared KINKS: READY FOR THE NEW WAVE. (Indeed, with the mere substitution of the word "Clash" for "Kinks," such accounts might seem more evocative of the summer of '77 than the spirit of '64.)

The man behind all this noise was described in *Melody Maker* as "a highly intelligent, quietly spoken twenty-year-old with a sincere, almost passionate belief in what he's doing." Ray Davies was quoted as saying that "when I was in art school, what I got out of it was color, expression. Now I find you turn out a bad song for the same reason you turn out a bad painting—insincerity. If you're sincere, if you do what *you* want, you can't do a bad thing . . . .

"We're not very good-looking as a group, but we like to think we've got something different because we're not trying to create anything false—what image we've got is ourselves. It hasn't been created for us." Actually, the major difference between the Kinks' image and those of their "manufactured" contemporaries was that the Kinks did most of the manufacturing themselves; they were certainly not short on gimmicks. "We wear hunting jackets, in dark pink," said Ray. "We imagine ourselves as characters out of the Dickens novel." They also wore frilly shirts and comported themselves like Edwardian fops (onstage, as John Mendelsohn has noted, Ray was wont to "let his guitar dangle unplayed at the waist while gesturing controversially with a right hand affixed to his right arm by the limpest of right wrists")—all of which provided a ridiculous contrast to the raw, earsplitting sounds emanating from the Kinks' amplifiers. Dave distinguished himself by sporting *the* longest hair—parted severely down the middle—in all of pop. There was also that business with the letter *k*—though that, no doubt, *was* the doing of some crafty press agent.

Unlike the Kingsmen, the Kinks succeeded in matching their

Dave was to rate "Tired of Waiting" the third milestone in Kink history because "it was a change of style for us; we got a bit posher! Our material started to get more melodic after that." On the group's subsequent *Kinda Kinks* LP, "chunka-chunka-chunk" largely gave way to poignant ballads such as "Something Better Beginning"—wherein Ray finds himself a brand new lover, but, instead of exalting over his good fortune, wonders mournfully: "Is this the start of another break-up . . . ?"

By this time, *NME*'s readers had voted the Kinks Britain's second most popular new group (after the Stones), and *Melody Maker* had gone so far as to suggest that the Kinks were Britain's third most popular group, new or old (after the Beatles and the Stones)—leading the cocky young Dave to predict that the Kinks would shortly "take over" from the Stones. *Melody Maker* reported that Mick Jagger and Keith Richards "retaliated" by "leaking" a story (which was actually printed in a major Fleet Street daily) that one of the Kinks had six toes on each foot. Such was the carefree spirit of the British pop scene in those halcyon days.

Unlike the Stones, the Kinks had seen their first three British hits crack the Top Ten in America, where the *You Really Got Me*

LP had also done quite well (even if Reprise Records' liner notes did misspell the names Quaife and Avory); a sequel called *Kinks-Size* (built around a British EP of the same name) had done even better. Phrases such as "Goin' Kray-zee with Those Four Kute Kut-ups the Kinks!" had duly materialized on the cover of *16 Magazine*, which was shortly to name the boys from Muswell Hill "honorary presidents of the fabulous 16 Club." America was kalling, and on June 17, 1965, the Kinks landed.

The nubile natives accorded Ray, Dave, Pete, and Mick the same high-decibel reception previously meted out to the Beatles, the Dave Clark Five, and Herman's Hermits; nonetheless, the Kink Invasion seems to have been an unmitigated disaster. Part of the problem, perhaps, was the conspicuous absence in the Kinks' baggage of a positive outlook toward America. "We are not feeling unduly excited about our [U.S.] success," Quaife had confided to *Melody Maker* prior to the trip. "Britain first always!" *NME* was subsequently to report that the American way of life made Ray "so depressed that he locked himself in his hotel room and refused to come out until Rasa [the German girl he had recently married] was flown out to join him." Dave, for his part, took exception to "people shouting corny things like 'Are you a Beatle or a girl?'—as if you couldn't be anything else."

Somewhere along the way, the punches started flying. It remains unclear whether this misconduct merely occurred in the presence of a dues collector from the American Federation of Television and Recording Artists or whether said official was actually the target of certain delinquent Kink fists. Be that as it may, the Federation promptly enacted a ban against future Kink visitations, which would remain in effect until 1969. At the time, Ray disclaimed any interest in a return visit, but his group's protracted absence from these shores doubtless played a part in the steadily declining American sales of subsequent Kink waxings.

Even in their native land, the Kinks acquired an unwelcome reputation as the most compulsive brawlers in pop. One British tour actually had to be canceled after a Kinks concert came to a premature end when Mick Avory scored a direct hit with a cymbal hurled at Dave Davies's head. The guitarist was rushed to hospital, where he received ten stitches; "fortunately," Quaife reported in *NME*, "they have not had to shave his head." Avory attempted to pass the incident off as part of the Kinks' new act: "The idea was to wave stuff and generally go mad." It seems that the main cause of this internecine friction was the erratic behavior of the younger Davies sibling. Ray, however, took pains to assure the readers of *Melody Maker:* "Dave will develop . . . he's eighteen now. Don't forget, it all happened very quickly for him."

The Kinks had other problems that summer. Their next single, "Everybody's Gonna Be Happy," was a relative failure; then producer Shel Talmy had a falling-out with co-manager Larry Page, engendering a running controversy over whether a subsequent single would be the Talmy-produced "See My Friends" or the Page-produced "Ring the Bells"—or, indeed, whether any further Kinks product would be permitted to escape the net of suits and countersuits.

Eventually the dispute was resolved in favor of Talmy and "See My Friends"—which also did relatively poorly on the charts, but emerges in retrospect as perhaps the first full flowering of Ray Davies's songwriting genius. "See My Friends" was also about three months ahead of its time, in that it took the hypnotic distortion and repetition of the Kinks' earlier hits a logical step further to recreate a conscious approximation of an Indian drone. A year before George Harrison bought his first sitar, Ray had told his first *Melody Maker* inquisitor: "I like going to Indian restaurants and listening to the records there. I like the drone they got." And when the Kinks stopped over in Bombay (en route from the wildly successful Australian tour Dave was to list as his fourth milestone), the environment moved Ray to write *the* first Raga Rock song. "We stayed at a hotel by the sea, and the fishermen came up at five in the morning and they were all chanting." In Ray's yearning ode to friends out of reach "playing across the river," the "river" is actually the Indian Ocean.

"One thing does bother me," Dave was shortly to complain in *Melody Maker*. "We didn't get any credit for making a very Indian-sounding record with 'See My Friends.' Since then, over the last six months, groups have all been doing this Eastern thing." Typically, however, Ray failed to pursue his own innovation after it became fashionable; his quasi-Indian drone was to resurface only once (on *Face to Face*'s "Fancy").

But in the annals of Kinky perversity, this was small potatoes when set against Ray's decision to relegate the most important songwriting departure of his career to an obscure British EP called *The Kwyet Kinks*. Throughout 1965, of course, Dylan, Folk Rock, and "social commentary" had been all the rage, but with "A Well Respected Man" Ray Davies was the first to transmute these influences into a style and a setting that were English to the core. (Ironically, the song was a big hit not in Britain, but in America, where Reprise had the sense to issue it as a single.) To a muted Folk Rock backdrop, Ray sketched his damning portrait of a smug young suburban commuter who works nine to five and "gets the same train every time," and who adores the girl next door almost as much as the smell of his own sweat, but whose adulterous parents "know the best about the matrimonial stakes." The lyric lacked the subtlety and compassion of its successors, but Ray Davies—little though he yet seemed to realize it—had found his calling.

And so we find Ray Davies at the beginning of 1966 and the crossroads of his checkered career, still "Top of the Pops" on

"We imagine ourselves as characters out of a Dickens novel."—Ray Davies (Reprise Records/Peter Kanze Collection)

his home turf. Yet among all the idols of that time and place, Ray was surely the quirkiest. Even as Swinging London approached its legendary zenith, Davies was telling reporters, "I don't dig the 'in' clubs too much, or go to all the parties." Instead, he claimed to divide his spare time between writing songs and such quixotic pursuits as writing letters to newspapers "protesting that we don't see enough of Ravi Shankar's drone player on the [TV] screen. I think he's fab." Isolation, Ray declared in *Melody Maker,* was "a nice thing. When you are alone you can get into things that are interesting, which with other people around you can't." That these confessions made for such good copy moved him to comment: "If I was a butcher they wouldn't write about me in the *Meat Trades Journal* as the most antisocial butcher. But this is a funny business. I'm not a great mixer and somehow an image has been built up around it."

According to *Rave,* Ray's North London home was decorated almost entirely in orange. His dress sense was equally unorthodox. As *NME*'s Keith Altham once observed: "He manages to wear a turquoise jacket with a pink shirt and striped tie and make it all look incredibly correct." His daily routine, Ray told *NME* some years later, consisted of a 7:00 A.M. breakfast of raw eggs, followed by a stint of songwriting and a long nap. "Then I get up again, have a little worry and a cry, get that out of my system and try to do a bit more work. The day goes very quickly."

Unlike all other pop stars (including his brother Dave), Ray preferred his trusty bicycle to any flashy or fancy car: "What would I do with a Rolls? Anyway, driving frightens me to death. I'd rather ride a horse." He neglected to keep up with the pop scene, and was rumored to own but three non-Kink albums (one apiece by Dylan, Sinatra, and Bach). When his old gramophone broke, he didn't even bother to fix or replace it.

Above all, he was, as one 1966 *Melody Maker* front page blared it, RAY—THE PATRIOT KINK: "I hope England doesn't change. I'm writing a song now which expresses how I feel. I hope we don't get swallowed up by America and Europe. I'm really proud of being British."

All the above and more was soon to be reflected in (or between) the lines of Ray's own songs. But for the Kinks' first 1966 album, Davies brought to a stunning conclusion that sequence of power chords with which "You Really Got Me" had first bludgeoned an unsuspecting world. *The Kink Kontroversy* was the band's first LP to boast an overall consistency in quality and style; it also offered resounding evidence of the Kinks' incorrigible eccentricity. Never had there been an album so loud and yet so sluggish.

In *Kontroversy,* those trademark piledriver chords are slammed out by all four boys in slow motion unison, like an over-manned rhythm section on an overdose of barbiturates. The very occasional solo parts tend to emanate not from Dave's chalk-against-the-blackboard fretwork, but from the tinnily miked tinklings of "Sessionman" Nicky Hopkins's piano; and Ray's own plaintive wailing is all but drowned in the surging, impenetrable murk. Even without any Indian instruments, the rock-solid *Kontroversy* droned far more hypnotically than any of the would-be Raga Rockers who were beginning to chase after the Quiet Beatle's hobbyhorse.

Ray's words—or what could be heard of them—were also noteworthy. He had begun writing about himself, and sounding oddly bemused and ironic (even world-weary) for a twenty-one-year-old pop star. "I'm on an island, and I've got nowhere to swim." "Woncha tell me, where have all the good times

gone?" "Times are pretty thin, and you can't win." But . . . "You just can't stop it, the world keeps going round."

The Kink Kontroversy also included the relatively upbeat "Till the End of the Day," which was to remain the group's concert opener for years, and which sounded so exactly like "All Day and All of the Night" that the Kinks' own record company would mislabel it as such on their subsequent live LP. Henceforth, however, there was to be no more looking back. Ray told *NME*: "After 'See My Friends' I said we're not going back to the same sound, and I meant it. . . . We're not making inferior records like 'Set Me Free' anymore."

He then resumed the role of social commentator with the hit single "Dedicated Follower of Fashion." This time the object of his sarcasm was no well-respected suburban stuffed shirt, but, rather, the trendy London Mods who comprised part of the Kinks' own audience: "In matters of the cloth he is as fickle as can be . . . ." During a *Melody Maker* "Think In" with The Who's Pete Townshend, the words "Dedicated Follower of Fashion" triggered these remarks from pop's preeminent Mod: "The Kinks record is fantastic, and I like Ray Davies because he's married and he's still hip. . . . I think Dedicated Followers of Fashion are great . . . I used to be one myself. They are bank clerks who earn fair wages, who've got nothing better to do than dress well."

According to Dave Davies, "Dedicated Follower" 's satirical patter had been modeled after the work of the popular prewar music-hall comedian George Formby. "We both think Formby was brilliant," said Dave, but he later allowed that "Dedicated Follower" was his least favorite of Ray's songs. Its weakness is its threadbare melody, which *Disc* aptly described as "tripe."

On the next single, however, the music was fully up to the words, and those were Ray's best yet. "Sunny Afternoon" hit the airwaves just in time for the first unfurlings of the beach blanket, and on first hearing this lazy, good-timey melody (complete with the choirboy falsetto harmonies that were to become a Kinks trademark) seemed merely a perfect evocation of summertime fun. Bur further listenings revealed that "Sunny Afternoon" was actually a bittersweet and highly ironic narrative about (in Ray's words) "the 'Well Respected Man' after he lost all his money."

Since last heard from, it transpires, said gentleman (for whom Ray has acquired a touch of compassion) has had even his yacht repossessed by the insatiable taxman; his "big fat mama" has turned against him; and to add insult to injury, his girl friend has absconded with his car and run home "to her ma and pa [rhymes with 'car'] telling tales of drunkenness and cruelty." Crying in his beer, our protagonist demands (in the deceptively relaxed drawl that Ray was to make use of in so many of his best performances) not one but "two good reasons" to justify his continued existence. Ultimately, however, he arrives at the philosophical realization that since "all I've got's this sunny afternoon" he might as well lie back and enjoy it.

Later cited by Dave Davies as Kink Milestone Number Five—presumably because it was the group's first fully realized post-"chunka-chunk" masterpiece—"Sunny Afternoon" scored the Kinks their third British Number One and ended up fifth in *NME*'s tally of the year's greatest hits. In America, the tune would be fondly remembered by local kultists as the Kinks' last AM radio smash for many a moon.

"Sunny Afternoon" was to reappear as the featured track on the Kinks' watershed album, *Face to Face.* In *NME* that June, Ray had enthused about the "great new idea" he had dreamed up to give the promised eighteen selections a veneer of con-

LP, U.S.A., 1966 (Reprise)

EP, France, 1966 (Pye)

LP, U.K., 1965 (Decca)

LP, U.S.A., 1968 (Reprise)

tinuity: "I want to link up every track with additional sounds and musical interpolations. We've got thunderstorm effects, bongos, a metronome, Mick plays 'Whistling Rufus' on a shepherd's pipe . . . ." (This, mind you, was a full year before *Sgt. Pepper*.)

Pye, however, wouldn't hear of it, and issued *Face to Face* with "only" fourteen tracks, which, despite the insertion of some of Ray's sound effects, did not "segue."* Davies was at least permitted his own cover painting, of a "theatrical mask with the head lifted up and butterflies fluttering out from the inside—huge butterflies all over the cover." (Ray seems to have had a butterfly fixation, as they were also all over his 1966 lyrics.) Even in its truncated form, *Face to Face* was (with the possible exception of the Beatles' *Revolver*) the most ambitious and literate record the British pop scene had yet produced.

The album offers wryly understated Davies commentary on such unlikely subjects as a "Party Line," a "Session Man," a "Holiday in Waikiki," and a "Most Exclusive Residence for Sale"—into which last Ray invests so much pathos that for two minutes and forty-nine seconds the listener is almost convinced that the For Sale notice on the grounds of a stately old home constitutes one of the world's poignant tragedies. Similarly, the moving "Rosie Won't You Please Come Home" has Ray taking the part not of a teenage runaway, but of her mother! (Which brings to mind "Two Sisters"—recorded around the same time but released on the subsequent *Something Else*—in which Sybilla's "smart young friends," "luxury flat," and freewheeling life-style are ultimately deemed less fulfilling than the house-wifely drudgery Priscilla must endure while raising her little children.) Another highlight of *Face to Face* is "Rainy Day in June," Ray's sole venture into apocalyptic doom mongering, which he delivers with such Kinky lyrical twists as "the demon stretched his crinkled head and snatched a butterfly"—to the

---

* Casualties included "A Girl Who Goes to Discotheques," "The Reporter," "Fallen Idol" (about a pop has-been), and "Lilacs and Daffodils" (the only known Kinks recording sung by Mick Avory).

synchronized beat of prerecorded thunderbolts.

Like the last few Beatles albums, *Face to Face* inspired a spate of British cover versions, including the Pretty Things' "House in the Country" and Gates of Eden's "Too Much on My Mind." The most commercially successful of these was Herman's Hermits' "Dandy," which nonetheless did little justice to the philandering ladies' man whom Ray addresses on *Face to Face* with such a subtle blend of censure, envy, and admiration.

Even prior to coming into his own as a lyricist, Ray had established himself as one of the most in-demand young tune-smiths on the London pop scene. Sonny and Cher had covered "Set Me Free," and "Who'll Be the Next in Line" had launched a new group called the Knack (not the last band of that name to do a Kinks song!). Unrecorded Davies originals were snapped up by artists ranging from the Honeycombs to Peggy Lee (who recorded "I Go to Sleep," which would turn up fifteen years later on the Pretenders' second album). Davies was also commissioned to write a single (titled "Kinda Kinks") for instrumental bandleader Ray McVay, and to provide new songs for the Animals ("I'm Not Like Everybody Else") and the Seekers ("This Is Where I Belong"). (When these last two selections went unreleased, the Kinks reclaimed them.) Ray even master-minded an orchestral LP of his own compositions, titled *Kinky Music* and nominally credited to the Larry Page Orchestra. "It's all my own arranging," Ray told *Melody Maker*. "I picked the musicians and A&R'd the session. This album is part of my ambition."

Perhaps inevitably, such ambitions began to conflict with the grind of the Kinks' traveling road show, which, Ray frankly declared, "has got so stale and boring." In the spring of 1966 he suffered a nervous breakdown. "My trouble," he told *Rave* soon after, "is that I'm a composer trying to do my work in theaters [and] ballrooms. . . . I've got some great ideas about French-Spanish influences that I want to experiment with, [and] a jazz-slanted LP . . . but I have no time to complete all these things." During his convalescence, Ray was replaced on a series of continental dates by Mick Grace from the Cockneys, inspiring rumors that the Kinks' leader was actually quitting the band.

In September, Pete Quaife announced *he* was quitting to settle with his fiancée in Copenhagen. His replacement, originally touted as ex-Hollie Eric Haylock, proved to be John Dalton from Mark 4, whom *NME* described as "softly spoken and covered all over in blue tattoos depicting the Crucifixion." Two months later, however, Pete changed his mind and was welcomed back to the fold—only to have his leg fractured by an overenthusiastic Parisian mob.

In early 1967, Ray confirmed long-standing reports that he planned to bow out of stage performance to become a "Brian Wilson figure." "A substitute will have to take my place on [tour]," he told *NME*. "There just isn't time to make personal appearances and work on the Kinks' records. . . . This kind of situation hinders my songwriting, and it's obviously a handicap to the group. I still intend to sing on the . . . records." This brought a sharp rejoinder from the Kinks' co-manager (and former lead singer) Robert Wace, who accused *NME* of spreading "rumors . . . put around by people with some sort of axe to grind." Next issue, Ray wearily backtracked: "It is difficult to find a substitute for a lead singer, so I will appear on all Kinks shows."

It was during this period that a full complement of Kinks was captured in the flesh for *The Live Kinks* album. Hysterical in every sense of the word, this high-voltage Scotland performance is decidedly slovenly, and all but drowned out by the ongoing screech of fan mania. But as Ray noted a decade later in the fanzine *Dark Star*: "It was a good example of what it was like at a concert then; I think it may have historic value. You've got to understand that for two or three years I never heard myself playing—no monitors. And with that audience, it was just a wall of sound."

The Live Kinks did offer at least two memorable moments: Ray charming the screeching girls into singing a good portion of "Sunny Afternoon" all by themselves, and the band's utterly incongruous rendition of television's *Batman* theme (which was eventually to engender the Kinks' latter-day hit "Superman"). In later years, audience singalongs and unlikely musical interpolations were to become staples of every Kink concert. (And already Ray was beginning to add skiffle chestnuts such as "Put Another Nickel In" to the group's repertoire, along with Dave's favorite selections from Dylan's *Blonde on Blonde*.) With all its faults, *The Live Kinks* was a far better and more authentic recording than the Stones' *Got Live If You Want It!*—and until the 1977 release of *The Beatles at the Hollywood Bowl*, those remained the only two such documents widely available.

Meanwhile, the Kinks followed "Sunny Afternoon" with a string of classic British hit singles, all of which eluded the American Top Forty. With its prominently wheezing trombone, "Dead End Street" was a precursor of Kinks to come; intimations of Punk may also be gleaned from its stark depictions of a working-class family trapped in a dismal present with no hope for the future. But the narrator of "Dead End Street" is more bemused than angry, and (like his upper-class counterpart in "Sunny Afternoon") ultimately resolves to make the best of what little he's got: "Pour the tea and put some toast on . . . ." *Melody Maker* raved: "If it didn't sell a single copy, the Kinks would deserve some kind of award for this. The stomping traddy beat completely defies all current trends, and this alone makes it stand out like a gem in a sea of mud."

Next came what some kultists consider *the* most beautiful pop song ever written. "Waterloo Sunset" is certainly the most poignant of all Davies compositions; yet, as ever, Ray deftly combines aching nostalgia with wry irony: "As long as I gaze on Waterloo Sunset, I am in paradise." (Waterloo, remember, is a rather grimy industrial section of London, best known for its railway station.) As in "See My Friends" (or, perhaps, "I'm on an Island") the singer uses the river (in this case the dirty old Thames) as a metaphor for his own sense of isolation from the "millions of people swarming like flies round Waterloo Underground." But even as he stands alone, "to look at the world from my window," he has the compassion not to begrudge the good fortune of those who, like Terry [Stamp] and Julie [Christie], are able to cross to the other side of the river, "where they feel safe and sound." (In *NME*, Ray revealed that he originally wrote the song as "Liverpool Sunset," "but the Beatles came up with 'Penny Lane' and so that was the end of that. . . . I suppose 'Waterloo' has stuck in my mind because I used to walk over Waterloo Bridge several nights a week on the way to art school.")

The music is as economical as the lyric, and supremely melodic; and the contrapuntal harmonies remain among the most exquisite in rock. (On occasions such as this, the Kinks confounded the usual modest estimates of their musical acumen.) "Waterloo Sunset," quite simply, epitomizes all the qualities that have led his dedicated followers to acclaim Ray Davies as a genius, and those who can hear it and yet remain unmoved are clearly not destined to join that select congregation.

"Waterloo Sunset" was also to provide a fitting finale for *Something Else by the Kinks,* whose other highlights included Ray's loving evocations of "Afternoon Tea" and "Lazy Old Sun." The album gets off to an infectious start with a somewhat more ambivalent tribute; in "David Watts" Ray's fellow misfits instantly recognized that archetypal golden schoolboy on whom the fates had bestowed such an unfair abundance of brains, brawn, charm, *and* good looks. With the Summer of Love now in full bloom, *Melody Maker*'s reviewer noted: "At the last check Ray wasn't wearing a bell, so that may seriously invalidate the Kinks' contribution to pop. If you can forgive this aberration, you might find *Something Else* is one of the best albums of the year."

The London Underground's arbiters of "progressive music" did indeed regard the Kinks (if at all) as a thoroughly old-fashioned singles band wallowing in thoroughly old-fashioned sentiments. With guitar heroes on the rise, revolution in the air, acid in the bloodstream, and the Blues about to Boom, the last thing British hippies wanted to hear about was afternoon tea, holidays in Blackpool, or even the travails of the little man on Dead End Street—or, for that matter, a style of music that tapped the very cultural heritage they were so avidly rejecting. The boys in the band did little to repair the damage, with Pete Quaife confessing in *Melody Maker* that his group "just let the whole flower power, LSD, love thing flow over [our] head. . . . It changed a lot of good blokes, who everybody rated, into creeps. . . . You still can't beat going to the pictures, a couple of pints, and a fag [cigarette]. The Kinks all agree that Sunday dinner is the greatest realization of heaven." (The group's next single even featured a snappy chorus of "Roast beef on Sundays—all right!")

Something Else was also the album on which Dave Davies came into his own. Since 1965 he had, in the manner of George Harrison, been allowed a self-composition—just one—per Kink kollection; on *Something Else,* however, Dave was accorded three, one of which—"Death of a Clown"—was released as a Dave Davies solo single. In the best tradition of a drunken pub singalong, "Death of a Clown" is both rousing and sentimental, and Dave leads the chorus with a strangled-sounding voice that is in its way as instantly recognizable as that of his brother (who contributed some of the verses' doomed carnival imagery—e.g., "The trainer of insects is crouched on his knees/and furtively looking for runaway fleas").

"People used to think that all I wanted to do was to get stoned and just coast along within the group without offering very much," Dave told *Melody Maker*. "This record will change that, I hope." Indeed, "Death of a Clown" surprised almost everyone by reaching number three in Britain. (It also spawned the first of the Kinks' plagiarism lawsuits, with the brothers D. charging that the Eurovision Contest winner "La La La" had lifted its infectious "la la la"'s directly from the chorus of "Death of a Clown.") On the strength of this one song, Dave's individual clout was such that *Melody Maker* reported he was "forming a group to play a series of solo dates in Britain and on the continent. He is not, however, quitting the Kinks." A solo LP was also said to be imminent.

Meanwhile, with the other Kinks still backing him in the studio, Dave concocted a follow-up single called "Susannah's Still Alive," which *NME* described as "the tale of an unwanted lady who finds solace in liquor" (booze being to Dave's songs what butterflies were to Ray's) and "an excellent pop record—well produced and very commercial." *Melody Maker*'s Chris Welch also tipped "Susannah" as a "hit of resounding proportions.'' In the event, however, it failed to pass number twenty.

A successor, ''Lincoln County'' (which strongly reflected Dave's Dylan fixation), was launched with full-page trade ads, and interviews in which the artist declared: ''This is the first record I've done on my own that I've really believed in. . . . People *must* like it . . . I will give up if people don't.'' But ''Lincoln County,'' as Dave later put it, ''died a terrible death,'' and even though he did try again with ''Hold My Hand,'' that fared just as poorly. Nonetheless, word of a pending solo album resurfaced regularly in the pop press—in 1973, for example, *NME* reported that ''Dave Davies has been recording solo tracks in the studio, with a view to putting out a solo album in the New Year''—until the very idea became something of a running joke among kultists.*

(Dave was to confound the skeptics by finally releasing *AFL1-3603* in July 1980—and by racking up respectable U.S. sales into the bargain. A year later, he issued a sequel called *Glamour.* Each album is a solo tour-de-force, with Dave playing almost every instrument.)

The Kinks, meanwhile, followed ''Waterloo Sunset'' with a single that was very nearly as characteristic of Ray Davies's world view and very nearly as good. While summer songs and even spring and winter songs had long been rock music staples, ''Autumn Almanac'' was perhaps the genre's first ode to the ''season of mists and mellow fruitfulness.'' By turns jaunty and melancholic, ''Autumn Almanac'' celebrates such seasonal pleasures as sweeping leaves in the sack, gorging oneself on ''toasted butter currant buns,'' and playing ''football on a Saturday''—even as the singer rues his ''poor, rheumatic back.'' If none of this sounds like standard rock & roll fare, neither will the song's second premise: ''This is my street, and I'm never going to leave it.'' (Some of ''Autumn Almanac'''s melody, incidentally, materialized when Ray played backward a tape of a discarded tune called ''My Street''). *Melody Maker*'s reviewer, for one, deemed it ''time Ray stopped writing about gray suburbanites going about their fairly unemotional business. It's becoming boring.'' Nonetheless, ''Autumn Almanac'' gave the Kinks yet another massive British hit.

It was the next single, ''Wonderboy,'' that snapped the golden chain. Oddly enough, *Melody Maker* had tipped this one to ''powee and zonk to the top,'' with *NME*'s Derek Johnson rating it ''as catchy as anything [Ray] has written . . . a charming, philosophic song . . . even more commercial than 'Autumn Almanac' or 'Waterloo Sunset.' Deserves to be big—and will be!'' Advising the listener that ''life is only what you conjure,'' Ray warmly endorses a retreat into childlike fantasy as Dave and Pete chirp their trusty ''la-la-la''s for two uninterrupted minutes. But those connoisseurs who deemed ''Wonderboy'' the Kinks' most irresistible popcorn yet were confounded by a record-buying public whose indifference accorded the group its first resounding British flop.

The Kinks continued to make singles for the British market throughout 1968 and 1969 (most of which Reprise no longer even bothered to release in America), but only the supremely melodic and moving ''Days'' made even a token impression. The subsequent ''Plastic Man'' was crippled at the starting gate when the BBC refused to sully the airwaves with the ''obscene'' phrase ''plastic legs that reach up to his plastic bum.'' As far as

Ray Davies was concerned, however, the Kinks had already outgrown their incarnation as Top of the Pops wonderboys. Henceforth, they were to be known as an album band.

The next album the Kinks recorded was the legendary ''great lost Kinks album,'' *Four More Respected Gentlemen*, which was actually assigned a Reprise Records serial number (RS 6309) before Ray scrapped the project at the last minute. ''It was going to be an LP about manners and things,'' he later revealed in *NME*. ''Table manners. What a joke that all is. The album got mixed in with *Village Green* and we decided to finish *Village Green* instead. And instead of having two albums, I tried to put as many tracks on one album as possible.'' (Though most copies of *Village Green* did indeed pack an unprecedented fifteen selections, there existed, to add to the confusion, a first British edition containing a different lineup of only twelve tunes.)

Ray had first conceived *The Village Green Preservation Society* as a possible solo album, loosely modeled after *Under Milk Wood*, the Dylan Thomas verse drama about the inhabitants of a sleepy Welsh village. The Kinks recorded some of the material as early as the start of 1967, at which time the song ''Village Green'' was promised for a great lost Kinks EP. When the album finally appeared in September 1968, it was perhaps the first rock LP on which, as Ray told *Melody Maker*, ''all [the songs] are related in a way. I hope [the overall concept] will be self-explanatory if people are interested enough to listen. Sometimes I wonder if they really do listen.''

As it happened, not many did; so all but the most rabid kultists missed out on the self-contained world of Davies's Village Green. The songs themselves were either portraits of that little world's inhabitants, or descriptions of popular local attractions (''The Last of the Steam Powered Trains'') or activities (''Sitting by the Riverside,'' ''People Take Pictures of Each Other'' [''. . . just to prove that they really existed'']). ''The title track,'' Ray once said, ''is the albums' national anthem''; at the time he told *Melody Maker*: ''Somebody mentioned to me that the Kinks do try to preserve things—we are all for that looking back thing. I thought it would be a nice idea to try and sum it up in one song. All the things in the song are things I'd like to see preserved.''

Village Green's memorable characters include a biker (''Johnny Thunder''), a prostitute (''Monica''), a suspected witch (''Wicked Annabella''), and a former wonderboy who's grown fat, married, and boring. (''Do You Remember, Walter?'' Ray explained in *Melody Maker*, ''is about the way that we try to hang on to things that we like, even people. Walter was a friend of mine; we used to play football together every Saturday. Then I met him again recently after about five years, and we found we just didn't have anything to talk about.'') Above them all, detached and impassive, is the Big Sky, to which (whom) all the people look for guidance and salvation. ''But Big Sky's too big to sympathize,'' Ray sings, in the closest he ever came to a theological statement. ''Big Sky's too occupied.''

Village Green was the first LP Ray produced without Shel Talmy; the production is unassuming in the extreme, with embellishments kept to a minimum. ''Miniatures'' might be an apt description of the predominantly acoustic songs, few of which run much past two minutes. In his ecstatic *Rolling Stone* appreciation, Paul Williams likened Ray Davies to Erik Satie, the French composer best remembered for his sparse, satirical, and eccentric piano vignettes.

At one point on the Kinks' album, Ray sings that ''American tourists flock to see the Village Green'' (where they duly burble ''Darn it, isn't it a pretty scene?''). But in the real world, Amer-

---

* *Dave did in fact record an album's worth of material with the Kinks around the time of ''Susannah'' (including the tracks ''Creeping Jean,'' ''This Man He Weeps Tonight,'' and ''Groovy Movies''), but, he says, ''my heart wasn't in it.''*

LP, U.S.A., 1969 (Reprise)

LP, U.S.A., 1969 (Reprise)

LP, U.K., 1970 (Pye)

LP, U.S.A., 1973 (RCA)

ican trade publications like *Cash Box* didn't even bother to review the album, which subsequently failed to make so much as a token showing on *Billboard*'s Top 200 LP chart. (Even *Something Else* had climbed to number 153.)

At this point, however, Warners/Reprise (which had previously let such klassics as *Kontroversy* and *Face to Face* go out of print) finally took note of the rave reviews in the "alternative" press and took steps to salvage the Kinks' standing. On August 23, 1969, a full-page ad appeared in *Rolling Stone* under the bold headline GOD SAVE THE KINKS: "The above, dear groovies, is our grab-'em watchword for a new promotion here at Reprise. A brilliant stratagem to make [the Kinks] the household words they were in the days of 'You Really Got Me' and 'Dedicated Follower of Fashion' and 'Sunny Afternoon.'"

As part of this campaign to garner due recognition for the Kinks and their neglected *Village Green* masterpiece, readers were offered—for a mere two dollars—a Kinks "goody box." This contained not only *Then Now and Inbetween* ("an astoundingly spiffy stereo album put together especially for this promotion"), but also such treats as a "God Save the Kinks" button, "a baggieful of grass supposedly imported from the aforementioned Village Green," and—the clincher—"a mind-bending puzzle made from the cover of the . . . critically acclaimed but commercially disastrous [*Village Green*] album."

The Kinks, for their part, agreed to tour America as soon as the American Federation of Television and Recording Artists might be persuaded to lift its four-year ban. In the meantime, John Dalton was invited to rejoin the Kinks following the definitive departure of original bassist Pete Quaife. "The first time I found out he had left," Mick Avory told *NME*, "was when I read about it in your paper, and saw the picture of him with his new group [Maple Oak]." Quaife ungraciously allowed that he was fed up with playing "bubble gum" and wanted to try something more progressive—on the order of Simon and Garfunkel. Before long, however, Pete was asking his former colleague to boost Maple Oak's fortunes with a Ray Davies original. But the resultant single, "Son of a Gun," went nowhere, and Quaife

presently abandoned the music business and Mother England for a kareer as a graphics designer in Copenhagen.

While these komplications were being sorted out, Ray accepted invitations to branch into the worlds of film scoring and outside record production. After furnishing the theme song for *Till Death Do Us Part* (which was to be followed by a score for *The Virgin Soldiers,* wherein David Bowie made his cinematic debut), Ray flew to America to produce the LP *Turtle Soup.* Howard Kaylan was to recall in *Rolling Stone* that he and his fellow Turtles had been "Kinks freaks," and had thought "it would be really far out if Ray Davies produced us. . . . [But] as much as we respected him—and he did a good job on the album, no doubt about that—we were so together that we didn't let him change anything."

In October 1969, the Kinks at long last returned to the American stage—though hardly in triumph; they were billed second to Spirit at the tour's Fillmore East debut. Nonetheless, kultists turned out in force, to witness perhaps the most untogether show Bill Graham ever presented on that legendary New York stage. As would prove the case at subsequent club dates (such as one I caught at the Boston Tea Party) the band was woefully out of tune, out of time, and evinced difficulty in remembering the words to their own klassic British hits—for which they largely substituted endless and inept instrumental workouts attached to such lesser works as "Last of the Steam Powered Trains." A painfully shy Ray Davies did his utmost to avoid the spotlight at all times, leaving Dave to handle the announcements and sing most of the songs (giving one's non-kultist companions the clear impression that the lead guitarist was also the leader of this motley crew). At the time, however, few aficionados would admit to any shortcomings; the important thing was that the Kinks were back. Upon returning to London, Ray told *NME* that he had "been overwhelmed by the response. I expected people not to know what we've done in the past three years."

The U.S. tour immediately preceded the release of a new album, which *Melody Maker* hailed as "Ray Davies' finest hour" and "a pop cavalcade that is beautifully British—to the core." *Arthur (or the Decline and Fall of the British Empire)* was originally conceived as the score for a TV musical of the same name, written in collaboration with novelist Julian Mitchell. The story line centers around Arthur Morgan ("a plain simple man in a plain simple working-class position") and his relationships with the various generations of his family. The play was set on the day prior to the departure of Arthur's son and daughter-in-law for the promised land of Australia.

Though cost overruns caused Granada TV to shelve the project, the Morgans' dialogue was to have been interwoven with the Kinks' musical flashbacks to seminal events both in the life of Arthur Morgan and in the history of the declining British Empire. These included the Golden Age of Victoria ("Victoria," which kicks off the proceedings with a stirring declamation by Ray/Arthur: "Long ago, life was clean; sex was bad and obscene"), the senseless carnage in the trenches of World War I ("Some Mother's Son"), and the London Blitz of World War II ("Mr. Churchill Says"). Through it all, Arthur doggedly struggles for "a better life and a way to improve his own condition." Following the postwar realization of the working-class dream of a Socialist England—where "things would be more equal and be plenty for everyone"—he is finally rewarded with his own suburban "paradise," complete with a car in the garage, a TV, and a hefty mortgage. "Shangri-La" is one of Ray's most achingly beautiful melodies, and even its more biting lyrics ("You're in your place and you know where you are/in your

Shangri-La'') are sung with a quiet compassion. ''Shangri-La'' was originally released as a British 45; according to Dave, ''that was the best single we ever did—but it was a flop.'' Such was also the fate—in Britain—of *Arthur* itself, which Dave was to list as the last of his six Kink milestones. Ray blamed the failure on Pye's persistence in viewing the Kinks as a singles band, and its endless Kink retrospectives on the Marble Arch budget label. ''We'd spend a year making an album called *Arthur*,'' he complained in *Dark Star*, ''and the following week they'd bring out a Marble Arch record for tuppence. And of course, if I wanted a Kinks record, I'd buy the cheap one.''

In America, however, Reprise seemed more attuned to Ray's vision, and *Arthur* sold better than any Kinks record since the 1966 *Greatest Hits* package. Indeed, the twelve songs' cohesive story line and use of dialogue rendered *Arthur* eminently marketable as a ''rock opera,'' at a time when the only other such item available was The Who's recent *Tommy*. Yet all the operatic hype also engendered insinuations that the Kinks were cashing in on The Who's success—which Ray, typically, dismissed with the words: ''I haven't even heard *Tommy*.''

But in terms of American mass appeal, the record that really propelled the Kinks back into the major leagues was their next single. Indeed, ''Lola'' was so chockablock with AM radio hooks that one suspects Ray could have pulled off a U.S. ''comeback'' at a much earlier date, had he really wanted to. The droll lyric recounts a young man's first sexual encounter—with a luscious creature who, much to his bewilderment, ''walked like a woman and talked like a man.'' Ironically, the BBC's threatened ban of ''Lola'' stemmed not from the song's unorthodox subject matter, but from the ''free advertising'' a reference in the original lyric would have accorded to Coca-Cola. The Kinks, meanwhile, had returned to the U.S. concert trail, obliging Ray (as he recalled in *Dark Star*) ''to fly back from America, get off the plane, go into the studio, and say 'cherry

''Isolation is a nice thing.''—Ray Davies (RCA Records)

cola' instead of 'Coca-Cola.' Then I got back on the plane and flew back. Then they said, 'Oh, could you do it again, it's not quite right.' So I got back on the plane and flew back [to London] again.''

At the time, the Kinks were reduced to playing tiny New York dives like Ungano's, but the massive success of ''Lola'' ensured that henceforth the group could top the bill at larger venues such as Carnegie Hall and the Palladium. It also bolstered Ray's confidence as a performer; and—in keeping with the sexually ambiguous image ''Lola'' had conferred upon him—he increasingly took to ''camping it up'' onstage. Once again, the Kinks, in their own quirky fashion, were a step ahead of the times, though others (notably David Bowie) were to prove far more adept at turning sexual ambivalence into a marketable commodity.

Notwithstanding what Kink kronikler John Mendelsohn called ''Ray's acceleratingly queenly stage manner,'' Davies is a twice-married man who has always considered the details of his private life to be nobody's business but his own. Nonetheless, Davies's songs regularly took issue with the way society reduces the broad range of human emotions to a stark choice between normal and abnormal, or straight and gay. In 1978 he told *Rolling Stone*'s Fred Schruers: ''Sexuality's something I haven't worked out yet. People's roles get confused at a very early age because they have this sexual thing thrust on them. You're immediately pigeonholed. You might be a normal person pushed to extremes because you've been crushed by the rules, by whatever other people call you. And you might be having a rebellion against what you really are.''

''Lola'' was included on the Kinks' next concept album, which amounted almost to a musical autobiography. *Lola Versus Powerman and the Moneygoround Part One*, Ray explained, ''tells the story of us on two planes—one as businessmen, the other as people.'' Many of the songs chronicle the various stages of a rock star's career, from the struggle for recognition (''Denmark Street'') to Making It (''Top of the Pops'') to the grind of touring (''This Time Tomorrow''). (''Lola'''s place in this scheme makes little sense, unless it is viewed as the hit single with which the saga's protagonists made the Top of the Pops.) The Kinks' most recent series of lawsuits were explicitly documented in ''Moneygoround,'' which mentions by name such former associates as Robert (Wace), Larry (Page), and Grenville (Collins) and implicitly suggests that these gentlemen had absconded with more than their fair share of the group's income. (For much of the Seventies, Ray would manage his own affairs, saying: ''I just feel that if you write a song like 'Village Green,' how can you justify having a heavyweight steamroller organization behind it?'')

Toward the end of the album, railings against the rat race give way to yearnings for an escape from same in the wistful ''Got to Be Free'' (originally used in the TV play *The Long Distance Piano Player*, in which Ray made his acting debut) and the whimsical ''Apeman,'' wherein Davies allows that he can only ''feel at ease . . . in a coconut tree,'' and whose infectious banana-boat singalongs scored the Kinks yet another hit single. Though much of *Lola Versus Powerman* was musically uneven, the presence of ''Apeman'' and ''Lola'' made the LP one of the Kinks' all-time biggest American sellers.

While Ray busied himself with a sequel called *Kinks Part Two: Continuing the Saga of Lola Versus Powerman*, the group's first full-length movie soundtrack was released as their next British album. *Percy* (the film) represented the nadir both of British comedy and of repressed British sexuality; its plot con-

The Kinks circa 1971 (from l.): Ray, John Dalton, Dave, John Gosling, and Mick (RCA Records)

cerned the world's first penis transplant, occasioning ninety minutes' worth of coy and puerile jokes. The Kinks' contribution ranged from undistinguished instrumentals to incongruously wistful ballads such as "God's Children" and "The Way Love Used to Be" (when one made love with one's own God-given equipment). In America, however, Reprise decided that the Kinks' rising American star would be better served by shelving *Percy* in favor of the forthcoming *Lola Versus Powerman II*.

But that eagerly awaited LP never materialized, and when the Kinks did resurface with an all-new concept, both Pye and Reprise were left out in the cold. Upon ascertaining that the group's contracts were running out, RCA Records—desperate to build up a credible roster of rock acts after having missed the boat during the British Invasion and the birth of "Woodstock Nation"—wooed Ray Davies into their high-powered embrace to the sweet tune of $1 million.

In December 1971 RCA celebrated the new alliance with an ostentatious bash at New York's Plaza Hotel, where Britain's leading music journalists were ensconced after being flown in at company expense. According to *NME*'s John Wells, "the more liberal might have called [the party] a raving transvestites/homosexuals/sex maniacs jamboree. . . . The guest list included Alice Cooper, the Cockettes, Andy Warhol and entourage, and most of New York's other deviants" (not to mention The Who's Keith Moon and John Entwistle). Wells overheard RCA executives discussing not only their strategies for restoring the Kinks to their rightful place in the rock firmament, but also their plans to transform the hitherto obscure David Bowie into an international household word.

To complete the songs for the Kinks' RCA debut, Ray, with pen and notebook in hand, flew from London to Los Angeles and then straight back; according to *Melody Maker*, "the sole purpose of the £300 return flight was to incarcerate himself in the sky in order to write songs." "I don't really like flying," Ray informed the newspaper, "but I can't concentrate on the ground. There are too many distractions like strikes and things. The only way I can finish these songs is in the air. . . . I won't be taking any luggage."

As usual, a loose thematic thread was evident when the songs surfaced as *Muswell Hillbillies*. Each explored some aspect of life in the Kinks' native district: the old-timers' sense of alienation from a world that seems to have passed them by ("I'm a twentieth century man but I don't want to die here"); the slum dwellers' subjugation to the urban-renewal schemes of government bureaucrats ("Here Come the People in Grey"); and, as always, the small pleasures of the working-class Briton ("Have a Cuppa Tea," "Holiday"), along with his secret fantasies and his hopeless dreams ("I'm a Muswell hillbilly boy, but my heart lies in old West Virginia").

Muswell Hillbillies was the Kinks' most political album thus far, though in "Uncle Son" the conventional rhetoric of Conservatives, Liberals, and Socialists is all dismissed with the same detached skepticism. None of it is ever going to make a whit of difference in the life of simple, good-hearted Uncle Son, whom Ray addresses with wistful irony: "They won't forget you when the revolution comes. . . ." Davies's philosophy is perhaps best described as libertarian. "I try to write about freedom," he once said, "to work out what freedom is."

In keeping with its title, *Muswell Hillbillies* experimented with a more American, country-flavored sound; it also marked the inauguration of an official Fifth Kink, balding keyboardist John Gosling (known as "John the Baptist" to other band members). *Muswell Hillbillies* furthermore made extensive use of the horn section that was to accompany the Kinks on subsequent albums and tours, contributing to the latter's vaudevillian atmosphere (and keeping a promise Ray had made at the very beginning, "to augment the group to form a big band"). And though professional kultists like John Mendelsohn felt the Kinks were patronizing their new American audience by forgoing subtlety and understatement for a more obvious and commercial approach, many of the new songs proved to be highly effective vehicles for Ray's flamboyant new stage persona. During the tragicomic "Alcohol," for instance, he was wont to spray the front rows with beer in the course of his shambling impersonation of the

"Oh demon alcohol, sad memories I can't recall . . ."
(Freelance Photo Guild Richard E. Aaron)

"sinner who used to be a winner"—until punters took to smuggling in their own ammunition, obliging Davies to cower out of range of his fans' booze while completing his dramatic performance.

The Kinks themselves acquired a dubious reputation as rock's most inebriated performers; never a tight band to begin with, they now evinced difficulty remaining upright throughout their concerts. Shortly before *Muswell Hillbillies*' release, the Kinks gave a memorable performance at New York's Philharmonic Hall, where, as *Rolling Stone* reported, "Ray Davies potted around the stage, hovered precariously over the edge, and finally collapsed among a bank of amps. Several equippies tried to rescue him, but Davies seemed unaware of his predicament and continued singing from the horizontal. Brother Dave glowered nearby. None of the Kinks did very well that night—singing out of tune and forgetting lyrics—but it didn't stop the fans [surging] onto the stage for the encore." Indeed it didn't, for aficionados no longer came to Kinks shows expecting faithful reproductions of Kink vinyl. What the boys almost invariably delivered was a rollicking good time. "What's the point of going on stage," said Dave, "and just standing there? We joke and have a laugh, and [the critics] couldn't see why."

It was in this spirit that the Kinks tirelessly crisscrossed America, massacring their greatest hits and interspersing these with ghastly renditions of "Baby Face," "Mr. Wonderful," and "The Banana Boat Song," to pick up a whole new generation of fun-loving fans. Even Ray's erratic behavior seldom detracted from the effectiveness of his showmanship; the vulnerability went hand in hand with the outrageousness, and as he told *NME:* "I *do* come on rather flash on stage, but I feel the audience really knows me and my songs. They know I'm isolated,

"It wasn't called heavy metal when I invented it"—Dave Davies (Ron Gott)

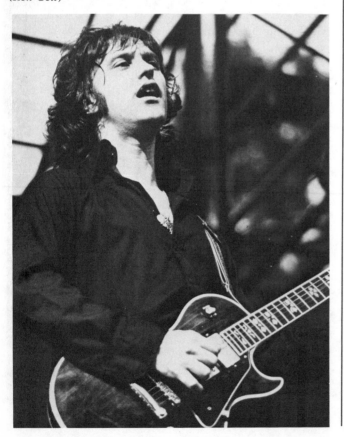

even though I'm dressed up in all those clothes. They see me weak and wandering—and they're like that too."

Ray chronicled one of these American tours on the Kinks' first double album, *Everybody's in Showbiz,* half of which was live. "The album shows what it's like for a band on the road in the States," Avory told *NME.* "We did a film when we were over there, and [Ray] noticed how people wanted to get in on it and do their own little party piece . . . everybody wants to be a star. . . . Basically the album is saying that we are all actors in one way or another."

But, except in his truly poignant and sweeping tribute to Hollywood's "Celluloid Heroes," Ray seems to have left his perceptiveness, compassion, and sense of humor back in England when he composed his American journal. The album could (and should) have followed in the tradition of countless travelogues wherein English writers discourse wittily upon the curious customs of the natives; but *Everybody's in Showbiz* delivers instead one long whine against American food, motels, and "motorways" (that's British for "highway"—Ray had yet to master the native dialect), and against the unreasonable demands this barbaric culture makes on such sensitive performers as Raymond Douglas Davies.

Several months later—in June 1973—Ray went so far as to announce—on stage, no less—that he was "fucking sick of the whole thing, sick up to here with it," and was "quitting the Kinks." This outburst took place during the Kinks' desultory third-billed performance at London's White City Stadium, and was later attributed to the fact that Ray's wife, Rasa, had run off with their two daughters, causing an overwrought Davies to go several nights without sleep just prior to the show. *Melody Maker* ran a touching full-page editorial by Roy Hollingworth (headlined "Thank You for the Days, Ray") begging Davies to reconsider.

Shortly thereafter, Ray confirmed reports of an imminent British Kinks tour, telling *Melody Maker:* "Several weeks ago I wrote a letter to the world; it turned out to be a letter to me. But I do feel that I made a decision . . . to change the format of the band." In its review of the tour's first show, the paper described Davies as an "incomparable clown prince" who "could be likened to a bottle of vintage French wine [that] tastes better with maturity."

Davies soon disclosed that his ideas for changing the Kinks "format" centered upon "a presentation based around our *Village Green* album." *NME* reported that "Ray will be attempting to present that show as a musical . . . [and] the new album will be an elaborated return to the theme of *Village Green.*" That LP, he later added, "was like a rough sketch" for his new project, for which he had "spent five years storing up ideas." When the first of *Preservation*'s two "acts" appeared in late 1973, fellow RCA recording artist Lou Reed's eyes all but misted over as he gushed: "Oh, oh, it's so fantastic." Critics such as *NME*'s Mitch Howard were almost as enthusiastic: "Ray Davies continues to show us that it is possible to write about the way the world affects ordinary people, to delve into politics, and still produce good songs. . . . *Preservation Act One* comes as a great relief. At least someone is writing real songs about real people living in a rather damp little island off the North of Europe, drinking cups of tea, going to work, hoping things get better. . . ." "No, it didn't run up massive sales," Ray noted in the same publication a few months later. "I suppose I was disgusted—I mean, I really worked hard on it, but maybe that's a reward in itself. I was unhappy when people hadn't heard it. That's all I care about, really."

Ray as Preservation's *Mr. Flash* (*Chuck Pulin*)

If the lyrical themes in *Preservation Act One* harked back to the *Village Green* album, the format duplicated that of *Arthur*. The first "act" of Ray's magnum opus is a collection of loosely related songs, which present a cast of characters ranging from a happy-go-lucky Tramp ("That's me," Ray confided) to a pompous Vicar, who, to a seedy Salvation Army–like brass accompaniment, offers the rules of cricket (which, after all, boasts "honor . . . character . . . and it's British") as a metaphorical guide to "the game of life." These gentlemen are presently eclipsed by *Preservation*'s arch-villains (and arch-rivals), the moralistic politician Mr. Black and Demolition King Mr. Flash.

Preservation Act Two (a double LP) was previewed in England with a single, "Mirror of Love," a demo Ray recorded largely on his own. *NME*'s newest writer, Chrissie Hynde (who would subsequently make her mark with the Pretenders, scoring both a massive British hit with Ray's "Stop Your Sobbing" and an intimate relationship with her longtime hero), rhapsodized:

> "You're a mean and obscene lover but I would have no other": yet another Kinks single that positively reeks of white trousers and loafers. Raymond Douglas Davies is the only songwriter I can think of who can write such personal material (and he is always *very* personal) and never get embarrassing. One of the true romantics of our time. "Mirror of Love" is perfect for listening to under the shade of a verandah, sipping iced tea. . . . God save the Kinks!

But except in this and a few other instances, something went dreadfully wrong between Acts One and Two. Part of the problem, perhaps, was that as a songwriter Ray was obviously more comfortable in the pastoral setting of the Village Green than in its later manifestation as Scrapheap City. Mostly, however, Davies seems to have got carried away by his own conceptual

ambitions; in *Act Two* the songs themselves are subsumed to the demands of a very explicit (and very contrived) story line. Ian McDonald's *NME* review was harsh, but generally on target: "In attempting a rock equivalent of *The Threepenny Opera*, Davies has merely created a drawn-out sequence of sociopolitical platitudes . . . supported by music of little overall cohesion and no individual personality whatsoever."

The Kinks presented a condensed version of *Preservation* on their next U.S. concert tour, complete with film clips and costume changes. These shows were a typically ramshackle production that dispensed with many of the albums' more epic aspirations. As Dave Hickey reported in *Rolling Stone*: "The affair is not profound—just a goofy, Kinkified blend of *1984* and *A Clockwork Orange*. . . . It makes good, pointed fun of vanity and hypocrisy; fun that's not easily made." Six years later, Ray told *Melody Maker*: "It was one of those things that would have been great if we'd persevered with it and been able to keep it on the stage, improving it. But because of the lack of success of the records we had to go on to the next one."

The "next one" was actually an outgrowth of a televised musical comedy called *Starmaker* that had been shown in Britain on September 4, 1974—only a month after *Preservation Act Two*'s release. Ray wrote, scored, and starred in the program, wherein a Star desperate for artistic inspiration switches places with an ordinary Norman, inheriting the latter's nine to five office job, nagging wife, and tastelessly decorated flat. ("Those ducks, ducks, ducks on the wall!") But the Star quickly tires of

. . . as a Schoolboy in Disgrace (*Chuck Pulin*)

. . . as the Headmaster in Schoolboys in Disgrace (*Chuck Pulin*)

Norman's mundane existence, even as the wife (played by June Ritchie) loses patience with his recollections of a more glamorous previous incarnation: "You're not a star, Norman. You're just a plain ordinary little bloke. . . . I've had enough of your ridiculous fantasies." Finally, we are told, "Norman decides to stop living out his fantasy of being a rock star and accept reality. This is the end for Norman, but not for us, because there will always be someone ready to take his place—after all, everybody's a star!"

NME's Charles Shaar Murray deemed *Starmaker* "insulting" in its patronization of both "the Common Man" and the audience; he also (with ample justification) dismissed its songs as "glib, shallow, and superficial. . . . 'I'll never get an album out of this,' moans the Star at one point. Right on, Ray. Neither will you." But of course Ray did, though he changed the title to *Soap Opera*. The Kinks, furthermore, took the musical on the road, and while it may not have worked as a TV play—or, for that matter, as a record—*Soap Opera* did make for an exceptionally entertaining evening with the Kinks. Indeed, the very fact that *Soap Opera* and its successor, *Schoolboys in Disgrace*, were such desperately thin gruel as "concept albums" made them far more manageable than *Preservation* in the context of so-called rock theater. For the *Schoolboys* show, the Kinks struck further ridiculous poses, appearing in school uniforms to engage their wildly partisan and increasingly school-age audience (who could readily identify such characters as the sadistic headmaster and "Jack the Idiot Dunce") in a madcap romp through the nostalgically recalled misadventures of "the happiest days of our lives."

RCA enjoyed respectable U.S. sales for the two original cast albums, but still had a long way to go toward recouping its million-dollar investment. The Kinks, however, failed to renew their contract when it expired in 1976. Despite speculation that they might record for their own recently launched independent label, Konk,* Ray struck a deal with Arista Records' Clive Davis, well-known for his ability to resuscitate flagging careers.

Unlike his RCA counterparts, Davis was a tough taskmaster. All Kink product would have to pass his commercially attuned scrutiny; further concept albums were out of the question. He even played Davies some songs by professional tunesmiths, with the suggestion that the Kinks try recording them. Ray promised he would—if he couldn't come up with anything better himself.

Ray rose to his challenge with the nine straightforward and highly commercial originals that were to appear in early 1977 as *Sleepwalker*. This high-voltage recording was heavily promoted with such catchy slogans as "At last—the Kinks are back—and they're better than ever!" (as if they'd ever been away!) and quickly outsold any of the RCA albums. Meanwhile the group tightened up its act, dropping the horns and female singers and replacing the disgruntled Dalton and Gosling with a pair of ace veterans, former Pretty Things keyboardist Gordon Edwards and ex-Argent bassist Jim Rodford (the latter was briefly preceded by Andy Pyle, and the former was eventually replaced by Ian Gibbons). With Dave and Mick having attained a solid mastery of their instruments, the Kinks finally sounded like a band of old pros.

This may have run counter to Ray's early dictum—"As soon as we become professionals we'll be ruined"—but Ray himself was no longer the neurotic, xenophobic, and painfully vulnerable figure who had once reigned over Kinkdom. Around the time he turned thirty, Davies responded to an *NME* reporter's inquiry about his "own little world": "It's not a little world anymore. It started off a little world, but there are infiltrators. When you say 'little world,' it makes me think I'm mentally not all there."

The main infiltrator was that very country which had once inspired such fear and loathing on the Village Green. America was now the setting for most of the Kinks' professional activities, and in the late Seventies Ray went so far as to take an apartment on New York's Upper West Side. He even began writing in American, to sing of "gas" and "bars" and "the subway" as opposed to "petrol," "pubs," and "the Underground."

Which is not to say that he lost any of his flair for showmanship, or that the Kinks' Arista albums lacked ingenious, original, and amusing songs. In any case, Ray certainly Gave the People What They Wanted: 1978's *Misfits* (which spawned a square promotional EP in a round cover) sold even better than *Sleepwalker;* 1979's *Low Budget* (which spawned the disco-tinged hit "Superman") scored the Kinks their first gold-certified LP since their 1966 *Greatest Hits* collection; and 1980's live double album *One for the Road* (which spawned the first rock video cassette) fared better still. Unlike other Sixties "survivors," the formerly unfashionable Kinks entered the Eighties as fashionable as they were popular; many New Wave bands—such as Squeeze—emulated Davies's social commentary and sparse arrangements, while other artists revived his old songs.

On *One for the Road,* the Kinks reclaimed most of the obscure Davies tunes that had recently been made famous by

---

* Konk's small roster included both Claire Hamill and Tom Robinson's acoustic trio, Cafe Society. Ray later claimed that his short-lived label anticipated by several years the ideals of such post-Punk independents as Two-Tone. Yet he took legal action to thwart the Tom Robinson Band's emergence on EMI. Davies later said he did so because "I was interested in the gamesmanship of it all. . . . I genuinely like him . . . but it's a back-stabbing business." After Robinson added "Tired of Waiting for You" to his onstage repertoire and recorded a message to Davies titled "Don't Take No for an Answer," Ray finally relented.

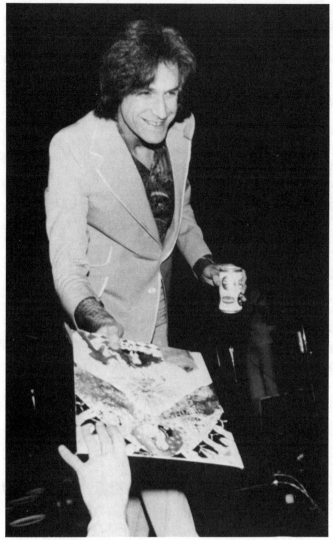

(Chuck Pulin)

There's been a lot of talk about "dinosaurs" these past few years. It's got to the point where many longtime rock fans (who prefer the term "survivors") might reluctantly vote in favor of banning some of their aging heroes to a remote cave. All concerned could then be spared a great deal of embarrassment, and the fantasies of our collective adolescence would be left forever intact.

The Kinks, nowever, are one "Sixties" act that has never had to face the dilemma of living up to (or living down) an identity forged from teen anthems like "My Generation" and "(I Can't Get No) Satisfaction." Following several rewrites of his first youthful Power Popper, "You Really Got Me," Ray Davies grew up almost overnight. Most of the understated narratives he penned in the latter half of the Sixties are not only timeless but ageless. Even his voice was almost that of a little old man. Davies might well have soldiered on into the next century, writing and singing such wry and poignant ditties as "Waterloo Sunset," "Autumn Almanac," and "Days," and nobody would have ever called him a dinosaur.

Yet now that he's actually approaching that age when people tend to grow partial to sweeping leaves into a sack, pasting snapshots in the family picture book, or just sitting by the fire in their Shangri-Las, the songwriter who once immortalized these small pleasures has regressed into a second rock & roll childhood. And every move in that direction has been matched in kind by guitar-hero poses and great, greasy riffs from kid brother Dave Davies.

Despite what he sings in one of his catchy new compositions, "Predictable" was always the last word anyone would have used to describe Ray Davies. His late-Seventies metamorphosis, however, was no mere kinky whim, but, rather, a conscious determination to, uh, *Give the People What They Want*. After seventeen years and some twenty-odd albums, Davies feels entitled to sing at Madison Square Garden. And Big Sky knows he deserves to.

But the real surprise here is that the Kinks are manifestly enjoying their reincarnation as Born Again rock & roll superstars. On *Give the People What They Want*, at least, they seldom sound tired and jaded, or even bored with their more hackneyed riffs. And their pleasure is passed on to the listener.

Not that the Kinks are entirely innocent of pandering; as a Davies character study, "Killer's Eyes" is dead obvious. "De-

the likes of David Bowie ("Where Have All the Good Times Gone"), the Pretenders ("Stop Your Sobbing"), the Jam ("David Watts"), and the Knack ("The Hard Way"). These and other vintage delights were refurbished (some might say adulterated) with a heavy metal wallop, and interspersed with such rabble-rousing pronouncements as "Rock bands will come, rock bands will go, *but rock & roll goes on forevvaaah!*" Despite all its Kink klassiks, *One for the Road* was hardly a representative encapsulization of the group's distinguished career; it is, however, a revealing record of how and why the Kinks at last achieved the mass recognition that had long been their due. It was performances such as this—hundreds upon hundreds of grueling one-night stands—that had hammered home to America's rock & roll multitudes the fact that the Kinks boasted a track record equal to those of the Stones or The Who. "We've really worked hard in the U.S. Played everywhere nearly," Ray told *Time* magazine—whose coverage was in itself testimony that the Kinks, too, had finally become an institution.

In summing up the latter days of Kinkdom, I have little more to add to a short piece I wrote for *Rolling Stone* about my heroes' 1981 offering, *Give the People What They Want:*

Giving the people what they want . . .
(Freelance Photo Guild/Ebet Roberts)

The Kinks circa 1979 (from 1.): Gordon Edwards, Ray, Dave, Mick, Jim Rodford (Arista Records)

stroyer'' (wasn't that the title of a Kiss record?) is positively brontosauruslike in its heavy-handed appropriation, à la 1979's ''Catch Me Now I'm Falling,'' of a familiar mid-Sixties riff. (This time, though, Davies has had the taste to select the Kinks' own ''All Day and All of the Night''—the tune Jim Morrison nicked for ''Hello I Love You.'') And when it comes to nuances like rhyme and meter, this notable craftsman has grown notably careless; even when he sings ''Here's hoping that the verses rhyme,'' they don't, quite.

Then again, that in itself may be a deliberate stroke of Davies irony. For make no mistake, Ray has not turned such an idiot dunce as to utilize a phrase like ''Give the people what they want'' without a sly wink and a smile (particularly when the song of that title specifies such vintage Roman crowd pleasers as ''bring on the lions and open the cage''; indeed, the irony there is downright bitter). In any case, Davies's curse is that he's too incurably quirky to qualify as a successful hack. Even when he does kowtow to mass taste, he just can't help being unique. Who else could or

would routinely deliver a line like ''Excuse me, is this your tooth?'' And who else would use what sounds like a marimba to complement a very proper, very English ''Art Lover'''s account of his predilection for very young girls?

Give the People What They Want even concludes with a special treat for the long-suffering Kinks kultist. Musically and lyrically, ''Better Things'' is of a piece with 1968's ''Days,'' the important difference being that the better days are said to be ahead now, instead of irretrievably behind. Dusting off his old crabbed, quavery voice, Ray Davies almost sounds vulnerable again as he ventures: ''I hope tomorrow you'll find better things.''

Same to you, old friend. Some of *Give the People What They Want* may sound pedestrian back to back with *Face to Face* and all those, and the words probably won't qualify as timeless literature and all that. But compared with most of the other yo-yos heard around my dial lately, tunes like ''Around the Dial'' and ''Yo-Yo'' certainly provide an exhilarating noise—delivered with a lightness of touch that hardly suggests the stomp of a dinosaur. They're funny and they're fun; and that, I'll venture, should be enough until Ray Davies gets around to writing a *Preservation Act Three.*

THE KINKS' HITS

U.S. Singles

1964	You Really Got Me (**7**); All Day and All of the Night (**7**)
1965	Tired of Waiting for You (**6**); Set Me Free (**23**); Who'll Be the Next in Line (**34**); A Well Respected Man (**13**)
1966	Till the End of the Day (**50**); Dedicated Follower of Fashion (**36**); Sunny Afternoon (**14**)
1967	Dead End Street (**73**); Mr. Pleasant (**80**)
1970	Victoria (**63**); Lola (**9**); Apeman (**45**)
1977	Sleepwalker (**48**)
1978	Rock & Roll Fantasy (**30**)
1979	(Wish I Could Fly Like) Superman (**41**)
1980	Lola (live version) (**81**)

U.S. LPs

1964	You Really Got Me (**29**)
1965	Kinks-Size (**13**); Kinda Kinks (**60**); Kinks Kinkdom (**47**)
1966	The Kink Kontrovery (**95**); The Kinks' Greatest Hits (**9**)
1967	Face to Face (**135**); The Live Kinks (**162**)
1968	Something Else by the Kinks (**153**)
1969	Arthur (**105**)
1970	Lola Versus Powerman and the Moneygoround (**35**)
1971	Muswell Hillbillies (**100**)
1972	The Kink Kronikles (**94**); Everybody's in Showbiz (**70**)
1973	The Great Lost Kinks Album (**145**); Preservation Act One (**177**)
1974	Preservation Act Two (**114**)

1975	Soap Opera (**51**); Schoolboys in Disgrace (**45**)
1976	The Kinks' Greatest—Celluloid Heroes (**144**)
1977	Sleepwalker (**21**)
1978	Misfits (**40**)
1979	Low Budget (**11**)
1980	One for the Road (**14**); Second Time Around (**177**)

(BY DAVE DAVIES)

1980	AFLI-3603 (**42**)

U.K. Singles

1964	You Really Got Me (**1**); All Day and All of the Night (**2**)
1965	Third of Waiting for You (**1**); Till The End of The Day (**8**); Everybody's Gonna Be Happy (**17**); Set Me Free (**9**); See My Friends (**10**)
1966	Dedicated Follower of Fashion (**4**); Sunny Afternoon (**1**); Dead End Street (**5**)
1967	Waterloo Sunset (**2**); Autumn Almanac (**3**)
1968	Wonderboy (**36**); Days (**12**)
1969	Plastic Man (**31**)
1970	Victoria (**33**); Lola (**2**); Apeman (**5**)
1972	Supersonic Rocket Ship (**16**)

(BY DAVE DAVIES)

1967	Death of a Clown (**3**); Susannah's Still Alive (**20**)

THE BRITISH INVASION

The Who

PICTURE YOURSELF OUTSIDE a condemned RKO cinema on Third Avenue and Fifty-eighth Street, standing in a shuffling line of boys with greased-back hair and girls with tresses piled high; there's a chill in the morning air, and the Summer of Love is still months away. The marquee reads MURRAY THE K'S EASTER SHOW, and you are about to witness the latest in a long series of all-star spectaculars produced and compered by New York's most renowned disc jockey. Long before his incarnation as self-proclaimed "Fifth Beatle," Murray Kaufman had been making rock & roll history with these marathons, which presented some twelve acts in rapid succession, each performing nothing but its famous hits—all two or three of them. But it is now March 1967, and this Easter Show will be Murray the K's last.

When the doors open at noon, you fork over your two fifty and scurry into the theater to claim a front-row seat. As the RKO slowly fills with teenyboppers and greasers from across the river, you must sit through two hours of documentaries on such gripping topics as Australian farm technology. Finally, the screen goes dark, and into the spotlight sashays Murray the K, snapping his fingers and rapping a mile a minute about his OUTASITE show, about the INCREDIBLE Mitch Ryder and the Detroit Wheels, and the FANTASTIC Wilson Pickett. . . . "It's what's happening, baby! *Aaahh-vayy!!*" he brays, cupping a hand to an ear, and the throngs respond in kind: *"aahh-vayy!!"*

One of the first warm-up acts is a new British trio called the Cream, who offer one straight pop song ("I Feel Free") and one dazzling display of virtuoso British Blues ("Spoonful"). When Messrs. Clapton, Bruce, and Baker take their leave, few in the audience venture so much as a polite smattering of applause; they're all too busy conversing with their neighbors, gobbling popcorn, and waiting for Ryder or Pickett.

Well, almost all: in the front rows there's a small contingent of girls who've managed to get their hands on import copies of *Rave* magazine, hands now at the ready with Beatlemania jelly beans and stuffed animals. And when old Murray introduces yet another group as hailing "direct from England . . ." there is a buzz in the front rows, a shiver of anticipation, and then a lusty squeal: ". . . *The Who!!*" To most in this audience, however,

"Nippers with big noses and small genitals trying to make the front page of the Daily News*"—Pete Townshend (1.) with Roger Daltrey, John Entwistle, and Keith Moon. (RDR Productions)*

the name promises nothing but a running joke ("Who? The Who. The *Who??*). Yet their wandering attention is arrested by the blinding flash of the first smoke bombs ever to be detonated on a New York concert stage. Out of the wings with a flying leap comes a tall, lanky guitarist with a comically large nose, resplendent in a Union Jack jacket, slashing out the most ear-wracking Power Pop chords anyone in the crowd has ever been subjected to. The spotlight slices through the smoke, revealing a golden-haired dandy twirling a microphone like a lasso from its long length of wire, seemingly oblivious to the hail of teddy bears and candy from the doting Anglophiles in the front rows. Behind him a baby-faced dervish in a bull's-eye T-shirt flings himself at the largest drum kit in the Northern Hemisphere. The singer hurls the microphone into the air with one hand, catches it with the other, and sneers: "You think we look pretty good toge-*thah*!/ You think my shoes are made of lea-*thah*!. . ." As more smoke bombs go off, the guitarist's flailing gathers such speed that his Union Jacketed arms begin to resemble a windmill in a hurricane. Judging from the noise he makes, the young drummer's hands must be moving faster still. In their frenzied competition for the audience's attention this four-man band is like a three-ring circus; only the bass player disdains to join in the fray, instead lurking in the shadows immobile as a stone. The punters in the front rows shriek like banshees, but for the first time in the history of the British Invasion the "screamagers" are drowned out by the sheer volume of the music itself. Most everyone else just sits there with his or her mouth hanging open.

The guitarist chucks his instrument twenty feet in the air, catches it, and The Who follow "Substitute" with an equally kinetic "So Sad About Us"—after which they slow the pace ever so slightly for the current single, which many in the audience actually recognize, as it is the first Who number to receive airplay on the likes of Murray the K's own WINS. The whimsical "Happy Jack" is accompanied by a film (hardly anyone's tried that before, either) which culminates in the larger-than-life black-and-white Who slapping custard pies into one another's faces.

And then the coup de grace: "My Generation," which the *Rave* readers instantly recognize as England's most notorious youth anthem since "Satisfaction." "Why don't you all fff-fff-fade away/ don't try dd-dig what we all sss-ssayy. . . ." The singer lashes the floor with his microphone; the guitarist unstraps his instrument and rams its neck against the massive bank of amplifiers until they topple like dominoes. The music degenerates into cacophony and chaos, with only the stalwart bassist hanging on to some semblance of melodic or rhythmic continuity. As the singer grinds a microphone to smithereens, the drummer knocks his cymbals and snares pell-mell, sending his two great bass drums rolling across the stage. The guitarist bludgeons the floorboards with his instrument and stomps on it with both feet. All the while his performance is transmuted into lethal shrieks of feedback from such amps as remain operative—until that climactic moment when he snaps the guitar's neck clear off its body. Flinging aside the splintered fragments of his instrument, Peter Townshend storms off the debris-strewn stage, followed by singer Roger Daltrey, bassist John Entwistle, and drummer Keith Moon, to a standing ovation from some two thousand young New Yorkers who until that day had hardly even heard of The Who. . . .

Ten minutes was all it took, and for this particular fan these will always remain the most thrilling ten minutes in rock & roll memory. At the time, white pop shows this side of Haight-Ashbury tended to consist of little more than cuddly wind-up toys in matching suits, or—far worse—of would-be "entertainers" from the Las Vegas school of show biz. The Rolling Stones, of course, had undertaken the first radical step of making themselves the embodiment of all the aimless anger and adolescent angst that had always been implicit in this music, yet

rarely personified in the stars themselves. But it was The Who who first transmuted these elements into full-scale Pop Theater.

Their onstage rites of violence and destruction were the stuff of instant pop mythology: primitive heroics as vulgar and flashy as anything ever perpetrated by the comic-book heroes of the Golden Age of Rock & Roll, but augmented with such futuristic trappings as smoke, film, and flashing lights, and the loudest PA advancing technology could muster (not to mention some of the most powerful music the British Invasion had yet conjured). For an impressionable lad attending his first Who concert, the experience was nothing less than a revelation.

From that day, I considered The Who to be the spirit of Pop incarnate. As one of those oddballs who frequented Manhattan newsstands that stocked British rags like *Disc* and *Rave*, I had already got my pudgy little hands on the group's hard-to-find records. So naturally (me living but six blocks away, and enjoying a spring recess from school) I spent most of my waking

*Townshend with his collection of broken guitars (**Photo Trends**)*

hours over the following week ensconced in one or another of the Fifty-eighth Street RKO's plush crimson seats. The show ran for seven days, three times daily, and once having paid the price of admission one could tarry from morning till the end of the day—through endless replays of Mitch Ryder, Wilson Pickett, and such promising local favorites as the Blues Project and Simon and Garfunkel (not to mention the same dreary documentaries, ad nauseam)—for the sole purpose of experiencing once, twice, and eleven times again those ten magic minutes of The Who.

Such was The Who's American debut. Though they never set foot outside New York City—and lost a small fortune in decimated equipment*—what Townshend called the "endurance

---

* Over the course of their twenty-one mini-concerts, The Who utterly demolished five guitars, four speaker cabinets, twenty-two microphones, and sixteen individual pieces of percussion.

113

test'' of their cameo performance on Murray the K's Easter Show engendered enough notoriety to make ''Happy Jack'' the group's first U.S. Top Forty hit (beating out current entries by both Ryder and Pickett). (The group also gave some memorable press conferences, for which the guitarist donned ''an electric jacket with flashing light bulbs.'' ''We worked hard at propaganda,'' Townshend told *New Musical Express* upon The Who's return to London, ''and I had two stock quotes which everybody wrote down. They were: 'We want to leave a wound' and 'We won't let our music stand in the way of our visual act.' '')

In June The Who returned to America for the historic Monterey Pop Festival, once again upstaging a formidable array of ''big name'' stars (an epic moment preserved on celluloid [*Monterey Pop*] for a million more potential converts to witness in the luxury of their own local air-conditioned cinemas). A month later The Who undertook their first cross-country U.S. tour second-billed to the hapless Herman's Hermits (a mismatch comparable only to the selection of fellow Monterey showstopper Jimi Hendrix as opening act for the Monkees). Within a year, The Who would outgrow their status as an Anglophile's cult band to become *Rolling Stone* cover-story fodder and an instant sellout at the Fillmores East and West—though it wasn't until after the 1969 release of their magnum opus *Tommy* that they finally joined the Beatles and the Rolling Stones in the ranks of the certified-platinum heavies.

When The Who exploded into America's consciousness, it was as a full-blown apparition. Few U.S. teenagers knew what the group's clothes or stance or song lyrics were supposed to signify; all that really mattered was that The Who were weird and wonderful and British. In England, by contrast, The Who's original impact closely reflected that of the larger phenomenon of the Mods.

In the mid-Sixties, young Americans were vaguely aware of Mods, if at all, only in conjunction with their nemeses, the Rockers—demented rival youth gangs on scooters and motorcycles, constantly staging epic battles at seedy seaside resorts like Brighton, Margate, and Hastings. The stereotypical Mod was an immaculate dandy with blow-dried hair; his adversary, a greasy oaf decked out in leather and chains. But those well-publicized hoodlum holocausts really marked the grand finale for the Golden Age of Mod, and by the time Americans had heard of Carnaby Street, that erstwhile Mod fashion mecca had long since degenerated into a tourist trap, even as *Datebook* began calling its English insert ''Mod Magazine.'' For according to those who were part of the original movement, much of the Mods' attraction had been that of a secretive and mysterious cult; they deliberately confounded and eluded the media with their constantly shifting preferences in matters of the cloth, the dance floor, and even such trifles as their favored brand of cigarette. The Mods represented the ultimate in trendiness, and (until the street corners were finally co-opted by TV's *Ready Steady Go* and our friends Messrs. Townshend, Daltrey, Entwistle, and Moon) their tastes were dictated from within their own ranks, not by slimy, scheming businessmen or even a charismatic deejay or pop star. Before any facet of the Mod style could be pinned down in the national press, it was by definition already passé; as Nik Cohn once put it, ''If you got caught in last night's sweater, you were finished, you were dead.''

This cult began as something of a reaction to that of the Teddy Boys, the first young Britons to establish an identity all their own. Around the middle of the previous decade, demographics and a booming postwar economy had turned Britain (no less than America) into a playground for unprecedented numbers of adolescents with unprecedented amounts of disposable income and leisure time. These singular circumstances set the stage for the introduction of products and styles (most notably rock & roll itself) strictly geared to a previously unheard-of ''youth market.'' In England the most extreme manifestation of the new youth consciousness was the Teddy Boys, so named because they affected a modified Edwardian look. (The very idea of working-class scum parodying the aristocracy was subversive enough; before long rock & roll stars would be desecrating the very flag with their Union Jack garb!) Apart from their drape jackets and oily hair, the Teds were best known for such idiosyncrasies as slashing cinema seats with razor blades during screenings of jukebox musicals like *Rock Around the Clock*. They were Britain's own juvenile delinquents, its first ''rebels without a cause,'' and their unsavory example inspired thousands of younger urchins—such as John Lennon and George Harrison—who studiously emulated the Teddy Boy image.

The forerunners of the Mods were equally restless working-class youths who were nonetheless repelled by the crude and garish Teds. Styling themselves ''Modernists''—after the modern jazz they then favored over the Fifties rock & roll so dear to the hearts of the Teds (and, subsequently, of their Sixties counterparts, the Rockers)—these young dandies aspired to the new and the sophisticated. Disdaining the backwardness and stuffiness of British mores and culture, the Modernists identified strongly with both America and the Continent—the one for its flashiness and speed, the other for its style and class. They were particularly drawn to the music of black America, and by the time the Modernist monicker was shortened to Mod, their interest in modern jazz had evolved into an affinity for the more danceable sounds of R&B and early soul music. From France and Italy, meanwhile, the original Mods derived their taste in films, hairstyles, and—above all—clothes.

Dapper and well-tailored, the Mod was able to blend unobtrusively into the respectable workaday world of nine to five. Though he felt as indifferent to the prospect of a ''straight''

Mods converge on Brignton (*RDR Productions*)

career as the Fifties Teddy Boy or the late-Sixties hippie, the Mod's addiction to snappy clothes necessitated a steady source of income. On the job, he might almost pass for a sober and industrious citizen (some subtle telltale quirk notwithstanding —the way his tie was knotted, perhaps, or a three-inch-high collar or two-tone mohair suit). But the Mod—memorably dubbed "noonday subversive" in an essay by Tom Wolfe— lived entirely for that magic moment when he might disappear, somewhere on the way home from work or shcool, into his "noonday underground" world of coffee bars, boutiques, and certain select street corners.

For the Mods, style *was* substance; image was everything. To qualify as a Mod, one had to conform to extremely exacting codes with respect to such basic functions as standing and walking. One was expected to hold a cigarette a certain way and to straddle a scooter at a precisely prescribed angle. Mods were forever posing, and their narcissism was such that girls were largely deemed unnecessary in this overwhelmingly male milieu. The average Mod was a peacock who preferred to dance alone, with his fellows, or with his irresistible reflection in the mirror.

But though they often patronized boutiques—such as those on Carnaby Street—that had long been the province of flamboyant homosexuals, Mods weren't necessarily gay. That many appeared to be simply asexual has often been attributed to their fondness for Drynamil, an amphetamine better known as "purple hearts." "There is no other drug that gives you such a bang, such an up," Peter Meaden—the Andrew Oldham crony and Mod-about-town who "discovered" The Who—told *Sounds'* Barbara Charone. "The high combined with the music gave you the energy to stay up for three days running. You felt great. You could dance, you had courage, confidence. . . . The Mod thing was actually a guy's thing; at the time all the little girls were screaming for the Beatles. Drynamil lowered your sex drive so you didn't have to desperately search for a girl to pull. You were independent."

PETE TOWNSHEND: The Mods were a real movement. It cut across all class lines, but it was working-class London originally. The Beatles were no more Mod than Elvis Presley. Mod clothes were . . . fairly plain, but they had to be just so: the exact length of hair, the style of shoe. . . . One outfit might be twelve quid, a week's wages, and the next fucking week you'd have to change the whole lot. Nobody ever figured out how the fashions started, any more than they ever figured out how it was decided that on a certain bank holiday all the Mod kids in London would converge on a certain beach town.

It only lasted a couple of years, really. In '66 it got very locked into this television program called *Ready Steady Go,* where the producers got the Ace Faces, the trendsetters, to go on television. It was a network show, so Mod fashions spread all through England overnight. And it wasn't the same anymore, because in the real Mod scene nobody would tell you. . . . It was incestuous, secretive. Difficult to be a real up-to-the-minute Mod, 'cause no cunt would tell you where to get the clothes. It wasn't something you decided to be, you just were. (*Rolling Stone,* 1974)

PETER MEADEN: I had this dream of getting a group together that would be the focus, the entertainers for the Mods: a group that would actually be the same people onstage as the guys in the audience . . . an actual representation of the people. (*Sounds,* 1975)

A Rocker is consoled by his mum following a run-in with Mods (RDR Productions)

After clothes and pills, music constituted the third focus of the noonday underground. Obsessed as they were with nuances of style, the Mods were notorious for discovering and popularizing (and then, as often as not, discarding) heretofore obscure forms of music. Mods were at the vanguard of London's R&B cognoscenti, and though many automatically disparaged British R&B the day the Rolling Stones made the hit parade, others still comprised an important audience for local R&B combos such as The Who—none of whose members yet considered himself a Mod when the group was approached by Ace Face Peter Meaden and his financial backer, a Jewish doorknob manufacturer named Helmut Gordon.

Roger Daltrey, however, looked the part in his "French crew cut," and according to Meaden, "Townshend identified with the Mod scene immediately." Their fast-talking co-manager strenuously coached his new protégés in Mod fashions and attitudes, and even persuaded them to change their name to the High Numbers. Under this rubric, the group was contracted to cut two Meaden compositions—"I'm the Face" and "Zoot Suit"—as a single for Fontana Records.

PETER MEADEN: The name was perfect. I dreamt of it one night. High—being a little high—and Numbers was [Mod slang] for the general crowd. There was a hierarchy situation with the Mods, and the name High Numbers gave them a step up the hierarchy. (*Sounds*, 1975)

DAVID BOWIE: [They] wore stuff that was five months out of date as far as we [Mods] were concerned, but we liked them 'cause they were kind of like us. They were our band. . . . Until the High Numbers they were pretty much a Rolling Stonesy type band, and it was only when they realized that most of their audiences were Mods that they looked to see what we were wearing. (*NME*, 1973)

PETE TOWNSHEND: "I'm the Face" was "written" by our then-manager, Peter Meaden, fashioner of our Mod image. He pinched the tune of "Got Love If You Want It" by Slim Harpo and changed the words to fit the groovy group. (*Rolling Stone*, 1971)

FONTANA RECORDS PRESS RELEASE: The first *authentic* Mod record . . . a hip, tailored-for-teens R&B oriented shuffle rocker . . . with a kick in every catchphrase for the kids of the fast-moving crowd . . . [to] cause an immediate rapport between [the High Numbers and] thousands of young people like themselves. In a nutshell—they are of the people. (August 1964)

On "Zoot Suit," Meaden had Daltrey bragging: "I'm the snappiest dresser right down to my inch-wide tie." Like "I'm the Face," it was essentially a catalogue of Mod buzz words, such as "Faces" (fashion leaders who would initiate a new look) and "Tickets" (the Faces' lowly followers). Musically, however, it was "too ordinary"—as the Merseys pointedly noted in the "Blind Date" review that gave the High Numbers their first notice in *Melody Maker*—and the single was a flop.

To progress beyond the London club circuit, the group plainly needed managers with more extensive connections, resources, and vision than the doorknob manufacturer and the pill-popping Ace Face. At this convenient juncture, an ambitious pair of assistant film directors happened to be scouring the clubs for a group of dynamic unknowns to spotlight in their projected documentary film on pop music. In the autumn of 1964, this quest brought Kit Lambert (son of the classical composer Constant Lambert) to the Railway Tavern in suburban Harrow, where he witnessed the High Numbers' mesmeric effect upon a back room packed with perspiring Mods. The next night Lambert dragged his partner Chris Stamp (brother of film star Terence) to the boys' performance at Watford Trade Hall. Four days later, the group had acquired its second pair of managers.

KEITH MOON: Kit and Chris. They went round together, and they were as incongruous a team as we were. You had Chris on one hand [*goes into unintelligible East London cockney*]: "Oh well, fuck it, jus, jus, whack 'im in-a 'ead, 't 'im in ee balls an' all." And Kit says [*slipping into a proper Oxonian*]: "Well, I don't agree, Chris; the thing is—the whole thing needs to be thought out in damned fine detail." These people were perfect for us, because there's me, bouncing about, full of pills, full of everything I could get me 'ands on—and there's Pete, very serious, never laughed, always cool, a grass-'ead. I was working at about ten times the speed Pete was. And Kit and Chris were like the epitome of what we were. (*Rolling Stone*, 1972)

Though the new managers agreed that The Who was, after all, a snappier name than the High Numbers, Lambert and Stamp energetically pursued Meaden's original game plan of linking the group with the Mod phenomenon. According to Moon, the boys "were sent to Carnaby Street with more money than we'd ever seen in our lives, like a hundred quid each. . . . We weren't into clothes, we were into music. Kit thought we should identify more with our audience. Coats slashed five inches at the sides. Four wasn't enough. Six was too much. Five was just right."

Townshend, meanwhile, embarked on his first attempts to capture the band's chosen milieu in songs of his own composition. Though Pete's Mod anthems proved less artlessly blatant than Meaden's, their very success—along with that of The Who's Mod image—played a role in transforming the noonday underground just as surely as they defined it. And to many longtime Mods, the public unveiling of what had once been secret and mysterious was to rob the cult of its very meaning, not to mention its glamour. Soon *Ready Steady Go* would begin transmitting Mod fashions into millions of British households; already, the Mods had been introduced as wanton hooligans to the readers of Britain's sensational dailies. In the spring of 1964 some of the thousand Mods who descended upon the seaside town of Clacton turned rowdy and got into a scuffle with the police. A few Rockers also chanced to be involved in the incident, and in the willfully garbled media reports, the story was played up as a Mod-Rockers confrontation (which it wasn't) under screaming front-page headlines like DAY OF TERROR BY SCOOTER GROUPS. *The Daily Mirror*'s account began: "The Wild Ones invaded a seaside town yesterday—one thousand fighting, drinking, roaring, rampaging teenagers on scooters and motorcycles." According to one news broadcast, Clacton's housewives spent the following day "sweeping up the glass from their broken windows."

These shameless distortions of both the scope and the nature of the violence at Clacton insured that real riots would soon follow. All over England, arrogant pilled-up Mods and loutish hard-boozing Rockers suddenly perceived one another as mortal enemies, and their ranks were swelled by thousands of bored kids itching for a fight. Throughout the following year, the British press gloried in lurid accounts of seaside hooliganism—tales that required little embellishment from Fleet Street.

Some of the original Faces tried to dissociate themselves from the sensationalized violence and commercial exploitation with which their movement seemed increasingly tainted, hoping to continue as before under the rubric of "Stylists." But the noonday underground could never recapture its status as an elusive and exclusive cult. "Mod" had become public property, the province of a million dedicated followers of fashion all across the U.K. And its pre-eminent symbol was that loud, flashy pop group whose stage act, every bit as chaotic and violent as the clash of Mods and Rockers in a sleepy seaside town, offered the same exhilarating release, yet drew no blood and left no bruises.

Peter Dennis Blandford Townshend (born May 19, 1945), Roger Harry Daltrey (March 1, 1945), and John Alec Entwistle (October 9, 1944) grew up in the vicinity of Shepherd's Bush, a working-class section of West London. All three attended the Acton County Grammar School, where Pete and John became close friends and fellow members of a traditional jazz band, playing, respectively, banjo and trumpet. Entwistle graduated to tax collecting, and Townshend enrolled in Ealing Art College.

The diminutive Daltrey, meanwhile, had taken a job as a sheet-metal worker after getting kicked out of school for smoking. He played lead guitar in a band of his own, and invited Entwistle to join as bassist. When the original rhythm guitarist left, John dragged in Pete. Eventually Daltrey decided to drop the guitar and concentrate on vocals and harmonica. Townshend

Entwistle and friend at London's legendary Mod mecca (RDR Productions)

even thought they existed, would always talk about my nose. . . . Whenever my dad got drunk, he'd say: "Look, son, you know looks aren't everything. . . ." He's ashamed of me because I've got a big nose and he's trying to make me feel good. I know it's huge and of course it became incredible and I became an enemy of society. (*Rolling Stone,* 1968)

So I used to think: "I'll bloody well show them. I'll push me huge hooter out at them from every newspaper in England. . . ." My whole absurdly demonstrative stage act was worked out to turn myself into a body instead of a face . . . I wanted people not to have to bother looking at my head if they didn't like the look of it. (*Evening Standard,* 1968)

When I wrote the first five or six hit songs for The Who I was *completely* and *totally alone.* I had no girl friend, no friends, no nothing—it was me addressing the world. That's where the power of the early stuff comes from. (*Rolling Stone,* 1980)

Until Townshend commenced writing, Daltrey tended to dominate The Who; but for most of their career The Who were a real *group,* as only the Beatles also were: four parts of a greater whole, each part indispensable to the unique "chemistry" that the group generated. The Who's astrological birth signs even corresponded to the ancient elements: Townshend was earth (Taurus); Daltrey, water (Pisces); Entwistle, air (Libra).

The Who found their fire around the same time they acquired their Mod image, when a surf-music fanatic from Wembley named Keith Moon (a Leo born August 23, 1946) materialized at the Oldfield Hotel resplendent in "dyed ginger hair and a ginger cord suit," to catch The Who's already notorious act. "They were outrageous," he recalled in *Melody Maker.* "Pete looked very sullen. They were a bit frightening." Nonetheless, the young drummer—whose talent and energy could hardly be contained by his present group, the Beachcombers—asked to sit in.

KEITH MOON: They said go ahead and I got behind this other guy's drums and did one song—"Road Runner." I'd had several drinks to get me courage up and when I got onstage I went arrrgg*Ghhhhh* on the drums, broke the bass drum pedal and two skins and got off. I figured that was it. I was scared to death.

Afterwards I was sitting at the bar and Pete came over. He said: "You . . . come 'ere." I said, mild as you please: "Yesyes?" And Roger, who was the spokesman then, said: "What are you doing next Monday?" I said: "Nothing." I was working during the day, selling plaster. He said: "You'll have to give up work . . . there's this gig on Monday. If you want to come, we'll pick you up in the van." I said: "Right." . . . And that was it. Nobody ever said: "You're in." They just said: "What are you doing Monday?" (*Rolling Stone,* 1972)

Even more than the rest of The Who, Keith Moon played as if possessed. The sounds issuing from his oversized kit often seemed to belie the fact that he owned but one pair of hands. Manic Moon played at an awesome speed, but he never sounded busy, or merely flashy and loud. Always of the opinion that "drum solos are fucking boring—they detract from the group identity," Moon (as John Entwistle once put it) "made the drums sing; he played along with every instrument in the band." Moon was one of the few rock drummers to earn the admiration of such jazz titans as Buddy Rich; according to *Rolling Stone's* Greil Marcus: "No drummer in a true rock & roll band has ever been given—has ever seized, perhaps—as much space and presence as Moon used in those first years, likely because no other drummer has ever been able to carry the weight. . . . [He had] an ability to hear—and then play—what no one had heard before. And because Moon, a genius if any

was promoted to lead guitarist, but, he once told *NME,* "I couldn't play properly, so built up a style around chords." They started out playing Beatles songs, then switched to the blues. The drummer was Doug Seaden, an old man of thirty who never quite fit in. They called themselves the Detours, until Townshend's art-school roommate Richard Barnes rechristened them The Who.

PETE TOWNSHEND: We knew we were going to become stars. We entered the business to become stars, not to make a day-to-day business out of it. That's what was so exciting [then], everyone worked to be as big as the Beatles. (*NME,* 1970)

Pete grew up surrounded by music: his mother was a singer, and his father, Clifford (himself the son of a variety performer), had been a sax player with the RAF Dance Orchestra before forming a leading postwar dance band called the Squadronaires. "My father was essentially a pop musician in his day. I hate to think what would have happened if I had been brought up in a classical family! . . . 'Rock Around the Clock' did it for me . . . I decided the guitar was what I wanted. My granny got me my first guitar and it was a very, very bad one indeed, though it cost her a lot. . . . I fought tooth and nail with it for a year and finally gave up." He switched to banjo until the advent of the Shadows made the guitar the preferred status symbol among Britain's youth.

Nonetheless, the main catalyst for Townshend's early career wasn't the influence of any particular group or pop star. It was his nose.

PETE TOWNSHEND: It was huge. At that time, it was the reason I did everything. It's the reason I played the guitar . . . the reason I wrote songs. . . . When I was in school the geezers that were snappy dressers, and got chicks like years before I musician in rock deserves the name, arrived in The Who full-grown, he gave the rest of the band, Townshend in particular, the freedom to grow. He was their line to the source.''

Under the aegis of Lambert and Stamp, The Who made its first important breakthrough at London's Marquee Club. The jazz-and-R&B joint where the Rolling Stones had given their first performance was now a prestigious Mod watering hole, and The Who's managers managed to wrangle a spot on Tuesday night (the week's slowest), on the understanding that they themselves would have to handle the promotion. Having already squandered much of their savings on The Who's Carnaby Street outfits, Kit and Chris poured another £300 into posters and handbills with which to inundate the metropolitan area—especially the band's supposed stronghold of Shepherd's Bush. The eye-catching white-on-black posters sported, in the upper-left corner, the high-contrast image of ''Birdman'' Pete poised to strike his Rickenbacker, while huge white letters across the bottom blared the memorable slogan: THE WHO. MAXIMUM R&B.

Stamp and Lambert even handed out dozens of complimentary tickets to selected Mods on Shepherd's Bush street corners, but when the big night arrived rainy and miserable, only an estimated sixty-nine citizens straggled into the Soho club. Undeterred, The Who pulled out all the stops; Daltrey demolished his microphone, Moon broke four drumsticks, Townshend attacked his amplifier with the neck of his guitar until the amp spluttered into silence, and the Marquee's management offered them a residency on the spot. On sixteen subsequent Tuesdays, before an increasingly packed house, The Who built up a small legend.

KEITH MOON: We opened up Tuesdays—and we blew open the doors of the Marquee to rock. . . . The Marquee had influence . . . the managers and promoters and press could see us [there]. They had a very discerning audience there, and it helped us to develop our musical ideas. The club also had a mystique about it, especially on me as a drummer. . . . We always played our best there. We were finding our feet—and the Marquee put us on our feet. (*Melody Maker*, 1973)

''Maximum R&B'' notwithstanding, Lambert and Stamp realized that if The Who were to make any lasting impact, they would have to come up with something more original than ''Road Runner'' and ''Smokestack Lightning.'' Townshend was induced to begin writing songs of his own (his first effort, ''It Was You,'' landed on a B-side by the Fourmost).

PETE TOWNSHEND: I wasn't keen [on writing] . . . I was very much into an image thing. I lived and breathed image. That was the key word in those days. Then I heard ''You Really Got Me'' and instantly knew that the Kinks had filled the hole we wanted to fill. . . . I wrote ''I Can't Explain'' just for The Who and it remains one of the best things I've ever done. It was based on ''You Really Got Me,'' just didn't have the modulations. I was influenced more by the Kinks than any other group. (*NME*, 1970)

The Who were similar to the Kinks in many respects, at least during their mutual Swinging London heyday. Both Townshend and Ray Davies were art-school oddballs channeling their neuroses into uniquely brilliant songs. The careers of both foursomes were to take a parallel course, from the primeval grand slam of ''You Really Got Me'' and ''I Can't Explain'' through the offbeat, lightfooted, and very British humor of, say, ''Sunny Afternoon'' and ''I'm a Boy''—at which point both Townshend

and Davies would develop an obsession with ambitious concept albums. The Who, however, were far more extroverted, and the three other members of the band were much more distinctive musicians and personalities than their counterparts in the Kinks.

At the outset of their careers, both groups also shared the same producer. Indeed, ''Can't Explain'''s Kinky sound was one of the factors that attracted Shel Talmy to The Who. Like the Kinks, The Who were obliged to cement the relationship by recording Talmy's ''Bald Headed Woman.'' And The Who, too, were bedeviled at their first recording session by the presence of Talmy's favorite studio guitarist. (''I really wasn't needed,'' Jimmy Page assured Who fans. ''Just straightening up riffs, that's all. Just two guitarists doing it instead of one.'')

PETE TOWNSHEND: [Talmy] was a great believer in ''making groups who are nothing stars.'' He was also a great believer in pretending the group didn't exist when they were in the recording studio. . . . However, dear Shel got us our first hits. So he was as close to being God for a week as any unworthy soul has been. Of course it was a short week; I quickly realized that it was really the brilliant untapped writing talent of our lead guitarist, needless to say myself, that held the key to our success. (*Rolling Stone*, 1971)

Talmy arranged for the release of ''I Can't Explain''/''Bald Headed Woman'' on the Brunswick label—a subsidiary of British Decca—whose faith in The Who was such that they originally pressed a mere thousand copies. Once again, it was left to Lambert and Stamp to pound the pavements on The Who's behalf. They bamboozled a friend at *Ready Steady Go* into booking The Who, and then contrived to pack the TV studio with enthusiastic cult followers from the Marquee Club. Not to be outdone, *Top of the Pops* proceeded to select "I Can't Explain" as a "tip for the top." Meanwhile, Kit and Chris had made use of their movie-directing talents (and their ever-dwindling savings accounts) to create a short film about The Who, which also wound up on the British airwaves. Four months after its release, "I Can't Explain" finally inched into the Top Ten. (In the U.S., *Shindig* also aired a film clip of The Who doing "Can't Explain"—with extensive closeups of every band member save the one with the large nose—and the American Decca single climbed all the way to number 93.)

Suddenly, The Who were happening, and the London pop weeklies wanted to know all about them.

> He sat tensed in a hard-backed chair, dressed in a Carnaby Street blue jacket and with a blond, Mod hairstyle that showed dark at the back. And he spoke slowly and uncertainly. "I never want to grow old," he said. "I want to stay young forever."
> This was my introduction—via vocalist Roger Daltrey—to the weird and way out group called The Who.
>
> from *NME*'s first feature story on The Who

The boys' measurements and favorite colors were duly recorded for *NME*'s "Life Lines" series, in which the bassist's name was given as "John Browne" (as short-lived an affectation as his High Numbers pseudonym, John Allison). Under "professional ambition," Townshend scrawled: "Die young."

NME also revealed that in their desperation to concoct a follow-up to "I Can't Explain," Pete and Roger locked themselves away in the wee hours before the morning of the recording sessions. The result was "Anyway Anyhow Anywhere," an instant anthem for the Drynamil set: "Nothing gets in my way, not even locked doors. . . ."

PETE TOWNSHEND: I was lying on the floor listening to a Charlie Parker record when I thought up the title. (It's usually title first with me.) I just felt the guy was so free when he was playing. He was a soul without a body, riding, flying, on his music. . . . The freedom suggested by the title was restricted by the aggression of our tightly defined image when I came to write the words. In fact, Roger was *really* a hard nut then, and he . . . toughened the song up to suit his temperament. (*Rolling Stone*, 1971)

The accompanying music was an altogether unprecedented eruption of jet-scream feedback, interspersed with Morse code bleeping and what has been called rock's first "abstract" guitar solo. To mark the occasion, Lambert orchestrated an explosion of sorts in the group's sartorial style; the fastidiousness of the original Mods gave way to military regalia, bull's-eye T-shirts, and—most strikingly of all—jackets and shirts cut from the very flag of Her Majesty's realm. (The Who's irreverent trivialization of the Union Jack was soon to proliferate on coffee mugs and dish cloths available over the counter in every souvenir shop in London; the British flag would never be the same.)* Coached by Kit Lambert, The Who dubbed these visual assaults "Pop Art"—an all-purpose label that was also used to describe the group's new music; in its capacity as "the first Pop Art single," "Anyway Anyhow Anywhere" hit the stands complete with a yellow-and-orange Pop Art sleeve.

---

* After making the Union Jack their sartorial trademark, The Who found themselves the recipients of a bomb threat from militant Irish nationalists hours before they were due on a Dublin stage. The Who appeared as scheduled—wearing jackets tailored from the flag of Ireland!

PETE TOWNSHEND: Pop Art is re-presenting something the public is familiar with, like clothes. Union Jacks are supposed to be flown, we have a jacket made of one. . . . We stand for Pop Art clothes, Pop Art music, and Pop Art behavior. We don't change offstage, we live Pop Art. . . . We play Pop Art with standard group equipment. I get jet-plane sounds, Morse Code signals, and howling wind. (*Melody Maker*, 1965)

"Pop Art" was but one of the terms Townshend and Co. bandied about as they began spouting the most mystifying jargon and the most preposterous jive ever to be dutifully recorded in the pages of a teen magazine. If Pop Art was put forth as the greater cause for which each member of the group now claimed to spend £100 a week on clothes, then similar sums consumed by instrument repairs were to be squandered in the lofty name of "Auto-Destruction."

> The music is defiant, and so is their attitude. Their sound is vicious. . . . Townshend swings full circle with his right arm. He bangs out Morse Code by switching the guitar pick-ups on and off. Notes bend and whine. He turns suddenly and rams the end of his guitar into the speaker. A chord shudders on the impact. The speaker rocks.
> Townshend strikes again on the rebound. He rips into the canvas covering, tears into the speaker core, and the distorted solo splutters from the demolished speaker. The crowds watch this violent display spellbound.
>
> from The Who's first *Melody Maker* concert write-up

And during one such performance at the Marquee Club, Auto-Destruction acquired its definitive symbol when Townshend unintentionally broke his first guitar.

PETE TOWNSHEND: It happened by complete accident. . . . I was playing the guitar and it hit the ceiling. It broke, and it kind of shocked me, 'cause I didn't particularly want it to go, but it went. . . . I pounded all over the stage with it, and threw the bits on the stage, and I picked up my spare guitar and carried on as though I'd really meant to do it. Deep inside I was very unhappy because the thing had got broken, but it got around . . . people came up to me and said: "We heard all about it, man, it's 'bout time someone gave it to a guitar." It kind of grew from there . . . built and built and built until one day a very important newspaper came to us and said: "We hear you're the group that smashes their guitars up. Well, we hope you're going to do it tonight . . . if you do, you'll probably make the front page." . . . After that I was into it up to my neck, and have been doing it ever since. (*Rolling Stone*, 1968)

The Who made a conscious effort to appear no less mean and violent offstage, blaspheming and insulting as if they owned the world. Storming through adoring crowds, they tossed aside with venomous relish the clinging fans whom Pete characterized in *NME* as "stupid screaming little girls, morons, and idiots." But it was all just an act, and a short-lived one at that; as Moon later admitted: "For the first year we said a lot of things we didn't mean merely to create impact."

Indeed, a unique sense of solidarity was to develop between this band and its audience by the time The Who were set to join the Beatles and the Rolling Stones in the ranks of Britain's Big Three. The Beatles, of course, belonged to everybody: mums adored them, grown-up critics acclaimed them. The Rolling Stones, needless to say, were rock's pre-eminent symbols of "youthful rebellion," but they didn't really belong to anyone. The Who, however, proved to be the real outlaw heroes of the British Invasion: like the Rolling Stones, they were as restless and angry and iconoclastic as their audience; but The Who made themselves accessible, they were on our side, and they belonged to us. As Roger Daltrey once said, "The Who *are* their audience. There are no barriers between us and them. We're really just a big mirror." (No wonder The Who were to leave out the question mark when they titled the original lineup's last album *Who Are You*.)

All of this first became apparent when the follow-up to "Anyway Anyhow Anywhere" spoke directly for "the kids" as no pop song ever had before.

PETE TOWNSHEND: Our next single is really Pop Art. . . . It's anti middle-age, anti boss-class, and anti young marrieds. . . . The big social revolution that has taken place in the last five years is that youth, and not age, has become important. (*Melody Maker*, 1965)

ROGER DALTREY: "I'm not tryin' to cause a big ss-ss-sensation/just talkin' 'bout my gg-generation." (1965)

KEITH MOON: Pete had written out the words and gave them to Roger in the studio. He'd never seen them before . . . so when he read through them the first time, he stuttered. . . . Kit [Lambert] said [*Oxonian accent*]: "We leave it in, we leave in the stuttering." When we realized what'd happened, it knocked us all sideways. And it happened simply because Roger couldn't read the words. (*Rolling Stone*, 1972)

PETE TOWNSHEND: Spontaneous words that come out of the top of your head are always the best. I had written the lines of "Generation" without thinking, hurrying them, scribbling on a piece of paper in the back of a car. For years I've had to live by them, waiting for the day someone says: "You said you hoped you'd die when you got old in that song. Well, you are old. What now?" (*Rolling Stone*, 1971)

We don't mean it now . . . [but] we *did* mean it. We didn't care about ourselves or our future . . . even about one another. We were hoping to screw the older generation, screw the Rockers, screw the Beatles, screw the record buyers, and screw ourselves. We've been most successful on that last account. We really didn't want to end up jabbering in the pop papers about our hang-ups; we wanted to die in plane crashes or get torn to pieces by a crowd of screaming girls. It all began to change when Paul sang "When I'm 64." (*Melody Maker*, 1970)

I never wanted to write a big rock song like "My Generation." "Generation" was so *big*, it was almost Wagnerian. [Originally] I wrote it as a talking blues thing, something like "Talking New York Blues." Instead of New York, this would be "Talking 'Bout My Generation." Dylan affected me a lot. In fact, "Generation" started off as my folk-song single. (*NME*, 1971)

Beyond giving The Who their first massive hit, "My Generation" gave them their identity. Though the group had recently completed an album dominated by such Maximum R&B as "Smokestack Lightning," this, quite obviously, would no longer do, even at 33⅓. As The Who resolved to rerecord their first album almost from scratch, Lambert told *Melody Maker*: "Now the LP material will consist of hard pop"—courtesy, for the most part, of the composer of "My Generation."

PETE TOWNSHEND: I felt that the only way I was ever, ever, ever going to make myself felt was through writing, so I really got obsessed with writing rock songs and concentrated far more on that than on any other single thing in life. I used to go back after gigs and write and write. I must have two hundred or three hundred unreleased demos from the period of "My Generation" to "Pictures of Lily." (*NME*, 1972)

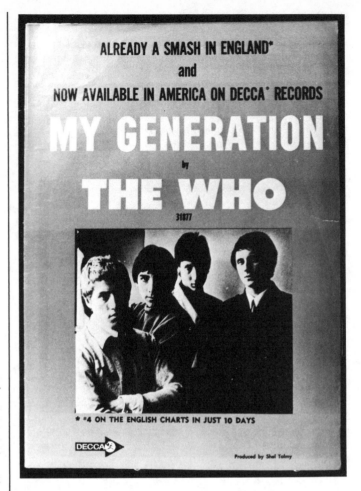

ALREADY A SMASH IN ENGLAND*
and
NOW AVAILABLE IN AMERICA ON DECCA* RECORDS
MY GENERATION
by
THE WHO
31877
* #4 ON THE ENGLISH CHARTS IN JUST 10 DAYS
DECCA
Produced by Shel Talmy

Named after their recent hit, The Who's revised LP debut was released in Britain in November 1965. Some of Townshend's titles speak for themselves: "Out in the Street" (which recycled "Anyway Anyhow Anywhere"'s dramatic intro) and the almost sentimental "The Kids Are Alright" (whose guitar solo was so "abstract" that it was expunged from the U.S. release, presumably because American Decca thought it was a recording error). Other selections—"The Good's Gone," "It's Not True"—were as exhilaratingly pigheaded as "Anyway Anyhow." Tough, raw, and uncompromising, *My Generation* was one of the few mid-Sixties albums that could and would sound wholly compatible with Britain's latter-day Punks upon its U.K. rerelease fifteen years later.

Soon after announcing "Circles" as the title of their next single, The Who summarily bolted from Decca to sign with their agent Robert Stigwood's new Reaction label (a precursor of Lambert's own Track Records). "Circles" then materialized on the B-side of *two* different "new" Who 45s. Reaction's entry featured "Substitute" as the A-side, and was produced by Townshend. Decca countered—rather wittily, one must admit—with the album track "A Legal Matter," for which the Talmy-produced B-side was incomprehensibly retitled "Instant Party." The BBC and the pirates all lined up behind either "A Legal Matter" or "Substitute," whose "controversial lyrics" ("I look all white but my dad was black") offered additional incentive for stations to select "A Legal Matter" until The Who provided them with a cleaned-up rendition.

At issue behind the Battle of the Who Titles—and the legal matters that were to bedevil The Who and their managers for some months—was the band's relationship with their producer.

Less docile than the Kinks, they took exception to Talmy's dictatorial ways and to the low royalty rate that accrued to them through his arrangement with Decca Records. Lambert and Stamp were also concerned about the indifference and incompetence American Decca had been lavishing upon The Who (on the U.S. version of their LP, *The Who Sings My Generation,* the liner notes revealingly advised: "If you liked The Who, you are sure to enjoy Len Barry").

The Who and Reaction were promptly enjoined from making any further recordings until the case had been settled—and also from selling any further copies of "Circles," which Talmy claimed was one of his productions. The Graham Bond Orchestra was tapped for a substitute B-side, titled, in Talmy's honor, "Waltz for a Pig." Eventually, Talmy was awarded a piece of The Who's future earnings ("Last time I saw Shel," Townshend told *Zigzag,* "he was gloating at our success"), and in America (where "Substitute" had appeared on the Atco label) the boys were returned to the clutches of Decca.

According to Townshend, "Substitute" (which started out as a parody of the Rolling Stones' "19th Nervous Breakdown") was a veiled description of the tensions and personality clashes that threatened to blow the group apart. Townshend envied Daltrey's good looks and physical agility; Roger seemed no less jealous of the songwriting prowess with which Pete appeared to have usurped the singer's original role as the group's leader and driving force. Perhaps Dippity-do (as he was called within The Who's circle, after his favorite brand of hair-setting gel) resented having become essentially Townshend's mouthpiece, the dumb blond Mod cast as the leading player in the fantasies of The Who's resident intellectual ("Bone" to his cohorts). At the same time, one of the key ingredients in The Who's violent and combustible image was the band members' habit of mincing few words in publicly discussing their mutual ill will.

PETE TOWNSHEND: I always used to work with the thought in my mind that The Who were gonna last precisely another two minutes. (*Rolling Stone,* 1968)

KEITH MOON: We really have nothing in common whatsoever apart from the music. (*Rave,* 1965)

ROGER DALTREY: Pete's got a bit of a chip because Moonie and I get all the birds whereas he, as the writer, was the most creative and thought he should have most of the attention. (*NME,* 1966)

PETE TOWNSHEND: Originally the group was run by the iron glove of Roger Daltrey . . . he used to be very tough and liked to get his own way, and if he didn't he'd shout and scream and stamp and in the end he'd punch you in the mouth. We'd all got big egos and none of us liked it. (*Record World,* 1974)

The British pop weeklies periodically ran reports of The Who's imminent breakup. In November 1965, for instance, *Melody Maker* announced that Daltrey had been replaced by Boz (of the Boz People). Chris Stamp dismissed the story as "absolute c-c-c-crap!" and Boz himself claimed to be insulted by the suggestion that he might deign to associate with mere "children playing with electronic toys." (Moon's response to that aside was: "But, after all, The Who are *rich* children playing with electronic toys.") But it was nonetheless true that Moon, Entwistle, and Townshend had had their fill of Daltrey's strong-arm tactics and had given him an ultimatum.

PETE TOWNSHEND: We all got together and politely asked Roger to leave. Kit Lambert intervened and said give him an-

other chance, and told Roger: "In the future if you want to make a point, it's got to be discussed sensibly, no more getting things done by violence." Roger said: "From now on I'll be Peaceful Perce." And I don't think he's ever raised his voice since. Roger had to modify himself from the inside, which is the hardest thing to do. I think it shows how much he cared about the group. (*Record World,* 1974)

But Townshend also tended to assert his authority in ways Entwistle and Moon found uncongenial. Following a May 1966 performance during which Pete "accidentally" struck Keith on the head with his guitar, the drummer and the bassist informed reporters that they were quitting The Who.

JOHN ENTWISTLE: Keith and I decided we'd go off and form a band with Richard Cole, who used to be our chauffeur. I said, okay . . . I'm gonna write all the stuff and Keith's gonna play drums and we're gonna be a big band—making much more

LP, U.K., 1965 (Brunswick)

LP, U.S.A., 1966 (Decca)

Single, France, 1966 (Polydor)

EP, U.K., 1966 (Reaction)

money than The Who would ever make. I was gonna call the band Led Zeppelin and I'd designed a cover of an R/101 Zeppelin going down in flames [which] I was gonna do in black and white. . . . [Then] Cole went to work for Jimmy Page, and you can see where our Zeppelin went. The name comes from [when] local bands used to meet at the local bar after our gigs and ask "How'd you go over tonight?" We'd say "We went down like a lead zeppelin." (*Rolling Stone,* 1974)

Once again, of course, a reconciliation was effected, after which the motley foursome managed to arrive at a permanent truce whose terms Townshend summed up in a *Time Out* interview five years later: "We have different basic ethics of how to live our lives, and they don't cross. Deeply written in Who philosophy is the fact that each member of the group thinks the other guy's way is total bullshit but it's-alright-by-me."

As a show of democracy, Daltrey, Moon, and Entwistle were encouraged to write two songs apiece for the band's first Lambert-produced album. According to Townshend, "my reign was over and the group was becoming a group. It was only then that we started to work together."

In the event, Daltrey managed only one song, the unmemorable "See My Way." Moon contributed the novelty instrumental "Cobwebs and Strange" (on which he and Roger played, respectively, tuba and trombone—for the first time in their lives); Keith also wrote and sang (in his high little would-be Beach Boy voice) "I Need You," which proved to be considerably less powerful than its originally announced title, "I Need You Like I Need a Hole in My Head." But the album's real surprises were "Whiskey Man" and "Boris the Spider"—wherein the band member popularly known as "the quiet one" asserted his presence for the first time.

JOHN ENTWISTLE: I don't say anything simply because Pete does all the nattering. Invariably we are asked "What is Pop Art?" or "Why do you smash your guitars?" and I'm just not interested. . . . I'm more concerned with our sound onstage and in what I'm playing . . . I think the group would fly off if they didn't have one solid person to keep it all together. (*Melody Maker*, 1966)

(*MCA Records*)

But if "the Ox" (as he was called within The Who's circle) had gone largely unnoticed by the press and even the fans, such was not the case among his fellow pop musicians, who voted him their favorite bassist in a March 1966 *Melody Maker* survey. The only Who member to place in this exclusive poll, Entwistle was heard to moan: "Why do I only get fan mail from bass guitarists, and not from girls?"

Nonetheless, Entwistle was to develop a genuine mystique, thanks to such quirky creations as his imaginary drinking buddy ("Whiskey Man") and the stickily dispatched Boris (whose namesake cousin Entwistle would subsequently encase in glass and keep on prominent display at home). Both songs were infused with a unique sense of the macabre and the perverse, for which Entwistle's own lugubrious, deadpan voice proved a perfect vehicle. (In those days, the mellowing Daltrey still refused to take part in any of Entwistle's compositions.)

PETE TOWNSHEND: Politics or my own shaky vanity might be the reason, but "Boris the Spider" was never released as a single and could have been a hit. It was *the* most requested song

we ever played onstage . . . and it was Jimi Hendrix's favorite Who song. Which rubbed me the wrong way, I can tell you. John introduced us to "Boris" the same way I introduced us to our "Generation": through a tape recorder. We assembled in John's three-by-ten-feet bedroom and listened incredulously as the strange and haunting chords emerged. Laced with words about the slightly gruesome death of a spider, the song had enough charm to send me back to my pad writing hits furiously. (*Rolling Stone*, 1971)

Townshend's own major contribution to the album was his first "mini-opera," "A Quick One (While He's Away)." As was often the case in those days, the original brainwave emanated from Kit Lambert, who encouraged Pete to string six different songs together to create pop's first extended narrative. The story line was as preposterous as the concept, with Daltrey singing the part of a forsaken damsel whose "man has been gone for nigh on a year." Entwistle, cast as Ivor the Engine Driver, offers her candy and lures her home—whereupon Townshend, as the cuckolded lover, finally returns to forgive her transgressions. The saga ends with all members of the love triangle chanting in three-part harmony the words "You are forgiven"— providing a soaring and triumphant climax not only for the mini-opera and the album, but also for The Who's stage act.

The record itself was called *A Quick One*—the first in a long series of cleverly ambiguous LP titles. In *NME* four years later, Townshend called the album "still about our best; we really discovered The Who's music for the first time, and that you could be funny on a record."

In 1966 and '67, Townshend and The Who hit their stride with a string of massive British hits that featured the same delicious blend of offbeat humor, vintage Who Power Pop, and bizarre concepts that teetered between grandiosity and sheer dottiness. "I'm a Boy," which preceded *A Quick One,* was purportedly excerpted from another Townshend pop opera, to have been set at a time in the future when parents could order the sex of their children, "and this woman orders four girls and one turns out to be a boy, so she pretends it's a girl." All the pent-up frustration and aggression of the pilled-up Mod was convincingly transferred to this hapless twenty-first-century lad railing against his enforced transvestism, and yearning for such male prerogatives as "cut[ting] myself [to] see my blood/ I wanna come home all covered in mud." Though it made absolutely no impact in America (possibly because Decca reportedly forgot to send review copies to *Cash Box* and *Billboard*), "I'm a Boy" scored The Who their first and only Number One on *Melody Maker*'s domestic hit parade.

The next single was the one that "broke" The Who Stateside at the time of their first visit, causing Decca to tack it onto the band's second album and rechristen the package in its honor. "Funny thing about 'Happy Jack,'" Moon commented in *Melody Maker*, "it's the one record we didn't think would go in the States at all." The Who had actually intended to record a different single specially for the American market, but never got around to it.

PETE TOWNSHEND: My father used to play saxophone in a band for the season on the Isle of Man when I was a kid. . . . I played on the beach a lot, and "Happy Jack" is my memories of some of the weirdos who used to live out on the sand. (*NME*, 1966)

That this nostalgic evocation of childhood innocence and cruelty ends with an incongruous yelp of "I saw ya!" can be traced to one of "Moon the Loon"'s vintage escapades.

PETE TOWNSHEND: Keith, you see, is very annoyed at not being allowed to sing; he's got an awful voice, really terrible. So when we [overdub] the voices, he feels left out, and, being Keith, he pisses about. On that particular session, we stuck him in the engineer's booth so we could do them—but that didn't work because he kept pulling funny faces at us through the glass, so that we'd laugh in the middle of the take. To stop him, we made him crouch down under the panel so that we couldn't see him—and just as we were finishing, he lifted his head up . . . so I yelled out "I saw ya!" and we left it on. (*Zigzag*, 1972)

The subsequent "Pictures of Lily" was yet another fond Townshend memory, this time concerning the joys of teenage masturbation. The punchline, of course, is that the object of the singer's onanistic fantasies turns out to have been dead for two generations. Accordingly, the British ads for "Pictures of Lily" incorporated a generous selection of ancient sepia girlie snaps.

PETE TOWNSHEND: I hope we get lots of letters of protest. . . . Really it's just a look back to that period in every boy's life when he has pin-ups. The idea was inspired by a picture my girl friend had on her wall of an old vaudeville star, Lily Bayliss. It was a 1920s postcard, and someone had written on it: "Here's another picture of Lily, hope you haven't got this one." It made me think that everyone has a pin-up period. John Entwistle and I used to swap "dirties" when we were kids at school—we used to get a kick out of buying [them] at tawdry little newspaper shops. . . . This stage is a very real part of a young person's life. When I was fourteen I got a bus pass for school without my age on it, and forged "sixteen" on it so I could get into X films. (*NME*, 1967)

The Who's next British single (never issued in the U.S.) was conceived, recorded, mixed, mastered, and released in a matter of some twenty-four hours. The endeavor was well publicized in ads and press releases that proclaimed: "The Who consider Mick Jagger and Keith Richard scapegoats for the drug problem, and as a protest against the savage sentences imposed upon them at Chichester yesterday, The Who are issuing the first of a series of Jagger-Richard songs to keep their work before the public until they are again free to record themselves." As might be expected, The Who's renditions of "The Last Time" and "Under My Thumb" were sloppy, angry, and urgent. (They also featured Townshend doubling on bass, as Entwistle was at sea, honeymooning on the *QE II*. This left Pete the group's last bachelor; he was to marry a year later.) Though the guitarist later admitted that the Stones tribute was basically another of Lambert's publicity stunts, the gesture served to enhance The Who's ever-growing reputation as rock's most passionate and idealistic standard bearers.

Despite Townshend's status as one of British pop's foremost "stars," he was also one of its most star-struck fans. By 1967, he had established himself as rock's resident philosopher, the most articulate observer and commentator ever to hold forth from the bright side of the floodlights. His interviews were wont to fill many pages of fine print (*NME* eventually took to attaching such irreverent headlines as TOWNSHEND DRONES ON); and no songwriter of Pete's caliber has ever dwelt so extensively, or with such insight, on rock & roll per se. Nor have any of his contemporaries seemed quite so obsessed with rock history or with their own place therein.

PETE TOWNSHEND: I've got tons of old *NME*s at home, and have a good old read at them whenever I can. It's great looking back over the years. (*NME*, 1966)

Rock & roll is enormous. It's one of the biggest events in history. . . . It's shear realisticness. It's like suddenly everybody getting hung up on a bum trip: mother has just fallen down the stairs, dad's lost all his money at the dog track, the baby's got TB. In comes the kid with the transistor radio, grooving to Chuck Berry. He doesn't give a shit about mom falling down the stairs. He's with rock & roll. That's what rock & roll says to life: I'm hip, I'm happy, forget your troubles and just enjoy! . . . this is the biggest single thing it has to offer. At the same time it can have content—if one desires content in something as incredible as [rock] is already. (*Rolling Stone*, 1968)

We're the only rock band on the face of this planet that knows what rock 'n' roll is all about. (*Time Out*, 1971)

(If that last comment exudes an excess of braggadocio, it should be noted that in the next breath Townshend dismissed The Who's latter-day performances as "a circus act." In any event, a strong case can be made that The Who *were* rock & roll's definitive band.)

Single, U.S.A., 1967 (*Decca*)

Single, Germany, 1968 (*Polydor*)

LP, U.S.A., 1967 (*Decca*)

LP, U.S.A., 1967 (*Decca*)

Townshend, of course, was always a sucker for "content," even as he affirmed The Who's allegiance to "Power Pop . . . the kind the Beach Boys played in the days of 'Fun Fun Fun,' which I preferred [to 'Good Vibrations']." The Who's ultimate response to the spirit of '67 was one of rock's first attempts at a thematically linked concept album. *The Who Sell Out* paid tribute to the only genuine rock & roll radio the U.K. had ever known: Radio London, which, along with the rest of the "pirates," had recently been capsized by the Blue Meanies of the House of Commons. "You don't realize how good something like the pirates are until they've gone," Pete remarked in *Melody Maker*, "so to give our album that ethereal flavor of a pirate radio station we incorporated some groovy jingles. And so The Who sell out."

This was the nearest Townshend and Co. ever got to Pop Art in the academic sense of the term; indeed, *The Who Sell Out* qualifies as the aural equivalent of an Andy Warhol soup can. Individual tracks are linked together by bona fide Radio London jingles (including such gems as "Radio London reminds you—join the church of your choice!"), or by Townshend and Entwistle's own sardonic commercials for Heinz baked beans, pimple cream, and a Charles Atlas body-building course. Some of the songs themselves, notably "Odorono," present extended narratives in the same vein.

Many of the selections, however, had been written and recorded before Townshend arrived at his weird vision of Radioland. "Armenia City in the Sky" was contributed by Pete's protégé Speedy Keen (soon to claim a British Number One hit as part of the Thunderclap Newman trio with his Townshend-produced composition "Something in the Air"). "Silas Stingy" was Entwistle's self-mocking response to being called a miser by the rest of the band for having saved up his pennies to buy a house in which he might settle down with his family. "Rael" was a fragment of another pop opera Townshend claimed to be working on, this one, he told *NME*, "about 'over-spill' when the world population becomes so great in years ahead that everyone is assigned to their one square foot of earth."

PETE TOWNSHEND: I had dithered tremendously with "Rael" . . . and intended for it to be written for full orchestra and be genuine opera. Looking back, I can't quite remember where The Who as a group fitted in, because I had Arthur Brown [another Townshend discovery from this period] lined up as the hero. . . . The story was running into about twenty scenes when Kit Lambert reminded me that while I was pretending to be Wagner, The Who needed a new single. What did I have? I had "Rael." Thus "Rael" was edited down to about four minutes—still too long for a single in those days, ironically . . . [and] it was squeezed up too tightly to make sense. Musically it is interesting because it contains a theme which I later used in Tommy for "Sparks" and the "Underture." That music was written in 1966. (*The Story of Tommy*, 1977)

Sell Out also featured the song that ultimately took "Rael"'s place as the next Who single: "I Can See for Miles," which remains (as of this writing) The Who's only American Top Ten hit. Highlighted by vintage Who guitar feedback and fuzz, gloriously arrogant lyrics, and Moon's most abandoned recorded performance—rim shots scattered helter-skelter, with a resounding crash from his bass drum on every beat—"I Can See for Miles," wrote *Melody Maker*'s reviewer, "marks the return of The Who as a major freak-out force."

But for all their intrinsic excellence, these tracks hardly jelled with the album's overall concept; and in any case the barrage of ersatz commercials and Radio London jingles peters out shortly after Side Two gets underway. *The Who Sell Out* could have been a tour de force, but the band was apparently too busy blitzing the States to see it through properly. In years to come, the lads themselves would hold diametrically opposed views of their romp through Radioland, with Moon calling it his all-time favorite Who LP even as Entwistle grumped (in *NME*): "Do you remember that dreadful thing *The Who Sell Out*? I never wanted to do that. It was done mainly for America. What a load of rubbish!"

Still, *Sell Out* evinced a light, humorous touch that would prove conspicuously absent from all subsequent Who albums. And after "I Can See for Miles," Townshend evidently lost his knack for penning classic British hit singles (The Who's highest-charting 45 during the Seventies was to be a reissue of "Substitute"). The reason in each case was Pete's having grown entirely serious about composing a full-length pop opera, to be released as The Who's next album.

The band did release three singles in 1968, all of which smacked of the throwaway. The U.K. follow-up to "Miles" was actually an overt "comedy track" about the dog races so dear to the hearts of the English populace. On the British chart sweepstakes, however, "Dogs" limped miserably, and was never released in America, where the honors went to "Call Me Lightning." Like the subsequent "Magic Bus," this was a rather mundane evocation of the Golden Age of Rock & Roll, culled from Pete's large collection of discarded demos. "I can no longer sit down with a straight face and write like that," he told *NME*, "though I was quite serious at the time. . . . In America we have to find instant hits, and that's what 'Magic Bus' is."

In the event, neither "Bus" nor "Lightning" (with its twenty-odd choruses of "Dum dum dum durang") duplicated the Stateside success of "Miles." Nonetheless, The Who's strenuous legwork on the U.S. concert circuit had finally begun to pay off.

PETE TOWNSHEND: The first major trip to the States is always treated as a group's big next step. They wave happily from the top steps of a DC-10 and set off to make their fortune. A couple of months later, after the most grueling and exhausting work they have ever done in their lives, they return triumphantly home and start to tell lies. "It was great!" "We made thousands!" It went terribly, and they lost thousands. A terrible indignity to have to suffer, especially if your angry British fans start making meat off your lies and tell you off for deserting them for money. (*Melody Maker*, 1971)*

By mid-1968, however, even U.S. rock fans unfamiliar with The Who's records had got wind of the group's reputation as in-concert dynamos. American Decca was particularly anxious to cash in on this notoriety with a live album, to which end The Who recorded their concerts at New York's Fillmore East on April 1. But Townshend felt dissatisfied with the results and subsequently burned the tapes. With no word from The Who of an imminent studio album—other than some Townshend-Lambert gibberish concerning a "pop opera" that threatened to keep the band incarcerated in the studio for nigh on a year—Decca lost all patience and pulled a fast one.

PETE TOWNSHEND: So in the end, in desperation, they got us to do this photo session, which they said was for a publicity handout, of us farting around with this absurd bus. It [the resultant Decca LP *Magic Bus: The Who on Tour*] was a culmination of all the most terrible things American record companies ever get up to. Just exploitation. They didn't care about [the pop opera], they just wanted to exploit The Who while The Who were big—though we weren't that big then—and make a few bucks, because who knows what may happen tomorrow. Plus the fact that they made it look like a live album. (*NME*, 1972)

Disregarding the existence of a double album's worth of uncollected Who 45s (including the British EP *Ready Steady Who*, featuring five songs—among them "Batman" and "Barbara Ann"—performed on a special edition of *Ready Steady Go*), Decca compounded the *Magic Bus: The Who On Tour* fiasco with random repeats from the two previous albums. "They have lived to regret it," Townshend reported in *Rolling Stone* four years later, "but not to delete it."

---

* Charges that The Who had sold out to America finally prodded Townshend into firing off a letter to **Melody Maker**: "All right! The game's up! I admit it. Not only do we charge too much for entry to our performances, but we all made it in the first place by sleeping with record company executives. . . ." The newspaper awarded Pete a free LP for writing the best letter of the week.

"Lightning" and "Bus" notwithstanding, Pete announced in *NME* at the beginning of 1968 that The Who's next single was to be a Pop Art operetta about "a boy and a girl in a plane crash, and as the plane goes down they begin to talk about the things they value in life. . . . There's a reincarnation angle to it." That the two young passengers are Mods is implied by the contents of their luggage: "Separates and lingerie, seven pairs of shoes. . . ." The noise of what Townshend called "a real Pop Art plane crash" is followed by chords that were to sound hauntingly familiar when "Glow Girl" finally surfaced on the *Odds and Sods* compilation in 1974. The song ends with the cry: "It's a girl, Mrs. Walker, it's a girl!"

When Townshend recorded "Glow Girl"'s Pop Art plane crash, The Who's own baggage was still heavily laden with Mod trappings. But then he killed off "Glow Girl" itself, appropriating its last line for the opening salvo of the first full-scale "pop opera" ever to see the light of day. In so doing, Pete Townshend effectively killed off The Who's Mod incarnation, to set the stage for a deaf, dumb, and blind boy named Tommy.

Like John Lennon and Brian Jones, Townshend went through a phase of eating acid for breakfast. "I couldn't write, play, or listen to music without being stoned," he once said, and such bizarre visions as "I'm a Boy" and "Rael" had doubtless been aided and abetted by LSD. But though his forthcoming magnum opus would provide a soundtrack for the LSD trips of a million young "seekers," *Tommy* was conceived in the aftermath of Townshend's own abandonment of all controlled substances.

PETE TOWNSHEND: What shook me about acid was when I took what turned out to be STP. . . . It was after the Monterey Pop Festival, and I spent more time outside my body looking inside myself than I've ever spent—it was like a hundred years . . . and it was on an airplane over the Atlantic. (*Zigzag*, 1972)

(John Rowlands)

A few weeks later, Townshend was "zapped" by Meher Baba (1894–1969), a purported member of that select group of "avatars," or divine messengers, that also included Krishna and Jesus Christ.

PETE TOWNSHEND: When I walked in on Meher Baba—or when he walked in on me, rather—there was absolutely no doubt in my mind that this was a real solid manifestation, and that there was no need to look further for any overall all-pervading meaning in life because it could all come from Baba. (*Time Out*, 1971)

His forty-year vow of silence notwithstanding, Baba might strike the uninitiated as an improbable avatar, with his triple chin, buffoonish grin, a cauliflower nose to rival Townshend's, and his pronounced fondness for lachrymose country & western ballads. But if Meher Baba's personal attributes ranged from the sublime to the ridiculous, this only endeared him further to his devotees. Baba lovers affected little of the solemnity of comparable Hindu-based cults; indeed, their Master's favorite motto was "Don't worry, be happy." By the same token, the urge to preach to nonbelievers was agreeably absent in most Baba followers (which may be one reason their avatar has remained a relatively obscure figure in the cosmic marketplace). "The only advice I'd give," Pete told *Time Out*, "[is] not to fuck about too much with dope, because it might put your head somewhere you don't want it to go. And I say that from experience."

KEITH MOON: Roger smoked, but that was it. The rest of us . . . went through the bloody drug corridor. . . . [Then] we stopped fucking about with the chemicals and started on the grape. Drinking suited the group a lot better. When we started drinking, that's when it all started getting together. (*Rolling Stone*, 1972)

PETE TOWNSHEND: One minute I was freaked out on acid; the next minute I was into Baba. And the fascination with opera . . . was happening at the same time. (*The Story of Tommy*, 1977)

Henceforth, all of Townshend's writing was to be infused with a spiritual quality few of his peers have equaled. It wasn't just that his commitment to Baba proved to be a permanent one (as opposed to, say, the Beatles' flirtation with the Maharishi). Townshend's real accomplishment in this respect was his insistence on fashioning his sermons and confessions in the context of gut-level rock music. (Unlike a George Harrison, Pete did not reflexively abandon the rock & roll nitty gritty for Indian instruments or quotes from the Bhagavad Gita when evoking his spiritual aspirations in a pop song format.) From the start, Townshend had approached rock almost as a religion, and he continued to do so even after he "got religion" in the more conventional sense. His subsequent work eloquently demonstrated that unalloyed rock & roll could be as valid a spiritual medium as any.

This revelation, however, did not come overnight. In grappling with the ideas that were eventually to coalesce as *Tommy*, Townshend tried his hand at forms as various as a thousand-word poem called "Amazing Journey" (some of which was preserved in the song of that title) and a "Hesse-like novel." In March 1968 Townshend informed *Melody Maker* that the opera itself would be called *The Amazing Journey*, adding: "I'd really like to call it *Journey into Space*, but there may be problems because of the old radio show."

As he then pictured it, Townshend's amazing journey would have chronicled the spiritual discoveries of an ordinary young man in two parallel sagas—one set on the level of day-to-day "reality," the other on the more rarified plane of cosmic consciousness.

PETE TOWNSHEND: Sometime later, [it] struck me that having a two-pronged concept was very cumbersome. Having to have one song about what was really happening to a person, and another about what appeared to be happening, was too much of an oscillatory way of going about things. I had to find some way of making the illusion of life organic and graspable by someone listening to the story. . . .

[The hero] became deaf, dumb, and blind when I realized that there was no way to get across, musically or dramatically, the idea of our ignorance of reality, as I had learned it to be from reading Meher Baba. Baba talked of our lives being led in an "illusion"; that we were dreaming; that reality was Infinite; and that we would realize that Infinity only through denying the lust, greed, and anger of the material world, through love, and starting our journey "back" to God.

I realized there was a parallel in the shape of the autistic child. . . . This was a straightforward analogy because . . . the illusion that we live in is one where our senses are fully functioning . . . but there are whole chunks of life which escape us. We don't really know who we are [or] how we got here . . . we don't understand life itself or what motivates it, we can't accept death and we feel it to be unjust (although it is part of the wheel of life). So I decided that the hero had to be deaf, dumb, and blind, so that, seen from our already limited point of view, his limitations would be symbolic of our own. (*The Story of Tommy*, 1977).

Townshend developed his unlikely hero's character in prose passages, one of which captured the bedridden thirteen-year-old boy's response to a visit from his parents:

I could hear it all. It was faint and even slightly reverberant in my head. I heard my father talk to me, he would talk to me often, obviously not believing that any of his words were getting through, but talking to me nonetheless. . . . I could hear all of them, all of the time, yet it was impossible for me to know what they meant when they said, "He can't hear a word we're saying!" for I couldn't even distinguish between the spoken word and odd noises in the room, they all sounded so natural, all arrived as simple vibrations of the air. I hadn't left that room since I was brought home from hospital at seventeen months. Aware of everything, I could not translate anything I heard or saw or felt. I couldn't co-ordinate the muscles of my body to move . . . I was just aware of being aware, so to speak, solid and non-active. . . . I had the power, the power, the power to stop the barrage, the unending, incessant bombardment of my soul by these relentless stimuli. So I did, slowly at first, but then faster and faster as I grew used to my new talent. Each tiny change in consciousness was a revelation to me, so green to any kind of change at all in my childhood years.

After renaming the work *Deaf Dumb and Blind Boy*, Townshend sat down with *Rolling Stone*'s Jann Wenner for the first extensive public airing of his ideas.

PETE TOWNSHEND: The album concept in general is complex. . . . We've been talking about doing an opera . . . we've been talking about a whole lot of things . . . and we've condensed all these ideas, all this energy and all these gimmicks . . . into one juicy package. . . . It's a story about a . . . deaf, dumb, and blind boy [who] is played by The Who, the musical entity. He's represented musically . . . he's seeing things basi-

cally as vibrations which we translate into music. . . . When you listen to this music you can actually become aware of the boy, and aware of what he's all about, because we are creating him as we play. . . . The boy sees things musically and in dreams and nothing has got any weight at all . . . he feels his father's touch, but he just interprets it as music. His father gets pretty upset that his son is deaf, dumb, and blind; he wants a kid that will play football and God knows what. One night he comes in and he's drunk and he sits over the kid's bed . . . trying to get through to him . . . and he starts to say: "Can you hear me?" . . . The kid won't respond, he just smiles. The father starts to hit him, and at this moment the whole thing becomes incredibly realistic. On the one side you have the dreamy music of the boy wasting his nothing life. And on the other you have the reality of the father outside, uptight, but now you've got blows, you've got communication. The father is hitting the kid . . . and the kid doesn't catch the violence. He just knows that some sensation is happening. He doesn't feel the pain, he doesn't associate it with anything. He just accepts it.*

A similar situation happens later on in the opera, where . . . an uncle comes in . . . a bit of a perv, you know . . . and starts to go through a scene with the kid's body. The boy experiences sexual vibrations, sexual experience, and again it's just basic music . . . it's got no association with sleaziness or undercover or any of the things normally associated with sex. . . . Slowly but surely the kid starts to get it together out of this incredible simplicity in his mind. He starts to realize he can see and he can hear and he can speak . . . all the time it's been there in front of him. . . . The music has got to explain what happens, that the boy elevates, and finds something that is incredible. To us it is nothing to be able to see and hear and speak, but to him it's absolutely incredible and overwhelming. This is what we want to [convey] musically. (*Rolling Stone*, 1968)

"I just lived with the story . . . and started to write songs," Townshend recalled a decade later. "I got Tommy's name from midair, but it suited. The middle letters were *om* which was aptly mystical, and it was an English name associated with the war and heroism."

The story still required a beginning and a conclusion. Why was the boy deaf, dumb, and blind in the first place? And what use did he make of his spiritual powers after he regained the use of his senses? Townshend decided to subject the infant Tommy Walker to a severe trauma: Captain Walker, missing in action during the First World War, reappears in 1921 to discover his wife in flagrante delicto. Mrs. Walker and her boyfriend respond to this intrusion by summarily bumping the captain off. Young Tommy, present at the scene of the crime, is then advised in no uncertain terms: "You didn't see it, you didn't hear it, won't say nothing to no one. . . ." Tommy is so shattered by the experience that he is literally struck deaf, dumb, and blind.

Before recovering his vision and hearing, the adolescent Tommy emerges from his coma to become a "Pinball Wizard," exercising with consummate skill his undamaged sense of touch. (Townshend later admitted that his already farfetched melodrama was given this ludicrous twist "as a ploy to get [rock scribe] Nik Cohn, who is an avid pinball player, to be a little more receptive to my plans for a Rock Opera." The notoriously cynical and antiprogressive Cohn duly passed advance word that *Tommy* was "brilliant . . . as good as anything [Townshend] has done, meaning . . . as good as anything anyone has done.")

The boy's Cousin Kevin was eventually cast as the villain of this vignette.

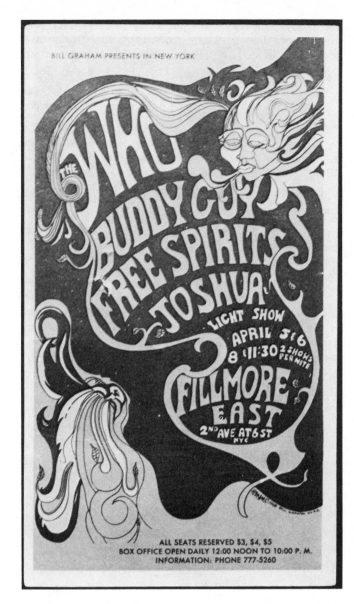

WHO
THE
BUDDY GUY
FREE SPIRITS
JOSHUA
LIGHT SHOW
APRIL 5 & 6
8 & 11:30 2 SHOWS PER NITE
FILLMORE EAST
2ND AVE AT 6 ST
NYC

ALL SEATS RESERVED $3, $4, $5
BOX OFFICE OPEN DAILY 12:00 NOON TO 10:00 P.M.
INFORMATION: PHONE 777-5260

When it becomes evident that the one visual stimulus to elicit any response from Tommy is his own reflection in the mirror, Mrs. Walker smashes the glass in exasperation—and the boy is miraculously cured! He becomes an overnight sensation, picking up a large youthful following as he preaches about his Amazing Journey. Tommy's subsequent metamorphosis from holy fool to a veritable Rock & Roll Messiah is stage-managed by his crafty Uncle Ernie, who turns the Tommy phenomenon into an organized cult. Tommy's fans are compelled to forswear weed and bottle, and to simulate his Amazing Journey by sealing their bodily orifices with eyeshades and corks to engage in endless rounds of pinball. Eventually they rise up in unison with a great cry of "We're not gonna take it!" and leave their fallen idol to face the divine music alone in Tommy's genuinely stirring "Listening to You . . ." swansong.

Lambert, of course, was thrilled with the entire concept, and egged Pete on at every turn. Though Daltrey would later confess that he "didn't know what [Tommy] was about until it had been out three months," Townshend did his best to involve the others in Tommy's creation. Entwistle was given the congenial assignment of composing the episodes about Cousin Kevin and Uncle Ernie, and Moon was also to receive a songwriting credit, though he didn't write a note. Townshend subsequently re-

vealed that upon expressing his delight with Moon's loony notion that Tommy's religious retreats be modeled after England's working-class "holiday camps," Keith announced that he would compose the sequence himself. To forestall this alarming possibility, Townshend scurried home to whip off "Tommy's Holiday Camp"—which he then magnanimously credited to the man who had inspired it.

As the marathon recording sessions got underway, Townshend found himself caught in a tug of war between Lambert—"who wanted to bring in hundreds of fucking French horns and all that"—and the rest of the band, who had reason to wonder what "all that" had to do with The Who. His own grandiose visions notwithstanding, Townshend agreed that the group's identity remained paramount, and that it was imperative Tommy be reproducible onstage. In the end, the double album incorporated only one French horn—masterfully wielded by John Entwistle—which ushers in the Overture with a Beethoven-like blast.

When the album was released two weeks later, Melody Maker's Chris Welch called it "an important facelift to the battered image of pop." (The paper subsequently named Tommy "Pop LP of the Year," saying: "One can imagine it lasting as long as music.") NME, however, deemed the music a "disappointment" and the lyrics downright "sick."

PETE TOWNSHEND: It was rated where it shouldn't have been and wasn't rated where it should have been. It *should* be rated as a successful attempt to tell a story in rock music. . . .

We were going down the drain; we needed challenging after putting out corny singles like "Magic Bus" and "Dogs." Making Tommy really united the group, and that was the best thing about it. The problem is that it has elevated the group to heights they haven't attained. (NME, 1970)

As had been the case with Sgt. Pepper two years earlier, it was in America that the acclaim and the controversy reached truly epic proportions. Vice-President Agnew singled out "Acid Queen"—the song in which the comatose Tommy is subjected to an LSD trip—as a corrupting influence on the young, and strongly advised radio stations to ban it. Leonard Bernstein, on the other hand, extended The Who his august seal of approval. Albert Goldman of The New York Times hailed Tommy as "a work of innovative power and philosophical profundity," "a powerful steel blade blowing all the bull out of the current atmosphere . . . [to] suck in great draughts of clean, cool, electric-spark-smelling ozone, like a heart-expanding whiff from a giant popper." Goldman went on to note that Tommy's leitmotif—the "See me, feel me, touch me, heal me!" refrain—"sounds the current generation's most urgent demand."

The funny thing was, Tommy wasn't even an opera. Many of the songs were third-person narratives; among those that weren't, only Tommy's own lines (sung by Daltrey) were consistently handled by a particular member of The Who. (The words of Tommy's mother, by contrast, are alternately voiced by three different members of the group.) Strictly speaking, Tommy was a cantata, or perhaps an oratorio. Needless to say, however, "the world's first Rock Cantata" hardly carried the same authoritative ring as "the world's first Rock Opera." In the best tradition of "Pop Art" and "Auto-Destruction," Lambert and Townshend had now managed to snow both America's Rock Biz *and* its cultural Establishment.

PETE TOWNSHEND: Tommy was definitely a result of image building. I mean, I'd spent two years writing the thing, but it was still more of an image idea than a musical idea. And it was the whole thing of being taken up in the States as a musical masterpiece that threw us. From selling 1,500 copies of *The Who Sell Out*, right, we were suddenly selling 20 million or whatever of *Tommy*. It was the ridiculous to the sublime. It had to have repercussions. Christ Almighty, we thought, here we are being told we are musical geniuses and all we are is a bunch of scumbags. (*NME*, 1971)

If parts of the album sounded uncharacteristically muted and lyrical, *Tommy* metamorphosed onstage into an hour-long barrage of Power Pop. (The Who's concert renditions dispensed with Pete's acoustic guitars and John's French horn, along with the slower numbers "Christmas," "Cousin Kevin," "Sensation," and "Welcome.") When The Who presented *Tommy*'s world premiere on May 10, 1969—about two weeks before the album's appearance—Chris Welch reported in *Melody Maker*: "A lot of the story line escapes the memory owing to The Who's partially successful attempt to make the audience deaf, dumb, and blind."

In that spirit, The Who took *Tommy* on the road. Donning a fringed leather jacket, Roger abandoned his Dippity-do, sprouted long golden ringlets, and struck the Olympian poses that were to earn him the epithet "Greek God" Daltrey. No longer did the singer seem, as one reviewer had unkindly put it, "The Who's weakest link." To millions of new converts who flocked to see rock's latest international superstars, the bare-chested, moon-eyed Roger *was* Tommy.

The Who's electrifying emergence at the top of the rock pile also brought its share of misadventures. During *Tommy*'s American premiere at New York's Fillmore East, the theater caught fire and Townshend was arrested for assaulting the police officer

who interrupted The Who's performance. Pete struck again while playing *Tommy* to four hundred thousand charter members of Woodstock Nation as the sun rose over Yasgur's Farm:

KEITH MOON: Abbie Hoffman jumped onstage at Woodstock and started protesting, and the kids didn't cheer until Pete whacked him with his guitar. If he wants to protest, let him do it on a soap box—not on our stage. (*NME*, 1970)

ROGER DALTREY: Woodstock was a nightmare. We got there at six, and we didn't go on till six the next morning. (*NME*, 1970)

JOHN ENTWISTLE: And somebody put LSD in our water just before we were due onstage. (*Crawdaddy*, 1974)

Milking the Pop Opera hoax for all it was worth, The Who then proceeded to rock the sedate halls of New York's Metropolitan Opera House and a series of similar venues on the Continent.

PETE TOWNSHEND: We were playing in fucking opera houses . . . [which] are very small; there are fifteen hundred people usually and you could see every face. . . . Only about a hundredth of the kids who wanted to see us could; we'd go in and play and like the first twenty rows would be Polydor [Records] people, or Prince Rainier and his royal family. . . . I just thought it was the biggest hype bullshit I had ever heard of . . . say there's an old guy in a bow tie out there, he's come to write up a review in some opera paper and . . . just sits there with his fingers in his ears. It's impossible to work when someone's doing that. (*Rolling Stone*, 1970)

In 1971 The Who finally tried to abandon *Tommy* for a new stage act, but they were never able to shake off the Frankenstein monster Townshend had raised.

PETE TOWNSHEND: About once every two weeks I receive a letter from an amateur dramatic society, a school, or a college, and occasionally from theatrical impresarios, for permission to [perform] *Tommy*. (*The Story of Tommy*, 1977)

Townshend's deaf, dumb, and blind boy was adopted by troupes as illustrious as Les Grands Ballets Canadiens and the Seattle Opera Company. Then a fast-talking New Yorker named Lou Reizner hit upon the 64-million-dollar notion of turning the rock opera into a *real opera*, sung by *rock superstars* to the accompaniment of a sixty-four-piece *orchestra*. Reizner conjured an additional character—the Narrator—to take care of all the third-person songs, and "because Lou's such a persuasive guy," Townshend told *NME*, "I just found myself getting involved."

While Wil Malone scored Pete's ditties for the London Symphony Orchestra, Townshend and Reizner rounded up the likes of Ringo Starr (as Uncle Ernie), Steve Winwood (the Stepfather), Maggie Bell (the Mother), John Entwistle (Cousin Kevin), and Rod Stewart (the ousted Pinball Wizard). Reizner had originally eyed Stewart for the leading role, but Narrator Townshend was so distraught at the prospect of "people comparing Rod's interpretations to Roger's" that he persuaded Daltrey to step back into the deaf, dumb, and blind boy's shoes.

Indeed, the production's most impressive feature was the resonance and authority Daltrey's voice had attained since the appearance of the original Who album. The bloated rearrangements, however, often sounded closer in spirit to Mantovani than to The Who. The orchestral *Tommy* is perhaps best savored as an audacious triumph of unadulterated kitsch, though

Single, U.S.A., 1969 (Decca)

LP, Spain, 1971 (Polydor)

A U.S. single from **The Who Live at Leeds,** *never accorded a general release*

Single, France, 1971 (Polydor)

at the time even so acerbic an observer as *NME*'s Roy Carr pronounced it "a truly monumental achievement . . . in the same way that *Sgt. Pepper* was." Townshend, for his part, thought it was "just great to sit here and hear the London Symphony Orchestra playing a piece of my music."

These words, however, were belied by Pete's actions during Reizner's live presentation benefiting the Stars Organization for Spastics. Originally scheduled at London's Albert Hall, the opera was obliged to relocate to the Rainbow Theater when the management came to the last-minute conclusion that *Tommy*'s content was "unsavory." On December 9, 1972, two thousand punters found that they'd paid fifty dollars each to witness less an opera than a series of superstar ego trips. Oblivious to their purported dramatic roles, Stewart cavorted as if he were fronting the Faces instead of the London Symphony Orchestra; Keith Moon (substituting for Ringo) pranced about in a leather jockstrap; and Entwistle just stood there wondering what to do with his hands. Though Daltrey at least played his part with distinction, the Narrator distinguished himself by insulting the conductor, missing his cues, and fluffing his lines. Pete concluded the performance by wiping his behind with the lyric sheet he had been holding all the while. Though a spokesman later claimed that Townshend had been suddenly seized by stomach cramps, one wondered whether he wasn't simply sick of *Tommy*.

Many longtime fans were; they could never forgive the deaf, dumb, and blind boy for delivering their cult heroes to the masses. But *Tommy*'s—and Pete's—Amazing Journey was far from over. From the beginning, both Townshend and Lambert had operated with the words "soon to be a major motion picture" very much in mind.

PETE TOWNSHEND: Kit Lambert started with The Who for the sole purpose of making a movie. And it's something he desperately wants to do before he's ready to die. . . . When I suggested we might have another bash at talking about a movie

of *Tommy*, he literally jumped for joy and leapt around the room and kissed me and hugged me and took me out to dinner. . . . That's how much Kit wants to make a movie. (*Crawdaddy*, 1971)

Yet they insisted that the film be made on a bottomless budget, by a top director, with Pete calling the shots. In 1974, an irresistible combination of resources and talent finally materialized in Robert Stigwood and Ken Russell. A director whose reputation for flamboyance was comparable to The Who's own, Russell's credits included films about such musical luminaries as Mahler and Tchaikovsky. He was also recommended by his appraisal (in *NME*) of Townshend's Rock Opera as "the greatest work of art the twentieth century has provided."

For his all-star cast, Russell drew in equal measure from the jukebox (Elton John, Eric Clapton, Tina Turner) and the silver screen (Ann-Margret, Oliver Reed, Jack Nicholson). Townshend later said he had wanted a larger quota of rock & rollers (including Lou Reed or David Bowie as the Acid Queen!) and fewer professional actors who couldn't sing rock if their lives depended on it. Once again all of The Who became deeply embroiled in the project, with Daltrey and Moon performing so superbly (as Tommy and Uncle Ernie) that both would subsequently develop acting careers. Entwistle, however, settled for a behind-the-scenes role as musical arranger.

According to Townshend, scoring the film was the most monumental job of his career. The decision not to use any dialogue obliged Pete to rewrite half of his original songs and to add several new ones to tie up loose ends. The tune "1921," for instance, was changed to "1951" (Tommy, after all, could hardly have made his mark as a pinball wizard and rock & roll Messiah had he been born during the *First* World War!); the father's murder was made far more explicit, and followed by the Narrator's declamation (in "Amazing Journey") "Now he is deaf! Now he is dumb! Now he is blind!" instead of "Deaf, dumb, and blind boy, he's in a quiet vibration land."

But the lyrics' newfound clarity and internal consistency were accompanied by a commensurate decline in musical inspiration. The revolving cast of session musicians that supplemented— and often replaced—Pete, John, and Keith on the soundtrack was no substitute for the real McCoy. And the sound of Ann-Margret making cocktail-hour pap of "1921" and "Christmas" was enough to make a Who freak gag.

For some viewers, that might seem an appropriate reaction to the whole of Russell's preposterous, excessive, and self-indulgent extravaganza, a *Tommy* as colossally kitsch as Reizner's. Ann-Margret writhing about in two-hundred gallons of baked beans, indeed! What had this to do with our collective Amazing Journey of five years earlier, with the acid and the mysticism, and their attendant ideals and revelations?

PETE TOWNSHEND: I think to a great degree you've got to live with the fact that [The Who] sold out. (*The Story of Tommy*, 1977)

CHRIS LEAN [merchandising director]: The combination of big film stars and top rock performers is unique. We're undertaking one of the biggest merchandising operations in years . . . there'll be *Tommy* T-shirts, *Tommy* badges, *Tommy* patches, *Tommy* sweatshirts, *Tommy* belts, *Tommy* shoulder bags, *Tommy* mirrors, *Tommy* neck pendants, and *Tommy* ties . . . [and] they will all be for sale. (*Melody Maker*, 1975)

PETE TOWNSHEND: Many Who fans feel the *Tommy* film is not what The Who are about, or even what *Tommy* is about. In fact, it is exactly what it is about. (*The Story of Tommy*, 1977)

He was at least half right. The original *Tommy,* after all, had been nothing if not preposterous and excessive. These are among the very qualities to which it owed its greatness; without them there would have been no Who in the first place—nor, for that matter, could there have been any such thing as rock & roll.

But if Townshend's original Rock Opera was largely a triumph of sheer chutzpah, what it lost in subsequent incarnations was its innocence, the purity of inspiration with which it had been conceived. Then again, by the mid-Seventies that could also be said of the rock biz in general, and even of The Who.

What to follow *Tommy?* The Who marked time in 1970 with a long-overdue live album, whose cover artwork parodied the spate of bootlegs that had preceded it. Though *Live at Leeds* consisted essentially of the non-*Tommy* segment of The Who's *Tommy* stage act, it came across as something of an about-face, a "return to the roots." Highlights included Eddie Cochran's "Summertime Blues" and Johnny Kidd's "Shaking All Over" (one of Britain's few bona fide pre-Beatles rock & roll classics), along with The Who's traditional "My Generation" finale and "Magic Bus" encore.

(John Rowlands)

PETE TOWNSHEND: We've gone for the hard stuff. The first number of the show, "Heaven and Hell," was something written by John Entwistle which I was very keen to get on, but it didn't come out well enough. . . . What hits you when you listen to [*Live at Leeds*] is how much you need to see The Who . . . there's all kinds of bits where sticks are obviously in the air when they're supposed to be on the drums and arms are spinning where they are supposed to be playing solos . . . but I'm just going to put it out anyway. (*Rolling Stone,* 1970)

Melody Maker then announced that "The Who and Track Records are to wage war against the rising price of records . . . [with] an EP of four completely new songs ['Postcard,' 'Now I'm a Farmer,' 'Naked Eye,' and 'Water'] available at 9s. 3d., the current price of singles." But the EP never materialized

because, as Townshend later admitted, "the tracks weren't really very good." Most eventually surfaced on the 1974 outtakes compilation *Odds and Sods.* Pete, meanwhile, applied his ample imagination to the problem of a sequel to *Tommy.*

PETE TOWNSHEND: You break down people's preconceptions . . . by doing something like *Tommy* . . . but the thing which broke down their fucking preconceptions instigates a new lot. It really did escape me that in fact the first thing people are going to want to hear after listening to *Tommy* is, of course, *Tommy* again. (*Rolling Stone,* 1970)

Townshend finally rose to the occasion with a blueprint for a concept album, theatrical event, and feature-length film, all rolled into one. This time, however, he seems to have overreached himself.

PETE TOWNSHEND: *Lifehouse* was originally a science fiction concept with a concert at the heart of it [and] a story about an approaching army heading toward this concert and busting in at the climax. . . . At one point I was imagining a ten-week concert, not just with The Who but with lots of other musicians as well. It was set in the future and this was a sort of illegal concert which they were trying to track down and stamp out. Like an expunged church: the lost art of rock & roll. When they finally break in, the concert has reached such a height that the audience are about to disappear. It was kind of a nutty idea. (*NME,* 1980)

We were . . . investigating a new kind of rock theater. The idea was to get two thousand people and keep them in a theater [London's Old Vic, which The Who actually booked for this purpose] with us for six months [until] characters would emerge from them. . . . But getting the idea through to film people is impossible. (*Melody Maker,* 1971)

JOHN ENTWISTLE: I never understood what that [*Lifehouse*] was all about. (*Rolling Stone,* 1971)

PETE TOWNSHEND: Roger [was] ringing me up every day, trying to dissuade me from doing the project, saying what we really needed to do is to work on the road. We eventually gave up, and, to put it quite frankly, just went back into the old mold. We went into the studio, I picked out a few of the numbers [from *Lifehouse*], we recorded them. (*Crawdaddy,* 1971)

Lambert, at least, was crestfallen at *Lifehouse*'s abortion, after which he and The Who drifted apart. On the *Who's Next* album, longtime engineer Glyn Johns inherited the role of producer.

PETE TOWNSHEND: Kit still has bigger ambitions for us. But what we want is to be able to justify ourselves to each other as musicians. We are at the point where the last thing we're thinking about is image. Yet Kit's still talking about concerts on the moon. (*NME,* 1971)

Lifehouse notwithstanding, *Who's Next* was presented as an old-fashioned grab-bag of unrelated songs. Though Townshend would later tell *Melody Maker* that the LP wasn't strong enough and should never have been released, many critics still consider *Who's Next* to be the band's finest album. Propelled by the ARP synthesizer that had become Townshend's latest obsession, tracks like "Baba O'Riley" certainly sounded unassailably "progressive."

PETE TOWNSHEND: This is the way we expected most of the music in the film to sound. (*Melody Maker,* 1971)

["Baba O'Riley"] was a number I wrote when I was doing

these experiments with tapes on the synthesizer. Among my plans for the concert at the Old Vic was to take a person out of the audience and feed information—height, weight, astrological details, beliefs, and behavior—about that person into the synthesizer. The synthesizer would then select notes from the pattern of that person. It would be like translating a person into music. On this particular track I programmed details about the life of Meher Baba, and that provides the backing for the number. (*NME*, 1971)

Synthesizers also predominated on another extended piece, the anthemlike "Won't Get Fooled Again," which was to garner more FM airplay in America than any other Seventies rock "classic," with the possible exceptions of Eric Clapton's "Layla" and Led Zeppelin's "Stairway to Heaven."

PETE TOWNSHEND: "Won't Get Fooled Again" [is] not an anti-Establishment song, more an anti-anti song. It's anti people who are negative. . . . I wrote [it] at a time when I was getting barraged by people at the Eel Pie commune. They live opposite me, and there was like a love affair going on between me and them. . . . At one point there was an amazing scene where the commune was really working, but then the acid started flowing and I got on the end of some psychotic conversations and I just thought "oh, fuck it!" I don't really want to be talking to people about things flying around in space. I'm very old-fashioned, I'm twenty-six, I've seen it all and done it all in a lot of ways, and I've come full circle to being right in the middle of the road. And that's not as boring as it sounds. (*NME*, 1971)

According to Townshend, The Who had virtually completed a follow-up album in May 1972, but it sounded too much like "a shadow of *Who's Next*" for his liking. Some selections—"Join Together," "Relay"—were issued as singles; others—like "Is It in My Head" and "Love Reign O'er Me"—were held in reserve when Pete began to receive glimmerings of a new magnum opus.

PETE TOWNSHEND: I said we needed an album, [but] couldn't keep treading water. . . . I got this idea for a project out of The Who having been going for ten years . . . an album [to] encapsulate everything The Who had ever done with a big sort of flourish, so we could really start afresh. (*Melody Maker*, 1973)

ROGER DALTREY: The Who don't just go in and record ten songs 'cause we need an album. Every [Who] album has always been far more than that. (*NME*, 1973)

PETE TOWNSHEND: We want something really big. *Tommy* lasted for three years as a stage act; *Who's Next* lasted three months. So now we are after something for the main body of the stage act—something like *Tommy*. (*Disc*, 1972)

In mid-1973 Townshend announced (in *NME*) that he was obsessively at work on "a new Rock Opera." Once again he intended to devote four sides of vinyl to chronicling the spiritual awakening of an adolescent boy. Only this time the boy was named Jimmy, and Jimmy was a Mod.

PETE TOWNSHEND: It's about teenage life. And funnily enough, all those real classics—"Generation," "Substitute," "I'm a Boy"—were good because I'm *good* at writing about teenage life. . . . I'm finding myself writing about being kicked out of home, parents not understanding, first drug use, first screw. . . . I shouldn't call this an opera 'cause it's even less of an opera than *Tommy* was, but what I'm trying to do is get the

writing to reflect the change in The Who's character, [to] start out with a sort of "Can't Explain" '65 feel . . . [and] end with an incredible amount of synthesizer. (*NME*, 1972)

As it turned out, even the beginning of *Quadrophenia* was awash in synthesizers, and (quotes from the High Numbers' "I'm the Face" and "Zoot Suit" notwithstanding) none of the music sounded remotely like The Who of 1965. Neither did *Quadrophenia* bear much resemblance to *Tommy*. "The main difference," said Pete, "is that it's not a story—more a series of impressions [and] memories."

Nonetheless, the hero of Townshend's impressionistic odyssey is indeed the archetypal Mod of "I Can't Explain" and "My Generation." "Magically bored on a quiet street corner," Jimmy is frustrated, inarticulate, violent, and confused. A pill head and a Who freak, he stoically endures his menial job in the greater cause of improving his wardrobe: "My jacket's gonna be cut slim and checked, maybe a touch of seersucker. . . ." Thus resplendent in his Mod uniform, Jimmy rides off on a "GS scooter with [his] hair cut neat" to battle Rockers on Brighton Beach.

"Me folks had let me down, rock had let me down, women had let me down, work wasn't worth the effort, school isn't even worth mentioning," Jimmy declares in the prose passage Townshend included on the LP sleeve. "But I never felt that I'd be let down by being a Mod." His illusions, however, are shattered when he discovers that the Ace Face who had rallied the charge at Brighton is employed as a lowly bellboy at a nearby hotel. Thus stripped of his identity, smashed out of his skull, Jimmy finally attains some sort of spiritual catharsis and self-reconciliation clinging to a rock off Brighton Beach in the pouring rain.

PETE TOWNSHEND: He's no longer got to be tough and a winner, or a daredevil, to earn other people's respect. He's just realized the emptiness of those labels stuck on what is just a spiritual desperation which everybody has. . . . It's not the miracle cure of *Tommy*, it's just the reverse. He's being stripped of all excuses, and in the last song . . . [he's] on his knees, but stronger crying in the rain than he ever was drinking gin, knocking back pills and kicking Rockers and whatever it was he thought was the meaning of life. (*Melody Maker*, 1973)

ROGER DALTREY: There's no doubt who is the best rock & roll writer after listening to this one. [*Quadrophenia*] really is amazing. (*NME*, 1973)

None of The Who had ever sounded so good, or played so well; Entwistle's incomparably melodic bass work and painstaking horn overdubs were especially noteworthy. But there were moments where *Quadrophenia* didn't quite ring true, when Townshend was obviously using Jimmy as a mouthpiece for his own spiritual hobbyhorse. (In "The Dirty Jobs," for instance, Pete has the Mod ruminating about his "karma"—a word that did not enter the English language until 1967.) But apart from the pitfalls—endemic to concept albums—or forcing individual songs to fit a larger scheme, the most contrived aspect of *Quadrophenia* is the premise behind the title itself.

PETE TOWNSHEND: ["Quadrophrenia"] is sort of a jokey expansion of "schizophrenia," but it's a bit of a mouthful with the extra *r*. *Quadrophenia* is something of a pun on "quadrophonic" as well. The whole album has been put together as a quadrophonic composition . . . stereo is a bit of a compromise. (*NME*, 1973)

The "characters" in this "opera" are the four sides of Jimmy's split personality, each of which is supposed to be embodied in a member of The Who: "a tough guy, a helpless dancer" (Daltrey); "a romantic, is it me for a moment?" (Entwistle); "a bloody lunatic, I'll even carry your bags" (Moon); and "a begger, a hypocrite, love reign o'er me" (Townshend). Each is represented by his own theme song, and though these are superbly set forth in *Quadrophenia*'s instrumental interludes, where they ultimately coalesce into a unified whole, the extra lyrical baggage proved to be a bit more than Pete's Mod odyssey could cope with.

For The Who, the most disappointing aspect of *Quadrophenia* was that it simply didn't work as a concert centerpiece. This was partly attributable to the show's reliance on prerecorded tapes of Townshend's synthesizers, Entwistle's horns, and sundry sound effects. *Rolling Stone* reported that The Who's second performance of their magnum opus collapsed in disaster "when the tape synch warning signal on Moon's headphones came in about fifteen seconds out of step with the band. Townshend realized it couldn't be held together [and] exploded—dragged [the sound engineer] over the sound deck, knocked an amp over and stormed offstage. After raging about the dressing room for half an hour, he cooled off enough to come back. But *Quadrophenia* was abandoned for the night, and instead The Who ran through a selection of golden oldies."

Quadrophenia ultimately became an endurance test for the band. Audiences, in turn, were left utterly baffled by Daltrey's long-winded introductions—to which Townshend would frequently take exception, interrupting Roger with his own interpretations. One night Entwistle cut them both short with a curt "Fuck it!"

ROGER DALTREY: We tried to make it another *Tommy*, and it was my fault because I especially tried to get that kind of feel into the act again. . . . By the beginning of [1974] . . . it got very oppressive. We knew we weren't really communicating. (*NME*, 1974)

Though the album was a critical and commercial success, reaching number two on both sides of the Atlantic, Townshend's brave and often brilliant attempt "to encapsulate The Who with a big flourish" signally failed to realize two of his originally stated goals. *Quadrophenia* neither presented The Who with a new stage act, nor flushed the past out of their system so they might "really start afresh."

For the remainder of the decade, The Who's output ranged from nostalgic flashbacks (including the two outtakes compilations, 1974's *Odds and Sods** and 1979's *The Kids Are Alright*) to rock & roll confessionals on the quandaries of the Aging Superstar trapped in his own past. *The Who by Numbers* (1975) is a brutally honest and altogether fascinating self-portrait, with Townshend lacerating himself as "a faker," "a paper clown," "a failure," and "nothing but a well-fucked sailor" in "How-

Moon the Loon proudly displays his gold record for Quadrophenia *(RDR Productions)*

ever Much I Booze (There Ain't No Way Out)." Roger, in turn, reacted against Pete's own anger and defeatism by attacking with genuine fury lyrics like "Goodbye all you punks, stay young and stay high/just hand me my checkbook while I crawl off to die." In the absence of Townshend's synthesizers, *By Numbers* was The Who's sparest and hardest-hitting LP since *My Generation*.

Nonetheless, the group's recorded output between 1971 and 1978—*Quadrophenia, Odds and Sods,* the *Tommy* soundtrack, and *By Numbers*—added up to an implicit acknowledgment that The Who were no longer "happening." They had turned into

---

* Compiler John Entwistle described Odds and Sods *as "a parallel 'Oo album . . . a potted history of what The Who* might *have released as their greatest hits." His original track lineup included such singles as "Join Together," "Water," and "I Don't Know Myself."*

(Dave Kleinwaks)

museum pieces, a status that Pete alternately reveled in and reacted against. Meanwhile, the rapidly aging Townshend, Entwistle, and Moon (if not the supernaturally well-preserved Daltrey) came to appear more and more incongruous as the embodiment of the fantasies that The Who had been so spectacularly successful at evoking; such, it seems, are the long-term risks of relying so heavily on "image." And so The Who were to wind up, by the turn of the decade, at the top of the New Wave's "dinosaur" hit lists.

Pete, at least, had seen it coming, even before the appearance of *Quadrophenia:*

PETE TOWNSHEND: To use very blunt terminology we're becoming less of a rock band and more of a circus act. . . . The group felt that we were better waving the banner for The Who and the Sixties . . . because we weren't capable of doing anything new. . . . I thought that we *were* capable of getting [*Lifehouse*] together and working on new formulas . . . [with] synthesizers and all the technical things that are available, but also using a whole other sort of new energy from within the group. Combining it all in one fell swoop, we could really sort of capture what was going on. I think maybe the group isn't capable of doing it now, though it was wrong not to try. But then I think The Who are The Who are The Who, and we're very much stuck with that. If we want to do anything different, we are going to have to break up, because we've got too many preconceptions of ourselves, and are too much ingrained in our own history and our own way of doing things—which admittedly works, but it's not changing at the same rate that the audience needs the change. (*NME,* 1972)

I don't know why Jagger and people like that are still able to get up on stage and prance about like idiots. It is very difficult to write like an enthused child, which is how rock should be written . . . if you don't feel like an enthused child all the time, or if you're not a showman and can't switch it on and off like a light bulb. . . . A lot of [rock stars] are noble savages. I've never been like that, there's always been something missing. (*NME,* 1973)

If a strong sense of mutual loyalty precluded The Who's breakup, each member nonetheless carved himself a small niche as a solo performer by the mid-Seventies. The first to do so was John Entwistle, who, like George Harrison in the Beatles, had accumulated a large backlog of songs. "It's too late for me to get my name pushed forward within The Who," he told *Melody Maker,* "so I have to try and do it outside the group." Nineteen seventy-one's *Smash Your Head Against the Wall* and 1972's *Whistle Rymes* treated connoisseurs of "Boris the Spider" and "Fiddle About" to uninterrupted orgies of voyeurism and voodoo, though the music was plainly too lumbering and lugubrious for the hit parade.

JOHN ENTWISTLE: My face on the cover [of *Smash Your Head Against the Wall*] looks like the death mask of a mongol. I went to my doctor and asked him for a chest X-ray on which I could superimpose my face, hidden behind a misted-up piece of sickly green plastic. So he said, "Haha, what you need is one of a heart disease patient, I have just the thing for you." The fellow's long since dead, I hope. (*Rolling Stone,* 1971)

In 1972 Entwistle formed a group to perform his solo material in concert. After Ro-Ro tested the waters with a series of free concerts at English universities, John changed the act's name to Rigor Mortis and released an album of Fifties rock & roll parodies called *Rigor Mortis Sets In.*

JOHN ENTWISTLE: What I'm really saying is that rigor mortis has set in to rock & roll, and here's a group playing it. (*NME,* 1972)

ROGER DALTREY: The problem with John is, speaking completely honestly, that he hasn't got stage presence. Not in the way that he could ever front a group. (*Melody Maker,* 1973)

Entwistle changed his band's billing yet again, to Ox, under which rubric he issued 1975's *Mad Dog.* By this time, however, both John's inspiration and the public's interest seemed to have run their course. It was not until 1981 that he finally tried again, with the assistance of Eagles guitarist Joe Walsh. *Too Late the Hero* replaced its predecessors' perverse idiosyncrasies with straightforward, well-produced Product. Contemporary FM rock programmers duly responded—to give Entwistle his first solo hit.

The catalyst for both facets of Daltrey's solo career was his old friend *Tommy.* After claiming an unplanned British solo hit with his symphonically scored reading of "I'm Free" (from the Reizner production), Roger was persuaded by Adam Faith (the

(RDR Productions)

Roger Daltrey as Franz Liszt (Peter Kanze Collection)

Touring England with Traffic in 1967, for instance, Moon rigged up fellow drummer Jim Capaldi's timpani with invisible wires, so that when the moment came for Capaldi to attack them with a dramatic flourish, they suddenly levitated out of reach. A few months later Moon arrived for a *New Musical Express* interview an hour late—sporting a crown, robe, and scepter. ''Matters of state, you know,'' apologized the self-styled prince. The tales of Moon the Loon multiplied as the poses and pranks grew ever more elaborate. In 1971 an *NME* interviewer recalled waiting at Moon's country estate for the drummer's belated entrance:

> The gleaming Mercedes skidded to a halt. . . . The electronically operated driver's window slid down and a Luger pistol was poked through, pointing directly at me from behind a pair of dark glasses, and topped by a chauffeur's cap a face peered and the heavily accented voice demanded: ''Vy are you here? Who do you vish?''
> My first reaction was to change my underpants, but as a small dark figure emerged and cordially asked, ''Spot of brandy, old chap?'' I realized that I was in the right place. . . . ''Herr'' Keith Moon laughed his maniacal laugh.
> Keith eased himself into an antediluvian armchair and swapped the top half of his uniform for a smoking jacket, put on a pair of carpet slippers, reached out to the phonograph, and placed the steel handle on an ancient 78. As the quavering sounds of a soprano voice singing ''Rose Marie'' hissed and crackled . . . Keith sat acting the retired colonel from the rubber plantations of India, muttering: ''It'll never come back, this music, never come back. Ah, this long-haired stuff nowadays! All balderdash, I tell you. . . .'' He assumed a gracious pose and placed a cigarette at the end of a foot-long holder.

early British pop star turned producer) to cut a new album in the same lush vein. Most of *Daltrey*'s songs were composed by the heretofore unknown Leo Sayer, and provided Roger with a new identity as a successful middle-of-the-road pop balladeer. Subsequent LPs like *Ride a Rock Horse* (which tapped the songwriting talents of Argent's Russ Ballard) were more rock oriented, yet remained as slick as The Who were not. *One of the Boys* (1977) actually featured some Daltrey originals—one of which, ''The Prisoner,'' had been inspired by the autobiography of the convicted armed robber John McVicar. Roger then snapped up the rights to the book, to produce and star in the 1980 movie *McVicar* (whose soundtrack was issued as Daltrey's fourth solo LP). Roger had previously been cast in Russell's irreverent *Lisztomania,* as the composer Franz Liszt, and in Richard Marquand's occult saga *The Legacy,* as a man who chokes to death on a chicken bone without even eating it.

Keith Moon also metamorphosed into a movie star, supporting David Essex and Mae West in, respectively, *Stardust* and *Sextette.* In 1974 he briefly distanced himself from his more patriotic cohorts to pursue the hedonistic existence of a superstar tax exile in Los Angeles. There he perpetrated an embarrassing solo LP called *Two Sides of the Moon.* As an individual artist, however, Keith is better remembered for the elaborate practical jokes that had long before won him the title of ''England's last great eccentric.''

PETE TOWNSHEND: There's something about Moon arriving in a pink Rolls-Royce with the windowscreen smashed, in a red velvet jacket with egg stains down the front, smoking a cigarette in a thousand-quid diamond holder, which spells ''Star'' to me. . . . Moon was born a star, is a star, and will always be a star—even when he's begging for pennies down by the river bank, he'll still be a bigger star than Bryan Ferry, Mott the Hoople, and David Bowie all rolled into one. (*NME,* 1974)

Keith Moon backstage at Carnegie Hall (Chuck Pulin)

Soon afterward, Moon got himself up as a bald vicar to arrange his own mugging on Oxford Street at the hands of the Bonzo Dog Band's Viv Stanshall and Larry "Legs" Smith. "How dare you! I've never been so outraged in my life!" screamed the vicar, as the two Al Capone impersonators unceremoniously dumped their victim into the back of a Rolls-Royce. Clerical legs flailing through the vehicle's open window, they drove away—with the police in hot pursuit.

New Yorkers fondly remember Moon officiating as MC at a Sha Na Na concert at Carnegie Hall, which Nancy Lewis covered for *NME:*

> Mr. Moon sauntered onstage in full drag—with an outrageous black wig, a rather low-cut gold lamé evening gown, short gold boots, and a long cigarette holder. A most stunning, voluptuous creature to be sure! Keith introduced [opening act] Cheech and Chong as "two extremely versatile lads—I've just come from their dressing room, so I should know!" Keith reappeared after intermission as the perfect English gentleman in top hat and tails . . .

Moon was most notorious for his habit of systematically demolishing hotel rooms during Who tours (with Townshend as his frequent accomplice). But the group was seldom banned from the scenes of their devastation; the hotels were generally reimbursed far in excess of the property's value. The fun-loving drummer was also apt to drive Rolls-Royces into swimming pools, or to dance onto tables of exclusive restaurants for the express purpose of waving his pecker in Bianca Jagger's face.

But Moon's penchant for living at the limits eventually exacted its toll. By the mid-Seventies, he was hopelessly addicted to drink and pills, and rapidly losing his looks and even his musical chops; much of his old fire was conspicuously ab-

sent from 1978's *Who Are You*. And on the morning of September 7, 1978, after attending Paul McCartney's birthday celebration for Buddy Holly, Keith Moon conquered his insomnia with thirty-two Heminevrin tablets, and never woke up.*

PETE TOWNSHEND: We all feel very weird; Keith has always appeared so close to blowing himself off in the past that we've become used to living with the feeling. But this time . . . he hasn't thrown himself off the balcony and landed in one piece. (*Rolling Stone,* 1978)

JOHN ENTWISTLE: He actually believed himself indestructible . . . I've seen him tumble down thirty stairs and get up as if nothing had happened and begin a conversation. (*Rolling Stone,* 1978)

PETE TOWNSHEND: We are more determined than ever to carry on, and we want the spirit of the group to which Keith contributed so much to go on. (*Rolling Stone,* 1978)

Before long, Townshend began to suggest that Keith's death might actually give The Who a new lease on life, by allowing them to experiment with a completely new format. Moon was indeed replaced, and if anyone could fill his shoes, Kenney Jones was surely the most qualified candidate; Kenney, after all, had been Keith's counterpart in the Small Faces, the second most popular Mod group after The Who, and Moon was both his favorite drummer and a close friend.

But with Moon's departure, the alchemy was lost and the magic circle irrevocably broken, and Townshend's visions of a new beginning for The Who proved to be little more than a mirage. The band returned to America in 1979 to offer a well-oiled, note-perfect program of their greatest hits that would have done any other group proud, but was no substitute for the spontaneity and chaos of yore. Though Jones played his role flawlessly, one had the uneasy feeling that it really wouldn't

---

* Other pivotal figures in The Who story fated to "die before they got old" were former managers Pete Meaden and Kit Lambert (not to mention the eleven victims of the tragic riots preceding The Who's Cincinnati appearance on December 3, 1979). Lou Reizner, meanwhile, succumbed to a fatal heart attack.

Keith Moon, hours before his death, partying with Kenney Jones—the drummer who was to replace him (RDR Productions)

Single, Japan, 1980 (Polydor)

Single, U.K., 1979 (Polydor)

Face Dances LP, U.S.A.,
1981 (Warner Bros.)

Single, U.S.A., 1981
(Warner Bros.)

have made much difference had Roger, Pete, and John also been replaced by trained impersonators. No new material was attempted; this might almost have been a Broadway show called *Whomania*.

The task of putting The Who's glorious past in order now seemed to absorb most of the survivors' energies. The first two books to roll off the presses of Townshend's Eel Pie Publishing were *The Story of Tommy* and *Mods!* In 1979 the newly formed Who Films Ltd. released *The Kids Are Alright* (a fascinating patchwork documentary of the group's career) and Franc Roddam's stark and realistic *Quadrophenia*. With Townshend and Daltrey plainly too old to show their faces in a movie about teenage Mods, the only pop star in evidence was the Police's Sting (as the bellboy). The film was well received in Britain, where it triggered the so-called "Mod revival."

In 1977 Townshend declared (in *The Story of Tommy*): "I'm just not interested in punks on the street anymore; I'm not interested in baggy white trousers, and kids with their hair cut off. I'm too old for it." Before long, however, Pete developed an intense, albeit ambivalent, involvement with the emerging New Wave, whose abrupt rejection of "dinosaurs" like The Who must have reminded him of Tommy's "We're Not Gonna Take It" downfall. He seemed by turns fascinated, threatened, and challenged, unsure whether he might play the role of elder statesman and father figure or was simply doomed to the status of a "boring old fart." He sheepishly deleted "My Generation" from The Who's act when the Jam's Paul Weller (who began as a shameless Townshend clone) made some disparaging remark; yet the most powerful song in The Who's recent repertoire— "Who Are You"—was inspired by Pete's encounter with Paul Cook and Steve Jones of the Sex Pistols at the Speakeasy Club, following a torturous eleven-hour business meeting with ex-managers Lambert and Stamp and the ubiquitous Allen Klein.

PETE TOWNSHEND: I had two whiskies and went completely bananas. I went around hitting people and practically got myself arrested. . . . Someone said: "That's one of the Sex Pistols,"

and I turned around and went *aarrrh!* . . . Whereupon I started to preach . . . shouting at them: "You've got to take over where the 'Oo left off!" And they said: "The Who aren't breaking up, are they? They're our favorite group!" And I'm going: "I'm disappointed in you!" . . . The next day I woke up in a doorway with a policeman kicking me. He said: "Wake up, Pete . . . if you can get up and walk away you can sleep in your own bed tonight." So I staggered home on the Underground. I was sad about it afterwards because I felt I was spending all my time behind a desk while the Sex Pistols were out enjoying the dream. (*Melody Maker,* 1977)

As The Who's maestro—and Daltrey's ventriloquist— Townshend never felt any desperate need for a solo outlet until 1980. His 1972 effort, *Who Came First,* consisted of heartfelt devotional songs Pete had privately distributed among Meher Baba devotees, and was only accorded a general release after bootleggers got into the act. *Rough Mix* (1977) was an equally unassuming collaboration with Ronnie Lane, another Small Faces veteran, whom Pete had turned on to Baba.

In *Empty Glass,* however, Townshend found a common ground between his devotional music and the more commercial approach he had formerly reserved for the group, to assert a strong identity distinct from that of The Who. He brought a fresh, positive perspective even to his inescapable treatises on the Aging Rock & Roller; he sounded as if he had come to terms with the New Wave and was taking pleasure in making music again. Even in *NME*—which had turned positively vitriolic in its rejection of the Sixties' standard bearers—Paul Morley called Townshend "touchingly sincere":

[He] has to be respected for his convincing, almost radiant response to the past few years. . . . Townshend is thrilled by rock and roll, but he's not shrinking behind its mythical properties, he's not embalmed in it. He's *using* it. Listening to *Empty Glass* . . . I realize that Townshend is near to madness; recklessly curi-

(Dennis Zentek)

ous, a bit of a bore, half mystical, half playful. That I'm seeing A Fool rather than A Legend or A True Artist is one of the many virtues of the LP. . . . If all those gods and idiots who had their futures assured by our gullibility and starvation prior to Punk took as much notice of [Punk's] implications as Townshend, then they wouldn't be so ridiculed and reviled now. There would be a proper place for them; they wouldn't be just perpetuating something treacherous. . . .

Empty Glass is no radical, stunning work. It's patchy, and there are things missing. . . . [It] is an old man giving himself a new lease on life, finding significance in survival, purpose in just getting up and doing it, and satisfaction in conviction. Pete Townshend belongs in the here and the now and the tomorrow.

Not bad for an ''old man'' of thirty-five!

The Who, but contrast, never sounded so bland and dispirited as on 1981's *Face Dances*. More than ever it seemed that if Pete Townshend was to produce truly vital new work, he would have to do it on his own. By the Eighties, however, the boys in the band had gone through so much together that it was almost too late for them to part ways.

Keith Moon once vowed that The Who never would break up. ''We'll finish up coming onstage in our wheelchairs,'' he told *NME* in 1970. ''By that time John'll be about twenty stone [280 lbs] and he'll have to be hauled onstage like a piece of equipment. . . . Roger's hair will be down to his feet like the curtain at the West Ham Odeon; it will go up to reveal an old cracked face. . . .'' Townshend, for his part, likened The Who to a successful marriage. More than any other rock band, The Who—and, by extension, their fans seemed destined, for better or worse, to grow old together—almost like a real family.

(followed by their highest chart positions, as listed in *Billboard*)

THE WHO'S HITS

U.S. Singles

1965	I Can't Explain (93)	
1966	My Generation (74)	
1967	Happy Jack (24); Pictures of Lily (51); I Can See for Miles (9)	
1968	Call Me Lightning (40); Magic Bus (25)	
1969	Pinball Wizard (19); I'm Free (37)	
1970	See Me, Feel Me (12); Summertime Blues (27); The Seeker (44)	
1971	Won't Get Fooled Again (15); Behind Blue Eyes (34)	
1972	Join Together (17)	
1973	The Relay (39); Love, Reign O'er Me (76)	
1974	The Real Me (92)	
1976	Squeeze Box (16)	
1978	Who Are You (14)	
1979	Long Live Rock (54); 5:15 (45)	

(BY ROGER DALTREY)

1973 Giving It All Away (83)
1975 Come and Get Your Love (68)
1977 Avenging Annie (88)
1980 Free Me (53); Without Your Love (20)

(BY PETE TOWNSHEND)

1980 Let My Love Open the Door (9); A Little Is Enough (72); Rough Boys (89)

U.S. LPs

1967 Happy Jack (67)
1968 The Who Sell Out (48); Magic Bus—The Who on Tour (39)
1969 Tommy (4)
1970 Live at Leeds (4)
1971 Who's Next (4); Meaty Beaty Big and Bouncy (11)
1972 Tommy (orchestral version) (5)
1973 Quadrophenia (2)
1974 Odds and Sods (15); A Quick One/Sell Out (185)
1975 The Who by Numbers (8); Tommy (sound-track) (2)
1978 Who Are You (2)
1979 The Kids Are Alright (8); Quadrophenia (soundtrack) (46)

(BY ROGER DALTREY)

1973 Daltrey (45)
1975 Ride a Rock Horse (28)
1977 One of the Boys (46)
1980 McVicar (soundtrack) (22)

(BY JOHN ENTWISTLE)

1971 Smash Your Head Against the Wall (126); Whistle Rymes (138)
1973 Rigor Mortis Sets In (174)
1975 Mad Dog (192)

(BY KEITH MOON)

1975 Two Sides of the Moon (155)

(BY PETE TOWNSHEND)

1972 Who Came First (69)
1977 (With Ronnie Lane) Rough Mix (45)
1980 Empty Glass (5)

U.K. Singles

1965 I Can't Explain (8); Anyway Anyhow Anywhere (10); My Generation (2)
1966 Substitute (5); A Legal Matter (32); I'm a Boy (2); Happy Jack (3); The Kids Are Alright (41)
1967 Pictures of Lily (4); The Last Time/ Under My Thumb (44); I Can See for Miles (10)
1968 Dogs (25); Magic Bus (26)
1969 Pinball Wizard (4)
1970 The Seeker (19); Summertime Blues (38)
1971 Won't Get Fooled Again (9); Let's See Action (16)
1972 Join Together (9)
1973 Relay (21); 5:15 (20)
1976 Substitute (7); Squeeze Box (10)
1978 Who Are You (18)
1979 Long Live Rock (48)

(BY ROGER DALTREY)

1973 Giving It All Away (5); I'm Free (13)
1977 Written on the Wind (46)

THE BRITISH INVASION

Pink Floyd

The Pink Floyd in 1967 (from l.): Roger Waters (crouching), Nick Mason, Syd Barrett, and Rick Wright (RDR Productions)

Q UEEN ELIZABETH HALL, London, May 12, 1967: The ads promised "GAMES FOR MAY: Space-age relaxation for the climax of spring—electronic compositions, color and image projections, girls, and THE PINK FLOYD." The absence of a warm-up band is still virtually unheard of, especially considering that the Floyd have thus far issued but a single 45. Yet a whole new breed of British youth seems to have crawled out of the woodwork for the occasion, resplendent in caftans and floral jackets, love beads and bells, their faces painted blue, yellow, and green. They have come to witness Britain's first liquid light show—and to hear songs about inner and outer space, tales of gnomes and scarecrows and Jupiter and Saturn interspersed with sound effects and "free form" electronic interludes, panned around the staid concert hall via Britain's first quadrophonic PA. As the supersonic mayhem reaches a crescendo, the bass player begins hurling potatoes at an oversized gong. The singer/guitarist, shrouded in a cape, waves his arms in the air, catching the spotlight to cast great menacing shadows on the screen behind. Toward the end, roadies toss armloads of daffodils into the audience while thousands of bubbles float overhead. The next day the hall's management finds that the bubbles have left indelible rings on the seats, and that daffodil petals have been ground into the carpets, and they ban the Pink Floyd from playing there again. The Floyd's singer/guitarist, for his part, declares: "In the future, groups are going to have to offer more than just a pop show. They're going to have to offer a well-presented theater show."

Nassau Coliseum, Long Island, February 24, 1980: Pink Floyd parlay their current Number One concept album *The Wall* into the most spectacular rock extravaganza ever staged. An estimated $1.8 million worth of equipment and props includes giant grotesque puppets representing *The Wall*'s characters; surreal animated films; a life-size model airplane that soars over the arena before crashing in flames; and a gigantic inflatable pig glowering over the multitudes through searchlight eyes. Most of all, there is the great white wall itself, approximately sixty yards wide and forty feet high, constructed by an army of roadies brick by cardboard brick, until the band and all its elaborate paraphernalia are completely blocked from the view of twenty thousand gawking young New Yorkers . . . .

Pink Floyd—Roger Waters, David Gilmour, Rick Wright, and Nick Mason—have always been recognized as Britain's foremost "progressive" band. Composed of former architecture students, Pink Floyd specialized not in mere songs, but in monumental edifices that filled one, then two, and finally (in the case of their Great *Wall*) four long-playing sides.

To some Floyd freaks, these constructions served as mystic oracles and/or space shuttles, probing far-flung vistas of space and time. With their "high tech" sound textures and their droning, dreamlike improvisations, Pink Floyd LPs supplied *the* ideal ambience for the audiophile to gloat over his three-thousand-dollar sound system and the more chemically inclined to explore his alternate states. Some sci-fi and fantasy buffs preferred to utilize the Floyd's predominantly instrumental meanderings as extraterrestrial background Muzak: eerie enough to read H. P. Lovecraft by, a suitably futuristic accompaniment to Heinlein or Asimov, an epic score for the desert dynasties of *Dune*. (The Floyd were once supposed to provide just that for a movie version of Frank Herbert's magnum opus.) To curmudgeon rock scribe Nik Cohn, Pink Floyd were simply "boring beyond belief."

For their part, Pink Floyd "always thought there was more to playing rock & roll than playing 'Johnny B. Goode,'" and their progressive credentials at least were never in question. Indeed, the Floyd's trademark combination of hypnotic bass/drum throb, soaring slide guitar figures, and celestial organ backdrops (augmented by temple gongs, synthesized white noise, and sound effects galore) seems so remote from rock's roots in American jazz, blues, and country music that one might query whether they were playing rock & roll at all. In any case, Pink Floyd certainly passed a key litmus test of musical progressivism: nobody has ever sold so many albums while remaining so doggedly oblivious to the medium of the three-minute single. Between 1967's "See Emily Play" and 1980's "Another Brick in the Wall," the Floyd failed to rack up even one Top Ten hit on either side of the Atlantic; yet their 1973 offering, *Dark Side of the Moon*, remained on *Billboard*'s U.S. album charts for over four hundred weeks—far longer than any other LP in rock history.

What's more, Pink Floyd's space-age dirges—which foreshadowed both "Eurodisco" and "Synth Rock"—have registered a truly phenomenal impact on non-English-speaking lands where Johnny B. Goode and his successors have traditionally left the populace unmoved. In countries like France, *Dark Side of the Moon* is the best-selling rock LP of all time. Strains of Pink Floyd can often be heard wafting down the narrow medieval streets of remote Italian or Moroccan villages, where the young British or American visitor will find that if a new acquaintance owns but one rock record or tape, that album will almost certainly be *Dark Side of the Moon*.

Nobody else, moreover, has sold so many records, yet remained so thoroughly anonymous, as Waters, Gilmour, Wright, and Mason. Except on the first and third albums, the band's faces (and often its name) were omitted from the packaging in favor of drawings or photographs (usually masterminded by the record-sleeve design company "Hipgnosis") every bit as off-the-wall as the music within: a cow in a pasture (*Atom Heart Mother*); a businessman consumed by flames, genially shaking hands with his double (*Wish You Were Here*); the aforementioned inflatable pig soaring amidst the belching smokestacks of London's Battersea power station (*Animals*). Pink Floyd's faceless components could—and sometimes did—walk unrecognized among the audiences at their own marathon concerts. Onstage, their demeanor was decidedly statuesque: ensconced in headphones like bored sound engineers, Pink Floyd deliberately allowed themselves to be upstaged by their elaborate visual effects. "Their life-style," confided *The Wall*'s producer Bob Ezrin, "is interchangeable with the president of just about any bank in England." Interviews were a rarity except in the early days; according to Gilmour: "We don't need the music press and they don't really need us." The Floyd succeeded in creating an invisible wall between themselves and the general public long before they got around to building the cardboard one.

The words "Pink Floyd" ultimately suggested less a group of four earthy "stars" than a corporate brand name (consider the nonexistent chart ratings of Gilmour's, Wright's, and Mason's turn-of-the-decade solo efforts—even as *Dark Side of the Moon* continued to break all records for hit-parade longevity). Always an enigma, Pink Floyd might even be described as an abstraction; the musicians created a chimera with a seeming life of its own. For the most part, Pink Floyd's spectacular aural achievements speak for themselves, and little need be added about the self-effacing wizards lurking behind the, er, wall.

But the greatest enigma of all—whose story lies at the root of

---

Pink Floyd in the early Seventies (from 1.): Nick Mason, David Gilmour, Roger Waters, and Rick Wright (Harvest Records)

Syd Barrett as a teenager (John Steele Collection)

Pink Floyd's history—was a charismatic figure named Syd Barrett. A twenty-one-year-old rock & roll visionary whose feverish imagination gave birth to the entire Pink Floyd concept (including the name), his voice, guitar, and songs dominated the records that propelled the Floyd to prominence during 1967's Summer of Love and still remain the last word in British psychedelia. Like his followers in the London Underground— and countless Pink Floyd enthusiasts ever since—Syd exhibited a ravenous appetite for chemical enlightenment. (The rest of the Floyd, by contrast, nurtured a secret preference for alcoholic beverages.) More than that—and more than any other rock star who ever trafficked in psychic brinkmanship or merely fashionable "decadence"—Barrett embodied the tenets laid down a century earlier by a sixteen-year-old Arthur Rimbaud: "A Poet makes himself a visionary through a long, boundless, and systematic disorganization of *all* the senses. All forms of love, of suffering, of madness . . . he exhausts within himself all poisons, and preserves their quintessences."

In Barrett's case, the distinction between visionary and psychotic evaporated all too quickly, until his erratic behavior forced him to abdicate following the triumph of his group's debut album. Though Pink Floyd carried on in his absence, scaling the heights of critical and commercial acceptance against all odds, the phantom presence of the madcap Barrett continued to fascinate, inspire, and haunt them.

Like Waters and Gilmour, Roger Keith Barrett grew up in the genteel university town of Cambridge, where he was born on January 6, 1946. He seems to have enjoyed a picture-book middle-class English childhood, complete with a stint in the Boy Scouts. Apart from camping and sports, young Roger's interests included drama, painting, and—above all—music. His father, a respected pathologist, was a classical music buff, and musical get-togethers round his prized piano were an important feature of his five children's upbringing. The idyllic picture, however, was abruptly shattered by Dr. Barrett's death in 1960.

By this time, Roger had acquired his first guitar, and the nickname Syd. He developed a keen interest in American blues and jazz, and became an early fan of both the Beatles and the Rolling Stones. One of his closest friends was another aspiring guitarist named Dave Gilmour, with whom Syd regularly traded licks and ideas. If Gilmour boasted a superior technique, Barrett was more musically inventive; each learned a great deal from the other. After gigging as an acoustic duo at a Cambridge club called the Mill, Syd and Dave spent a summer together bumming around France, playing for small change and sampling marijuana for the first time. Another longtime friend and associate, Storm Thorgerson of Hipgnosis, remembered Syd as a "bright extrovert kid. Smoked dope, pulled chicks—the usual thing. He had no problems on the surface."

Having demonstrated great promise as a painter—Gilmour and Thorgerson both say he was "a great artist"—Barrett won a scholarship at London's Camberwell School of Art. In 1965, to the sorrow of his doting mother, Syd left Cambridge for a flat in the big city. Among his new neighbors were a man said to be London's sole supplier of a strange new drug called LSD—and Roger Waters, a familiar face from Cambridge High School and the Mill, who presently invited Barrett to join his fledgling R&B band.

Like his protagonist in *The Wall,* George Roger Waters (born September 9, 1944) lost his father to World War II and was raised with some severity by his schoolmarm mother. Prior to Barrett's arrival, the bass-toting disarmament activist had formed a group called Sigma 6 (later the Architectural Abdabs, Screaming Abdabs, or just plain Abdabs) with drummer Nicholas Berkeley Mason (born January 27, 1945), a fellow architecture student from the Regent Street Polytechnic, and keyboardist Richard William Wright (born July 28, 1945), a former classmate who had transferred to the London College of Music. When Barrett plugged in, the band already boasted a traditional jazz-oriented guitarist named Bob Close.

Though Waters, Mason, and Wright were conscientious students who viewed the group as little more than a hobby, Syd's painting career was rapidly eclipsed by visions of pop stardom; he abruptly stopped working on canvas and set out to make "music in colors" instead. Already well-doused with LSD, he became obsessed with Eastern mysticism, supernaturalism, and ESP. His induction into the band seems to have triggered the departure of the more conventional, albeit technically more accomplished, Close, who failed to share Syd's fascination with the possibilities of guitar feedback and distortion. Almost by default, Barrett found himself fronting a group, which he rechristened the Pink Floyd Sound, after a pair of Georgia blues musicians named Pink Anderson and Floyd Council. (The "Sound" soon fell by the wayside, though the band continued to be known as "the" Pink Floyd until the 1970s.)

The quartet's repertoire, performed mostly at pubs and parties, consisted of the usual R&B winners—"Road Runner," "Louie Louie," and the Rolling Stones' Greatest Hits— distinguished only by Barrett's spasmodic "freak out" interludes. Before long, however, garbled reports began filtering in from America's West Coast of a revolutionary new youth subculture presided over by a revolutionary new breed of rock & roller. Bands with hair down to their elbows and far-out names like the Jefferson Airplane and the Grateful Dead were reputed to weave lysergic improvisations for hours on end, buttressed by "psychedelic" light shows and great quaffs of electric Kool-Aid. Because none of these legendary figures had yet come out with a record, the London cognoscenti were unable to hear (let alone see) precisely what all the hoopla was about. But this hardly impaired their resolve to duplicate the Haight-Ashbury magic on their own turf.

The result was a distinctly British "Underground"—which

Tony Tyler of *New Musical Express* was to recall as the "Age of Aquarius—brown rice, King Arthur, Pyramidology, UFOs, Tolkien, flowers, peace, light, and Krishna the goat placidly munching on organic carrot"—and whose definitive soundtrack would be furnished by none other than Syd Barrett and the Pink Floyd.

This subculture first surfaced in a series of Sunday-afternoon happenings at London's ever-pivotal Marquee Club. "Spontaneous Underground" was a British variation on the San Francisco Be-In—part costume ball, part jam session, and part anarchic free-for-all. Though the afternoon's entertainment generally encompassed a rock band or two, these were hardly the sole focus of attention. Movies flickered on the walls throughout the performances, and little distinction was made between player and audience. Customers were encouraged to dress as outlandishly as possible and to contribute to the general racket with such "found" instruments as transistor radios and lavatory plungers, or by usurping the stage to bellow their own poetry.

"We've always thought there was more to playing rock & roll than playing 'Johnny B. Goode.' " (RDR Productions/Dezo Hoffmann)

Occasionally someone like Donovan, accompanied by a troupe of sitar players, would also materialize in the spotlight. Promotion was limited to word of mouth and the occasional cryptic handbill, e.g.:

> TRIP bring furniture toy prop paper rug
> paint balloon jumble costume mask
> robot candle incense ladder wheel
> light self all others march 13th 5 p.m.
>
> marquee club 90 wardour street w1
> 5/-

The above, in fact, constitutes the sole surviving record of the Mad Hatter's tea party at which the Pink Floyd made their Marquee Club debut, complete with layers of formerly gratuitous feedback now recognized by both Syd Barrett and the Spontaneous Subterraneans as Acid Rock.

The Pink Floyd were quickly accepted as a fixture of Spontaneous Underground, and encouraged to stretch out each number for as long as half an hour so as not to interrupt the slow, sinuous swaying peculiar to would-be dancers who have indulged in LSD. (Listeners also had the option of stripping down to their underwear to roll about in great heaps of pink jelly that the management had thoughtfully placed on the Marquee Club's floor.)

After about a dozen such Sundays, the Floyd were "discovered" in their natural habitat by a would-be Brian Epstein. According to Roger Waters (in a 1973 *Zigzag* interview), a Mr. Jenner "approached us and said, 'You lads could be bigger than the Beatles'—and we sort of looked at him and replied in a dubious tone, 'Yes, well, we'll see you when we get back from our hols,' because we were all shooting off for some sun on the Continent."

Pete Jenner was a professor at the London School of Economics whose only involvement with the music business had been via the short-lived avant-garde jazz label DNA. Long disdainful of commercial pop music, Jenner—who by his own admission "hardly knew about the Beatles, even"—changed his tune when he noticed that rock was spawning an avant garde of its own, and concluded that a progressive pop group could prove just the vehicle with which he might make his fortune and still keep his principles intact. Jenner's first overtures were made to New York's Velvet Underground, whom he had heard on tape, but a trans-Atlantic conversation with Lou Reed revealed that the band's affairs were already being handled by one Andy Warhol.

Shortly thereafter, Jenner took a break from correcting exams to check out the Marquee's Spontaneous Underground. "And there on the stage," he would recall to *Zigzag*'s Pete Frame, "was this strange band playing a mixture of R&B and electronic noises . . . and I was really intrigued because in between the routine stuff like 'Louie Louie' and 'Road Runner' they were playing these very weird breaks—so weird that I couldn't even work out which instrument the sound was coming from. It was all very bizarre and just what I was looking for: a far-out, electronic, freaky pop group."

Jenner was startled to learn that the Floyd had no management or agency, minimal equipment (most of it home-made, or hopelessly decrepit), and so few gigs lined up that they were on the verge of calling it quits. Accordingly, Jenner roped his friend Andrew King into co-managing the Floyd in a six-way partnership called Blackhill Enterprises.

Jenner also encouraged his new clients to emphasize their unique instrumentals at the expense of the R&B chestnuts, while Barrett took it upon himself to furnish the Floyd with songs of their own. As Nick Jones noted in the band's first *Melody Maker* write-up: "'Psychedelic' versions of 'Louie Louie' don't come off, but if they can incorporate their electronic prowess with some melodic and lyrical songs—getting away from dated R&B things—they could well score in the near future."

"The fact that Syd was a songwriter changed the whole thing," Mason told *NME* years later. "We could have spent years playing old Stones and Bo Diddley tunes, and . . . wouldn't have achieved anything." Jenner is said to have demanded that Barrett's material be as weird as the band's instrumental breaks, yet melodic and lyrical enough for the hit parade (in short, he wanted to have his cake and eat it too), and Syd rose to the occasion with a string of infectious pieces of stoned English whimsy, influenced in equal measure by Lewis Carroll, C. S. Lewis, and LSD (e.g., "Sitting on a unicorn . . . swimming through the starlit sky . . . hey-ho! here we go, ever so high!"). "His inventiveness was quite astounding," Jenner remembered. "All those songs . . . were written in the space of about six months."

During the summer of 1966, the Pink Floyd acquired another regular gig when the Free School—Alternative London's first community organization—began sponsoring "light and sound workshops" at Notting Hill's All Saints Church, under the aegis of Jenner's close friend John Hopkins. Five years hence, Rick Wright was to reminisce (in *NME*): "Those early days were purely experimental for us and a time of learning and finding out exactly what we were trying to do. Each night was a complete buzz because we did totally new things and none of us knew how the others would react to it."

At one of the All Saints shows, some American pals of Timothy Leary's elected to project slides onto the group in time with their music. This was a revelation to the Floyd and their managers, who immediately set about constructing the United Kingdom's first light show. In the absence of any blueprints from San Francisco's Fillmore Theater, Jenner and King improvised a home-made device from sundry slabs of lumber, bits of colored perspex, and hardware store spotlights operated by domestic light switches.

In October, Hopkins launched Britain's first Underground rag, *International Times* (or *IT*), with a mass celebration at the Roundhouse, an abandoned railway warehouse in North London. "There was virtually no electricity other than an ordinary domestic power supply," Jenner told *Zigzag*'s Frame, "so our puny light show looked magnificent in all the darkness." Paul McCartney and Marianne Faithfull were in attendance (dressed, respectively, as an Arab and a nun), as were director Michelangelo Antonioni (in town to film his Swinging London movie, *Blow-Up*), and two-thousand anonymous citizens in caftans and antique military regalia; each was ceremoniously handed a sugar cube upon arrival. Jenner called it "the most epochal party you could ever see, and the bands got noticed—particularly the Floyd, who blew up the power during their set and consequently ended the evening's entertainment. That in itself—to be cut off in the middle of 'Interstellar Overdrive'—was a bummer, but at the same time it was incredibly dramatic." The band received its first national press in *The Sunday Times*'s coverage of the event, which drily noted that "a pop group called the Pink Floyd played throbbing music while a series of bizarre colored shapes flashed on a huge screen behind them. Someone had made a mountain of jelly which people ate at midnight and another person had parked his motorbike in the middle of the room. All apparently very psychedelic."

The Floyd returned to the Roundhouse on December 3 as part of a Majority Rule for Rhodesia benefit, dubbed "Psychodelphia versus Ian Smith"—"Bring your own happenings and ecstatogenic substances," advised the posters, "drag optional"—and yet again for a New Year's Eve "Giant Freakout All Night Rave," where the Floyd's *son et lumière* upstaged both the Move (who decimated three TV sets and a car) and The Who (who took their own turn at blowing the power, triggering one of Townshend's legendary tantrums).

Alternative London found its permanent vortex at the enterprising John Hopkins's new Tottenham Court Road club, UFO, whose tiny stage would serve as a launching pad for the likes of the Soft Machine, Arthur Brown, Procol Harum, Tomorrow, and Tyrannosaurus Rex. But it was the Pink Floyd who presided over the December 23 opening-night festivities, and who would remain *the* house band of both UFO and the London Underground in general. "I suppose you could describe us as the movement's house orchestra," said Waters a few months later, "because we were one of the first people to play what they wanted to hear." The band's UFO performances, Mason would tell *Zigzag*, were often supplemented by "some mad actors, a couple of light shows, perhaps the recitation of some poetry or verse, and a lot of wandering about and cheerful chat-

ter." UFO—which Barrett dubbed "a microcosm of what was to happen later"—served as the prototype for two other London Underground meccas, christened (in Professor Tolkien's honor) Gandalf's Garden and Middle Earth.

It was only a matter of time before conservatively dressed record executives materialized amidst the clouds of sweet-smelling smoke to gingerly pick their way through the sprawling freaks. The Floyd duly signed with the highest bidder, EMI's Beecher Stevens, who later told writer Rick Sanders that he "classified them as weird but good," yet felt that "one of the boys, and some of the people around them, seemed a bit strange, which is one of the reasons I wanted Norman ['Hurricane'] Smith [an EMI staff producer, formerly George Martin's—and the Beatles'—engineer] . . . to keep a firm hand on the sessions."

The Floyd's first single, however, was produced independently, prior to Smith's installment, by Jenner's friend—and UFO's musical director—Joe Boyd. The result was the most auspicious recorded debut by any of the artists featured at length in this book: a hook-laden piece of whimsy about the twilight adventures of a transvestite sex pervert. According to Waters (in *Zigzag*), "Arnold Layne" and his "strange hobby" weren't just figments of Barrett's bizarre imagination: "Both my mother and Syd's mother had students as lodgers, because there was a girl's college up the road. So there were constantly great lines of bras and knickers on our washing lines, and Arnold, or whoever he was, had bits and pieces off [them]. . . . He stopped doing it after a bit, when things got too hot."

Melody Maker was suitably impressed: "First outing from the colorful Pink Floyd with an amusing and colorful story about a guy who got himself put inside because he screwed up whilst learning of the birds and the bees. . . . Without a doubt, a very good disc. The Pink Floyd represent a new form of music to the English pop scene so let's hope the English are broadminded enough to accept it with open arms." Oddly enough, "Arnold Layne" triggered a fit of prudery among the ultra-hip pirates of Radio London, who banned the ditty even as the staid old BBC accorded it precious airplay. "Arnold Layne just happens to dig dressing in women's clothing," Syd retorted. "A lot of people do—so let's face up to reality!" His B-side, meanwhile, had run afoul of EMI; as Waters remembered in *Zigzag*: "We had to change all the lyrics because it was about rolling joints. It was called 'Let's Roll Another One' and we had to change the title to 'Candy and a Currant Bun.'"

"Arnold" made the Top Twenty. A follow-up, "See Emily Play" (originally called "Games for May" in commemoration of the famous Queen Elizabeth Hall concert), materialized, supposedly "Kubla Khan"–style, after Barrett dozed off in a forest. "Emily" got to number six. The Pink Floyd had arrived in a big way, just in time for the Summer of Love.

"We are simply a pop group," Waters insisted (in *NME*). "But because we use light and color in our act, a lot of people seem to imagine we are trying to put across some message with nasty, evil overtones." The pop weeklies, for their part, greeted the Floyd as harbingers of the New Age. *Melody Maker* called them "Britain's top psychedelic group . . . a cacophony of sound played to a background of multi-colored lights." According to *NME*, the boys themselves came off as "remote, mystical creatures, simply because few people could see them properly. 'It sometimes makes it very difficult for us to establish any association with the audience,' said Roger. 'Apart from the few at the front, no one can really identify us.'"

Despite their personal remoteness and their Underground

stance, the Floyd proved amenable to most of the initiation rites traditional to fledgling British pop stars. They cheerfully listed their measurements, hair and eye colors, brothers' and sisters' names, schools, and "age entered show business" for *NME*'s "Life Lines" series—which also informed readers that Nick Mason's hobbies included sailing and riding; that Roger Waters's favorite food was "cream doughnuts"; and that Rick Wright's "professional ambition" was "to hear my own symphony performed at Festival Hall." Even Syd Barrett—the only member to leave several blank entries—allowed that he owned a "cat named Rover."

"Suddenly they were stars," Jenner recalled in a radio interview with deejay Mike Sparrow, "[which] became a very difficult thing for everyone to cope with. Most of all Syd, because from then on everyone was saying: 'Is that the next single?'" The current single's success, meanwhile, "instantly put the Floyd on the 'Hit Band' circuit, which was mad! . . . People expected them to do a thirty-minute set, a string of hits, and most of all 'See Emily Play.'"

The Floyd, however, perversely declined to perform the famous ditty. "We could go on doing the same numbers, which is very pop star," Waters later told *Melody Maker*. "But that's not what the Pink Floyd are all about. It's about taking risks and pushing forward." Nonetheless, as Wright put it, "outside London nobody wanted to know." The uncompromising crew was therefore subjected to the wrath of the philistines. "They were pouring pints of beer onto us from the balcony," Waters told *Zigzag*. "That was most unpleasant, and very dangerous too. . . . The worst thing that ever happened to me . . . was a penny, which made a bloody great cut in the middle of my forehead. . . . Happily, there was one freak who turned up who liked us, so the audience spent the [rest of] the evening beating the shit out of him, and left us alone."

From Jenner's perspective, "the first indication that things were going to be a bit difficult" came when the Floyd were booked onto television's *Top of the Pops* for the three consecutive weeks of "Emily"'s sojourn in the Top Ten. The boys made their first appearance impeccably turned out in the King's Road's best satins and velvets. During the second performance, however, Barrett's opulent finery looked as if he had slept in it throughout the intervening week. And for the third *TOTP* taping, Syd arrived as the picture of flamboyant elegance—only to disappear into the dressing room and don a set of smelly old rags for the cameras.

"Shortly after this," said Jenner, "we had to do a radio show [*Saturday Club*] to promote the single . . . and Syd just walked out and said 'I never want to do that again.' . . . We had to pull the band off the road, and everybody have a holiday. . . . Up to that point [Barrett] was just a delight, one of the nicest people. It was from that point on that people started saying he was a bit weird."

PINK FLOYD FLAKE OUT! blared the front-page headline in *Melody Maker*. "Lead vocalist and songwriter Syd Barrett is suffering from 'nervous exhaustion' and the group have withdrawn from all engagements booked for the month of August. As a result they have lost at least £4,000 in work."

Tales of Barrett's increasingly erratic behavior became legion. One account had him locking up a girl friend for a week, periodically shoving biscuits under the door so she wouldn't starve. At one point during the sessions for the Floyd's first LP, he reportedly announced he was going to the bathroom; after he failed to emerge, the lavatory was found utterly demolished—but Syd had vanished for the day.

"He was 100 percent creative, and very hard on himself," co-manager Andrew King would tell *Sounds*. "He wouldn't do anything unless he thought he was doing it in an artistic way." Barrett applied his unique flair even to the usually humdrum process of mixing the album: "He would throw the levers on the board up and down apparently at random, making pretty pictures with his hands." The result can be heard in pieces like "Interstellar Overdrive," where instruments careen from speaker to speaker with dizzying abandon. (According to Jenner [in *NME*], "Overdrive"'s explosive chord progression emerged from a discussion he'd had with Barrett about the latter's favorite West Coast group, Love. "I was trying to tell him about this Arthur Lee song I couldn't remember the title of, so I just hummed the main riff. Syd picked up the guitar and followed what I was humming chord-wise. The chord pattern he worked out [became] the main riff for 'Interstellar Overdrive.'")

Piper at the Gates of Dawn
LP, U.K., 1967 (*Columbia*)

Single, Holland, 1968
(*Columbia*)

LP, U.K., 1970 (*Harvest*)

LP, U.K., 1970 (*Harvest*)

Originally called *Astronomy Domine*, the LP was retitled *The Piper at the Gates of Dawn*, after a chapter of Kenneth Grahame's *The Wind in the Willows*. Its release (on August 1, 1967) elicited many comparisons with *Sgt. Pepper*; and these, for once, were justified. *Piper*, as Jenner recalled, "was made at the same time as *Pepper*, at EMI['s Abbey Road studios], and I think that was *not* a coincidence! We used to go down and hear what was wafting out of the doors, and I daresay a bit of that went on the other way as well!"

Like Lennon-McCartney, Barrett set stream-of-consciousness fantasy to catchy melodies and commercial pop hooks, often tempering childlike wonder with grown-up irony. He had his Eastern influences, too; "Chapter 24," for instance, fuses devotional chanting with messages from the *I Ching*. As a guitarist, Syd was similarly innovative and expressive—not to mention unpredictable. Without warning, his melodic breaks give way to harsh dissonances, and straightforward strumming to an almost jazzlike improvisation, with little regard for such trifles as key and time signatures. Barrett worked wonders with echo boxes and the wah-wah pedal, and, perhaps most impressively, turned the slide guitar (previously associated mostly with the blues) into an integral component of his space odysseys.

Though *Piper* was criminally butchered in the U.S. by Capitol (which omitted "Flaming," "Bike," and "Astronomy Domine," the latter still unavailable Stateside in its original studio glory), the LP made a highly favorable impression on discriminating dope fiends and Anglophiles. On October 26, the Floyd landed at, fittingly enough, San Francisco's Fillmore West to launch their first American invasion. Among other things, they found that the West Coast music scene was hardly as "extraordinary and mind-blowing and trippy" (Waters's phrase) as they had imagined it—the Floyd having long since surpassed their supposed American prototypes in the art of breaching rock's outer limits. Indeed, many of the local bands had been galvanized by *Piper*; Alice Cooper even had Syd and the boys over to dinner—rock's most ersatz psychopath thereby gaining an intimate glimpse of the genuine article.

"Syd was definitely from Mars," Cooper's guitarist Glen Buxton informed Kris DiLorenzo of *Trouser Press*. "They'd fly a thousand miles, get to the gig, he'd get up onstage and he wouldn't have a guitar. . . . Sometimes they'd have to fly back and pick [it] up." The tour, said Waters, "was an amazing disaster. Syd by this time was completely off his head."

During an appearance on Dick Clark's *American Bandstand,* where the Floyd were supposed to mime to their "See Emily Play" single, they found that "Syd wasn't into moving his lips that day." Then came *The Pat Boone Show,* wherein the antiseptic Fifties idol's vain attempts to coax a word out of Barrett were rewarded with the disconcertingly blank stare that Waters would characterize (in his famous ode to Syd) as "a look in your eyes, like black holes in the sky." At this point Andrew King canceled all remaining dates and sent the boys home.

Barrett did come up with a follow-up to "Emily": "Apples and Oranges," an oblique paean to "shopping at shops" ("their most psychedelic single yet," said *NME*) that was never issued in the U.S. and flopped dismally in the U.K. "Couldn't care less," said Syd, who had wanted the single to be "Jug Band Blues"—the number that Jenner would call "the ultimate self-diagnosis on a state of schizophrenia," citing lines like "I'm most obliged to you for making it clear that I'm not here, and I'm wondering who could be writing this song. . . . " (This would prove the only one of three new Barrett compositions salvageable for the second Pink Floyd LP; the other two were called "Scream Your Last Scream" and "Vegetable Man.")

"He was wearing lipstick, dressing in high heels, and believing he had homosexual tendencies," Dave Gilmour told *NME*'s Nick Kent. "We all felt he should have gone to see a psychiatrist, though someone in fact played an interview he did to R. D. Laing, and Laing claimed he was incurable."

On the original lineup's last British tour (supporting Barrett's idol Jimi Hendrix), Syd was wont to let his arm dangle limply from his trademark mirrored Telecaster, or play a single chord throughout the set. One such night, frantically arranging his "obligatory Hendrix perm" just before the Floyd were due onstage, Barrett is said to have crushed the contents of a jar of Mandrax tablets and poured the crumbs of his favorite "downs" onto his head along with a tube's worth of Brylcream. Under the heat of the spotlights, the dribbling mess gradually transformed Barrett's face into a melting death mask.

Sometimes he refused to leave the tour bus altogether, allowing Dave O'List from the bottom-billed Nice to deputize for him. That they actually could more or less "manage without Syd" proved a revelation to the rest of the group.

In *Rolling Stone* a decade later, Gilmour remembered Barrett as "the brightest, wittiest, and most popular guy I knew. Whether acid or success acted as the catalyst, I couldn't tell, but gradually he was just not in the same world as you and I. You would ask him questions and get an answer to something else entirely."

Barrett then announced that he was bringing in a pair of his court jesters—a banjo player and a saxophonist—to turn the Floyd into a six-piece. But Waters, Wright, and Mason had other ideas. In March 1968, *Melody Maker* reported that "a new singer and guitarist has joined the Pink Floyd, increasing their lineup to five. He is twenty-one-year-old David Gilmour, a childhood friend of the Floyd's Syd Barrett and Roger Waters." According to Jenner, Gilmour (who had been working as a male model) was a fine technician who lacked a distinctive style of his own, but could do "very effective takeoffs" of guitarists like Jimi Hendrix. "So the band said: 'Play like Syd Barrett.'"

"So we were teaching Dave the numbers," Mason told *Zigzag*, "but Syd came in with some new material. The song went 'Have You Got It Yet?' and he kept changing it so no one could learn it." "It was a real act of mad genius," added Waters. "I didn't suss it out at all. I stood there for an hour while he was singing . . . trying to explain that he was changing it all the time so I couldn't follow it. He'd sing 'Have you got it yet?' and I'd sing 'No, no!'"

"I thought the only way that we could carry on together was for him to be still a member of the group, still earn his fair share of the money, but not to come to gigs at all, be a sort of Brian Wilson figure if you like, write songs and come to recording sessions. . . ."

But Jenner and King, who felt that Barrett *was* the Floyd, took exception to the proposed downgrading of his status in the group. The upshot was that Syd was eased of the Floyd, and the Floyd was eased out of the Blackhill partnership after its co-managers decided to place their bets on Barrett's proposed solo career. (They subsequently took on another budding legend from the London Underground called Tyrannosaurus Rex—but that tale belongs in the next section of this book.)

Barrett's departure, on March 2, 1968, did not prevent him from turning up at Floyd gigs, standing in front of the stage and leveling his catatonic stare at his hapless replacement. Even so, Gilmour would go to heroic lengths to facilitate Barrett's re-emergence on a pair of solo LPs in 1970. The first half of *The Madcap Laughs* was produced by Malcolm Jones, head of EMI's new "progressive" label, Harvest (to which the Floyd themselves had been rerouted). When Jones gave up in despair, Gilmour and Waters volunteered to replace him, bringing along the Soft Machine and Willie Wilson (from Quiver) for instrumental support. (The second LP, *Barrett,* would be co-produced by Gilmour and Wright, Waters having said, "I can't cope with *that* again!," and with Humble Pie drummer Jerry Shirley complementing the Floyd boys' own instrumental work.) "I thought the sessions were actually rehearsals," reported the Soft Machine's Robert Wyatt. "We'd say, 'What key is that in, Syd?' and he'd reply 'Yeah' or 'That's funny.'" Sometimes Barrett's overconsumption of Mandrax caused him to fall off his stool or get his fingers entangled in his guitar strings.

Barrett's solo work is similar in structure and content to his Pink Floyd songs, only much of the method seems to have gone out of his madness. In comparison with *Piper, The Madcap*

Laughs and *Barrett* often sound flat, listless, offhand, and awkward. "It's all [still] going on in his head," Shirley told *Trouser Press*'s DiLorenzo, "but only little bits of it manage to get out of his mouth. . . . Sometimes he can sing a melody absolutely fine, and the next time round he'll sing a totally different melody, or just go off-key." Syd's solo material still yields brilliant flashes of fantastic imagery, or (to use his own phrases) "clover honey pots of mystic shining seed" and "moaned magnesium proverbs and sobs." But the visions have turned desperately bleak: "Cold iron hands clap the party of clowns outside. . . ." "Light misted fog, the dead waving us back in formation. . . ." "A broken pier on a wavy sea. . . ." Occasionally, however, the phantasmagoria gives way to lucid commentary on the artist's own confused mental state: "Inside me I feel so alone and unreal . . . ." "Please lift a hand . . . I tattooed my brain all the way."

Accompanied by Shirley and Gilmour (on bass), Barrett performed some of the material on "progressive" radio programs and at a London music festival, after which he moved back to his mother's house in Cambridge. He subsequently announced he was planning a third album—to consist of "twelve jolly good singles"—but none ever materialized. Though his solo LPs would go unreleased in the U.S. until 1974, a *Rolling Stone* writer who tracked Barrett down in Cambridge reported that he looked "hollow-cheeked and pale, his eyes reflect[ing] a permanent state of shock. He has a ghostly beauty which one normally associates with poets of old." Like his own songs, Syd seemed alternately lucid and elliptical. He said he felt "full of dust and guitars" and, at twenty-five, afraid of getting old. "I think young people should have fun, but I never have any." Nonetheless, he insisted he was "totally together," adding: "I'm not anything that you think I am anyway."

Barrett made his last public appearance at the Cambridge Corn Exchange in February 1972 with a makeshift band called Stars, consisting of bassist Jack Monck and ex-Tomorrow, Pretty Things, and Pink Fairies drummer Twink; but both gig and group collapsed in a shambles before the eyes of a rapidly dwindling crowd. Syd eventually moved back to London, to be sustained by royalties from the Floyd's classic first album.

In retirement, the Piper's ever-growing legend was fanned by one of the most zealous cults ever known to rock & roll. The appearance in 1972 of a Barrett fanzine called *Terrapin* (after a song from *Madcap*) triggered an overwhelming response from Syd freaks in some fifteen countries, including Brazil, Israel, and the U.S.S.R. Despite its increasing reliance on fan poetry and artwork and Syd Barrett crossword puzzles, *Terrapin* eventually ran out of old clippings and lyrics to reprint. As editor John Steele was forced to note in one of his last (and slimmest) issues, "the Society cannot keep on functioning if there is nothing new to report, and people tire of old records, no matter how amazing they may be." Yet there would be little further news about Syd Barrett, other than the occasional tragicomic anecdote, such as the one about his visit to a King's Road boutique, where he selected three different sizes of the same pair of trousers, claiming they all fit him perfectly.

To some extent, Barrett's latter-day cult resembles that of the late Jim Morrison, vicariously feeding upon the bizarre escapades of a brilliant and charismatic countercultural icon who evidently let himself be ruled (and eventually destroyed) by the weirder implications of his own art and public image. Barrett's story, in any case, certainly provides a cautionary tale of the toll that the glamorous Rock Biz exacts from its most sensitive and creative innovators. Indeed, these two interrelated themes—the exploitative tendencies of the music industry, and the artist's descent into madness—would permeate Pink Floyd's subsequent work (and occasionally prod them into forgoing their robotistic aloofness for the very human emotions of, respectively, anger and compassion). By the same token, Syd Barrett's ongoing mystique and importance derived in part from his unwitting influence on the albums that, after his departure, would establish his former group as one of the world's leading rock bands. "It couldn't have happened without him, but on the other hand it couldn't have gone on with him," said Waters.

Jenner, along with most people familiar with the Floyd, not only couldn't imagine the band amounting to much without its singer/songwriter/guitarist, but also supposed that the general public would share these sentiments and refuse to take the new lineup seriously. They were wrong on both counts. Barrett had already furnished the Pink Floyd blueprints, which (at least from a commercial standpoint) might be more successfully developed by a group of astute technicians than by the mercurial

Mason, Gilmour, Waters . . .

. . . and Wright (Ron Gott)

visionary who had dreamed them up in the first place. What's more, in 1968 Syd's name still meant little outside the London Underground, even among the masses of people who *had* heard of the Pink Floyd and their extraordinary reputation. If Waters, Gilmour, Wright, and Mason could manage to deliver the goods, who would be any the wiser?

The second phase of the Floyd's career got off to an inauspicious start with a Wright-bylined "It Would Be So Nice," which *NME* dubbed "Kinks-like jogging good time." Like the Kinks' "Lola" it ran afoul of the BBC's censors for giving free publicity to a commercial enterprise (*The Evening Standard*), obliging the Floyd to spend £750 to change a single word ("Evening" to "Daily") for the deejay copies. But as Waters caustically told *Zigzag*: "Nobody heard it [anyway] because it was such a lousy record."

LP, Holland, 1969 (*Columbia*)

Atom Heart Mother *LP, 1970* (*Harvest*)

Dark Side of the Moon *LP, 1973* (*Harvest*)

Single, Japan, 1980 (*CBS*)

"At that period we had no direction," added Mason. "We were being hustled to make hit singles. There's so many people saying it's important you start to think it is." But after the subsequent "Point Me at the Sky" made an equally dismal showing, Pink Floyd resolved to abandon the medium altogether, to become exclusively an album act. "We've never been a singles band," Wright later told *NME*. "'Arnold Layne,' which was a great single I thought, and 'See Emily Play,' which wasn't . . . are the only two we've ever had."

On 1968's *Saucerful of Secrets*, Waters and Wright each appropriated a familiar slice of Barrett songwriting territory, with Richard plumbing for the childhood memories ("Remember a Day," "See Saw") and Roger claiming the cosmos ("Set the Controls for the Heart of the Sun," "Let There Be More Light"). (Waters would later cite as his "greatest regret" the fact that the Floyd didn't do the music for Kubrick's *2001: A Space Odyssey*.) Syd can be heard on "Remember a Day" and his own exercise in schizophrenia, "Jug Band Blues"; but on the extended instrumental title track, the disjointed freak-outs of

"Interstellar Overdrive" have, under Gilmour's stewardship, given way to a more homogenized and ethereal brand of Space Rock. (The change was also facilitated when Wright began to alternate his Farfisa organ—then standard among rock keyboardists—with the churchier-sounding Hammond.) Though *NME*'s reviewer complained of "basically good tracks being ruined by the now mandatory bit of extended psychedelic electronics," the British consumer rated *Saucerful* (which reached number nine) very nearly as mind-blowing as *Piper* (which had peaked at number six). Pink Floyd's reputation as "the band who ate asteroids for breakfast" had survived unscathed; soon the boys would even be able to up their fifty-dollar-a-week salaries and settle some of their awesome debts.

During this period, the Floyd subjected themselves to a back-breaking regimen of one-night stands in Britain and on the Continent. In June 1968 they launched a new London tradition by staging Hyde Park's first free rock concert. Nine months later, at a London Festival Hall concert titled "More Furious Madness from the Massed Gadgets of Auximenes," Pink Floyd inaugurated their "sensurround" Azimuth Coordinator. "What's inside the box is a secret," Waters told *Melody Maker*, "but as you push the joystick around you can fade in and out of speakers placed all around the hall." The Azimuth (my dictionary defines the word as "a great circle intersecting a celestial body . . .") was but the most legendary component of an arsenal of machinery that by 1975 would occupy two whole floors of an Islington chapel.

As far as the music was concerned, however, Wright insisted (in *NME*): "We don't have any specially built instruments; we use normal instruments, apart from the VCS3, which anyone can buy. One of the myths about the Pink Floyd is that they have all this amazing electronic gadgetry, when in fact we all use the same as any other group. It's our technique of using them in a different way." He then proceeded to list their "normal" equipment: "a Kelsey Morris PA using Phase Linear amps and the mixer built by Alan and Heath; Hi Watt amplifier through WEM cabinets; sinsondecho machines; Farfisa organ; Fender electric piano; Fender guitars; Ludwig drum kit; four-track machine; and seven quadrophonic speakers."

At considerable expense, the Floyd not only lugged all this equipment to, and around, America (where they had yet to become a household word), but took the additional financial gamble of insisting that there be no other act on the bill. Yet as Gilmour would report in *Melody Maker*: "We rented the Fillmore ourselves, and it sold out. Originally Bill Graham, who runs the place, offered us a forty-minute spot with three other groups."

In 1969 the Floyd breached *Billboard*'s top hundred for the first time with the double album *Ummagumma*. (The title seems to refer to Frank Herbert's *Dune*, wherein the sage wizards are called "umma"). Ironically, these LPs offered little in the way of new Floyd music, one capturing live rehashes of such sci-fi oriented material as "Set the Controls" and "Astronomy Domine" ("Overdrive" was dropped at the last minute), while the other gave each member of the group half a side to indulge in solo experiments. The most intriguing (and/or least tedious) of these was Waters's otherwise lilting "Grantchester Meadows," wherein the nagging sound of a bee buzzing from one side of the headphones to the other is likely to prod the listener into swatting the air with his *Ummagumma* sleeve. "I've always felt that the differentiation between sound effects and music is a load of shit," Roger told *Zigzag*. "Whether you make a sound on a guitar or a water tap is irrelevant."

"Ticking away the moments that make up the dull day . . ."
(*Chuck Pulin*)

With Waters increasingly calling the shots (and writing the tunes), Pink Floyd shored up their avant-garde credentials by embellishing a series of arty Continental films with what *NME*'s Roy Carr and Nick Kent termed "their distinctive brand of instant cosmic epiphany soundtrack Muzak." Director Barbet Schroeder's *More* (1969) and *The Valley* (a.k.a. *Obscured by Clouds*, 1972) each spawned a soundtrack album, though Antonioni wound up using only three numbers from the Floyd's original full-length score for 1970's *Zabriskie Point*. The band also furnished music for German and Dutch TV shows about the moon landing and began scoring a proposed psychedelic cartoon series about "a boy in space" called *Rollo,* masterminded by Alan Aldridge—for which the requisite wealthy backers never materialized.

Then there was the Floyd's much-touted score for a Roland Petit ballet based on the works of Proust. But, as Waters told *Zigzag,* "it never happened. First it was Proust, then it was Aladdin, then it was something else. We had this great lunch . . . with Nureyev, Roman Polanski, Roland Petit, some film producer or other . . . to talk about the projected idea of us doing the music, and Roland choreographing it, and Rudy [Nureyev] being the star, and Polanski directing this fantastic ballet film. . . . Everybody just sat there drinking this wine and getting more and more drunk, with more and more poovery going on around the table, until someone suggested Frankenstein and Nureyev got a bit worried. . . . I was just sitting there, enjoying the meat and the vibes, saying nothing. . . ."

". . . with Roland's hand upon your knee," added Mason.

". . . and when Polanski got drunk enough he started to suggest we make the blue movie to end all blue movies, and then it all petered out into cognac and coffee and then we jumped into our cars and split."

In September 1971, by way of compensation, Pink Floyd were selected as the first rock group to play at the Montreux Classical Music Festival. This honor stemmed from their recent *Atom Heart Mother* (a.k.a. the "Cow Album"), a whole side of which was devoted to an extended composition by the Floyd and electronic experimenter Ron Geesin, wherein the band is complemented by a large brass section and choir. The title, said Mason, "came from a headline about a pregnant woman who had been kept alive with an atomic pacemaker. There's a con-

nection between the cow and the title if you want to think of the earth mother, the heart of the earth." Side two included a little-noticed tribute to Ray Davies called "Fat Old Sun" (which even opens with tolling bells lifted from the Kinks' "Big Black Smoke") and a montage of sizzling frying-pan effects called "Alan's Psychedelic Breakfast," which later made the Floyd squirm with embarrassment. Nonetheless, the album gave them their first British Number One, and also did well in America—where Capitol, having finally recognized the Floyd's potential, plastered the famous cow across forty-foot billboards and mailed plastic inflatable udders to influential deejays and critics.

The *Atom Heart* experiment led the Floyd to attempt another lengthy piece—this time without a collaborator—to fill a whole side of 1971's *Meddle.* "Echoes," Mason told *NME,* "was a specific attempt to do something by a slightly different method." Without having composed anything in advance, they booked a studio for a month. "Anytime that anyone had any sort of rough idea, we'd put it down." At the end of the month, "we'd got thirty-six different bits and pieces that sometimes cross-related and sometimes didn't. 'Echoes' was made up from that."

The Floyd premiered "Echoes" at a May 1971 "Garden Party" at London's Crystal Palace, as a fifty-foot inflatable octopus rose out of the lake and fireworks exploded overhead. Unfortunately, the music's volume was such that the real fish in the water were unable to survive the trauma.

The famous inflatable pig plugging the Animals *album and tour in Central Park* (*Chuck Pulin*)

And then the masterpiece. "It was all basically Roger's idea," Gilmour related in *NME.* "We'd all written [melodies] beforehand, and then Roger got the theme and the words together" (Waters, like Davies and Townshend before him, having become an incurable devotee of the Concept Album). As early as February 1972, the song cycle they still called *Eclipse* had been installed as the Floyd's concert centerpiece; it took them over a year to perfect, record, and release it as *Dark Side of the Moon.*

Ba-bump, ba-bump, ba-bump, goes the steady beat of the human heart. "I've been mad for fucking years," a deranged voice is heard to mutter. *Ba-bump, ba-bump . . .* the heartbeat is joined by the relentless ticking of a clock and by rhythmically synchronized cash registers, foreshadowing the two key songs (and villains of the piece) "Time" and "Money." Demented laughter gives way to unearthly screams, before relaxing into the familiar Floydian swirl of "Breathe"—which respite is followed by footsteps racing from speaker to speaker and the synthesized pyrotechnics of "On the Run." . . . The album plays out to the lilting, wide-eyed strains of "Eclipse"—the lunatic on the grass, "remembering games [of May?] and daisy chains and laughs . . . ." The psychotic mutterer, however, gets in the final word: "There is no dark side to the moon really; as a matter of fact, it's all dark." *Ba-bump, ba-bump, ba-bump.* . . .

Throughout much of the proceedings, saxophonist Dick Parry provides an alternate lead to the standard Floyd keyboards and guitar, in much the same way that Clare Torry and Doris Troy boost the boys' somewhat thin vocals. The production—wrought by the Floyd themselves, with the assistance of star engineer Alan Parsons—is worthy of any audio buff's wet dreams.

Honed past perfection, the accompanying stage show swept across the United States during the spring of 1973 with a full complement of dry ice, strobe sparks, and multicolored smoke. An enormous round screen provided cinematic counterpoint to the songs; gongs burst into flames; a balloon giant flashed green eyes; a floodlit balloon moon hovered overhead. And *Dark Side of the Moon* rose with helium velocity to Number One. "Quite suddenly," Gilmour marveled, "we've been able to sell out fifteen-thousand-seaters every night."

But *Dark Side of the Moon* would prove an impossible act to follow. Though Clive Davis of CBS, brandishing vast sums, immediately spirited them away from Capitol in the U.S., it took the Floyd over two years to devise a sequel. In the meantime, a backlash was developing among the critical elite back home, with *NME*'s Nick Kent blasting their "facile, soulless music" as "Orwellian":

> One can easily envisage a Floyd concert in the future consisting of the band simply wandering on stage, setting all their tapes into action, putting their instruments on remote control and then

"Another Brick in the Wall"'s Schoolmaster takes the stage (Dennis Zentek)

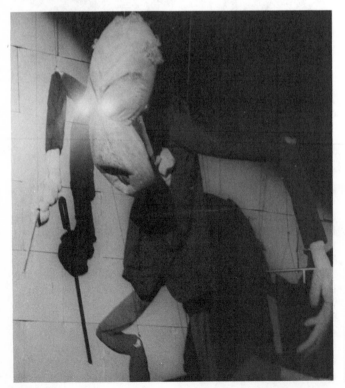

walking off behind the amps to talk about football. . . . Still, the Floyd can content themselves on one score. They are definitely the quintessential English band. No other combine quite sums up the rampant sense of doomed mediocrity inherent in this country's current outlook. "Hanging on in quiet desperation is the English way. . . ."

In 1978 Gilmour admitted (in *Melody Maker*) that the Floyd's post–*Dark Side* malaise almost culminated in a breakup. "*Wish You Were Here* was very indicative of our state of mind at the time. It was a terribly, terribly difficult record to make, simply because no one was really into it, everyone was very confused. . . . I think it's powerful because of that." *Wish You Were Here* consists of the nine-part Barrett tribute "Shine on You Crazy Diamond," interpolated with the highly pertinent title song and the anti–Rock Biz diatribes "Welcome to the Machine" and "Have a Cigar." With uncanny timing, as the Floyd were preparing the final mix of "Crazy Diamond," the madcap himself materialized, an obese, shaven-headed apparition barely recognizable as Syd Barrett.

A few days later the band left for America with their thirty tons of equipment and twenty-member crew ("a monstrous machine," conceded Gilmour). It was during this tour that Waters conceived the notion of physically building a wall across the stage: "People con each other that there is no wall . . . between performer and audience, so I thought it would be good to build one."

The Floyd's next album, however, was the stark, truly Orwellian vision of *Animals* (1977), which divvied up the whole human race into three unflattering categories: "Pigs," "Sheep," and "Dogs." The latter two selections had actually been part of the band's repertoire for years, under the respective titles of "Raving and Drooling" and "You've Gotta Be Crazy." According to Gilmour, "The *Animals* concept didn't come up until the album was three quarters finished . . . [when] Roger realized how close the lyrics were." During the cover photo sessions at Battersea Power Station, *Animals*'s trademark forty-foot inflatable pig floated out of control and was carried by prevailing winds over Heathrow Airport (much to the bemusement of the air traffic controllers) before finally touching down in faraway Kent.

Following the obligatory *Animals* tour, Pink Floyd again vanished from view, to their respective tax exiles in the Greek islands (Wright and Gilmour) and the south of France (Mason), while Waters (who dwelt in Switzerland) constructed his great *Wall*.

The Wall (1979) consists of two LPs' worth of anguished, angry *songs* (as opposed to predominantly instrumental mood pieces) that chronicle the life of a rock star/curmudgeon named "Pink Floyd," whose personality closely reflects Waters's own—except that "Pink" is gradually transformed into a raving psychopath under the cumulative pressures of childhood repression and Rock Biz "success." "On the simplest level," Waters explained to deejay Jim Ladd, "whenever something bad happens, he isolates himself a bit more—i.e., symbolically, he adds another brick to his wall to protect himself." By the end of side two, "Pink" is completely bricked in (metaphorically)—as are the Floyd (literally) at the climax of the first half of their stage spectacular.

"He then becomes susceptible to the worms. The worms are symbols of negative forces within ourselves, [of] decay. The worms can only get at us because there isn't any light or whatever in our lives." The second part of the album, show, and preconceived film spinoff (which would be directed by Alan

Parker, and star the Boomtown Rats' Bob Geldof) evokes Pink's breakdown before and during an arena concert. His mind begins to wander, Waters reported, "in 'Nobody Home,' [where] he slips back to 1968, and [in 'Vera'] he's going all the way back to the war. . . . There are people banging on the door going 'Come on, it's time to go! . . .' They've come to get him to the show, and he's in no state, so they get this doctor to get him standing up so they can wheel him onto the stage." The drugged stupor brought on by the doctor's injection is evoked by "Comfortably Numb"—ironically, the only selection among *The Wall*'s otherwise stark narratives to recall the Space Rock that made the Floyd famous.

Once onstage (emerging from behind the wall in the show), "Pink" metamorphoses into a ranting ultra-rightist (advocating capital punishment for those afflicted with Negroid features, homosexual tendencies, or acne), and the concert itself becomes a Fascist rally (with the crowd's "Pink Floyd! Pink Floyd!" chant turning into "Hammer! Hammer!"). "The idea is that we've been changed from the lovable old Pink Floyd that

we all know and love into our evil alter egos." Finally the protagonist suffers a total breakdown, hallucinating the Gilbert and Sullivan–esque "The Trial," wherein all the villains of his past—his mother, schoolmaster, and wife—sit in judgment. But though "Pink" "thinks that the worst thing that can happen to him is that he be exposed . . . in fact it's the best thing."

Actually, Waters is as sane as they come, which may be why ninety minutes' worth of *The Wall*'s prosaic lyrics and deliberately constructed symbols could never hope to approximate the genuine psychodrama of any one song on *The Madcap Laughs* or *Barrett*. The man behind *The Wall* is no visionary artist either; he remains, to the end, an architect.

Nonetheless, *The Wall* represented a departure for the Floyd, as courageous as it was spectacular; no longer could Pink Floyd be typecast as bloodless and invulnerable robots propelled by atom hearts. Waters, paradoxically, built his tangible Wall for the express purpose of exposing the real human being that had so long been obscured by the figurative one.

And at the end of "The Trial" the real Wall, too, comes crashing down (to appropriate fire-and-brimstone effects), leaving Pink Floyd to wander among the rubble, blowing childlike melodies through woodwinds—like pipers at the gates of dawn.

Pink Floyd and surrogates piping through the rubble of The Wall (Dennis Zentek)

(followed by their highest chart positions, as listed in *Billboard*)

PINK FLOYD'S HITS

U.S. Singles

1973   Money (**13**)
1980   Another Brick in the Wall (**1**)

U.S. LPs

1967   Piper at the Gates of Dawn (**131**)
1970   Ummagumma (**74**); Atom Heart Mother (**55**)
1971   Relics (**152**); Meddle (**70**)
1972   Obscured by Clouds (**46**)
1973   The Dark Side of the Moon (**1**); More (**153**); A Nice Pair (**36**)
1975   Wish You Were Here (**1**)

1977   Animals (**3**)
1979   The Wall (**1**)

(BY SYD BARRETT)

1974   The Madcap Laughs/Barrett (**163**)

(BY DAVID GILMOUR)

1978   David Gilmour (**29**)

U.K. Singles

1967   Arnold Layne (**20**); See Emily Play (**6**)
1979   Another Brick in the Wall (**1**)

T. Rex

THE SAGA OF MARC BOLAN (a.k.a. T. Rex) is one of a spunky little dreamer who looked and played the part of an elvish minstrel; whose bizarre voice and songs were dismissed by critics as a fleeting novelty or, worse, a bad joke; and whose most laughable trait of all was a near-mystical belief (shared only by his wife and his producer and a very few others) in his own importance and destiny—in short, a surefire loser who played by rules all his own and went on to become the biggest pop star in Britain.

Following his own obscure paths, Mr. T. Rex always seemed to end up in the right place at the right time. He was a genius—not so much at writing words and music (though much of that was indeed extraordinary) as at, simply, acting out the role of the pop genius. Marc Bolan was, among other things, one of the greatest charlatans ever known to rock—and that's no gibe; in pop at its most dynamic, image and implication have always counted for as much as the actual content of the music. Bolan's triumph was in part one of form over matter, style over substance—and, one might add, what style!

His first five LPs, for example, were laced with references to such imaginary peoples and places as the Dworns, the Lithons, and Rarn—giving his original Tolkien-nurtured cult following the distinct impression that young Marc was the creator of pop music's first elaborately detailed fantasy world. But Bolan was mostly just dropping exotic names; though the pieces were enthralling enough in themselves, they never quite added up. Marc certainly had a flair for imagery and alliteration, but he was something of a sphinx without a secret. And despite his extravagant claims as a composer and guitarist, he remained unwilling or unable to add more than a handful of chords to his musical arsenal.

No matter. By 1971 Marc Bolan promised to become the new decade's equivalent to the Sixties' Big Three—the Beatles, the Rolling Stones, and Bob Dylan—all rolled into one. "T. Rextasy" erupted as the biggest phenomenon Britain had witnessed since Beatlemania, and various ex-Beatles anointed the five-foot-five "Glitter King" their heir. As poster pinup, he supplanted Jagger as the stuff teenage dreams were made of; as electric bard with a style and bandwagon all his own—the press

Marc Bolan (Chuck Pulin)

dubbed it "Glam Rock"—he looked to be the real "new Dylan."

But the very fact that Bolan himself had always known it would happen something like this proved to be his undoing. Self-confidence turned to smugness, outrageousness to exhibitionism. All the charming quirks that had made his songs so special seemed to evaporate, and the music became colossally self-indulgent. Though at his peak Marc meant as much in Britain as almost any of the pop heroes chronicled in this book, his story offers our sole major instance of a U.K. phenomenon failing to cross the Atlantic as scheduled. Then, even at home, Bolan's star burned out almost as quickly as it had risen. Overweight and alcoholic, the "national elf" went into eclipse.

But in the wake of the Punk Rock/New Wave renaissance—which Bolan's own music had foreshadowed—he managed to shed a few pounds and pull himself and his act back together. Then, on the verge of a surefire comeback, Marc Bolan was killed instantly when his car crashed into a tree. The date was September 16, 1977—two weeks before his thirtieth birthday.

Aside from the fact that this was almost precisely the sort of classic rock & roll death Nik Cohn had notoriously wished upon the Rolling Stones, the macabre ironies seemed endless. One image that had recurred in so many of Marc's songs—even, anachronistically, in some of the early prehistoric fantasies—was that of the fast car, though he himself, for all the Rolls-Royces he bragged of owning, had never learned how to drive. Bolan also had a lyrical fondness for trees: "Our lives are merely trees of possibilities. . . ."

One of the greatest of all rock & roll legends, Marc Bolan will still have his revival—even if, alas, he himself won't be around to enjoy it.

As far as Marc Bolan was concerned, he was born a star. "When I was younger, I certainly thought I was a superior kind of being. And I didn't feel related to other human beings," he would tell a *New Musical Express* reporter. "I was always, like, the leader of all the things I did, but very solitary. I created a world where I was king of my neighborhood. I was very into clothes . . . forty suits when I was a kid, but never any friends."

This unusual child was born in the working-class London suburb of Hackney, on September 30, 1947, with the ordinary Jewish name Mark Feld. Sid, his father, drove lorries (trucks); Phyllis Feld ran a Soho fruit stall.

"I used to read a lot," said Marc; and by the time he was kicked out of school for truancy at fourteen, he had already developed the obsessions that he would one day combine into a distinctive pop formula: Greek mythology, British romantic poetry, and the French teenage prodigy Arthur Rimbaud ("the first poet that really rocked me; when I first read him I felt like my feet were on fire")—all in tandem with such twentieth-century forms of instant communication as movies ("I think I've seen every horror film that's ever been made") and, above all, rock & roll. As a stripling, Marc's favorite of his parents' records was "Ballad of Davy Crockett" by Bill Hayes; his initiation into rock came when Mr. Feld brought home "another record by that chap you like." But the name on this disc was Bill *Haley,* and the title, "Rock Around the Clock." Marc had been handed his calling.

His indulgent parents were soon talked into buying him a guitar and drum kit, and presently Marc was writing his first songs with a neighborhood lad named Keith Reid (future lyricist for Procol Harum). And as his mother would remember in a 1972 *Record Mirror* "special" on her son, "He'd come back after seeing Cliff Richard or Gene Vincent or the others of that time and he would say: 'Look—that's how I'll be one day.'"

In the meantime Marc sharpened his visual image and cultivated a talent for hustling strategically placed people. As a fifteen-year-old representative of the burgeoning Mod movement, he managed to attract the notice of *Town* magazine, which translated his wardrobe and outlook into a feature article: "Where is the goal towards which he is obviously running as fast as his impeccably shod feet can carry him? It is nowhere.

He is running to stay in the same place, and he knows that by the time he has reached his mid-twenties the exhausting race will be over and he will have lost. . . ." A stint modeling suits for John Temple followed, though Marc was not yet above washing dishes at Wimpy's for a few extra quid.

Then he gadded off to Paris and, by his own account, ended up living for five months with a practicing wizard (to whom Marc would pay tribute in his first record). "I learned by watching him," Marc would tell *The Evening Standard*'s Ray Connolly years later. "And I went on studying magic from books for two years. It's a very powerful thing. . . . I saw someone levitate. He was standing on the floor and he raised himself eight feet in the air. I've also done magical rites and conjured up demons. I've also seen flying saucers. . . ."

At the very least, Marc had developed his wildly fertile imagination, which would manifest itself not only in the enchanted visions of his poetry and lyrics, but also in a near-pathological tendency to exaggerate and fantasize about himself. In 1973 he would actually admit as much to Penny Valentine of *Sounds,* adding with an impish grin: "I feel that my credibility as a poet allows me to make things up." Indeed, much of Marc's charm derived from his ability to deliver (in song as well as in speech) the most preposterous lines with perfect aplomb. Nonetheless, many Bolan statements—including some found here—should be taken with the proverbial pinch of salt.

Back in England and "sick of modeling and living off wizards," Marc began to write songs in earnest. His method then, and always, was to scribble away in a manic frenzy of inspiration and then move on to the next endeavor. "He was never one of those people who'd sit for days and days working out lines and words," his future wife, June, would recall (in *Marc Bolan: A Tribute*). "It just happened like a force flowing out of him."

Marc himself was wont to boast of his ability to crank out a song in twenty minutes flat: "My guardian angel does all the writing; I'm sure it isn't me." This procedure often worked fine, but in the beginning, before Marc had developed an instinctive knack for the pop form (and toward the end, when inspiration was supplanted by the demon alcohol and sheer megalomania), the results could be grim indeed.

Over the three years preceding the release of his first album, Marc created a vast reservoir of original songs (which he would still be tapping for his fifth LP, *T. Rex*). Armed with his acoustic guitar and notebooks filled with his childlike scrawl, Marc set out to become a pop star. He hung around the appropriate pubs and ferreted out the scribes for *Melody Maker* and *NME,* telling all who would listen of his plans to join Presley, Dylan, and the Beatles atop rock & roll's Mount Olympus. "We metaphorically patted him on the head, bought him a Coke, and sent him away," Keith Altham has recalled. "A nice lad, but obviously

The child star at eighteen, after committing his "Wizard" to wax (Photo Trends)

with a marble missing! Yet there was something disturbing about his obsessive belief in his future, and I remember feeling that there was more to this ego freak than met the eye."

Marc tried on various personae for size; billing himself as Toby Tyler, he came on like a Dylan/Donovan folkie, complete with denim cap. But young Toby failed a recording test at EMI (which would one day distribute a label called T. Rex Wax Company) and went back to being Mark Feld. Finally the American record producer Jim Economides took the eighteen-year-old troubadour under his wing, secured a contract with Decca, and taped "The Wizard" at the unmagical hour of nine in the morning with a full orchestral accompaniment. When the singer/songwriter received the acetate, he was disconcerted to find scribbled upon it the name "Marc Bowland," which Decca thought would sell more records than plain old Mark Feld. After some wrangling the moniker was modified to Bolan.

Marc recorded one more Decca flop before being adopted by Yardbirds manager/producer Simon Napier-Bell. Those early recordings were delivered in a piping vibrato marginally less grating than chalk striking a blackboard the wrong way. When toned down a notch, however, Bolan's wobbly warble would become—if still by no means everyone's cup of tea—certainly one of the most distinctive voices in the business. Love it or hate it, Marc's sound was hard to ignore.

In early 1967, Columbia (U.K.) issued its sole Bolan single, "Hippy Gumbo," which proved no more successful than its predecessors; perhaps the "gay" message ("It seemed right/ that I should dig him all the night") was ahead of its time. (Marc in fact tended more toward the ladies, but he was also the sort to try anything at least once.) "The only interesting thing that came out of that ['Hippy Gumbo'] period was watching the Yardbirds work," Marc would tell *NME*'s Danny Halloway four years later.

But then Simon Napier-Bell had a brain-wave: One of his other acts, John's Children, had the looks and the pose down pat, and had already caused a stir with their nude publicity shots. ("We've got a pretty wild act," said one of the boys. "We undress each other onstage.") All they lacked was someone with a modicum of creative talent.

"It was decided John's Children needed a kind of Pete Townshend," Marc told Halloway. "I was sort of brought in to be the writer. They resented that incredibly because they wrote songs, which weren't very good, unfortunately." Despite the friction, Bolan scored a minor success for the group with his song "Desdemona"—though the line "lift up your skirt and fly" kept the single off the BBC playlist. "A lot of people dug that record. Pete Townshend really dug it . . . it really felt like it was going to explode."

John's Children were sent to Germany as opening act for their Track Records stablemates The Who. To hear Bolan tell it in a 1972 *NME* story, Townshend and Co. "had us taken off the tour in the end because we upstaged them. Not with music, just with the visual thing. I used to have a chain whip at the time. I'd chain up the whole bank of amplifiers and drag them across the stage and whip the guitar. I couldn't play, but I used that whip really well." (He would resort to it again years later, during the course of a slide back down the rock Olympus.)

"Next I went in to record the next song, which was called 'Mid-Summer Night's Scene' . . . we did it in one take and it sounded good. . . . I heard it the next day and it was a totally different thing. Simon had overdubbed all these 'oobie-doo's.'" Throwing a mid-summer night's scene of his own, Bolan quit the band.

Which is where our tale really begins.

When Marc Bolan finally did emerge as a minor local folk hero during London's Summer of Love, he arrived as if out of nowhere, a messenger from another time and place, wrapped in a homemade cape and strumming an acoustic guitar, a seeming stranger to technology but intimately acquainted with the older forms of magic. "I come from a time when the burning of trees was a crime," he sang. "My people were fair and had sky in their hair. . . ."

Looking every bit the part, delicate elvish features framed by ringlets of black curls, he lisped and stuttered and wailed and shrieked—often in a strange, unearthly accent that would render the all-important lyrics incomprehensible. (Fortunately, these would be printed on nearly all his LP releases.) Sometimes Bolan's poetic flights would give way to pure scat. For his entranced cult following, Marc offered a welcome antidote to all the lysergic noise being aired at the time, but in a sense Bolan was carrying *Magical Mystery Tour* and the science-fiction mumbo jumbo of *Their Satanic Majesties Request* (not to mention the widespread infatuation with astrology, sitars, natural foods, and *The Lord of the Rings*) to their illogical conclusion.

And yet we *need* fantasy—in direct proportion to the extent we feel choked by our own material progress. More than ever we need to get back in touch with the spirits of a purer and simpler age—with the questing heroes and the wizards and the dragons—to retrieve the archetypes from the very roots of our own culture, even if we may now contact them from our claustrophobic urban towers only via our headphones and mass-market paperbacks and color TVs. This became most apparent during the mass rebellion among the youth of the Sixties (who also turned to cultures, such as India's, that did not yet appear to have been raped by twentieth-century materialism), but the trend has never really been reversed: in the book world, the fantasy market is still booming.

Bolan was acutely aware of all this and made his original pitch accordingly. As he would write in the preface to his own book, *The Warlock of Love:*

> We hide behind the masks of the Orient,
> because the sullen, lumbering shapes of
> the western world strike fear and terror
> into our limbs, and all is ungrown.
> Legends we long for and legends there are
> in the east of our heads.

Bolan's sole musical accomplice then was Steve Peregrine Took, who had changed his name from Porter to that of the youngest of the four hobbit heroes of *The Lord of the Rings.* Sporting shades and a scraggly beard, Steve hardly resembled "Pippin," yet he provided Bolan with a moody and magnificent foil. A fine percussionist, he could make a pair of ratty old bongos gallop like Shadowfax carrying the hobbit Peregrine Took and the wizard Gandalf full-speed toward Minas Tirith; and as Marc would acknowledge even after their relationship turned sour: "He was a very good singer. Whatever I sang, he immediately found a harmony for it."

Bolan christened his duo Tyrannosaurus Rex because, he would tell *Disc,* "of the things that happened long ago that are

---

Tyrannosaurus Rex: Marc Bolan and Steve Peregrine Took (Ron Gott)

unbelievable and that people should be open and wise about. Imagine, forty-foot monsters used to walk on the earth where there are now motorcars and council houses.'' The apparent delicacy and vulnerability of both Rex's music and the singer/songwriter himself seemed to belie the fierce name, but Marc would insist (in *Melody Maker*): "[Elves] are not two-inch fey creatures—they're very powerful scientific sorcerers . . . so to me, Tyrannosaurus Rex was never a lame, camp, faggy sort of number. It was a very powerful prehistoric force."

In 1967, when Marc, not yet twenty, found his eighteen-year-old sidekick through an ad in London's underground rag *The International Times,* the sound he envisaged for his next band was in fact as overpowering as the name Tyrannosaurus Rex implied. With a full drum kit still at Steve's disposal, and Marc retaining the electric guitars he had wielded with John's Children, the pair recruited a pipe-smoking bassist and an ulcer-plagued lead guitarist ten years their senior. But as Steve would tell *NME,* the guitarist took to "knocking my drum kit around, knocking my cymbals over, thought he was Pete Townshend. . . . We decided we couldn't play with these other two cats. I sold my drum kit [to pay the rent on a flat he was now sharing with Bolan], got some bongos, and that was that." In any case, Track Records had decided to repossess Marc's equipment, obliging him to revert to his £12 acoustic guitar.

One of Tyrannosaurus Rex's earliest and most influential fans was Radio London disc jockey John Peel, who had frequently included Bolan's "Hippy Gumbo" on his eclectic playlists. After the government's 1967 crackdown on the offshore pirate stations, Peel was to be hired as the BBC's token hipster. In the meantime, he held forth as emcee in the new London club Middle Earth and duly installed Bolan and Took as house troubadours. Peel subsequently insisted that Tyrannosaurus Rex appear at all his engagements across Britain, and regularly invited them to perform their music on his Radio One program. (Bolan and Peel billed these shows "Oak, Ash, and Thorn," a phrase from *The Hobbit.*)

All this publicity helped to attract crowds of adoring flower children to Middle Earth and similar venues such as the London UFO; and the music-biz heavies soon followed. These included producer Denny Cordell's brilliant twenty-year-old protégé, Tony Visconti—memorably described by David Bowie's then-manager as a "New York draft-dodging anarchist"—who was scouting talent for Cordell's new label, Regal Zonophone.

"The three hundred people there were absolutely hypnotized," Visconti recollected in *NME,* "and I was one of them. I found Marc to be quite an incredible person, and . . . I guess he liked me because he came to see me at the office. Denny liked Rex a lot, but never thought they'd make it. So he said: 'They'll be our token underground group.' "

Bolan, for his part, favored Regal Zonophone over even the likes of Apple Records because—ironically, in light of Rex's future history—Cordell was willing to let them focus on albums instead of singles. Visconti was assigned all production responsibilities, and from then on, he says, "dedicated my life to T. Rex" (as he called them from the start). Even such later clients as David Bowie would remain a second priority on the Brooklyn whiz kid's agenda.

Tyrannosaurus Rex rose out of the sad and scattered leaves of an older summer. During the hard, gray winter they were tended and strengthened by those who love them. They blossomed with the coming of spring, children rejoiced and the earth sang with them. It will be a long and ecstatic summer.

John Peel's liner notes for the first Tyrannosaurus Rex LP

153

The album was recorded on a budget of just £400—about a thousand dollars. With overdubbing and other production effects kept at a minimum, Visconti and Tyrannosaurus Rex faithfully reproduced the skeletal sound of the duo's live performances. But this austerity hardly extended to a lyric sheet largely inhabited by solid silver genii and gazelle girls striding through palaces—with some stilted contemporary references to "mind-blowing visions" and "acid words" and a few "Hare Krishna"'s thrown in for good measure. On subsequent albums Bolan was to dwell more exclusively in his self-contained dream world, but the first LP offers such incongruities as "Mustang Ford" and "Hot Rod Mama," along with the young vegetarian's droll sketch of a lady butcher: "Graceful fat Sheba works with a meat-cleaver, sweating behind the meat counter."

LP, U.K., 1968
(*Regal Zonophone*)

LP, U.S.A., 1969
(*Blue Thumb*)

Peel was easily persuaded to lend his well-known speaking voice to a Bolan "children's story" included at the end of the program. (A second Peel reading was held in reserve for Rex's third LP.) Lacking any discernible plot, Marc's fairy tales free-associate in much the same manner as his rhymed song lyrics: "[He] let his molish imagination skip to and fro over sunken galleons and pirate pictures of rusted doubloons and deep-water cabins stacked to the brim with musty muskets and goldfish gauntlets. . . ." Like all subsequent Tyrannosaurus LPs, the package sported a dedication (in this case a C. S. Lewis reference): "To Aslan and the Old Narnians." Bolan gave his debut album one of pop history's longest-ever titles: *My People Were Fair and Had Sky in Their Hair, but Now They're Content to Wear Stars on Their Brows.*

The LP sessions also produced a catchy and relatively upbeat single called "Debora," whose lyrics previewed Bolan's unique blend of evocative imagery and sheer nonsense. The small but fanatical Tyrannosaurus Rex cult snapped up both single and album when they appeared in mid-1968, sending "Debora" into the lower reaches of Britain's Top Fifty, and *My People Were Fair* as high as number fifteen, according to the tabulations of *New Musical Express.* A second single quickly followed—"One Inch Rock," in which Bolan recounts his seduction by an enchantress who reduces him to the height of one inch and places him in a can with an equally bite-size girl. "They both get bored," explained Marc, "and do a dance"—the One Inch Rock.

"One Inch Rock" scored another minor success for Tyrannosaurus Rex, but until Bolan finally altered the name and the lineup, the band would remain the exclusive property of the British underground's postadolescent, Tolkien-toting LSD buffs. The duo was often likened to Donovan (at one point Rex performed as his opening act) and, especially, to that other pair of acoustic mystics, the Incredible String Band. But Bolan's

musical resources were considerably more limited, and he came across as even more bizarre and unworldly.

Nonetheless, while the Incredibles served up an eclectic mish-mash of *existing* philosophies, mythologies, and styles of folk music, by the next Tyrannosaurus Rex LP Bolan was weaving a spell distinctly his own. However crude and inaccessible Rex may have seemed in 1968, Marc's bold individualism enabled him to forge a unique style and image that would ultimately prevail over those of his more broadly gifted fellow flower children. Meanwhile, the second album, *Prophets, Seers, and Sages: The Angels of the Ages* showed Bolan thoroughly immersed in his idiosyncratic world of myths and dreams, which he had now swept clear even of such quaint twentieth-century artifacts as Mustang Fords and Hot Rod Mamas.

Tyrannosaurus Rex's eccentric appeal probably came closest to that of original Pink Floyd leader Syd Barrett, whom Bolan acknowledged at the time as a key influence, along with Bob Dylan, Pablo Picasso, Salvador Dali, and C. S. Lewis's *Chronicles of Narnia.* "What the Pink Floyd do electronically," Bolan declared, "we do acoustically." Years later he would describe Barrett as "one of the few people I'd actually call a genius . . . he inspired me beyond belief."

In those days Rex and Pink Floyd were both managed by Blackhill Enterprises—which is where Marc met his future wife, June Child, whose combination of music-biz savvy and utter devotion to Bolan and his work would prove a major asset to his

(*Ron Gott*)

career. The couple shared a cold-water flat near Notting Hill Gate for two years before finally getting married in 1970.

During that time, Tyrannosaurus Rex established itself as a fixture of the era's open-air celebrations, and continued to regale the faithful at small venues across Britain. (Some of these performances were enhanced by the pantomime routines of a young would-be pop singer named David Bowie.) In short, Tyrannosaurus Rex was bopping along merrily. But that wasn't quite enough for Marc Bolan, who would confide to *Melody Maker*'s Chris Welch that he "wanted successful records (or books) to make life a little more exciting, rather than bum along in dedicated obscurity."

Nineteen sixty-nine's *Unicorn* proved to be the most imaginative and impressive of all the Bolan/Took albums—and also the last. For the first time, Visconti and the boys fully tapped the resources of the recording studio, enhancing Marc's multi-tracked acoustic guitars and newly acquired harmonium with Steve's overdubbed bass, piano, and drum kit, to create a sound strangely reminiscent of Phil Spector—by way of the rinky-dink Kinks of *The Village Green Preservation Society*. *Unicorn* also made use of distortion, sound effects, and *Revolver*-style backwards tapes, but in such a seemingly ingenuous way that the LP retained all the homemade charm of its predecessors. And, oddly enough, the electric guitar was still nowhere to be heard.

Yet, despite tighter, catchier melodies such as "The Seal of Seasons," "Catblack (The Wizard's Hat)," and "The Misty Coast of Albany," commercial potential remained slim. These were still the days when, as *NME*'s Nick Logan put it, "the name Tyrannosaurus Rex on a record signaled its instant dismissal to disc jockeys' rejection piles." (Nonetheless, when a Tyrannosaurus Xerox called "In the Summertime" took Mungo Jerry all the way to Number One, Bolan "realized there was nothing to stop us from being bigger.")

Unicorn's lyrical landscapes are peopled with such singular

characters as "the darkly ghostish host, haggard vizier of the moats" and "the husky hag of early darkness in her hoods of snowy grey." This quirky masterpiece was the first Tyrannosaurus Rex album to appear in the U.S. (on the tiny Blue Thumb label), where it was soon relegated to the bargain bins. To promote the record, Bolan embarked on the first—and most disastrous—of all his ill-fated attempts to conquer America. As supporting act for the Turtles, he did at least befriend Howard Kaylan and Mark Volman (a.k.a. Flo and Eddie), whose shrieking harmonies would one day furnish a key ingredient in the T. Rex success formula.

But Took and Bolan had been growing apart; at this point, said Marc, "we didn't communicate at all." Bolan, despite his spaced-out image, shunned psychedelics and even pot, seldom touching anything stronger than the occasional glass of wine. Took, however, was dropping acid almost daily. According to June Bolan, "He became just like a vegetable, and onstage . . . would suddenly start taking his clothes off and beating himself with belts." In a 1972 *NME* feature, Steve would recall with relish: "I took my shirt off in the Sunset Strip where we were playing and whipped myself till everybody shut up. With a belt, y'know, a bit of blood. . . . I mean, Iggy [Pop] Stooge had the same basic approach."

Such escapades hardly helped the acoustic duo's music to come across in an optimum light, and at the end of the tour Steve eloped with an American girl to sighs of relief all round. "I was obliterated for months afterward, I was totally chemicalized," he said. In October 1969, Britain's music weeklies confirmed that the original Tyrannosaurus was extinct.

Took attributed much of the friction to his thwarted desire to contribute his own ideas and songs. "Instead of being on the fantasy part of the trip, they were about what happens to the kids on the street. But the record company started objecting to words like 'breast' or 'drugs,' and it frustrated me greatly."

"He wanted to be like a front man," said Bolan, also in a 1972 *NME* story. "He thought he wasn't contributing enough, and he wanted to contribute. But I sincerely believe that had he contributed what he wanted to do, it would have killed the group stone dead."

The two also differed in that Took was a wild-eyed radical who (in Bolan's words) "wanted to burn down the city and put acid in the waterways," while Marc was merely determined to become a star. "For a while, Marc was a good hippy," said Steve. "Like, we used to sit around and rap about what needed changing. I know he doesn't do that now. The trouble is that after you've had two or three hits you find yourself socializing with a different type of person—other people with hits, or managers of groups with hits. While I was lying about smoking dope, Marc would be checking these people out."

Two years after his exit from Tyrannosaurus Rex, journalists would refer to Took as the Pete Best of the Seventies. Like the Beatles' former drummer, Steve would be dredged up by the usual music-biz sharks once his old group turned into a national phenomenon, but again to no avail. Bolan himself could wax extremely catty on the subject of his ex-partner; when asked Took's whereabouts, he once replied: "In the gutter somewhere."

In fact—after playing bass in a band with the Tolkien-derived name Shagrat, and "a bit of boogying around with the [Pink] Fairies"—Steve wound up in a dingy basement flat, with a mattress on the floor and dead rats in the hallway, nursing his modest ambitions: "Basically, all I want to do is sit under an orange tree, play my guitar in the sun, get stoned, and dig the smells and colors.'' Following innumerable comeback attempts—all jinxed by his irrepressible self-destructiveness—Steve Peregrine Took, too, would die young, choking on a cocktail cherry on October 27, 1980.

Prior to the split, Bolan had already ventured out on his own to produce a sixty-three-page volume of poetry. Though he later claimed that *The Warlock of Love* ''took me about two weeks to write''—which he attributed to his previous incarnation as a Celtic bard—this torrent of free-associative, free-verse fantasy always remained Marc's proudest accomplishment. The poems reflect the themes and style of his words on *Unicorn*, though some suffer from the absence of the discipline imposed by the song lyric form.

The unkind might dismiss *The Warlock of Love*—along with similar efforts authored by Dylan, Donovan, and Jim Morrison (whom Bolan once called his favorite singer)—as a monumental self-indulgence peculiar to Sixties rock stars with literary pretensions. Yet even if such pieces as ''The Fluted Floors of Dagamoor'' fail to bring Marc's private mythology into clearer focus, his images of ''wisdom mist and foul fingering fog'' or ''skull juice curdled like an overripe cheese'' testify to a brilliant imagination and verbal flair. At their best, Bolan's couplets effectively blend winsomeness and whimsy:

> I wish you Earth's rich moss fulfillment
> in your bluebell chiming plight.

In the wake of T. Rextasy, *The Warlock of Love* would, to its author's vast delight, get snapped up to the tune of forty thousand copies to become Britain's best-selling book of poetry.

In late 1969, Marc's first order of business was to recruit a new partner with whom to put down the songs written on that ill-starred tour of the States. After want ads in the music rags for

''a gentle young guy who can play percussion'' failed to produce a suitable candidate, a friend steered Bolan toward Notting Hill Gate's Seeds restaurant, where a young artist and musician named Micky Finn was engaged decorating the macrobiotic watering hole with psychedelic murals.

Finn's credits included stints as painter (under The Fool's aegis) of the Beatles' Apple Boutique and as drummer with a band called Hapsash and the Coloured Coat; but Bolan hired him primarily on the strength of his aquiline good looks and their instant personal rapport. Both were obsessed with UFOs, Fellini films, and Fifties rock & roll; and Mr. Tyrannosaurus Rex is also said to have been impressed by Micky's mammoth motorcycle. Musically speaking, Finn was no Steve Peregrine Took; according to Bolan, ''He couldn't sing at all at that point and his drumming was not really very sophisticated, *but* we jammed for about four hours. I never jammed with Steve.''

When the new Rex holed up in the Welsh countryside to get their act together, Marc brought his electric guitar out of the closet for the occasion. The next album, *A Beard of Stars,* showed him shifting musical gears. The words were less purple, the melodies stronger, and the sound more commercially oriented. Yet the riffing of the born-again electric warrior was still fairly crude and generally kept subordinate (with the unfortunate exception of the high-voltage freak-out ''Elemental Child''). By and large, *A Beard of Stars* simply added a dollop of punch and volume to the usual Tyrannosaurus Rex preoccupations.

Nonetheless, the album had staked out a new musical direction, which the star-bound Bolan would feel impelled to follow to its logical destination. ''After a few years you get sick of sitting cross-legged on a stage,'' he would later tell *NME*. ''I wanted to boogie. I wanted to get out of my little room on Portobello Road. People really think I fell out of the sky and landed on a mushroom holding my acoustic guitar. But before that I was yer actual heavy guitarist. I wanted to get back to that.''

Marc's next move was to shake off some of his act's dinosaur and hippie connotations by abandoning the ''Tyrannosaurus,'' which, he claimed, ''the BBC always had difficulty in pronouncing.'' Bolan and Co. were now set to take on the new decade with a snappy new name: T. Rex.

When the first T. Rex single, ''Ride a White Swan,'' appeared in October 1970 (on Denny Cordell's newly formed Fly label), Marc threatened to chuck his music in favor of a literary career should ''Swan'' fail to take off. But—though his electrified *Beard of Stars* had sold no better than its predecessors—Bolan deployed every trick in the books of Agadinmar to load the dice against T. Rex's premature retirement.

Not only was his new record a trend-setting three-for-the-price-of-two ''maxi single''; it was also touted, cannily enough, as a ''triple A-side.'' And when T. Rex hit the road to promote it, Marc insisted that all tickets be kept down to 50p ($1.25)—a popular attention-getting device in a time of soaring concert prices, not to mention one eminently suited to the duo's low overhead.

But it was in the music itself that this wily conjurer pulled out all the stops. On one of the tracks—''Summertime Blues''—Marc let down his corkscrew hair to positively flaunt his rock & roll roots; yet, to be doubly perverse, he and Micky performed the Eddie Cochran classic (the first of a bare handful of nonoriginal Bolan releases) with the traditional Tyrannosaurus acoustic guitar plus bongos. ''Is It Love?'' reversed that equation in an early sample of electric Bolan boogie that wedded archetypal T. Rex chunka-chunk bar chords to Marc's warbled delivery of his most succinct lyric to date: "Is it love that makes us rock? . . . We're gonna rock, gonna rock with love."

Those other two "A-sides" notwithstanding, it was indisputably "Ride a White Swan" that made the first T. Rex single a smash, and Marc Bolan a star. Like the best of Buddy Holly and the Crickets—whom "Swan" invokes right down to the infectious handclaps—Bolan's musical accomplishment here is slight yet perfect. A trebly Les Paul tosses off the poppiest of hooks by the second, yet there's no mistaking the elf himself in the whimsical lyrics and delivery. Bolan's cauldron still bubbled with the spells and potions of his mythical land of Beltane, but now these had finally been boiled down to the ultimate magic of a two-and-a-half-minute instant radio classic.

Marc's reputation for mumbled esoterica tended at first to keep the record off the BBC playlists, but when a single airing on Radio One reportedly sparked two thousand orders, Bolan's "Swan" at last took flight. It reached number four in *NME*, began to slip, and then enjoyed a resurgence, peaking at number two some five months after its release.

"Ride a White Swan," said Tony Visconti (in *International Musician and Recording World*),

> was a hit he was aiming for; believe me, he didn't want to be that cultish. . . . All those weird singles like "King of the Rumbling Spires" [the very last Rex recording to feature Took, and the first to feature Marc's electric guitar] were attempts at Number One records. The only difference on "Ride a White Swan," which made it, was that for years I was asking Marc to use some strings. I asked my boss, David Platz, how many strings we could afford, and he said four. So we used these four violinists . . . putting a little glistening thing on the top, and that seemed to do it. . . . Marc always had it in him to make hit records—he just needed the right elements, and finally we invented the T. Rex formula.

The subsequent *T. Rex* LP offered pared-down Tyrannosaurus motifs presented in a revved-up style (plus more from those four violinists)—and Mr. Marc Bolan poised at the crossroads of his career, with both his confidence and his guitar chops considerably enhanced. This album is far more accessible than any of its predecessors, yet the spirit of Tyrannosaurus Rex lingers intact; indeed, *T. Rex* features superior retreads of Marc's early singles "The Wizard" and "One Inch Rock," and fully half the album's contents had been copyrighted by 1968. Marc and Micky run the gamut from taut toe tappers to lush ballads, all sparked by that inimitable magic touch—"She bathes in thunder, the elves are under her" . . . "A shape that was golden and crimson extended a claw to my frame" . . . "light up the wind with all the kings inside you . . ."—the finest lines in Rex phantasmagoria telegraphed in eminently catchy two-minute tunes. Though Marc's trademark warble is still very much in evidence, his delivery has shed its grating edge, and one can actually hear what he is singing about.

In short, this is the Rex LP that best represents the full sweep of Marc's talents, and the one that this particular Bolan buff would bring to that electrically wired desert island so frequently invoked by rock critics.

It also marked Bolan's American debut on the Warner Brothers/Reprise label, the first indication that T. Rex might ever amount to anything across the big water. *Rolling Stone,* which had always ignored Bolan, now chimed in with encouraging words, lauding in particular Marc's "fascinating ability to intermingle vocal and instrumental sounds—the vocals often go into a feedback guitar imitation." To *Rolling Stone* boss Jann Wenner, Bolan shot back a handwritten note, sprinkled

T. Rex: Micky Finn and Marc Bolan (Globe Photos)

with dime-store stick-on stars and the telltale signs of a would-be bard who had never learned to spell:

> Jan
> thank you for useing our name in rolling stone, we have a nice scene here but its a small Land so were looking forward with winged hearts to meeting american heads & playing & speaking for anybody with ears. I've enclosed some poems & pictures in case there of use to you
>
> all my love as a freind
> marc bolan of t. rex

One of the *T. Rex* selections, "The Children of Rarn," was supposed to reappear as the title track of a magnum opus Bolan had been working on for two years. *The Children of Rarn* was to represent the culmination of all Bolan's excursions into the realms of prehistoric dreamscapes and heroic fantasy, and his first attempt to fashion these into a coherent narrative—a true pop epic, and Marc's own *Sgt. Pepper* or *Tommy.*

Bolan envisaged *Rarn* as a double album, set "in prehistoric earth before the dinosaurs were heavy creatures," and telling of a cataclysmic war provoked by such evil forces as "trolls from Marrow Mound [who] live on bones," "Lithons old as earth [who] knew no death, know no birth," and "Dworns, devil-born . . . machine-god kings." Marc explained to the newly attentive *Rolling Stone* that "'Dworn' is actually a two-sided word—it's a man but it's also a machine, which in fact was a prehistoric motorbike which worked on solar power. It has solid ivory wheels, a golden base, and two gazelle horns to steer. It could go about eight hundred miles per hour."

In the end, the god Rarn intervenes to save the seven-foot Peacelings, and then—exacting a price reminiscent of the last part of *Lord of the Rings*—"changes the name from Beltane to Earth in a shower of rain" as "the creatures of legend disappear through the gate" and the Peacelings themselves are reduced to the status of ordinary mortal men.

But the only trace we have of this fabulous endeavor is the handful of demos Marc recorded in Visconti's apartment, which have been issued posthumously on a Cube Records compilation called *Marc.* Though *Rarn*'s key songs had all been written by 1971, the project also called for elaborate arrangements, as well as linking passages, both musical and verbal. Bolan would never finish painting his masterpiece, for he was now too busy turning himself into a pop megastar: "There's always time to be Pasolini, but only a few short years in which to become a teenage idol."

As Marc and Micky plugged the *T. Rex* album on their cut-rate tours—whose division into acoustic and electric segments recalled Bob Dylan's controversial period of transition some five years earlier—Bolan began to yearn for a heavier rhythm section. "So Tony Visconti did some gigs on bass," he would tell *NME*, "and I was getting more and more into the electric thing. That was really what the kids wanted, you see. And I was doing the older things, and most of the people that were coming to see us had never even heard of the older things. And I worked with Tony, and I said: 'I *must* have a bass player.'

"One day later we had Steve Currie.* Then it was bass, hand drums, and me, and it sounded fine. But then I realized, after 'White Swan,' that it had to have a drum kit, and . . . I said: 'I must have a drummer now, or I'm never going to play again.' I got very dramatic. And suddenly it was all there, and I thought: 'Man, I've got a band.'"

Currie was a failed medical student turned ship broker whom Bolan had recruited through the *Melody Maker* classifieds, and the drummer, Bill Fyfield, was a former Sunday-school teacher. Fyfield had played with the Epics and, more recently, a Visconti-produced band called Legend—which prompted Marc to change the drummer's name to Bill Legend—and Currie had worked in a jazz-rock outfit dubbed Rumble. Bolan kept his two new cohorts on a salary of £30 ($75) a week; though this would be raised to £100, neither Legend nor Currie ever received a percentage of the T. Rex Number One hits that followed in their wake.

The first link in that golden chain was "Hot Love." Released in February 1971, this combined a clichéd twelve-bar blues structure with a good-timey sound and an unprecedentedly smooth production (complete with Flo and Eddie and creamy strings). Marc's voice and lyrics remained distinctive, but for the first time they connected directly to the erogenous zones of his fellow mortals: "Well she ain't no witch/ and I love the way she twitch, ah ha."

Bolan called "Hot Love" "cosmic rock." *NME* called it "very commercial," adding: "You will feel compelled to sing along. The very simplicity of the number is the key to its assured popularity—plus the contagious bounce beat that's emphasized throughout by handclaps." But the first of many such letters to *NME* called it "a terrible mistake" and "teenybop trash"; another fan wrote *Melody Maker*: "John Peel's ecstatic summer of Tyrannosaurus Rex has come to an end. An ultra-cool autumn bears T. Rex. . . . Gone are the mellow tones of 'Strange Orchestras,' the weird tales and sounds we love. Who would have thought Marc would transform into a Hendrix-style guitarist screaming and gyrating?" Concluded *MM*'s Chris Welch: "'Once he was fair and had stars in his hair' is the dismal chorus of the woeful cherubs who write in childlike hand of the magical change which has befallen their fairy king."

"Everything I'm doing now is a risk," claimed Marc. "I am very self-destructive. The risk is that 'Hot Love' could have died a death and we could have blown the whole thing." In fact, "Hot Love" was firmly lodged at Number One within a few weeks of its release.

---

* *Currie, too, was fated to die in a car crash, in 1981.*

"I watched them play 'Hot Love' on *Top of the Pops*," Bolan marveled to an *NME* reporter. "There they were dancing away in their little hot pants and that really turned me on. Because they probably didn't know anything about me or who I am, but they are digging that record."

Yet instead of basking in his rising star at home, Bolan slogged through his second American tour—as a supporting act playing to audiences who didn't know anything about him and by all accounts remained indifferent. "We got heckled at the Fillmore and I insulted two people in the front row. I said: 'Instead of you ----- we could be at home playing to people who want to see us.'" But, as always, Marc preferred to dwell on the silver lining, insisting in *NME* that "more people knew of the band than we expected. If we had done any better it would have felt hyped. . . . It tightened us up, tightened me up a lot. It was like a battle and I feel we won." By contrast, when T. Rex went back on the road at home in May, Marc began to draw squeals from his increasingly young (and large) audiences; there were even a few small-scale riots.

July 1971 brought another instant British chart topper; in London's pubs and boutiques that summer, one seemed to hear little else but "Get it on, bang a gong, git-t on." "Get It On" remains Marc's strongest claim to a bona fide rock & roll classic. (Nearly a decade later it was being covered by disco acts and adopted by Blondie as a concert encore.) It also provided the archetype for years of soundalike T. Rex hits: sustained notes from Tony Visconti's string department hovering ominously over adamant-hard rock music (in this case an adaptation of the Chuck Berry song "Little Queenie," which is briefly quoted in the fadeout), with Flo and Eddie vamping out of some imaginary Fifties rock & roll horror show, and Bolan's fey voice spouting, in almost the same heavy breath, imagery from both Greek legend ("got the teeth of the Hydra upon you") and Juvenile Delinquent Row ("you got a hubcap diamond-star halo"). This heady concoction even made the Top Ten in America (where it was retitled "Bang a Gong" in deference to a current hit by Chase called "Get It On")—a feat Bolan would never manage to duplicate.

"Get It On" also set the tone for (and was included on) the next T. Rex LP, *Electric Warrior*. Discussing this album with various *NME* correspondents, Marc said: "Every record I dug as a kid I got now. I see my place as writing things like 'Quarter to Three' or 'Runaround Sue' but with better words. At the time those words were a groove, but we've all got over that now. We're a different generation . . . living on a different sort of planet."

Years before the emergence of the Ramones and Elvis Costello, nearly every track on *Electric Warrior* incorporated sly references to the landmarks and clichés of pop history, from Elvis Presley and the Schlock Rock classic "Duke of Earl" to the counterculture's favorite film, *2001: A Space Odyssey*. "Jeepster," said Bolan, "is very positively meant to sound like a Sun record . . . like [Presley's] 'Mystery Train.'" According to *Rolling Stone* critic Ben Gerson: "What Marc seems to be saying on *Electric Warrior* is that rock is ultimately as quaint as wizards and unicorns, and finally, as defunct. It is a self-contained, completed form."

For an example, Gerson cited "Monolith," dubbing it "Stanley Kubrick meets the Duke of Earl." Bolan himself said: "The song is not in fact 'Duke of Earl' but it could be any of those songs. The main thing with that song is the lyrics, because the lyrics are not anything to do with that period. To put them [lines like "lost like a lion in the canyons of smoke"] against that kind of backdrop was an idea that just made me smile.''

Bolan insisted that ''there is more feeling on [Electric Warrior] than on every other album put together. I have never been so excited about putting out a record . . . if we are ever going to get a Gold Album worldwide this is it. It is instant hum-the-songs, but the words are such that no way can it be called a sellout.'' Indeed, Warrior is a T. Rex classic, chock-full of unforgettable Power Pop hooks and melodies. The words still bear traces of Bolan's unique imagination and poetic flair, and he has never sung better. Temporarily kept at bay by strong Number One albums from Rod Stewart, John Lennon, and Led Zeppelin, T. Rex's tour de force finally claimed Britain's top LP slot in the last week of 1971.

In his new role as pop star extraordinaire, Bolan was a natural; he clearly adored every minute, every facet of the business. Claiming he spent £500 a week on clothes, Marc was seldom seen in the same outfit twice. The capes that June had formerly stitched for him out of old blankets now gave way to multicolored suits of silk and satin—occasionally outfitted with batlike wings—along with fabulous furs and jewelry, the likes of which had rarely adorned a twentieth-century heterosexual male. Bolan made the rest of the band conform to his singular dress code, despite all their attempts to lose the suitcases on tour; the T. Rex camp's motto became: ''Anyone caught wearing a T-shirt gets shot at dawn.''

Marc's adorable pixie features—such obvious fodder for the teen pinup magazines—were accentuated with heavy makeup and a sprinkling of silvery stars. ''I am my own fantasy,'' Marc boasted; and he proceeded to both launch and personify what the press would soon tag Glitter (or Glam) Rock. Whatever Bolan did, his growing hordes of guitar-toting imitators and Rextatic fans slavishly copied; as NME's Roy Carr has written: ''He prompted the male populace to discover the hitherto unknown delights of Woolworth's cosmetics counter''—though the sexual implications of all this were to remain safely closeted until their canny exploitation by Marc's old pal David Bowie. In any case, Bolan's glittering image—coupled with his infectious hits—brought flair and fun back to a British music scene stifling under the reign of the heavy-metallurgist bone crunchers, the pompous classical/rock fusionists, and the ''Power to the People'' brigade.

Marc proved to be an equally outrageous interviewee, a master at manipulating the press. He had every angle covered; whether the reporters came from the sophisticated music weeklies, the Sunday supplements, or the teen fan magazines, all were certain to bring back a lively story expressly tailored to their needs. He would discuss his exquisite bone structure, or dispense handy tips for girls hoping to catch his eye, if that's what the journalists wanted; but if it was a creative genius they were after, he would talk of the five books he'd just finished writing, or a forthcoming T. Rex film ''about a cosmic messiah, a messenger from God who has to check up on planet Earth. He's visually very incredible and has to adapt to be able to walk about. We will be filming his reaction to all the shit that we take quite naturally, like garbage on the telly and mass murders and all the rubbish he has never seen before. When he left Earth it was a Garden of Eden with potential gods, and in the story God has not returned to the planet since then. He expects a race of gods and what he finds is this mess.''

On other occasions Bolan would nonchalantly liken his guitar playing to that of the late Jimi Hendrix, or his poetry to Keats. The provocative headlines blared from Melody Maker and New Musical Express: I WAS A SUPERIOR KIND OF BEING . . .

LENNON COPIED ME . . . I'M AS GOOD AS TOWNSHEND AND HE KNOWS IT.

The letters, naturally, came back fast and furious: ''Who the hell does Bolan think he is?'' . . . ''When T. Rex are even one tenth as good as The Who, he can pat himself in the face with a cricket bat.'' All, of course, excellent grist for the star maker's mill. (Townshend's own response was: ''I've always dug Marc Bolan and he knows it, and he also knows that I'd let him get away with murder because of what he's doing for rock & roll.'')

Britain's relatively compact size, and the fact that all its communications media are centralized in one city, make it far more fertile ground for instant phenomena than the United States. T. Rex became so successful so quickly that there were bound to be detractors in any case. The most common charge

Bolan flanked by superstar cronies Elton and Ringo (Globe Photos)

leveled against Bolan by the posthippie tastemakers and semi-intellectual heavies was that he had ''sold out.''

True, Marc underwent his metamorphosis from flower child and cult hero to electric warrior and teen idol at a time when the rock world was at its most self-conscious, and its music critics at their most elitist. Yet it is doubtful that the anti–T. Rex faction had ever really understood and appreciated Bolan's work in the first place. Through all the changes, Marc had remained uniquely himself; only now he was getting more successful at it.

As he would later tell Keith Altham, one of his NME allies (and subsequently T. Rex's publicist): ''It was that transformation from what people thought was 'the Little Elfin Prince and the Summer Toadstool' to an electric rock star in just over a year that freaked everyone out. . . . [But] if there's going to be any kind of revolution in pop music it must come from young people. If you ignore them, you're cutting yourself off from the life force of rock. . . .

''I suppose I'm a sort of teenage idol but I'm not a teenybop idol. What people do with you in their own minds you can't stop, but I think of myself as an idol only in the same way that George Harrison once was, and I'd be very upset if the press wrote me off as anything less than a musician and a poet.''

My own favorite T. Rex memory remains a performance at an August 1971 Woodstock-style "Festival of Progressive Music" in Weeley, England. The bank holiday weekend was almost over; the sun had just set; and much of the audience, still caught up in the boozy high spirits of Rod Stewart and Co., was clamoring for yet another Faces encore. Enter into the spotlight a tiny satin-clad figure, electric guitar and sense of irony firmly in place as he claimed the microphone: "I'm Marc Bolan. You've seen me on *Top of the Pops*. I'm a big star." Cheers from the faithful clashed with jeers from a coalition of juiced-up Faces fans taking exception to their heroes' second billing to the renegade Tyrannosaurus, and stringy-haired pot smokers who'd read of his sellout to the teenyboppers. Bolan proceeded to drown them all out with a high-wattage new T. Rex car anthem titled "Cadillac." The tense atmosphere really did recall Dylan's controversial electric debut at the Newport Folk Festival six years earlier—and Bolan, alternately playing the strutting punk and the winsome troubadour, certainly delivered the goods that night. "I *demand* a reaction," he would later declare. "They can either love me or hate me, but I won't have apathy."

Yet a month later, in the less charged ambience of Amsterdam's Concertgebouw, the child star failed to impress. One endless clumsy jam followed another, until the finale, "Get It On," gave way to Marc jerking a tambourine up and down the neck of his guitar, faster and faster, ultimately climaxing with the tambourine's ejaculation into the front rows. Maybe Bolan did that at Weeley, too—I can't remember—but viewed from the perspective of the polite, sophisticated Dutch audience it all seemed downright narcissistic and silly. At least the youth of Amsterdam—as attuned as anyone on earth to underground culture, and especially British "progressive" rock—knew of Bolan's accomplishments and were willing to give him a fair hearing. In the American heartlands, where T. Rex remained little more than a one-hit wonder, their frequent in-concert sloppiness would prove fatal.

Back home, however, it hardly mattered anymore. Having mesmerized the youth of Britain with his Number One singles and his pretty face, Bolan was packing auditoriums with glitzed-up kids for whom he could do no wrong. "I will do anything, anytime, for, to, or with you (delete whichever is inapplicable)," read one of his thousands of fan letters. "Please send me any food, nail cuttings, clothes, anything you may have touched." The end of 1971 brought the payoff of a decade of struggles and intrigues—and on a scale that staggered even the longtime true believers. The obscure bard of the flower-power fringe was now the focus of the first bona fide teenage phenomenon Britain had seen since Beatlemania, for which Fleet Street coined the word T. Rextasy.

In a long *Melody Maker* feature headlined THE PROPHET OF THE NEW GENERATION, Michael Watts reported:

> In the space of a month fans put out of action no less than eleven cars in which the band traveled. Without exception they stripped the vehicles of everything that could be taken away as a souvenir; windscreen wipers, mirrors, door handles—all went. To get away from concert halls means running a gauntlet of hands that pull at the body like young piranha fish. The cars are not just means of transport; they're getaway vehicles. The roadies are not just there to lug equipment; they're bodyguards. Police guard the hotels where the group stays. . . .
>
> John Lennon . . . and Paul McCartney . . . both see in T. Rex their own successor in the creation of audience mania. Ringo told me six months ago that he thought the band was "fantastic" and "one of his favorites" while comparative outsiders on the tour

were fascinated by the phenomenon. Tony Smith, one of the biggest rock promoters in this country . . . promoted this last T. Rex tour and says it's the story of the Stones and Beatles all over again: "It's been amazing from the point of view of audiences. Marc speaks to a whole new generation of young kids, whose average age seems to be about fifteen. . . ."

Bolan's own doorstep became the site of round-the-clock vigils. "I never before understood why people have dark windows in cars," he said. "I do now. It can be fun."

The two-inch front-page headline in *NME* was simply REXMANIA. "In scenes of hysteria and confusion unparalleled since early days of Beatlemania, thirty-three people fainted and one girl was taken to hospital after falling off the balcony in her excitement. . . ." In the same January 1972 issue, *NME* reported T. Rex's sweep of its annual Readers' Poll. Bolan's outfit had scored half of the six most popular singles, the most popular album (*Electric Warrior* actually finished in a dead heat with John Lennon's *Imagine,* at 2,229 votes apiece), and the top

LP, 1972 (T. Rex Wax Company) Single, Germany, 1973 (Ariola)

world and British vocal group awards. According to Derek Johnson's analysis of the poll results: "When posterity looks back upon 1971, there is little doubt that T. Rex and Rod Stewart will emerge as the two big names and dominating influence in pop music."

In yet another stroke of astonishing luck, all this happened just as Bolan's record company and management contracts were due to expire. Tony Secunda was brought in to negotiate with EMI one of the most lucrative deals in British recording history—which specified that Marc's product appear on his own T. Rex Wax Company label—though shortly afterward Bolan dismissed Secunda and misguidedly assumed his own managerial duties. Fly Records responded by releasing "Jeepster" as a hit single, which was followed by a Number One compilation LP called *Bolan Boogie* and then a Tyrannosaurus Rex maxi single featuring "Debora," which would reach number seven on its second go-round.

Meanwhile, Marc bought an office building on New Bond Street, leasing space to the likes of Pink Floyd and running his own empire—with the assistance of a flamboyant publicist named B. F. Fallon and, of course, June Bolan—from a vast room reportedly filled with mirrors and little else in the way of decorations or furniture but a rocking horse.

The first T. Rex Wax Company maxi single—"Telegram Sam"—rolled up advance orders of mid-Sixties Beatles proportions. Both "Sam" and the subsequent "Metal Guru" were instant British Number Ones, and prime cuts on the next T. Rex LP, *The Slider.* Bolan described this album in *NME* as "a new sound, softer but harder, like liquid concrete" and "by far the best thing we ever did." Nonetheless, *NME*'s Charles Shaar Murray (a self-professed Tyrannosaurus Rex fan) would give

Bolan his first truly devastating review upon *The Slider*'s July 1972 appearance:

> The catalogue number of the new T. Rex album is BLN-5001, which is not surprising since "Telegram Sam" was MARC 1. This latest burst of megalomania is singularly unfortunate, coming as it does attached to an album which is startlingly bad by any conventional critical standards . . . dangerously close to a total artistic collapse. . . .
>
> There's nothing wrong with repeating yourself musically . . . [or even] with repeating other people. . . . But what makes *The Slider* such a colossal drag is that Marc is currently repeating himself repeating other people. . . .
>
> The lyrics are lame, slipshod, flabby, and lacking in all care for the use of language. Maybe the connections, obvious to a zapped-up mind like Marc's, are just too much for a hidebound music industry hack like myself to comprehend . . . most of the way it's alternate lines of sword & sorcery and neon city racetrack imagery.

(There were in fact fewer of the former lines than ever, though the one track Murray did find worthy—"Ballrooms of Mars"—extensively paraphrases H. P. Lovecraft.) Needless to say, Murray's fusillade drew howls of fury from *NME* readers. Bolan's own response was: "Why should I worry about what a few pretentious mentally stunted students in their twenties are saying?"

Bolan was to do far worse than *The Slider*. If its lyrics were less carefully wrought than *Unicorn*'s, or even *Electric Warrior*'s, they remained much more imaginative than your average Top of the Pops fare; and if *Warrior* and "Hot Love" qualify as classics of the rock & roll pastiche, then so do the likes of "Rock On," "Baby Boomerang," and "The Slider" itself. Marc's guitar playing—often overdubbed umpteen times—has never been more impressive; and Visconti's production is flawless.

The Slider, however, did display some warning signals. For one thing, the little bopping elf had really come to view himself as the hottest stud in the galaxy. (He once attributed "about 98 percent" of his popularity to his sex appeal.) Even the acoustic ballads tend to degenerate into—or climax with, according to one's perspective—orgasmic grunts and sighs. (On stage in New York that fall, Bolan would even embroider the winsome "Spaceball Ricochet" with such verbal sallies as "Gimme some head/fill my boots with lead.") On occasion (e.g., "Rabbit Fighter"), Marc could pull this stance off; but usually his posturing was enough to make the unsmitten gag. He seemed to have forgotten Michael Watts's astute *Melody Maker* analysis of his appeal to pubescent girls: "[Marc] is projecting not sex but romance, for who can take seriously the idea of sex trips in association with a young man who's twenty-four but looks sixteen, stands little more than five feet tall, and wears spangles round his eyes. . . . Sex is there, but it's sex courtesy of the Magic Prince. She'll wake up in the morning to a kiss from Marc."

Then, too, *The Slider* is marred by an excess of rock-star name dropping. Bob Dylan is cited in three different songs, as "a natural born poet," "a hobby with the learned ones," and an authority on eldritch Lovecraftian horrors. John Lennon and Alan Freed also get mentions; and the cover photo is credited to Ringo Starr—though it was in fact taken by Tony Visconti, who was none too pleased about the deliberate mixup.

It apparently meant a lot to Marc to have his name associated with those of established stars. He avidly sought out such longtime heroes as Dylan, Lennon, and Ray Bradbury—who

would often remember their encounters with Bolan far less vividly than he did. Bolan did become close to Starr, who agreed to direct a T. Rex documentary film and subsequently invited Marc to play on the *Ringo* album. Other frequent companions included such peers as Elton John and, later, Steve Harley of Cockney Rebel.

"On an early press release," Elton recalled in *NME*, "I said I detested pretentious groups like Tyrannosaurus Rex. Then I met Marc one day in a record shop and he sent me up about it. Marc comes [over] quite a lot . . . to relax. I didn't know what to send Marc for a Christmas present so I sent him that life-size picture of me, the one with a dartboard for a head. Then, when it was my birthday, he outdid me—sent a twenty-seven-foot blow-up of himself which came in a great big van, plus the silver disc for 'Jeepster.'"

Marc's long-standing relationship with David Bowie, however, had turned into a vicious rivalry—albeit one invented entirely by Bolan himself, together with the journalists who

Souvenir program for the film Born to Boogie, *directed by Ringo Starr*

egged him on. Bolan's and Bowie's careers had always been somewhat interwoven; after David's stint miming at Tyrannosaurus Rex shows, Marc was among the first to convince him that "Space Oddity" would be a big hit. It was; and Bolan played guitar on Bowie's follow-up single, "The Prettiest Star." David subsequently pastiched Marc's music on "Black Country Rock," wrote a song about him called "Lady Stardust," and then paid specific tribute to T. Rex in the lyrics of "All the Young Dudes."

Nonetheless, after T. Rex launched the Glitter Rock bandwagon for dozens of utterly dispensable imitators, Bowie's ascendancy gave Bolan his first serious competition. The critics generally acknowledged Bowie as the superior artist; *NME* at one point dubbed him "the thinking man's Marc Bolan." As their mutual producer, Tony Visconti, put it (in *Marc Bolan: A Tribute*): "Marc brought in the 'Glam' thing, but David took it a step further . . . [and] came out with these beautiful bizarre costumes from Japan, designed by a top Japanese designer. Marc couldn't think on that level. There was always this envy, this jealousy."

Soon the likes of *NME* were printing rambling Bolan monologues on the subject of his arch-rival: "I think it's much too soon, with no disrespect to David, to put him in the same class as me . . . he's still very much a one-hit wonder, I'm afraid. . . . Really, I've always thought Mott the Hoople were bigger than David. . . . I've never heard a David Bowie album. . . . I think maybe he's been sucked into something that's unhealthy for him . . . you can't create an image, it's only what you are.''

Then again, Bolan's interviews were growing stranger in other respects. In September 1972 he told *NME*'s Keith Altham: ''Sometimes I feel all these things are a part of something I'm meant to go through in some weird, fatalistic sort of way. I honestly feel it could all end tomorrow. Not the band thing—I mean *life*. . . . Now I feel I'm writing out of a sense of desperation, as if I'm not going to be around that much longer.'' (One distraught fan was moved to write the editor: ''You have knocked Marc Bolan, criticized him, and abused him. . . . You will be the very people to write an obituary to him and lament and say 'Why did he have to die?' Yes, he's going to die soon. It'll be *your* fault.'')

Though the reaction of some critics was indeed turning sour, T. Rextasy ran rampant throughout 1972 in such places as Germany, Japan, and, of course, Britain. The hysteria reached its pinnacle during a pair of concerts held at the ten-thousand-seat Wembley Empire Pool on March 18. Tony Tyler's extensive *NME* coverage of the event began: ''He was a poem in silks, satins, and embroidered velvets. A soft cap, sewn with astrological stars, clung to his curly locks. Silken breeches encased his legs, where gleaming hose fell away to reveal silver-buckled shoes. Spangled dust, artistically arranged beneath his lustrous eyes, glittered, reflecting the powerful lighting in visionary flashes. He was an arch-priest of High Camp. He was beautiful.'' And then the punchline: ''And he, incredibly, was only a photographer at Saturday's staggering T. Rex concerts at the Wembley Pool.''

Tyler described the shows as ''a religio-sensual experience'' inspiring ''a crush of climactic mania, unsurpassed since the Beatles.'' Bolan's ''unmitigated triumph'' was ''demonstrated by the near-mesmeric control he had over [his audience], by the ease with which he pulled the strings and they responded. . . . He need only twitch a satined rear to bring forth a surge of thousands against the crash barrier, the metal warping visibly beneath the pressure. He had the power, and he used it. . . . Bolan puts everything into the stage act, camping it up, strutting, pigeon-chested, across the stage, with superb arrogance.'' Tyler also reported that Ringo Starr ''captured the entire concert in living color, completely unnoticed by the crowd.''

The film, *Born to Boogie,* additionally incorporated *Magical Mystery Tour*–style ''surrealist'' episodes and sequences of Marc hobnobbing with Ringo and Elton. The Rextatic teenagers made it an instant box-office draw, but more discriminating viewers such as *NME*'s Nick Kent found it ''a bad, often atrocious film. Cheap, pretentious, narcissistic, and noisy.''

All along, Bolan was convinced that the film would provide the key to T. Rex's American breakthrough. He told *Words and Music*'s Bob Harris: ''The movie will totally explain to America what the phenomenon we are in England is. Until people really saw *A Hard Day's Night*, they just didn't believe what goes on.'' But *Born to Boogie* was never shown in the U.S.—nor, for that matter, was there ever an American breakthrough for T. Rex.

Everyone had taken it for granted that Marc would eventually duplicate his British success in the United States; all his superstar compatriots since the Beatles had done so, even if it took The Who several years to turn the trick. ''Get It On (Bang a Gong)'' had been a smash, and *16 Magazine* was printing

Bolan joined onstage by his oversized cardboard effigy
(*Chuck Pulin*)

Marc's picture, while at the other end of the spectrum of rock journalism *Rolling Stone* had been following Bolan's career since its mid-1971 headline *Tyrannosaurus Enters Rock Age.* On March 16, 1972, a photograph of Bolan appeared on page one (perhaps the fact that it had been snapped by Ringo had something to do with it), and Michael Thomas' lengthy feature, headlined T. REX IS GONNA FUCK YOU INTO THE MICK JAGGER GAP, began:

It was berserk all over England and Europe. Theaters were stampeded, limousines were ripped and rent and stove in, a dozen were lost forever, and one night in Birmingham twenty girls fought over a glass T. Rex left on stage and a lot of them got cut up grappling over the shards and shatters. . . .

Bolan's been lurking in London for a long time, and there's always been something ominous and alluring about him—he had all his moves down, and he had a lot of nerve and cocky talk and puppy flash and he had a lot of secret knowledge too, and, as he says, he finally had to *do it,* and do it fucking big. . . . He's done it in England and Europe and he's about to do it here as sure as tyrannosauruses once roamed the earth and pterodactyls flew overhead. . . .

Like a sinister little angel out of the densest and most exotic prison visions of Jean Genet, with glitter round his eyes and stars in his hair and dressed in satin and sequins and girl's shoes from Anello and Davide's, Marc is the Queen of the Hop, right in the middle of the Mick Jagger gap.

The story went to vivid (if somewhat credulous) lengths on such topics as Marc's stint as a sorcerer's apprentice and his more recent forays into writing occult fiction. Thomas even revealed the plot of one Bolan short story, an unlikely fusion of H. P. Lovecraft and Little Richard, ''about some sorcerer calling up spirits out in the primeval marshes; he's interrupted by a colleague, and it turns out neither of them know what they're doing except that they can feel a draft, something's happening, and sure enough out of the eternal mire emerges a creature beyond all description and all it says is: AWOP-BOPALUBOPAWOPBAMBOOM.''

But Bolan did not ''do it here,'' despite the million dollars Warners sank into his promotion. Maybe all the hype backfired; when T. Rex played the Academy of Music in 1972, all the New York scenemakers were out in force, expecting a Bowie-style extravaganza, and all they got were a pair of twenty-seven-foot cardboard cutouts of Marc flanking the stage while the real Bolan dished out his boogie jams and flounced around as if he were still in front of the screamagers at Wembley. A few of the concertgoers began shouting for Ziggy Stardust, and it was all downhill from there.

The status of T. Rex in America during the Seventies, ironically enough, resembled that of Tyrannosaurus Rex in Britain during the Sixties. Bolan did acquire a Stateside cult following; *Words and Music*'s 1972 poll, for instance, placed him fourth in the songwriter and male singer categories, and "Get It On" and *Electric Warrior* were voted best single and second-best album. A thirteen-year-old New Jerseyite named Natalie McDonald launched a fanzine called *Electric Warrior* to keep the flame burning for hundreds of Rextatic U.S. subscribers.

But Marc's crowning ambition—to achieve true stardom in America—went unfulfilled. Perhaps he was too English; but then who could be more English than the Kinks? Or, for that matter, than Bolan's literary inspiration, J. R. R. Tolkien?

More likely, Bolan was a casualty of the polarization that had set into the American music scene around 1967. Though the Beatles had made their first impact largely among unsophisticated young teenagers, by *Sgt. Pepper* time few self-respecting Beatles freaks would admit anything but scorn for the "teenybopper" sounds of, say, the Monkees. Bolan's evolution resembled the Beatles' in reverse, though he clung to a vestige of credibility in Britain, where at least some of the music journalists gave him due credit for his past accomplishments. In America, Bolan seemed unable to choose between the AM and the FM listeners, between the readers of *16 Magazine* and those of *Rolling Stone*—audiences that were just about mutually exclusive. So he fell, as the saying goes, between two stools.

Nonetheless, the main reason T. Rextasy never reached epidemic proportions on these shores is simply that by the time Marc had really focused his sites on America, most of the

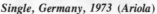

Single, Germany, 1973 (Ariola)   *Single, Germany, 1973 (Ariola)*

qualities that had made his songs and his band so successful in England in the first place were rapidly fading away.

Over the following year—through the end of 1973—the monster British hits continued to roll fast and furious from the T. Rex Wax factory: "Children of the Revolution," "Solid Gold East Action," "20th Century Boy," "The Groover."

By and large, each new single arrived to mounting critical jeers. Of "Children of the Revolution," *NME* declared: "Bolan doesn't realize he's run a good thing into the ground. The main riff, augmented by Visconti's strings, tediously grinds through the side. Along the way Marcy-poo shouts a few nursery school lyrics." Bolan heatedly pleaded innocent to charges that he was repeating himself: "Everyone has revamped 'Telegram Sam' and 'Get It On' except T. Rex." He insisted that "Solid Gold" was "very, very different . . . [and] five times faster than anything we've done"; and, minting a new label for each release, he dubbed "20th Century Boy" "erection rock." ("Every young man in the twentieth century's a superstud and the record's meant for him.") The critics, however, were right in saying the T. Rex singles sounded alike. They were wrong in taking Bolan so severely to task for it.

All those singles were, in fact, snappy variations on the most basic rock & roll themes—classic clichés, if you like, with the inimitable Bolan touch. Years later Marc would proudly cite his encounters with such budding Punks and New Wavers as the Ramones—who, he claimed, attributed their original inspiration to records like "Solid Gold Easy Action." By that time, the Ramones' repetitive, tongue-in-cheek "minimalism" was garnering rave reviews from some of the very critics who used to charge that Bolan's rock & roll hits were too simple and all sounded the same. Once again, Bolan was ahead of his time.

That said, there was indeed something rotten in the state of Marc; the megalomania was taking its toll. Having outsmarted the critics for so long, Bolan was past the point of listening to advice from anyone—not even Tony Visconti or the members of the band. Though Marc could still "get it on" at 45 rpm when he made the effort, his immersion in the business side of T. Rex—and above all with his own image—soon left his actual musical development in a state of sad neglect. Convinced, however, that every idea that popped into his head merited instant immortalization on T. Rex company wax, Bolan embarked on the most unlistenable series of albums ever spawned by a major rock artist.

The hideously self-indulgent packaging of 1973's *Tanx* said it all. Swathed in satins and furs, the former flower child glowers astride a model tank, whose cannon protrudes from Bolan's crotch like a heavy metal phallus. Likenesses of 119 more tanks clutter the double sleeve—a fixation with violent images and implements that continued on such releases as *Bolan's Zip Gun*.

(RDR Productions/Bill Orchard)

Bolan's answer to the government's curb on private vehicles during the 1973 energy crisis (Photo Trends)

And the music itself is just as lethal. Gone is the naive simplicity that had always enabled Marc to turn even his limitations to advantage; instead, *Tanx* bogs down in umpteen overdubs of masturbatory guitar workouts and tape loops. The occasional snatches of actual melody—"Broken Hearted Blues," "Highway Knees"—are lost in the miasma of Bolan's Heavy Metal sludge, or strangled by the boozy growl that has largely replaced the charming vibrato of yore.

Nor does *Tanx* offer so much as a hint of the inspired doggerel that Bolan used to skim so effortlessly from his subconscious, and which his uncomprehending critics had dismissed as drivel. Now the words truly *were* drivel; *NME*'s James Johnson rested his case on "Shock Rock" (changed from "Cock Rock" at EMI's insistence): "an abomination made utterly banal by the two lines of lyrics, something about 'oh baby pretty baby you're my girl' and 'if you know how to rock then you don't have to shock'—which are just repeated a few times."

Bolan himself touted *Tanx* as "a gospel album," though the only faint gospel touch is provided by the black girls attempting to fill the shoes of Flo and Eddie—whose departure presaged the complete disintegration of the old winning team. Over the following year all the key figures in Marc's personal and professional life—June Bolan, Tony Visconti, and Micky Finn—finding him next to impossible to live and work with, were to follow suit. Drummer Bill Legend was among the first to go; his replacement was Davey Lutton.

In Visconti's absence even the singles were to lose their snap and stop selling, while Finn's departure (to a self-owned antique store on the King's Road) would impair a T. Rex image already sagging under the weight of one alcoholic paunch.

As if to add insult to injury, the Stateside failure of *Tanx* prompted Warners to drop Bolan like an old brown shoe (ostensibly as part of an "austerity campaign" whose other casualties included Roxy Music). According to a spokesman for the label, "promoting Marc in the States cost a fortune. Press ads, radio ads, TV ads wherever he played, taking on additional people to work on his publicity—we just haven't made enough money off him to justify what we were having to spend."

So what was the story with "Swan king, the elf-lord"? Perhaps it had already been told in the Greek myths Marc once held so dear—particularly in that of Narcissus, the beautiful

youth who falls in love with his own image in the water and, stooping to embrace it, drowns—or of Icarus ("I sussed a scene from Icarus," went one old Tyrannosaurus ditty), who soars heavenward on fragile manmade wings that eventually carry him too close to the sun and melt, leaving him to plunge to his doom.

Well, not entirely: Bolan's star was to go down, but never all the way out. He could always be counted on for at least the occasional lively interview and minor British hit. And one day he would start to pull the pieces together again.

It was Marc's romantic entanglement with one of his backup singers that finally caused June to call their marriage quits. In time, Gloria Jones—formerly a producer for Motown Records—would in a sense fill the roles of Visconti and Finn as well as June's. *The* Gloria Jones, as she was billed on the albums, took to playing the clarinet onstage (alongside new keyboardist Dino Dines) and assumed full member status in T. Rex—whose sound her influence helped point in a soul/disco direction. In September 1975 Gloria bore Marc a son named Rolan Seymour Bolan; the proud father helped deliver the baby himself.

By that time T. Rextasy had ebbed to a cult of memories, kept alive by a handful of the most zealous fanatics ever to be spawned by rock & roll. As early as 1973, Marc had seemed, despite all the bravado, to sense that his position was sliding, and resorted to his flair for staging headline-grabbing PR stunts.

With the release of "The Groover" that summer, the Glitter King was back on page one—announcing his abdication. He told reporters for, respectively, *NME* and *Music Scene*: "Glam Rock is now as dead as a doornail. . . . I'm into denim. I'm going back to Woodstock." "I'm an artist, and I feel insulted to be involved with anyone who sticks makeup all over his face . . . but I still see people with stars under their eyes, like the Sweet, and I just can't believe they've got the balls to do it, seeing as I did it five years ago . . . it just seems a trifle desperate." Now look who's talking!

After "Truck On (Tyke)" failed to make the Top Ten that autumn—"a planned thing; the listings I got are so incredible I

(RDR Productions)

wanted something not so good to happen to compare it against''—the subsequent ''Teenage Dream'' was marketed as ''Marc Bolan's first solo single,'' despite the fact that both records featured the same T. Rex personnel. But ''Teenage Dream'' fared even worse on the charts, following its annihilation by such critics as *NME*'s Roy Carr, who wrote: ''Zinc Zimmerman and the Hidden Riders of Mars step clumsily on some cold turkeyburgers when cranking out this amazingly inarticulate mean teen lament.'' Mr. Carr was pointing up the suspicious similarity between the titles of Bolan's imminent LP *Zinc Alloy and the Hidden Riders of Tomorrow* and Bowie's *Ziggy Stardust and the Spiders from Mars*—though in fact Marc had coined his metallic alias during his Tyrannosaurus days, when he told an interviewer: ''If I get a hit I'm changing my name to Zinc Alloy and I'll wear an aluminum suit.''

Recorded on the run in six different countries, the new album proved to be as sorry a mess as *Tanx*, despite (some might say because of) Gloria's infusion of ''Interstellar Soul.'' That was one of the *Zinc* song titles, and even those were often daunting (''Painless Persuasion v. the Meathawk Immaculate''). So were Marc's references, à la the Beatles' ''Glass Onion,'' to his own past triumphs (''Metal Guru's in the loo with my glue . . .'').

Mr. Alloy took his Hidden Riders on their first British tour in over a year; *NME*'s Julie Webb was there opening night:

> Looking not so much the elongated Elf as the Porky Pixie, Marc Bolan returned to Glasgow's Apollo Theatre amid uncontrolled hysteria, deafening screams and seat-vaulting Rextatics. . . . But taken as a musical experience it was dire. Never, I thought, have so many screamed at so little. A teenage dream turned nightmare.
> And yet it started so well. Bolan's entrance was stunning—a huge star picked out in lights at the center of the stage with Bolan wedged against it; a superstructure at the back of the stage with the letters T. REX shining out in hundreds of bulbs. . . .
> And in the middle of it all a decidedly plump Bolan—the man who claims Glam Rock is dead wearing white trousers with glitter motifs, and a shimmering silver and black satin cloak.

The performances commenced with the mechanical star's elevation from a prone to a vertical position, catapulting Bolan into the opening thunder of ''20th Century Boy.'' At the end of the inevitable extended ''Get It On'' finale, Marc attacked his guitar with a large whip, which he then hurled into an amp (a dummy) that duly exploded. Thank you and good night.

In late 1974, Bolan brought his star, whip, and exploding amps on a last-ditch American campaign, during which T. Rex alternated between small clubs and second-billing to the likes of Three Dog Night. For his debut on Casablanca Records, Bolan attempted to manufacture straightforward commercial sounds expressly for the American marketplace. ''Looking back on it, I think *Zinc Alloy* was rather messy and overproduced, but this new one is much tighter. It's more vibrant, full of energy, and much more dancy.''

Light of Love actually included three tunes from the *Zinc* LP (which had gone unreleased in the U.S.), but the eight new cuts did indeed dispense with the obnoxious clutter. Unfortunately, they weren't particularly distinguished either; even the words were now standard Fifties clichés (''Will you love me/like you said in your let-ter?''). That proved insufficient to ingratiate T. Rex with Top Forty program directors, and *Light of Love* was soon cast into the cutout bins. (In Britain, the new material surfaced on *Bolan's Zip Gun,* which fared little better than the American version.) Marc would never again tour the States, nor would he see any of his subsequent records released in this country.

Single, France, 1974 (EMI)

Single, France, 1976 (EMI)

LP, U.K., 1975 (T. Rex Wax Company)

Maxi-single, U.K., 1977 (T. Rex Wax Company)

Bolan himself, however, joined Beverly Hills's growing community of British rock star tax fugitives. He soon grew desperately homesick, and a move to Monte Carlo failed to improve his morale. (''I did nothing but sit in the sun and drink brandy all day.'') In his last year, finally deeming the Inland Revenue's tax bite preferable to exile—perhaps in part because his income had dwindled considerably—Marc was to return to his beloved London.

Nineteen seventy-five's *Futuristic Dragon* opened promisingly with the title track. ''Deep beneath an ancient shadow, stunned with age and too much wisdom . . . ''—the lines were reminiscent of Tyrannosaurus Rex, but Bolan's demented recitation—to searing feedback and a discofied beat—was something else entirely. (He even had an elaborate dragon constructed as a stage prop for the next British tour.) But, apart from his two-line ''boogie mind poem'' ''New York City,'' it was all downhill from there; ''Ride My Wheels'' and ''Dreamy Lady'' were neither very good disco nor very good T. Rex; certainly Marc, unlike David Bowie, never accrued much commercial mileage from this particular bandwagon.

The growing pile of substandard Bolan product was joined by *The Beginning of Doves,* a collection of demos and outtakes from the days of John's Children and very early Tyrannosaurus that Bolan had unsuccessfully tried to squelch in court. Future Pretenders star Chrissie Hynde, still an *NME* reviewer, used the occasion to defend a man who remained her hero, if not her colleagues':

> The poor guy ain't even dead yet, and already they're releasing sloppy first takes and rejects. Maybe they're trying a new approach and have decided to play on the fact that the press slag him off at every possible opportunity.
> Well, I ain't gonna jump on your bandwagon. I *like* Bolan. Shocking, isn't it? Twenty aborted attempts from the past—oh thank you, Track Records. Bolan needs this release like he needs barbed wire underpants. . . .

165

T. Rex's last U.S. tour, 1974 (Billy Charas)

Look, world, give this man a break. Bolan's made some great music (listen to *Warrior* again to refresh your memory).

With an eye toward broadening his career, Bolan undertook his first brief foray as a British TV personality, interviewing Keith Moon, Mrs. David Bowie, and Marvel Comics creator Stan Lee. According to Bolan, Lee was devising a comic starring Mr. T. Rex himself, but this seems to have had as little grounding in "the real world" as the movie Marc incessantly talked of doing with David Niven, supposedly titled *Obsession*.

"Dandy in the underworld, when will he come up for air? . . ."
(RDR Productions)

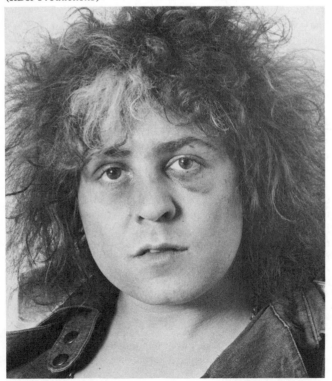

("I play a psychotic who has sexual problems and sells dope. I kill three people and end up in a nuthouse, so altogether it's quite a lovely role.") And, as always, new volumes of his writings—poems, horror stories, autobiography—were said to be on their way to press. But all that materialized was a handful of painfully weak singles. Bolan seemed to have well and truly pissed it all away.

Then came Britain's Punk Rock explosion, and suddenly, grooving along at the center of the action, there appeared a familiar waiflike figure, sporting shortish slicked-back hair and a well-cut Italian suit. While delighting the tabloid journalists with tales of his self-emancipation from "a twilight world of drugs, booze, and kinky sex," a slimmed-down Bolan settled into his self-proclaimed role of an "elder statesman" of rock & roll—"the Godfather of Punk if you like," he told *The Sun*'s Bob Hart. "Underneath this veneer of brilliantine, and behind this perfect profile, lurks a lad who understands perfectly what the Punk movement is all about. And I think it's what we all need."

The twenty-nine-year-old elder statesman would even be awarded his very own monthly column in *Record Mirror*, excerpts from which follow:

I love the raw-edged energy and freshness New Wave has brought to the British rock scene. The music of now is *noise*, be it beautiful, elaborate, complex, clean or bestial, primitive, political or raw. It's a wild mixture of the lot, such cute noise from those Gibson and Fender toys. . . .
No matter how much they might shout about "giving someone a good kicking" it is basically just talk because they don't do it—it's all show biz and good for grabbing the headlines. The papers loved to hear me mouthing off about how I was a better guitarist than Hendrix or a better showman than Townshend but that is just part of the game.
The Pistols are a bloody good mirror. Anyone who thinks things are not in a mess just does not look around. . . .
And so to the saddest news of the month—the death of Elvis Presley. Often badly promoted, badly advised, and obscenely produced in his last years—or so it seemed to me—he was led down the drain by whoever stuck him on the treadmill of those terrible Hollywood musicals and tried to turn him into a sort of male Jayne Mansfield. It's sad that he's gone but probably better that he went before he turned into the Bing Crosby of rock 'n' roll. . . .

Marc's regard for the young New Wavers was often mutual. Many had gotten hooked on rock & roll in the first place by the T. Rex hits that may well have provided the blueprint for the new power chords. Bolan signed the Damned—one of the first British Punk bands—as the opening act for a T. Rex comeback tour. "I was introduced to them," he explained, "because one of them had the good taste to wear a Marc Bolan T-shirt."

All his old sidekicks save Dino Dines having departed—even Gloria was concentrating on promoting her solo LP *Vixen*, which featured the songs and guitar of her lover—Marc assembled a new band with Miller Anderson on second guitar, Herbie Flowers on bass, and Tony Newman on drums. The latter pair were crack session musicians, best known, ironically, for their work with David Bowie. According to most accounts, the 1977 T. Rex concerts were tight and highly professional—qualities conspicuously lacking in Bolan's heyday.

The *Dandy in the Underworld* LP, whose release coincided with the tour, vanquished any remaining doubts. Though it has its quota of string-synthesizer horrors, most of the tracks are catchy straight-ahead rock & roll in the best T. Rex tradition.

"Dandy in the Underworld" itself, perhaps the finest song Bolan ever wrote, evokes Marc's own fall from grace: "Distraction he wanted, to destruction he fell . . . when will he come up for air?"

Bolan reportedly put down enough material for yet another album, but until the red tape is cleared, *Dandy in the Underworld* remains his swan song. If the rest of the LP didn't quite break any new musical ground for T. Rex, the *Dandy* album at least ends Bolan's recorded history on a strong, upbeat note.

For his British public, the closing episodes of the Marc Bolan story took the form of a six-week TV series called *Marc*. This proved a resounding success, with host Bolan introducing such promising newcomers as the Boomtown Rats to the Wednesday afternoon audience. David Bowie flew in from overseas especially for the occasion of *Marc*'s final installment, premiered a new song called "'Heroes,'" and sang, played, and bantered with his longtime friend.

Just days after that public reconciliation, following a late night on the town, Gloria drove Marc home in his purple mini. Only a few blocks from their destination—at six o'clock on the morning of September 16, 1977—she lost control of the wheel, and the car smashed into a chestnut tree.

Bowie and Bolan on the British TV miniseries **Marc** (*Photo Trends*)

"Ride a White Swan" remembered at Golders Green Crematorium, September 20, 1977 (*Photo Trends*)

T. REX'S HITS

(followed by their highest chart positions, as listed in *Billboard*)

U.S. Singles

1971	Ride a White Swan (**76**); Hot Love (**72**)
1972	Bang a Gong (Get It On) (**10**); Telegram Sam (**67**)

U.S. LPs

1971	T. Rex (**188**); Electric Warrior (**32**)
1972	The Slider (**17**); My People Were Fair . . . /Prophets . . . (**113**)
1973	Tanx (**102**)

U.K. Singles

1968	Debora (**34**); One Inch Rock (**28**)
1969	King of the Rumbling Spires (**44**)
1970	Ride a White Swan (**2**)
1971	Hot Love (**1**); Get It On (**1**); Jeepster (**2**)
1972	Telegram Sam (**1**); Metal Guru (**1**); Children of the Revolution (**2**); Solid Gold Easy Action (**2**); Debora/One Inch Rock (**7**)
1973	20th Century Boy (**3**); The Groover (**4**); Truck On (Tyke) (**12**)
1974	Teenage Dream (**13**); Light of Love (**22**); Zip Gun Boogie (**41**)
1975	New York City (**15**); Dreamy Lady (**30**)
1976	I Love to Boogie (**13**); London Boys (**40**); Laser Love (**41**)
1977	The Soul of My Suit (**42**)

David Bowie

WHEN DAVID Bowie makes his New York debut on September 28, 1972, he remains very much an unknown quantity. None of his singles or LPs has yet surfaced on the U.S. charts; a few weeks earlier, his name was still unfamiliar to at least 99 percent of what's still called the counterculture. Yet David Bowie's concert is the hottest ticket in town. The sidewalk outside Carnegie Hall is jammed with kids desperate to get in and scalpers willing to help them for a price. The aura of mystery and drama is heightened by a circling searchlight that beams great arcs of white light through the midtown sky. Assorted RCA Records personnel, transvestites, and Famous People—including Andy Warhol—grandly file through the clutching riffraff. Nobody knows quite what to expect.

At nine P.M. the PA blares the opening strains of Walter (a.k.a. Wendy) Carlos's synthesized Beethoven's Ninth (from the *Clockwork Orange* soundtrack). The whole hall begins to flicker as a brilliant strobe light catches the outlines of about four or five spiky-haired space invaders toppling all over the stage, plugging in instruments. They are joined by a thin white figure sporting an orange-and-green body suit and suspiciously yellow hair, and holding (incongruously enough) an acoustic twelve-string guitar. Barely missing a beat of Ludwig Van, David Bowie and the Spiders from Mars blast off.

The "Hang on to Yourself" opener, like much of what follows, is culled from the recently issued *Rise and Fall of Ziggy Stardust and the Spiders from Mars*—a futuristic concept album about a messianic space-age rock & roll superstar. Bowie, however, is not here merely to sing and play selections from his latest LP; the whole premise of his show is that the singer *is* Ziggy, and that his accompanists are the very same Spiders from Mars cited in the album title—an elaborate theatrical conceit such as has never before been attempted on the rock concert stage.

Ziggy, moreover, delivers a real show: a carefully choreographed extravaganza of light and sound whose myriad theatrical touches include several costume changes and a pantomime sequence wherein Bowie uses his flattened palms to create the

"You tell me what it means and I'll agree . . ." (*Photo Trends/ Richard Imrie*)

illusion of imprisonment behind a wall of glass. Bowie and his guitarist, Mick Ronson, also add a new dimension to rock's aggressively macho Guitar Hero iconography when the singer crumples to his knees to grasp his platinum-haired Main Man's buttocks in supplication to Ronson's metal machine.

The boys in the band play hard and loud, fast and flashy, but after about seven numbers Bowie and Ronson perch on stools for an acoustic respite from the futuristic razzle-dazzle. Just once, Bowie even lets slip his brittle, alien persona, giving a dramatic solo reading of Jacques Brel's "My Death" which transforms the theatrical ambience to that of a Continental cabaret—though some of this feeling ultimately resurfaces in an altogether different context on Ziggy Stardust's almost Edith Piaf–like swansong, "Rock 'n' Roll Suicide." And when Bowie/Ziggy sings "Give me your hands," and the first ten rows reach out in unison to do just that, you know that the Seventies have finally found their long-awaited star. . . .

Bowie, his manager Tony deFries, and RCA Records had planned this last epiphany months in advance, orchestrating it with an almost military precision. Though David had yet to earn a nickel for either RCA or deFries's Main Man enterprises, vast amounts of cash were invested in perpetrating the illusion that this extraterrestrial rock & roller had fallen to earth a full-blown Superstar, the Seventies equivalent of the Beatles, the Stones, and Dylan rolled into one—or, to be more precise, the (more or less) flesh-and-blood embodiment of the imaginary Ziggy Stardust. As Charles Shaar Murray relayed back to *New Musical Express:*

> To RCA, no act has higher priority than Bowie, except one Elvis Presley*. . . . There's a traveling circus of hairdressers, equipment men, trouble-shooters, camp followers, and court jesters, and the whole deal revolves around a deceptively delicate twenty-five-year-old androgyne named David Bowie.
> Bowie is an industry. And like all industries, he is protected, and swaddled, and handled with care. The security is so tight that on one gig the support band were evicted from the backstage area by rent-a-cops two minutes before they were due onstage.

Meanwhile, back in England, Bowie's old friend Marc Bolan had already established his own credentials as the glittering prophet of a new rock & roll decade. And just as the Stones, ten years earlier, couldn't have happened without the Fab Four, so, too, David Bowie (whose imagery provided a sci-fi counterpart to Bolan's swords and sorcery) couldn't have happened the way he did had it not been for the precedent of T. Rex.

Bolan's major contribution in this regard was to transmute the fantasy and make-believe inherent in so much late-Sixties British music (including his own) into unadulterated escapism and Glamour. He turned rock back into pop and presented a new generation of 45 rpm addicts with a bona fide teen idol of their own. In refreshing contrast to his contemporaries' dour virtuosity, the androgynous pixie was all style and image. He flaunted makeup and glitter and outlandish costumes (some of whose components had been manufactured with the ladies in mind); he gave British kids a glorious excuse to dress up and party. Their American contemporaries, meanwhile, were rapidly succumbing to the flamboyant horror-show theatrics of a man named Alice Cooper. As David Bowie was to declare at one of his first major press conferences: "It's going to be a brave new world, and we either join it or we become living relics. . . . Alice Cooper, Marc Bolan, myself, Iggy Pop, Lou Reed—we all anticipated it almost a few years too early. Now we're all emerging at the same time, which is interesting. There is a wave of the future and the kids have begun to discover that wave. . . . They may not know what to make of us, but they are eager to reach out anyway."

Rock & roll, always celebrated for breaching bourgeois taboos, had never been so outrageous—or (with the Stones, to name but one example, well into their orgiastic jet-setting mainliner phase) so decadent. But for all the androgyny, promiscuity, and general perversity that Seventies rock had come to promulgate, one forbidden fruit remained resolutely unplucked.

---

* *Presley and Bowie, incidentally, shared a January 8 birthdate.*

THE ZIGGY FLASH
Bowie symbol for *Ziggy Stardust.* Later used in Bowie's makeup on the *Aladdin Sane* album cover. Fantastic as pendant or key ring.

OFF-THE-SHOULDER SHIRT
Black shirt with the Bowie logo emblazoned across the front in Diamond Dust.

When *Melody Maker* sent Michael Watts to interview David Bowie in January 1972, the editors probably envisaged the story as a piece of filler for the back pages. Despite his new RCA contract and favorably reviewed *Hunky Dory* album, Bowie's seven years of performing and making records had netted him only one hit, and even that had been back in 1969. Yet when the article appeared, it was on page one, with the two-inch headline OH YOU PRETTY THING!

How did he do it? Simple: "David's present image is to come on like a swishy queen, a gorgeously effeminate boy. He's as camp as a row of tents, with his limp hand and trolling vocabulary. 'I'm gay,' he says, 'and always have been. . . .'" This was the one thing to which no rock star had ever quite owned up. In a single bold stroke, Bowie supplied the press with a goldmine of controversy and thrills, and they, in turn, all put his picture on the cover.

Even more than T. Rex, Bowie (whose music was of a piece with his public image) represented a triumph of sheer, glorious style over mere "substance." Taking the implications of Bolan's brand of Glitter Rock to their logical conclusion, David had his hair coiffed, and his face made up, as painstakingly as any Hollywood starlet's. And engaging the talents of top European and Japanese designers, he assumed the role of rock's leading fashion model, previewing outfits as stylish as they were bizarre.

A trend which should probably be attributed to Bowie was the frequent presence of brightly colored hair. There was a person with a bold kelly-green stripe running through his/her shoulder-length mop, and there were several mellow boys with patches of light blue. . . .

from *NME*'s account of Bowie's Carnegie Hall concert

Along with the instant notoriety, Bowie's avowed sexual propensities provided the fledgling superstar overnight with a loyal hard-core following among gays. As the first of his ilk to claim a place in the rock pantheon, Bowie was an inspiration (if not a revelation) to thousands of sexually ambivalent youths. He was also accorded generous coverage by homosexually oriented publications such as *After Dark,* which ran a Bowie cover story even before the Spiders' first American invasion got underway: "David's hand rests on his hip while he's belting out his tunes. The lights playing on his innocent, unlined face color him an unearthly green. . . . More unearthly than his face is his crotch, which seems unusually large, almost inhuman. . . ."

Bowie's homosexual aura doubtless turned the stomachs of many strictly heterosexual youngsters (and certainly failed to endear him with the aggressively T-shirted and beer-bellied U.S. rock critical establishment). But when parents began echoing the sentiments of *The Daily Express*—which likened Bowie to "a Soho stripper" and blasted his influence as "unwholesome"—hordes of basically straight kids decided to purchase his records without further delay.

Bowie flicked open the closet doors for a host of sexually ambiguous singers and songs. These included several Bowie protégés—such as Mott the Hoople, to whom he bequeathed the gay-youth anthem—as it then seemed—"All the Young Dudes." Camp Rock became *the* novelty of 1972, and the British pop weeklies took great delight in coining headlines like THE SWISHIEST STAR and IS BOWIE FAGGED OUT?

Yet all these intimations of lavender were but Bowie's novel variation on the old Trojan horse. It was impossible to pigeonhole David Bowie. "I'm not about to wave a banner for Gay Lib," he demurred. He even had a wife.

NME: How does it feel to be married to the man who everybody in the world and his dog Eric think is the world's king faggot?

ANGELA BOWIE: I think it's great. I love it. It all depends on your knowledge of gay culture, of which I can happily say I'm a member.

Some of David's audience found the existence of even a pink-haired Mrs. Bowie reassuring, as if all the gaiety was simply good clean fun, and after the show David removed his glitter and went home to his wife and kid.

Over the long run, however, Bowie demonstrated that he viewed sexuality in much the same light as fashion, art, music, stardom, and almost every other facet of his life and career, each of which presented a vast spectrum of potential roles and experiences. Refusing to be chained to any one specific identity, Bowie strove continually to reinvent himself as alternately homo-, hetero-, and bisexual, in much the same way that he could (and would) reinvent himself as a Mod revivalist, a soul singer, a Continental crooner, a movie star, or a film director; the bisexual space oddity just happened to be the persona through which we first made Mr. Bowie's acquaintance. Like his "hero" Andy Warhol, Bowie was open to anything; if something or someone happened to engage his attention, he was apt to reshape his personality and style (and even his extraordinarily malleable physical features) accordingly. "I'm a person of diverse interests," he told Dick Cavett in 1974; "I 'glit' from

Bowie at New York's Radio City Music Hall, Valentine's Day, 1973 (Chuck Pulin)

one thing to another. ['Glit'] is like flit; it's the Seventies version."

Previous rock icons—notably Bob Dylan, but to some extent the Beatles and even Bolan—had retained the public's fascination and their own artistic vitality by constantly revamping their public image and musical style. Bowie elevated such transformations to a fine art, an end in themselves, rather than a means to an end, let alone a natural process of evolution. David Bowie was a chameleon by profession.

As early as 1972, Bowie was describing himself as "a collection of other people's ideas" or "a photostat machine with an image." He disliked the label "rock star" and preferred to style himself an "actor" (some of his early-Seventies releases include the credit "produced by Ken Scott assisted by the Actor"). The theatrical quality of his extravaganzas notwithstanding, Bowie most resembled an actor (not to mention a scriptwriter or a director) in the manner with which he was wont to slip into, and then discard, a new persona as casually as he might select an outfit from his legendary wardrobe.

Bowie's first leading role, of course, was that of Ziggy. He played the part brilliantly—as did his supporting cast of musicians, technicians, makeup artists, and empire builders—especially when you consider that the magnificently produced *Ziggy Stardust* LP was nothing less than the blueprint for Bowie's own novalike emergence.

Side one sets the stage with vignettes of a decadent planet "Five Years" from total collapse, with a benevolent "Starman" watching from the sidelines, wondering whether to intervene. Side two traces Ziggy's rise from an androgynous laughingstock (''Lady Stardust'') to a bonafide ''Star,'' and, ultimately, his breakdown and fall (''Rock 'n' Roll Suicide''). On the surface the album offered nothing specifically new; the music was a highly processed mélange of latter-day Beatles, T. Rex, and Velvet Underground, set to a combination of sci-fi imagery (much of it yielded by *A Clockwork Orange* and Arthur C. Clarke's *Childhood's End*) and standard Sixties rock clichés (up to and including ''freak out . . . far out . . . blow your mind''). Indeed, *Ziggy Stardust* was positively loaded with clichés. Which (Ziggy's ''serious'' content notwithstanding) was exactly the point.

Unlike, say, Lennon, Dylan, or Townshend, Bowie did not purport to be ''authentic.'' The aesthetic distance he placed between himself and his medium, and from which remove he cleverly manipulated rock & roll's vocabulary and mythology, is what really made him far more ''camp'' than a Marc Bolan, and what qualified him as both the archetypal Seventies rock star and the first harbinger of the New Wave. As he told *Rolling Stone* a full year before the rise of *Ziggy Stardust,* ''I think [rock] should be tarted up, made into a prostitute, a parody of itself. It should be the clown, the Pierrot medium. The music is the mask the message wears—the music is the medium, and I, the Pierrot, am the message.''

The Rise and Fall of Ziggy Stardust and the Spiders from Mars was not the Seventies' *Sgt. Pepper, Blonde on Blonde,* or *Tommy*; it was (as they would say in the *Beatlemania* ads) an incredible simulation. Rock stars, Bowie declared at the time, were ''the original false prophets. We want all the adulation but we've got nothing to say. They keep asking me: 'What do you represent?' I don't know.''

. . . during his metamorphosis from Ziggy Stardust to Aladdin Sane (*Chuck Pulin*)

To his fans, Bowie offered, above all, a pretext to live out their fantasies as surely as he did his. And when he returned to New York on Valentine's Day, 1973, to descend from the remote ceiling of Radio City Music Hall in a glass-domed UFO, hundreds of sequined Martians trailing orange and purple feather boas tottered squealing down the aisles on nine-inch heels, and littered the stage with a bisexual shower of valentines. This time the folks back home got to see it all on TV, and hear the Channel 2 news reporter solemnly intone: ''Do you know where *your* children are tonight?''

David Robert Jones was born in the derelict, blackening South London district of Brixton on January 8, 1947. Eight years later, his father, Haywood—a public-relations officer for an orphanage—briefly moved the family to the countryside in his native Yorkshire before resettling in the ''better'' suburban London neighborhood of Bromley.

David early inherited an affinity for jazz and Beat literature (especially Kerouac's *On the Road,* which he later said first made him ''want out'') from his bohemian older half-brother, Terry, whose precarious mental balance would lead to his incarceration in the ''mansions cold and gray'' of which Bowie sings in ''All the Madmen.'' At twelve, David began studying the saxophone, which he played in his first group. George and the Dragons made their public debut at a Bromley Technical High School Christmas pageant arranged by David's art teacher, a Mr. Frampton (whose son Peter also put in an appearance with his combo, the Little Ravens).

At sixteen, David dropped out of Bromley Tech for a brief stint as a commercial artist at an ad agency. ''I wanted to prove myself in some field as an artist,'' David would recall in 1979, ''but I didn't think I was a very good painter. So I went into music.'' (Nonetheless, he would draw heavily on his background as a visual artist in shaping his myriad public images.)

By this time, David's attraction to the emerging Mod subculture had steered him from jazz to pop and R&B, and a chance meeting at a Brixton barber shop led to the formation of a quintet called the Hooker Brothers (later the King Bees). The rhythm guitarist, one George Underwood (also an aspiring painter), got it into his head that David was eying his girl friend. He retaliated with a single knockout punch that landed an unconscious David Jones in the nearest emergency ward and permanently paralyzed his left pupil. This mishap provided the young saxophonist-turned-singer with his most distinctive facial attribute—one permanently dilated gray eye set in unearthly contrast to its naturally blue companion.

But his relationship with the King Bees and Underwood survived intact (the latter eventually furnished artwork for the *Hunky Dory* album). David set about honing his hustling skills, even presuming to petition washing-machine tycoon John Bloom to invest some of his vast fortune in the booming pop scene—specifically, Davie Jones and the King Bees. Impressed with the lad's chutzpah, Bloom put David in touch with his friend Leslie Conn, who worked for the Beatles' music publisher, Dick James. Conn became the King Bees' manager, securing them a contract with Decca Records and a BBC-TV appearance—as he would for his other teenage Mod client, Marc Bolan. (Dick James, however, pursuing his perennial quest for the Next Beatles, dismissed both David and Marc out of hand.)

In June 1964, Decca's Vocalion Pop subsidiary issued Davie Jones and the King Bees' first and only single, pairing the ersatz R&B of Conn's own ''Liza Jane'' with Paul Revere and the

Raiders' "Louie Louie Go Home." According to the obligatory press release: "Davie's favourite vocalists are Little Richard, Bob Dylan, and John Lee Hooker. Apart from the saxophone he also plays guitar. He dislikes Adam's apples and lists as his interests Baseball, American Football, and collecting Boots. A handsome six-footer with a warm and engaging personality, Davie Jones has all it takes to get to the show business heights, including talent. . . ." But the single flopped, Decca dropped the King Bees, and the group broke up.

David then joined an outfit called the Manish Boys, with whom he recorded his second single, this one for Parlophone. "I Pity the Fool" (backed with David's first self-composition, "Take a Trip") was produced by Shel Talmy of Kinks and Who fame, and augmented by the nimble fingers of Talmy's favorite session guitarist, Jimmy Page. After forming yet another band,

David at age nineteen (Popperfoto)

David cut one more Parlophone single with Talmy. "You've Got a Habit of Leaving" was strongly reminiscent of The (circa 1965) Who, for whom David Jones and the Lower Third (a.k.a. the Buzz) were wont to open at the Marquee Club (outside which young Jones was known to spend the night in an old ambulance).

It was at one such show that David captured the imagination of music publicist Kenneth Pitt, ending the latter's long search for the Now Generation's answer to Tommy Steele, the one pre-Invasion British pop star who had successfully made the transition to stage and screen. David, for his part, seems to have been impressed by Pitt's former association with the popular singer, songwriter, actor, and playwright Anthony Newley, whom David greatly admired—and who would provide the model for his first startling metamorphosis.

Soon after becoming David's manager, Pitt caught wind of the impending Monkees TV series, and advised his new client to adopt a pseudonym so as not to be confused with the Prefab Four's Davy Jones. As the name Bowie (as in bowie knife) had always appealed to him in any case, David gladly adopted it as his new surname. "I was into a kind of heavy philosophy thing," he would tell author William S. Burroughs in their 1974 *Rolling Stone*–sponsored get-together. "I wanted a truism about cutting through the lies. . . ."

The David Bowie moniker made its bow on the labels of three 1966 Pye singles. "Can't Help Thinking About Me," "Do Anything You Say," and "I Dig Everything" were all undistinguished Bowie originals that reflected the continuing influence of such Mod faves as the Kinks and The Who, and ("Can't Help Thinking"'s front-page *NME* ad notwithstanding) all resounding flops.

It was at this point that Pitt commenced reshaping his handsome young protégé in the "legitimate" image of Tony Newley—though not without some resistance. "When I wanted David to be extrovert, he wanted to be introvert," Pitt would recall in *NME*. "When I wanted him to wear beautiful clothes, he wanted to wear dirty clothes. Once he was so scruffy that a casting director I sent him to called me [to complain]." Nevertheless, Bowie accepted an invitation to settle into his benefactor's swanky London pad among the rare Victoriana and Oscar Wilde first editions—enabling Pitt to boast, years later, that he was the only man on earth to have lived with both James Dean and David Bowie.

The first of umpteen "new" Bowies was unveiled in December 1966 after David signed with a recently established Decca subsidiary called Deram. The singles "Rubber Band"/"London Boys" and "The Laughing Gnome" were followed by an album (released the same week as *Sgt. Pepper*) which on first hearing sounds like the antithesis of the emerging pop progressivism. In retrospect, however, the show-tune patter on *David Bowie* may be seen as an early manifestation of the artist's theatrical proclivities. And if one can overlook the "light musical arrangements" (as *NME* charitably called them), the *David Bowie* LP (which forms the nucleus of the 1973 collection *Images*) reveals an impressive command of the social commentary and Edwardian whimsy that Ray Davies had recently made his forte. The Deram material ranges from "London Boys" (an unusually poignant glimpse behind the glamorous facade of the Mod subculture) and "When I Live My Dream" (a mainstream ballad that garnered awards at two European song festivals) to "The Laughing Gnome" (an inane novelty tune—complete with sped-up voices à la Chipmunks—that would return to haunt Bowie as a best-selling 1973 reissue).

Under Pitt's aegis, Bowie also made his cinematic debut in a fifteen-minute film called *The Image,* followed by a bit part in *The Virgin Soldiers* and a prominent role in a TV commercial for Lyons Maid's "Pop Ice Cream" bars. But David subsequently failed his audition to play alongside Peter Finch and Glenda Jackson as the young bisexual in *Sunday Bloody Sunday*'s love triangle.

Another of Bowie's assignments during this period was to provide English words for a French song called "Comme d'Habitude." Unfortunately for David, these were not attached to the demo sent Frank Sinatra, at whose instigation Paul Anka then proceeded to supply a new lyric titled "My Way." (Bowie—never one to let a good chord sequence pass unstolen—would eventually rework the tune in "Life on Mars?")

Bowie also carried on a longtime flirtation with Tibetan Buddhism, later describing himself in retrospect as "a terribly earnest Buddhist" who once spent several weeks at a Scottish monastery for Tibetan exiles. On the verge of having his head shaved to take his monastic vows, David suddenly "decided this wasn't for me and vanished completely." Nonetheless, the experience profoundly shaped Bowie's subsequent work and career—wherein he sought to dramatize the essentially Buddhist concept that there is no true "self," only endless layers of fluctuating and ephemeral images disguising the ultimate reality of nothingness. (The calculated manner in which he demonstrated this, however, could not have been more Western.)

Bowie as Virgin Soldier, 1969. (Photo Trends)

Bowie is said to have acquired his next obsession after hearing his song "When I Live My Dream" used in a performance by Lindsey Kemp's mime troupe. After the show David introduced himself and offered to supply Kemp with new musical scores in exchange for pantomime lessons. In 1973, Kemp—Scotland's ultracamp answer to Marcel Marceau—told *Crawdaddy*: "I taught him to exaggerate with his body as well as with his voice, and the importance of looking as well as sounding beautiful. Ever since working with me he's practiced that, and in each performance he does his movements are more exquisite. . . . He learned to free his body . . . [which] is what I endeavor to teach anyone who studies with me. . . . Everybody has that dove flying about inside them, and to let it free is a fabulous experience."

In January 1968 David appeared in a BBC-TV play called *The Pistol Shot*, where he became friendly with his co-star Hermione Farthingale (the subject of Bowie's uncharacteristically heartfelt "Song to Hermione"). The two took a flat together and formed a multimedia mime group called Feathers, which, like their relationship, lasted about a year.

Pitt, meanwhile, had decided to showcase his former roommate's multivarious talents in a short film intended for TV. Titled *Love You Till Tuesday* after the most jauntily Newleyesque tune on Bowie's LP, the film called for some new material that might lend itself to visual representation. One viewing of Kubrick's latest movie was all it took for Bowie to pop up with "Space Oddity," which he described as "a mixture of Salvador Dali, *2001*, and the Bee Gees."* "I never felt at home in the Sixties," he later insisted. "I was writing about space . . . when everybody else was writing about peace and love."

"Space Oddity," whose beguiling melody and futuristic ambience provided the requisite commercial sweetener for a profound statement about alienation, scored a major breakthrough for David Bowie; its astronaut hero, Major Tom—who ultimately resolves to sever communications and float off into space rather than return to his native planet—was hardly a run-of-the-mill rock & roll space cadet. But the song went unreleased for the next year, while the film took up permanent residency on Pitt's shelf, following the BBC's devastating query: "But *who*'s David Bowie?"

Bowie, however, was encouraged by the reaction of his old friend and associate Marc Bolan—then coming into his own as a London Underground cult hero—who pronounced "Space Oddity" a surefire hit. The two developed an intimate relationship which Marc later characterized as "the Greek idea of two warriors . . . being very close—they didn't actually screw each other on the battlefield, but mentally they were really into each other—and they had wives who bore them children." Bolan's guitar can be heard on "Karma Man" (one of David's last Deram recordings), while Bowie, in turn, began augmenting Tyrannosaurus Rex performances with his pantomimes.

Bolan and his producer, Tony Visconti, were also instrumental in radicalizing Bowie's attitude toward the music business, his middle-of-the road image, and (indirectly) Kenneth Pitt. Discarding his Tony Newley persona, Bowie recast himself in the "Unwashed and Somewhat Slightly

---

* *Bowie's infatuation with* 2001: A Space Odyssey *would be subsequently reflected in the "Thus Spake Zarathustra" drumrolls at the end of both "Width of a Circle" and "Life on Mars?"*

Dazed'' image of Bob Dylan, acquiring a Zimmerman perm and a harmonica, which last he duly wore about his neck in a rack as he strummed at his acoustic twelve-string guitar.

When "Space Oddity" finally landed him his fifth recording contract—with Philips/Mercury—Bowie sought to recruit Visconti as his producer. Visconti was favorably impressed by the Dylanesque material Bowie was currently cranking out; the only song he *didn't* like, in fact, was "Space Oddity." So Gus Dudgeon wound up producing the single, though David—much to Visconti's surprise—still insisted that Tony produce the subsequent LP (which, incidentally, also utilized the services of an unknown keyboardist named Rick Wakeman).

According to Bowie, the single's release was delayed a further two months "because the record company were waiting to cash in on the American moon landing." And cash in they did: "Space Oddity" made the Top Five, netted its creator an Ivor Novello "special award for originality," and subsequently resulted in Bowie's being voted the fourth-best "new disc

LP, U.S.A., 1967 (Deram)

LP, U.K., 1969 (Philips)

LP, U.K., 1971 (Mercury)

LP, Germany, 1971 (Mercury)

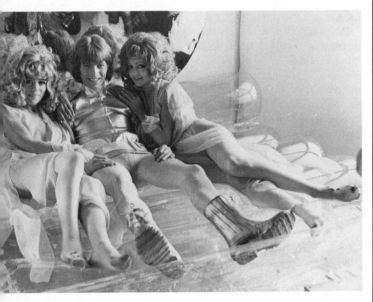

Bowie as Space Oddity in an unreleased TV movie, 1969 (Photo Trends)

singer" in *NME*'s 1969 Readers' Poll. (David, meanwhile, had presented one of his first copies of "Oddity" to his longtime idol Pete Townshend. "I said, 'scuse me Mr. Townshend, would you play this at your convenience and tell me what you think?'" Bowie recalled in *Rolling Stone* a decade later. "Funnily enough, when he came to the studio to work on [1980's *Scary Monsters* LP] he said: 'By the way, I've been meaning to tell you. About that single—it should do all right!'")

Bowie's second album—like its predecessor, titled *David Bowie* in the U.K., but renamed *Man of Words/Man of Music* in the U.S. and *Space Oddity* on RCA's 1972 worldwide rerelease—drew critical raves from both sides of the Atlantic. Nancy Erlich of *The New York Times* called it "a complete, coherent, and brilliant version . . . one of the few proofs that what used to be rock and roll is now a limitless form of expression." She concluded prophetically: "The day will come when David Bowie is a star and the crushed remains of his melodies are broadcast from Muzak boxes in every elevator and hotel lobby in town."

"Memory of a Free Festival"—whose rhapsodic chant "sun

machine is coming down, and we're gonna have a party . . ." supplied the ignition for many an acid trip—particularly endeared Bowie to a small international coterie of LSD buffs. The piece commemorated a festival David had staged in his capacity as founder/director of an "Arts Laboratory"—"my chief occupation," he told *Melody Maker* at the time—in Beckenham, the South London neighborhood where he then lived. "We started [it] with poets and artists who just came along. It got bigger and bigger and now we have our own light show and sculptures, etc. And I never knew there were so many sitar players in Beckenham."

Overall, the *Space Oddity* album's most remarkable quality is that each of its songs tells a distinct story. Though four years later Bowie would call "Oddity" and "Cygnet Committee" "the only songs to come out of that period that I still have a feeling for," one may discern the artist's theatrical bent in even the more pedestrian numbers. But the album got lost in the shuffle of Christmastime product—partly because Bowie, instead of devising a suitable follow-up to his first hit, had vanished from the public eye.

His father died the same week "Space Oddity" entered the Top Ten; to Bowie, "the juxtaposition was like a pantomime, a comic tragedy." In the meantime, the up-and-coming pop star had been booked all over the country as an opening act for Humble Pie (starring David's former schoolmate Peter Frampton). "I went on in front of gum-chewing skinheads," he told *Melody Maker* three years later. "As soon as I appeared, looking a bit like Bob Dylan in curly hair and denims, I was whistled and booed. I had cigarettes thrown at me—isn't that awful? If turned me off the business. I was paranoid, and I cut out." Apart from the flop single "The Prettiest Star" (which featured Bolan on guitar), Bowie offered no new product in 1970.

When he eventually returned to the stage, it was as the leader of a short-lived ensemble called Hype, who performed in bizarre costumes that "[made] us look like Dr. Strange or the Incredible Hulk." The lineup included a lead guitarist named

Mick Ronson, recruited from "a band called the Rats who played blues all night," along with Visconti on bass and John Cambridge on drums. The latter were eventually replaced by Ronson's co-Rats Trevor Bolder and Mick "Woody" Woodmansey to complete the lineup that would catapult into the world's consciousness as the Spiders from Mars. (In the meantime, they dubbed themselves Ronno and Arnold Corns, under which alias Bowie and friends issued his rough drafts of "Moonage Daydream" and "Hang on to Yourself.")

The dedicated, adaptable, and self-effacing Ronson proved the perfect foil for Bowie, both onstage and in the studio. In a 1973 *Melody Maker* interview, Ronson described their partnership as "an invisible link which puts us on the same level of thought . . . we supply each other with inspiration, we never argue, and I think we'll always stay together. I'd never leave him, but if we did split I'd give up whatever I was doing to go back to him if he needed me."

If the cover and contents of 1971's *The Man Who Sold the World* are any indication, Bowie seems to have spent most of 1970 growing his hair out and listening to his Velvet Underground records. In 1976, he would describe *The Man* as "the most drug-oriented album I've made. That was when I was the most fucked up." The Dylan persona and peace/love trappings had given way to a manically heavy Velvet sound, replete with searing feedback and an even heavier set of elliptical nightmare images (mostly written after the music had been captured on tape) that plumbed the darker regions of sexual ambiguity and contemporary urban psychosis. Bowie subsequently acknowledged the Velvets as his "biggest influence," comparable to that of Chuck Berry on the Rolling Stones, and added: "I'd like to think I'm playing my rock & roll in [Lou Reed's] tradition." (A few months later, Reed would move to London and join forces with Bowie in a mutual admiration society, accompanying his disciple onstage during numerous Ziggy-era performances.)

One may also, in songs like "The Man Who Sold the World" and "Supermen," discern an echo of William S. Burroughs. The key concept here is "control"—both self-control (the calculated suppression of emotion) and mind control (the manipulation of the masses in the exercise of absolute power). Bowie's preoccupation with these parallel themes shaped the manner in which the self-described "iceman" prefabricated his own public image—and then proceeded to manipulate his public accordingly. "I stripped myself down," Bowie recalled in 1976, "chucked things out and replaced them with a completely new personality . . . when I saw a quality in someone that I liked, I took it. I still do that, all the time. It's just like a car, man, replacing parts."

The Man Who Sold the World was the spiritual predecessor of *Ziggy Stardust,* though a much more impenetrable work, lacking the pop hooks, panache, and gimmicks with which *Ziggy* would snare the proletariat. Nonetheless, *The Man* garnered some exceptional notices in America's countercultural rags, with *Rolling Stone*'s John Mendelsohn calling it "one of the year's most interesting albums" and "an experience that is as intriguing as it is chilling." *Rock* went so far as to anoint Bowie "the most singularly gifted artist making music today. He has the genius to be to the Seventies what Lennon-McCartney, Jagger, and Dylan were to the Sixties."

The original cover of *The Man Who Sold the World* earned Bowie a certain notoriety by depicting the solitaire-playing artist lolling on a settee in a *dress,* the Queen of Diamonds dangling from his limp right hand. "Why does David Bowie like dressing up in ladies' clothes?" queried the *Melody Maker* headline—prompting Bowie to retort: "They were *men's* dresses. They didn't have big boobs or anything like that. Sort of a medieval sort of thing. I thought they were great."

Though Mercury hurriedly substituted a less controversial sleeve for the U.S. market, Bowie insisted on wearing his "man's dress" when he promoted the album during his first (nonperforming) American visit. In Texas, he reported, "one guy pulled out a gun and called me a fag. But I thought the dress was beautiful." In San Francisco, Bowie informed KSAN-FM's listeners that *The Man Who Sold the World* was in fact a concept album about a shaven-headed transvestite.

Be that as it may, he was now a happily married father. American expatriate Angela Barnett had first eyed David in 1969, when she accompanied a talent-scouting record executive to a Feathers performance. She liked it—even if her date didn't—and became David's constant companion after they

David, Angela, and Zowie Bowie (RDR Productions)

met at a press reception for King Crimson (led by Bowie's future collaborator Robert Fripp). Partly to resolve Angie's visa problems, she and David quietly married on March 20, 1970. Their son, Zowie Bowie, was born the following June.

Anxious to extricate David from his legal ties with Ken Pitt, Angie steered him in the direction of a megalomaniacally ambitious twenty-seven-year-old lawyer named Tony deFries. Though his knowledge of the music business was strictly limited to its legal red tape, deFries apparently took a close listen to Bowie's two Philips/Mercury albums and concluded that David was "potentially bigger than Dylan." Accordingly, deFries (to be unaffectionately known within the rock biz as Tony Deep Freeze) decided to abandon his legal practice and become Bowie's manager. "The way I think about David," he confided, "is as a building. . . . He has the potential—in my hands, anyway—to create the income to make a building on Sixth Avenue. . . . He is the beginning, potentially, of an empire syndrome."

At the time, the public knew Bowie (if at all) as a one-hit wonder, or a bit player from sundry bygone youth subcultures. DeFries, however, insisted that David was a Star: "Bowie is not another Rod Stewart or Cat Stevens. David Bowie is from the Marlon Brando/James Dean school of superimages. . . ." DeFries treated his client accordingly (swanky hotels, limousines, and champagne at every stop), and made his preposterous pronouncements with such aplomb that journalists were willing to give him the benefit of the doubt. The rock media, for their part, were as desperate as ever for fresh infusions of controversy and flash with which to titillate their readership. Bowie offered, in one irresistible package, both lurid headlines ("I'm gay . . .") and food for thought ("the thinking man's Marc Bolan," *NME* tagged him, rather to Marc's own annoyance). DeFries and Bowie, in short, each acted out his chosen role with a thoroughness and precision worthy of the man who sold the world.

In constructing his "Main Man" empire, deFries's first coup was to buy out David's Philips/Mercury recording contract and place him with RCA (Bowie's sixth label in as many years). The relationship was inaugurated at the end of 1971 with *Hunky Dory,* whose title reflected Bowie's avowed state of mind at the time: "I've become optimistic about things, which I never used to be." Then again, *Hunky Dory* may simply have manifested Bowie's desire to launch the next phase of his career with the most commercial piece of product he could possibly devise.

Hunky Dory's airy-fairy persona, McCartneyesque music, and whimsical pastiches certainly make for an incongruous interlude between *The Man* and *Ziggy.* One pictures the iceman of a year later ruing such embarrassingly human (if not downright gauche) vignettes as his sentimental lullaby to Zowie ("Kooks") or his plea to Bobby to bring it all back home again ("Song for Bob Dylan"). "If Dylan was no longer going to unite us, I would at least try to lead the way," said Bowie. But *Hunky Dory*—which opened with "Changes," Bowie's closest ever approximation of a signature tune—also presented the surrealistic panoramas of "Life on Mars?" (to be answered in the affirmative next time round), the enigmatic "Bewlay Brothers" (an impressionistic evocation of Terry and David Jones); "Quicksand" (Bowie's "chain reaction" to "the bliss and the calamity of America"); and his affectionate Lou Reed impersonation about female impersonators, "Queen Bitch." And there were strong intimations of *Ziggy Stardust* in the lyrics of "Oh! You Pretty Things" (even if the ditty *sounded* like Beatle Paul and was first recorded by Peter "Herman" Noone, who probably didn't listen to the words very carefully), wherein Bowie proclaimed that the human race was about to be supplanted by an extraterrestrially sponsored "homo superior"—appearing in the guise of androgynous rock & roll teenagers driving their mamas and papas to distraction with their alien habits. ("Oh! You Pretty Things" would later inspire Pete Shelley's 1981 Electropop dance classic "Homosapien.")

Hunky Dory was accorded rave reviews, with *NME*'s Daniel Halloway declaring: "David Bowie is a million different people and each one is a bit more lovely than the one before. But for Christ's sake don't think he's a hype or a gimmick. Instead, enjoy him for what he is: a surreal cartoon character brought to life for us all to enjoy."

This time, however, the world began to take heed. Bowie, having just made his sensational *Melody Maker* confession, lost little time in adopting the iconography of yet another Kubrick film—*A Clockwork Orange*—for his *Ziggy Stardust* songcycle, whereupon all the world became his stage. At year's end Bowie

would be voted Britain's third-ranking male singer in *NME*'s Readers' Poll; a year after that he was firmly ensconced at Number One.

On August 16, 1972, Bowie unveiled his new alter ego at London's Rainbow Theater. His opening act—the heretofore unknown Roxy Music—having departed to a standing ovation, the theater was engulfed by the synthesized strains of Ludwig Van,* after which Bowie materialized in a cloud of dry ice, warbling "Lady Stardust," as the face of Marc Bolan flashed onto a screen behind him. Subsequent chapters of Ziggy's rise and fall were complemented by Lindsay Kemp's troupe of pantomimists. Lou Reed, lurking in the wings behind shades, alternately chewed his maroon-tinted fingernails and appraised the ongoing proceedings: "Amazing! Incredible! Stupendous! The greatest thing I've ever seen."

Reed's own career was about to receive the proverbial shot in the arm from Bowie's production (with Ronson) of the LP *Transformer*—a title more descriptive of the producer than the singer—whose classic "Walk on the Wild Side" gave Uncle Lou the only Top Twenty hit of his entire checkered career. In much the same vein, British rock's foremost patron of the arts dredged Iggy Pop out of oblivion and rescued Mott the Hoople from a premature breakup by presenting the band with "All the Young Dudes." (Had he issued it himself, this last anthem would have given Bowie his first British Number One. Instead, he released the equally gay—but far less stirring—"John I'm Only Dancing," wherein the singer assures his boyfriend that he has no untoward designs on a female dance partner.)

The resurrection of Lou, Iggy, and the heretofore swaggeringly macho Mott the Hoople as avatars of the polymorphously perverse Glitter/Glam/Camp Rock movement was facilitated by their annexation to the Main Man empire. All, however, presently grew disgruntled and detached themselves from Deep Freeze's indifferent embrace. Like Presley's Colonel Parker, deFries was essentially a one-artist manager.

The rise of Ziggy Stardust was followed by further Tom Parker comparisons when deFries abruptly ensconced his client in a gilded cocoon, secured round-the-clock by burly black bodyguards who felt few qualms about manhandling the prying intruder or ripping the film right out of the unauthorized photographer's camera.

Bowie, of course, was—as deFries himself put it—"a lot brighter than Elvis"; his Presley-like retreat from public display went beyond mere managerial myth mongering. On one level, Bowie was acting out the implications of songs written years before. Nonetheless, many of the rock scribes cried foul, with Nick Kent (in *Creem*) blasting Bowie and his entourage as "rigid, tyrannical, and humorless": "To be a real star you've got to project some kind of human warmth, and Bowie is studiedly inhuman on the most pretentious and superficial level, just as Tony deFries, for all his cigar-chomping Colonel Parker affectations and outright manipulativeness, remains more a caricature of that sort of tyro than the real thing. It may look like good business (though that remains to be seen) but it sure ain't good rock 'n' roll."

More and more, the would-be superstar did seem to be taking at face value what Ziggy had first instigated in the tongue-in-cheek name of "camp." An undeniable arrogance and fatuity

---

* Bowie's use of classical music as a prelude to his performances was to be emulated by many of his imitators and admirers, with Mott the Hoople plumbing for Holst's "Jupiter" (from **The Planets**), Steve Harley and Cockney Rebel for Ravel's **Bolero**, and the Rolling Stones for Copland's "Fanfare for the Common Man."

began to creep into Bowie's few remaining press interviews. "We must not leave the young behind," he would admonish reporters. "I repeat that." Or: "I've been around the world and I think I've discovered who's controlling the world. And, do you know, I've never been so scared in all my life." He was even overheard cutting short the compliments of a stoned admirer—"That was a great rock & roll concert . . ."—with the stern rejoinder: "You didn't see a *rock & roll* concert . . . you saw a *David Bowie concert!*".

As Bowie grew increasingly remote, his appearance, too, turned ever more unearthly. His naturally light-brown hair changed from yellow to carrot orange; as his stalwart supporter Charles Shaar Murray noted in *NME*, "His eyebrows have vanished, replaced by finely sketched red lines. He's wearing red eyeshadow which makes him look faintly insect-like. . . ."

Single, Italy, 1973 (RCA)

LP, 1974 (RCA)

Single, Japan, 1973 (Pye)

Single, Germany, 1978 (RCA)

Bowie capped his red-letter year by previewing his eagerly awaited *Ziggy* sequel. "The Jean Genie"'s basic British R&B sound provided an incongruous setting for the lyrics' protagonist, a hybrid of Iggy Pop and Jean Genet. "Lindsay Kemp did the most fantastic production of *Our Lady of the Flowers* a couple of years ago," Bowie explained, "and it's always been in the back of my mind."

Most of the rest of the album constitutes a diary of Bowie's first American tour with the Spiders, who are augmented here by the cocktail-hour piano of Mike Garson. The opening track, "Watch that Man," describes the bizarre partygoers Bowie entertained at his Plaza suite following his triumphant New York debut—including yet another paranoia-inducing Man, who "talks like a jerk but could eat you with a fork and spoon." The music sounds like an outtake from the Stones' recent *Exile on Main Street;* elsewhere on the LP, Bowie breathes new controversy into Jagger-Richards's "Let's Spend the Night Together" by switching the AC to DC.

"Panic in Detroit," Bowie's vision of the Motor City reduced to rubble, was inspired by Detroiter Iggy Pop's fond

reminiscences of his gum-chewing, gun-toting teenage hoodlum comrades. "Cracked Actor" zeroes in on the mutually exploitative nocturnal hijinks of Hollywood's smacked-out hustlers and their aging show-biz johns. "Drive-In Saturday" materialized on the train to Phoenix (Bowie, for all his spaceman impersonations, had always refused to travel by air) when he espied "the moon shining on seventeen or eighteen enormous silver domes." "I couldn't find out from anyone what they were," he told *Circus*. "But they gave me a vision of America, Britain, and China after a nuclear catastrophe. The radiation has affected people's minds and reproductive organs. . . ." In an attempt to reacquaint themselves with the mechanics of sexual intercourse, the survivors resort to a study of ancient porno flicks.

Upon his return to London, Bowie happened to pick up Evelyn Waugh's *Vile Bodies,* and the whole concept fell into place. "The book dealt with London in the period just before a massive, imaginary war. People were frivolous, decadent, and silly. And suddenly they were plunged into this horrendous holocaust . . . still thinking about champagne and parties and dressing up. Somehow it seemed to me they were like people today. . . ." The song Bowie was inspired to write, "Aladdin Sane" (subtitled "1913-1938-197?"—the years preceding the world wars), provided him with a name for both the album and his fun-loving new doppelgänger, all of which were to draw somewhat mixed notices. Reviewing the album in *Melody Maker*, Chris Welch opined: "The title is a pun, of course, and a deadly accurate one: the lyrics are more intense, more strung out . . . than anything he's done before—splintered nightmare images of a journey across America. . . . There is much to dazzle the eye and ear, but little to move the mind or heart. It is clever, but icy cold. . . ." Nonetheless, *Aladdin Sane*, capitalizing on Bowie's momentum, rose posthaste to Number One in Britain, where it outsold any other album released in 1973.

The first unmistakable signs of a backlash from the British music press came in the wake of Bowie's May 12 performance

Bowie with Lou Reed and Mick Jagger, on the night of his "retirement" (RDR Productions)

at an enormous exhibition hall in London's Earl's Court, which had yet to be properly refurbished for rock concerts. Less than half the seats offered an unobstructed view of the stage, causing dissatisfied customers to run amok and disrupt their Main Man's well-oiled extravaganza. The pop weekly headlines ranged from ALADDIN DISTRESS TO BOWIE BLOWS IT! *NME*'s Nick Kent savaged the program from start to finish: "The sound from the PA was the equivalent of David Bowie's 'Hang on to Yourself' played on a transistor radio coming from the next room." Bowie's customary "Rock 'n' Roll Suicide" finale gave Kent the impetus for a resounding conclusion of his own: "And there he was: the little man in the red spaceman suit, exhorting his aficionados to 'Come give me your hands.' It was beautifully symbolic in a way, because that gig was a formidable batch of nails for the coffin in which the whole Bowie mystique will soon be placed and solemnly laid to rest. And all the costume changes and mime poses in the world won't compensate for that, sweetheart."

But Bowie, as always, had an ace up his sleeve (this one borrowed from Frank Sinatra and Bob Dylan). In the meantime, the *Aladdin Sane* tour, as Bowie proudly noted, "played to 137,000 people, which is more than any act has played to on a single tour of Britain." And when the caravan returned to London for a climactic July 3 performance at the Hammersmith Odeon, David played his ace. With film director D. A. Pennebaker's cameras rolling, Jeff Beck having put in a guest appearance to duel with an awestruck Ronson, Bowie elicited gasps from the crowd with the dramatic announcement: "This show will stay the longest in our memories, not because it's at the end of the tour, but because it is our last show."

"That's it. Period," Bowie would subsequently tell Charles Shaar Murray. "I don't want to do any more gigs . . . from now on I'll be concentrating on activities that have little to do with rock." But *NME*'s Roy Carr (who deemed Bowie "a singing boutique who only appeals to outrageous fashion freaks") dismissed the announcement as "the most calculated publicity stroke since Elvis took up arms . . . in the service of Uncle Sam."

Melody Maker's Roy Hollingworth, at least, hoped that David would prove as good as his word:

> Bowie has saved himself, and by doing that has hopefully saved the futures of his few million followers. They are already weird. Given time they would have gone mad.
>
> Bowie, whether he knew it or not, created a monster. We were all ready to drink from the cup of decadence. Trouble is, few knew when to stop.
>
> [Standing] in the foyer of the Hammersmith Odeon [are] a dozen Bowie look-alikes . . . sneering and posing, and altogether awful. They sneer upon those who they feel don't look as good as they do. . . .
>
> Do you really think that perversion is fun? Think about it. If what Bowie did on stage became a reality on the street, it would not be very pleasant.

Bowie, in fact, was back onstage within six months, performing to a select audience at his old haunt the Marquee Club, for a special edition of NBC-TV's *Midnight Special*. He previewed his new LP, *Pin Ups*, which was to prove his last record with the Spiders from Mars,* and played the genial host to such Sixties faves as Marianne Faithfull and the Troggs. David's myriad costumes proved as striking as ever; one even

En route to Paris and **Pin-Ups** *(Keystone Press Agency)*

incorporated a disembodied pair of gold-painted hands, clutching at his breast like a surrealistic bra. (A third hand was hastily removed from his genitals at the request of the TV team.) He donned green leotards to perform Sonny and Cher's "I Got You Babe" as a duet with Marianne Faithfull, who impersonated a nun for the occasion.

Along with the TV special, *Pin Ups* represented Bowie's closest approximation of a sentimental journey. Such excursions had recently come into vogue among rock's creatively stifled superstars; unlike, say, the John Lennon of *Rock 'n' Roll*, however, Bowie's roots proved to lie not in Fifties Americana, but in the London pop scene of the mid-Sixties as exemplified by such artists as the Kinks, The Who, the Yardbirds, Them, and "Syd's" Pink Floyd—better known to Americans as the British Invasion.

Pin Ups provided Bowie with a pretext for reveling in one of his favorite pastimes—role playing. At its best, the album sheds a perverse new light on the original songs and artists: the acid whimsy of Syd Barrett's "See Emily Play" is transmuted into a barrage of calculated dementia, and The Who's "I Can't Explain" is taken at half-speed to eerie effect, slowed down (in Nick Kent's phrase) from "amphetamine '65 to Mandrax '73."*

David's decision to part with the Spiders first revealed deFries's infallibility when Main Man launched Mick Ronson's solo career with the same hype and fanfare it had previously accorded Bowie. The campaign backfired badly when Ronson, for all his versatility as a musician and arranger, failed to establish a distinct personality of his own. Ronson was ultimately left to return to a more congenial supporting role, alongside the likes of Ian Hunter and (in 1976) Bob Dylan. Bolder and Woodmansey, meanwhile, met with little success in

---

* On **Pin Ups**, *drummer Woodmansey's place is taken by Aynsley Dunbar, who had played on the original version of the Mojos' "Everything's All Right" almost a decade before Bowie's remake.*

* *A remake of Bowie's own 1966 Mod B-side, "The London Boys," was dropped at the last minute.*

their attempt to perpetuate themselves as Spiders from Mars.

At the end of 1973, *NME* revealed that Bowie had spent much of the previous year devising "a musical adaptation" of George Orwell's *1984* as "a spectacular Broadway-style revue" intended for London's West End. Bowie had already previewed the intended title song on his *Midnight Special,* but ran into an unforeseen snag when Orwell's widow denied him the rights to the book. Bowie then rewrote the script as *Diamond Dogs,* under which title he released the revue's proposed musical content as his next LP.

Dogs was preceded by the snappy single "Rebel Rebel," which provided Bowie's heterosexual female admirers with an "All the Young Dudes"–style anthem of their own. The musical setting, as Roy Carr noted in *NME,* was "a premeditated rewrite of the entire 'Satisfaction' formula. . . . [Presumably] Bowie didn't want to cover a Stones hit for *Pin Ups,* preferring as he's done to update the contents, matter, and notation of their biggest-ever hit." Bowie pinched another of the Stones' ideas when Jagger confided that the Belgian artist Guy Peeleart (who had just produced the brilliant book *Rock Dreams* with Nik Cohn) was furnishing a cover for their next LP. David instantly hired Peeleart to do the same for *Diamond Dogs*—which, to Mick's displeasure, materialized several months before *It's Only Rock 'n' Roll.*

"Rebel Rebel" and Peeleart's stunning cover notwithstanding, *Diamond Dogs* (which Main Man billed as "the album of the century!") indicated that David had lost much of his sense of perspective and humor. The production and arrangements, along with most of the instruments, were all credited to one "Bowie" (his Christian name having been withdrawn from circulation on all new "Bowie" product and Main Man literature). The result was a fairly turgid and impenetrable performance of the writer's most ambitious song cycle to date. *1984*'s storyline is only intermittently recognizable in Bowie's evocation of a post-Holocaust New York, where gangs of roving "peoploids" stake out their domain on "the highest of the sterile skyscrapers," periodically roaming the streets below to scavenge for food among "rats the size of cats" and copulate with fellow pedestrians. *Diamond Dogs* represented a distillation of all *Ziggy*'s fashionable doom-mongering and "decadence," with none of the latter's wit, panache, and flawless execution. More than ever before, *Dogs* also reflected the influence of William S. Burroughs, with whom Bowie held his *Rolling Stone* tête-à-tête around this time. Though aficionados remain divided over its merits, *Diamond Dogs* undoubtedly qualifies as Bowie's most *unpleasant* work.

His next move was to salvage his "Broadway-type spectacular" (minus the dialogue)—only, instead of staging it in a London West End theater, he took it on the road across America, less than a year after his vaunted "retirement" (an implicit acknowledgment of the fact that Bowie was by no means as popular in the U.S. as in Britain, and if he wanted to become a megastar on this side of the Atlantic he would have to promote his new product like ordinary mortals). "The Year of the Diamond Dogs" tour was certainly the most theatrical, spectacular, and expensive production Bowie (or any other rock performer, for that matter) had ever staged, even if his new Halloween Jack persona eschewed glitter for an Yves St. Laurent suit, blue sweater, and suspenders.

Mark Ravitz's elaborate set (loosely based on Fritz Lang's film *Metropolis*) transformed the arena stage into the ravaged cityscape of *Diamond Dogs,* and each number was a set piece, choreographed by Tony Basil (with the band, now led by

guitarist Earl Slick, kept hidden behind a screen). There was a movable catwalk, from which Bowie, wrapped in a trench coat, crooned "Sweet Thing" and "Candidate" under the glare of a streetlight. For "Cracked Actor" he donned a cape and shades, to address the skull that he clutched at his crotch. During the sophisticated, S&M-flavored dance routines of "Diamond Dogs," David's backup singers tied him up with their "leashes." "Big Brother" was highlighted by a giant mirrored pleasure dome; but the pièce de résistance was "Space Oddity," for which Bowie entered an actual space capsule, hoisted over the cheering throngs by a glorified cherrypicker as he sang his first hit into a red telephone.

Mike Garson added to the program's "legitimate" show-biz ambience, particularly in the jazzy piano interludes with which he linked each number to the next. As the tour progressed, however, the music began to foreshadow Bowie's next metamorphosis; his vocals became tinged with the Philadelphia International soul he had been soaking off the American airwaves, and his band, in turn, acquired a nascent disco bounce. When "the Year of the Diamond Dogs" reached Philly—where the show was immortalized for the *David Live* album*—Bowie made a pilgrimage to Sigma Sound studios, and began concocting a "plastic soul" record of his own. And when he resumed his grueling concert schedule, the cityscape was replaced altogether by a chorus of fat, sassy blacks.

"Just working with a band and singing is a new kind of fulfillment," Bowie declared at the time, cultivating the impression that the actor had finally shed his masks to reveal the "real" David Bowie (though there were to be several more of these as well). But his blue-eyed soul revampings of

---

* An ironic title, in light of the ban on Bowie's Christian name during the actual tour.

"The year of the Diamond Dogs . . . ," 1974 (*John Rowlands*)

"Suffragette City" and "The Jean Genie"—complete with interjections of "Awl-raght!" and "Unh-hunh!"—were less than convincing. When he returned to New York's Radio City Music Hall, the near-silence that followed his perennial "Rock 'n' Roll Suicide" finale was almost deafening; there were certainly none of the usual cries for "more!"

Bowie's problems stemmed less from his choice of musical style, or even the absence of costumes and props, than from his utter listlessness. He had been driving himself past the breaking point, and the strain was compounded by the legal ramifications of his decision to part ways with Main Man and deFries. ("I grew to dislike their attitude, so I just said goodbye.") Nonetheless, Bowie achieved what he had set out to accomplish: his Philly album, released as *Young Americans* in March 1975, scored him his first American Number One single.

Co-produced by his old friend Tony Visconti, *Young Americans* was as slick as *Diamond Dogs* was not, and represented Bowie's first attempt to manufacture unadulterated Product. But the crowning touch was added only at the eleventh hour, when a meeting with John Lennon bore fruit in a remake of the Beatles' "Across the Universe," and "Fame"—the off-the-cuff disco smash that they based on a riff Bowie's new guitarist Carlos Alomar had dreamed up for David's concert renditions of the Flares' 1961 R&B hit "Foot Stomping."

The nomadic D.B.'s next move was to L.A., where he hobnobbed with the Tinseltown celebrities, indulged in all the usual superstar excesses, and became the Thin White Duke: a Continental aristocrat cum Cracked Actor. "I want to be a Frank Sinatra figure," he announced, "and I will succeed." On *Station to Station* (1976) Bowie's unctuous and cadaverous

Bowie's self-portrait (RCA Records)

crooning often comes across as the iceman's impersonation of a romantic balladeer; occasionally, however, a genuine yearning actually to *feel* the emotions he is feigning cuts through the artifice, hinting at a romanticism (that of the outsider longing to rejoin the human race) far more profound than any known to Tin Pan Alley.

To the disco funk of last year's model, *Station to Station* adds a heavy, Teutonic grandeur; the album is Bowie's vision of Europe—particularly the Germany of the Thirties—viewed from the remote vantage point of Los Angeles, and through the distorting prism of cocaine. Bowie's 1976 interviews reeked of crypto-Fascist delusions—e.g., "I'd be an excellent dictator, very eccentric and quite mad . . . I'll bloody lead this country and make it a great fucking nation"—reflecting what he later called a fascination "with the *mythology* involved [in] the magical side of the whole Nazi period," which, he later conceded, was "not something to be dealt with unless you're in a stable frame of mind." But this was only one manifestation of Bowie's desperate search for spiritual meaning in the city he would remember as "the armpit of the universe." He also acquired a crucifix, and in *Station to Station* the daunting Aryan superman persona momentarily crumbles as David delivers himself of an actual *hymn* called "Word on a Wing," wherein the emotion doesn't sound counterfeit at all.

During this period, Bowie also enacted his first leading cinematic role in Nicolas Roeg's *The Man Who Fell to Earth*. He proved the perfect choice for the part of the stranded extraterrestrial who dons a human mask and, instead of achieving his mission to obtain water for his own parched planet, succumbs to the temptations of power in this world. Beyond Thomas Newton's obvious kinship with such erstwhile Bowie "space invader" personas as Ziggy Stardust, David had

"I wouldn't mind being the first English president of the U.S. I'm certainly right wing enough" (Steven Blau Collection)

written extensively about superhuman miracle workers and the corrupting influence of power in both *Ziggy* and (especially) *The Man Who Sold the World*.

Bowie also invested a great deal of energy in scoring *The Man Who Fell to Earth*, so was extremely perturbed when the producers settled instead on an eclectic soundtrack dominated by Stomu Yamashta and ex-Papa John Phillips. But, as Bowie told *NME* in 1980, the experience "did prompt me in another area—to consider my own instrumental capabilities . . . [which] I hadn't really done before. . . . That's when I got the first inklings of trying to work with [fellow ex-Glitter Rocker, and former Roxy Musician, Brian] Eno," whose recent *Another Green World* LP, with its incandescent instrumentals and

"The return of the Thin White Duke . . .," 1976 (John Rowlands)

experimental recording techniques, had given Bowie much listening pleasure.

In the meantime, he took the Thin White Duke ("a very nasty character indeed," he admitted later) on a concert tour of America, Britain, and the Continent. His 1976 presentation was a study in stark simplicity, with monochromatic black-and-white sets flooded throughout by harsh white lighting. Bowie, short hair slicked severely back, performed in a conservative white shirt and black trousers, boots, and vest (with a convenient side pocket from which to extract a Gitane cigarette at every opportunity). "That whole *Station to Station* tour was done under duress," he recalled in *NME*. "I was out of my mind totally, completely crazed."

Still fixated on the mystique of Fascism, Bowie gravitated toward Berlin, where he rented a flat in the ramshackle Turkish neighborhood of Neukölln. "And of course the first thing that happened to me when I got [there] was that I really had to face up to it, because . . . I was meeting young people of my age whose fathers had actually been SS men. . . . I came crashing down to earth" (to become, like Thomas Newton, increasingly recognizable as a member of the human race).

Bowie then entered what he later called his "withdrawal period," renouncing (in no particular order) Fascism, super-stardom, narrative songwriting, and his whole premeditated approach to making and selling his music. Rock and disco gave way to stream-of-consciousness electronics; slick production to random studio experimentation; and cohesive lyrics to free-form word association, cut-ups, nonsense syllables, and (in many cases) bona fide instrumentals. Tony Visconti recalled Bowie's invitation to produce a record "so radical that it's probably not going to be released. Are you willing to waste a month's time? It might prove the best album I've made or the worst, because I have never done this before, but I'm sick and tired of being a rock star and have this desire to compose music a bit deeper." When RCA heard the results, Bowie recalled in *NME*, "the one comment I received from them was 'Can we get you another pad in Philadelphia?'—so that I could do another *Young Americans*." As he declared in *Rolling Stone*, however, he was now "prepared to relinquish [record] sales, by sticking to my guns about the kind of music I really wish to make."

Low (1977)—with Bowie's profile on the cover perpetrating a visual pun—consists of quirky, predominantly instrumental mood pieces,* the mood being one of somber introspection, psychic withdrawal, and rampant claustrophobia ("pale blinds drawn all day, nothing to read, nothing to say . . ."). Late 1977's *"Heroes"* (which inaugurated Bowie's collaboration with guitarist Robert Fripp) repeats the *Low* format (vocals on side one, instrumentals on side two, with little to interest U.S. radio programmers), but it is somewhat more expansive—particularly in the title track, whose epic sweep qualifies it as possibly the greatest song Bowie (and/or Eno) ever wrote. "'Heroes'" ("I felt that the use of quotes indicated a dimension of irony about . . . the whole concept of heroism") was inspired by a young couple who met every afternoon by the Berlin Wall, beneath the shadow of an East German guard tower, some fifty feet from the studio where Bowie was recording his album. In "'Heroes,'" both his words and his vocal evince an aching compassion (reminiscent of Lou Reed at his very best) for the heroism of those in desperate circumstances who (like Reed's junkies and transvestites)

---

* The two last selections, "Weeping Wall" and "Subterraneans," originated in Bowie's abortive **Man Who Fell to Earth** score.

"We can be 'Heroes' . . . ," 1978 (Ron Gott)

The title's broadest implication, however, is that Bowie no longer felt constrained to focus, at any given time, on one specific style, character, concept, or even vocation. His latter-day discography could and would encompass both a collaboration with platinum megastars Queen ("Under Pressure") and a narration of Prokofiev's *Peter and the Wolf* (accompanied by Eugene Ormandy and the Philadelphia Orchestra); he also seemed relatively content to concentrate on *music* when making records, and to channel his aspirations as an actor into a series of highly acclaimed stage and screen performances.

Though these last were preceded by a starring role in David Hemmings's Weimar Berlin fiasco *Just a Gigolo* (which Bowie called his "thirty-two Elvis Presley movies rolled into one"), his celebrated 1980 Broadway debut in Bernard Pomerance's Tony Award–winning play *The Elephant Man* surpassed all expectations. The story of John Merrick enabled Bowie to explore further a key theme from *The Man Who Fell to Earth* and many of his own songs—"seeing what sort of juxtapositions you get . . . [when you] shove [a] pure 'new' spirit into the middle of sordid society"—and he skillfully drew upon his background in mime to convey his character's hideous deformities. This time, however, David's every move was scrutinized by exacting theater critics with little sympathy for the publicity stunts of rock & roll stars—and even they came away impressed. (*The New York Times* called him "splendid.")

Bowie as the Elephant Man (© 1981 by Susan Cook)

nonetheless manage to extract a glimmer of purpose or even beauty from their doomed lives.

The relatively uncommercial content of *Low* and *"Heroes"* notwithstanding, Bowie could still fill twenty-thousand-seat halls on his 1978 world tour (captured for posterity on the *Stage* album). Though the first half of the program was dominated by his last two LPs, he proved perfectly amenable to delivering his greatest hits (including most of *Ziggy*) after intermission, and in the absence of any spectacular props or special effects he turned out the most relaxed and polished performances of his entire career.

For *Lodger* (1979), Bowie and Eno eschewed the ethereal instrumentals of their previous collaborations, electing instead to experiment within the framework of the three-minute pop song. On "Boys Keep Swinging," each of the musicians was instructed to switch to an unfamiliar instrument; guitarist Carlos Alomar, for instance, was placed behind the drum kit. Bowie and Eno also created an entirely different song—the romantic ballad "Fantastic Voyage"—by taking "Boys'" frenetic chord changes at half-speed. The tune to "Move On" was derived from "All the Young Dudes" played backwards, and "African Night Flight" emerged when the same treatment was given the rock standard "Suzie Q." Basic tracks were recorded, then summarily erased after new layers had been overdubbed, leaving the songs with wholly unanticipated textures.

As the title suggests, *Lodger* constitutes an impressionistic journal of Bowie's recent world travels (he referred to the album as *Travel Along with David Bowie*) and draws from the musical idioms of places as various as Kenya, Turkey, and Jamaica (the latter two fused into the one song "Yassasin"). No longer affecting the role of exotic alien in *our* midst, this "lodger" looked, dressed, and acted the part of the unassumingly stylish, well-spoken, globe-trotting English artist, blending as unobtrusively as possible into the genuinely exotic *terrestrial* surroundings that he now scoured for inspiration.

Single, Spain, 1979 (RCA)

Single, Spain, 1979 (RCA)

12" Single, U.K., 1980 (RCA)

"Crystal Japan" Single, Japan, 1980 (RCA)

There were no further Bowie "personas" as such, perhaps because he no longer felt the need to sell himself in a single distinctive package. As his 1978 concerts demonstrated, he now had no qualms about drawing from any or all of the sundry periods or styles that comprised his brilliant legacy. Bowie's 1980 British Number One, "Ashes to Ashes," was a direct sequel to his first hit; a decade later, "Space Oddity"'s astronaut hero resurfaces as a junkie. "'Ashes to Ashes,'" David told the *Soho News,* "is about the dissolution of the great dream that brought Major Tom to space in the first place. Ten years later, everything has soured, because there was no reason to put him up there in the first place—just a technological ego trip."

The repercussions of Bowie's legacy, meanwhile, had profoundly influenced every major phase of the emerging New Wave. The early Punks' deliberately unconvincing dye jobs; Elvis Costello's sly manipulation of the vocabulary of rock & roll; Gary Numan's high-tech futureworlds; and the "pretty boys" of 1981—all sprang virtually full-blown from the head of Ziggy Stardust. David Bowie was the one established rock star whom nobody called a Boring Old Fart.

Bowie actually placed himself at the vanguard of the New Wave video revolution when he channeled his erstwhile attempts to create a new form of musical theater into a series of visual complements to *Lodger* and 1980's *Scary Monsters.* Unlike most rock videos, Bowie's brilliantly edited images added a whole new dimension to his songs. "Ashes to Ashes," for instance, presented surreal juxtapositions of Bowie as a spaceman, a deep-sea diver, and a clown, who walks alongside a black sea in the company of his garrulous mum. Bowie's videos, like his songs, and, finally, like the artist himself, functioned as magnificent Rorschach tests, yielding endless possible interpretations, yet none in particular. As British rock's "hero" of a thousand faces told an earnest German lady interviewer who attempted to press him on the "meaning" of his video images: "You tell me what it means and I'll agree."

(followed by their highest chart positions, as listed in *Billboard*)

DAVID BOWIE'S HITS

U.S. Singles

1972	Starman (**65**); The Jean Genie (**71**)
1973	Space Oddity (**15**)
1974	Rebel Rebel (**64**)
1975	Young Americans (**28**); Fame (**1**); Changes (**41**)
1976	Golden Years (**10**); TVC 15 (**64**)
1977	Sound and Vision (**69**)
1980	Fashion (**70**)

U.S. LPs

1972	Hunky Dory (**93**); The Rise and Fall of Ziggy Stardust and the Spiders from Mars (**75**); Space Oddity (**16**); The Man Who Sold the World (**105**)
1973	Images 1966–1967 (**144**); Aladdin Sane (**17**); Pin Ups (**23**)
1974	Diamond Dogs (**5**); David Live at the Tower Philadelphia (**8**)
1975	Young Americans (**9**)
1976	Station to Station (**3**); Changesonebowie (**10**)
1977	Low (**11**); "Heroes" (**35**)

1978	Prokofiev's Peter and the Wolf (narrated by Bowie (**136**); Stage (**44**)
1979	Lodger (**20**)
1980	Scary Monsters (**12**)

U.K. Singles

1969	Space Oddity (**5**)
1972	Starman (**10**); John I'm Only Dancing (**12**); The Jean Genie (**2**)
1973	Drive-In Saturday (**3**); Life on Mars? (**3**); Sorrow (**3**); The Laughing Gnome (**6**)
1974	Rebel Rebel (**5**); Knock on Wood (**10**); Diamond Dogs (**21**); Rock 'n' Roll Suicide (**22**)
1975	Space Oddity EP (**1**); Young Americans (**18**); Fame (**17**); Golden Years (**8**)
1976	TVC 15 (**33**)
1977	Sound and Vision (**3**); "Heroes" (**24**)
1978	Beauty and the Beast (**39**); Breaking Glass EP (**54**)
1979	Boys Keep Swinging (**7**); D.J. (**29**); John I'm Only Dancing (Again) (**12**)
1980	Alabama Song (**23**); Ashes to Ashes (**1**); Fashion (**5**); Scary Monsters (**20**)

THE BRITISH INVASION

The Next Wave

TWELVE YEARS AFTER THE start of the British Invasion, rock & roll seemed, once again, a spent force. One might almost say it had come full circle, back to the pre-Beatle Dark Ages. But unlike the Founding Fathers from the Golden Age of Rock & Roll, the superstars spawned by the Sixties simply wouldn't just f-f-fade away. What's more, nobody would let them: certainly not the rock biz moguls whose fortunes depended on what was now a multibillion-dollar industry; nor the fans, clinging to the vestiges of their receding adolescence, to Summer of Love mirages, and to the occasionally warranted conviction that these icons were Great Artists. Accordingly, the living legends settled into comfortable ruts; each year or so they'd crank out a variation on the old platinum-certified formula, then promote the product on a tour of the world's leading sports arenas, reduced to the size of performing fleas in the eyes of the sitting ducks on the twelve-dollar bleachers.

Rock, by and large, had turned back into Show Biz, yet this time around the freshness and innocence of the shoo-be-doo/lang-doo-lang/ da-doo-run-run days was nowhere in evidence. Many of the British Invasion's "survivors" appeared to have metamorphosed from teen-dream pinups cum countercultural prophets into jaded tax exiles, trading in on past glories to join the international jet set and fill Hollywood gossip columns with accounts of million-dollar recording contracts, divorces, and "palimony" suits—not to mention hair transplants and blood transfusions.

The Top Forty, in turn, was usurped by the "mellow" sounds of "L.A. Rock" (or: music by and for laid back ex-hippies going through "heavy changes" in their suburban hot tubs) and by the slick, mechanical disco rhythms that eventually threatened to supersede rock altogether (and whose most penetrating messages were "I wanna funk with you all night" and "Shame, shame, shame, shame, shame on you if you can't dance too . . ."). Such was the Spirit of '76 as America's so-called Me Generation celebrated the bicentennial of the thirteen colonies' revolution against Britain to a soundtrack by the Eagles and Jackson Browne, by KC and the Sunshine Band and the resuscitated, discofied Bee Gees.

In the Mother Country, however, revolution was truly in the

"We're into chaos, not music"—Johnny Rotten of the Sex Pistols (RDR Productions)

air, if not yet on the airwaves: a bona fide rock & roll insurrection that promised to purge British pop of mid-Seventies complacency and nostalgia and return the music to the streets, to the kids, and to the moment. Originally dubbed Punk Rock, this insurgency gradually acquired the less disturbing label "New Wave" as it broadened its musical base and popular appeal.

Punk Rock stripped the music of all niceties, subtleties, and frills—back to rock & roll's three primeval chords, thrashed out at breakneck speed with the volume and treble controls of battered-up amps dialed past the threshold of pain. Anyone could play Punk Rock, and anyone did; thousands of new bands sprang up virtually overnight, most of them practically interchangeable, recharging those three magic chords in a machine-gun volley that threatened to level the superstars' vaunted pedestals, reconsecrate rock & roll as a force for subversion and anarchy, and put fear and loathing back into the hearts of upstanding citizens. . . .

In the end, however, these shock troops' main contribution was (as the Psychedelic Furs' Richard Butler put it) to "break down barriers in the business . . . so bands could be adventurous again." New Wave, by and large, substituted sophisticated irony for Punk rage, though it continued to withhold the comforting illusions of the rock "mainstream." It eventually encompassed so many disparate styles and trends that "New Wave" became little more than an all-purpose label attached to any new young performer of a vaguely unconventional and/or "minimalistic" bent (playing anything from 1950s rockabilly to 1960s Jamaican ska to 2001 electropop). Thanks to the Punk insurrection, more of these artists than ever before were given the opportunity to make themselves heard. The result was a surfeit of great noise such as Britain hadn't experienced since the days of its Invasion—not to mention a welcome infusion of hot young blood.

By the same token, however, New Wave produced few towering figures comparable—in terms of influence or mass appeal—to the Beatles, Stones, Kinks, Who, Floyd, Bolan, or Bowie at their respective primes. Partly for this reason, no New Wave artist or group has been selected as the subject of a major section of this book, though the most celebrated and influential British New Wave acts will be found in "The British Hot Hundred," and a chronological history of British New Wave music may be gleaned from the "British Rock Diary." What follows here is a brief romp through latter-day British Rock.

Both "Punk Rock" and "New Wave" were well-worn labels long before the advent of the safety-pin brigade. In the early Sixties, the latter term was applied to young upstarts in such diverse fields as film and jazz; *Melody Maker* (still primarily a jazz rag) routinely blared headlines like THE NEW WAVE: IS IT KILLING JAZZ? A year later, it had already adapted the phrase to suit such post–Mersey Beat pop groups as the Kinks. Soon any new rock act that purported to be a step ahead of the game was likely to be tagged New Wave (e.g., the 1968 Mercury Records ad campaign on behalf of "the New Wave sounds of Blue Cheer and Spanky and Our Gang").

"Punk Rock," meanwhile, entered the vernacular at the end of the Sixties to describe the rash of American garage bands that had sprung up between 1965 and 1967 in emulation of the raunchier elements of the British Invasion. Groups like Sam the Sham and the Pharaohs ("Wooly Bully"), ? and the Mysterians ("96 Tears"), Shadows of Knight ("Gloria"), and Count Five ("Psychotic Reaction") took their cues from the Rolling Stones, the Kinks, The Who, Them, and the Yardbirds; none could sing or play a lick, but they made up for it with sheer spunk and zest, each band managing one classic piece of Top Ten trash before getting chucked back onto the scrap heap. In the early Seventies, a few revisionist critics decreed that Sixties Punk Rock had actually epitomized the spirit of rock & roll, but the vogue quickly waned. In a 1974 interview with *New Musical Express*'s Nick Kent, Bryan Ferry of Roxy Music (earlier described in *NME* as "one of Britain's most provocative and entertaining New Wave bands") suggested that the piece be headlined PUNK ROCK—I EAT IT FOR BREAKFAST. "Nah," said Kent. "Punk Rock was last year's thing."

Though Roxy's arty decadence would prove anathema to the early British Punks, the group's obsession with visual style and

Ferry's own brand of deadpan crooning—whereby he reinterpreted pop artifacts ranging from Leslie Gore's ephemeral "It's My Party" to Bob Dylan's apocalyptic "A Hard Rain's a-Gonna Fall" with precisely the same measure of sardonic detachment—would both be rehabilitated as key ingredients in the "new" New Wave.

Roxy, for their part, started out under the spell of the Velvet Underground, the Andy Warhol protégés whose music shared much of the original Punk Rock spirit. Unlike other Sixties garage band ringleaders, however, the Velvets' Lou Reed was a certifiable rock & roll visionary. While his "progressive" contemporaries decked themselves out in flowers and Nehru jackets, Reed was dispassionately chronicling the underbelly of New York City life in songs about kinky drugs and hard-core perversion. Resolutely unfashionable, uncommercial, and unprofessional, the Velvets transmuted Reed's three-chord monologues into interminable barrages of searing noise.

Another "seminal" late-Sixties proto-Punk band was the Stooges, who hailed from Detroit. Though less arty than the Velvet Underground, the Stooges' music was just as loud and anarchic, a fitting backdrop for the idiot nihilism of their G-stringed singer. Iggy Stooge (a.k.a. Pop) regularly vomited onstage, smeared his hunky torso with peanut butter and shards of broken glass, bared his buttocks to the audience (occasionally inserting a broken drumstick), and hurled himself into the front rows for rounds of mutual abuse with selected admirers. Like Lou Reed, Iggy was dredged out of obscurity in the early Seventies by David Bowie and found a wider audience among the Glitter bugs. Which brings us to the New York Dolls.

Though they arrived in time for the Glitter Rock bandwagon resplendent in cheap makeup, secondhand rhinestones, and tottering high heels, the Dolls would be best remembered as the first real embodiment of the Punk aesthetic. They were the most shamelessly ersatz Rolling Stones imaginable, with Jagger lookalike David Johansen and Keith Richards clone Johnny Thunders carrying their inept impersonations to the point of sheer burlesque. The Dolls wrote ghastly but true-to-life songs called "Trash" and "Personality Crisis" and turned the amps up all the way. The very fact that they were just fucked-up rock & roll kids from the suburbs pretending to be the Rolling Stones was precisely what so endeared them both to New York's jaded scenemakers and critics—and to a handful of similarly dissolute working-class British teenagers. "I was very impressed by their ordinariness and how bad they were," the Sex Pistols' Sid Vicious would recall.

The Dolls helped launch a thriving local music scene that centered around Max's Kansas City and a fetid hole-in-the-wall on the Bowery known as CBGB's. Leading lights included Blondie, whose style derived from early-Sixties "girl groups"; the comic-book-moronic, leather-jacketed Ramones; Patti Smith, who ululated her poetry to the crude accompaniment of a solitary electric guitar; and Television, whose spiky-haired bassist, Richard Hell, originated the shredded T-shirt look.

Though record-buying America remained indifferent to the Dolls, many British observers were riveted. These included one Malcolm McLaren, whom Johnny Thunders hailed as "the greatest con man I've ever met." In 1975, McLaren took over the Dolls' management and vainly attempted to revive their flagging career by dolling them up in Red Army uniforms and draping the stage with Communist flags. When the Dolls broke up, McLaren returned to his King's Road boutique, where he proceeded to adapt the sartorial fashions of the new New York rockers for his own unsavory purposes.

Though he changed his emporium's name from Let It Rock to the more memorable Sex, McLaren's X-rated T-shirts, bondage baubles, and fetishistic rubber wear were expressly designed to arouse outrage and nausea instead of hard-ons. The boutique soon became the preferred watering hole for growing numbers of teenage malcontents who adopted the Sex look as their own. Most felt little kinship for the Sixties counterculture and its increasingly bloated icons, but they nonetheless enjoyed an occasional bash at drum kits and guitars. So McLaren decided to assemble a band of Sex regulars and perpetrate on his home turf what he had failed to achieve in New York with the Dolls.

Their Sex regalia notwithstanding, guitarist Steve Jones, drummer Paul Cook, and bassist Glen Matlock (replaced much later in the game by Sid Vicious) were all ordinary, pleasant-looking kids. The search for a suitably gangrenous front man ended when "a teenaged amphetamine hunchback with green hair and rotting dentures to match" (to quote Julie Burchill and Tony Parsons's so-called "Obituary of Rock & Roll") slouched into Sex sporting a slashed-up Pink Floyd T-shirt with the words "I HATE" scrawled above the venerable space cadet's name. Induced to audition for the band by miming to Alice Cooper's "School's Out" in front of the Sex jukebox, John Lydon was hired on the spot. McLaren, christening his new Frankenstein monster, tacked the unsettling word "Pistols" onto the equally controversial name of his shop, while Lydon assumed the moniker "Johnny Rotten" in deference to the state of his teeth.

It was altogether fitting that British Punk should have been, to some extent, the by-product of a boutique; it always had at least as much to do with fashion as with music. Dubbed "confrontation dressing" by McLaren's associate, Vivienne Westwood, Punk outfits made use of such singularly mundane components as plastic clothespins, razor blades, tampons, fragments of household appliances, garbage bags, and lavatory chains. The subculture found its best-known symbol in the quintessentially utilitarian safety pin, which served both to stitch the bits and pieces together and as a distinctive ornament in its own right, worn variously through ear, cheek, or nipple. Fabrics and designs were selected for their sheer tackiness: lurex and plastic, tiger stripes and mock leopard skin. Carrying the application of beauty aids to ostentatious extremes that deliberately foiled their original purpose, Punks of both sexes routinely dyed their hair jet black, snow white, bright purple, pink, or green (or some intricate combination thereof), while prodigious amounts of makeup transformed faces into "abstract portraits: sharply observed and meticulously executed studies in alienation" (to quote Dick Hebdige's *Subculture*).

Punks also gloried in such obvious symbols of violence and unpleasantness as military uniforms, guerrilla outfits, and even the dread swastika. This last was favored purely for its shock value (rather than as a manifestation of any actual political convictions) in much the same spirit as the Punks adopted the paraphernalia of sexual fetishism.

Indeed, the Punk subculture—and the Sex Pistols in particular—could hardly have been less sexy. In his first big *Melody Maker* write-up, Johnny Rotten yawned: "Sex . . . is so easy nowadays. By the time you're twenty you just think—another squelch session. . . . I don't believe in love, and I never will. It's a myth brought on by Micky Most & Co. to sell records. . . . Love is what you feel for a dog or a pussy cat. It doesn't apply to humans, and if it does it just shows how low you are."

Like the Mods twelve years earlier, Punks preferred to dance with members of their own sex, or, better yet, alone—though, unlike Mod, Punk was not a stag party. (Indeed, one of Punk Rock's most positive contributions would be the decimation of the music's ubiquitous sexual stereotypes.) Displays of affection were hardly facilitated by the Punks' peculiarly staccato, robotlike dances, the most notorious of which was the pogo. Jumping up and down, hands clenched to the sides, as if interacting with an imaginary ball rather than another human being, pogoists in crowded clubs often extracted additional pleasure from the act of stamping on one another's feet.

Johnny Rotten looks bored. The emphasis is on the word "looks" rather than, as Johnny would have you believe, on the word "bored." His safety-pinned-together clothes fall around his slack body in calculated disarray. His face is an undernourished gray. . . . This malevolent, third generation child of rock 'n' roll is . . . the elected generalissimo of a new cultural movement scything through the grass roots disenchantment with the present state of mainstream Rock. You need look no further than the letter pages of any recent rock weekly to see that fans no longer silently accept the disdain with which their heroes, the rock giants, treat them. . . . There is a growing, almost desperate feeling that rock music should be stripped down to its bare bones again, taken by the scruff of its bloated neck and given a good shaking.

from *Melody Maker*'s first feature on Punk Rock, by Caroline Coon, July 28, 1976

"I look at myself as one of the most sexless monsters ever"—Sex Pistol Sid Vicious (Freelance Photo Guild/Ebet Roberts)

Within weeks of their formation, the Sex Pistols, ignoring all the usual forms of career advancement, began gate-crashing gigs at colleges. Cultivating an image as anarchistic, nihilistic, and confrontative as its name, the band achieved instant notoriety and a rapidly growing following. The Pistols' example inspired a rash of like-minded combos, including Siouxsie and the Banshees (early camp followers of the band) and the Clash (assembled by McLaren's erstwhile cohort Bernie Rhodes).

Behind-the-scenes Svengalis like McLaren and Rhodes notwithstanding, the raison d'être of the Punk/New Wave explosion was ordinary kids taking matters into their own hands, making the most of their limited resources and abilities (and dispensing with the usual middlemen and go-betweens) to create their own music and fashions—on, by, and for "the street." They even had their own alternative press: scabrous, scatological fanzines called *Sniffin' Glue, Ripped and Torn,* and *Vomit,* whose typing errors were deliberately left uncorrected in the final proof to reinforce the aura of immediacy and urgency, the sense that these, no less than the music they promulgated, were bulletins red hot from the battle zone. (The Punk fanzines were especially fond of "ransom note" typography, wherein each character was drawn from a different type face—usually newspaper headlines—a technique that paralleled the cut-ups of Punk fashion and was to be appropriated both on numerous record sleeves and in the Sex Pistols' own logo.) It was *Sniffin' Glue* that perhaps best summed up the spirit of Punk Rock—in a diagram of three guitar chords, bearing the legend, "Here's one chord, here's two more, now form your own band. . . ."

The vortex of the emerging Punk Rock scene was a cluster of crummy London dives, such as the 100 Club (and, later, the perennially pivotal Marquee), which stressed the music's immediacy—and de-emphasized traditional barriers between musician and fan—by keeping stages close to the floor and dispensing with seats so that customers might dance, press up close to the action, indulge in gobbing [spitting] matches with one another and the performers, and occasionally surge onto and usurp the stage itself. Audience participation was an all-important element of Punk Rock; punters were encouraged to express their displeasure as freely as their approval, and to revel in the sense that any of them could take the stage and do just as well as (if not better than) the featured act.

Two-tone Steve (his hair is black on top, white at the sides) was on a bass he picked up for the first time the night before. Sid Vicious, Johnny Rotten's friend and inventor of the pogo dance, was on drums. He had one rehearsal. A mature gent called Marco was lead guitarist. . . . The sound is what you'd expect from, er, novices. But Sid, with miraculous command, starts his minimal thud and doesn't fluctuate the beat from start to finish of the, er, set. Against this rough corrugation of sound, Siouxsie, with the grace of a redeemed ghoul, rifles the senses with an unnerving, screeching recitative [of "The Lord's Prayer"]. . . . The audience, enjoying the band's nerve and audacity, eggs them on, gets bored, has a laugh, then wonders how much more it can take. Twenty minutes later, on a nod from Marco, Sid just stops. The enthusiastic cheering is a just recognition of their success. If the Punk Rock scene has anything to offer, it's the opportunity for anyone to get up and experience the reality of their wildest stage-struck dreams. The bar-flies are horrified.

"God, it was awful," says Howard Thompson, an A&R man from Island. But Siouxsie is not interested in contracts. "The ending was a mistake," she says. "I thought we'd go on until they pulled us off."

from Caroline Coon's *Melody Maker* account of Siouxsie and the Banshees' debut at the 100 Club Punk Rock Festival on September 20, 1976

Despite the Punk Rockers' resolute amateurishness, many developed into remarkable performers. At the festival at the 100 Club (by this time the only London venue that would book the Sex Pistols), Ms. Coon saw Johnny Rotten

prying open the nether reaches of his personality and presenting audiences with . . . dark fragments from his psyche. Once he moved over the stage squirming and jiggering around like a spinderly geigercounter needle measuring radio activity . . . [but now his] deathly, morgue-like stance sets skin crawling, and his lyrics are as suffocating as the world they describe. He wears a bondage suit . . . dangling with zips, chains, safety pins, and crucifixes. He is bound around the chest and knees, a confinement symbolizing the urban reality he sees around him.

In New York, where Punks were mostly well-educated and pushing thirty, this might have passed for an ironic pose. But while the likes of Patti Smith and Television pictured

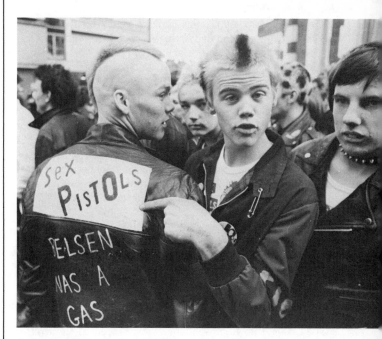

A Punk vigil for the late Sid Vicious (Photo Trends)

themselves the spiritual heirs of Rimbaud and Verlaine, the Sex Pistols dismissed all dead poets as "disgusting old farts." Britain's working-class Punks were often unsophisticated louts, and proud of it. They would have felt little in common with either the ideologically motivated critics or the fashion-conscious gay blades and former Disco buffs who were to form the vanguard of the British New Wave's limited U.S. constituency.

Unlike most of their American counterparts and imitators, Britain's Punks had more to complain about than just rock's domination by the legendary figures they derided as "BOFs" (Boring Old Farts). The Welfare State was in tatters; inflation, recession, and unemployment had reached their direst levels since the Great Depression. In June 1976 alone, some one hundred thousand British teenagers were obliged to go straight from school to an idle and purposeless life on the dole. As Johnny Rotten would snarl on the Pistols' most notorious anthem ("God Save the Queen"), "No future for you, no future for me. . . ."

It was during the long hot summer of '76 that Punk exploded

into the national consciousness. For once, Britain was feeling the pangs of a genuine, extended heat wave; almost three months passed without a single rain shower. By August the dry, sunny weather—initially welcomed as a heaven-sent antidote to the country's myriad crises—had become a national disaster in its own right, engendering failing crops, water rations, and a specially appointed Minister of Drought. As if this weren't enough, the annual Caribbean festival in London's Notting Hill inexplicably erupted in violence. British TV viewers were horrified by the familiar specter of angry young brick-throwing blacks chasing policemen down sweltering streets; only this time the flickering images did not originate in distant and barbaric lands like South Africa and the U.S.A. The chickens of the British Empire had come home to roost—in the guise of a growing immigrant community, disillusioned by the lack of opportunities, even as the underemployed whites vented their resentment at "Nignogs" and "Pakis" for taking such jobs as they could scrounge.

It was at approximately this juncture that Britain's citizenry was introduced, via the daily tabloids, to the crowning horror: the Punks. ("They wear torn and ragged clothes held together with safety pins. They are boorish, ill-mannered, foul-mouthed, dirty, obnoxious, and arrogant. They like to be disliked. They use names like Johnny Rotten, Steve Havoc, Sid Vicious, and Rat Scabies. . . .") Taking all the Punks' confrontational posturing at face value, the British media launched an orgy of "youth menace" headlines surpassing those of the Mod/Rocker era. As had been the case twelve years earlier, the press's exaggerated reports of youth cult violence quickly turned into a self-fulfilling prophecy, and Punk's ranks were swelled with so-called bandwagon jumpers whose "street credibility" remained doubtful.

The Punk Rockers delighted in their media image as harbingers of Western Civilization's decline and fall—which they consciously strove to embody and dramatize. The Pistols' first single was titled "Anarchy in the U.K."—a three-minute blitzkrieg of angst-powered noise that opened with an unsettling cackle and concluded with the succinct Punk manifesto: "I wanna be an anarchist . . . get pissed . . . destroy!"

The Clash, Tom Robinson, and others proceeded to turn this aimless nihilism into a more overtly political stance, making common cause with movements like Rock Against Racism, and partly dispelling the Punks' image as latter-day skinheads whose idea of a night on the town was beating up Pakis and queers.

Like many of their contemporaries, the Clash was particularly drawn to the music of Britain's West Indian community. Unlike McCartney, Clapton, and the Stones, who had previously patronized reggae mainly for its lazy, shuffling rhythms, the Punks were equally enamored with the lyrics' apocalyptic graffiti and revolutionary rabble rousing. The influence of reggae (and its Sixties precursor, ska) on Britain's New Wave proved comparable to that of R&B on the first wave of the British Invasion.

Relatively apolitical pop groups—notably the all-blond Police—continued to adapt Jamaican accents and rhythms, making reggae "safe" for wholesome white tots much as the Beatles had sanitized black American music on their early LPs. Bands like the Clash, however, appropriated in toto what Dick Hebdige calls reggae's "exotic and dangerous aura of forbidden identity, its conscience, its dread, and its cool." Their recordings made use of Jamaican studio techniques—notably "dub"; and they even indulged in a Kingston street look,

complete with narrow "sta-prest" trousers, pork pie hats, and khaki battle jackets stenciled with legends in arcane patois.

By this time the Clash had launched their recording career with the single "White Riot," which went beyond expressions of solidarity with the Notting Hill carnival's unruly Negroes to agitate for a "white riot—a riot of my own!" In July 1981, such Punk Rock broadsides would seem altogether prophetic when an epidemic of multiracial street clashes tore through over twenty-five decaying British cities. By that time, however, New Wave music could also be credited for having furthered more racial understanding than perhaps any other force in British society. Just as sexually mixed bands like Siouxsie and the Banshees, X-Ray Spex, and the Pretenders (not to mention female outfits like the Slits and the Raincoats) had redefined

The Two-Tone Specials (Two-Tone Records)

women's role in a heretofore white- and male-dominated medium, such "Two-Tone" bands as the Specials, the Beat, and the Selecter (whose lineup even included a black woman) provided both the music world and Britain as a whole with admirable examples of biracial harmony.

That these last-named ska revivalist bands all emerged on the Specials' own Two-Tone Records also offers a prime instance of the New Wave's enterprising do-it-yourself spirit. Instead of waiting for the corporate giants to see the light (and having to kowtow to their demands once they did), many of the leading New Wavers hitched up with independent labels—or, like the Specials, formed their own operations from scratch. Even from a commercial standpoint, many of the New Wave "indies" achieved an extraordinarily high batting average; the first such label, Stiff Records, snapped up Nick Lowe, the Damned, Elvis

Costello, and Ian Dury—all of whom had accumulated a sheaf of rejection letters from established companies. (Needless to say, these last came running as soon as Punk hit the national front pages, with CBS grabbing the Clash and EMI the Sex Pistols—whom they subsequently dropped like the proverbial hot potato.)

Apart from restoring to the 45 rpm record its pre-*Pepper* popularity and prestige, the new wave of small labels was also instrumental in introducing (or reintroducing) the rock biz to such marketing and merchandising gimmicks as colored vinyl, the picture disc, and the picture-sleeve single—soon to be followed by six-inch singles, five-inch singles, bonus flexidiscs, and special editions of albums released on several ten-inch discs packaged together in a picturesque box—all of which also reflected a growing awareness (and exploitation) of rock & roll's "collectability." In addition, the Punk Rockers and their immediate successors were among the first to recognize video's potential, both as a marketing tool and as a visual extension of the music.

The advent of Punk amounted to a bloodless coup in the rock & roll U.K. The venerable pop weeklies—especially *NME*—embraced the revolution wholesale, adopting much of Punk Rock's inherent dogmatism and gratuitous negativity, and sharply curtailing their reverent coverage of the old guard (which apostasy, in turn, would jolt people like the Stones out of their comfortable doldrums; BOFs like Ian Hunter and Pink Floyd's Nick Mason even went on to produce albums by, respectively, Generation X and the Damned). As if to soften the blow, however, "Punk" had gradually metamorphosed into "New Wave" by the time groups like the Boomtown Rats, the Jam, and the Police began collecting their first British Number Ones.

Now that they prevailed (in Britain, if not elsewhere), the New Wavers found themselves in the quandary of successful revolutionaries everywhere. Would they, too, find the perquisites of power—or stardom—irresistible, and/or allow themselves to be defanged and co-opted by the rock biz and the media? After all, such BOFs as the Stones, The Who, and Pink Floyd had been every bit as radical in their day. Yesterday's revolutions, don't you know, inevitably become tomorrow's Establishment.

The early Stones and Who, however, had never turned up their noses at the prospect of fortune and fame. Punk Rockers, by contrast, had their own rhetoric to contend with in the event that they "sold out"—or merely perpetuated their careers. Punk was made to self-destruct; the Sex Pistols, at least, had the integrity to do just that, at the climax of their one and only American tour. None of which deterred the tattered remnants of the movement (not to mention the bandwagon jumpers who bought their regulation Punk threads at high-priced chichi boutiques) from clinging to the subculture's surface trappings as unthinkingly as the aging hippies had clung to theirs—a situation that moved the Pretenders' Chrissie Hynde to comment: "Johnny Rotten's whole idea when he hit the streets in a ripped-up jacket covered in safety pins was to flip the bird at anyone who was establishment, including the hippies who were establishment by this time. . . . People walking around four years later with safety pins in their lapels couldn't be farther from what he started out to instigate." Some of the New Wave's other leading lights, meanwhile, settled down to become stars; the Police (to name but one example) cheerfully played twenty-thousand-seat venues (though the yellow-haired threesome also took advantage of their low overheads to

venture unprecedented tours of Africa, the Near and Far East, and Latin America).

The aftermath of Punk brought an ever more dizzying proliferation of new record labels and specialty shops, new recording artists, and new trends. Nineteen seventy-eight saw a short-lived resurgence of tuneful "Power Pop," and even a "Mod revival" (triggered, ironically, by the film of The Boring Old Who's *Quadrophenia*). The other extreme of the New Wave's ever-widening spectrum was filled by the bleak "industrial" sounds of Joy Division and the abrasive funk of the Gang of Four, Delta 5, and John Lydon's new band, Public Image Ltd., whose music was at once eminently danceable and ideologically correct. In 1979 the next wave seemed to be the aforementioned Two-Tone ska revival; in 1980 it was Electropop (a.k.a. Technopop and Synth Rock), whose most commercially successful proponent was Gary Numan.

By resurrecting Bowie's extraterrestrial bisexual persona

The Police—Sting, Andy Summers, and Stewart Copeland—during the Indian stop of their innovative tour of Africa, the Near East, and the Orient (RDR Productions)

before a bank of synthesizers, Numan helped to popularize the bloodless computer-world sound of Germany's Kraftwerk and such like-minded British combos as Ultravox, the Human League, and Simple Minds. By 1981, yet another "London Underground" had begun to coalesce at a disco called Billy's (and later the Blitz) where deejays Rusty Egan and Steve Strange regaled flamboyantly attired young Bowie clones with a well-chosen mix of the new Electropop and the Glitterbug classics of T. Rex, Roxy Music, and the Main Man himself. The publicity thus generated sufficed to score Blitz's house band, Spandau Ballet, a licensed label deal with Chrysalis after fewer than a dozen gigs.

Dubbed "New Romantics" and "Futurists" by the press, Spandau Ballet and similar acts—Duran Duran, Visage (the band formed by deejays Egan and Strange), Classix Nouveaux, Orchestral Manoeuvres in the Dark, Depeche Mode, and Soft Cell (who registered a Number One with their cover of Gloria "Mrs. Bolan" Jones's "Tainted Love")—generally strove to sound, look, and act as much like Mr. Bowie as possible. For all the music's synthetic sheen and programmed-for-dancing rhythm boxes, the vaunted "New Romanticism" had less to do with sound than with fashion. (The doyenne of New Romantic fashion, incidentally, was none other than Vivienne Westwood, Malcolm McLaren's former partner in Sex.) While frilly collars, kilts, lace, and bouffants proliferated on the drab London landscape, the charts were reclaimed by a horde of pretty boys, as bisexual as Ziggy Stardust, as "decadent" as you please. These were the "passionate bright young things" of "Aladdin Sane"; rather than herald the Apocalypse with dreary doom mongering, better simply to go out in style, dancing and looking good. When times get *really* hard, escapism and glamour always win out in the end.

As had been the case with earlier New Wave trends, the emergence of the Blitz kids was accompanied by a distinct sense of déjà vu (at least for those old enough to remember Ziggy and Aladdin). Indeed, most post-Punk rock & roll was consciously predicated upon the music's own past (if only—as had been the case with the likes of the Sex Pistols—as a deliberate reaction *against* that past). The British New Wave's obsession with golden oldies was usually filtered through a Pop Art sensibility, whereby any and all of rock's historical artifacts (as they now became) were contemplated, appropriated, and discarded with the unwavering detachment of an Andy Warhol. Elvis Costello, for instance, not only peppered his recordings with subtle references to the songs, riffs, and production techniques of groups like the Beatles, but even parodied mid-Sixties music-biz conventions on his record sleeves' artwork, typography, and liner notes.

Rock & roll seemed to have become compulsively incestuous and self-referential, an elaborate "in" joke. The New Wave turned on its head all the conventional wisdom as to what was hip and what wasn't. The innocent vapidity of British Invasion–era groups like the Dave Clark Five suddenly seemed far more amusing than the ambitious posturings of a Moody Blues or an Emerson, Lake, and Palmer. The hideous stain on John Paul Jones's reputation was no longer his brief membership in Herman's Hermits, but his ongoing involvement with Led Zeppelin. And the Fab Four's greatest album, it went without saying, was *Meet the Beatles*. This New Wave esthetic was hardly conducive to the emergence of original artistic masterpieces, which, depending on one's own perspective, may or may not have been a bad thing.

The U.S. rock scene, however, cannibalized itself with far less panache than the British. The new generation of American rock consumers—born too late to remember the British Invasion firsthand, and weaned on the rock mythology of their older brothers and sisters (or even their parents!)—seemed content to experience secondhand the "Classic Rock" of the Beatles, Stones, Who, and Floyd and generally evinced little

yearning for a rock culture of their own. Squeezed by the economy, major record labels were equally content to rely on proven superstars and forgo the expense of boosting new ones or of perpetuating the careers of marginally commercial artists. At even the most "progressive" FM stations, programmers completed the vicious circle by tightening their playlists accordingly.

In 1979, Stiff Records' general manager proclaimed: "The British are coming again. America's fallen way behind the times, and American youth are fast asleep. We're going to wake them up; we're bringing rock & roll back to America!" But the new British Invasion—partly for the reasons outlined above—never registered much impact outside the New Wave dance clubs that proliferated in a handful of major U.S. cities. Though Britain's economy was in far worse shape than America's, the U.K.'s relatively small size lent itself far more readily to establishing new artists and/or independent labels on a national scale. Such relatively commercial New Wave acts as did "make it" in America—e.g., Elvis Costello, the Police, the Pretenders, and Squeeze—did so by dint of grueling coast-to-coast itineraries, which in turn earned them the "label support" that finally put them over the top. Otherwise, New Wave music (both the British and homegrown varieties) generally remained the exclusive property of an elite audience of dance-club habitués.

By derailing many of rock's aspirations (or pretensions) to Timeless Art, the New Wave movement generally sought to return the music to its original function as a strictly *popular* culture. Yet even on that level, the New Wave's importance (at least in America) was somewhat marginal, simply because, by and large, the music wasn't very popular. Among those who did pay attention, however, New Wave engendered a new willingness to redefine rock, retrace its origins, recapture its original energy, and approach the business of making and selling music with a new vitality.

The New Wave also contributed in no small measure to the splintering of the rock "community" into a profusion of cults, subcults, and revivals. By the Eighties, there were few new superstars on the horizon, and fewer of the old ones' records were turning platinum. In place of a relatively homogeneous counterculture, rock in the early Eighties presented the consumer with an almost endless choice of genres, ideologies, fantasies, and styles. The new global rock supermarket was liberally stocked with product drawn from four different decades and myriad nationalities; fresh novelties like Afro-Caribbean Rock and Beatnik Rock thrived side by side with the Rolling Stones and Pink Floyd, as did Disco with Heavy Metal, Rockabilly with Ska, Punk with Psychedelia, and Futurism with the past. Rock in the Eighties offered its constituency only one, final promise—the opportunity for every man or woman, boy or girl, to plug into the reality of his or her choice.

## PART TWO

Adam and the Ants

It may turn out that 1981 will be remembered as the Year of The Ant in British pop. Adam Ant landed five singles and two LPs in the U.K. Top Fifty—not bad for a gimmick-oriented "Blitz" band.

The roots of Ant's incredible rise from third-rate S&M punk freak show to Top of the Pops teenybop hysteria began with the teenage fascination of one Stuart Goddard, a glitter-rock enthusiast who copped a Marc Bolan autograph to start, and wrote a term paper on Bryan Ferry (subject: "artist important to the twentieth century") before heading off, as all fledgling rock stars must, to art school.

Goddard left art school in 1976 (at age twenty-one) when Punk was in its infancy and flamboyantly renamed himself Adam Ant. The early Ants (who later founded Bow Wow Wow) created a fearsome, unholy, metallic racket while Adam flirted with themes of perversion, Teutonism and fetishes. They were critically reviled, but managed to attract a rabid cult following. A goofily Gallic one-off single, "Young Parisians," stiffed miserably on Decca Records; the Ants soon were dropped and subsequently signed to Do It, a small independent label, who issued their debut LP, *Dirk Wears White Socks,* in August 1979.

The Ants soldiered on in semiobscurity until Adam forged a pact with Sex Pistols mastermind Malcolm McLaren (who would go on to steal Adam's backup group, and, some would say, his ideas about integrating African and American Indian rhythms with pop music to form Bow Wow Wow).

Adam teamed with guitarist/composer Marco Pirroni, and a dual drum section, and recorded *Kings Of The Wild Frontier. Kings* melded Burundi beats, Indian war whoops, Sergio Leone melodrama and some slightly turgid heavy metal for a sound that was as original and unique as Adam's buccaneer clothing, braids and war paint. *Kings* yielded smash singles with the title track, "Dog Eat Dog," and "Antmusic," and constant video exposure made Antmusic the hottest teenage fad since 1980's Gary Numan. The non-LP stopgap single "Stand and Deliver" provided the Ants with their first Number One single in the summer of '81.

(Epic Records)

Adam Ant
(vocals)
Marco Pirroni
(guitar)
Kevin Mooney
(bass)
Terry Lee Miall
(drums)
Merrick
(drums)

Kings proved to be one of the major dance-floor hits of 1981, and the LP eventually cracked the U.S. Top Fifty with virtually no commercial radio play. Trend-crazy New Yorkers could be seen strutting around in Adam's pirate-inspired fashions, and even the big names of the fashion world promised more flounces, ruffles and frills for the fall.

In the final analysis, though, Adam and the Ants' success, past and future, depends largely on the persona and charisma that Stuart Goddard fashioned in homage to the teen idols he once adored. "If you give me a choice of seeing a rock band or seeing Liberace," he has said, "I'd be in the front row for Liberace. From him I can learn."

(DAVID KEEPS)

U.K. Hit Singles

1980 Dog Eat Dog (**4**); Ant Music (**2**)

The Animals

Eric Burdon
(vocals)
Alan Price
(keyboards)
Hilton Valentine
(guitar)
Chas Chandler
(bass)
John Steele
(drums)

In the summer of 1964, an obscure quintet from Newcastle-on-Tyne became the first British group after the Beatles to score an American Number One hit. That noteworthy achievement, however, was no more remarkable than the single itself. "House of the Rising Sun" featured an ominous guitar riff, a voice blacker than Jagger's, and a swelling gospel organ that came together in a climax of gibbering frenzy. The Animals boasted as authentic an R&B sound as any band in Britain. In the wake of "House of the Rising Sun"'s surprise ascendancy, the Animals were whisked over to New York, unveiled at the Paramount Theater, and duly mobbed on Broadway.

Notwithstanding their subsequent string of classic rock & roll hits, however, the Animals remained an excellent club band, never quite able to adapt to the larger stage. In the dives of Newcastle, Price recalled, "we used to play everything from the blues to Chico Hamilton, and it used to swing like the clappers. When we had a Number One with 'Rising Sun,' that was it. We should never have gone on. . . . It was sweat and tears for seven years to get some respect and make it. And when it finally did happen, it all happened too fast."

The Animals began life around 1961 as a straight jazz trio, the Alan Price Combo, featuring Chandler and Steele. Over the following year, the addition of Valentine and Burdon inspired a change in musical emphasis (to R&B) and billing (to the Kansas City Five). This name, however, made little impression on audiences, who persisted in calling the group "the animals" on account of the tubby singer's demeanor and the indigent musicians' ill-matched street clothes.

For the black-voiced Eric Burdon, not being a Negro amounted to a personal tragedy. In 1965, *NME* revealed the existence of "a large diary in which Eric has written out hundreds of lyrics by artists like Mose Allison and Chuck Berry. On the first page he has written the word *Blues* in his own blood. He had cut his finger especially for it." Burdon applied a similar fanaticism to most of his pursuits, notably boozing and brawling.

Alan Price, on the other hand, was among the first British musicians to develop a Bob Dylan fetish, and his electric arrangements of two traditional songs from Dylan's first LP—"House of the Rising Sun" and "Baby Let Me Take You Home"—became highlights of the Animals' act. These were the two numbers that particularly impressed producer Mickie Most during the Newcastle Club-a-Go-Go performance that convinced him to present the Animals with an EMI recording contract.

Because his superiors found "Rising Sun" "too long and boring," "Baby Let Me Take You Home" was selected as the Animals' first release. Following the record's moderate success, Most and the Animals were allowed to cut "Rising Sun" as a sequel. Because the single ran four and a half minutes long, the Animals were denied the opportunity to plug it on British TV, though the pop programs reversed their policy after the disc hit Number One. Something of a fluke, "House of the Rising Sun" proved a tough record to follow. Albums presented no problem; like the Stones,

the Animals simply drew from their R&B-dominated club repertoire. (In many instances, such as "Around and Around" and "She Said Yeah," the two groups' discographies overlapped.) Unlike the Stones, however, the Animals had no consistent knack for defining their sound and image through the medium of the three-minute hit single. The next two 45s illustrated their dilemma: "I'm Crying," an original composition, was undistinguished; and their version of John Lee Hooker's "Boom Boom" was too uncompromisingly bluesy for the Top Forty airwaves.

The commercially astute Most took matters in hand by scouring Tin Pan Alley, turning up such teen anthems as "We Gotta Get Out of This Place" and "It's My Life." For many fans, the welding of the group's raw R&B sound to classic Brill Building hooks resulted in the Animals' finest moments. But Burdon frankly detested songs like "It's My Life"—as he made plain in interviews even as the tune was climbing the charts—and the band resisted the Animals' conversion into a "manufactured" product. When their contract with EMI and Most ran out in late 1965, the Animals defected to Decca Records and former Dylan producer Tom Wilson.

By this time, Alan Price had handed in his notice, pleading doctor's orders and fear of flying. Though Burdon's megalomania was not officially given as a factor, each of the other Animals presently made his excuses until by the end of 1966 the singer was left with a cast of faceless sidemen and the billing he had long coveted: Eric Burdon and the Animals. During this transitional period, he continued to score minor hits: e.g., "Inside Looking Out," "Don't Bring Me Down," and "See See Rider."

In 1967, Burdon, like many of his peers, underwent a dramatic metamorphosis. Britain's finest blues hollerer repudiated his past, telling *Melody Maker:* "It wasn't me that was singing. It was someone trying to be an American Negro. I look back and see how stupid I was."

Newly decked out in paisleys and love beads and relocated in California, Eric was determined to be as sensitive and relevant, as cosmic and mind-blowing, as Donovan and Ravi Shankar and *Sgt. Pepper's Lonely Hearts Club Band*. ("We should hand the country over to the Beatles," he told *NME*.) His old crusader's zeal remained undimmed, only now it was directed toward universal brotherhood (*We're all one/ The wind, the rain, the sun*) and understanding (*No matter how ugly you are/ There is no such thing as ugly*). A pair of timely hit singles proselytized for "San Francisco Nights" and "Monterey," the pop festival where "young gods"—such as Burdon himself—"smiled upon the crowd."

Feedback and freakouts, light shows and smoke bombs, Raga Rock and stream-of-consciousness mixed metaphors: Eric Burdon and the Animals did it all, and did it badly. The acid visions of *Winds of Change* and *The Twain Shall Meet* gave way to the barbiturate stupor of *Love Is,* after which Burdon resolved to become a Negro again. He discovered, and sang with, the spectacularly successful all-black funk band War in a short-lived liaison that produced one large hit, "Spill the Wine," and the albums *Eric Burdon Declares War* and—what else?—*The Black Man's Burdon*. He subsequently formed the Eric Burdon Band, whose recorded repertoire included heavy retreads of old Animals hits such as "It's My Life."

While other pop stars merely embraced trends, Eric Burdon aspired to personify them—though he often ended up parodying them. Yet for all his gullibility, he always remained *a soul whose intentions are good,* as he had testified on "Don't Let Me Be Misunderstood," one of the original Animals' greatest hits.

Even as Eric Burdon devoured trends, Alan Price—whose departure from the Animals amounted to the first nail in the group's coffin—doggedly ignored them. In late 1965 he formed the Alan Price Set, whose six-man lineup boasted two saxes and a trumpet in lieu of the usual guitars.

Though Price had been the most articulate and musically gifted of the Animals, he was viewed as essentially a background figure, with none of the charisma of the front man. To the surprise of many, Alan proved to be a compelling and stylish performer in his own right, with an easy charm and a strong voice not unlike Eric Burdon's.

The Alan Price Set promptly cracked the British Top Ten with the bluesy rocker "I Put a Spell on You." Alan then proceeded on an unexpected, but commercially successful, tangent with such traditional vaudevillian pop as "Hi Lili Hi Lo."

The Alan Price Set scored one massive British hit with "Simon Smith and His Amazing Dancing Bear," penned by American songwriter Randy Newman. Price—whose earlier infatuation had manifested itself in his role as a hanger-on in the 1965 Bob Dylan tour documentary *Don't Look Back*—became as ardent a booster of Newman's work as he had once been of Dylan's. The difference was that in 1967, Newman was far from fashionable.

Following the Set's breakup in 1968, Price made frequent appearances with Georgie Fame, hosted TV shows, and scored plays. Price returned to the international limelight in 1973 with his witty and infectious score for Lindsay Anderson's film *O Lucky Man.* This assignment, and its highly acclaimed outcome, gave Price the confidence to pursue his songwriting talents. *Between Today and Yesterday* (1974) was an inspired concept album that explored his working-class roots. But Price's frankly cynical philosophy (sometimes expounded in a *Melody Maker* column) could also, when directed at his own career, work to his music's detriment. Subsequent albums smacked of sheer product; when he recaptured the British airwaves at the end of the decade, it was with a beer commercial sung to the tune of "O Lucky Man."

Of the other original Animals, Hilton Valentine (the group's heartthrob) also attempted a solo career, with the 1969 LP *All in Your Head.* Chas Chandler, however, took note of the fact that his years of rock stardom had netted him the grand total of three thousand dollars, two bass guitars, and one London flat—so the canny lad decided to make his fortune managing other rock stars. His first discovery—made in a Greenwich Village dive called the Cafe Wha—was Jimi Hendrix, whom Chandler imported to London and introduced to Noel Redding and Mitch Mitchell. After the Jimi Hendrix Experience slipped from his grasp, Chas applied his magic touch to a group called Slade.

Those two bass guitars were taken out of mothballs only twice during the following decade: in December 1968, when the original Animals gave a one-shot hometown reunion concert; and a full eight years later, when they descended on Chandler's country estate to make a comeback album, *Before We Were So Rudely Interrupted,* that sounded like a collection of outtakes from the first two Animals LPs.

(NICHOLAS SCHAFFNER)

U.S. Hit Singles

1964 House of the Rising Sun (**1**); I'm Crying (**19**); Gonna Send You Back to Walker (**57**)
1965 Boom Boom (**43**); Don't Let Me Be Misunderstood (**15**); Bring It On Home to Me (**32**); We Gotta Get out of This Place (**13**); It's My Life (**23**)
1966 Inside Looking Out (**34**); See See Rider (**10**); Don't Bring Me Down (**12**); Help Me Girl (**29**)
1967 When I Was Young (**15**); San Francisco Nights (**9**)
1968 Monterey (**15**); Sky Pilot (**14**); White Houses (**67**); Anything (**80**)

(BY ALAN PRICE)

1966 I Put a Spell on You (**80**)

U.S. Hit LPs

1964 The Animals (**7**)
1965 On Tour (**99**); Animal Tracks (**57**)
1966 The Best of the Animals (**6**); Animalization (**20**); Animalism (**33**)
1967 Eric Is Here (**121**); The Best of Eric Burdon and the Animals, Vol. II (**71**); Winds of Change (**42**)
1968 The Twain Shall Meet (**79**); Every One of Us (**152**)
1969 Love Is (**123**); Greatest Hits (**153**)
1973 Best of the Animals (**188**)
1977 Before We Were So Rudely Interrupted (**78**)

(BY ALAN PRICE)

1973 O Lucky Man (**117**)
1977 Alan Price (**187**)

U.K. Hit Singles

1964 Baby Let Me Take You Home (**21**); House of the Rising Sun (**1**); I'm Crying (**8**)
1965 Don't Let Me Be Misunderstood (**3**); Bring It On Home to Me (**7**); We Gotta Get out of This Place (**2**); It's My Life (**7**)
1966 Inside Looking Out (**12**); Help Me Girl (**14**); Don't Bring Me Down (**6**)
1967 When I Was Young (**45**); San Francisco Nights (**7**); Good Times (**20**)
1968 Sky Pilot (**40**)
1969 Ring of Fire (**35**)

(BY ALAN PRICE)

1966 I Put a Spell on You (**9**); Hi Lili, Hi Lo (**11**)
1967 Simon Smith and His Amazing Dancing Bear (**4**); The House That Jack Built (**4**); Shame (**45**)
1968 Don't Stop the Carnival (**13**)
1971 Rosetta [with Georgie Fame] (**11**)
1974 Jarrow Song (**6**)
1978 Just for You (**43**)
1979 Baby of Mine (**32**)

ARGENT: See The Zombies

Bad Company

Paul Rodgers
(vocals)
Simon Kirke
(drums)
Boz Burrell
(bass)
Mick Ralphs
(guitar)

Free, a much-troubled blues-based combo that scored a major 1970 U.K./U.S. hit with "All Right Now," provided the initial musical pairing of Paul Rodgers and Simon Kirke, who would go on to form Bad Company in 1974.

Londoners Kirke and Paul Kossoff (guitar) left the blues group Black Cat Bones after seeing Middlesborough-born Rodgers singing with Brown Sugar in a northern London pub. Sixteen-year-old whiz-kid bassist Andy Fraser was recruited from John Mayall's Blues Breakers, and the fledgling act was touted by Alexis Korner, a founding father of British blues.

Korner named the group and hooked them up with Chris Blackwell of Island Records, who eventually arranged the group's debut gig in the spring of 1968. Free developed a loyal club following in the final year, but their early LPs received only moderate interest from the public and press until "All Right Now," which rocketed into the American Top Five in the autumn of 1970.

But the group was unable to continue its hit-making momentum, breaking up for the first time in 1971 to pursue solo projects. Kirke and Kossoff recorded a 1971 Island LP with Texan keyboardist John "Rabbit" Bundrick (later a Who sideman) and bassist Tetsu Yamauchi (who'd join the Faces).

In early 1972, the original Free regrouped for a tour, an inconsequential LP (*Free at Last*), and the hit single "A Little Bit of Love." Fraser departed and was replaced by Bundrick and Yamauchi. Paul Kossoff, suffering from a drug habit that would contribute to his death in 1976, quit Free after recording one more LP, *Heartbreaker* (1973).

Rodgers and Kirke teamed with founding Mott the Hoople member Mick Ralphs and King Crimson bassist Boz Burrell, debuting as Bad Company in March 1974. Ralphs, who wasn't getting along with Mott mainman Ian Hunter, found a formidable and charismatic vocalist in Rodgers, who could handle tunes like his chart-topping "Can't Get Enough" with swaggering style.

Led Zeppelin manager Peter Grant signed them to Zep's Swan Song Records. In 1974 their self-titled debut LP went to Number One, and a string of hard-rocking hit LPs carried them through the decade.

(DAVID KEEPS)

U.S. Hit Singles

1974	Can't Get Enough (**5**)
1975	Movin' On (**19**); Good Lovin' Gone Bad (**36**); Feel Like Makin' Love (**10**)
1976	Young Blood (**20**); Honey Child (**59**)
1977	Burnin' Sky (**78**)
1979	Rock 'n' Roll Fantasy (**13**); Gone Gone Gone (**56**)

(BY FREE)

1970	All Right Now (**4**); Stealer (**49**)

U.S. Hit LPs

1974	Bad Company (**1**)
1975	Straight Shooter (**3**)
1976	Run with the Pack (**5**)
1977	Burnin' Sky (**15**)
1979	Desolation Angels (**3**)

(BY FREE)

1970	Fire and Water (**17**)
1971	Free Highway (**190**); Free Live! (**89**)
1972	Free at Last (**69**)

(BY PAUL KOSSOFF)

1975	Backstreet Crawler (**191**)

U.K. Hit Singles

1974	Can't Get Enough (**15**)
1975	Good Lovin' Gone Bad (**31**); Feel Like Makin' Love (**20**)

(BY FREE)

1970	All Right Now (**2**)
1971	My Brother Jake (**4**)
1972	Little Bit of Love (**10**)
1973	Wishing Well (**7**)

Badfinger

Pete Ham
(guitar, keyboards, vocals)
Tom Evans
(bass, vocals)
Joey Molland
(guitar, vocals)
Mike Gibbons
(drums)

The soap opera saga of Badfinger, the hard-luck group that blossomed and withered in the Beatles' shadow on Apple Records in the late Sixties and early Seventies, had its beginnings in the Welsh seaport of Swansea during the British beat music boom of the mid-Sixties. The original lineup of the band, then called the Iveys, had Pete Ham and David Jenkins on guitars, Ron Griffiths on bass and Mike Gibbons on drums. In April 1966, they were spotted at a Swansea ballroom by an aging former bandleader named Bill Collins, who soon became their manager.

The group moved to London in December 1966; Collins, meanwhile, had a plan for helping the Iveys make it big. He had once played in a Thirties dance band with Paul McCartney's father, Jim, and he used this connection to bring the band to McCartney's attention at around the time of the *Sgt. Pepper* sessions.

Jenkins left the group in early 1968 and was replaced by Liverpudlian Tom Evans. The Iveys were making a favorable impression in London. Ray Davies even expressed interest in producing the group, though nothing came of it. With encouragement from Beatles road manager Mal Evans, the Iveys submitted tapes to McCartney just as the Beatles were preparing to launch their Apple label. McCartney's response, Evans later recalled, was "'Yeah, it's good, but there aren't any singles on it.' Then Derek Taylor [the Apple press officer] got both Lennon and Harrison to listen to it, and so they signed us.''

With the band's well-developed sense of pop melody and harmonies reminiscent of the Fab Four's own early days, it seemed only natural that the Beatles should take the Iveys under their wing. But the band's potential was not realized immediately. The first single, released in November 1968, was an emotional ballad called "Maybe Tomorrow"; it reached number sixty on the U.S. charts. An album with the single as the title cut, produced chiefly by Mal Evans, was released by Apple in Europe only in the summer of 1969 and sold poorly. Nobody was satisfied. Even the group's name was a sore point. Much discussion followed, with McCartney suggesting the name Home and Lennon characteristically proposing Prix. Finally, Apple executive Neil Aspinall came up with Badfinger. Meanwhile, Griffiths left in April 1969 and another Liverpudlian, guitarist Joey Molland, came aboard.

Things really began to take off for Badfinger when McCartney had the group score the Ringo Starr/Peter Sellers film *The Magic Christian.* McCartney produced the sessions and even donated a song, "Come and Get It." Released as a single, "Come and Get It" made the Top Ten on both sides of the Atlantic. An album, *Magic Christian Music* (consisting of old tunes salvaged from the *Maybe Tomorrow* LP and some new tunes) came out in the spring of '70 and sold well in the U.S., where Badfinger would continue to enjoy its greatest commercial and critical acceptance.

McCartney may have given Badfinger its first boost, but the band subsequently concentrated on original material. Preceded by the classic hit single "No Matter What" the LP *No Dice,* produced mostly by Beatles engineer Geoff Emerick, was chock full of lovely melodies and ear-catching harmonies.

The Beatles connection continued, with Badfinger members playing on the sessions for Harrison's *All Things Must Pass,* Lennon's *Imagine* and Ringo Starr's single, "It Don't Come Easy." And, in August 1971, Harrison invited them to participate in his all-star Concert for Bangla Desh at Madison Square Garden. Mostly they strummed away on acoustic guitars, but Ham did join Harrison in the spotlight for "Here Comes the Sun."

Straight Up, the third Badfinger album, boasted two superstar producers. George Harrison turned a Pete Ham tune called "Day After Day" into a million-selling hit single that sounded like a Harrison record. The rest of the LP was produced by Todd Rundgren, and while *Straight Up* became Badfinger's best-selling LP, the band members had grown fed up with producers pushing them around. Molland later called Rundgren "an arrogant asshole and egomaniac who had no respect for our ideas."

By this point Apple Records was in its death throes, and the individual members of Badfinger weren't too well off themselves. An ill-advised management contract had been signed after *No Dice,* and the musicians were kept on low salaries. They would see little of the money they earned. *Ass,* Badfinger's last album under its Apple contract, wasn't released until the end of 1973, a few weeks before the group's Warner Bros. debut album was due out.

(*John Rowlands*)

The latter album (released under the title *Badfinger* because the label forgot to include the intended title *For Love Or Money*) showed a dispirited and disillusioned group of musicians at work. Things looked more promising when their much-improved second Warners LP, *Wish You Were Here,* was released in the fall of 1974. It jumped right on the charts without a single or much promotion. Then, suddenly, someone at Warner Publishing began asking questions as to the whereabouts of the advance money given to Badfinger. It was supposed to be in an escrow account, but it couldn't be found. The band members didn't have it and their manager wasn't talking. So Warners immediately pulled the album from release and sued.

The group members were devastated. Finally, Pete Ham came to the realization that Badfinger had been taken for a ride. On April 23, 1975, Tom Evans, who had been with Ham the night before, was awakened by a call from Ham's girlfriend. Pete Ham had hung himself in his garage/studio at the age of twenty-seven, leaving behind a note that cursed Badfinger's management and the music industry.

Penniless and unable to work as Badfinger because of litigation, Molland, Evans and Gibbons went their separate ways. Finally, Evans and Molland re-formed Badfinger in 1978 in California with a couple of American musicians. Their 1979 album, *Airwaves,* didn't do all that well, and Badfinger again disappeared until early 1981, when a new album, *Say No More,* was released on the Atlantic-distribution Radio Records label.

The fact that Joey Molland and Tom Evans kept at it after all those years showed that either they were a bit thick or they truly had rock & roll souls. Anyone who's ever really listened to a Badfinger record knows it's the latter.

(BILL KING)

U.S. Hit Singles

1970	Come and Get It (**7**); No Matter What (**8**)
1972	Day After Day (**4**); Baby Blue (**14**)
1979	Love Is Gonna Come at Last (**69**)

U.S. Hit LPs

1970	Magic Christian Music (**55**); No Dice (**28**)
1971	Straight Up (**31**)
1973	Ass (**122**)
1974	Badfinger (**161**); Wish You Were Here (**148**)
1979	Airwaves (**125**)

U.K. Hit Singles

1970	Come and Get It (**4**)
1971	No Matter What (**5**); Day After Day (**10**)

The Bay City Rollers

(*Arista*)

Oh, it happened all right—the screams, the fainting, the smashed police barricades and the crazy tartans, or, as *The New York Times* put it, "the mayhem and frenzy of Rollermania." But when it was all over, two facts about the Bay City Rollers' career were painfully evident: First, Rollermania never caught on much outside the British Commonwealth. And second, the Rollers were no different from dozens of other teen idols whose fans outgrew them.

The group got its start in Edinburgh in 1967 when Alan and Derek Longmuir, brothers in their mid-teens, formed a band called the Saxons. After the usual number of personnel changes, the group found a home at Edinburgh's Top Storey Club and changed its name to the Bay City Rollers (it was chosen by sticking a pin into a map of the U.S. The pin hit Bay City, Michigan).

After linking up with manager Tom Paton, the group landed a recording contract and began signing up permanent personnel—guitarist Eric Faulkner and singer Les McKeown in 1972, and guitarist Stuart "Woody" Wood soon thereafter. They were all set to conquer the world.

Capitalizing on their Scottish origin, the quintet took to wearing clothes with strips of tartan plaid sewn to them: blue jeans rolled halfway up the leg with tartan cuffs, short-sleeved shirts with tartan collars, plaid suspenders, and the like. The gimmicks, and the Rollers' youthful appearance and enthusiasm (not to mention Paton's savvy), all worked the way they were supposed to, and by 1975 there was something approaching true mania in Great Britain.

While a hyperactive band of press agents produced daily reports of Roller goings-on and other "fab fax," the English tabloids discovered a ready fund of sensational stories: 17,000 crush concert barriers in Essex! More than 500 fans need medical attention at London show! Eric and Derek collapse onstage! To many, it was all reminiscent of a decade earlier, when Beatlemania had been in full flower.

Oddly, it was the persistent—and unjustified—comparisons to the Beatles that first tainted the Rollers' success. Perhaps "backlash" is too strong a term,

but to some rock fans, the word "mania" deserved to be attached to only one group—and that group wasn't the Bay City Rollers.

At any rate, it was time to conquer America. With an Arista recording contract, a U.S. single ("Saturday Night") and management by Sid Bernstein—who'd set up Beatle tours—the Rollers crossed the Atlantic for TV appearances. New York braced itself for mob scenes and provided lavish police protection for a limousine motorcade in June 1975. The turnout of fans was less than expected, however, and the Rollers found themselves waving at some barricades with only a handful of fans behind them. After a few TV shows, they headed back home; real American concerts would wait until the next year.

The American tour began in August 1976. *The New York Times* reported: "Yes, they can sing and play and aren't just puppets in the hands of their record producers . . . [but] they simply don't have the sort of blazing passion for rock that the Beatles did." And so it went—screams from the teenyboppers in city after city and a kind of genial so-what shrug from the critics. By 1977, even the teen magazines had found a hotter idol—Shaun Cassidy—to feature in photo spreads.

Part of the problem with the Rollers was that their hit records seldom rose above the level of pleasant pop-light fluff. Best of the early British hits was the first, "Keep on Dancing." The albums were stuffed with filler, and each, in its own way, failed to rise above the mediocrity of the material. The Rollers' catalogue is an inglorious record of the careers of what was basically a bunch of nice guys in tartans.

(HENRY McNULTY)

Leslie McKeown
(vocals)
Stuart Wood
(guitar)
Eric Faulkner
(guitar)
Derek Longmuir
(drums)
Alan Longmuir
(bass)

U.S. Hit Singles

1975	Saturday Night (**1**)
1976	Money Honey (**9**); Rock 'n' Roll Love Letter (**28**); I Only Want to Be with You (**12**); Yesterday's Hero (**54**)
1977	Dedication (**60**); You Made Me Believe in Magic (**10**); The Way I Feel Tonight (**24**)

U.S. Hit LPs

1975	Bay City Rollers (**20**)
1976	Rock 'n' Roll Love Letter (**31**); Dedication (**26**)
1977	It's a Game (**23**); Bay City Rollers/Greatest Hits (**77**)
1978	Strangers in the Wind (**129**)

U.K. Hit Singles

1971	Keep On Dancing (**9**)
1974	Shang-A-Lang (**2**); Summerlove Sensation (**3**); All of Me Loves All of You (**4**); Remember (Sha-La-La) (**6**)
1975	Bye Bye Baby (**1**); Give a Little Love (**1**); Money Honey (**3**)
1976	Love Me Like I Love You (**4**); I Only Wanna Be with You (**4**)
1977	It's a Game (**16**); You Made Me Believe in Magic (**34**)

Be-Bop Deluxe

Bill Nelson
(guitar, vocals)
Andy Clarke
(keyboards, synthesizer)
Charles Tumahai
(bass)
Simon Fox
(drums)

Be-Bop Deluxe was all about the world of the future. Guitarist/singer Bill Nelson was a well-read, independent-thinking chap from Yorkshire whose fables of panic in the world owed more to the French surrealist cinema of Jean Cocteau than to any antecedents in the world of rock. Except, perhaps, for Jimi Hendrix, with whom Nelson shared a restless, eloquent expressiveness on the guitar.

Be-Bop Deluxe made music that was treasured by a fanatical cult following, yet barely known outside that cult. In the U.S., they never had what could be termed a hit record. But that was beside the point. Be-Bop Deluxe was one of those nobly brainy bands—in a league with Peter Hammill & Van der Graff Generator, Steve Harley & Cockney Rebel, and Gentle Giant—whose talents were sometimes overshadowed by those fortunate few who were able to parlay their Art Rock inclinations into mass acclaim (i.e., David Bowie, Roxy Music, King Crimson).

Bill Nelson genuinely and relentlessly looked for new avenues of expression. To this end, Be-Bop Deluxe made exquisitely abstruse concept albums; flashed shots from Fritz Lang's sci-fi epic *Metropolis,* along with lots of lasers and lights, at their audience; and incorporated synthesizers and all manner of odd noise into their music—all before such strategies had become terribly common. And Nelson & Co. always undertook such experiments with taste and dignity. Indeed, Be-Bop Deluxe often took the idea of unruffled élan, of detached suave, to extremes: often the entire quartet would appear decked out in double-breasted suits, and Nelson himself was rarely photographed without a coat and tie.

Having established such a formal decorum, he'd deliver unsettling visions of the future—a world of dehumanization and technological ecstasy. Be-Bop's debut album, *Axe Victim,* was an ambitious record that (to quote a label bio) "expressed the belief that any totally dedicated artist becomes a prisoner of his creations. In Nelson's case, it was his guitar music that was making him an 'axe victim.' "

Heady stuff, that, and not your typical Bay City Rollers fare. *Axe Victim* became a brisk-selling import, and the demand eventually prompted its Stateside release. But it was their third album, *Sunburst Finish,* that really began turning heads. Nelson was at his flashy best on *Sunburst Finish,* and the LP gave the band a clutch of songs that became Be-Bop classics, such as "Fair Warning." The cover, which was a silhouette of a naked woman holding a burning guitar above her head, said much about the Be-Bop aesthetic. The burning guitar symbolized the point at which art reaches such an intensity as to burst into flames and consume itself. *Sunburst Finish* was, alas, the closest that Be-Bop Deluxe would come to realizing this sort of intensity.

Actually, Be-Bop seemed to grow somewhat tamer on subsequent releases, or maybe Nelson rendered his aesthetic more subtle and implicit. The next album, *Modern Music,* was very nearly their commercial breakthrough. With its appealing melodies, the LP was an eminently listenable meditation on the subject

Bill Nelson (**Ron Gott**)

of "modern music." One side was a suite of short songs linked together à la *Abbey Road;* indeed, it was a kind of *Abbey Road* moved a few decades up the road.

Their obligatory double live album, *Live! In the Air Age,* was notable more for the white vinyl it was pressed on than as a definitive statement of this band's live capabilities. But *Drastic Plastic* was another revelation; the band was now exploring guitar/synthesizer minimalism in a more abbreviated song format. This fascinating new tangent, unfortunately, turned out to be their last.

Nelson, tired of touring and the wasted energy it takes to maneuver in the business of rock, disbanded Be-Bop Deluxe. He embarked on a solo career on which he called all the shots. A couple of solo LPs elicited the customary praise from Nelson stalwarts, and a 1981 single, "Living in My Limousine," got considerable votes in a U.S. critics' poll as Single of the Year. Though Bill Nelson and Be-Bop Deluxe were not knighted with success in conventional terms, they were much appreciated by an adoring cadre of fans who tuned in to their engrossing futurist wavelength, and their influence continues to be felt today.

(PARKE PUTERBAUGH)

U.S. Hit LPs

1976 Sunburst Finish (**96**); Modern Music (**88**)
1977 Live! In the Air Age (**65**)
1978 Drastic Plastic (**95**)

U.K. Hit Singles

1976 Ships in the Night (**23**); Hot Valves EP (**36**)

(BY BILL NELSON'S RED NOISE)

1979 Furniture Music (**59**)

Jeff Beck

Guitar fans can argue forever as to who brought the instrument to its popular solo forefront or who "invented" feedback. But no one can deny British invader Jeff Beck his contribution to the lexicon of rock. The term used worldwide for flash guitar technician extraordinaire has eight letters—and it's pronounced Jeff Beck.

Jeff Beck was the scruffy long-haired guitarist of a London-based band called the Tridents. In 1965 he joined a soon-to-be-famous quintet, the Yardbirds. The Yardbirds have their own history, though suffice it to say that Beck contributed greatly to their most stellar artistic and popular moments.

After Beck's departure from the Yardbirds, he set out on a solo career under the guidance of producer and British pop starmaker, Mickie Most. Beck released three commercially aimed singles from April 1967 to April 1968. However, hidden on the B-sides of two poorly sung ditties and an instrumental version of the MOR hit "Love Is Blue" were pure gold. There was the classic "Beck's Bolero," a Jimmy Page–penned reworking of Ravel's original, featuring Beck, Page, Nicky Hopkins on piano, John Paul Jones on bass, and Keith Moon on drums and midinstrumental howl.

Performing on "Rock My Plimsoul" and "I've Been Drinking," the other B sides, were the musicians soon to be known as the Jeff Beck Group. Joining Beck on guitar were Micky Waller on drums, Ron Wood (now a Rolling Stone) on bass guitar, and a little-known vocalist, Rod Stewart. When Nicky Hopkins, the most famous session pianist in rock, joined a few months later, the Jeff Beck Group were untouchable.

Between the band's first tour and Hopkins's entry came *Truth*. Though it was recorded prior to the band's U.S. tour, Epic, Beck's record label, had no interest in releasing the LP. It was only after Mickie Most's assistant, Peter Grant, telegraphed a rave review of Beck's first U.S. performance at the Fillmore East to Epic's president that the classic Beck album would reach the public ear. On *Truth*, Beck essayed blues tunes, rockers, a reworking of the Yardbirds'

(Ron Gott)

"Shapes of Things," the aforementioned "Bolero," and even "Ol' Man River" and "Greensleeves."

Drummer Waller was replaced by Tony Newman, and the band recorded *Beck-Ola*, a disappointing disc in comparison to *Truth*, though not without its moments. The group embarked on another tour in '69, but disbanded prior to their scheduled stop at Woodstock. The question "What British group was advertised to appear at Woodstock but didn't show?" has since become a favorite of trivia buffs.

While Rod and Ron went off to join the Faces, Jeff was planning his next group—slated to include Vanilla Fudge bassist and drummer Tim Bogert and Carmine Appice. But Beck, a hot-rod fancier who drives even faster than he plays guitar, was involved in a crash that put him out of commission for over a year.

By the time Beck recovered (1971), Bogert and Appice had formed Cactus and were unavailable. Beck recruited drummer Cozy Powell, bassist Clive Chaman, singer Bob Tench, and keyboardist Max Middleton, releasing *Rough and Ready* in late '71 and *The Jeff Beck Group* in spring '72, the latter produced in Memphis by Steve Cropper. The second Jeff Beck Group was a disappointment to fans and to Beck, and by August of '72 they no longer existed.

But by then Cactus didn't exist either, permitting the formation of the "dream band" Beck, Bogert and Appice, who released its only studio album, *Beck, Bogert and Appice*, in March 1973 (*BBA Live in Japan* was released only in that country). The power trio did not live up to expectations. Bye bye, BBA.

In 1965, Yardbird's rhythm guitarist Chris Dreja said of Jeff Beck, "He is 1975." He could have made it as a fortune teller, 'cause 1975 *was* the year of Jeff Beck.

With Middleton back on keyboards, Phil Chenn on bass, Richard Bailey on drums, and George Martin producing, Beck created *Blow by Blow*, a tour de force of jazz-rock fusion that proved that the idiom did serve a purpose. Beck defined fluidity for guitar players, while still displaying ample flash chops for the rockers.

Beck's '75 tour was a split bill with the Mahavishnu Orchestra, and there Beck met synthesizer pro Jan Hammer, with whom he recorded *Wired* and toured in 1976.

For the next three years, Jeff played with his cars. But by late 1980, he cut *There and Back*. Though almost half the album was older material recorded with Jan Hammer, Jeff still rang through.

Given his temperament and his history of erratic hirings and firings of musicians, Jeff Beck was often called the "bad boy" of rock. He was an arrogant punk before punk took on a capital *P* and musical significance. He was ahead of his time, and had no relation to time. He was voted "rock guitarist of the year" in jazz magazine polls and "jazz guitarist of the year" in rock magazine polls. No other guitarist fit so little into any mold, or created so many molds to then abandon. And his fans loved him for it.

(KAREN ROSE)

U.S. Hit LPs

1968 Truth (**15**)
1969 Beck-Ola (**15**)
1971 Rough and Ready (**46**)
1972 Jeff Beck Group (**19**)
1973 Jeff Beck, Bogert and Appice (**12**)
1975 Blow by Blow (**4**)
1976 Wired (**16**)
1977 Jeff Beck with the Jan Hammer Group Live (**23**)
1980 There and Back (**21**)

U.K. Hit Singles

1967 Hi Ho Silver Lining (**14**); Tally Man (**30**)
1968 Love Is Blue (**23**)
1973 I've Been Drinking (**27**)

Black Sabbath

Ozzy Osbourne (vocals)
Tony Iommi (guitar)
Geezer Butler (bass)
Bill Ward (drums)

Black Sabbath represented the serpentine underbelly of the Woodstock Generation. They projected all the warmth and good cheer of a Hell's Angels' brawl. Their credo could have been "death by decibels": they were louder than a sonic boom and not nearly as subtle. To attend one of their concerts was about as pleasurable an experience as a Gestapo interrogation. And when you left, you could be sure you wouldn't hear a thing for days. Somehow, they became one of thc top-drawing groups of the early to mid-Seventies, and their songs, with their dime-store aura of demon possession and gloomy incantation, grabbed the attention of a younger audience whose sensibilities were way out of kilter with the Beatles-fed generation that came of age in the Sixties.

Black Sabbath began in 1968 as Earth—four lads from Birmingham with a chip on their shoulder the size of a heap of coal slag. They began cultivating their graveside manner from the first, setting pachydermal guitar chords and Baskerville-hound baying against a flimsily conceived backdrop of black magic and exorcism. Their spelunking into the darker realms of the supernatural struck a resonant chord with many of the disenchanted progeny of the early Seventies, for Black Sabbath took off like a pack of broom-riding witches on Walpurgis Night. Over here, they were headlining both Fillmores before you could say "Bill Graham, I hex thee," and their first two albums especially (*Black Sabbath* and *Paranoid*) became indispensable tracts for the legions of the doomed.

All of this folderol over a band with so limited a musical acumen and an almost illiterate grasp of words and ideas was a source of great vexation to the rock press. "Black Sabbath is making it big this year and no one knows why," said *Rolling Stone* in 1971. Others were more to the point: one grumpily avowed that Black Sabbath played "predictable acid rock that went nowhere," while another hated their music "with an indescribable loathing." The very idea of a serious analysis of a Black Sabbath record was a joke in itself.

Black Sabbath, meantime, laughed all the way to the (blood) bank. Well, maybe they didn't *laugh:* "If we come across doomy and evil," said guitarist Tony Iommi, "it's just the way we feel." On the strength of such muddled hymns to paranoia as "War Pigs," "Electric Funeral," "Iron Man," and "Sabbath Bloody Sabbath," the band's first six albums went gold. Black Sabbath's thundering, end-of-the-world noise-making was an appropriate soundtrack to the tension-ridden Vietnam War era, those years when gas got hard to come by and venerable Western economies started to come unglued. Many an impressionistic teen was bait to be swayed by vague messages of apocalypse and reminders of mortality. So too could he be overwhelmed by the stupor-inducing properties of barbiturates and other downers, which had lately become de rigueur for concertgoing and "partying."

Despite the tragic purple haze that seemed to settle over a formerly joyous, exuberant music form, even the critics—some of them, anyway—looked for something to like in Black Sabbath after a while. Comically, there was a certain hip cachet involved in proclaiming *Master of Reality* or *Volume 4* a powerful masterpiece of heavy metal. Still, the scribes eventually lost interest, as did the record- and pill-gobbling hordes, and Black Sabbath settled into a less than comfortable middle age of making records for those holdouts who crawled out from under rocks for their annual clubbing of the eardrums.

When Ozzy Osbourne left to go solo toward the end of the decade, hardly a tear was shed and nary a beat was missed. Ronnie James Dio, a singer whose sub-illustrious credentials included charter membership in Richie Blackmore's Rainbow, was Osbourne's replacement, and Black Sabbath lumbered gracelessly into the Eighties. Osbourne, meanwhile, kicked off his new career by biting the head off a live dove at a press conference. He contracted no life-threatening infection from this stunt. More's the pity.

(PARKE PUTERBAUGH)

U.S. Hit Singles

1970 Paranoid (**61**)
1972 Iron Man (**52**)

U.S. Hit LPs

1970 Black Sabbath (**23**)
1971 Paranoid (**12**); Master of Reality (**8**)
1972 Black Sabbath—Vol. 4 (**13**)
1974 Sabbath Bloody Sabbath (**11**)
1975 Sabotage (**28**); We Sold Our Soul to Rock 'n' Roll (**48**); Technical Ecstasy (**51**)
1978 Never Say Die! (**69**)
1980 Heaven and Hell (**28**)

U.K. Hit Singles

1970 Paranoid (**4**)
1978 Never Say Die (**21**); Hard Road (**33**)

BLIND FAITH: See Clapton, Eric, and Traffic

Bonzo Dog Band

The Bonzo Dog Band was that rarity in rock music: an intentionally funny group. For some reason, rock and comedy have never quite hit it off; perhaps the earnestness required for the former precludes irreverence. The Bonzos sidestepped the issue by hardly being a rock group at all. Closer at first to the English trad jazz revival than anything else, they were linked to the British Invasion set through their backgrounds (mid-Sixties London art schools) and a surreal sense of humor. What others wouldn't (or couldn't) put into their music, the Bonzo Dog Band wallowed in.

They formed in 1965 as the Bonzo Dog Doo Dah Band, whimsically named after a George E. Studdy cartoon that was all the rage in England in the Twenties. Their music, too, drew on that decade for inspiration; the first recordings, in 1966, were of period esoterica like "I'm Gonna Bring a Watermelon to My Baby Tonight" and "My Brother Makes the Noises for the Talkies." In appearance, though, the Bonzos were thoroughly modern: loud bellbottoms and double-breasted jackets, and (as time went on) an incredible variety of LSD-inspired costumes.

Mining a unique musical field—camp dementia—the band quickly attracted attention, and with their first album, *Gorilla* (1967), the Bonzos were off and running. By now they had dropped the Twenties oldies for their own time- and brain-warped tunes, composed by Viv Stanshall and Neil Innes. In addition to the Betty Boop snap of "Jollity Farm" and "Mickey's Son and Daughter," *Gorilla* also looked back (or forward) (or both) to rock with the parodies "Death Cab for Cutie" and "Piggy Bank Love."

Their versatility paid off in late 1968, when "I'm the Urban Spaceman," a harmless ditty written by Innes (and produced by Paul McCartney under the pseudonym Apollo C. Vermouth), went to number five on the British singles charts. With a second album (*The Doughnut in Granny's Greenhouse*, retitled *Urban Spaceman* in the U.S.) and hit 45 behind them, the band was shoved up the music industry's ropes. The band's lineup stabilized with Stanshall (a leader among anarchists), Innes, saxophonist/prop technician Roger Ruskin Spear, saxophonist Rodney Slater, bassist Dennis Cowan and drummer/transvestite tapdancer "Legs" Larry Smith. A colorful bunch.

More albums (*Tadpoles, Keynsham*) followed, and although there were no more smash hits, the Bonzo Dog Band retained a rabid following. They even came to the U.S., winning over audiences who had no idea what they were in for. Live, the band was a nonstop carnival of costume changes—Spear as a bear, Stanshall as a powdered, wigged clown with grotesquely false breasts—flashing, exploding dummies and maniacal music.

The Bonzos were way too eccentric for the big time, of course, but their own relentless creativity did them in more than mass indifference. An act like theirs required intense effort, and by 1969 the strain was showing. The band split in 1970 amid rumors of "musical differences," and although they reunited two years later for one last album (*Let's Make Up and Be Friendly*), it just wasn't the same.

Time has only certified the Bonzos' position as rock's most lovable lunatics. Stanshall may have been a little *too* involved; he suffered a nervous breakdown in the Seventies, but has since bounced back (more or less) with the multimedia *Sir Henry at Rawlinson End*. Innes hooked up with the Monty Python troupe after an attempted solo career. The others have remained marginally in touch with the rock world, but we'll have to look elsewhere for pop mayhem in the Eighties. The Bonzo Dog Band was one of a kind.

(SCOTT ISLER)

Vivian Stanshall
(vocals)
Neil Innes
(piano)
Roger Ruskin Spear
(saxes, devices)
Rodney Slater
(horns)
"Legs" Larry Smith
(drums)
Sam Spoons
(percussion)
**Vernon Dudley
Bohay-Nowell**
(bass)

U.K. Hit Singles

1968 I'm the Urban Spaceman (5)

The Boomtown Rats

Bob Geldof (Columbia Records)

Bob Geldof's musical career began with the demise of his career as an Irish correspondent to the staid U.K. rock weekly *Melody Maker*. A disgruntled reader, apparently unamused by Geldof's scathing criticism, wrote to request that he kindly "shut up or do better." The loquacious, self-promoting Geldof, whom the press would dub "the Mouth" and "Modest Bob" in short order, rose to the challenge and created a sensation throughout Ireland in 1975 and 1976.

Early publicity stunts included letting live rats loose during their performances, but by the time the group had signed to Ensign Records, Geldof was a sophisticated master of boldfaced statement-mongering. His most celebrated remark made exceptionally honest "good copy" and nearly distinguished the Rats from the supposedly antimaterialistic ranks of the punkers. "I know that most of the bands I know have *privately* told me that they agree with what I say, that I'd like to be rich, famous, and get laid," he told *New York Rocker* in 1978.

The Rats' self-titled debut appeared in 1977.

Bob Geldof
(vocals)
Johnny Fingers
(piano)
Gerry Cott
(guitar)
Garry Roberts
(guitar)
Pete Briquette
(bass)
Simon Crowe
(drums)

Mercury Records picked it up for American release, but even though the band sounded like an accessible Jagger/Bowie fusion, the New Wave guilt-by-association prevented them from achieving U.S. airplay for British hits like "Mary of the Fourth Form" and Geldof's philosophical anthem, "Looking After No. 1."

While the band failed to achieve the street credibility of the Clash and the Sex Pistols, they did create well-crafted, cleanly produced pop songs, which, in tandem with Geldof's outsized persona and slick showmanship, quickly established them in Britain's pop pantheon. "Rat Trap," from the Rats' second LP, *A Tonic for the Troops,* became the first New Wave single to reach the coveted Number One spot in the British charts, setting a stage for a U.S. signing to Columbia Records.

Columbia sponsored an extensive personal promotional visit for Geldof and the perpetually pajama-clad Johnny Fingers in 1979. During this tour, Geldof read an account of a California schoolgirl who went on a shooting spree because she didn't like Mondays, and the Rats' first bona fide U.S. hit was born. "Mondays" appeared on *The Fine Art of Surfacing,* and Geldof mounted an expensive, critically raspberried stage show that included a massive lighting structure that echoed the gigantic tick-tack-toe board from *The Hollywood Squares.* While the critics' reactions cooled considerably, the English record-buying public made "Mondays" a million seller.

The Boomtown Rats' fourth LP, *Mondo Bongo,* marked a more eclectic departure from their previous rock & roll efforts, yielding a U.K. smash with the reggaefied "Banana Republic" and a U.S. disco hit in "Up All Night." In the summer of '81, guitarist Gerry Cott left the group. The Boomtown Rats continued as a five-piece, pursuing Geldof's intention to achieve "ultimate individual freedom . . . to buy out of this society because I don't like it."

(DAVID KEEPS)

U.S. Hit Singles

1980 I Don't Like Mondays (**73**)

U.S. Hit LPs

1979 A Tonic for the Troops (**112**);
The Fine Art of Surfacing (**103**)

U.K. Hit Singles

1977 Looking After No. 1 (**11**);
Mary of the Fourth Form (**15**)
1978 She's So Modern (**12**); Like Clockwork (**6**);
Rat Trap (**1**)
1979 I Don't Like Mondays (**1**);
Diamond Smile (**13**)
1980 Someone's Looking at You (**4**);
Banana Republic (**3**)

Arthur Brown

Arthur Brown was the "son of Necromancer Mordo of Cornwall, Chief Druid of a moonworship cult," according to the press release issued by Track Records. Actually he was the offspring of a perfectly respectable English couple, but to see him onstage, bedecked in flowing robes, his face streaked with colorful paint, and a flaming headdress set atop his head, one might be more inclined to believe Track's account of his ancestry.

Brown, a former philosophy student at the University of Reading, began merging his bluesy singing style with theater-of-the-absurd shenanigans in 1966, while performing on the French club circuit. Initially, he confined his Dada-esque approach to wearing conventional clothes in unconventional ways—i.e., backwards, inside out, and upside down—but by 1967 he was giving full rein to his outrageousness, when he was lowered by crane, his head engulfed in a flaming helmet, on to the stage of the Windsor Jazz Festival.

In the summer of '68, The Crazy World of Arthur Brown had an international hit with "Fire," a single that was produced by Pete Townshend. Shortly after the release of "Fire," an album, *The Crazy World of Arthur Brown,* was issued, and it, too, fared well in the charts. Unfortunately, Brown was never able to take full advantage of this success, as his band disintegrated in early '69 under the duress of an American tour.

Though there was talk of Brown's desire to change his image, when he did finally resurface a year later, his penchant for the bizarre remained unabated.

Brown's comeback gig at the Marquee Club in April 1970 was enlivened with the usual flames, strobe lights, and costume changes (which included a brief dash about the stage stark naked). However, psychedelia began taking a nose dive in popularity, and audiences grew increasingly less responsive to Brown's pioneering blend of theater and rock. Though Brown recorded three albums with his group Kingdom Come, his career never regained momentum, and the band split up in 1973. In the mid-Seventies he released a solo album, *Dance,* and was last glimpsed by a wide audience performing with his usual frenetic wildness as the priest in Ken Russell's film version of *Tommy.*

(ELIZABETH SCHAFFNER)

(*Henry McNulty Collection*)

U.S. Hit Singles

1968 Fire (**2**)

U.S. Hit LPs

1968 The Crazy World of Arthur Brown (**7**)

U.K. Hit Singles

1968 Fire (**1**)

The Buzzcocks

Pete Shelley
(guitar and vocals)
Steve Diggle
(guitar and vocals)
Steve Garvey
(bass)
John Maher
(drums)

Pete Shelley

In the spring of 1976 a bored young songwriter named Pete Shelley pinned a notice to a college bulletin board in Manchester seeking like-minded comrades to form a group. The lone respondent to this philosophy major's plea, one Howard Devoto, became the Buzzcocks' lead singer. With the addition of bassist Steve Diggle and a gangly sixteen-year-old drummer, John Maher, the Buzzcocks were set for their debut gig supporting the Sex Pistols in July 1976.

Gigs and tours with both the Pistols and the Clash followed, and in December 1976, the Buzzcocks became the first Punk band to form their own label (New Hormones), releasing an EP entitled *Spiral Scratch*. It was a primitive recording that sold an incredible number of copies for an unknown band. With Devoto leaving after only eleven gigs to form Magazine, Diggle moved from bass to guitar. Steve "Paddy" Garvey succeeded him as bassist in November 1977.

The Buzzcocks signed to United Artists in 1977 and released the instantly banned single "Orgasm Addict," which briefly charted anyway. Devoto, meanwhile, formed the core of Magazine with bassist Barry Adamson, drummer John Doyle, keyboardist Dave Formula, and guitarist John McGeoch. Critics swooned over this Manchester double threat, focusing attention on this northern industrial center that would soon make it the "second city" of the U.K. New Wave. Deserved praise was lavished on the Buzzcocks as standard bearers of a new pop sound that integrated the aggressiveness of dueling guitars and the pure pop appeal of addictive hooks, harmonies, and choruses.

Pete Shelley approached the pop idiom with a brace of humorous, unconventional love songs—anathema to most Punkers—heavily laden with a sparkling sense of irony and wit.

A matter-of-fact bisexual, Shelley explained "I try to keep the lyrics I write ambisexual. I enjoy writing songs that do not exclude anyone. The only people they exclude are people who don't know anything about love," he told *NME*. The Buzzcocks' second release, "What Do I Get?" began their string of memorable singles hits.

While Devoto and Magazine received a critical thumbs-up, they never matched the commercial success of the Buzzcocks. Following well-received American tours and numerous attempts at Top Thirty singles, Magazine disbanded in mid-1981.

But just as a major commercial breakthrough seemed imminent, the seeds of dissipation had begun to blossom for the Buzzcocks as well. Throughout 1980 the individual band members pursued various solo projects; and in the spring of 1981, to no one's surprise, a press release made the split official. Later that year, though, Pete Shelley's striking "Homo-sapien" single (and subsequent LP) demonstrated that at least one 'Cock had survived the dismemberment with his creative juices intact.

(DAVID KEEPS)

U.S. Hit LPs

1980   A Different Kind of Tension (**163**)

U.K. Hit Singles

1978   Have You Ever Fallen in Love (With Someone You Shouldn't Have) (**12**); Promises (**23**); Love You More (**34**); What Do I Get (**37**); I Don't Mind (**55**)

1979   Everybody's Happy Nowadays (**29**); Harmony in My Head (**32**); Spiral Scratch EP (**31**)

(BY MAGAZINE)

1978   Shot by Both Sides (**41**)

Eric Clapton

Probably no single rock artist—with the possible exception of the various ex-Beatles—has been saddled with so hyperbolic a tag as that which attached itself to the retiring young guitar virtuoso from Ripley, Surrey, in the mid-1960s. "Clapton Is God" read the London graffiti. Ever since, Eric Clapton has alternately disappointed and exhilarated critics and fans as he has proved to be just the contrary—all too human. Still, few question his status as one of rock music's most talented and distinctive guitarists.

Keeping track of Clapton's career over the years has been a rather involved proposition, as he has flitted from one group to another. Born March 30, 1945, this bricklayer's son actually got a rather late start in music, seriously taking up guitar at age seventeen. Caught up in the bewitching sounds of such black American blues players as Muddy Waters, Big Bill Broonzy, and Robert Johnson, he found his stained-glass studies at Kingston Art College filling less and less of his time.

After being kicked out of school, Clapton played in an R&B group called the Roosters (former musical home of Rolling Stone Brian Jones) in early 1963 before joining the Yardbirds in October 1963.

Nicknamed "Slowhand," the young blues purist remained in the band through its hit single "For Your Love." Next up was a year-long stint with John Mayall's Blues Breakers. It was during this period that Clapton's reputation as the best of the new breed of British guitar heroes was solidified. Still, he wasn't satisfied. A trip to Greece and a short flirtation with a band called the Powerhouse (including Stevie Winwood) provided respites from the Blues Breakers.

In the meantime, Clapton had become acquainted

with bassist Jack Bruce, a classically trained Scotsman who had played with Alexis Korner's Blues Inc. and the Graham Bond Organization before gigging with the Blues Breakers. One night the drummer from the Bond group, one Peter "Ginger" Baker, sat in with Clapton and Bruce; and the Cream, so to speak, rose to the top.

Although Cream, the first of the power trios, only lasted from July 1966 to November 1968, its influence is still felt, especially in the heavy metal resurgence of the Eighties. The group originally was conceived as a classic blues trio, but what Clapton, Bruce, and Baker ended up with was, for the most part, a commercial, heavy, improvisational rock sound.

Revisionists have since viewed the band as overrated and self-indulgent (indeed, their long solos in concert often veered into the realm of the latter). But much of its studio work holds up quite well. The first album, *Fresh Cream* cracked both the U.K. and U.S. charts. *Disraeli Gears* was the top-selling album of 1968, and the double LP *Wheels of Fire* didn't lag too far behind. The trio even managed a gold single in "Sunshine of Your Love."

Soon, however, Clapton's restlessness—aided somewhat by a stinging review in *Rolling Stone,* Bruce and Baker's inability to get along, and the group's hectic touring schedule—led to Cream's demise. "They just worked us too hard," Bruce has said. "By the time we were a success, we were all fed up with each other." So Cream said goodbye onstage at the Royal Albert Hall on November 26, 1968, and with the *Goodbye* album in March 1969. A particular highlight of the latter was "Badge," a song co-authored by Clapton and his pal George Harrison. Clapton had already helped out Harrison with the guitar solo on "While My Guitar Gently Weeps."

Clapton and Baker immediately moved into a "supergroup" called (appropriately, as it turned out) Blind Faith. They were joined by Stevie Winwood from Traffic and Rick Grech of Family. Blind Faith lasted less than a year and made one album (albeit a million-seller) before breaking up after a strenuous U.S. tour. Even while the group was ostensibly together, Clapton couldn't resist flying off to Toronto in June 1969 to gig with John Lennon's impromptu Plastic Ono Band and sitting in with an American soul-rock aggregation known as Delaney and Bonnie and Friends.

When Blind Faith parted company (with Baker moving into the short-lived Ginger Baker's Air Force), Clapton decided to join and help finance a Delaney and Bonnie tour in early 1970. His first solo album, *Eric Clapton* (recorded with Delaney and Bonnie and Friends), was released later that year, yielding a hit single in his cover of J. J. Cale's "After Midnight." Clapton's brief time as a sideman with the Bramletts convinced him he could put together another group, but this time an anonymous "nonsupergroup."

The result, in May 1970, was Derek and the Dominos, featuring Clapton, Carl Radle, Bobby Whitlock, Jim Gordon, and, very briefly, Dave Mason. In the studio, Duane Allman of the Allman Brothers Band joined Clapton on twin lead guitars for one of the most memorable musical moments of the Seventies—*Layla and Other Assorted Love Songs.*

As brilliant as the album—particularly the title cut—was, it did not sell that well at first. This poor reception, along with Clapton's heroin addiction and the fact that Pattie Harrison broke off a love affair with him to return to her husband and his best friend, made 1970 a less than happy year for Slowhand. In fact, after

Cream: Eric Clapton, Ginger Baker, Jack Bruce (Atco Records)

Derek and the Dominos split in April 1971, Clapton's only public performances for the next two years would be George Harrison's Concert for Bangla Desh and Leon Russell's Rainbow Theatre show, both in 1971. Clapton retreated to his Surrey home to fight his addiction. A "comeback" concert organized for him in January 1973 by another friend, Pete Townshend, proved a bit premature. But a year later an acupuncture treatment had him off heroin and ready to return—with Pattie Harrison now by his side to stay.

By April 1974, the first Eric Clapton Band was assembled. That spring, Clapton returned to Miami to cut *461 Ocean Boulevard.* While he toured the U.S., his remake of Bob Marley's "I Shot The Sheriff" went to Number One.

But the low-key Clapton reflected in the album's lyrics, with their religious overtones, was not to everyone's liking—especially onstage. Instead of thrilling the crowd with Cream-like solos, Clapton seemed content to spend most of his time in the background. Indeed, for a while it seemed as if the fire that had burned in his early playing had died out. *461 Ocean Boulevard* was followed by a succession of aimless recordings. On the all-star *No Reason to Cry* Clapton seemed like a guest on his own album. Sales were disappointing.

He returned to the groove—at least commercially—with the country-oriented *Slowhand* in November 1977, from which came the Top Five single "Lay Down Sally." The next two albums, *Backless* and the live-in-Japan *Just One Night,* continued in the same laid-back vein, with Clapton's playing so restrained as to be almost invisible.

Surprisingly, *Another Ticket,* released in the winter of 1981, broke the mold. It was a delightful sampler of Clapton's musical tastes, with his instrumental and songwriting presence more in evidence than anything he'd done in years. Finally, everything seemed to be falling into place. He had married Pattie Harrison in the spring of 1979. He had his best band in years, including Albert Lee, Dave Markel, Chris Stainton, Henry Spinetti, and Gary Brooker of Procol Harum. He had a hit single in "I Can't Stand It." And he had a lengthy U.S. tour ahead of him. But a few shows into that tour, Clapton was hospitalized with severe stomach ulcers. The tour was canceled, and he was ordered by doctors to take the rest of the year off.

And what of his cohorts from the days of glory? Ginger Baker built a studio in Africa and made a few unsuccessful solo albums. And Jack Bruce continued to make generally under-noticed albums, though several collaborations with Robin Trower have given him a higher profile.

(BILL KING)

U.S. Hit Singles

1970 After Midnight (**18**)
1972 Let It Rain (**48**)
1973 Bell Bottom Blues (**78**)
1974 I Shot the Sheriff (**1**);
Willie and the Hand Jive (**26**)
1976 Hello Old Friend (**24**)
1978 Lay Down Sally (**3**); Wonderful Tonight (**16**)
1979 Promises (**9**)
1980 Tulsa Time/Cocaine (**30**); Blues Power (**76**)

(BY CREAM)

1968 Sunshine of Your Love (**5**); White Room (**6**);
Anyone for Tennis (**64**)
1969 Crossroads (**28**); Badge (**60**)

(BY DEREK AND THE DOMINOS)

1971 Bell Bottom Blues (**91**)
1972 Layla (**10**)

U.S. Hit LPs

1970 Eric Clapton (**13**)
1972 History of Eric Clapton (**6**);
Eric Clapton at His Best (**87**)
1973 Clapton (**67**); Eric Clapton's Rainbow
Concert (**18**)
1974 461 Ocean Boulevard (**1**)

1975 There's One in Every Crowd (**21**);
E.C. Was Here (**20**)
1976 No Reason to Cry (**15**)
1977 Eric Clapton (**194**); Slowhand (**2**)
1978 Backless (**8**)
1980 Just One Night (**2**)

(BY CREAM)

1967 Fresh Cream (**39**); Disraeli Gears (**4**)
1968 Wheels of Fire (**1**)
1969 Goodbye (**2**); Best of Cream (**3**)
1970 Live Cream (**15**)
1972 Live—Vol. 2 (**27**); Heavy Cream (**135**)

(BY DEREK AND THE DOMINOS)

1970 Layla (**16**)
1973 In Concert (**20**)

U.K. Hit Singles

1974 I Shot the Sheriff (**9**)
1975 Swing Low Sweet Chariot (**19**);
Knockin' on Heaven's Door (**38**)
1977 Lay Down Sally (**39**)
1978 Promises (**37**)

(BY CREAM)

1966 Wrapping Paper (**34**); I Feel Free (**11**)
1967 Strange Brew (**17**)
1968 Sunshine of Your Love (**25**);
Anyone for Tennis (**40**)
1969 Badge (**18**); White Room (**28**)

(BY DEREK AND THE DOMINOS)

1972 Layla (**7**)

The Clash

Leading figures in the 1977 Punk explosion, the Clash's peculiar blend of hazy agitprop and searingly heartfelt music kept them at the center of raging controversy ever since the group's formation. Many rock fans felt that rock & roll and politics couldn't and shouldn't mix; on the other hand, radical left wingers railed that the group's views were phony and superficial. But the *British Patriot,* the magazine for members of Britain's right-wing organization, the National Front, obviously thought otherwise when it called the Clash "the most left-wing of the contemporary groups" and advised its readers to "[keep] an eye out for posters that advertise Clash concerts so that they may be removed from walls and boardings and reconsigned to the gutter where they will reach the most appropriate clientele."

The Clash was formed in May of 1976. With the exception of Paul Simonon, who was an utter novice on bass, the members of the band had considerable experience behind them. Guitarist Mick Jones and drummer Terry Chimes had played in the famed proto-Punk group London S.S., and singer Joe Strummer had led the legendary London pub group the 101ers. Originally, the Clash had a fifth member, guitarist Keith Levene, who surfaced several years later with Public Image Ltd.

Joe Strummer
(vocals, rhythm guitar)
Paul Simonon
(bass guitar)
Mick Jones
(lead guitar)
Nicky Headon
(drums)

Paul Simonon, Topper Headon, Joe Strummer, Mick Jones (RDR Productions)

Instrumental in the group's formation and choice of direction was Bernard Rhodes, the Clash's manager. As Joe Strummer told *Melody Maker* in 1977: "He's had a load of influence—especially at the start. He put the group together. And he also put us on the right track—mainly about song content." Rhodes was a close friend of the Sex Pistols' svengali, Malcolm McLaren, and his PR tactics and political inclinations were no less outrageous and iconoclastic. According to Jerry Dammers of the Specials (a group that was managed by Rhodes when they went under the name of the Coventry Automatics), one proposed publicity stunt was to have the Clash hold up a bank. If they got away with it, Rhodes reasoned, they'd have all that money. And if they got caught? Well . . . it would be *great* publicity.

After touring extensively throughout England, the Clash landed a lucrative recording contract with CBS. Some fans saw their signing with a major label as a betrayal of Punk. One disgruntled proponent of this theory asserted that "Punk died the day the Clash signed with CBS."

The band recorded its debut album, *The Clash*, in three weekend sessions. Released in April 1977, it entered the British charts at number twelve. Along with *Never Mind the Bollocks, Here's The Sex Pistols*, *The Clash* stands as the ultimate statement of Punk intent and is considered by some to be the group's best album. Unlike the Sex Pistols, whose reaction to a grim situation was a defeatist nihilism, the Clash's music was infused with a rebellious optimism, as well as a good deal of wit and warmth.

Shortly after the band finished recording the album, drummer Terry Chimes, unnerved by the ever-increasing violence at Punk gigs, quit the group. The Clash were effectively put out of action for several months while they auditioned 206 drummers, finally settling on Nicky "Topper" Headon, an old friend who'd briefly passed through London S.S.

During the band's absence, the accolades heaped on them began to reach ludicrous proportions. Stories of their antiauthoritarian stance, coupled with their genuine generosity and friendliness to their fans, brought about a rabid hero worship to which members of the rock press were not in the least bit immune. Accordingly, the Clash discovered that their popularity had dropped considerably with the English constabulary. Their tour bus was repeatedly stopped and searched on the flimsiest of pretexts, and band members were arrested and fined quite stiffly for crimes as innocuous as forgetting to return a hotel key.

In November 1978 the band's second album, *Give 'Em Enough Rope*, was released. Though well received upon its release, *Give 'Em Enough Rope* is in retrospect the Clash's least successful record. Producer Sandy Pearlman, best known for his association with Blue Oyster Cult, managed to turn the thrashing vitality of the Clash into a bland heavy-metal blast, rendering Strummer's vocals unintelligible by burying them deep in the mix.

Since Epic Records had deemed the first album "too crude" to be released in the U.S. (where it consequently became the best-selling import ever), *Give 'Em Enough Rope* was the Clash's Stateside debut. (Epic Records eventually released *The Clash* in a somewhat altered form in 1979.) Although the Clash's American following was not terribly large, they made up for their lack of numbers by an almost religious fervor. Tom Carson explained in *Rolling Stone*: "To their fans, they're not just the greatest rock & roll band in the world—they're the last hope, the only group that still seems to promise that rock & roll can make a difference."

The Clash gave their debut American performance in San Francisco on February 7, 1979, coincidentally (some thought prophetically) fifteen years to the day

that the Beatles first arrived in the U.S. Of the final show of the tour, at New York City's Palladium, Tom Carson wrote in *Rolling Stone* that "the Clash unleashed one of the most staggering performances I've seen. It was music of heroic grandeur, epic sweep, and visceral force. . . . Listening to them, one not only believed in the world at war they sang about, but also wanted to enlist, on their side, on the spot."

During the remainder of '79, the Clash started work on their third album, toured England, and, in September, traveled to the States for a second tour. In October, the quasi-documentary film *Rude Boy* opened in England, despite attempts by the Clash to block its release (according to Strummer, the group objected to the way blacks were depicted). Shot mostly in '78, the film told the story of a disaffected youth, Ray Gange, a one-time friend of Strummer's, who aspires to be a roadie for the Clash. He attains this goal but then loses the job due to his general laziness and his predilection for the bottle. While flawed and somewhat boring, *Rude Boy* contains excellent footage of the band playing live and recording songs for *Give 'Em Enough Rope*.

In January 1980, the Clash released a two-record set for which they took a cut in royalties so it could be sold for little more than a single album. On *London Calling*, the group sounded more relaxed and diversified than usual, but not with a whit less bite or anger. Finally, the diamond had emerged from the rough; producer Guy Stevens captured the Clash at their most spontaneous and playful.

London Calling reached a wider audience, sweeping into the American Top Thirty. In England, however, a backlash began brewing. Again, the tiresome claim that "the Clash sold out Punk" was raised, as well as a new epithet, that the group had become "Americanized." During a summer tour of Europe, matters reached an unpleasant and disillusioning climax. Joe Strummer explained to Roy Carr of *NME*: "Punk Rock has just hit Europe in a big way, but it's totally worthless. It's nothing but a complete 1976 revival . . . just another fashion. It's become everything it wasn't supposed to be. I was emotionally shattered . . . completely disheartened to see what's happened to the seeds of what we've planted. If those pricks and kids like them are the fruits of our labors, then they're much worse than those people they were meant to replace." During a gig in Hamburg, the Clash were repeatedly jeered at until Strummer, driven beyond the point of endurance, hit one of his tormentors over the head with his Telecaster. A near-riot occurred and Strummer was hauled off by police.

The Clash returned to England, where rumors of the band's breakup were being bandied about by the rock press. Fortunately, they were unfounded, and in late 1980 *Sandinista!* was released. The sheer length of this triple album was initially off-putting to many fans and critics. Containing thirty-six songs, well over two hours of music, and listing for only $14.98, it showed the Clash in a myriad of musical guises: disco-rap, calypso, rockabilly, the inevitable reggae-dub, gospel, jazz, and even a waltz. It was the Clash Variety Show in another sense, including guest appearances by such diverse artists as Ellen Foley, Mikey Dread, Lew Lewis, and Timon Dogg. The record was marred by a few self-indulgent tracks and some of the political lyrics smacked of empty rhetoric, but the majority of *Sandinista!* has the creativity, intensity, and passion of the Clash at their best.

(ELIZABETH SCHAFFNER)

U.S. Hit LPs

1979	Give 'Em Enough Rope (**128**); The Clash (**126**)
1980	London Calling (**27**); Black Market Clash (10-inch) (**74**)

U.S. Hit Singles

1980	Train in Vain (Stand by Me) (**23**)

U.K. Hit Singles

1977	White Riot (**38**); Complete Control (**28**)
1978	Clash City Rockers (**35**); (White Man) in Hammersmith Palais (**32**); Tommy Gun (**19**)
1979	English Civil War (**25**); Cost of Living EP (**22**); London Calling (**11**)
1980	Bankrobber (**12**)

Joe Cocker

Joe Cocker reigned as one of rock's most distinctive vocalists during the late Sixties and early Seventies, covering material that ranged from Bob Dylan and the Beatles to "Bye Bye Blackbird." No matter what the song, though, his style remained consistent: raw, soulful vocals backed by top-notch musicianship.

Chris Stainton, Alan Spenner, Bruce Rowland, and Henry McCulloch (known collectively as the Grease Band) provided the licks for Cocker's first chart-topping British single in 1968, "With a Little Help from My Friends." Taking a cue from the hit song, Cocker's like-titled debut LP included a little help from such friends as Jimmy Page and Steve Winwood. The disc was well received on "underground" rock stations and, combined with a powerful performance at Woodstock, helped establish Joe Cocker as both a front-line album artist and a highly acclaimed concert act.

Writer-producer-performer Leon Russell (one of Delaney and Bonnie's friends) hooked up with Cocker in 1969, coproducing the followup album, *Joe Cocker!*. Once again surrounded by a talented supporting cast (including Russell on piano, organ, and guitar), Cocker applied his gutsy vocals to another mixed bag of material. The combination worked perfectly and *Joe Cocker!* became a certified American hit, ranking as one of *Billboard*'s top ten albums of 1970.

On the concert front, Leon Russell was also instrumental in organizing the musicians for Cocker's biggest-ever swing through America: the 1970 Mad Dogs & Englishmen Tour. From March to May, an entourage of forty-three musicians (and other hangers-on) traveled from coast to coast in an elaborate showcase for both Cocker and Russell. The tour resulted in an excellent rock documentary film, a double-album "soundtrack," and Cocker's two biggest American singles: "The Letter" and "Cry Me a River." However, instead of serving as his catapult to further rock superstardom, the tour left Joe Cocker both physically and emotionally drained. Ironically, it was Leon Russell who rode the momentum to superstardom, while Cocker pulled back from the limelight.

Though he soon resumed recording, Cocker was unable to recapture his "Mad Dogs" success and had only one more big hit in the 1970s ("You Are So Beautiful"). Despite the lack of subsequent chart success, Joe Cocker continued in fine voice, closing out the decade with another "cast of thousands" effort, *Luxury You Can Afford*.

One of the most unusual moments in Cocker's career took place in late 1976, when he appeared on NBC's *Saturday Night Live* to sing "You Are So Beautiful." As he launched into a followup number, *Saturday Night*'s John Belushi stepped on camera dressed as a Joe Cocker lookalike (a caricature that Belushi had first developed on stage in Chicago and New York, complete with exaggerated guttural voice and mock-spastic hand gestures). Prototype and clone traded stylized movements perfectly as they belted out a lively version of "Feelin' Alright" for a delighted, if somewhat confused, audience.

(WALLY PODRAZIK)

(*Freelance Photo Guild /Ebet Roberts*)

U.S. Hit Singles

1968	With a Little Help from My Friends (**68**)
1969	Delta Lady (**69**)
1970	The Letter (**7**); Cry Me a River (**11**); She Came in Through the Bathroom Window (**30**)
1971	High Time We Went (**22**); Black-Eyed Blues (**95**)
1972	Midnight Rider (**27**); Feeling Alright (**33**); Woman to Woman (**56**)
1973	Pardon Me Sir (**51**)
1974	Put Out the Light (**46**)
1975	You Are So Beautiful (**5**); It's a Sin When You Love Somebody (**95**)
1978	Fun Time (**43**)

U.S. Hit LPs

1969	With a Little Help from My Friends (**35**); Joe Cocker! (**11**)
1970	Mad Dogs & Englishmen (**2**)
1972	Joe Cocker (**30**)
1974	I Can Stand a Little Rain (**11**)
1975	Jamaica Say You Will (**42**)
1976	Sting Ray (**70**)
1977	Joe Cocker's Greatest Hits (**114**)
1978	Luxury You Can Afford (**76**)

U.K. Hit Singles

1968	Marjorine (**48**); With a Little Help from My Friends (**1**)
1969	Delta Lady (**10**)
1970	The Letter (**39**)

Cockney Rebel

Steve Harley
(vocals)
Jean-Paul Crocker
(electric violin, guitar)
Paul Jeffreys
(bass)
Milton Reame-James
(keyboards)
Stuart Elliot
(drums)

With much fanfare was this pretender to David Bowie's glittery throne launched, months before he even had a record out. A former journalist, Harley (née Steven Nice) went on the dole, dropped "a *lot* of acid," made the pilgrimage to the Isle of Wight to hear Bob Dylan ("I was overawed, enraptured"), and plotted a new career. The cocksure and arrogant would-be pop star told *NME:* "Success in the rock & roll business I regard as a very mild challenge. I mean, I'm very upset that standards are so low. I guess it'll take us about nine months to be appreciated for our true worth—which is about two years ahead of our time." Within four months of forming Cockney Rebel, Harley's relentless hustling had scored him a five-figure advance from EMI.

Riding the new wave of Glam Rock, Steve invested Cockney Rebel with a lot of calculated mystique: rouge, makeup, and velvet suits for the boys. Though he was actually a most charismatic performer—simultaneously projecting both arrogance and vulnerability—the British music press very quickly suspected it had been taken for a ride by a manipulative charlatan.

Reviewing *The Human Menagerie* for *NME*, Roy Carr plunged in the knife. Dismissing Rebel as "an effete hype" and "the ultimate poseurs' party band," he wrote that their debut LP's contents "smack of a bygone era when rock became punch drunk from an overdose of psychedelics." Carr concluded: "By the way, Steve—when you're finished with it, David Bowie would like his voice back, and Bryan Ferry his vibrato. You can keep the clothes."

From then on it was open warfare between Harley and the U.K. pop weeklies—especially *NME*. A face-to-face confrontation with Roy Carr caused the critic to conclude (in print) that Steve belonged in a padded cell. "I've never heard of a pioneer that didn't suffer," Harley had lectured him. "They kick the one who does it first, and then pat the copyists on the back shouting 'New Wave!' . . . . I've got something you haven't got, because God has blessed me and I'm trying to share it with you. *I'm* doing *you* a favor."

Cockney Rebel's second album, *The Psychomodo*, offered some of Harley's most powerful work. Cockney Rebel did have a distinctive sound, with Crocker's manic violin often giving way to the sweep of a full orchestra and choir as Harley gibbered his "surrealistic" visions of sinking ships and suicide trips. Though even Steve's admirers weren't always sure what he was driving at—and, very likely, much of

it was bogus—*The Psychomodo*'s intensity was undeniable, and oddly engrossing.

By now, however, Harley was feuding with his own band. In September 1974 he summarily fired all but drummer Stuart Elliot, and had his erstwhile cohorts' names and photograph removed from the U.S. edition of *The Psychomodo*. A new lineup—henceforth billed as Steve Harley and Cockney Rebel—was assembled, comprising keyboards player Duncan Mackay, bassist George Ford, and former Family guitarist Jim Cregan. Though musically more accomplished and versatile than their predecessors, the new Rebel would never quite manage to duplicate *The Psychomodo*'s carnival of dementia. Nonetheless, Harley's new work could be extremely enjoyable—and even moving—when he had something coherent to say and would sing it straight from the heart. The poppish "Make Me Smile" (from *The Best Years of Our Lives*) was a U.K. smash ("It must have hurt [*NME*'s] feelings to have to put us at Number One"); and *Timeless Flight* offered at least one transcendent moment in "All Men Are Hungry." Songs like this—and the Commie-baiting "Red Is a Mean, Mean Colour"—almost justified Harley's claims to literary preeminence.

But following the failure of 1976's gimmick-ridden *Love Is a Prima Donna* (and Cregan's defection to Rod Stewart), Harley dropped the Cockney Rebel tag altogether and moved to California. Like his good friend Marc Bolan—who, along with Gloria Jones, guested on Steve's first "solo" LP *Hobo with a Grin*—Harley had never realized his dream of Stateside stardom. *Hobo* (coproduced by Michael Jackson) was obviously devised with the American market in mind, yet this slick slew of discofied ditties only served to alienate Harley's cult following and put the ex-Rebel in the lamentable position of one who had sold out and then failed to find a buyer.

(NICHOLAS SCHAFFNER)

Steve Harley (EMI Records)

U.S. Hit Singles

1976   Make Me Smile (**96**)

U.K. Hit Singles

1974   Judy Teen (**5**); Mr. Soft (**8**)
1976   Make Me Smile (**1**); Mr. Raffles (**13**)
1976   Here Comes the Sun (**10**); Love Is a Prima Donna (**41**)
1979   Freedom's Prisoner (**58**)

Elvis Costello and the Attractions

Elvis Costello
(vocals, guitar)
Steve Nieve
(keyboards)
Pete Thomas
(drums)
Bruce Thomas
(bass)

In the mid-Seventies, the enterprising founders of Stiff Records, Jake Riviera and Dave Robinson, placed ads in the English music papers asking for tapes from unsigned artists. The first tape they received (and the best, according to Robinson) was from a bespectacled

twenty-one-year-old songwriter calling himself Elvis Costello, whose vehemently bitter lyrics about the harrowing underside of romance were set to catchy, hook-filled music strongly reminiscent of early Sixties pop.

In July 1977, after releasing two successful Costello singles, Stiff issued *My Aim Is True*. With production duties handled by Nick Lowe (who subsequently has gone on to produce practically all of Costello's work) and musical backing provided by Clover, a West Coast group, *My Aim Is True* was a stunning debut album and was warmly received by critics and fans alike. Monty Smith of *New Musical Express* claimed that Costello "possesses more understanding of the stark realities of modern love than many of the vacuous songsmiths who assume they have their fingers on the pulse of what goes on behind closed doors."

In the States, critical reaction was equally enthusiastic. *Rolling Stone* selected the album as one of the top five albums of 1977, and American radio stations, in an unusual display of astuteness, gave the LP generous airplay, undoubtedly aiding it in becoming the first New Wave album to break into the Top Fifty. A year later, commenting on this U.S. success, Costello was typically sour: "Well, of course, Americans have never produced one decent home-grown rock & roll band, so when they're confronted by the real thing, they tend to get a little overexcited." (*NME* 1978)

Costello originally kept himself shrouded in Garbo-esque inaccessibility; he actually inserted a clause into his recording contract that he did not have to meet with the press. When he finally lifted his ban on interviews and met with Nick Kent of *NME*, he made the now-famous assertion: "The only two things that matter to me, the only motivation points for me writing all these songs, are guilt and revenge." As the rather booze-soaked interview continued, Costello revealed that he kept a little black book filled with names of people he felt had done him wrong (mostly record company executives who had rejected his early work) and with whom he planned to settle the score when the suitable time arose. Costello clarified the intentions of his lyrics, saying: "I'm talking about being a complete loser. That's something totally new to the rock idiom, which by its nature is totally immature and totally macho-oriented in its basic attitude."

Costello was extremely reluctant to divulge any information about his personal life, but within the ensuing months the story unfolded. His real name was Declan MacManus and he had grown up within a musical family. His father, Ross MacManus, had been a singer with the Joe Loss Orchestra, and was voted Tenth Best Singer in the 1961 *Melody Maker* Readers' Poll. As a boy, Elvis had frequently accompanied his father to recording studios, where he witnessed sessions of pivotal Sixties groups such as the Hollies, the Beatles, and the Stones. Prior to signing with Stiff he played in a bluegrass band, Flip City, while supporting himself as a computer programmer.

At the end of 1977, conflicts between the two founders of Stiff caused Riviera to dissolve his partnership with Robinson, pursuing instead a career as manager of Costello and Nick Lowe. This left Costello temporarily without a label; eventually he signed with Radar Records in Britain, having already committed himself to Columbia in the States.

Early in 1978, *This Year's Model* was released. Costello's second album was more cohesive and confident, a development that was largely due to the acquisition of the Attractions. Gone were the Pub Rock overtones that had dulled the needling menace of Costello's lyrics. *This Year's Model* introduced a more minimalist but highly inventive sound; the creepy-crawly organ work of Steve Nieve was

(*Ron Gott*)

particularly suited to Costello's neurotic persona.

This Year's Model sold moderately well and culled ecstatic reviews, but it was *Armed Forces,* released the following year, that put Costello over the top in the U.S. Originally titled *Emotional Fascism,* the album dealt with Costello's usual obsession, the power struggle within relationships, but on this record the struggle was depicted in global terms. The ominous lyrics made frequent allusions to espionage, the military, and imperialism, constructing a world view that was sinister and despairing. In contrast, the production was luxuriously plush, making *Armed Forces* more accessible perhaps, but sacrificing the dynamic clarity of *This Year's Model*. Which didn't deter record buyers in the least. *Armed Forces* entered the British record charts at number two and became the first British New Wave product to crack the American Top Ten.

The fall of 1979 found Costello in the studio producing the Specials' debut album. Seemingly influenced by this experience, Costello carried the rough "live" sound of *The Specials* over to his next LP. *Get Happy!!* could hardly have been more stylistically different from its predecessor. Much of the inspiration for *Get Happy!!*'s marathon twenty songs derived from R&B and Motown soul, making this the most danceable Costello offering so far.

In the latter part of 1980, Columbia released *Taking Liberties,* a compilation of singles and album outtakes that had never been issued in the U.S. Though the album was a hodgepodge of material recorded at varying times in Costello's career, *Taking Liberties* was a surprisingly cohesive and most enjoyable LP. Barely four months later, the sixth Costello LP was in the stores. On *Trust,* Costello flaunted his formidable ability to write many different kinds of music, but the crowning glory here was the manner in which the evocative lyrics were delivered. The Costello croon was looser and more powerful than ever before, and his timing was deliciously masterful. Toward the end of 1981, the man who once claimed "my ultimate ambition in life is to be an irritant" released *Almost Blue,* an album of his favorite country & western songs.

In his review of *This Year's Model*, Nick Kent of the *NME* wrote: "Like Townshend and Dylan before him, Costello knows that the true essence of rock as potent music is as a vehicle for frustration." And like Townshend and Dylan before him, Costello is faced with the dilemma of which direction to take once that frustration has been alleviated, for the man who once sang about being a "complete loser" was now anything but that. Yet, *unlike* the aforementioned artists (in particular Townshend), Costello never allowed himself to be pigeonholed by either the music press or his audience. That, and his breathtaking ability to create so prolifically and in such a wealth of styles, insures Costello a permanent place as a consistently exciting rock & roll innovator.

(ELIZABETH SCHAFFNER)

The Damned

Dave Vanian
(vocals)
Brian James
(guitar)
Rat Scabies
(drums)
Captain Sensible
(bass)

The Damned were Punk's groundbreakers; if they couldn't always be the best at something, at least they would be the first ones to have a crack at it. Among the major bands in the Class of '76, the Damned had the first single out ("New Rose," on the then-fledgling independent label Stiff), were the first Punks to tour America, the first to break up, and the first to reunite.

Infantile theatricality was a Damned hallmark; their amphetamine-laced, sloppy MC5/Stooges power rock was merely a suitable backdrop for Dave Vanian's Bela Lugosi posturings and the unpredictable antics of tutu-clad Captain Sensible (formerly Ray Burns), who once finished a typically raunchy set at CBGB's in the buff. Drummer Rat Scabies (born Chris Miller) frequently challenged audience members to duke it out in midperformance, while Brian James, the comparatively "quiet one" of the group, flailed away at his guitar amid the hail of spit, beer, abuse, and miscellany that enthusiasts sent hurling at the band.

The Damned, in fact, were instrumental in encouraging the quaint English custom of "gobbing" upon performers. While other Punk stars shunned the practice, admonishing their peers to "grow up," the Damned frequently engaged themselves in all-out war with their phlegmatically anarchistic audiences. Unlike some of their sloganeering contemporaries, the Damned's polemic centered around sophomoric obnoxiousness and goofy costuming. A far more serious gaffe—agreeing to audition for a local council to determine the suitability of their act for the community—isolated them from their peers and saw them unceremoniously dumped from the Sex Pistols' "Anarchy" tour.

Damned, Damned, Damned, their debut LP, was a fair seller on both sides of the Atlantic, and contained a classic single, "Neat Neat Neat." An American tour, booked, incredibly enough, by the prestigous William Morris Agency, proved an unqualified disaster, with the boisterous outfit completely alienating the press and damaging equipment and relations in every club they played.

Back in Blighty, a second guitarist called Lu was added and the Damned recorded the ironically titled *Music For Pleasure* LP, which was savaged by the critics and public alike. The darkest hour had seemingly arrived and guitarist James split to form a short-lived psychedelic revival band (later he'd fulfill a fantasy by playing with Iggy Pop). Rat Scabies formed the barely remembered White Cats, and the Damned were no more.

Vanian, Scabies, and Sensible knocked around, jokingly, as the Dimmed before hooking up with bassist Algy and inking with Chiswick Records for the 1980 release of *Machine Gun Etiquette*. This album marked a propitious rebirth for the Damned, with a more mature attitude, both musically and emotionally. Sensible moved into the guitar spot, co-composing their first hit single, the deliriously poppy "Love Song." By 1981, the fortunes of the Damned had reversed, and they transcended joke-band notoriety to become a solidly respectable commercial combo.

(DAVID KEEPS)

CREAM: See Clapton, Eric

The Dave Clark Five

Dave Clark
(drums, vocals)
Mike Smith
(vocals, keyboards)
Lenny Davidson
(guitar)
Rick Huxley
(bass)
Dennis Payton
(saxophone)

On January 18, 1964, Dave Clark & Co. were handed the luckiest break in showbiz. The Beatles' "She Loves You" and "I Want to Hold Your Hand," after breaking all British sales records, at long last vacated the Number One position. The record that happened to follow them there was the DC5's "Glad All Over"—a decidedly lightweight entry by comparison. But no matter: the twenty-two-year-old

Clark—a film stunt extra whose cautious band members were still holding down full-time day jobs—was immediately cast as Beatle-beating giant killer, a deceptive image that proved particularly catching in an America still reeling from the Fab Four's initial impact. Though groups such as Gerry and the Pacemakers had already enjoyed multiple British Number Ones, Dave's was the first to mop up across the Atlantic in the Beatles' wake.

If later invaders contrived to make the Beatles seem relatively tame, the Dave Clark Five did just the opposite. The quintet appeared in identical starched white shirts and black dinner jackets, with little white hankies peeping out of their breast pockets. Their hair was always firmly parted to one side, and none of them was ever seen to perspire. The blurbs on their first U.S. LP made disparaging reference to "their strangely hair-cutted colleagues" and predicted that "the Tottenham Sound of the Dave Clark Five is on its way towards overthrowing the reign of the Beatles in this country as well."

If Clark's troupe of well-mannered London suburbanites couldn't quite live up to *that* billing, they weren't more than half bad either. Though their attempt to film a *Hard Day's Night* of their own—*Having a Wild Weekend*—flopped dismally, they never attempted to be anything more or less than confectioners of unadulterated junk-food pop. And, as if *Highway 61 Revisited* and *Revolver* had never happened, the DC5 kept cranking out the same succulent and successful formula while everyone else was undergoing all those "heavy changes."

But *Sgt. Pepper* finally did them in. After all those years of instant access to the American Top Twenty, the monotonous Tottenham Sound was snapped off as abruptly. And the Dave Clark Five were never heard from again on these shores. (Until twelve years later, that is, when the New Wave yearnings for infectious, unself-conscious, pre-*Pepper* trash suddenly turned "Glad All Over" and "Bits and Pieces" into must-listening.)

Handsome Dave was no dummy. He played the equivalent, rolled into one, of not only drummer Ringo and heartthrob Paul, but also Brian Epstein and George Martin. Clark managed, produced, and ran the whole show (with considerable musical input from Mike Smith). At the height of late Sixties anti-Mammon countercultural fever, Dave baldly insisted: "We're all in it to try and make money." He made a pile.

After the bubble burst, Clark tried his hand at acting; the original Five disbanded only days before the Beatles, too, officially called it quits.

(NICHOLAS SCHAFFNER)

U.S. Hit Singles

1964	Glad All Over (**6**); Bits and Pieces (**4**); I Knew It All the Time (**53**); Do You Love Me (**11**); Can't You See That She's Mine (**4**); Because (**3**); Everybody Knows (**15**); Anyway You Want It (**14**)
1965	Come Home (**14**); Reelin' and Rockin' (**23**); I Like It Like That (**7**); Catch Us If You Can (**4**); Over and Over (**1**)
1966	At the Scene (**18**); Try Too Hard (**12**); Please Tell Me Why (**28**); Satisfied with You (**50**); 19 Days (**48**)
1967	I've Got to Have a Reason (**44**); You Got What It Takes (**10**); You Must Have Been a Beautiful Baby (**35**); A Little Bit Now (**67**); Red and Blue (**89**)
1968	Everybody Knows (**43**)

U.S. Hit LPs

1964	Glad All Over (**3**); Dave Clark Five Return (**5**); American Tour (**11**)
1965	Coast to Coast (**6**); Weekend in London (**24**); Having a Wild Weekend (**15**); I Like It Like That (**32**)
1966	Dave Clark Five's Greatest Hits (**9**); Try Too Hard (**77**); Satisfied With You (**127**); More Greatest Hits (**103**)
1967	5 by 5 (**119**); You Got What It Takes (**149**)

U.K. Hit Singles

1963	Do You Love Me (**30**); Glad All Over (**1**)
1964	Bits and Pieces (**2**); Can't You See That She's Mine (**10**); Thinking of You Baby (**26**); Anyway You Want It (**25**); Everybody Knows (**37**)
1965	Come Home (**16**); Catch Us If You Can (**5**); Reelin' and Rockin' (**24**); Over and Over (**45**)
1967	Everybody Knows (**2**); You Got What It Takes (**28**)
1968	Red Balloon (**7**); No One Can Break a Heart Like You (**28**); Live in the Sky (**39**)
1969	Good Old Rock 'n' Roll (**7**); Put a Little Love in Your Heart (**31**)
1970	Everybody Get Together (**8**); Here Comes Summer (**44**); More Good Old Rock 'n' Roll (**34**)

Deep Purple

Deep Purple were among the first and foremost British bands to profit from the creation of heavy metal; they were a band for the soporific Seventies. Their first major hit, the haunting "Hush," a Top Five hit in the summer of 1968, set a trail that would eventually lead to platinum-plus records and massive arena performances.

Deep Purple grew out of the late-blooming English psychedelic era. Jon Lord and original bassist Nicky Semper emerged from a combo called the Flowerpot Men, while Ritchie Blackmore toured with the legendary Screamin' Lord Sutch, whose histrionics would have made a well-suited match to the bombastic wizardly Blackmore eventually unleashed. Drummer Ian Paice had a Beat band background, and singer Rod Evans simply turned up in open auditions.

This quintet recorded three LP's—*Shades of Deep Purple, Deep Purple,* and *The Book of Taliesyn*—which were released Stateside on Tetragrammaton, an obscure label founded by comedian Bill Cosby that eventually went bankrupt. The group signed to Warner Bros., and their first LP for the label, *Deep Purple with the Royal Philharmonic,* marked a change in lineup, with singer Evans and bassist

Jon Lord
(organ)
Ian Paice
(drums)
Ritchie Blackmore
(guitar)
Ian Gillan
(vocals)
Roger Glover
(bass)

Semper replaced by Ian Gillan and Roger Glover. The album sold well enough in the U.S., but established an intellectual, symphonic image that the band quickly wished to jettison. The 1970 release, *In Rock,* succeeded brilliantly with a new, hard rock sound that kept the disc in the U.K. Top Twenty for an astonishing fifty weeks. The group had its first platinum LP with *Machine Head,* which contained the 1972 smash hit "Smoke on the Water." Deep Purple had remade itself into a maxi-decibel riff machine, flaunting a brutalizing macho showmanship that saw Blackmore smashing and igniting his axe. Their incendiary live show was captured on the double LP, *Made in Japan.* Further personnel changes followed, with Glenn Hughes and David Coverdale replacing Glover and Gillan respectively after the release of *Who Do We Think We Are?* Around this time, the band began to face stiff competition from younger groups who had been spawned by the heavy metal monster Purple had forged. *Burn* and *Storm Bringer* found Deep Purple leveling out, both creatively and commercially. Blackmore split in 1975 to form Rainbow, a heavy metal behemoth of no fixed personnel.

American guitarist Tommy Bolin (ex-James Gang) replaced Blackmore for the final Deep Purple studio LP, *Come Taste the Band.* The group disbanded in July 1976. Gillan resurfaced as a U.K. hitmaker, and Coverdale fronted Whitesnake, a heavy metal combo that built a large British following.

(DAVID KEEPS)

U.S. Hit Singles

1968 Hush (**4**); Kentucky Woman (**38**)
1969 River Deep—Mountain High (**53**)
1970 Black Night (**66**)
1973 Smoke on the Water (**4**);
Woman from Tokyo (**60**)
1974 Might Just Take Your Life (**91**)

(BY RITCHIE BLACKMORE'S RAINBOW)

1979 Since You've Been Gone (**57**)

U.S. Hit LPs

1968 Shades of Deep Purple (**24**)
1969 The Book of Taliesyn (**54**); Deep Purple (**162**)
1970 Deep Purple/The Royal Philharmonic
Orchestra (**149**); Deep Purple in Rock (**143**)
1971 Fireball (**32**)
1972 Machine Head (**7**); Purple Passages (**57**)
1973 Who Do We Think We Are? (**15**);
Made in Japan (**6**)
1974 Burn (**9**); Stormbringer (**20**)
1975 Come Taste the Band (**43**)
1976 Made in Europe (**148**)
1980 Deepest Purple/The Very Best (**148**)

(BY RITCHIE BLACKMORE'S RAINBOW)

1975 Ritchie Blackmore's R-A-I-N-B-O-W (**30**)
1976 Rainbow Rising (**48**)
1979 Down to Earth (**66**)

(BY WHITESNAKE)

1980 Ready an' Willing (**90**); Live . . . in the Heart
of the City (**146**)

U.K. Hit Singles

1970 Black Night (**2**)
1971 Strange Kind of Woman (**8**); Fireball (**15**)
1972 Never Before (**35**)
1977 Smoke on the Water (**21**);
New Live and Rare (**31**)
1978 New Live and Rare II (**45**)

(BY RITCHIE BLACKMORE'S RAINBOW)

1977 Kill the King (**44**)
1978 Long Live Rock 'n' Roll (**33**);
L. A. Connection (**40**)
1979 Since You've Been Gone (**6**)
1980 All Night Long (**5**)

(BY WHITESNAKE)

1980 For Your Loving (**13**)

Dire Straits

Mark Knopfler
(lead guitar, vocals)
David Knopfler
(rhythm guitar)
John Illsey
(bass)
Pick Withers
(drums)

Dire Straits' arrival in 1978 came as a breath of fresh air on a scene that was growing distressingly redundant. Punk, for all intents, had gone down with the Sex Pistols' stormy demise in America. New Wave was then but a gleam in Deborah Harry's big blue eyes. And the old-guard Seventies supergroups, made silly by the honesty of the Punk challenge, had only their dry ice to hide behind.

Out stepped Dire Straits, and they blew everybody away. This they accomplished without gimmickry or contrivance, but by virtue of real songs and a high level of musicianship. In fact, with their sensuous lyric imagery, sinewy guitar lines and taut, economical group playing, you might even be tempted to think you were revisiting hidden stretches of Highway 61.

Dire Straits was, in effect, a vehicle for the talents of Mark Knopfler. He penned the seductive lyrics. He was the lead guitarist, unraveling improvised single-note lines that teased the melody, stinging lightly and skittering fluently across a range of moods.

He also sang the songs in a dusky voice that's subtly effective in its understatement.

A former journalist and English teacher, Knopfler migrated to London in '77 with his acoustic guitar in tow. He taught some songs he'd written to his guitar-playing younger brother, David, and David's roommate, bassist John Illsey. Session drummer Pick Withers rounded out the band.

Influential London DJ Charlie Gillett played a three-song demo tape of theirs (including an early take of "Sultans of Swing") on his *Honky Tonkin'* show. Three interested record companies phoned the station during the broadcast, and listener response was overwhelming. In short order, they were in the studio with producer Muff Windwood (Steve's brother) recording *Dire Straits.* The album became an immediate favorite overseas. It took a while longer to break in an American market generally wary of British imports at that point, but a momentum built, owing to heavy FM airplay. To many American ears, Dire

Straits represented a welcome respite from the Punk onslaught and a harking back to the venerable songwriting tradition of Dylan and the Sixties folk scene. Who could resist? Knopfler cleaved his guitar lines with the precision of a diamond cutter, and the songs had a rich, smoky quality—from the haunting "Down by the Waterline" to "Sultans of Swing." The latter—a percolating tune about a gang of jazz old-timers with a stubborn devotion to Dixieland—became their first hit.

On their infrequent tours, Dire Straits offered no discernible image, save for a complete *lack* of image. They'd stand stock still and play, insisting that they be judged on talent, not personality. Their low-key manner only made them more likable.

In early 1980, the usual sibling rivalries, heightened by the close quarters of a tour situation, prompted David Knopfler's exit. Abetted by two new members, Dire Straits returned with renewed vigor and a remarkable album, *Making Movies*. Like the title suggested, Knopfler's new songs possessed a sweeping cinematic quality—a sense of drama, of romance and

high stakes—that recalled Hollywood's finest moments. This time out, Knopfler's pen seemed to move more to the sway of Bruce Springsteen's urgent here-and-now scenarios than to Bob Dylan's abstruse imagery. As a *Rolling Stone* reviewer observed: "If *Making Movies* really were a film, it might win a flock of Academy Awards."

(PARKE PUTERBAUGH)

U.S. Hit Singles

| 1979 | Sultans of Swing (**4**); Lady Writer (**45**) |
| 1980 | Skateaway (**58**) |

U.S. Hit LPs

| 1979 | Dire Straits (**2**); Communiqué (**11**) |
| 1980 | Making Movies (**19**) |

U.K. Singles

| 1979 | Sultans of Swing (**8**); Lady Writer (**51**) |

Donovan

It was early 1965, and Bob Dylan was the hottest American import since cheeseburgers. The British music industry that had a decade earlier manufactured a pallid Elvis clone named Tommy Steele now—presto!—conjured a frizzy-haired youth sporting the initial *D* and a harmonica round his neck, strumming earnest songs against war and injustice and a debut hit about blowing in—sorry, catching—the wind. Bob himself arrived in Britain for his *Don't Look Back* tour, and all the reporters demanded his opinion of the local pretender to the Dylan throne. "Who's this Donovan?" snapped the big D. "I'd never even heard of him until yesterday." Dylan, however, was cordial when the two were introduced at a party; but when they took turns playing their latest compositions, Bob's "It's All Over Now, Baby Blue" clearly slashed Donovan's ditty to ribbons.

If that's how the Donovan saga seemed to begin and end in the view of contemporary cynics, the young Scot's very real talent and sweetness soon prevailed over all the hype. Born in Glasgow on May 10, 1946, and raised in Hatfield, England, Donovan Leitch had tramped around the country with his chum Gypsy Dave, playing for small change, before being pounced upon by talent scouts from Southern Music, BBC-TV's *Ready Steady Go,* and Pye Records.

He quickly developed the best ear for composing catchy, pleasant melodies this side of his close colleague, Paul McCartney. As Dylan hammered home his hard-bitten, elliptic tracts from Desolation Row, Donovan turned East and went medieval, sprouting magic mushrooms, flower power, and sitars, harpsichords, and celestial strings galore. With Mickie Most in the producer's box, Donovan became one of the most commercially potent acts around. Shrouded in flowing robes and a perpetual haze of incense, Donovan as much as anyone else personified the spirit of 1967's Summer of Love.

Donovan always appeared to see himself, above all,

as a poet. If some of his material seems silly after all these years, much of it still stands up. Take the untypically realistic "Young Girl Blues," a portrait of a jaded innocent killing time ("It's Saturday night . . . feels like a Sunday").

The New Dylan at eighteen and Prophet and Pied Piper in his own right at twenty-one, Donovan was perhaps a bit out of his depth. He couldn't handle his chemicals, and the law caught up with him. He then not only joined the Beatles at the Maharishi's Indian retreat but even packaged his new records with pictures of His Holiness and appended antidope propaganda. "I call upon every youth to stop the use of *all* Drugs and heed the Quest to seek the Sun . . . thy humble minstrel, Donovan."

If that wasn't enough to make his natural constituency gag, the new "high on life" Donovan albums soon unaccountably degenerated into so much filler—though evocative singles such as "Hurdy Gurdy Man" and "Atlantis" continued to score hits. Meanwhile, Donovan published a book of poems (*Dry Songs and Scribbles*), which mostly read like the work of fourteen-year-old female Donovan fans; scored a few films; and settled down with his new wife, Linda Lewis, formerly Brian Jones' girlfriend.

In 1972, Donovan forecast his own major comeback: "Saturn is out of my planets now and I feel good." But neither the recruitment of early Rolling Stones producer Andrew Loog Oldham nor a contract and heavy push from Clive Davis's Arista Records could derail the swift slide into obscurity. Donovan, having filled the twenty-thousand-seat Madison Square Garden in 1971, found himself playing the two-thousand-seat Avery Fisher Hall on his next visit. The time after that he was relegated to the 400-seat Bottom Line.

Sad to say, his songwriting magic seemingly did evaporate. One of his later efforts, *7-Tease,* was a painfully pedestrian concept album about the state of the Seventies in light of the preceding golden decade. It was even worse when Donovan tried to stage it as Bowie-style rock theater.

Yet whether or not Donovan ever gets reacquainted with his muse, he deserves, at the very least, a cherished place in the acid-addled memories of reformed hippies everywhere. *Sunshine Superman* and *Mellow Yellow* rank among the most delightfully imaginative albums of their kind.

(NICHOLAS SCHAFFNER)

U.S. Hit Singles

1965	Catch the Wind (**23**); Colours (**61**); Universal Soldier (**53**)
1966	Sunshine Superman (**1**); Mellow Yellow (**2**)
1967	Epistle to Dippy (**19**); There Is a Mountain (**11**); Wear Your Love Like Heaven (**23**)
1968	Jennifer Juniper (**26**); Hurdy Gurdy Man (**5**); Lalena (**33**)
1969	Susan on the West Coast Waiting (**35**); Atlantis (**7**); Barabajagal (**36**)
1970	Riki Tiki Tavi (**55**)
1971	Celia of the Seals (**84**)
1973	I Like You (**66**)

U.S. Hit LPs

1965	Catch the Wind (**30**); Fairytale (**85**)
1966	Sunshine Superman (**11**); The Real Donovan (**96**)
1967	Mellow Yellow (**14**); Wear Your Love Like Heaven (**60**); A Gift From a Flower to a Garden (**19**); For Little Ones (**185**)
1968	Donovan in Concert (**18**); The Hurdy Gurdy Man (**20**); Like It Is (**177**)
1969	Donovan's Greatest Hits (**4**); Barabajagal (**23**); Best of Donovan (**144**)
1970	Open Road (**16**)
1973	Cosmic Wheels (**25**)
1974	Essence to Essence (**174**); 7-Tease (**135**)

U.K. Hit Singles

1965	Catch the Wind (**4**); Colours (**4**); Turquoise (**30**); Universal Soldier EP (**14**)
1966	Sunshine Superman (**2**)
1967	Mellow Yellow (**8**); There Is a Mountain (**8**)
1968	Jennifer Juniper (**5**); Hurdy Gurdy Man (**4**); Atlantis (**23**)
1969	Barabajagal (**12**)

Ian Dury

(*Boloks Photography /Judi Lesta*)

Ian Dury is one of the great archetypes of British rock & roll, but it's hard to think of him as a trailblazer. Is he the epitome of the music-hall tradition in Anglo rock? Yes, but others were there before him—the Beatles, the Kinks, and even Herman's Hermits come to mind. Was he among the first and best of the early-Seventies Pub Rockers? Yes again, but that period of his career is barely remembered—Nick Lowe and Brinsley Schwarz have a much closer identification with the pub scene than Dury does. Was he a prototype of Punk fashion and safety-pin chic? Well, he *did* dress that way early on, but as a fashion force I'd put him about equal to Sitting Bull vis à vis Bow Wow Wow or Adam and the Ants.

But an archetype he remains: is there another rocker so very much *sui generis?* In Britain his face is as familiar as a TV star's; his figure, an oddly Dickensian mixture of the genially shabby and the faintly sinister, is certainly worthy of a class of its own. And his songs could be no one else's—despite the fact that his music is nominally Chas Jankel's or Davey Payne's or Mickey Gallagher's, even without the vocals the songs just have to be Dury songs. And add the words—there's just no one around to match his flair in that department. He's the only rocker I know whose words consistently outstrip the music, however fine that often is—when I buy a new Dury record it's a Dury's verbal play I want to hear, and it's only when the words have been dealt with that the rest of the song begins to fall into place. With the work of the New York–style rappers or the Jamaican toasters, the words are most often an afterthought, an added overlay—a witty new texture in the fabric that's been cut to order for dance. Kurtis Blow and Grandmaster Flash are easy to enjoy, but who would want to read (hear) their words if the music weren't there to be danced to? But with Dury it's the other way

around—it's the verbal play that counts, and the music is there to supply a backdrop. And the rhythm that's so eminently danceable is there to start with in the words.

Ian Dury was born in London's East End in 1941. Stricken with polio as a child, he spent a good deal of time in hospitals and homes for the handicapped. Later, in the Fifties, he discovered rock & roll pretty much from the ground up; his first rock idol was Gene Vincent—"Sweet Gene Vincent," as Dury's fine homage would have it. In the grand tradition of British rockers, Dury entered art school—the Royal College of Art; unlike most, he actually took his degree. For a while, he even made a living in the field, teaching at both his alma mater and the University of Canterbury.

In 1970, when he was close to thirty, Dury's abiding love of rock & roll flowered into Kilburn and the High Roads, one of the first and finest of the pub bands that cropped up in early-Seventies London—a reaction, much as Punk was to be in '76, to the overbloated, overproduced music that passed for rock in the contemporary scene. (Dury later claimed, rather self-deflatingly, that pub rock was simply another excuse to get pissed.) The Kilburns played beery, good-time rock & roll with a music-hall ambience and a Cockney accent. In songs like "Billy Bentley" and "The Upminster Kid," Dury pioneered his offbeat, off-color scenarios and his theory of song lyric as catalog—names and places strung together as artfully as a fine strand of pearls. Kilburn and the High Roads became cult favorites and reaped glowing notices from the press (John Lydon was an early fan, and surely a great deal of his showmanship was picked up from watching Mr. D.). The Kilburns peaked in '73; later, personnel changes and shaky finances caused the band to split. The lone Kilburn album (*Handsome*, released on Pye) fails to show them at their best.

Dury lay low for a while—he even applied to

Harrods for a job as elevator operator. But in 1977—abetted by musical whizkid Chas Jankel—he concocted a group of demo tapes and took them to old pub mate Dave Robinson, coboss at Stiff. The results were the brilliant "Sex and Drugs and Rock and Roll," released in September and an instant classic, and the next month's *New Boots and Panties*, which charted briefly, disappeared, then returned with a vengeance to spend most of '78 firmly ensconced in the Top Thirty. Single and album received the sort of ecstatic press that would invite suspicion if the product weren't so damned unassailable. The Stiff road tour that autumn, with Nick Lowe, Dave Edmunds, Elvis Costello, et al., established Dury and his new group, the Blockheads, as one of the tightest, loosest, and wittiest ensembles around. And the singles that rocked the charts in '78 and '79—"Hit Me with Your Rhythm Stick" and "Reasons to Be Cheerful (Part Three)"—enthroned Dury as a rock-disco king with a sizable crossover audience among his subjects.

Dury's second album for Stiff—his first as Ian Dury and the Blockheads—was released in June '79. *Do It Yourself* hit number two in the course of its four-month tenure in the charts—quite a success, if not one to match *New Boots*. But musically and verbally there was no letdown at all—Jankel's arrangements were varied and inventive, and Dury's nimble wit allowed for dextrous and unpredictable shifts between the raucous and the refined, the mordant and the mellow. When early in 1980 Chas Jankel parted with Dury to pursue a solo career, the remaining Blockheads—augmented by Wilko Johnson of Dr. Feelgood fame—stepped in to fill the breach. The first post-Jankel singles disappointed

at the charts, and the album *Laughter* was indifferently received by critics and public alike.

Nineteen eighty-one brought the flip side of the 1980 coin: the Blockheads disbanded and Jankel reentered the scene. (Ironically, his biggest success during his absence was another man's hit—Quincy Jones's Top Ten cover of Jankel's "Ai Non Corrida.") Dury had parted with Stiff and signed to Polydor, and the reconciled duo flew to the Bahamas to collaborate with the ubiquitous reggae glamour team of Sly Dunbar and Robbie Shakespeare. When the single "Spasticus Autisticus" emerged in the late summer of '81, it enjoyed the questionable distinction of being blacklisted by the BBC and later deleted by Polydor for its allegedly offensive lyrics. The Upminster Kid of Kilburn days may have picked up a title (*Lord Upminster* was the new album's name), but a healthy part of him remained the incorrigible schoolboy whose pranks demanded a spanking. He's been drubbed a bit by the critics, too, but he's a survivor, and it's likely that when he's a Grand Old Man of rock & roll, he'll be a dirty one, with his wits as sharp as ever.

(PATRICK DILLON)

U.S. Hit LPs

1978	New Boots and Panties	(**168**)
1979	Do It Yourself	(**126**)

U.K. Hit Singles

1978	What a Waste (**9**);	
	Hit Me with Your Rhythm Stick (**13**)	
1980	I Want to Be Straight (**22**)	

Electric Light Orchestra

Jeff Lynne
(vocals, guitar)
Bev Bevan
(drums)
Richard Tandy
(keyboards)
Mik Kaminski
(violin)
Melvyn Gale
(cello)
Hugh McDowell
(cello)
Kelly Groucutt
(bass)

The Electric Light Orchestra (or ELO, as it is more commonly known) is an oddity. It didn't just evolve; it was on the drawing board long before it became a reality. Before even a note was recorded, ELO was given a mission: to unite rock and the classics and to preserve the kind of music the Beatles would have made if they'd been forever frozen in their "I Am the Walrus" period.

ELO had its beginnings in the Move, a Birmingham-based band led by a brilliant multi-instrumentalist named Roy Wood. The Move had enormous success in Great Britain from 1967 to 1972, with a number of songs hitting the Top Five.

By the early Seventies, guitarist Jeff Lynne had been recruited from the Idle Race. Lynne, whose own music frankly mirrored the Beatles' style, had a big impact on the Move's sound from the outset, partly because the group had been pared down to a trio of himself, Wood, and drummer Bev Bevan. Lynne's "Do Ya" and "Down on the Bay" were ferocious rockers, and Wood's "Chinatown" and "California Man" were some of the best songs he ever wrote.

Still, the days of the Move were numbered. While the group's contract required that the Move stay intact for a while, Wood and Lynne began charting another course for the trio. A new type of music would be played, and the group would even take a new name

reflecting both rock and the classics: the Electric Light Orchestra.

At first, it was hard to figure out whether a genuinely new group had been born or whether the old one had just adopted a new pose. The record label on the band's first release in 1972 read "Move Enterprises Ltd. presents the services of the Electric Light Orchestra." The album cover showed the three members of the Move all gussied up in eighteenth-century garb, but the liner notes listed five group members—Bill Hunt on horns and Steve Woolam on violin were the additions.

The music was experimental and somewhat crude, with classical riffs smeared over rock melodies and vice versa. The music also showed the differences in style that were to split ELO down the middle. Lynne's songs, such as "Mr. Radio" and "10538 Overture," were Beatlesque and rock-oriented, while Wood's, like "Whisper in the Night" and "The Battle of Marsden Moor," were experimental, aggressive, and more in tune with the classics. Still, "10538 Overture" made the British Top Ten and got some exposure in America.

ELO had been created, but it wasn't really working. Wood wanted to try a more radical marriage of destructo-rock and the baroque, while Lynne opted for a more popular, commercial sound. Wood adored

Elvis Presley and Phil Spector, while Lynne worshipped Lennon and McCartney. Something had to give. The ''something'' was Roy Wood who, with better grace than you'd suppose, left ELO in the hands of Jeff Lynne and went off to form a new band, Wizzard. Drummer Bev Bevan stayed behind with Lynne.

The second and third ELO albums moved closer to Lynne's dream of Beatledom. The melodies were more refined, the musical craziness was mostly gone, and a string section (comprised of classically trained symphony musicians) became part of the group. The hit records, however, had a hard edge: ''Showdown'' and ''Ma-Ma-Ma Belle'' were nasty and cutting, and a strangely appropriate remake of Chuck Berry's ''Roll Over Beethoven'' featured shouted vocals.

It wasn't until the fourth album, *Eldorado,* that ELO's unified orchestral style emerged. At last, the crunchy guitar inherited from Wood was gone, and Lynne gave up Chuck Berry remakes forever. This wasn't just an album; it was ''a symphony by the Electric Light Orchestra,'' the cover declared, and the record featured an overture, a finale, and a cut called ''Illusions in G Major.'' All songs were written by Lynne, and the band now numbered seven.

ELO developed a science fiction aura about this time, and the next several albums all began with a whooshing of synthesizers that seemed to indicate that the music had arrived from some distant galaxy. The group's fifth LP, *Face the Music,* gave them their first solid American hit singles with ''Evil Woman'' and ''Strange Magic.'' ELO was off on the path to success. A whole string of hits followed, including ELO's first gold record, ''Telephone Line.'' The band adopted a logo, a circular ELO monogram that looked as if it had been swiped off a jukebox.

The 1979 album *Discovery* saw the group take a tentative step into rock-disco with ''Shine a Little Love.'' But the rest of the album was more Beatles cloning, and a rhythmic cut called ''Don't Bring Me Down'' (no relation to ''Don't Let Me Down'') garnered much FM airplay. ELO's late-Seventies tours were grand affairs, with a gigantic version of the ELO logo looming over the stage like a huge, hovering spaceship. Laser beams and all sorts of aural tricks added to the shows—or detracted from them, depending on your point of view; some concertgoers claimed that the group used prerecorded tapes at a supposedly ''live'' concert.

As the Eighties began, Lynne was calling ELO a quartet. The permanent members were Lynne, Bevan, Tandy, and bassist Kelly Groucutt, and strings would therefore be added by anonymous symphony musicians looking to do a little session work. ''I'm Alive,'' a spectacular cut from the soundtrack of the film *Xanadu,* was the decade's first offering from ELO.

(HENRY McNULTY)

Mike Kaminski and Jeff Lynne (Ron Gott)

U.S. Hit Singles

1973 Roll Over Beethoven (**42**)
1974 Showdown (**53**); Daybreaker (**87**)
1975 Can't Get It Out of My Head (**9**)
1976 Evil Woman (**10**); Livin' Thing (**13**); Strange Magic (**14**)
1977 Telephone Line (**7**); Do Ya (**24**)
1978 Turn to Stone (**13**); Sweet Talkin' Woman (**17**); Mr. Blue Sky (**35**); It's Over (**75**)
1979 Shine a Little Love (**8**); Don't Bring Me Down (**4**); Confusion (**37**); Last Train to London (**39**)
1980 I'm Alive (**16**); All Over the World (**13**); Xanadu (with Olivia Newton-John) (**8**)

U.S. Hit LPs

1973 Electric Light Orchestra II (**62**); On the Third Day (**52**)
1974 Eldorado (**16**)
1975 Face the Music (**8**)
1976 Olé ELO (**32**); A New World Record (**5**)
1977 Out of the Blue (**4**)
1979 Discovery (**5**); ELO's Greatest Hits (**30**)
1980 Xanadu (soundtrack) (**4**)

U.K. Hit Singles

1972 10538 Overture (**9**)
1973 Roll Over Beethoven (**6**); Showdown (**12**)
1974 Ma-Ma-Ma-Belle (**22**)
1976 Livin' Thing (**4**); Evil Woman (**10**); Strange Magic (**38**)
1977 Rockaria! (**9**); Telephone Line (**8**); Turn to Stone (**18**)
1978 Mr. Blue Sky (**6**); Wild West Hero (**6**); Sweet Talkin' Woman (**6**); ELO EP (**34**)
1979 Shine a Little Love (**6**); The Diary of Horace Wimp (**8**); Don't Bring Me Down (**3**); Confusion/Last Train to London (**8**)
1980 I'm Alive (**20**); Xanadu (with Olivia Newton-John) (**1**); All Over the World (**11**)

Emerson, Lake, and Palmer

If there is any such thing as a ''Seventies phenomenon,'' Emerson, Lake, and Palmer were it. Although they enjoyed fame both before and after that decade, it was during the Seventies that they had their greatest successes.

They had each performed for many years by the time of their first appearance together at the Isle of Wight Festival in 1970. Keith Emerson was a brilliant, classically oriented child pianist; not quite a prodigy, but good enough to have mapped out a career on the concert stage before he entered his teens. Along came rock & roll and things changed somewhat—but his

love of classical music remained. By 1967 he was playing keyboards with the Nice, a quartet that specialized in reworking jazz, classical, and show music in rock terms; there were no American hits, but a spirited version of Leonard Bernstein's ''America'' came close.

Greg Lake took his bass from the resort town of Bournemouth to London in the late Sixties and joined King Crimson, the mystico-classical-rock ensemble assembled by guitarist Robert Fripp. Although Lake spent less than a year with the band, he apparently learned a lot about turning classical themes into stirring rock music.

Keith Emerson (keyboards)
Greg Lake (guitar and bass)
Carl Palmer (drums)

Carl Palmer, a professional drummer since age sixteen, played in R&B pickup bands before briefly joining the Crazy World of Arthur Brown and helping found the short-lived Atomic Rooster.

From a marketing point of view, the union of E, L, and P made good sense. Emerson was the fun-loving intellectual, well versed in the classics but still willing to overturn an electric organ and stomp on it. Lake was the romantic, the one who crooned ballads about knights and their ladies. And Palmer was the muscle-man, a powerhouse drummer who could reduce an entire drum kit to smithereens.

And the trio knew exactly what kind of music they wanted to make: classical-rock, but without the Moody Blues' mellotrons and soupy strings. With one or two notable exceptions, they stuck to their original formula. Ironically, the first exception was their most substantial hit, "Lucky Man," a gentle, evocative tune by Lake. Despite some characteristic synthesizer whoops from Emerson halfway through, it was Lake's guitar and somewhat uncertain tenor voice that carried the song.

ELP's first success in their typical mode was *Tarkus,* a 1971 suite that took up an entire side of their second album. The lyrics were ultraobscure (something about prehistoric mechanical armadillos and pterodactyls, if the cover art could be believed) but the music was not. It was hyperactive, jet-propelled classical rock with a jazzy feel. The band featured *Tarkus* on its first American tour, and audiences were bedazzled. The trio could make more music than any sextet, with Emerson leaping from piano to organ, straddling synthesizer and harpsichord, and finally jabbing a Bowie knife into some unlucky instrument's innards. Although Greg Lake generally remained relatively subdued, Carl Palmer flogged his cymbals, snares, cowbells, tom-toms, hi-hats, and gongs into submission (his later drum kits would revolve, flash on and off, and explode). For sheer pyrotechnics, ELP's first tour won over America.

Their second hit single was more typical. It was a live version of "Nutrocker," a rocked-up segment of Tchaikovsky's *Nutcracker Suite* which had been a hit for B. Bumble and the Stingers ten years before. "Nutrocker" was stuck on the end of their third LP, *Pictures at an Exhibition,* a live reworking of the Mussorgsky/Ravel classical suite. That record showed ELP doing what they liked best—namely, having a rocking good time with "serious" music—but it contained nothing original. When an entirely original new album did come along in late 1972 (*Trilogy*), it disappointed many fans. ELP's 1973 release, *Brain Salad Surgery,* was better received.

The next year, the group put out a three-record live set, *Welcome Back, My Friends, to the Show That Never Ends.* Although it was basically a rehash of previous studio work, in a sense it was quite reflective of the band's current status. For by 1974, ELP were basically a touring band; they continued to sell out arenas, but they had no more hit singles and the albums weren't hitting the gold mark quite so effortlessly. ELP were still great fun to watch—Palmer's drums now went up and down, and lasers had been added to the show—but fans found that their newer music just didn't stand up well on the stereo.

For a while, the three found a way to pursue solo careers without actually breaking up the band. *Works, Volume I* gave them each one solo side, with the fourth being a group endeavor. The mistitled *Works, Volume II* didn't pursue the concept, instead being a grab bag of old singles and outtakes.

By 1979, Emerson, Lake, and Palmer were looking tanned and happy on the cover of their *Love Beach* LP (no more moody poses). But the music inside was just about the same as ever: a classical-rock suite called "Memoirs of an Officer and a Gentleman" and a few melodic Lake tunes, with the customary dose of rocked-up "serious" music.

In retrospect, the trio's remarkable consistency can be seen both as the group's key to success and its fatal flaw. They discovered early on what type of music their fans wanted and gave it to them over and over again, record after record.

But it's likely that ELP will not be remembered for their records. It was on stage that they really shone. With Emerson playing two instruments simultaneously, Lake strumming furiously and Palmer almost buried in a massive pile of drums, ELP gave the Seventies one of the most visually exciting acts of the decade.

(HENRY McNULTY)

Keith Emerson

U.S. Hit Singles

1971	Lucky Man (**48**)
1972	From the Beginning (**39**); Nutrocker (**70**)

(BY GREG LAKE)

1975	I Believe in Father Christmas (**95**); C'est la Vie (**91**)

U.S. Hit LPs

1971	Tarkus (**9**); Emerson Lake & Palmer (**18**)
1972	Pictures at an Exhibition (**10**); Trilogy (**5**)
1973	Brain Salad Surgery (**11**)
1974	Welcome Back, My Friends, To the Show That Never Ends—Ladies and Gentlemen—Emerson, Lake and Palmer (**4**)
1977	Works—Volume I (**12**); Works—Volume II (**37**)
1978	Love Beach (**55**)
1979	In Concert (**73**)

U.K. Hit Singles

1977	Fanfare for the Common Man (**2**)

(BY KEITH EMERSON)

1976	Honky Tonk Train Blues (**21**)

(BY GREG LAKE)

1975	I Believe in Father Christmas (**2**)

The English Beat

The English Beat suffers from a split personality. In England, known simply as the Beat, they scored with three Top Five singles and a hit LP. In America, where they were forced to preface "English" to their name to avoid conflict with the next-to-unknown American band the Beat (much as Squeeze had initially been dubbed U.K. Squeeze), they failed to win a large public, despite the States' rampant Anglophilia.

Originally a quartet, the English Beat was formed in 1979 in Birmingham, that depressed industrial city in England's North. Ace "toaster" Ranking Roger, an early fan of the band's, was later made a full-fledged member. And the inimitable Saxa, who admitted to being at least fifty, was recruited from a Birmingham pub, making the Beat possibly the only band to bridge both the races *and* the generations.

With their integrated lineup and double-timed ska sound, the Beat was a natural for the Specials' Two-Tone label. Their first single, a cover of Smokey Robinson's "Tears of a Clown," was released by Two-Tone in late '79 and quickly entered the Top Five.

The Beat soon left Two-Tone to establish their own label, Go-Feet, via Arista. The debut Go-Feet single, "Mirror in the Bathroom," and the more politically minded double A-side, "Hands Off She's Mine/Stand Down Margaret," followed "Tears" into the charts. And the Beat's first LP, *I Just Can't Stop It,* hit the upper reaches of the British charts in the summer of 1980.

But when the album was released in the States that fall, it failed to score with the American public, though the music press gave it some fine notices. The band toured behind the record, leaving rave reviews—and raving crowds—in their wake. Still, the album remained stubbornly resistant to sales. In becoming the "English" Beat, the band lost something in translation.

Their followup album, *Wha'ppen,* didn't improve matters. Less spontaneous and more studied than its predecessor, it was something of a comedown from the amphetamine edge of their debut. In the fall of '81, with a fizzled single as carrion, the vultures of the British music press showed every sign of an imminent attack on its erstwhile darlings. Still, with the disintegration of the Specials and the Selecter and the increasing pop supercelebrity of Madness, only the Beat was keeping intact the promise of the early Two-Tone bands as 1981 clocked out.

(STEVE MIRKIN)

Dave Wakeling
(vocals, guitar)
Ranking Roger
(vocals)
Andy Cox
(lead guitar)
Everett Moreton
(drums)
David Steele
(bass)
Blockhead
(keyboards)
Saxa
(saxophone)

U.S. Hit LPs

| 1980 | I Just Can't Stop It (**142**) |

U.K. Hit Singles

| 1979 | Tears of a Clown/Ranking Full Stop (**6**) |
| 1980 | Hands Off She's Mine (**9**); Mirror in the Bathroom (**4**); Too Nice to Talk To (**7**) |

ENO, BRIAN: See Roxy Music

FACES: See Stewart, Rod; and Small Faces

Fairport Convention

"The bigger the tree, the deeper the roots . . ."

So goes an autobiographical snatch of lyrics from a tune on Fairport Convention's sixth album, *Angel Delight.* It accurately describes this enduring band's status as a family, one whose roots and branches extend far into the British folk-rock movement. If you look at the Fairport "tree" closely, you'll discover that this group and its many offshoots are almost single-handedly responsible for this extremely delightful genre.

"Folk-rock" is admittedly a weak tag to put on this music. Fairport has drawn upon much, much more in their fertile symbiosis, melding American rock, folk, and country influences to the sometimes haunting, ofttimes spirited traditional music of the British Isles. As one English music tabloid put it in 1971, "Fairport Convention and sister group Steeleye Span have together done more for folk in the past four years than anyone else has in forty."

Fairport Convention began as the Ethnic Shuffle Orchestra, and then renamed themselves after "Fairport"—guitarist and founder Simon Nicol's Muswell Hill abode. The first lineup featured Ian Matthews and Judy Dyble on vocals, with guitarists Nicol, Richard Thompson, and Ashley "Tyger" Hutchings supplying most of the songs and direction. At this early juncture, the group performed a fifty/fifty mix of tunes by American writers and their own folkish originals. Their lone album in this configuration was low-key, pleasant—and not terribly consequential.

With the departure of Dyble and arrival of angel-voiced Sandy Denny, Fairport found a distinctly natural and unfettered musical identity. Their next two albums—*What We Did On Our Holiday* (untitled in the U.S.) and *Unhalfbricking*—found them romping gleefully through songs salted with Cajun and Celtic influences, filtered through their own Byrdsy folk roots. Fairport's freewheeling enthusiasm and boozy good humor were irresistible. The piquant interweaving of guitars and mandolins and the rising chorus of voices were as enthralling as a sunny, leaf-blown fall afternoon. Fairport could also be serious and somber—as somber as the fables of the mistral, lonely life at sea or the spirits of lost souls haunting the moors that found their way into the group's repertoire. "A Sailor's Life" from *Unhalfbricking,* with its drone-like Eastern modality mounting steadily over the course of eleven lovely minutes, is the finest example of this.

Fairport also became known for breathing life into obscure Bob Dylan material, claiming for themselves such dusky gems as "Percy's Song," "Million Dollar Bash," and, best of all, "If You Gotta Go, Go Now," which they translated into French ("Si Tu Dois Partir").

Liege and Lief witnessed Fairport making a complete move into the electric-folk synthesis at which they'd dabbled previously. The thrust for this came from Ashley Hutchings, a great admirer of the Byrds who wanted Fairport to do for their own august

Sandy Denny
(vocals, piano)
Simon Nicol
(vocals, guitar)
Richard Thompson
(vocals, guitar)
Ashley Hutchings
(vocals, bass)
Dave Swarbrick
(vocals, violin, mandolin)
Dave Mattacks
(drums)

217

British folk heritage what Roger McGuinn and company did for the American folk tradition. *Liege and Lief* succeeded in every way, establishing Fairport in their home country as the foremost proponents of this quieter new wave.

Even as *Liege and Lief* was a work of consummate artistry that suggested newfound group cohesiveness, it accelerated the splintering of the original Fairport Convention. Ian Matthews had actually departed after the second album to form his own band, Matthews's Southern Comfort, which enjoyed modest success and even had an international hit with a cover version of Joni Mitchell's ''Woodstock.'' But Fairport also suffered a genuine tragedy when their talented young drummer, Martin Lamble, was killed in an accident involving the group's equipment truck.

As a band, Fairport Convention really found themselves left high and dry by the departure of key members Sandy Denny and Ashley Hutchings, who lit out for new territory. Denny formed Fotheringay and Hutchings assembled Steeleye Span, in which he pursued his formula of electricity, eclecticism, and tradition with great success.

The remaining Fairports—Richard Thompson, Simon Nicol and drummer Dave Mattacks—took on bassist Dave Pegg and violin and mandolin player Dave Swarbrick, whose jovial fiddling set Fairport Convention off on yet another tangent. *Full House,* the first album by the reconstituted band, was fine, if a bit hesitant vocally.

Richard Thompson thereupon dropped out to follow his own esoteric muse, leaving Simon Nicol the sole original member. The Nicol-Swarbrick-Mattacks-Pegg axis carried on, releasing several albums that, if they didn't scale the heights of Fairport's early output, were consistently entertaining and well crafted. Particularly memorable was *Babbacombe Lee,* a story album that spun the apparently true tale of an accused murderer who pleaded his innocence and could not be killed in several trips to the gallows.

With Simon Nicol's exit during the recording of *Rosie,* Fairport Convention was squarely Dave Swarbrick's one-man show. As a kind of nod to the past, Sandy Denny sang with Swarbrick's Fairport Convention on their live album (*Live Fairport* in the U.K., *A Movable Feast* in the U.S.), and became a full-fledged member for a second time on their 1975 album, *Rising for the Moon.*

All of these comings and goings were not indicative of ongoing internal strife. Rather, they were illustrative of Fairport Convention's philosophy of the band as a loose cooperative of British musicians of similar folksy inclination who would fall in and out of group projects as the mood struck.

Sandy Denny made a handful of solo records, of which *The North Star Grassman and the Ravens* is a haunting work of intense lyricism. Tragically, Denny died in 1979 after falling down a flight of stairs. Richard Thompson had been recording alone and with his wife, Linda Peters. Various other ex-Fairporteers have left their mark on countless projects. As for Fairport Convention itself—well, the name seems to have been retired (though one never knows . . .). Gone, but far from forgotten.

(PARKE PUTERBAUGH)

U.S. Hit LPs

1971	Angel Delight	(**200**)
1972	''Babbacombe'' Lee	(**195**)
1975	Rising for the Moon	(**143**)

U.K. Hit Singles

1969	Si Tu Dois Partir	(**21**)

Family

Family had three solid hit singles in England, performed a good deal in the United States, got some FM airplay here, and spawned a member of rock's first supergroup. Yet they were practically unknown in America.

Family—born 1966, died 1973—had three primary assets: the amazing voice of lead singer Roger Chapman, the songwriting team of Chapman and Whitney, and the ability to perform in almost any musical style. Jazz, hard rock, show biz, soft ballads, experimental music, pop—all were grist for Family's mill. And, in retrospect, it seems that the band's inability to settle in one musical groove is one reason it ultimately failed. Family's music was most often termed ''progressive rock,'' and that fit as well as anything.

Music in a Doll's House (produced by Dave Mason) introduced the record-buying public to Chapman's vocal cords; it's unlikely that anything similar had been heard before or since. By turns gruff and rumbling, shrill and vibrant, gentle and cooing, Chapman's voice was a remarkable instrument. Fresh from the British success of the first album, Family toured the United States in early 1969. By all accounts, it was a disaster, highlighted by a fist fight with promoter Bill Graham and the departure of bassist Rick Grech, who went off to join Blind Faith, the ''supergroup'' quartet.

Back in England, Family made a few more personnel changes and put out *A Song for Me.* That album and the next, *Anyway,* are quite typical of the mid-period band, with new recruit John ''Poli'' Palmer adding a jazz feel on piano while Chapman wailed away.

After another, slightly more successful U.S. tour in 1970 (no fights, no abrupt departures, no laryngitis), Family's promoters decided that the time was ripe to make a major move into the American market, and the album *Fearless* was given a big push. The unique, award-winning cover art (in which the faces of the group were blended) was striking enough, but it was the music that at long last began to raise a few eyebrows. Family toured again in 1972, opening in some cities for Elton John, and released *Bandstand,* which generated the English hit single ''Burlesque'' and was considerably more gentle than its predecessor. Simultaneous with the completion of *It's Only a Movie* in 1973, Family announced that it was splitting up. Founding members Roger Chapman and Charlie Whitney formed Streetwalkers, which had some British success in the mid-Seventies.

Roger Chapman
(vocals)
Charlie Whitney
(guitar)
Rob Townshend
(drums)
Jim King
(saxophone)
Rick Grech
(bass)

Roger Chapman

If any group is worthy of the mossy cliché "ahead of its time," certainly it is Family. Chapman's frequently nihilistic approach to rock singing would have come into its own with the late-Seventies arrival of Punk, and it's likely that Family's musical skills would have made the band standouts among the many New Wavers. But Family existed mostly in the early Seventies, when Tony Orlando, the Osmonds, Gilbert O'Sullivan, and Three Dog Night were chart-toppers. What chance did Family have?

(HENRY McNULTY)

U.S. Hit LPs

1972	Fearless (**177**);	
	Bandstand (**183**)	

U.K. Hit Singles

1969	No Mule's Fool (**29**)	
1970	Strange Band/The Weaver's Answer (**11**)	
1971	In My Own Time (**4**)	
1972	Burlesque (**13**)	

Fleetwood Mac

Fleetwood Mac: an all-English traditional blues band with an Elmore James bent, shifting slightly to pop to produce such Top Twenty hits as "Albatross," "Man of the World," "Oh Well," and "Green Manalishi."

Fleetwood Mac: a part-English, part-American pop act whose soft, mellow sound bears little resemblance to the blues but has led to such Top Ten hits as "Rhiannon," "Over My Head," and "Go Your Own Way."

Depending on where you call home, you are likely to recognize one of the above definitions as the correct description of Fleetwood Mac. Of all top British acts to make it across the Atlantic, only the Moody Blues dare compete with Fleetwood Mac in the category of Total Personality Change. Religious conversion, true love, outright fraud, dazzling success, and dismal failure—all are part of the soap opera that makes up this remarkable group's history.

Things began in 1967 when guitarist Peter Green, drummer Mick Fleetwood, bassist Bob Brunning, and guitarist Jeremy Spencer formed a traditional blues band. Both Green and Fleetwood had been with John Mayall's Blues Breakers, and Brunning was soon jettisoned to make room for another Mayall alumnus, bassist John McVie. Green took his own name, added Mick's surname and part of John's, and termed the quartet Peter Green's Fleetwood Mac.

By the time the first album came out, "Peter Green" had been dropped from the title and the record, entirely devoted to traditional blues, was called *Fleetwood Mac*. Success soon modified the group's blues orthodoxy. By late 1968, Fleetwood Mac found themselves in possession of the Number One song on the British charts not with a traditional blues number but with a moody instrumental called "Albatross." From that point, the band began to edge away from the blues.

Through 1969 and into 1970, the band was one of the most successful groups in England, although its music made little impact in the United States. Their albums sold quite well; *Then Play On* actually climbed into the British Top Ten in late 1969. Then, at the peak of the band's popularity, Peter Green left the group for religious reasons. He retired completely from the music business, and one account had him working as a gravedigger. Ironically, his composition "Green Manalishi" was a major hit for the band just as he was leaving.

The next year, Jeremy Spencer disappeared during

Mick Fleetwood
(drums)
John McVie
(bass)
Peter Green
(guitar)
Jeremy Spencer
(guitar)
Danny Kirwan
(guitar)
Christine Perfect McVie
(keyboards, vocals)

Mick Fleetwood, Peter Green, Jeremy Spencer, and John McVie (Keystone Press Agency)

an American tour. It turned out that he, too, had undergone a religious experience and had taken up with a community called the Children of God.

The rest of the band, now led by Fleetwood and Mac, carried on. Christine Perfect was lured away from Chicken Shack to do vocal and keyboard work, and a number of guitarists—Bob Welch, Danny Kirwin, Bob Weston, Dave Walker—came and went over the course of half a dozen albums. But the band couldn't seem to recapture its previous glory.

Different musical styles were tried. Depending on which of the early-Seventies Fleetwood Mac albums one happened to pick up, the music could be blues, mainstream rock, folk-tinged pop, or even a Buddy Holly tribute. Clearly, Christine McVie's (née Perfect) singing had given the band a new, identifiable sound, but success was still elusive. In 1973, it was not a new song but a reissue of "Albatross" that landed in the British Top Ten.

During the early Seventies, they did make some inroads on this side of the ocean. The rise of album-oriented radio probably had a lot to do with the rising American interest in the band. In 1974, however, Fleetwood Mac suffered the ultimate insult: a former manager started touring a group he called Fleetwood Mac. The bogus Mac bore no resemblance to any present or past configurations of the group.

When things were at their lowest, guitarist Welch left and was replaced by Lindsey Buckingham, an American guitarist, and his then-girlfriend, vocalist Stevie Nicks. This, it turned out, provided the magic spark, and Fleetwood Mac began to rise phoenix-like from its ashes to become the most stunning hitmakers of the decade. With a new symbol—a top-hatted penguin—and a fresher, more pop-oriented sound, the band released its eponymous 1975 album. This time, with a large American following and nearly ten years of experience to build on, the hit-making power was there. The dusky and mysterious "Over My Head" and "Rhiannon," the gently rocking "Say You Love Me," and other cuts from the album could be heard on the radio at any hour of the day or night in late 1975 and 1976. The next year saw the release of an even bigger LP, *Rumours,* which generated four monster singles.

Fleetwood Mac became a major concert attraction in the United States for the first time. Oddly, the group profited from the late-Seventies rise of Punk Rock and disco by providing a glossy, high-quality alternative to the nihilistic screaming of the Sex Pistols and the falsetto squealing of the Bee Gees.

The two-record set *Tusk* (1979) was an ambitious effort. *Tusk* experimented with different styles (e.g., Buckingham's "Not That Funny") and had some haunting entries (Nicks' "Beautiful Child"). The title track was an enormous departure, incorporating African drums and chants and a college marching band. It became a substantial hit anyway and ended up being a popular number among, uh, college marching bands. Nicks' composition "Sara" was in the more typical mellow mode, and was also a major success.

Since then, the band took time off for solo projects, a double-live album serving as a stopgap. In 1981, Mick Fleetwood, Stevie Nicks and Lindsay Buckingham each put out solo records. Fleetwood's *The Visitor,* recorded in the African country of Ghana with native musicians, was by far the most unusual. Nicks' *Bella Donna* was backed up by the usual gang of West Coast studio props. And Buckingham's *Law and Order* was more endearingly off-the-wall pop music from Fleetwood Mac's irrepressible singer-guitarist.

(HENRY McNULTY)

U.S. Hit Singles

1970	Oh Well—Part I (55)
1976	Say You Love Me (11); Rhiannon (Will You Ever Win) (11); Over My Head (20)
1977	Go Your Own Way (10); Dreams (1); Don't Stop (3); You Make Loving Fun (9)
1979	Tusk (8); Sara (7)
1980	Think about Me (20); Sisters of the Moon (86)

U.S. Hit LPs

1968	Fleetwood Mac (198)
1969	English Rose (184)
1970	Kiln House (69)
1971	Black Magic Woman (143); Fleetwood Mac in Chicago (190); Future Games (91)
1971	Bare Trees (70)
1973	Penguin (49); Mystery to Me (67)
1974	Heroes Are Hard to Find (34)
1975	Vintage Years (138); Fleetwood Mac (3); Fleetwood Mac in Chicago (118)
1977	Rumours (1)
1979	Tusk (4)
1980	Fleetwood Mac Live (14)

U.K. Hit Singles

1968	Black Magic Woman (37); Need Your Love So Bad (31); Albatross (1)
1969	Man of the World (2); Oh Well (2)
1970	The Green Maharishi (10)
1976	Say You Love Me (40)
1977	Go Your Own Way (38); Dreams (24); Don't Stop (32); You Make Loving Fun (45)
1978	Rhiannon (46)
1979	Tusk (6); Sara (37)

Foghat / Savoy Brown

In the mid-to-late Sixties, a group of British groups dedicated themselves to strive for "authenticity"—authenticity meaning the ability to sound as much like a bluesman from the Mississippi Delta as a kid from the heart of London or Liverpool is able. Formed in 1966 by guitarist Kim Simmonds, the Savoy Brown Blues Band (later just Savoy Brown) shared this dedication with the likes of John Mayall, Fleetwood Mac, and a host of others.

The only difference was that fame and fortune of a modest sort awaited Savoy Brown on the opposite side of the Atlantic. Over the course of Savoy Brown's brief headlining heyday (1969–1971), their music veered a bit from straight blues to boogie, but to the ear of the beholder, all was in fine form. However, internally there were the clichéd "too many chiefs and not enough Indians," and Savoy Brown's best-known incarnation (featuring singer Chris Youlden) soon boogied and blew its last.

Kim Simmonds, legal heir to the Savoy Brown name, nonetheless has persevered with revised and updated Savoy Browns, performing to diminishing audiences.

The remaining sixty percent of Savoy Brown were left not only nameless but shy one guitarist. Recruiting lead guitarist Rod Price from another British blues

Rod Price
(guitar)
Lonesome Dave Peverett
(guitar, vocals, piano)
Tony Stevens
(bass)
Roger Earl
(drums)

band, Black Cat Bones, solved half the problem. A heated debate over a Scrabble board as to whether or not it was a "real word" gave the band the name Foghat. Real or not, Foghat would soon become a household word to teenage boys all over America. For Foghat, like their Savoy Brownish forerunners, were to be virtually ignored in the U.K., while achieving great success in the U.S.

In 1971, Foghat began recording their first album in England with Dave Edmunds at the boards of his Rockfield Studio. Midway through, the band was signed to America's Bearsville Records, who sent over their wizard/true star Todd Rundgren to assist. Foghat found the work of both men too ornate for their tastes. Finally, studio pro Nick Jameson was brought in to mix and dress down almost half the album. In Jameson, Foghat found a sympathetic producer, in addition to a substitute bass player when Tony Stevens, three years and three albums later, decided that "Road Fever" (the band's anthem) had taken its toll.

Foghat continued to tour endlessly and work hard, loving every minute of it. A more spirited group of rock & rollers could not be found. In order to pay what they felt were some overdrawn dues, Foghat staged a benefit at New York City's Palladium in late 1977 for the establishment of a collection of blues recordings at the Lincoln Center Library of the Performing Arts. Not only did the band raise quite a bit of cash for the Library, they exposed a few thousand fans to Muddy Waters, Otis Blackwell, and many other blues greats. Lonesome Dave got to jam with his idol, John Lee Hooker, a thrill that he admitted "took three weeks to get over."

Two years later, "Trouble Trouble" (the name of an early Foghat tune) reared its head with Rod Price's decision to leave the band. In 1981, after a full year of auditions, Foghat found Rod's replacement in Pennsylvania-born session guitarist, Erik Cartwright. Four-strong once more, the band took to the studio and then the road.

Foghat, it seems, will never be superstars—in over a decade of existence, their only glimpse of extra-musical notoriety was Britt Ekland's post–Rod Stewart fling with drummer Roger Earl. Yet on their music and energy alone, Foghat continued to fill arenas. Their eleventh album did well, as probably will their twentieth. "Gonna roll till I'm old, gonna rock till I drop," goes the credo from "Road Fever." Foghat delivers, and they're a band you can count on. Solid as rock.

(KAREN ROSE)

U.S. Hit Singles

1972	I Just Want to Make Love to You (**83**)
1973	What a Shame (**82**)
1976	Slow Ride (**20**); Fool for the City (**45**); Drivin' Wheel (**34**)
1977	I'll Be Standing By (**67**); I Just Want to Make Love to You [live] (**33**)
1978	Stone Blue (**36**)
1979	Third Time Lucky (First Time I Was a Fool) (**23**)
1980	Stranger in My Home Town (**81**)

(BY SAVOY BROWN)

1969	I'm Tired (**74**)
1971	Tell Mama (**83**)

U.S. Hit LPs

1972	Foghat (**127**)
1973	Foghat (**63**)
1974	Energized (**34**); Rock and Roll Outlaw (**40**)
1975	Fool for the City (**23**)
1976	Night Shift (**36**)
1977	Foghat (**11**)
1978	Stone Blue (**25**)
1979	Boogie Motel (**35**)
1980	Tight Shoes (**106**)

(BY SAVOY BROWN)

1969	Blue Matter (**182**); A Step Further (**71**)
1970	Raw Sienna (**121**); Looking In (**39**)
1971	Streetcorner Talking (**75**)
1972	Hellbound Train (**34**); Lion's Share (**151**)

Peter Frampton / Humble Pie

"Spittin', arse-kickin' rock & roll, man." Thus spake Steve Marriott, the diminutive leader of Humble Pie, the prototypical Seventies heavy band, once upon a time. If you should ever require a thumbnail description of these dinosaurs' dreary rock, blues, and blather, there it is, straight from the horse's mouth.

Basically, Steve Marriott's too nice a guy to slag too mercilessly. History should be kind and remember him as one of the founders of Mod, as the driving force and creative brains behind the Small Faces, and as someone who did a few nice things in Humble Pie's humbler moments. Which weren't too frequent, if truth be told, and all of which seemed to happen on their first several records.

Humble Pie started out as a good idea and a promising chemistry. As a member of the teenybop fave band the Herd in the mid-Sixties, the cherubic Peter Frampton was being jerked around by seedy management. Marriott, then the reigning king of Mod, preferred some sagely advice with avuncular concern. Namely, get out. He hooked up the Herd-less Frampton with a drummer he knew named Jerry Shirley. Then Marriott himself bailed out of the Small Faces and asked Frampton if he could join his still-evolving band. Marriott brought along bassist Greg Ridley, who'd jettisoned out of Spooky Tooth.

It was 1968. With all this talent culled from three of Britain's most favored bands, Humble Pie found themselves prey to Supergroup Fever in the year of Blind Faith. All eyes were upon them as they issued their first album, *Town and Country,* which turned out to be a quiet, acoustically flavored LP. The band, it seems, had tuned into The Band and *Music from Big Pink.* Tasteful, spare and lovingly crafted, *Town and Country* sounds fresh today.

Steve Marriott
(vocals, guitar)
Peter Frampton
(lead guitar, vocals)
Greg Ridley
(bass)
Jerry Shirley
(drums)

The news about Humble Pie's second long player, *As Safe as Yesterday,* wasn't quite so encouraging. "A monumental pile of refuse" carped one disgruntled hack; "it sounded as if the music had been strained through an old sock into a trash can" wrote another. *Rock On,* their fourth album, at least evidenced some finely honed hard-rock dynamics—and that was about as good as you were going to get from this band from now on.

The plot thickened with the release in 1971 of *Rockin' the Fillmore,* a record that ushered in a whole new school of clichés: i.e., titles with the word "Fillmore" in them; the phenomenon of the live double album; and a decade of leaden "boogie" and self-indulgent guitar solos. Still, it made Humble Pie stars of a sort to a kind of lowlife rock audience.

Peter Frampton left anyway, even before the gold plating had dried on his copy of *Rockin' the Fillmore.* "The Face of 1968" (which he was actually voted by Britain's adoring teenybop population) bailed out to be a frontman, and kicked off his new career with *Winds of Change,* an album that was pleasant beyond all expectation.

Humble Pie, meanwhile, were strutting and spitting their way across American stages with ever more cretinous excess. *Smokin'* (1972) went gold faster than you can say "rolling papers," and yielded a sizable hit in "Thirty Days in the Hole." *Eat It,* another double, was more stink-to-high-heaven boogie. There were others, though we shall not summon them here.

Frampton found the singles road a hard one, but he worked diligently at establishing his low-key persona to American audiences. He made a string of lush, lovely studio albums, and then—stardom! Platinum records! The cover of *Rolling Stone*—twice!! It seems that the old *Rockin' the Fillmore* formula worked in spades for Frampton. *Frampton Comes Alive* vaulted the girlish-looking singer-guitarist into the cherished inner circle of Seventies superstars. Frampton's amiable, fresh-faced brand of rock became a viable alternative to Led Zeppelitis: hard and heavy, with marshmallow. The overwhelming left-field success of *Frampton Comes Alive* served notice of the arrival of a new and younger audience for rock, the second wave after the first wave of the Sixties. Teenaged, carefree, and not too preoccupied with content or message, the new audience simply wanted to be entertained. And what more congenial a babysitter than Peter Frampton? This predilection for innocuous fare would continue into the Eighties, affecting the direction and the economics of the rock industry in a major way.

Frampton was a sentinel of the new blandness, but he was also a victim of an underlying fickleness. Just as quickly as he was hurtled into orbit, he cam crashing back to earth, with the miserable—albeit deserving—failure of his subsequent albums, especially *I'm In You,* that all-time treatise on what it means to be a soggy simpleton. Then there was the travesty of his leading role, with the Bee Gees, in Robert Stigwood's atrocious movie adaptation of *Sgt. Pepper's Lonely Hearts Club Band,* plus a messy public breakup with his longtime girlfriend—all of it well documented, yet thankfully forgotten by now.

Humble Pie died a howling death down in Boogieland, and Peter Frampton flaked out into the ozone. Is there a moral here? Is it that the Seventies weren't so hot a decade for our musical friends?

(PARKE PUTERBAUGH)

U.S. Hit Singles

1976	Show Me the Way (**6**); Do You Feel Like We Do (**10**); Baby, I Love Your Way (**12**)
1977	I'm in You (**2**); Signed, Sealed, Delivered (I'm Yours) (**18**)
1978	Tried to Love (**41**)

(BY HUMBLE PIE)

| 1971 | I Don't Need No Doctor (**73**) |
| 1972 | Hot 'n' Nasty (**52**) |

U.S. Hit LPs

1973	Frampton's Camel (**110**)
1974	Something's Happening (**125**)
1975	Frampton (**32**)
1976	Frampton Comes Alive! (**1**)
1977	I'm in You (**2**)

(BY HUMBLE PIE)

1971	Rock On (**118**); Performance: Rockin' the Fillmore (**21**)
1972	Smokin' (**6**); Lost and Found (**37**)
1973	Eat It (**13**)
1974	Thunderbox (**52**)
1975	Street Rats (**100**)

U.K. Hit Singles

| 1976 | Show Me the Way (**10**); Baby I Love Your Way (**43**); Do You Feel Like We Do (**39**) |
| 1977 | I'm in You (**41**) |

(BY THE HERD)

| 1967 | From the Underworld (**6**); Paradise Lost (**15**) |
| 1968 | I Don't Want Our Loving to Die (**5**) |

(BY HUMBLE PIE)

| 1969 | Natural Born Bugie (**4**) |

(*John Rowlands*)

Freddie and the Dreamers

The ex-milkman from Manchester is perhaps best remembered in America for frantically waving his arms in the air on such TV shows as *Shindig* and *Hullaballoo.* Garrity's merry antics, celebrated in his U.S. hit "Do the Freddie," were supplemented by the spectacle of his Dreamers—some of whom were going bald even then—heaving their right legs skyward in unison.

This silliest of all British Invasion-era groups also merits a footnote in rock history for having been the first band from outside Brian Epstein's managerial stable to make it big in England in the wake of the Beatles. At the end of 1963, the readers of *New Musical Express* voted Frantic Freddie number three in the "British Vocal Personality" sweepstakes.

By the time Americans latched on to the Fab Four,

Freddie Garrity
(vocals)
Roy Crewdson
(rhythm guitar)
Derek Quinn
(lead guitar)
Pete Birrell
(bass)
Bernard Dwyer
(drums)

however, the Dreamers' string of big British hits had already been broken. Even so, the belated success of their two-year-old recording of ''I'm Telling You Now'' turned them into an overnight Stateside sensation in the spring of 1965. They fizzled as fast as they had flared; four months and as many hits later, Freddie and the Dreamers had already made their last dent on *Billboard*'s Hot Hundred.

They continued to churn out records as late as February 1970, when they produced a budget-priced children's concept album called *Oliver in the Overworld,* tracing the adventures of a singing clock. After years on the British cabaret circuit, Garrity pursued a solo career as a children's TV personality.

(NICHOLAS SCHAFFNER)

U.S. Hit Singles

1965 I'm Telling You Now (**1**); I Understand (**36**); Do the Freddie (**18**); You Were Made for Me (**21**); A Little You (**48**)

U.S. Hit LPs

1965 Freddie and the Dreamers (**19**); Do the Freddie (**86**); I'm Telling You Now (**86**)

U.K. Hit Singles

1963 If You Gotta Make a Fool of Somebody (**3**); I'm Telling You Now (**2**); You Were Made for Me (**3**)
1964 Over You (**13**); I Love You Baby (**16**); Just for You (**41**); I Understand (**5**)
1965 A Little You (**26**); Thou Shalt Not Steal (**44**)

FREE: See Bad Company

Gang of Four

In late 1978, literally from out of left field, the Gang of Four sprang upon the English music scene, releasing an EP, *Damaged Goods,* on Fast Records. It combined the energy of early Punk with the rhythms of disco, adding a crucial third element of a positive socio-political program.

But positive should be taken not as mindless approval but rather the ability to form solutions. Countering the nihilism of early Punk, Gang of Four know too that intellect is not the only answer.

If the above seems especially complex, so are the Gang of Four. Educated in both art and politics, the Gang of Four saw music and life as dialectical relationships. The band was formed in 1977 by Jon King and Andy Gill, who were students at the University of Leeds Art School. The early Gang was an R&B based band but the arrival of bass-playing sessionman Dave Allen gave the band a funkier sound.

The band attempted never to repeat itself. Gang of Four's sound went from amphetamine funk with shouted, almost sloganistic lyrics, to slower tunes and chants that reflect the personal concerns of the lyrics.

Their records have received enthusiastic reviews, *Rolling Stone* calling *Entertainment!* ''the best debut by an English band since the Clash,'' *Melody Maker* describing *Solid Gold,* the follow-up LP, as ''an album of almost monstrous intensity.'' The only complaint critics had was that Gang of Four's intelligence sometimes lapsed into pretension. But any charges of pretense were dropped whenever Gang of Four played live.

They have been called a ''thinking man's rock band.'' In interviews, questions turn into forums for discussion. These friendly arguments sometimes grew into rows, one result being the defection of Dave Allen for ''personal reasons.'' He was replaced by Sara Lee, late of Robert Fripp's League of Gentlemen. And the Gang of Four continued to plumb the musical politics of everyday events and look for new forms of entertainment.

(STEVE MIRKIN)

Andy Gill
(guitars, vocals)
Jon King
(vocals)
Hugo Burnham
(drums)
Dave Allen
(bass)

U.K. Hit Singles

1979 At Home He's a Tourist (**58**)

Genesis

In the beginning, Genesis merely wanted to be pop songwriters, selling their ditties to other recording artists who would turn them into hits.

The group's core—Peter Gabriel, Tony Banks, Michael Rutherford, and Anthony Phillips—met as students in 1966. In short order, they were penning songs, though only pianist Banks had any real musical proficiency. Nonetheless, their demo tapes impressed pop wunderkind Jonathan King, who christened them Genesis and gave them their studio baptism. After a few flop singles they recorded their first album *From*

Genesis to Revelation in 1968, while on a school break. It was a best-forgotten affair, saddled with a cumbersome concept (''man's evolution'') and sunk by King's heavy-handed production.

Somewhat chastened, they retreated to the proverbial country cottage to ponder their future. The next summer Genesis emerged with an endearingly eccentric, though at times downright macabre, sound and vision. Their oddball world view found its way onto their next four albums—*Trespass, Nursery Cryme, Foxtrot* and *Selling England by the Pound.* Against a

Peter Gabriel
(vocals)
Tony Banks
(keyboards)
Steve Hackett
(guitar)
Michael Rutherford
(bass, guitar)
Phil Collins
(drums, vocals)

lush, near-orchestral backdrop, Gabriel would weave fanciful narratives. And what stories he'd tell! Giant hogweeds overrunning the earth . . . an eavesdropping lawnmower relating old folks' teatime gossip . . . the bizarre, *Dorian Grey*-like tale of murder, reincarnation, and desire of "The Musical Box." A scene from the latter, one of Genesis's signature tunes, adorns the cover of *Nursery Cryme:* on a surrealistic croquet green, a cherubic young girl is preparing to knock the disembodied head of a young man through a wicket with her mallet. No wonder one perplexed writer called them "a most peculiar band."

Nursery Cryme, their third LP, found Genesis in a lineup that would not change (except by attrition): Gabriel, Rutherford, Banks and newcomers Steve Hackett (guitar) and Phil Collins (drums). Around this time, the group began to animate its songs in concert. Peter Gabriel would don a different theatrical guise for every song—he'd appear as a giant sunflower in "Willow Farm," a glowing-eyed extraterrestrial in "Watcher of the Skies," an anguished old lecher in "Musical Box." (And to think that not much earlier he'd been so stage shy he wanted the whole group to perform *behind* a black curtain.) Gabriel's stagecraft became the focal point of their live shows; the other members positioned themselves inconspicuously in a semicircle near the rear of the stage. Hackett and Rutherford actually sat on folding chairs, so intent were they on the proper concentration. Despite the gasping superlatives of scribes and fans, Gabriel was self-effacing about it all: "I just poodle about and put on silly costumes."

In 1974, Genesis unveiled a two-record masterwork, *The Lamb Lies Down on Broadway.* Instead of the usual epic-length compositions, there were twenty-three titles, and the playing was considerably looser (for them). If the music had grown more accessible, Gabriel's lyrics were harder to crack than ever. *The Lamb* told a story—albeit elliptically—about Rael, a New York street punk, and his quest for spiritual self-discovery. As usual, Gabriel was unruffled by the general bafflement with which the work was greeted. How much one got out of it, he opined, depended on how much one put into it.

Coincident with the album's international release, Genesis embarked on a grueling six-month tour. The stage adaptation of *The Lamb* was a multimedia leviathan: supplementing the *de rigeur* costume changes and mime was the surreal accompaniment of 2000 slides and a host of special effects.

At tour's end, Gabriel dropped a bombshell: he was leaving the band. The British music press ran banner headlines and mourned the split. Critics predicted the imminent demise of Genesis, figuring Gabriel *was* Genesis. Four hundred singers were auditioned before Genesis decided not to replace their ex-leader; vocal chores fell to Collins. Gabriel went into seclusion. Genesis went into the studio.

A Trick of the Tail (1976) came as a complete surprise to everyone. Phil Collins's voice bore an uncanny similarity to Gabriel's, and the songs were rich, vivid miniatures (though they lacked the madcap dementia that was Gabriel's special contribution). *Wind and Wuthering* (1977) offered more of the same. Technical perfectionism had by now become an end in itself, and Genesis's musical collages were so seamless one could scarcely separate Steve Hackett's guitar lines from Tony Banks' synthesizer. Genesis sans Gabriel was regarded as awesomely accomplished by some, coldly sterile by others.

Having lost their visual focus, they compensated with a spectacular light show and a sea of dry-ice fog. Phil Collins strode out from behind his drum kit to sing front and center, and the band would use a temporary fifth member as drummer while on tour. (Collins, incidentally, led an offshoot project in his spare time, the jazz-rock band Brand X.)

When Steve Hackett departed following the live album, *Seconds Out,* the band continued as a three-piece (their next album was wryly titled . . . *and Then There Were Three*). The onus was now squarely on Tony Banks's keyboards, and Genesis suddenly seemed much less fun, a somewhat murky stew (though their 1980 album *Duke* was admittedly more spirited, a pleasant rebound). All three have also cut solo albums; among them, Phil Collins's *Face Value* was an unexpectedly snappy set, featuring horns by Earth, Wind & Fire. It became a big radio favorite in 1981, and Genesis's *Abacab,* which appeared later in the year, benefited further from Collins's more extroverted, upbeat input.

Gabriel, on the other hand, emerged from two years of hiding in 1977 with a vision that'd grown even more black-humored. Over the course of three solo albums—each of them titled *Peter Gabriel*—he described a desolate world, populated with dislocated individuals and flirting with apocalypse. With generous assistance from pals like Robert Fripp and synthesizer whiz Larry Fast, he fashioned a music that was stark and scarifying—like the world he saw around him. Without doubt, this oddball visionary has proved himself one of pop music's most fertile minds and incorrigible enigmas.

(PARKE PUTERBAUGH)

Peter Gabriel

U.S. Hit Singles

1977 Your Own Special Way (**62**)
1978 Follow You Follow Me (**23**)
1980 Misunderstanding (**14**); Turn It On Again (**58**)

(BY PETER GABRIEL)

1977 Solsbury Hill (**68**)
1980 Games without Frontiers (**48**)

U.S. Hit LPs

1973 Selling England by the Pound (**70**)
1974 Genesis Live (**105**); From Genesis to Revelation (**170**); The Lamb Lies Down on Broadway (**41**)
1976 A Trick of the Tail (**31**)
1977 Wind and Wuthering (**26**); Seconds Out (**47**)
1978 . . . and Then There Were Three (**14**)
1980 Duke (**11**)

(BY PETER GABRIEL)

1978 Peter Gabriel (**38**)
1980 Peter Gabriel (**22**)

U.K. Hit Singles

1974 I Know What I Like (In Your Wardrobe) (**21**)
1977 Spot The Pigeon (**14**);
          Your Own Special Way (**43**)
1978 Follow You Follow Me (**7**);
          Many Too Many (**43**)
1980 Turn It On Again (**8**); Biko (**38**)

(BY PETER GABRIEL)

1977 Solsbury Hill (**13**)
1980 Games without Frontiers (**4**)

Gerry and the Pacemakers

Ah, Gerry and the Pacemakers. Their sound is of another time, the mid-Sixties, when music was fun and we all held on to our dreams. The band was born in Liverpool and were friends of the Beatles. They played the same clubs and shared the same manager, Brian Epstein. Epstein brought them to the attention of producer George Martin, who was captivated by Gerry's wild antics and his rapport with the audience.

As luck would have it, the Beatles refused to record the song "How Do You Do It," so it was given to Gerry and the Pacemakers. Eager to record anything, they agreed. As Gerry reminisced, none of the Liverpool bands even thought about having a hit record; at that time just making money to live on was enough for them. But the bands did go into recording studios, and what came out was often magic. Gerry and the Pacemakers were the first English band to knock the Beatles out of their Number One spot on the British charts—with the song the Beatles had previously rejected. After that, two more Number Ones in a row followed ("I Like It" and "You'll Never Walk Alone")—and three in a row in the top spot on the British charts was a first for anyone.

In 1965, they starred in *Ferry Cross the Mersey*, a madcap movie for which Gerry wrote the soundtrack. The movie was fun, but it was the title song that set young girls' hearts to fluttering. We all longed to be on that ferry. The group continued to perform and have hit records, but they couldn't change with the times, and their sugar-sweet musical style seemed outdated in the drug-oriented late Sixties. They were no match for Sgt. Pepper or Jumping Jack Flash. So as other bands successfully conquered new heights, Gerry's words "This land's the place I love and here I'll stay . . ." became prophetic.

When the band began to appeal more to their followers' parents than to the teens, Gerry seized on this new audience and started to play the English cabaret circuit and appear on family-fare TV shows. It wasn't a comedown for him because he enjoyed the feedback from his audience—regardless of size—and became well-known to young kids and adults alike.

Today Gerry and his band are headliners at Sixties revival shows. And when the lights go down, the captivating pop sound recaptures days long gone. As Gerry invites us back on that ferry there are quite a few people who still dream of riding it someday.

(SUE WEINER)

Gerry Marsden
(guitar, lead vocals)
Freddie Marsden
(drummer)
Leslie Maguire
(piano)
Les Chadwick
(bass)

U.S. Hit Singles

1964	Don't Let the Sun Catch You Crying (**4**); How Do You Do It? (**9**); I Like It (**17**); I'm the One (**82**)
1965	Ferry Cross the Mersey (**6**); I'll Be There (**14**); It's Gonna Be Alright (**23**); You'll Never Walk Alone (**48**); Give All Your Love to Me (**68**)
1966	Girl on a Swing (**28**); La La La (**90**)

U.S. Hit LPs

1964	Don't Let the Sun Catch You Crying (**29**); Second Album (**129**)
1965	I'll Be There (**120**); Ferry Cross the Mersey (**13**); Greatest Hits (**44**)

U.K. Hit Singles

1963	How Do You Do It (**1**); I Like It (**1**); You'll Never Walk Alone (**1**)
1964	I'm the One (**2**); Don't Let the Sun Catch You Crying (**6**); It's Gonna Be Alright (**24**); Ferry Cross the Mersey (**8**)
1965	I'll Be There (**12**); Walk Hand in Hand (**29**)

Gary Glitter

Gary Glitter is a shining example of British pop eccentricity; a truly unremarkable, ungainly figure who has floated in and out of the public limelight for over twenty years. As a teenybait rock Liberace, his paunch swathed in silver lamé, he croaked his way through anthemic double-drummer numbers like "Do You Wanna Touch Me" and achieved his greatest success at the height of the Glitter/Glam Rock craze in the mid-Seventies.

Glitter was born Paul Gadd in Banbury, England on May 8, 1944, and began singing as Paul Raven at age fourteen, touring with Tommy Steele, Engelbert Humperdinck, and Cliff Richard. Two years later, in 1960, he signed to Decca and released his debut single, "Alone in the Night." His career coasted along in uninspired anonymity—he achieved a Middle Eastern hit with a cover of "Walk On By"—until he became a program assistant on the classic pop show *Ready Steady Go*, where he met Mike Leander, the man who scored the Beatles' "She's Leaving Home" and the Stones' "As Tears Go By." Leander later became his manager and co-writer of the big Glitter hits.

But there were still many career cul de sacs throughout the later Sixties. In 1967, under the name of Paul Raven, he signed to MCA Records and was featured on the soundtrack LP for *Jesus Christ Superstar*. As Paul Monday, he also covered the Fab Four's "Here Comes the Sun," which failed to catch fire.

In 1971 he signed with Bell Records and teamed with Leander to produce the monster hit "Rock and Roll Parts One and Two." Glitter's zany over-the-top stage persona, lurex outfits, and outrageous platform shoes instantly endeared him to the scores of teens whose

(*Epic*)

appetites for spectacle had been recently whetted by T. Rex, David Bowie, and Slade. But his appeal was not limited merely to the prepubescent set; his shrewd instincts and perverse pop theatricality crossed more than one generation gap and kept "Rock and Roll" at the top of the charts for an amazing fifteen weeks. A string of hits followed in the U.K., but his novelty in the U.S. market did not extend beyond the number seven spot for "Rock and Roll."

After more successful European hits, many of which became discotheque favorites, Glitter announced the first of many retirements in 1975, as his career was winding down in the trendless period between Glam and Punk. One would have expected that the Punks would have nothing but scorn for his schmaltzy, overblown personality, but most of the spiked-hair legions retained a perverse fondness for the Glitter legend. Electronic wizards the Human League successfully covered "Rock and Roll," and Adam Ant cited Glitter as an important influence. As polypercussive, rhythmic dance music forged to the forefront in late 1980, Glitter hit the comeback trail once again and released a greatest hits EP that found favor in New Wave dance clubs.

(DAVID KEEPS)

U.S. Hit Singles

1972   Rock and Roll Part Two (**7**);
I Didn't Know I Loved You (Till I Saw You Rock and Roll) (**35**)

U.K. Hit LPs

1972   Glitter (**186**)

U.K. Hit Singles

1972   Rock and Roll Parts One and Two (**2**);
I Didn't Know I Loved You
(Till I Saw You Rock and Roll) (**4**)
1973   Do You Wanna Touch Me (Oh Yeah) (**2**);
Hello Hello I'm Back Again (**2**);
I'm the Leader of the Gang I Am (**1**);
I Love You Love Me Love (**1**)
1974   Remember Me This Way (**3**); Always Yours (**1**); Oh Yes You're Beautiful (**2**)
1975   Love Like You and Me (**10**); Doing Alright with the Boys (**6**); Papa Ooom Mow Mow (**38**)
1976   You Belong to Me (**40**)
1977   It Takes All Night Long (**25**); A Little Boogie Woogie in the Back of My Mind (**31**)

Alex Harvey

Born in 1935, Alex Harvey has acquired the richly deserved title of Britain's "oldest living Punk." With his roguish humor, outrageous stage shows, and memorably gruff vocals, Harvey has been enlivening the English rock & roll scene from its earliest days.

Born in the slums of Glasgow, Scotland, Harvey tried his hand at thirty-six different jobs after leaving school at age fifteen. In 1954, he settled down to become a musician, playing in numerous skiffle groups before forming the Alex Harvey Big Soul Band in 1959. Popular in its own right, this band also backed up legendary rockers Gene Vincent and Eddie Cochran during their U.K. tours. Seven years and two LPs later, Harvey split up the Big Soul Band. Thereafter, Harvey landed the position of guitarist in the pit band of the London production of *Hair*. He stayed with the musical for five years, appearing on several cast recordings and also making a solo LP (*Roman Wall Blues*, 1969) with fellow denizens of the pit.

In the early Seventies, Harvey teamed up with a Scottish band called Tear Gas to create the Sensational Alex Harvey Band. With the use of props and stage sets, the group produced a madcap rock & roll vaudeville show of erratic musical quality but consistently outrageous fun. The Sensational Alex Harvey Band slowly acquired a cult following on both sides of the Atlantic, and the group's breakup in 1978, seven albums later, was much mourned.

Harvey, the ultimate rock & roll survivor, alternated announcements of his retirement with announcements of "comeback" engagements. His concerts remained a carnival of sight and sound: sea shanties, dirges, jazz and rock tunes are sung to the musical accompaniment of brass, strings, choirs, bagpipes, and Highland drummers, while dancing girls and interchangeable scenery complete the panorama.

(ELIZABETH SCHAFFNER)

(*Capital*)

U.S. Hit LPs

1975   The Impossible Dream (**197**); Live (**100**)

U.K. Hit Singles

1975   Delilah (**7**); Gambling Bar Room Blues (**38**)
1976   The Boston Tea Party (**13**)

(*On February 5, 1982, as this book was going to press, Alex Harvey died of a double heart attack.*)

Herman's Hermits

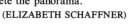

Of all the groups riding the first crest of the British Invasion, Manchester's Herman's Hermits catered the most unabashedly to the prepubescent crowd. They also ranked among the more successful; in 1965 and 1966 much of the American music biz lumped the Hermits into a Big Three with the Beatles and the Stones.

When producer Mickie Most set about turning

Peter Noone
(vocals)
Derek "Lek" Leckenby
(guitar)
Keith Hopwood
(guitar)
Karl Green
(bass)
Barry Whitwam
(drums)

Peter Noone (1.), 1967
(Henry McNulty Collection)

seventeen-year-old "Herman" into a recording star, Peter Blair Denis Bernard Noone's face was already familiar to millions of Britons through his television work as a child actor. As the Hermits' frontman, Noone effortlessly played the role of a wide-eyed waif. If the Hermits themselves (all also purportedly seventeen) couldn't really play their instruments, it hardly mattered. Onstage they were drowned out by squeals, and in the studio such chores were adeptly handled by the likes of future Led Zeppelin guitarist Jimmy Page and bassist John Paul Jones. The songs themselves were an astutely chosen selection of American rock & roll chestnuts ("Silhouettes," "Wonderful World") and English music-hall marshmallows ("I'm Henry the VIII, I Am"). Later Herman raided the songbooks of more fashionable contemporaries such as Ray Davies ("Dandy") and Donovan ("Museum"). In the same spirit Noone, after parting from the original Hermits in 1970, managed a minor solo comeback the following year with David Bowie's "Oh You Pretty Things," and attempted to duplicate the trick with another Bowie tune, "Right On Mother."

By 1980 the disposable pop of Herman's Hermits had returned to vogue, and Peter Noone resurfaced with the New Wave, fronting a Power Pop quintet called the Tremblers.

(NICHOLAS SCHAFFNER)

U.S. Hit Singles

1964	I'm into Something Good (**13**)
1965	Can't You Hear My Heartbeat (**2**); Mrs. Brown You've Got a Lovely Daughter (**1**); Silhouettes (**5**); Wonderful World (**4**); I'm Henry the Eighth, I Am (**1**); Just a Little Bit Better (**7**)
1966	A Must to Avoid (**8**); Listen People (**3**); Leaning on the Lamp Post (**9**); Dandy (**5**); This Door Swings Both Ways (**12**); East West (**27**)
1967	There's a Kind of Hush (**4**); No Milk Today (**35**); Don't Go Out into the Rain (You're Going to Melt) (**18**); Museum (**39**)
1968	I Can Take or Leave Your Loving (**22**); Sleepy Joe (**61**)

U.S. Hit LPs

1965	Introducing Herman's Hermits (**2**); On Tour (**2**); The Best of Herman's Hermits (**5**)
1966	Hold On! (**14**); Both Sides of Herman's Hermits (**48**); The Best of Herman's Hermits—Volume II (**20**)
1967	There's a Kind of Hush All Over the World (**13**); Blaze (**75**)
1968	The Best of Herman's Hermits—Volume III (**102**); Mrs. Brown, You've Got a Lovely Daughter (**182**)

U.K. Hit Singles

1964	I'm into Something Good (**1**); Show Me Girl (**19**)
1965	Silhouettes (**3**); A Must to Avoid (**6**); Wonderful World (**7**); Just a Little Bit Better (**15**)
1966	No Milk Today (**7**); This Door Swings Both Ways (**18**); You Won't Be Leaving (**20**); East West (**37**)
1967	There's a Kind of Hush (**7**)
1968	Something's Happening (**6**); Sunshine Girl (**8**); I Can Take Or Leave Your Loving (**11**); Sleepy Joe (**12**)
1969	My Sentimental Friend (**2**); Here Comes the Star (**33**)
1970	Years May Come, Years May Go (**7**); Lady Barbara (**13**); Bet Yer Life I Do (**22**)

(BY PETER NOONE)

1971	Oh You Pretty Things (**12**)

The Hollies

This will come as a surprise to all but the most hard-core fanatics, probably, but in the early Eighties, the Hollies were still together and making records. Not too many record buyers pay much attention to their latest works, preferring to wait for repackagings of their earlier material, such as 1981's *The Best of The Hollies* EPs. That sort of makes the band the Beach Boys of Britain: carrying on with a sound hopelessly lost in a time warp while fans clamor for the old stuff.

Ah, but what old stuff! Variously described through the years as "frothy," "cheerful," "fun," and "sparkling," The Hollies' brand of pop-rock is the kind of music that can elicit a smile from even the most hardened cynic. Bright, bouncy instrumentation combined with gorgeous harmonies to produce such unforgettable tunes as "Bus Stop," "Look Through Any Window," "Carrie-Anne," and "On a Carousel." That sound also made the Hollies one of Britain's most consistently successful chart acts in the late Sixties.

The genesis of the group came when two seven-year-old Manchester primary school students,

Allan Clarke
(vocals and harmonica)
Tony Hicks
(lead guitar and vocals)
Graham Nash
(guitar and vocals)
Bernie Calvert
(bass)
Bobby Elliott
(drums)

(Peter Kanze Collection)

Graham Nash and Allan Clarke, met and became friends. Later, they were inspired by the Everly Brothers and formed the Dominators of Rhythm, which in 1963 became The Hollies, after the American rocker who had such a tremendous influence on the British beat scene—Buddy Holly.

The Hollies' earliest recordings were basically the same American R&B tunes that they and every other British beat group had been playing for years: "Searchin'," "Stay," "Just One Look," "Memphis," etc. "Searchin'," in fact, was their first U.K. chart record, reaching number twelve in September 1963. "Just One Look" made it to number two in March 1964. Strangely enough, the only Hollies single to make it to Number One in Britain (they never topped the U.S. charts) was "I'm Alive."

It wasn't until the fall of 1966 that the Hollies made any significant showing in America. The big breakthrough came with "Bus Stop," which peaked at number five on both sides of the Atlantic. After that, the hits kept coming with regularity: from 1963 to 1970 they had an unbroken string of twenty-one Top Twenty hits in Britain.

The emphasis on singles in the early part of the Hollies' career typecast the band in a way the Beatles had avoided. But as the group's momentum solidified, their albums did become more ambitious, as is evidenced by the more sophisticated offerings of *For Certain Because, Evolution* and *Butterfly*. Still, the Hollies were essentially a fun group; nobody mistook their lyrics for serious statements. This bothered Nash, who desperately wanted to be taken seriously. He was the moving force behind such experiments as "Dear Eloise," "King Midas in Reverse," and "Wings," the beautiful shimmering tune the group donated to the *No One's Gonna Change Our World* charity LP. But the Hollies' record-buying public demurred, and Nash was bitterly disappointed when "King Midas" only made it to number eighteen in the U.K.

Nash was beginning to doubt his own abilities. Then former Byrds member David Crosby, whom he'd met when the Hollies played Los Angeles, made him a fateful offer. Nash was having no luck at trying to talk the other Hollies out of making an album of Bob Dylan songs (a creative step backward, he thought). It was December 1968, and he gave the Hollies a month's notice. They replaced him with Terry Sylvester of Liverpool's Swinging Blue Jeans.

Sure enough, in 1969 came *Hollies Sing Dylan*, featuring the group's new arrangements of Zimmerman classics. Some called the results disastrous. Others agreed with one critic who said that while the reworkings made no sense at all, they were "ravishing."

The Hollies returned to singing Hollies, with Sylvester taking Nash's place in the band's writing triumvirate with Clarke and Hicks. They had not lost the touch, as "Sorry Suzanne" and "He Ain't Heavy, He's My Brother" made clear.

The attention seemed to go to Clarke's head and, spurred on no doubt by Nash's success with Crosby, Stills, and Nash after leaving the Hollies, he announced in 1971 that he, too, was splitting. A Swedish singer named Mikael Rikfors was recruited to take over the lead vocals. But, ironically, it was Clarke's voice ringing out on "Long Cool Woman in a Black Dress," the Creedence Clearwater Revival–sounding single that soared up to number two in the U.S. in 1972, that gave the band's career a much needed boost.

Since Clarke's solo albums had gone unnoticed by record buyers, he decided to return to the fold after a year away. Early in 1974, the Hollies were back near the top of the charts with the ethereal ballad "The Air That I Breathe." Unfortunately, as of this writing that was the final Hollies hit. Their last tour of the U.S. was in 1975, and the band's last U.S. album was *A Crazy Steal* in 1977. When *A Crazy Steal* stiffed, they were left with no U.S. recording contract.

Clarke continued to maintain an on-again, off-again relationship with the Hollies. At last word, Clarke was both a solo artist and a recording and touring member of the Hollies.

Even if the Hollies did pass their prime, their place in British rock history is secure. Never before or since has any group so clearly and naturally defined the ingenuous charm of rock & roll at its most elemental and enjoyable level.

(BILL KING)

U.S. Hit Singles

1966	Bus Stop (**5**); Stop Stop Stop (**7**); Look through any Window (**32**); I Can't Let Go (**42**)
1967	Carrie-Anne (**9**); On a Carousel (**11**); Pay You Back with Interest (**28**); Just One Look (**42**); Dear Eloise (**50**); King Midas In Reverse (**51**)
1968	Jennifer Eccles (**40**); Do the Best You Can (**93**)
1969	Sorry Suzanne (**56**)
1970	He Ain't Heavy, He's My Brother (**7**); I Can't Tell the Bottom from the Top (**82**)
1972	Long Cool Woman (in a Black Dress) (**2**); Long Dark Road (**26**)
1973	Magic Woman Touch (**60**)
1974	The Air That I Breathe (**6**)
1975	Another Night (**71**); Sandy (**85**)

HUMBLE PIE: See Frampton, Peter

The Human League

Philip Oakey
(vocals)
Adrian Wright
(synthesizer)
Martyn Ware
(synthesizer)
Ian Craig Marsh
(synthesizer)

From the outset, Sheffield's Human League were a schizophrenic proposition; torn between Art and Pop, a synthesizers-and-voice-only combo surfacing in a noisy New Wave. Their debut single, "Being Boiled," attracted critical attention but their electronic pulsings and innovative live show—sparse, inert staging accompanied by "stereo" slide projections—defied the mythic conventions of rock & roll and ensconced them in a for-cultists-and-trendies-only pigeonhole.

They inked with Virgin Records in 1979 and released a startling debut LP, *Reproduction*, a prophetic swirl of synthesized rock and disco instrumentation that prefigured the electropop explosion of 1981. The Human League suffered the classic "second album syndrome" with the 1980 release of *Travelogue*, which, much to Virgin's dismay, failed to capture the audience Gary Numan had reached with a similar brand of synth-pop. Tension between the pop-single oriented Oakey/Wright axis and the art-inclined Marsh/Ware duo came to a head with the failure of the group's cover version of Gary Glitter's classic "Rock and Roll."

The group split amicably with Oakey and Wright maintaining the Human League moniker, while Marsh and Ware formed a musical corporation called the British Electric Foundation. Oakey recruited Ian Burden and ex-Rezillo Jo Callis on synthesizers and a pair of Sheffield disco dollies in order to honor contractual touring obligations. The new League, with a visual and visceral emphasis on love and glamour, joined forces with producer Martin Rushent in 1981 and recorded their first chart smash, "The Sound of the Crowd," which achieved wide play in Stateside discos throughout the summer of '81. "Sound" found its way onto their U.K. Number One album, *Dare*, which eventually yielded chart-busting singles with "Open Your Heart," "Love Action," and "Don't You Want Me."

Ware and Marsh's British Electric Foundation released a single called "(We Don't Need This) Fascist Groove Thang" under the name Heaven 17, and followed it up with a charting LP, *Penthouse and Pavement*, which contained disco hits with "Play to Win" and the title track. Though less commercially successful than their former partners, the British Electric Foundation—more a production company than a proper pop group—were far more ambitious and released a variety of records, cassettes, and compilations featuring collaborations with 1960s pop singers. (DAVID KEEPS)

The Incredible String Band

Mike Heron
(vocals, guitar, sitar, organ, dulcimer, harpsichord, recorder, harmonica, percussion)
Robin Williamson
(vocals, guitar, gimbri, sarangi, chahanai, oud, whistle, flute, bass, violin, piano, organ, percussion)

Say Incredible String Band to Britain's more hip record buyers and you will have said the first and last word on what popular music is all about.

New Musical Express, 1968

Take two exceptionally talented purveyors of traditional music from Scotland, immerse them in an underground cauldron of occult secrets, Eastern spells, and LSD in Swinging Sixties London and you have an approximation of what the Incredible String Band was all about.

The Incredibles began life as a folk trio and died a rock quintet. But most of the time they were just Mike and Robin in a category all their own, playing an array of instruments worthy of an ethnomusicology encyclopedia. Both brilliant songwriters, Heron differed from Williamson like Lennon from McCartney. As Steve Turner once wrote in *NME:* "The contrast was a good one—Williamson the poet and mystic whose voice barely lifted off the ground and Heron, more of a man of this world, with his down-to-earth rock-flavored music."

Heron's early musical development was characterized by the eclecticism for which he and Williamson would become famous. He went from a skiffle group to a "soul big band" to "an imitation Cliff Richard group" to singing Beatles songs in yet another band—after which he succumbed to the spell of Bob Dylan and went on the road as a solo artist. Then he met Robin Williamson and Clive Palmer, "who were doing British traditional music, but with a very odd approach—banjo and fiddle, you know. . . . They were looking for someone to play rhythm guitar, so they asked me to join. And that was the beginning of the Incredible String Band."

Moving from Edinburgh to Glasgow, the trio started an all-night club and began to draw crowds; Elektra's Joe Boyd heard their demo and signed them on the spot. Nine months on the national club circuit were followed by *The Incredible String Band* LP; then Palmer split for Afghanistan. It was now 1967.

In the hothouse of the emerging Underground, Heron and Williamson blossomed to the extent that they came to epitomize all that was best about that era. Though *The Incredible String Band* had won high praise from folk aficionados (and even from Bob Dylan), Heron and Williamson's debut as a duo, *The 5000 Spirits or the Layers of the Onion,* was the record that introduced all those Chinese, Arab, and Indian instruments and turned the Incredibles into cult heroes. Sporting a psychedelic cover by the same Fool who painted the Beatles' Apple Boutique, *Spirits* was described by Heron as "a vote of confidence in the flower power generation." Paul McCartney called it the album of the year.

Despite the exotic instruments, *Spirits* consisted of relatively straightforward songs about talking clouds and singing hedgehogs, plus Robin's poignant ode to "The First Girl I Loved" (memorably recorded—with a sex change—by Judy Collins). The subsequent *Hangman's Beautiful Daughter* found the Incredibles singing quarter tones, dispensing with rhymes, and taking bold liberties with conventional song structures. One of their metaphysical odysseys, "A Very Cellular Song," sprawled to eleven minutes-plus. ("I wrote most of it on one [acid] trip," said Mike.) Critical consensus rates *Hangman* the Incredibles' finest work, and it even made the British Top Five.

Around this time girlfriends Rose and Licorice were brought in to do menial musical chores onstage while Mike and Robin performed Incredible feats with twenty-odd instruments. Despite the heavy metaphysics, their late-Sixties concerts were delightfully loose, with balloons and incense contributing to the atmosphere of a Love-In. Heron's attributes included the widest grin this side of the Cheshire Cat; and when the traditional jigs began reeling from Williamson's fiddle, ecstatic flower children danced in the aisles. As *Melody Maker*'s Michael Watts wrote: "If any band is projecting pure love to its listeners, it is the Incredibles."

Particularly in America, the Incredibles remained a cult attraction. They made no concessions to the commercial mainstream, issued few singles, and even declined to perform familiar material in concert. Yet so prolific were they in their heyday that March 1969 saw

Robin Williamson (Ron Gott)

Mike Heron (Elektra)

the simultaneous release of two Incredible classics, *Wee Tam* and *The Big Huge*. Many of the songs were steeped in Biblical allusions and Hindu-derived beliefs in reincarnation and Maya (*all the world is but a play, be thou the joyful player*), yet the proceedings were seldom dour and very often disarmingly droll. Somehow it all worked.

But the Incredible String Band were very much a product of the Sixties; in retrospect it seems as if their magical mystery coach turned into an old pumpkin around the stroke of midnight December 31, 1969. Some observers blamed the Incredibles' abrupt transformation on their conversion to Scientology, a "church" founded by science-fiction pulp writer Ron Hubbard. In any event, there were no more *Hangman's Daughters, Wee Tams,* or *Big Huges.* An ambitious stage show, *U,* made for an entertaining evening at the Fillmore but thin gruel indeed as a double album. *U*'s main pantomimist, Malcolm LeMaistre, joined the band as bassist and singer; in 1972, with the addition of drummer John Gilston and saxophonist Gerald Dott, the Incredibles "went electric." Their slick new sounds, however, singularly failed to please, and in 1974, having become an embarrassment even to themselves, the String Band broke up.

Williamson and Heron had already produced "solo" endeavors, the former a book of poetry, *Home Thoughts from Abroad,* the latter an album called *Smiling Men with Bad Reputations* (featuring such surprise guests as John Cale and The Who). "Heron is a revelation as a rock singer," wrote *Melody Maker*'s Watts, but Mike's more recent efforts in the genre, as front man for a band called Reputation, attracted as little notice as Robin's solo work in a more traditional idiom. "Timeless" one decade, "anachronisms" the next. . . . The Incredible String Band may not mean much to the Eighties, but then perhaps the feeling is mutual. "I Was a Young Man Way Back in the 1960's" was a Williamson showstopper way back in 1967; Heron would join in on the chorus: *Hey, you young people, I just do not know/ I can't even understand you when you try to talk slow.*

(NICHOLAS SCHAFFNER)

U.S. Hit LPs

1968	The Hangman's Beautiful Daughter (**161**)
1969	The Big Huge (**180**); Wee Tam (**174**); Changing Horses (**166**)
1970	I Looked Up (**196**)
1971	"U" (**183**)
1972	Liquid Acrobat as Regards the Air (**189**)

The Jam

In 1977, when most Punk fans were happily pogoing to the vitriol of the Sex Pistols' "God Save the Queen," Paul Weller of the Jam was stoutly defending Her Majesty and announcing his plans to vote Conservative in the next election. Weller's reluctance to be involved in what he saw as the left-wing trendiness of the New Wave scene resulted in the Jam being dubbed "the acceptable face of Punk Rock" by the English music press.

Though the Jam had fierce driving energy and fast-paced music in common with the Punks, they owed equal allegiance to the Mods of the early Sixties. Weller was (and still is) obsessed with the style and music of the Mods. In particular, he was obsessed with the premier Mod group, The Who.

Appearing on stage in custom-tailored suits with a Union Jack hanging behind them, the Jam's clanging power chords from Weller's guitar and the leaps into the air of bassist Bruce Foxton evoked memories of The Who in their pre-*Tommy* days. Indeed, the resemblance was too striking for some listeners, who dismissed the Jam as shameless Who clones with little original to offer. Yet, though their music did have a somewhat familiar ring, the lyrics, with their searing indictment of society's injustices and hypocrisies, were nothing if not modern.

The Jam quickly proved that they were capable of turning out brilliant singles, but it seemed at first as if creating an entire album of the same quality might be beyond their grasp. Their first two LPs, *In The City* and *This Is The Modern World*, both released on Polydor in 1977, consisted mainly of undistinguished youth anthems delivered at breakneck speed. It wasn't until the Jam's third album, *All Mod Cons*, that Weller's songwriting talents fully emerged. Charles Shaar Murray of *NME* hailed it as "one of the handful of truly essential rock albums of the last few years." Fans concurred, voting *All Mod Cons* the best album of the year in the 1978 *NME* Readers' Poll.

By 1979, the Jam were firmly established as one of Britain's most popular bands. Their fourth album, *Setting Sons,* a darkly baroque record with interweaving themes of alienation, class conflict, lost idealism, and frustrated patriotism, earned the Jam their second U.K. gold record (the first had gone to *All Mod Cons*). And in March 1980, the Jam became the first artists in seven years to enter the British singles charts at Number One, with "Going Underground."

On the Jam's fifth album, *Sound Affects,* released in 1980, The Who took a backseat to the Beatles as an influence. In interviews Weller freely admitted that the Beatle's *Revolver* album had served as inspiration. (The uncharitable were quick to point out that in the case of "Start," the hit single from *Sound Affects,* Weller had received a bit more than inspiration from George Harrison's "Taxman.") *Sound Affects* was an amalgamation of the mid-Sixties psychedelic sound with the disco/funk of the late Seventies. The Jam capped a successful year by winning every conceivable category (including Weller as "Most Wonderful Human Being") in the 1980 *NME* poll.

Though the Jam acquired an enthusiastic cult following in the States, their songs, with references to such exclusively British phenomena as the class system, the welfare state, and the fading Empire, are simply too English to endear them to the majority of American rock fans. Speaking to *Trouser Press* in 1981, Weller seemed quite resigned to the Jam's limited popularity in America: "Our environment affects what we write and how we sound, and it is just a compromise to do anything other than that. That's why we'll never be successful outside of Britain."

(ELIZABETH SCHAFFNER)

Paul Weller
(guitar, vocals)
Rick Buckler
(drums)
Bruce Foxton
(bass guitar)

U.S. Hit LPs

1980	Setting Sons (137)

U.K. Hit Singles

1977	In the City (40); All Around the World (13); This Is the Modern World (36)
1978	News of the World (27); David Watts/"A" Bomb in Wardour Street (25); Down in the Tube Station at Midnight (15)
1979	Strange Town (15); When You're Young (17); Eton Rifles (3)
1980	Going Underground (1); Start (1)

Jethro Tull

The late Sixties and early Seventies were an era of pop myth making; day to day, the rock audience called for new giants, and giant killers. The issues were hotly debated in the streets and on the printed page. Who was better—Clapton or Hendrix? Who was faster—Beck or Lee? Who was bigger—Cream or Traffic?

Into the fray came Jethro Tull. Like some backwoods ruffians come to plunder the big city, they hit London in late '67. Led by a deranged-looking flute player, they flouted all conventions of musical decorum. In so doing, they turned a tepid, insular blues-rock scene completely topsy-turvy, and for the next ten years, Jethro Tull ruled the roost. The sight of Ian Anderson at center stage, perched storklike on one leg and blowing demonically on his flute, was a familiar one to a whole generation of concertgoers.

Back in 1967, though, Anderson & Co. were just another quasi-bluesy quartet gigging penniless around London. Prior to that, Anderson had been in the seven-member John Evans Band. When the Evans Band dispersed—most of them returning from London to their native Blackpool—Anderson and bassist Glenn

Ian Anderson
(vocals, flute, guitar, keyboards)
Martin Barre
(guitar)
John Evans
(keyboards)
Jeffrey Hammond-Hammond
(bass)
Barriemore Barlow
(drums)

Cornick stayed put in London. They met up with guitarist Mick Abrahams and drummer Clive Bunker. The foursome held their first rehearsal on Christmas Day 1967. Soon after, Anderson pulled a book off a friend's shelf; its author was Jethro Tull, an eighteenth-century agriculturalist who's remembered as the inventor of the seed drill. The group had a name.

Just as quickly, they were hammering out an identifiable sound. That sound was shaped by Anderson's unlikely choice of a lead instrument: the flute. It was all the more unlikely since he'd never picked up a wind instrument in his life. In any case, several months of apprenticing with Roland Kirk records found Anderson blowing in an enthusiastic, if unpolished, style.

Their first album, *This Was,* came out late in the year. It was a mix of straight blues and untraditional jazz-tinged pop, and served to pull Jethro Tull out of the pubs, graduating them to London's Marquee Club, where they more or less became the house band for a spell. But, as was growing obvious, Abrahams and Anderson could no longer co-exist in the same band. Abrahams left to form a new group, Blodwyn Pig, which stuck more closely to the blues-rock and big-band verities he favored. Jethro Tull settled on Martin Barre as his replacement.

Nineteen sixty-nine turned out to be a stellar year for the band. In between albums, they released a single, "Living in the Past," which scored in the Top Five. *Stand Up,* their second LP, went to Number One in England two days after its release and stayed there for eight weeks.

Stand Up is almost without argument Jethro Tull's greatest piece of music, a certifiable rock classic. Its ten songs were a tour de force of varied musical styles cast into witty, concise arrangements. Some of it was quite exotic for rock & roll. "Fat Man" was driven along not by guitars but by balalaikas. "Bourrée" brought Bach up to date. "For a Thousand Mothers" had a Near Eastern feel. "A New Day Yesterday," on the other hand, was pure Led Zep riff-rock. Unmistakably, this was a rock album, but rock salted with a potpourri of ingenious touches.

Tull toured heavily behind *Stand Up,* and thereupon began to earn a reputation as a must-see live band. Anderson played the demented master of ceremonies; decked out in a tattered full-length plaid overcoat, he'd lurch about on one leg, rolling his eyes, grimacing, thrusting out an arm, leering nastily at the crowd, muttering as if possessed. Almost from the moment of their arrival, Jethro Tull was headlining in the States.

The American public, young and old, got a glimpse of the band when they appeared on *Switched On Symphony,* a TV special that found the Los Angeles Philharmonic gamely trying to find common ground with assorted pop groups. The sole bright spot was Jethro Tull's "Bourrée," of which the *Los Angeles Times*'s classical-music critic wrote: "A clever fellow named Ian Anderson does marvelously obscene things to Bach, to a bourrée, and to a flute in one brief episode." *Life* magazine, in an issue with Spiro Agnew on the cover, devoted several pages to the group, noting approvingly that "despite appearances, Anderson is in the conservative camp as far as pop stars go: anti-liquor, anti-drugs, anti-groupies."

Anderson's sobering meditations on Christianity provided the substance for Jethro Tull's 1971 album. *Aqualung* took on organized religion ("one of the great moral tragedies of history," vouchsafed Anderson), finding the stern tenets of the church wanting in their lack of humanity. However little relish Anderson professed for the role, this antiestablishment broadside only further cemented his position as a generational spokesman. *Aqualung* expanded Tull's audience by leaps and bounds. The words were suitably heretical, while the songs were crunching, riff-heavy rockers, perfect for large arenas and less subtle than any music Jethro Tull had ever made.

Anderson was still playing the mad pied piper in a long jerkin-coat and medieval boots, and Tull was doing land-office business on the road. Yet, as an *NME* writer sourly observed, "Perhaps in response to the demands of American audiences, riffs rose to the point of overkill, Anderson's stage gestures simultaneously veering to the point of self-parody." There was more than a shred of truth to that. "Locomotive Breath" and "Wind Up," for example, would often go on for a half-hour or so, stretched out by guitar solos, flute improvisations, stage business, and so forth.

Thick as a Brick and *A Passion Play* came next. By now, a series of personnel changes found Ian Anderson and Martin Barre augmented by Jeffrey Hammond-Hammond, Barriemore Barlow, and John Evans. Except for Barre, all had been chums from Blackpool and had played together in the John Evans Band back in the mid-Sixties.

Anderson's latest projects both were continuous pieces of music spread over two sides. Again, they were ostensibly conceptual in lyric content. *Thick as a Brick* came elaborately packaged as a newspaper, its contents written entirely by Anderson, including a self-review of the record inside: ". . . their music spins a delicate web of sensitive sounds: sometimes lilting, sometimes soaring to form a brilliant backdrop for the meaningful lyrics and improvisational techniques. . . . One doubts at times the validity of what appears to be an expanding theme . . . but the result is at worst entertaining and at least aesthetically palatable." The LP went to Number One in the U.S., and an edit from side one made for a surprising hit single.

Passion Play was its labored, mannered follow-up. Jethro Tull was now playing rock chamber music, and the lyrics defied comprehension. One writer found it "an incredibly tiresome epic," while another carped that it "struggles under the weight of its pretensions." Perhaps harshest of all: "Anderson doesn't write mere songs anymore, he writes Homeric legends. Except he isn't Homer."

Licking his wounds, Anderson responded in a way no one expected. Citing "press abuse," he announced Jethro Tull's indefinite retirement. Like similar proclamations from David Bowie and Ray Davies, the breakup was short-lived, though. Soon enough, they were back in the studio, rehearsing material for *War Child.*

The mid-to-late Seventies found Jethro Tull touring, rehearsing, and recording fifty weeks out of the year. David Palmer, a classically trained keyboardist who'd orchestrated tracks on virtually every Tull album, became a permanent member, as did a new bassist, John Glascock. This lineup recorded a pair of delightful LPs, *Songs from the Wood* and *Heavy Horses,* that paid homage to their English folk roots and the rustic world of peasants and maidens.

In 1980, a few more albums down the road, Anderson dissolved the band, retaining only Martin Barre. With new recruits, he made his seventeenth album, *A.* On tour, Jethro Tull still sold out the large halls, though the records had stopped going gold and

Ian Anderson

platinum. Though the future of the band looked uncertain, one expected that Anderson, in his indefatigable way, would manage to keep himself occupied.

(PARKE PUTERBAUGH)

U.S. Hit Singles

1971	Hymn 43 (**91**)
1972	Living in the Past (**11**)
1973	A Passion Play (**80**)
1974	Bungle in the Jungle (**12**)
1975	Minstrel in the Gallery (**79**)
1976	Locomotive Breath (**62**)
1977	The Whistler (**59**)

U.S. Hit LPs

1969	This Was (**62**); Stand Up (**20**)
1970	Benefit (**11**)

1971	Aqualung (**7**)
1972	Thick As a Brick (**1**); Living in the Past (**3**)
1973	A Passion Play (**1**)
1974	War Child (**2**)
1975	Minstrel in the Gallery (**7**)
1976	M.U.—The Best of Jethro Tull (**13**); Too Old to Rock 'n' Roll, Too Young To Die! (**14**)
1977	Songs from the Wood (**8**); Repeat—The Best of Jethro Tull—Vol. II (**21**)
1978	Heavy Horses (**19**); Bursting Out (**21**)
1979	Stormwatch (**22**)
1980	"A" (**30**)

U.K. Hit Singles

1969	Living in the Past (**3**); Sweet Dream (**9**); Love Story (**29**)
1970	The Witch's Promise/The Teacher (**4**)
1971	Life's a Long Song (**11**)
1976	Ring Out Solstice Bells (**28**)

Joe Jackson Band

"Joe Jackson is a man who can hold his head up proudly in the morning and not have to worry whether his success is due to his good looks," wrote *New Musical Express*'s Charles Shaar Murray. And indeed, with his petulant baby face, his round balding head, and his extremely tall, gawky frame, Joe Jackson was a very odd-looking rock star. Yet out of this peculiarly shaped being came some of the best pop music of the late Seventies.

Jackson was a one-time percussion student at the Royal Academy of Music. In the mid-Seventies, he held a variety of jobs, one of which was serving as musical director and piano player at the Playboy Club in his hometown of Portsmouth. In 1978 he signed a publishing contract with Albion Music and, shortly afterward, a recording contract with A&M Records.

Jackson's first album, *Look Sharp*, received considerable airplay and became a substantial hit in America. Jackson wrote economical, witty, energetic songs, most often about the more negative aspects of romance.

I'm the Man, released in late '79, was Jackson's tour de force, evoking a wide spectrum of emotions, from the pointedly sardonic comment on merchandising of the title cut to the slyly ironic view of sexuality in "It's Different for Girls" and the passionate repudiation of the rock star life-style in "Don't Wanna Be Like That." Unlike *Look Sharp, I'm the Man* was successful on both sides of the Atlantic.

"This album represents a desperate attempt to make some sense of Rock and Roll. Deep in our hearts, we knew it was doomed to failure. The question remains: Why did we try?" Thus read the liner notes of the third and final LP by the Joe Jackson Band. *Beat Crazy,* despite a change of musical direction towards a more sensual reggae-dub sound, was as discouraged and dispirited as its liner notes, and a few months later the band broke up.

Joe Jackson resurfaced in 1981 with Jumpin' Jive, a band dedicated to reviving jazz music of the Forties Swing Era. Though some people predicated that this endeavor would deal a fatal blow to Jackson's

Joe Jackson
(vocals, piano, melodica)
Graham Maby
(bass guitar)
Dave Houghton
(drums)
Gary Sanford
(guitar)

(*Ron Gott*)

popularity, Jumpin' Jive was warmly received when it toured the States, and an album of the same name fared decently in the American charts.

(ELIZABETH SCHAFFNER)

U.S. Hit Singles

1979	Is She Really Going Out with Him? (**21**)

U.S. Hit LPs

1979	Look Sharp! (**20**); I'm the Man (**22**)
1980	Beat Crazy (**41**)

U.K. Hit Singles

1979	Is She Really Going Out with Him? (**13**)
1980	It's Different for Girls (**5**)

Elton John

If the Sixties were magic years for innovative rock groups, the Seventies turned out to be prime time for solo singer/songwriters. And of the dozens who attained stardom, none rose higher or stayed on top longer than Elton John.

He was a strange rock star, this pudgy, gap-toothed, balding, and bespectacled Englishman. At a time when guitar was king, he played the piano. When moodiness and introspection were in vogue, he played the clown with outrageous costumes and ninety pairs of glasses. When everyone else was worried about making a "statement," he didn't even write his own lyrics.

And yet throughout the Seventies, Elton John's canny, catchy pop-rock came to dominate—even to define—the music scene. You couldn't turn on the radio without hearing something by him. A third of his releases made the Top Twenty. His concerts were instant sellouts.

The bouncy little man in the foot-high platforms and pink feather boas had a long, hard climb to the top. Reginald Kenneth Dwight played the piano all during his childhood, but seemed an unlikely candidate for superstardom. Winner of a scholarship to the prestigious Royal Academy of Music, he turned aside the classics in his mid-teens and sold his soul to rock & roll.

The early rock years were spent as keyboardist in Bluesology, a professional backup band that eventually became Long John Baldry's backing unit. Reg Dwight might have continued for years playing obscure blues numbers, but he had other ideas. Taking the first names of Elton Dean (the band's sax player) and singer John Baldry, he answered a trade paper advertisement for a songwriter. "Elton John" could write the tunes, but not the words; poet Bernie Taupin could do the words, not the melodies—and rock history was made.

The first John-Taupin hit in America was "Your Song," a moody, melodic number about almost-requited love. Released at Christmastime, 1970, it became one of 1971's first big hits and put Elton John in the same league with the other soloists who were emerging at that time—Cat Stevens and James Taylor. "Friends," John's second U.S. hit, seemed to confirm his status as a thoughtful, sentimental balladeer.

Those who bought the Elton John albums, however, discovered quite a different kind of musician. Here was a fellow who wasn't afraid to attack the piano in a wild manner not unlike that of Jerry Lee Lewis. Elton would hammer at the keys on "Burn Down the Mission" and "Take Me to the Pilot." He gave a new, hard edge to ballads like "Country Comfort" (covered, significantly, by Rod Stewart) and "Border Song," and went all out on "Can I Put You On" and "Honey Roll." His third album, 11-17-70, was an equally energetic live recording, with only the most sparse backing.

Yet the softer tunes continued to get the airplay. "Levon" and "Tiny Dancer," the most melodic cuts from *Madman Across the Water*, were chosen as singles.

Elton's American tours changed all that. No bookish poet who murmured his songs from behind the Steinway, he was an outrageous rock & roller who wouldn't think twice of getting up to dance on the piano. He loved the Beatles; he adored the Stones; he thought Fifties-style rock was the greatest; and "Boogie!" was his battle cry.

Suddenly, a different sort of Elton John song was sent over the airwaves. "Crocodile Rock," a paean to the Golden Age of Rock, hit Number One in America in February 1973—his first single to do so. "Saturday Night's Alright for Fighting," "Bennie and the Jets," and "The Bitch Is Back" all were huge hits—and all showed the hard-hitting, unsentimental side of John and Taupin.

To be sure, Elton's prodigious output included many gentler songs. "Goodbye Yellow Brick Road" was the hit single from the double album of that name, which also included a hymn to Marilyn Monroe, "Candle in the Wind." Perhaps the oft-played FM radio favorite "Funeral for a Friend/ Love Lies Bleeding" sums up the two sides of Elton John best; the first half is a dreamy sonata, the second half a steamy rocker.

In the mid-'70s, he turned his talented hand to promotion. The soulful Kiki Dee and veteran English star Cliff Richard came under the Elton John umbrella; John's magic superstar name proved enough to fuel their middling careers. But as a backer, Elton's biggest find was Neil Sedaka, a pop-rock leftover from the early Sixties whose career had foundered. Neil's songs became immensely popular all over again on Elton's Rocket Records label.

By 1975, Elton John was at his peak—displaying his wild antics at their most outré as the Pinball Wizard in the film *Tommy;* hobnobbing with such celebrities as Billie Jean King, for whom he wrote "Philadelphia Freedom"; watching album after album sell millions of copies.

Since then—especially in the very late Seventies—things haven't gone quite so well. A hair transplant, attempted in 1978 to cover one of rock's most famous foreheads, didn't take; all photos of E.J. at that time show him with hats. In 1978, Elton "retired" from show biz, complete with a farewell concert; few doubted that he would be back soon, and so he was. That year, he also split with Bernie Taupin, and lyrical chores were handled by Gary Osborne (of the duo Vigrass and Osborne); since then, Taupin has returned to cowrite a few new songs. In 1979, Elton tried his hand at disco with a dismal album called *Victim of Love*. In the disappointing years of the late Seventies, he was a victim, all right—but the culprit was hype.

Elton John, however, is no mean talent, and a slump—even a prolonged one—isn't likely to finish him off. His first album of the Eighties, *21 at 33,* received wide critical approval and landed him a genuine hit single, "Little Jeannie." His 1981 album, *The Fox,* was again well-received, if a commercial dud.

(HENRY McNULTY)

(*MCA Records*)

U.S. Hit Singles

1970 Border Song (**92**)
1971 Your Song (**8**); Friends (**34**)

1972 Rocket Man (**6**); Honky Cat (**8**); Levon (**24**); Tiny Dancer (**41**)	**1976** Here and There (**4**); Blue Moves (**3**)
	1977 Elton's Greatest Hits Vol. II (**21**)

1972 Rocket Man (**6**); Honky Cat (**8**); Levon (**24**); Tiny Dancer (**41**)

1973 Crocodile Rock (**1**); Goodbye Yellow Brick Road (**2**); Daniel (**2**); Saturday Night's Alright for Fighting (**12**)

1974 Bennie and the Jets (**1**); Don't Let the Sun Go Down on Me (**2**); The Bitch Is Back (**4**)

1975 Island Girl (**1**); Philadelphia Freedom (**1**); Lucy in the Sky with Diamonds (**1**); Someone Saved My Life Tonight (**4**)

1976 Don't Go Breaking My Heart [with Kiki Dee] (**1**); Sorry Seems to Be the Hardest Word (**6**); Grow Some Funk of Your Own (**14**); I Feel Like a Bullet (In the Gun of Robert Ford) (**18**)

1977 Bite Your Lip (Get Up and Dance!) (**28**)

1978 Part-Time Love (**22**); Ego (**34**)

1979 Mama Can't Buy You Love (**9**); Victim of Love (**31**)

1980 Little Jeannie (**3**); (Sartorial Eloquence) Doncha Wanna Play This Game No More (**39**)

U.S. Hit LPs

1970 Elton John (**4**)

1971 Tumbleweed Connection (**5**); ''Friends'' (**36**); 11-17-70 (**11**); Madman across the Water (**8**)

1972 Honky Chateau (**1**)

1973 Don't Shoot Me I'm Only The Piano Player (**1**); Goodbye Yellow Brick Road (**1**)

1974 Caribou (**1**); Elton John—Greatest Hits (**1**)

1975 Empty Sky (**6**); Captain Fantastic and the Brown Dirt Cowboy (**1**); Rock of the Westies (**1**)

1976 Here and There (**4**); Blue Moves (**3**)

1977 Elton's Greatest Hits Vol. II (**21**)

1978 A Single Man (**15**)

1979 The Thom Bell Sessions (**51**); Victim of Love (**35**)

1980 21 at 33 (**13**)

U.K. Hit Singles

1971 Your Song (**7**)

1972 Rocket Man (**2**); Crocodile Rock (**5**); Honky Cat (**31**)

1973 Daniel (**4**); Goodbye Yellow Brick Road (**6**); Saturday Night's Alright For Fighting (**7**); Step into Christmas (**24**)

1974 Lucy in the Sky with Diamonds (**10**); Candle in the Wind (**11**); The Bitch Is Back (**15**); Don't Let the Sun Go Down on Me (**16**); Goodbye Yellow Brick Road (**36**)

1975 Philadelphia Freedom (**12**); Island Girl (**14**); Someone Saved My Life Tonight (**22**)

1976 Don't Go Breaking My Heart [with Kiki Dee] (**1**); Pinball Wizard (**7**); Sorry Seems to Be the Hardest Word (**11**); Bennie and the Jets (**37**)

1977 Crazy Water (**27**); Bite Your Lip (Get Up and Dance) (**28**)

1978 Ego (**34**); Part-Time Love (**16**); Song for Guy (**4**)

1979 Are You Ready for Love? (**42**)

Joy Division

Ian Curtis
(vocals)
Bernard Albrecht
(guitar, synthesizer)
Peter Hook
(bass)
Stephen Morris
(drums)

It is sadly, perversely ironic that Joy Division attained commercial status and across-the-board critical acclaim simultaneously with the rock & roll mythmaking of lead singer Ian Curtis, who committed suicide in May 1980 at the tender age of twenty-three.

Joy Division began as Warsaw, a predictably high-decibel punky thrash machine that emerged from the scene centering around Manchester's Electric Circus in 1976 and '77. They released an independent single, ''Ideal for Living,'' and contributed to a Virgin Records live compilation but failed to capture critical/cult attention until their association with the fledgling Factory Records and producer Martin Hannett, who immediately launched them with a new name (taken from the Nazi tag for the prostitutes' wings in concentration camps). Their debut LP, *Unknown Pleasures*, captured both the primitive energy of Warsaw and the sophisticated Hannett production style. It proved an evergreen independent release, selling steadily as Joy Division became headliners on the club circuit and critical raves filtered across the Atlantic.

Curtis's suicide occurred during the final stages of mixing the followup long-player, *Closer*, on the eve of a debut American club tour. The resulting press eulogies certainly helped push Joy Division into the public consciousness, and their undisputed classic, ''Love Will Tear Us Apart,'' a splendidly orchestrated, synthesizer-driven sorrow symphony, broke the U.K. Top Twenty and created a similar, though localized, sensation in American rock discos.

Joy Division's critical canonization was virtually simultaneous with the massive resurgence of interest in the Doors' charismatic Jim Morrison—an odd coincidence made even stranger by the vocal similarities between Morrison and Curtis and their mutual poetic fascination with isolation, alienation, and death. ''Love,'' in fact, was named best import single of 1980 by magazines as diverse as *New York Rocker*, *Village Voice*, and *Rolling Stone*.

The posthumous *Closer* exhibited greater maturity and musical sophistication and its gloomy atmospherics seem somehow frighteningly prophetic; Curtis's mournful croak blended perfectly with the band's dolorous melodies to express emotional turmoil in no uncertain terms. After Curtis hanged himself, the remaining members persevered as New Order. Their debut 45, ''Ceremony,'' ranked among the best independent releases of 1981.

(DAVID KEEPS)

U.K. Hit Singles

1980 Love Will Tear Us Apart (**13**)

King Crimson

Born in the basement of a seedy cafe in the West End of London during the winter of 1969, King Crimson was the brainchild of Robert Fripp, a young guitar wizard from Devon, and Pete Sinfield, a computer specialist with a knack for writing surrealist lyrics.

Their intent was to integrate rock with classical, jazz and avant-garde music. They wanted to jar their listeners' emotions, to take the rock & roll genre to extremes, at times even to the threshold of pain. The name King Crimson was invented by Sinfield as a synonym for Beelzebub, the prince of Hell.

Scarcely two months after their debut gig on April 28, 1969, at London's Speakeasy, King Crimson were hailed by critics and fans as the year's most exciting and innovative new band. Reviewers of their gigs reported having seen members of the audience literally burst into tears from the emotional impact of the music. The musicians in the band themselves admitted to being devastated by their own performances.

Robert Fripp, perched on a velvet-cushioned stool, unsmilingly evoked extraordinary sounds from his Gibson SG. He and guitar were the nuclei around which spun kinetic rhythms and piercing sax or flute solos from Ian McDonald.

The Court of the Crimson King, released in October 1969, contains songs of shattering intensity ("21st Century Schizoid Man") and melodic, jazzy, and psychedelic ballads. The album scaled the upper reaches of the British charts, and the band did a nine-week tour of the U.S. Upon their return Greg Lake and Ian McDonald quit the band because, to quote McDonald: "It is not happy music."

Undaunted by this misfortune, Fripp quickly replaced McDonald and Lake (the latter would soon become the "L" in ELP), and King Crimson completed its second album, *In the Wake of Poseidon,* the title referring to the end of the Piscean age and the dawn of the Aquarian. Released in the spring of 1970 *Poseidon* shows the emergence of Fripp as composer and soloist as well as Crimson's departure from conventional rock to a new avant-garde, jazz style. The third album, *Lizard,* was immediately intriguing for its medieval-style illuminated cover. Around the letter "I" in the word "Crimson" are painted the figures of the Beatles and Yoko Ono on a boardwalk. Musically, *Lizard* is dense and impressionistic, representing Crimson's furthest departure from popular music. In 1971, King Crimson put out two more albums, *Islands* and *Earthbound,* the latter a live recording not issued in the U.S.

In 1972 King Crimson underwent a dramatic transformation, emerging as a heavy space-rock band. This, the group's final incarnation, consisted of Fripp on guitar, John Wetton on bass, violinist David Cross, and former Yes drummer, Bill Bruford. This lineup released three albums—*Starless and Bible Black, Larks' Tongue in Aspic,* and *Red*—over the next two years.

While recording their last album, *Red,* Fripp underwent a personality crisis that compelled him to announce his and the band's retirement during a concert in New York's Central Park on July 5, 1974.

Two posthumous albums, one a European compilation called *R.I.P.* and the other a live album called *U.S.A.* (which features former Roxy Music violinist Eddy Jobson), were released in 1975.

After the breakup, John Wetton joined Uriah Heep and later reunited with Bill Bruford and Eddy Jobson in the band U.K. Ian McDonald and Mike Giles teamed up as McDonald and Giles. When this failed, McDonald helped form Foreigner, and Giles turned to session work.

Robert Fripp retreated to the Sherbourne Academy of Continuous Education in 1974. There he studied and practiced the wisdom of philosophers Gurdjieff, Ouspensky, and J. G. Bennett for three years.

In 1977, he returned to the music world to play guitar on David Bowie's *"Heroes."* Acting as a sort of musical godfather, Fripp subsequently produced or performed with such artists as Blondie, Daryl Hall, Peter Gabriel, and the Roches. He also collaborated with Brian Eno on the albums *No Pussyfooting* (1973) and *Evening Star* (1975).

In 1978, Fripp released his first solo attempt, *Exposure.* On it, he boldly attempted to expand the definition of rock music with synthesizers and tape loops and "found" music (dialogue or sounds recorded live and then transposed upon the music). *Exposure* was a diverse compilation that ranged from hard rock to jazz to hypnotic electronic treating of the guitar, which Fripp dubbed "Frippertronics."

With "Frippertronics" as his trademark, Fripp launched what he called "the Drive to 1981," during which time he released *God Save the Queen/Under Heavy Manners* (1979), and *The Power Must Fall* (1981). After occasionally performing his solo tape loops and guitar pieces in bookshops, churches, record stores, and even pizza parlors in Europe and America, Fripp decided to try his hand at bandleading again and formed the League of Gentlemen. With former XTC member Barry Andrews, bassist Sara Lee, and Johnny Toobad on drums, the League's repertoire consisted of short, danceable numbers over which guitars and keyboards intertwined. The League broke up in late 1980 after recording one album.

Then, as if to prove that all things run in cycles, Fripp re-formed King Crimson with first-time members Adrian Belew (guitar and vocals) and Tony Levin (bass), and a familiar face, Bill Bruford, back on drums. Throughout 1981, the new combo vigorously toured Europe and America, and their album, *Discipline,* in some ways was a musical continuation of the old King Crimson.

Fripp's idiosyncratic guitar playing, as well as his understated and accessible profile, have engendered a cult of Frippophiles. Their hero meanwhile took up residence in New York City, where he continued to sponsor and encourage young artists and musicians.

(TIMOTHY SCHAFFNER)

Robert Fripp
(guitar)
Pete Sinfield
(lyrics)
Ian McDonald
(alto sax, clarinet, flute, mellotron)
Greg Lake
(bass and vocals)
Mike Giles
(drums)

Robert Fripp (Polydor)

U.S. Hit Singles

1970   In the Court of the Crimson King,
       Part One (**80**)

U.S. Hit LPs

1969	In the Court of the Crimson King (**28**)
1970	In the Wake of Poseidon (**31**)
1971	Lizard (**113**)
1972	Islands (**76**)
1973	Larks Tongues in Aspic (**61**)

1974	Starless and Bible Black (**64**); Red (**66**)
1975	U.S.A. (**125**)

(BY ROBERT FRIPP)

1979	Exposure (**79**)
1980	God Save the Queen Under Heavy Manners (**110**)

Billy J. Kramer

Billy J. Kramer (née William Ashton) deserves a place in our Hot Hundred if only because he was, in a sense, *the* original British Invader. When manager Brian Epstein traveled to New York in November 1963 to rustle up a Capitol recording contract for the Beatles, he brought Kramer with him. Billy J. proceeded to flash his winning smile on *The Ed Sullivan Show*—some two months before anyone in America had heard of the Beatles—as a sort of dry run for the Fab Four's own historic appearance the following February 9.

Like his fellow Liverpudlian, Gerry Marsden, Billy Kramer began the decade working for British Railways—to metamorphose at lunch hour into a Cavern Club heartthrob. After the Beatles scored their EMI recording contract, Epstein began to picture himself as the tycoon of Mersey Beat and snapped up both Gerry and Billy J. He didn't, however, much care for Kramer's local backing group, the Coasters, so he linked him up with an established Manchester band called the Dakotas. According to *The Big Beat* (a 1964 U.S. British Invasion fanzine), "The marriage of the zing singing of Billy J. to the true-beat accompaniment of the Daks has proven a brilliant stroke on the part of Epstein. These boys just have to step onto the stage and the fans go wild!"

George Martin, however, recalled in his memoirs that though "Billy was certainly a very good-looking boy, when I listened to him I was forced to the conclusion that his was not the greatest voice in the world . . . but Brian was so keen that I agreed. I decided the only way I could ever make a hit out of him was always to double-track his voice . . . [and] where there was any offending phrase from the Kramer tonsils, I [overdubbed] a bit of [electronically treated] piano."

Nonetheless, Billy J. clicked massively with his first release, "Do You Want to Know a Secret?," a track off the Beatles' first LP. This was followed by three other Lennon-McCartney penned hits, "Bad to Me," "I'll Keep You Satisfied," and "From a Window." But though Kramer also successfully crooned the American songs "Little Children" and Burt Bacharach's "Trains and Boats and Planes," he was known primarily for his Beatles connections and his pleasant face, and never established a distinct style or identity of his own. By 1965, he was already a fading memory.

Like Gerry Marsden, Billy J. eventually became a fixture of Britain's cabaret circuit. He enjoyed a moment of recycled Stateside glory on Richard Nader's 1973 package tour, "The 1960s' British Invasion Revisited." Long plagued by drinking and weight problems, Kramer was back in the recording studios in 1981, attempting a comeback album. In the meantime, his sister, Elkie Brooks, established herself as a leading British singer.

(NICHOLAS SCHAFFNER)

U.S. Hit Singles

1964	Little Children (**7**); Bad to Me (**9**); I'll Keep You Satisfied (**30**); From a Window (**23**)
1965	It's Gotta Last Forever (**67**); Trains and Boats and Planes (**47**)

U.S. Hit LPs

1964	Little Children (**48**)

U.K. Hit Singles

1963	Do You Want to Know a Secret? (**2**); Bad to Me (**1**); I'll Keep You Satisfied (**4**)
1964	Little Children (**1**); From a Window (**10**)
1965	Trains and Boats and Planes (**12**)

Led Zeppelin

Robert Plant
(vocals)
Jimmy Page
(guitar)
John Paul Jones
(bass, keyboards)
John Bonham
(drums)

It's a fairly safe bet to say that right now, even as you read this, somewhere an FM radio station is airing "Stairway to Heaven," the classic staple by the most imitated, most successful British heavy metal outfit of the Seventies.

Jimmy Page formed Led Zep in 1968 to fulfill leftover contractual obligations caused by the sudden demise of the Yardbirds. Page had been wooed to join that group as early as 1965 (as a replacement for Eric Clapton), but recurring glandular fever and lucrative session work kept him off the boards until the departure of Yardbirds bassist Paul Samwell-Smith in 1966.

By the time he did join, Middlesex-born Page could claim an impressive list of sessions and hit singles (including work on "I Can't Explain," "Gloria," Tom Jones' "It's Not Unusual," and numbers by Petula Clark and Herman's Hermits) and a stint as house

Jones, Bonham, Page, and Plant (Chuck Pulin)

producer for Andrew Loog Oldham's Immediate label.

John Paul Jones was also a respected session man, having worked with the Rolling Stones, Lulu, Dusty Springfield, and even Shirley Bassey. He often crossed paths with Page, and they bandied the idea of forming a group while working on Donovan's *Hurdy Gurdy Man* with a young drummer named John Bonham.

Bonham, like his mate Robert Plant, was far less celebrated than the Page-Jones foundation, playing anonymously in embarrassingly named Birmingham area bands like the Way of Life and the Band of Joy (who backed Plant on solo singles for CBS). Page's search for "New" Yardbirds led him to second choices in Bonham and Plant after his initial selections, vocalist Terry Reid and B. J. Wilson (subsequently of Procol Harum), fell through.

Peter Grant, ex-pro wrestler and film double for Robert Morley, picked up the managerial reins (after considerable success with the pre-Animals Alan Price Combo and the Nashville Teens) and steered the group through Page's remaining contractual obligations, and the selection of a new name. The Whoopee Cushion and the Mad Dogs were rejected in favor of a variation on Keith Moon's jibe that the group would go down like "a lead balloon."

Early audiences, promoters, and critics were apathetic, but Grant scored a coup by signing the group to Atlantic Records without a demo tape (though certainly aided by their reputations and label mate Dusty Springfield's recommendation). Zeppelin, unhappy with their reception in native England, decided to concentrate on breaking in the U.S. Their self-titled debut LP, released in late 1968, drew critical raves back home and, despite mixed reviews, sold gold in the U.S. by early '69.

Led Zeppelin was a startling debut, integrating classic blues structures with heavy-metal blare and an incredible feel for dynamics, texture, and precision. Classic cuts like the Yardbirds' unrecorded "Dazed and Confused," an instant FM hit in the days of truly progressive radio, stood out of the eclectic brew.

Plant's leeringly sexual vocalizing on "Whole Lotta Love" scored another big hit and pushed *Led Zeppelin II* to the top of the charts on both sides of the Atlantic.

By 1970, with the release of *Led Zeppelin III,* the group had risen to the forefront of the genre they had so radically changed. Their third album contained the same hard-rock formulas of its predecessor, but also introduced partly acoustic, folk-styled material and hippie metaphysics that would come to the fore in the classic "Stairway" on 1971's *Led Zeppelin IV.*

Zep's 1973 American tour demolished the previous records established by the Beatles, hot on the heels of the enormous success of *Houses of the Holy.* The tour grossed an incredible $3 million (though just a drop in the bucket of their reported $30 million earnings for 1973). Considerably well-heeled, the group and manager Grant created their own record label, Swan Song, in 1974. Bad Company, Maggie Bell, and the Pretty Things were among their first signings.

Despite no LP or tour in 1974, Led Zep remained high in the annual critics' and readers' polls worldwide. By the 1975 release of the double LP *Physical Graffiti,* the group had built a reputation as one of the top international live acts, even though they had only once appeared on TV and never officially released a single in their homeland. Despite frequently reported hotel-smashing and groupie exploits, the group's stringent control on exposure and record releases helped create a "might never catch them again" mystique that often created riots at box offices when tickets were put on sale.

Their 1975 U.S. tour was a sensory assault incorporating neon lights, laser beams, and seventy-thousand watts to pump out the old faves and new hits like "Trampled Underfoot." An estimated fifteen thousand New York fans queued up for over twenty-four hours for their Madison Square Garden show, and in Boston a riot at the box office caused more than $75,000 damage.

Robert Plant's serious auto accident while vacationing in Greece (1975) slowed the band considerably and started a string of unfortunate incidents that some superstitiously stalwart Page fans have attributed to his increased fascination with the occult. The success of Led Zep enabled Page to indulge his mysticism, and he purchased a London occult bookstore, Equinox, along with Boleskine House, where turn-of-the-century black magician Aleister Crowley had lived.

Zep's popularity leveled off at the peak reached by *Physical Graffiti,* though the followup, *Presence,* was still a guaranteed platinum seller. But the rumblings of the New Wave and its inherent disenfranchisement of disgust with rich arena rockers and prima-donna stars like Plant, began to turn the heads of a new generation of potential fans. Constantly labeled "boring old farts," the group was regularly assaulted in the British rock press, and was even subjected to the lampooning of Californians Little Roger and the Goosebumps, who wedded the lyrics of the *Gilligan's Island* TV theme to the tune of "Stairway to Heaven" (an independent release, it was squashed by an injunction from Led Zeppelin).

More troubles followed—the tragedy of Robert Plant's son's death in 1978 and assault indictments against Bonham and manager Grant for the beating of a photographer—even while Zep stretched their stylistic boundaries in 1979's *In Through the Out Door.* But the death of drummer "Bonzo" Bonham after an all-night drinking bout in 1980 cast a pall over the group, and as of early 1982, they had neither played nor recorded as Led Zeppelin since.

(DAVID KEEPS)

LOVICH, LENE: See Stiff Records

Lulu

Lulu, 1981

Among the golden girls of mid-Sixties British pop—from the soulful stylings of Dusty Springfield to the middle-of-the-road Pepsi Generation anthems of actress-thrush Petula Clark—Lulu, the carrot-topped Mod songstress, most closely approached the rock energy of her contemporary British Invaders. Although she was relatively unknown in the U.S. until 1967, Lulu, born Marie MacDonald McLaughlan Lawrie, was already a local star in her native Glasgow by age thirteen.

Lulu fronted a group called the Gleneagles and was quickly signed to Decca Records after a microphone-breaking audition that was prompted by massive publicity in the Scottish *Daily Express*. She recorded her first hit, "Shout," in 1964, just as the Stones and Bealtes had begun their assault upon the British pop consciousness. By the time she was fifteen, the energetic, booming-voiced lass had left school and relocated to London, redubbing her combo Lulu and the Luvvers. As a teen sensation, Lulu boasted a boisterous honey-and-whiskey vocal style, a perky, earthy personality, and trendy Mod fashions.

Lulu and the Luvvers scored a string of chart hits, played a Command Performance for the Queen, warmed up for the Beatles on numerous occasions, and even appeared in a ridiculous teen movie titled *Gonks Go Beat*. But by 1967, Lulu decided to split with the Luvvers and pursue a career as a ballad singer. On a final tour with the Beach Boys she met James Clavell (author of *Shogun*), who cast her with Sidney Poitier in *To Sir with Love*.

Sir was a worldwide smash, but, far more important, an accurate depiction of the Mod scene and working-class youth in England. Lulu's heart-rending rendition of the title song eventually sold four million copies worldwide and stayed at the top of the U.S. charts for six straight weeks, longer than any previous single by a foreign female artist.

Her first and only tour of America followed *Sir*'s success, but she quickly returned to England, where she hosted a BBC-TV series and married Bee Gee Maurice Gibb. On one of her celebrated live music programs, Jimi Hendrix shocked a nation by stopping mid-tune, uttering "Fuck this," and launching into an impromptu ten-minute tribute to Cream. Lulu won the prestigious Eurovision Song Contest with "Boom Bang-a-bang" in 1969. Meanwhile, her marriage to Gibb foundered and eventually ended in a separation in 1973.

Soon afterward, she crossed paths with David Bowie, newly into his superstar ascendancy, and their mutual admiration resulted in a hit cover version of "The Man Who Sold the World" for Lulu. In 1975 she married hairdresser-to-royalty John Frieda and gave birth to a son, Jordan, two years later, all the while continuing to host BBC programs and performing in a London Palladium production of *Peter Pan*. In 1981 she appeared on U.S. TV in the syndicated Fifties rock & roll show *Let's Rock* and relaunched her U.S. recording career with an LP that contained the slickly produced, discofied MOR hit "I Could Never Miss You (More Than I Do)."

(DAVID KEEPS)

MADNESS: See Two-Tone Records

Manfred Mann

Manfred Mann
(keyboards)
Paul Jones
(vocals, harmonica)
Mike Vickers
(guitar, sax, flute)
Tom McGuinness
(bass)
Mike Hugg
(drums, vibes)

Manfred Mann's first and only U.S. Number One hit—a cover of the Exciters' "Do Wah Diddy Diddy"—made them, after the Beatles and the Animals, the third British group to top the American charts. (Manfred Mann was indeed a *group,* as album titles like *The Five Faces of Manfred Mann* would remind us, when they weren't given over to such belabored puns as *Mann Made.*) Like the Animals, Manfred Mann consisted of five R&B aficionados who hit the commercial jackpot with a series of teeny-pop singles—mostly concocted by the jinglesmiths of Denmark Street and the Brill Building—that the musicians themselves frankly disparaged.

Manfred Mann himself was born in South Africa with the name Michael Lubowitz. The jazz pianist with the trademark beard, clean-shaven upper lip, and horn-rim spectacles first made the London music scene in 1962, when he teamed up with Mike Hugg to form the Mann-Hugg Blues Brothers. By the summer of 1963, the group had acquired Vickers and a following at Soho's Marquee Club; their first unsuccessful single—an instrumental called "Why Should We Not"—was released on EMI's HMV label under the collective pseudonym of Manfred Mann. "Manny"'s next move was to recruit Tom McGuinness and Paul Jones; the latter had previously declined Brian Jones' invitation to sing with the fledgling Rolling Stones. At the time, the dashing and articulate would-be actor still felt loath to abandon his undergraduate studies at Oxford University for the pursuit of pop stardom.

The Manfreds' lucky break came in the first weeks of 1964, when their third single "5-4-3-2-1" was selected for the signature tune of *Ready Steady Go* and became a major British hit. Such sequels as "Hubble Bubble Toil and Trouble" perpetuated the Mann formula of using nursery-rhyme ditties for their singles fodder. That the Manfreds were all earnest blues and jazz buffs would only become apparent with some of their album tracks.

After coasting to international stardom on the strains of "do-wah-diddy-diddy-dum-diddy-do," Manfred Mann found a successful (if almost painfully obvious) followup in the Shirelles' "Sha La La." When the band toured America with Peter and Gordon in late 1964, Paul Jones' gyrations left many a damp seat in their wake.

Back home, Manfred Mann's 1965 EP *The One in the Middle* owed most of its phenomenal popularity to the inclusion of "With God on Our Side," one of the first rock treatments of a Bob Dylan song. Ever quick to discern a winning formula, Manfred Mann lost no time in issuing an excellent single of Dylan's little-known "If You Gotta Go, Go Now." Though the line ". . . or else you gotta stay all night" distressed Britain's censors, the record got to number two anyway. Dylan himself more than compensated for its American failure by stating that Manfred Mann did his songs better than anyone else in the business. This remark may have been just another of Dylan's Delphic throwaways, or a calculated jab at Roger McGuinn and the Byrds, but it furnished a great blurb for a decade's worth of Manfred Mann press releases.

By 1966, Paul Jones—like the Animals' Eric Burdon—had come to view the other members of his band as extraneous to his own stellar ambitions. Obviously unable to duplicate Burdon's trick of replacing all his cohorts while continuing to use the old group's name, Jones decided to go solo even as Manfred Mann's "Pretty Flamingo" topped the British charts. By this time, Vickers had already departed for a successful career as a "legitimate" musical arranger. With McGuinness now on guitar, Jack Bruce briefly filled the bassist vacancy before opting for the greener pastures of Cream.

Not one to give up so easily, Manfred found a new bass player in Klaus Voorman, the Beatles' longtime friend from Hamburg. The enormous void left by the man in the middle was admirably filled by Michael d'Abo, though his voice lacked the instant recognizability of Jones' raspy wailing.

Manfred Mann, meanwhile, continued as a well-oiled music machine, cranking out classic pop singles along with bland LPs that offered few vestiges of the old lineup's love affair with jazz and the blues. Mann made it clear that he was interested only in cutting hits; and, to the amazement of many, these kept surfacing in quantity. And quality: Manfred always had exceptionally good taste.

The sound of Manfred Mann "chapter two" was quintessential British pop—airy and frothy, full of falsetto harmonies and jangling guitars, with Manfred's organ punching out the melodic hooks in unison with one ubiquitous flute. The first d'Abo-sung single was "Just Like a Woman," from Dylan's hot-off-the-presses *Blonde on Blonde.* Just when it looked set to repeat its surprising British success in America, Columbia stole the Manfreds' thunder by releasing a single of Dylan's own rendition. After the excellent "Semi-Detached Suburban Mr. James" and "Ha Ha Said the Clown" crossed the Atlantic stillborn, Dylan came to the rescue with a copy of his then-secret *Basement Tapes.* Manfred Mann's classic recording of his "Mighty Quinn" returned them in triumph to the American airwaves.

But then d'Abo (composer of Rod Stewart's "Handbags and Gladrags") began to get the solo itch and even Manfred grew weary of life in the hit factory. In June 1969 he and Hugg finally disbanded the "Manfred Mann pop group" and began recording the album "we personally have been wanting to do for some years." *Manfred Mann Chapter Three* represented a jazz-rock fusion, with the former drummer playing piano and singing in a style reminiscent of Dr. John. The LP featured driving melodies liable to bursts of avant-garde cacophony, with the occasional heavenly choir eerily juxtaposed. It offered proof that the jazz-rock genre *could* be explored with taste and imagination; but it didn't sell, and neither did *Manfred Mann Chapter Three Volume Two.*

So in 1971 Manfred got back to business-as-usual with the formation of another rock group. With Mick Rogers on guitar and vocals, Colin Pattenden on bass, and Chris Slade on drums the new lineup—eventually dubbed Manfred Mann's Earth Band—set Manfred's own space-age synthesizer work to a heavy metal backdrop. It was all really rather pedestrian, but tireless gigging earned Mann a whole new following in the American heartlands. Manfred was among the first to view Bruce Springsteen as Dylan's Seventies counterpart, and, in the hands of the Earth Band, such Springsteen compositions as "Spirit in the Night" and "Blinded by the Light" became big hits.

In 1975, Rogers left and was replaced by two guitarists named Chris Thompson and David Flett. As of this writing, Manfred himself is still going strong—not bad for a professorial-looking South African jazz buff who has admitted: "I'm hardly the matinee idol, and I'm sure the public don't think of me as a personality." Yet over the course of two decades in pop music, the man left his byline on an awful lot of successful and/or interesting discs. "I sit and play those old records now and I think maybe they weren't bad after all . . . quite good even."

(NICHOLAS SCHAFFNER)

U.S. Hit Singles

1964	Do Wah Diddy Diddy (**1**); Sha La La (**12**)
1965	Come Tomorrow (**50**)
1966	Pretty Flamingo (**29**)
1968	Mighty Quinn (Quinn the Eskimo) (**10**)
1969	Fox on the Run (**97**)
1972	Living Without You (**69**)
1977	Blinded by the Light (**1**); Spirit in the Night (**40**)
1979	You Angel You (**58**)

U.S. Hit LPs

1964	The Manfred Mann Album (**35**)
1965	The Five Faces of Manfred Mann (**141**)
1968	The Mighty Quinn (**176**)
1972	Manfred Mann's Earth Band (**138**)
1974	Solar Fire (**96**); The Good Earth (**157**)
1975	Nightingales and Bombers (**120**)
1976	The Roaring Silence (**10**)
1978	Watch (**83**)
1979	Angel Station (**144**)

U.K. Hit Singles

1964	5-4-3-2-1 (**5**); Hubble Bubble Toil and Trouble (**11**); Do Wah Diddy Diddy (**1**); Sha La La (**3**)
1965	Come Tomorrow (**4**); If You Gotta Go Go Now (**2**); Oh No Not My Baby (**11**)
1966	Pretty Flamingo (**1**); Just Like a Woman (**10**); Semi-Detached Suburban Mr. James (**2**); You Gave Me Somebody to Love (**36**)
1967	Ha Ha Said the Clown (**4**); Sweet Pea (**36**)
1968	Mighty Quinn (**1**); Fox on the Run (**5**); My Name Is Jack (**8**)
1969	Ragamuffin Man (**8**)
1973	Joybringer (**9**)
1976	Blinded by the Light (**6**)
1978	Davy's on the Road Again (**6**)
1979	Don't Kill It Carol (**45**)

John Mayall

It has always been John Mayall's fate to be remembered less for what he did than for whom he did it with. Yet Mayall was as responsible as anyone for engendering not only the British Blues Boom of the late Sixties, but also a larger white audience for the genuine article.

Between 1965 and 1968, John Mayall's Blues Breakers served as a sort of finishing school for brilliant young unknowns. Some graduated to form the nucleus of Cream (Eric Clapton and Jack Bruce), Fleetwood Mac (John McVie, Mick Fleetwood, and Peter Green), and Colosseum (John Hiseman, Dick Heckstall-Smith, and Tony Reeves); others would find fame and fortune in groups as various as the Rolling Stones (Mick Taylor), Free (Andy Fraser), and Jefferson Starship (Aynsley Dunbar). The cynical might attribute Mayall's aversion to working with established musicians—and his band's revolving-door lineup—to sheer niggardliness: Clapton received standard session rates (and no royalties) for his work on the *Blues Breakers* LP (which many Clapton aficionados deem the most inspired of his entire career), and whenever the band crisscrossed Britain in a van, Mayall requested that his accompanists squeeze up front while he luxuriated behind them on a mattress. Yet Mayall was unusually scrupulous about awarding due credits (and royalties) to the indigent blues artists whose work he adapted.

Born in Manchester in 1933, Mayall formed his first blues group, the Powerhouse Four, upon leaving the army at the age of twenty-two, and cultivated the reputation of a thrifty eccentric by making his home in

a treehouse. In 1963, at the behest of Alexis Korner (who alone can match Mayall's record as midwife to Anglo-rock legends), the singer-keyboardist-harp virtuoso relocated in London, where he launched the first incarnation of the Blues Breakers. Mayall's band received national attention in 1965 when Yardbird Eric Clapton, casting off the mantle of Swinging London pop idol to supplicate himself to the Blues, replaced Roger Dean as Mayall's guitarist. Bassist John McVie and drummer Hughie Flint completed the *Blues Breakers* LP lineup.

On the subsequent—and equally outstanding—*A Hard Road* LP, Clapton and Flint were replaced by Peter Green and Aynsley Dunbar. When McVie and Green in their turn departed to form Fleetwood Mac, Mayall took on the services of the teenaged Mick Taylor and augmented the band with a horn section. *Crusade* (1967) was dedicated to the exploited blues masters, while *Bare Wires* (1968) replaced the Blues Breakers' trademark Chicago-style blues with a jazzier sound. After the *Wires* band broke up, Mayall scrapped the Blues Breakers moniker to record his impressions of California—*Blues from Laurel Canyon*.

In June 1969, Mayall took the radical step of forming a predominantly acoustic, drummerless band with Steve Thompson (bass), Johnny Almond (flute and saxophone), and Jon Mark (acoustic guitar). *Melody Maker*'s Chris Welch went so far as to call them "the most original, refreshing, and exciting group in Britain, nay the world." Despite its subtlety and delicacy, *A Turning Point* (recorded live at New York's Fillmore East) became Mayall's all-time best seller.

(*Ron Gott*)

To his credit, Mayall strove with each LP to explore a new facet of the somewhat rigidly proscribed genre he had made his own. *Jazz Blues Fusion* (1973) featured noted jazz trumpeteer Blue Mitchell; *New Year, New Band, New Company* introduced a woman, Dee McKinnie, on lead vocals (perhaps because Mayall's own voice was deteriorating). Nonetheless, many listeners found Mayall's latter-day waxings increasingly dull. Reviewing *USA Union* in *Rolling Stone,* Lester Bangs wrote: "If the Stones are speed and Van Morrison is fine red wine, Mayall in 1970 is pure Librium—safe, soothing, non-toxic, non-habituating, and very specific."

Mayall spent most of the Seventies in California. In January 1982, he scored his first Rock Biz headlines in a decade with a Blues Breakers reunion tour of Australia featuring Mick Taylor, John McVie, and drummer Collin Allen.

(NICHOLAS SCHAFFNER)

U.S. Hit Singles

1969 Don't Waste My Time (**81**)

U.S. Hit LPs

1968 Crusade (**136**); The Blues Alone (**128**); Bare Wires (**59**)
1969 Blues from Laurel Canyon (**68**); Looking Back (**79**); A Turning Point (**32**)
1970 The Diary of a Band (**93**); Empty Rooms (**33**); U.S.A. Union (**22**)
1971 Back to the Roots (**52**); Live in Europe (**146**); Thru the Years (**164**); Memories (**179**)
1972 Jazz Blues Fusion (**64**); Moving On (**116**)
1973 Down the Line (**158**); Ten Years Are Gone (**157**)
1975 New Year, New Band, New Company (**140**)

The Moody Blues

There are two separate and distinct chapters in the Moody Blues saga. One, involving the years 1964 and 1965, is the story of an average British Invasion quintet with one Top Ten song. The other, from 1967, onward, is the tale of a phenomenally successful mystico-classical band with a near-fanatic following and a secure niche in the history of popular music.

First things first. The Moody Blues came together in 1964 in Birmingham. Their first record, a Rhythm & Blues number called "Lose Your Money," did moderately well. But it was their second release—"Go Now," a rhythmic piano-based thumper originally cut by the bluesy Bessie Banks—that really caught on, spending six weeks in the American Top Twenty and hitting the Number One spot in England in early 1965.

After that brief brush with fame, bassist Clint Warwick left for parts unknown and guitarist Denny Laine also decamped (Laine turned up six years later in Paul McCartney's newly formed Wings). The Moodies, meanwhile, acquired Justin Hayward and John Lodge and went into seclusion. They issued no more records until late 1967, when they burst forth with the landmark *Days of Future Passed* album. Lots had happened since their 1965 success, and the Moody Blues synthesized it all on this one amazing record. It was a concept album like *Sgt. Pepper;* it was, like "A Whiter Shade of Pale," strongly linked to classical music; it was as cosmic as Donovan's "There Is a Mountain"; it had confident, inventive melodies and thick, rich harmony. In sum, the Moody Blues hadn't just made a hit record—they had created a whole new genre.

And after that, the formula never changed. Each Moody Blues album was basically a variation on the last one. Whether the sweeping orchestral sound was created by a Mellotron or the London Festival Orchestra, it was there, swelling and rolling in the background while the three- and four-part harmony took center stage. Often, the album's concept was explained in little spoken pieces of doggerel between the songs; the poetry was worse than the most pitiful Edgar A. Guest, but the fans didn't seem to mind and record sales soared.

Individual songs were, to be truthful, skillfully done. "Tuesday Afternoon" and "Nights in White Satin" qualify as classics. "Ride My See-Saw" was as close as the Moodies ever got to a stormy rocker, and "Isn't Life Strange" was lyrically beautiful. "I'm Just a Singer in a Rock and Roll Band" was pointed, witty, and wry.

In the mid-Seventies, the group temporarily suspended work at its hit factory while individual members did solo work, all of which was fairly inconsequential and sold poorly. Hayward and Lodge's *Blue Jays* LP was probably the best, and—surprise!—it sounded the most like the Moodies.

Having gotten the solo bug out of their systems, the quintet reunited toward the end of the Seventies and cut *Octave* (their eighth one, get it?). Their 1981 album *Long Distance Voyager,* was lush and luminous—and one of the biggest-selling records of the year.

Although the Moody Blues have typically been on the receiving end of critical brickbats, their unique contribution to rock music cannot be denied. Nobody else can build up a thick aural gumbo of strings and synthesizers, then slice through it with the piercing, steely whine of a guitar. Nobody else can assemble harmony, hack poetry, and outer-space orchestration and have it sound even halfway impressive. They have moved beyond cliché to the classic. What else would you expect to hear on your FM radio, in the pure, still hours before dawn as some late-night deejay cops a quick snooze, but the sonorous tones of the Moody Blues?

(HENRY McNULTY)

Mike Pinder
(keyboards)
Ray Thomas
(flute and vocals)
Graeme Edge
(drums)
Justin Hayward
(guitar)
John Lodge
(bass)

U.S. Hit Singles

1965 Go Now (**10**); From the Bottom of My Heart (**93**)
1966 Stop! (**98**)
1968 Ride My See-Saw (**61**)
1969 Never Comes the Day (**91**)
1970 Question (**21**)
1971 The Story in Your Eyes (**23**)

1972	Nights in White Satin (2); Isn't Life Strange (29)
1973	I'm Just a Singer (in a Rock 'n' Roll Band) (12)
1978	Steppin' in a Slide Zone (39); Driftwood (59)

(BY JUSTIN HAYWARD)

1978	Forever Autumn (47)

U.S. LPs

1968	Days of Future Passed (3); In Search of the Lost Chord (23)
1969	On the Threshold of a Dream (20)
1970	To Our Children's Children's Children (14); A Question of Balance (3)
1971	Every Good Boy Deserves Favour (2)
1972	Seventh Sojourn (1)
1974	This Is the Moody Blues (11)
1977	Caught Live + 5 (26)
1978	Octave (13)

(BY THE GRAEME EDGE BAND)

1975	Kick Off Your Muddy Boots (107)
1977	Paradise Ballroom (164)

(BY JUSTIN HAYWARD AND JOHN LODGE)

1975	Blue Jays (16)

(BY JUSTIN HAYWARD)

1977	Songwriter (37)

(BY JOHN LODGE)

1977	Natural Avenue (121)

(BY MICHAEL PINDER)

1976	The Promise (133)

(BY RAY THOMAS)

1975	From Mighty Oaks (68)
1976	Hopes Wishes and Dreams (147)

U.K. Hit Singles

1964	Go Now (1)
1965	From the Bottom of My Heart (22); I Don't Want to Go On Without You (33); Everyday (44)
1967	Nights in White Satin (19)
1968	Voices in the Sky (27); Ride My See-Saw (42)
1970	Question (2)
1972	Nights in White Satin (9); Isn't Life Strange (13)
1973	I'm Just a Singer (in a Rock 'n' Roll Band) (36)

(BY JUSTIN HAYWARD)

1978	Forever Autumn (5)

(BY JUSTIN HAYWARD AND JOHN LODGE)

1975	Blue Guitar (8)

MORRISON, VAN: See Them

Mott the Hoople

Mott the Hoople, who derived their name from a book by Willard Manus, was launched in late 1968 as a Buffalo Springfield soundalike band fronted by singer Stan Tippins. As such, Mott scored an Island Records contract, but their manager and producer, the late Guy Stevens, felt they needed a stronger identity. Tippins was demoted to tour manager, and former engineering apprentice Ian Hunter enlisted to croak into the microphone and jangle the ivories. In the name of "image," the homely Hunter was instructed to wear shades at all times, and was subsequently never seen in public without them.

For their self-titled debut LP, Mott the Hoople had the great good taste to base the cover on a surreal drawing by M. C. Escher (then just coming into fashion). They also had the glorious bad taste to record Sonny Bono's "Laugh at Me." Yet even at its most kitsch, *Mott the Hoople*—with its piano/organ combination and Hunter's Dylanesque mannerisms—sounded uncannily like *Blonde on Blonde*.

The hard-rocking but terminally sloppy *Mad Shadows* followed, whereupon Hunter decided that he "wanted to play guitar and get into the middle." Nineteen seventy-one's country-flavored *Wildlife* was, as Hunter later told the *Trouser Press*, "a total departure and the worst-selling album we ever did." Mott attempted to recapture the old formula with *Brain Capers*, but that, too, proved a flop. *Melody Maker* later characterized Mott's four LPs for Island

(Atlantic in the U.S.) as "two long fly balls, one home run still rising out of the park, and one miserable strikeout."

Though few bothered to buy their records, Mott the Hoople's rowdy and energetic concerts made them a popular concert draw in the U.K., and often sparked full-scale riots. After Mott wreaked their customary havoc on London's Albert Hall, the management decreed that no rock & roll would ever be heard there again. Despite such accomplishments, Ralphs resented Hunter's growing domination, and the band as a whole felt dispirited by the low record sales. On May 26, 1972, Mott announced their imminent breakup.

David Bowie, meanwhile, had just sent his recently composed "Suffragette City" to Mott for consideration as their next 45. As Hunter related in *NME*, Watts "phoned David to thank him for the demo, and told him the news." "You *can't* break up!" insisted Bowie. "This is ridiculous! We must stick together!"

When they met face to face, Hunter recalled in *Trouser Press*, Bowie was "shaking, real nervous. He thought we were real bikers." Hunter brusquely told him that Mott "needed something stronger." So Bowie presented Mott with "All the Young Dudes," Mott was duly snapped up by Columbia, and Bowie's production of the single was to outsell even the Main Man's own 45s.

The rise of Ziggy Stardust triggered Mott's own

Ian Hunter
(vocals, piano, guitar)
Mick Ralphs
(guitar, vocals)
Pete "Overend" Watts
(bass)
Verden Allen
(organ)
Dale "Buffin" Griffin
(drums)

Ian Hunter (*Chrysalis*)

metamorphosis from Sixties has-beens to avatars of Glitter and Glam—a hasty change of image that left the boys in the band tottering about on nine-inch stacked heels, resplendent in rhinestones and mascara, and camping it up like mad. Hunter's ridiculous attempts at pantomiming (à la Bowie) were alone worth the price of a ticket.

Because "All the Young Dudes" had all the hallmarks of a gay youth anthem, Hunter recalled, "we were considered instant fags. A lot of gays followed us around, especially in America." Mott rose to the occasion with a brace of originals in the same vein—"One of the Boys," "Sucker"—for the Bowie-supervised *All the Young Dudes* album.

Mott's ersatz glamour was further enhanced when they became the first rock band to play on Broadway (with the heretofore unknown Queen opening the bill)—even if Hunter's bland and repetitive book, *Diary of a Rock 'n' Roll Star*, managed to make touring America with a famous rock band sound about as glamorous as being an apprentice engineer.

Though 1973's self-produced *Mott* LP, which yielded a pair of U.K. hits in Hunter's "All the Way from Memphis" and "Honaloochie Boogie," demonstrated that the band had no further need of Bowie, internal friction got the better of Mott the Hoople. The departure of Verden Allen—who would end up driving a truck—was followed by Mick Ralphs' defection to Bad Company. Having concluded that Mott had become too stylized, and that his songs were being unfairly neglected, Ralphs literally came to blows with Hunter (ironically enough, during the recording of the latter's "Violence").

Mott's next LP, *The Hoople*, and their replacement guitarist, Ariel Bender (an alias for Luther Grosvenor, formerly of Spooky Tooth), both came across as pale Xeroxes of their predecessors. The eventual substitution of Bowie's celebrated former guitarist Mick Ronson promised to give Mott a new lease on life, but Watts and Griffin took exception to the manner in which cameras and spotlights tended to focus on the new recruit. Following Ronson's appearance on a few singles, Hunter suffered a nervous breakdown and handed in his notice (leaving Watts and Griffin to coast into obscurity in a new band called, simply, Mott).

Ronson worked with Hunter on the latter's self-titled solo debut, and they shared equal billing on a major U.S. tour. But the association collapsed when their respective managers, Tony deFries and Fred Heller, failed to come to terms on how the cash should be divvied up. Not that there was much to haggle over in

any case—Hunter and Ronson apparently suffered from low name recognition among audiences that had earlier flocked to Mott and Bowie concerts, and halls remained resolutely empty.

After wallowing in self-pity on a pair of solo disasters—*All-American Alien Boy* and *Overnight Angels*—Hunter reunited with Ronson for 1979's strong comeback, *You're Never Alone with a Schizophrenic*. By this time he had achieved due recognition as a godfather of the New Wave, whereupon Mick Jones of the Clash stepped in to produce Hunter's 1981 effort *Short Back and Sides*. An everyday nerd in shades who alternated punky aggression with a touching empathy for his audience—and who thought Sonny and Cher were of a piece with Bob Dylan—Ian Hunter, after all, had been ten years ahead of his time.

(NICHOLAS SCHAFFNER)

U.S. Hit Singles

1972	All the Young Dudes (**37**)
1973	One of the Boys (**96**)
1974	Golden Age of Rock and Roll (**96**)

(BY IAN HUNTER)

1979	Just Another Night (**68**)

U.S. Hit LPs

1970	Mott the Hoople (**185**)
1972	All the Young Dudes (**89**)
1973	Mott (**35**)
1974	The Hoople (**28**); Rock and Roll Queen (**112**); Mott the Hoople Live (**23**)
1975	Drive On (**160**)

(BY IAN HUNTER)

1975	Ian Hunter (**50**)
1976	All American Alien Boy (**177**)
1979	You're Never Alone with a Schizophrenic (**35**)
1980	Live—Welcome to the Club (**69**)

U.K. Hit Singles

1972	All the Young Dudes (**3**)
1973	Honaloochie Boogie (**12**); All the Way from Memphis (**10**); Roll Away the Stone (**8**)
1974	Golden Age of Rock and Roll (**16**); Foxy Foxy (**33**); Saturday Gig (**41**)

(BY IAN HUNTER)

1975	Once Bitten Twice Shy (**14**)

The Move

One of the most exciting bands of the late Sixties, the Move never managed to transpose their string of British hits to the American charts. Formed in February 1966, the Move started out performing covers of soul hits, to synchronized dance steps of their own creation, before taking advantage of the eclectic songwriting talents of guitarist Roy Wood. After building up a sizable following in Birmingham, the group set out to conquer London with the assistance

of their new manager, Tony Secunda, who was determined to make the Move a household word at all costs. Secunda persuaded the musicians to dress up in gangster suits and encouraged them to take The Who's auto-destruction act several steps further, demolishing TV sets, cars, and dummies of political figures onstage. Though privately the Move had doubts about some of Secunda's schemes, singer Carl Wayne dutifully told the *New Musical Express*: "It is our life's

Carl Wayne
(vocals)
Roy Wood
(guitar)
Ace Kefford
(bass guitar)
Bev Bevan
(drums)
Trevor Burton
(guitar)

Roy Wood (*United Artists*)

ambition to start a riot. People love violence. In our act we wreck cars and stick an axe through TV sets. The kids go wild. Within minutes they're right in there with us—WRECKING, SMASHING, breaking things up.''

Secunda's efforts were not in vain; the Move's exploits received strong coverage in the British music press throughout 1966 and '67. But, when news of the burgeoning West Coast psychedelic scene reached Secunda's ears, he abruptly changed tactics. The axes and gangster suits were replaced with caftans, love beads, and beatific press releases.

Secunda's biggest publicity coup was yet to come. For the Move's single ''Flowers in the Rain,'' Secunda had postcards printed up which featured a caricature of British Prime Minister Harold Wilson in a compromising position with his secretary. Wilson was not amused, and he successfully sued the Move for all the royalties from the single, which he donated to charity.

In April 1968, after four Top Five U.K. hits and a successful album, *The Move*, the band underwent its first change of lineup when Ace Kefford (''the singing skull'') left. Guitarist Trevor Burton switched to bass and Rick Price entered on guitar. In January 1969, the Move claimed their first Number One with ''Blackberry Way.'' Shortly afterward, just as the band was about to depart on its first U.S. tour, Trevor Burton turned in his notice with the words: ''I'm not playing this commercial shit anymore.''

The Move toured the States as a foursome in October '69. The group's one and only excursion to America (reportedly financed by Jimi Hendrix) proved a total disaster, and the group fled back to England before it was completed. Yet even back home, touring had become difficult as the musicians' reputation for destructiveness cost them numerous gigs. Thus ensued one of the more bizarre twists in the Move's history, as the band briefly metamorphosed into a cabaret act. This development suited Carl Wayne, whose heart had always been in this direction, but not Roy Wood, who loathed every moment. Things came quickly to a head and, after Wood engaged himself in a brawl with the audience one night, Wayne departed in a huff.

The Move's second album, *Shazam*, recorded while Wayne was still in the band, was released in February 1970. Containing only six tracks, *Shazam* careened eclectically from heavy metal raunch and Folk Rock to the intelligent, imaginative pop at which the Move were so adept.

Subsequently, Wayne was replaced by guitarist Jeff Lynne. Though the Move were to enjoy further hit singles and record two more albums (*Looking On* and *Message from the Country*), during the next few years, pivotal members Wood and Lynne were more preoccupied with their vision of a ''rock & roll orchestra.'' According to Roy Wood: ''If it had been left to us, Jeff and I would have knocked the Move on the head as soon as he'd joined, and we'd have got on with Electric Light Orchestra full steam ahead—but we were pressured not to.''

Roy Wood left ELO in July 1972 during the recording sessions of *ELO II*. He immediately formed Wizzard, a band roughly similar to ELO insofar that it utilized an unlikely assortment of instruments (sitars, celloes, tubas, trumpets, and harpsichords, to name a few) to produce a rampaging, unruly, and raucous music that slipped ably into various musical guises yet never lost touch with the more primal aspects of rock & roll.

English audiences responded to Wood's musical and visual rock & roll circus with an enthusiasm that put Wizzard in the Top Ten six times during the band's two-and-a-half-year career, which ended in February '75. Dispirited by the disintegration of Wizzard and plagued by contractual difficulties, Wood kept a low profile until April 1977, when he introduced his new band, Wizzo. Intended as jazz/rock fusion, Wizzo never duplicated the success of Wood's previous endeavors and disbanded less than a year after its formation.

In addition to one Wizzo and three Wizzard LPs, Roy Wood also found time to record three solo albums (*Boulders, Mustard,* and *On the Road*) wherein he displayed his talents for producing, arranging, and playing every instrument on every song. In 1980, Wood commenced work with a new group, Helicopters.

(ELIZABETH SCHAFFNER)

U.S. Hit Singles

1972 Do Ya (**93**)

U.S. Hit LPs

1973 Split Ends (**172**)

(BY ROY WOOD)

1973 Boulders (**176**)

U.K. Hit Singles

1967 Night of Fear (**2**);
I Can Hear the Grass Grow (**5**);
Flowers in the Rain (**2**)
1968 Fire Brigade (**3**); Blackberry Way (**1**)
1969 Curly (**12**)
1970 Brontosaurus (**7**)
1971 Tonight (**11**); Chinatown (**23**)
1972 California Man (**7**)

(BY WIZZARD)

1972 Ball Park Incident (**6**)
1973 See My Baby Jive (**1**);
Angel Fingers (**1**);
I Wish It Could Be Christmas Everyday (**4**)
1974 Rock 'n' Roll Winter (**6**);
This Is the Story of My Love (Baby) (**34**);
Are You Ready to Rock (**8**)

(BY ROY WOOD)

1973 Dear Elaine (**18**); Forever (**8**)
1974 Going Down the Road (**13**)
1975 Oh What a Shame (**13**)

Gary Numan

Far too many people have been exploited in pop and have nothing to show for years of success. It won't happen to me . . . I just don't think I owe anybody anything and I don't believe my fans made me either.

Gary Numan

Electronic pop's enfant terrible was born Gary Webb on March 8, 1958, adopting his present surname from the London Yellow Pages "during David Bowie's Berlin period." In the autumn of 1977 he formed Tubeway Army, whose 1979 debut LP consisted of year-old demo tapes. Numan's turn in the spotlight came with the smash success of his second LP, *Replicas*, which dominated the charts throughout the winter of 1979. Numan's striking futuristic persona, agreeably whining vocals, and hypnotically simplistic melodies clicked with British TV audiences and pushed the single "Are 'Friends' Electric?" to Number One.

Numan fashioned an enigmatic image—much the same as Bowie before him—that endeared him instantly to the hordes of barely pubescent teeny-boppers short on idols since the Punk explosion of '77. But the trendy British rock press, wary of any phenomenon they didn't themselves invent, entered into a combative stalemate with the equally paranoid artist. Numan rapidly developed a cynical, "ends justifies the means" stance of using rock as a stepping stone for further adventures in film, video, and jet piloting his now-affordable plane. The Man Who Never Smiles watched his newest batch of synthesizer sagas about technology and isolation, *Pleasure Principle*, and the single "Cars," reach Number One in the U.K. singles and album charts. Britain's year-end pop polls confirmed Numan's rapid ascendancy, naming him Best New Artist of the Year, as he surrounded himself with people he could trust:

(Atco)

his manager father, costumer/hairdresser mother, and press photographer brother. "Cars" and *Pleasure Principle* were released Stateside in January 1980, and "Cars" hit the Top Ten that May. *Pleasure Principle* lingered in the U.S. album charts for seven months while Numan conquered more territory (Japan, Europe, and Australia) and scored another U.K. Top Ten with "We Are Glass."

Telekon (1980) with its pulsating electro-rhythms and robotoid vocals, was less ecstatically received, and was followed up with two live LPs from Numan's '79 and '80 tours, coinciding with Numan's announcement that he would retire from live performances to concentrate on film and video projects.

And yet he seemed to have ambivalent feelings. "You see, in terms of fame," he told *Record Mirror* in the summer of 1981, "I don't get that much out of it, but I need it. It's like a paradox. Everything I do has equal and opposite feeling; I'm very, very shy and yet I can go on stage. I'm emotionally unstable almost to the point of treatment, and yet I can handle the whole business with a precision that is almost mechanical."

(DAVID KEEPS)

U.S. Hit Singles

1980   Cars (**9**)

U.S. Hit LPs

1979   Replicas (**124**)
1980   The Pleasure Principle (**16**); Telekon (**64**)

U.K. Hit Singles

1979   Are "Friends" Electric? (**1**); Cars (**1**);
           Complex (**6**)
1980   We Are Glass (**5**); I Die You Die (**6**);
           This Wreckage (**20**)

Mike Oldfield

Mike Oldfield was an unlikely star. His long brown hair cascaded to his shoulders, and his glazed-over eyes betrayed little emotion. He seemed subdued and more than a little vulnerable.

In fact, Oldfield was responsible for one of the best-loved pieces of music of the Seventies, *Tubular Bells*. It was a fifty-minute work of soaring virtuosity on which Oldfield played every instrument—some twenty of them, including glockenspiel, tympani, and "flageolet," as well as more conventional ones.

Oldfield's first musical experience came at age fourteen, when he played in a folk duo with his sister, Sally. Two years later, Oldfield signed on for a stint with Kevin Ayer's backup band, the Whole World. Toward the end of his stay with Ayers, Oldfield began mapping out a blueprint for *Tubular Bells*. He left the

band in late 1971 to record the opus, but label interest was nil until he approached Virgin Records, which was just setting up operations. With contract in hand, he fine-tuned his project, using Manor Studios at those odd hours when it was empty. Nine months and 2300 overdubs later, the album was finished, and in May 1973 *Tubular Bells* became Virgin Records' first release.

It was a best seller in America in early 1974. Many U.S. listeners were introduced to it via the movie *The Exorcist*, which employed parts of it as soundtrack music (as a single, "Theme from *The Exorcist*" was an odd Top Five hit). In Britain, the album charted for an unprecedented length of time, ushering in the U.K.'s ongoing love affair with Oldfield and his adventuresome music. *Tubular Bells* was dislodged from the Number One position a full sixteen months later only by Oldfield's second long player, *Hergest Ridge*, which was again a continuous piece of music with Oldfield playing all the parts.

All the while, he managed to maintain ties with his former bandmates, lending a hand to projects by Kevin Ayers, Lol Coxhill and David Bedford (who conducted the Royal Philharmonic in a fully orchestrated *Tubular Bells*). Oldfield's next record, *Ommadawn* (1975), took a year to complete and found him augmenting his one-man orchestra with such esoterica as African drummers and bagpipe players.

Despite their excellence, neither *Hergest Ridge* nor *Ommadawn* rose to the majestic heights of *Tubular Bells*. That album presented a new musical symbiosis—symphonic grandeur and rock instrumentation. The composition swam effortlessly through a range of moods and musical styles; one section culminated with master of ceremonies Viv Stanshall introducing the instruments and climaxed with the final ''plus—tubular bells!'' and their glorious pealing.

All this is not to say that Mike Oldfield—or anyone—could live up to the ridiculously inflated notices that followed its release. ''The most important composer of the decade'' was actually a shy young man who was ill-at-ease in the public eye. He rarely talked to journalists and, following *Ommadawn*, dropped out of sight for a while.

Tubular Bells has proved to be an enduring classic—and a recurring selling point for Oldfield's catalogue. In addition to the original LP, there's been *The Orchestral Tubular Bells* (1974); a completely remixed version of the original, included in the four-record compilation *Boxed* (1976); and a ''free live record—while supplies last'' of the composition, thrown in as a come-on for a later work, *Airborn* (1980). The latter record, incidentally, found Oldfield somewhat liberated from his compulsion to create two-sided masterworks. The side-long ''Platinum'' was downright succinct by comparison, and side two featured four discrete compositions. All of the pieces were, furthermore, sprightly and good-humored, a heartening change of pace from a kid with a mind-blowing imagination.

(PARKE PUTERBAUGH)

U.S. Hit Singles

1974	Tubular Bells (Theme from *The Exorcist*)	(7)

U.S. Hit LPs

1973	Tubular Bells	(3)
1974	Hergest Ridge	(87)
1975	Ommadawn	(146)

U.K. Hit Singles

1974	Tubular Bells	(31)
1975	In Dulce Jubilo/On Horseback	(4)
1976	Portsmouth	(3)
1978	Take 4 EP	(72)
1979	Guilty (22); Blue Peter	(19)

Graham Parker and the Rumour

Graham Parker
(vocals, guitar)
Martin Belmont
(guitar)
Brinsley Schwarz
(guitar, saxophone)
Bob Andrews
(keyboards)
Andrew Bodnar
(bass)
Stephen Goulding
(drums)

Graham Parker is like a lit stick of dynamite—he may be small, but when he detonates, look out. The wiry Parker just doesn't look as if he'd be physically capable of rocking out with the ferocity he always manages to muster. He stands all of five foot four and is somewhat frail-looking, yet behind his opaque shades lurks the mind of a man who's taking in everything around him and trying to make sense of the emotional consequences. In so doing, he became one of the most compelling songwriters of the late Seventies.

Parker has unceremoniously been lumped in with a host of other rockers of similar vintage as part of the New Wave phenomenon. Yet his roots go far deeper, and to typecast him so shallowly does him an injustice. In fact, Graham Parker and Elvis Costello are the missing link between two musical movements—Pub Rock and New Wave—without being inextricably wed to either of them.

Pub Rock was a roots-oriented music scene in which a whole fleet of English bands began reviving certain cast-off American musical styles—i.e., Chuck Berry-type rock & roll, Sun Records rockabilly, Memphis rhythm & blues, and the Band's rustic bop. Pub Rock was so-called because the groups would play at hole-in-the-wall clubs and bars as opposed to the large halls. The music was no-frills, down to earth, danceable, and lots of fun.

Graham Parker arrived on the pub-rock scene relatively late (1976) after sending a cassette tape of some of his songs to the Hope and Anchor pub in London, which was the hub for this music, even boasting its own studio. His tunes impressed some of the locals, and Parker—then working as a gas-station attendant—made the trek to London to cut a more professional demo.

Scooping up some of the unemployed pub-rockers on the scene, Parker suddenly found himself with the tightest band in the U.K., the Rumour. The rest is history: a record contract soon followed, and Parker's talents were much celebrated on both sides of the Atlantic. Graham Parker and Elvis Costello became the great white hope of the New Wave. Spluttering their angry lyrics to an urgent R&B beat, they were as undeniable as a slug in the chest, and made many of the established rock ''stars'' look pusillanimous and foolish by comparison. And Parker and Costello were no mere trendy pretenders to the throne who'd slashed and burned their way up front à la Johnny Rotten. You could in fact hear in them echoes of Elvis Presley, Van Morrison, Bruce Springsteen, and even Hank Williams.

His first two albums—*Howlin' Wind* and *Heat Treatment*, both released in 1976—mixed ebullient R&B and tough-minded lyrics. Both finished high on critics' year-end lists, and Parker was building a word-of-mouth reputation from extensive touring. His momentum was perhaps slowed down by *Stick to Me* (1977); the songs were fine, but a rushed production job made the record sound harsh and grating.

Curiously too, Parker's three-sided live album, *The Parkerilla*, seemingly caught the band on an off-night.

But his fourth studio LP, *Squeezing Out Sparks*, was a master stroke. The passion in Parker's lyrics was matched at every turn by the band's playing. *Squeezing Out Sparks* was one of those rare records where not a single false note was played.

Squeezing Out Sparks was Parker's unqualified triumph, and as with every new plateau, there were some growing pains and awkwardness. *The Up Escalator* was a lukewarm followup, the razor-edged emotionality seeming somewhat forced. Producer Jimmy Iovine had dressed Parker and band in finer rock trappings, but Parker's raspy voice sounded lost in these more studied surroundings and his discomfort showed.

Herewith, Parker parted ways with the Rumour, who had already been recording without him and backing up other singers, such as Carlene Carter and Garland Jeffreys. Parker's future direction seemed uncertain, but he could be counted on to continue to make good on his statement of intent: "All I want to do is send a shiver up people's spines."

(PARKE PUTERBAUGH)

U.S. Hit Singles

1977	Hold Back the Night	(58)

U.S. LPs

1979	Squeezing Out Sparks	(40)
1980	The Up Escalator	(40)

(BY THE RUMOUR)

1979	Frogs Sprouts Clogs and Krauts	(160)

U.K. Hit Singles

1977	The Pink Parker EP	(24)
1978	Hey Lord, Don't Ask Me Questions	(32)

Peter and Gordon

Following the Beatles' nine-week stranglehold on the Number One position of the U.S. charts, the next British record to go all the way—Peter and Gordon's "A World Without Love"—kept things more or less in the family. Not only did the harmonies have a Beatleish ring, but the song turned out to be a Lennon-McCartney original and Peter the brother of Paul McCartney's girlfriend Jane Asher. Though Peter and Gordon's LP tracks often sounded like Peter and Paul minus Mary, the duo continued to be supplied with hit singles in the form of such unrecorded Beatles compositions as "Nobody I Know," "I Don't Want to See You Again," and "Woman." This last was originally credited to one Bernard Webb, but after it clicked McCartney revealed that he had used the Webb pseudonym to find out whether it was his name or the music that made his songs sell. Peter and Gordon's string of hit singles also included pleasant revivals of chestnuts by Buddy Holly, Phil Spector, and Del Shannon. Later LPs veered towards syrupy "adult" pop.

With their well-scrubbed sound and image, the pair felt no need to disguise their background as classmates at a posh school for boys. By 1968 they had parted ways; Gordon Waller married the fiancée of the late, legendary Eddie Cochran ("Summertime Blues") and made unsuccessful solo records, while Peter Asher moved to the other side of the glass and became a producer and talent scout with the Beatles' Apple Records. Peter has gone on to launch himself into a whole new success story, as manager and producer of such Seventies stars as James Taylor and Linda Ronstadt.

(NICHOLAS SCHAFFNER)

U.S. Hit Singles

1964	A World Without Love (1); Noboby I Know (12); I Don't Want to See You Again (16)
1965	I Go to Pieces (9); True Love Ways (14); To Know You Is to Love You (24); Don't Pity Me (83)
1966	Lady Godiva (6); Woman (14); There's No Living Without You (50); To Show I Love You (98)
1967	Knight in Rusty Armour (15); Sunday for Tea (31); The Jokers (97)

U.S. Hit LPs

1964	A World Without Love (21)
1965	I Don't Want to See You Again (95); I Go to Pieces (51); True Love Ways (49)
1966	Woman (60); The Best of Peter and Gordon (72)
1967	Lady Godiva (80)

U.K. Hit Singles

1964	A World Without Love (1); Nobody I Know (10)
1965	True Love Ways (2); To Know You Is to Love You (5); Baby I'm Yours (19)
1966	Woman (28); Lady Godiva (16)

The Police

Sting
(vocals, bass)
Andy Summers
(guitar)
Stewart Copeland
(drums)

American drummer Stewart Copeland formed the Police with guitarist Henri Padovani in the adrenaline rush of Punk-happy early-1977 London. Eager to complete the lineup, Copeland spotted bassist Gordon (Sting) Sumner singing with the jazz-oriented Last Exit in Newcastle and enticed him to London. Later, a second guitarist, thirtyish veteran Andy Summers, was recruited, and the four-man Police played the Mont de Marsan Punk festival in France in September 1977—at a healthy distance from the top of the bill. Shortly thereafter, Padovani was dropped, unable to keep pace musically with his more experienced colleagues on the force.

The fledgling Police found themselves working with several strikes against them: in the do-it-yourself, every-man-a-musician climate of Punk, their collective experience and obvious musicianship were strangely off-putting. And they weren't kids, not by anyone's standards. Sting was a former schoolteacher; Summers had been a California flower child (collegiate variety) in the Sixties; and the well-traveled Copeland had a CIA agent for a dad—hardly the stuff of which street credibility was made.

The Police's first single, the independently released "Fall Out," was more or less straightforward Punk. Their second, the now-classic "Roxanne," showed the pronounced influence of reggae and jazz and a real sophistication; despite mediocre sales, it captured a good deal of attention and won the trio a contract with A&M. A third single, "Can't Stand Losing You," was an even neater Punk-jazz-reggae fusion, but again failed to stir up much of a storm. The Police's debut album, *Outlandos d'Amour,* released in fall 1978, was overshadowed by the simultaneous LP debuts of Siouxsie and the Banshees and X-Ray Spex.

When the band packed up and flew economy class to America in November, it must have seemed an amazingly foolhardy move. With zero support from A&M and only a rented van to transport them, they played a series of one- or two-nighters, with hardly a ripple of interest at New York's CBGB—the audience most likely to respond. But America, prodded by a few enterprising deejays, took a shine to "Roxanne," and *Outlandos,* released in the States early in 1979, made a steady climb into the Top Thirty of the American charts—a feat that none of the better-known British Punkers had yet achieved.

The Police made their first major tour of Britain that summer, and public indifference turned to frenzied adulation. "Roxanne" was rereleased and rose to the Top Ten; *Outlandos* climbed to number seven—six months after its release. A new single, "Message in a Bottle," and album, *Regatta de Blanc,* made rapid ascents to Number One. Sting played Ace Face in the movie *Quadrophenia* and became Britain's premier male rock & roll sex symbol.

The Police spent most of 1980 conquering uncharted territory in the name of rock & roll: Bangkok, Istanbul, Cairo, Bombay. . . . A third album, *Zenyatta Mondatta,* showed a broadening musical scope and a new responsiveness in Sting's lyrics (as ever, he wrote the bulk of the songs) and more than matched the commercial appeal of its predecessors. And album number four, *Ghost in the Machine*

(loosely inspired by the Arthur Koestler novel), showed an admirable willingness to experiment beyond the spare sound that had become the band's calling card.

In Britain, it's always in fashion to disparage the Police, especially among the hipper-than-thou London trendsetters; and to the British critics, commercial success is often the kiss of death. But it's a mistake to think (as it's often been thought) that the Police were mandatory target practice for the press. While the standard irrelevant objections to the band were periodically brought out to air, their music won them a good deal of—perhaps grudging—respect. "If ever a band passed through the twilight zone of the New Wave and came out with an original and distinctive sound of their own, it's the Police," said *NME* in September 1978, at the same time noting the "small but loyal following" the trio had managed to attract.

And their music and sound *are* distinctive—almost any Police song would be an easy guess in a game of Name the Band. Elements of Punk, jazz, reggae, and plain old r & r are held neatly in balance with an expertise that speaks highly of the band's professional discipline and "class." Though on record the Police may lack a certain visceral impact—they generate neither the gut-level excitement of Punk nor the deeper "inner" physicality of the best reggae—their live sets, fueled by Sting's undeniable front-man charisma, never fail to deliver. And Sting's songs have been covered by singers like Grace Jones and the Jamaican Sheila Hylton—whose Jamaican hit "Bed's Too Big Without You," produced by reggae rhythm aces Sly Dunbar and Robbie Shakespeare in an arrangement that sticks amazingly close to the Police's, stands as a remarkable tribute from the source of so much of the trio's inspiration. Whatever their flaws, the Police are no one-shot wonders.

(PATRICK DILLON)

The first pre-blond single.

U.S. Hit Singles

| 1979 | Roxanne (**32**); Message in a Bottle (**74**) |
| 1980 | De Do Do Do, De Da Da Da (**10**) |

U.S. Hit LPs

1979	Outlandos d'Amour (**23**);
	Regatta de Blanc (**25**)
1980	Zenyatta Mondatta (**5**)

U.K. Hit Singles

1978	I Can't Stand Losing You (**2**)
1979	Roxanne (**12**); Message in a Bottle (**1**);
	Fallout (**47**); Walking on the Moon (**1**)
1980	So Lonely (**6**); Six Pack [singles collection]
	(**17**); Don't Stand So Close to Me (**1**);
	De Do Do Do, De Da Da Da (**5**)

The Pretenders

Chrissie Hynde
(guitar, vocals)
Pete Farndon
(bass)
James Honeyman-Scott
(guitar)
Martin Chambers
(drums)

Chrissie Hynde grew up falling in love with rock & roll—not really that surprising for a teenager in the Rubber City wastelands of Akron, Ohio—and cut her teeth on British invaders like The Who, Rod Stewart,

and Jeff Beck. In 1973, Anglophile Chrissie flew to England and wound up writing reviews for *New Musical Express.* Her hatchet job on a Neil Diamond platter was followed by a feature story on Brian Eno (for which she posed in a leather miniskirt and bondage gear), which gained her some notoriety. Following a brief stint as a clerk in Malcolm McLaren's Kings Road boutique, Hynde sailed to Paris to sing in a band, a fiasco that drove her to exasperation when she discovered that the group had never even heard of her favorite native American rocker, Mitch Ryder.

In 1975, she returned to Cleveland and became part of an R&B outfit called Jack Rabbit, another short-lived affair that led her to move to Tucson and finally back to Paris. Six months later she returned to London, attracted by the underground rumblings of the newly emerging Punk scene. She jammed with Mick Jones before he formed the Clash and with members-to-be of the Damned, and even had a liaison with the tastelessly obscure Moors Murderers. A demo tape from that period caught the attention of Real Records mogul Dave Hill, who was impressed with an original composition, "The Phone Call." Chrissie sang backup for Johnny Thunders's solo LP and LPs by Chris Spedding and Mick Farren and set about auditioning members for her own band.

Bassist Pete Farndon introduced Hynde to Honeyman-Scott and Chambers, and the Pretenders covered Ray Davies's "Stop Your Sobbing" in January '79 with Nick Lowe producing. "Sobbing" made the Top Thirty before the group had actually begun performing. It was followed by "Kid," another Top Thirty hit. But it was "Brass in Pocket," with its bold, sexually assertive lyrics and Motown feel, that established the Pretenders as a pop force to be reckoned with. Released in November '79, it climbed to the top spot in the U.K. singles chart during the Christmas onslaught of seasonal slush by the likes of McCartney and Abba. The debut LP entered the charts at Number One in January 1980. In the U.S., *Pretenders* nearly sold platinum by the time the group arrived for their debut tour in the spring.

American audiences and critics alike warmed to the tough-but-tender Hynde image and her considerably soulful vocal and lyrical skills, and FM radio programmers had no trouble "selling" the sometimes

too thinly disguised heavy metal raveups of her band to their audiences.

Work on *Pretenders II* commenced in November 1980, and a Valentine's Day single, "Messages of Love," was released in the U.K. A five-track *Extended Play* was released in America to satisfy demand, including "Messages" and a previous Brit hit, "Talk of the Town." *Pretenders II* was released in September '81 and rapidly ascended the U.S. charts, despite a sound critical thrashing. Another sellout U.S. tour followed, with Hynde continuing her strongly individualistic approach to music and life.

(DAVID KEEPS)

U.S. Hit Singles

1980 Brass in Pocket (**14**); Stop Your Sobbing (**65**)

U.S. Hit LPs

1980 Pretenders (**9**)

U.K. Hit Singles

1979 Stop Your Sobbing (**34**); Kid (**33**); Brass in Pocket (**1**)
1980 Talk of the Town (**8**)

The Pretty Things

They were scruffy and unkempt. They would take old blues numbers by Slim Harpo and Bo Diddley and turn them into bone-splintering raveups. Some would say that if it weren't for the Rolling Stones, the Pretty Things would have been *the* R&B band in Britain. It wasn't for lack of talent or ambition that it didn't happen that way; perhaps they were just too raunchy for their own good.

The Pretty Things were born in 1964 alongside the Stones. Dick Taylor, a founding Stone and their original bassist, had quit that band when they went professional to continue his art-school studies. He formed the Pretty Things in 1964 with a schoolmate, singer Phil May. Things happened quickly for them: an original song, "Rosalyn," became an immediate hit and before they'd played their fifth gig together, they were appearing on *Top of the Pops*, the prestigious BBC showcase.

The Pretty Things were a sight to behold. While even the baddest of the bad boys, the Stones and the

Animals, were wearing hound's-tooth jackets and skinny wool ties, the Pretties dressed sloppily. Phil May could forthrightly claim he had the longest hair in rock & roll. In concert, they were loud and aggressive and crude, playing throttling rock & roll and leering slow blues.

They so offended gentrified British society that there was debate in Parliament over how to combat the menace to decency posed by such groups as the Pretty Things. One notorious concert tour of New Zealand in 1965 resulted in scandalizing headlines and rumors of wild behavior and trashings of venerable old opera halls. Capitalizing on their provocative image, the British media posed the question: "Would you let your daughter marry a Pretty Thing?"

In fact, there was some substance to the reputation. Greg Shaw noted: "They appeared onstage in their scruffiest street clothes, their hair matted in unkempt dreadlocks. The songs weren't merely played—they were attacked, as by a tribe of wild-eyed barbarians."

Phil May
(vocals)
Dick Taylor
(guitar)
Peter Tolson
(guitar)
John Povey
(keyboards)
Gordon Edwards
(guitar, keyboards)
Jack Green
(bass)
Skip Alan
(drums)

In reality, they seem fairly tame by latter-day standards. As for the unleashed fury of their rock and blues, they were merely enlivening their music with all the implied suggestiveness of their mentors.

Of their first three albums as raunch-rock barbarians, only the first was issued in this country. By 1966, their contract with the Fontana label had expired, and it proved to be a time of realignment. May and Taylor lost a few old members and added a few new ones, and the Pretty Things moved away from R&B to make a string of singles that evidenced a heavy psychedelic bent. Tunes like "Deflecting Grey" featured demented production work, such things as backwards tapes and special effects—hinting at a mind come unhinged. These deranged sides are some of the most prized collectables of the British Invasion.

Phil May & Co. continued to occupy a place in rock's creative vanguard via a pair of records—*S. F. Sorrow* and *Parachute*—that are widely recognized as the first rock concept albums. The former was based on an Orwellian short story by Phil May about an individual, Sebastian F. Sorrow, and his loss of self and eventual death in a soulless technocratic society. Pete Townshend reputedly listened to the album nonstop for the better part of a week, after which he sat down and composed *Tommy*. *S. F. Sorrow* was released in Britain sometime in early '68 but did not reach America until many months later, the Who's *Tommy* beating it out by a full three months in fact. Ironically, *S. F. Sorrow* was criticized for being derivative of Townshend's rock opera, until Townshend and May intervened to set the record straight.

Parachute was another groundbreaking effort, a musically adventurous slab of psychedelic hard-rock. But their U.S. distributor was the myopic Rare Earth label (an arm of Motown), and neither album got the sales or exposure it deserved. This despite the fact that the *Rolling Stone* critic's poll selected *Parachute* Album of the Year in 1971.

Another album, *Freeway Madness* (1972), again elicited critical raves and dead silence from the public. The Pretty Things never really got the push they merited until Led Zeppelin signed them to their Swan Song label. The Zeppelins cited the Pretties as a major influence, and Robert Plant said of them, "They have got this 'tomorrow's-just-around-the-corner' feel about what they do." The group made two albums for Swan Song, *Silk Torpedo* and *Savage Eye*, both splendid examples of hard-rock melodicism. Despite considerable expense on the part of Led Zeppelin and Swan Song, the commercial rewards once again did not compensate for the effort expended, and the Pretty Things disbanded in 1976. Out of left field, however, they regrouped in 1980, virtually intact and with founding member Dick Taylor back in the fold.

The Pretty Things are recognized as having been a major influence on the American Punk Rock of the Sixties and the British Punk movement of the mid- and late-Seventies. They've survived as long as the Rolling Stones. David Bowie considered them important enough to include two of their songs on his tribute to the Mod-era British R&B scene, *Pin Ups*. The Who and Led Zeppelin rate them as a large influence on their own work. Quite a lot of delightful music awaits those who have yet to discover the Pretty Things.

(PARKE PUTERBAUGH)

U.S. Hit LPs

1975 Silk Torpedo (**104**)
1976 Savage Eye (**163**)

U.K. Hit Singles

1964 Rosalyn (**41**); Don't Bring Me Down (**10**)
1965 Honey I Need (**13**); Cry to Me (**28**)
1966 Midnight to Six Man (**46**); Come See Me (**43**); A House in the Country (**50**)

Procol Harum

Like all truly special rock artists, Procol Harum acquired a devoted cult following, yet in their case this was hardly a cult of personality. Procol Harum represented a unique sound and mood, and the people who created it remained almost anonymous. The Procol Harum mystique was purely a matter of words and music, which were Gothic and gloomy, stately and somber—and more often than not, the classiest in the field.

Appropriately enough, Procol Harum began life as the figment of a poet's imagination. The name (gobbledegook Latin for "beyond these things") originally belonged to a Blue Burmese cat owned by a friend of twenty-year-old Keith Reid, who had just written a lyric titled "A Whiter Shade of Pale" that gave him premonitions of the rock & roll jackpot. Now Reid could juggle the pop surrealisms and non sequiturs of the day as inventively and wittily as anyone, but he wasn't a musician and couldn't sing.

Enter twenty-two-year-old pianist/composer Gary Brooker ("favorite music: baroque, New Orleans, Dylan"), introduced to Reid at a party. Brooker's

South End R&B group the Paramounts had been signed up to Brian Epstein's stable of artists, cut six singles and an EP for Parlophone, toured with the Beatles, and finally called it a day due to lack of real recognition. Eager to explore new horizons, Brooker now set Reid's morbid vision of flying ceilings and vestal virgins to his own haunting variation of Bach's "Air on a G String," and the pair knew they had a blockbuster on their hands.

Ads in the music rags produced four obscure backup musicians, of whom the most talented by far was twenty-one-year-old organist Matthew Fisher. The blend of piano and organ as featured instruments (originally found on Dylan's *Highway 61 Revisited*, but given a uniquely antiquarian flavor by Brooker and Fisher) lent the fledgling group a distinctive sound in a year when new sensations were at a high premium. In rapid succession, Procol Harum had a record contract, a single in the shops, one of the fastest-selling discs ever released, an almost instantaneous Number One. In December the readers of *New Musical Express* voted "A Whiter Shade of Pale" best record of 1967.

Keith Reid
(lyricist)
Gary Brooker
(vocals, piano)
Matthew Fisher
(organ)
Robin Trower
(guitar)
David Knights
(bass)
B. J. Wilson
(drums)

Procol Harum's was one of rock's true rags-to-riches stories, the moral of which was probably "too much too soon." Everyone involved promptly cracked under the strain of instant stardom. Tours had to be canceled and various Procols were hospitalized for exhaustion. Then Brooker concluded that guitarist Ray Royer and drummer Bobby Harrison were duds, and called in former Paramounts colleagues Robin Trower and B. J. Wilson to replace them. (Trower had formed, in the interim, his own trio, called the Jam.)

The lineup of Procol's most creative period was now complete, and the band reclaimed its haunted cathedral with a first album, *Procol Harum*, drenched in all the eldritch mystery of a Black Mass, and a magnificent second single, "Homburg." Perhaps on account of the bad publicity back home, Procol did most of their gigging in America and Europe. A Danish correspondent of *New Musical Express* summed up the ambience of one of their earliest concerts: "You may not be in the year 1967, but back in the Middle Ages. They wear hunting dress and boots, their colorful clothes reminiscent of knights and esquires at court centuries ago. What makes an even stranger impression is that they don't move even the tiniest little bit onstage. They are just there! Immobile . . . yet so moving."

Brooker, Fisher, Knights, Trower, and Wilson recorded two more inspired albums: *Shine On Brightly*, with its seventeen-minute self-mocking suite tracing a man's search for the meaning of life; and *A Salty Dog*, with its award-winning cover adaptation of the Player's Navy Cut cigarette packet design. The song "A Salty Dog," like many of Procol's finest, told of a futile quest—in this case, that of a mariner bound for the world's edge. For sheer sweep and grandeur it had no peer.

The group subsequently fell victim to what might be called the George Harrison "equal time" syndrome. Fisher and Trower wanted to write and sing as well as play, though as singers, at least, both were hopelessly outclassed by Brooker's mournful gospel-tinged vocals. Each was allowed two or three cuts on *A Salty Dog,* but Fisher still felt cramped and he went solo. Knights disappeared around the same time (later resurfacing with his own band, Ruby). Their places were taken by the last of the ex-Paramounts, Chris Copping, doubling on organ and bass. That early Sixties Rhythm & Blues band the Paramounts was now intact once more—in the guise of the arty, mysterious Procol Harum!

The Procol/Paramounts cranked up the volume and stuck together for the intermittently wonderful *Home* and the relatively tedious (and organ-less) *Broken Barricades*. (Upon the latter's release, Brooker commented: "Keith writes the lyrics, and whatever he's into, the group just follows along. Last year it was death. This year it's sex.") Then Trower, self-styled blues guitarist, got fed up with simulating screeches from the crypt and departed for a lucrative career as a musical clone of the late Jimi Hendrix. Temporarily replacing him with David Ball, Procol Harum picked up the pieces and took their act to Edmonton, Canada, where the hooked up with the local symphony orchestra for an experimental concert. Captured on vinyl, it became a huge surprise North American hit—as did the spinoff single, "Conquistador," a retread from the first LP.

So Procol Harum seemed to wield considerable clout when a new lineup incorporating Mick Grabham on guitar and Alan Cartwright on bass signed with Chrysalis Records. But the Blue Burmese cat that once provided their name had recently died, and the band itself would prove increasingly moribund. Reid's measure of the fine line between pretentiousness and self-parody seemed more and more precarious. And though the Chrysalis albums did boast the occasional gem and the band remained a deservedly popular U.S. concert draw—thanks largely to Wilson's remarkable drumming—Procol Harum was now an institution banking on past glories.

The unlikely presence of legendary Fifties producers Jerry Leiber and Mike Stoller for *Procol's Ninth* may have briefly revived Brooker and Reid's long-dormant inspiration; but with Procol's tenth and worst, *Something Magic,* it was painfully evident that this band's number was up. They promoted the album with a desultory tenth-anniversary tour showcasing incongruous Fifties-penned odes to the barroom and the bayou. They might just as well have been an aging British R&B group with a pedestrian name like . . . the Paramounts.

So maybe the talented Messrs. Reid, Brooker, and Wilson picked the right moment to put their dinosaur out of its misery. Better to keep intact the illusions that Procol Harum could once conjure as effectively as anyone. (In the early Eighties, Brooker was spotted in Eric Clapton's backup band, and Wilson in Joe Cocker's.)

(NICHOLAS SCHAFFNER)

U.S. Hit Singles

1967   A Whiter Shade of Pale (**5**);
        Homburg (**34**)
1972   Conquistador (**16**)

(BY ROBIN TROWER)

1976   Caledonia (**82**)

U.S. Hit LPs

1967   Procol Harum (**47**)
1968   Shine On Brightly (**24**)
1969   A Salty Dog (**32**)
1970   Home (**34**)
1971   Broken Barricades (**32**)
1972   Live in Concert with the Edmonton
        Symphony Orchestra (**5**)
1973   Grand Hotel (**21**);
        The Best of Procol Harum (**131**)
1974   Exotic Birds and Fruit (**86**)
1975   Procol's Ninth (**52**)
1977   Something Magic (**147**)

(BY ROBIN TROWER)

1974   Bridge of Sighs (**7**)
1975   For Earth Below (**5**)
1976   Live! (**10**);
        Long Misty Days (**24**)
1978   Caravan to Midnight (**37**)
1980   Victims of the Fury (**34**)

U.K. Hit Singles

1967   A Whiter Shade of Pale (**1**);
        Homburg (**6**)
1968   Quite Rightly So (**50**)
1969   A Salty Dog (**44**)
1972   Conquistador (**22**)
1975   Pandora's Box (**16**)

The Psychedelic Furs

Richard Butler
(vocals)
John Ashton
(guitar)
Roger Morris
(guitar)
Tim Butler
(bass)
Duncan Kilburn
(horns, keyboards)
Vince Ely
(drums)

Of all of Britain's post-Punk bands, the Psychedelic Furs most closely recaptured the original meaning of the words Punk Rock—as exemplified by those mid-Sixties American garage bands with psychedelic-sounding names (e.g., Question Mark and the Mysterians) whose inept attempts to Xerox the music of the British Invasion and its acid aftermath inadvertently resulted in a handful of rock & roll classics ("96 Tears," "Psychotic Reaction," et al). Or, as *The Village Voice*'s Robert Christgau averred: "We can thank them, I suppose, for emphasizing that Punk is the child of the hippie as well as its antithesis."

Be that as it may, the Furs were certainly the only band ever to have drawn its inspiration in equal measure from Jim Morrison, David Bowie, and Johnny Rotten. The components of the Furs' early music were as distinct as they were incongruous, creating the overall effect of a strange—and strangely fascinating—collage. Butler's stream-of-consciousness lyrics were as disjointed as the band's music; yet somehow it all worked, and the Psychedelic Furs' self-styled "beautiful chaos" emerged as one of the few British New Wave sounds to capture the American consumer's imagination.

"We Love You"—*not* coincidentally, the title of the Rolling Stones' most psychedelic 1967 single—was issued by CBS in late 1979 as the Furs' British debut, and promptly claimed the Number One slot on *Sounds'* "Alternative" singles listing. In March 1980, *The Psychedelic Furs* LP entered the U.K.'s national charts at number eighteen and went on to become a big-selling import in America. The response to the band's first U.S. tour that autumn prompted Columbia Records to rev up its starmaking machinery on the Furs' behalf; the band, in turn, slogged through forty dates in thirty cities (and committed themselves to two more similarly grueling tours over the following year).

That Americans were willing to listen in the first place may be attributed to vain hopes for a "psychedelic revival." But the Furs' second album hardly evoked a latter-day Strawberry Alarm Clock. Though the band's eclectic influences (psychedelic and otherwise) were still much in evidence, *Talk Talk Talk* was more a synthesis than a collage. The monolithic din was now pierced by lead guitar breaks and snatches of real melody ("We've learned to play in the last year or so," Butler admitted in *Trouser Press*); and *Talk Talk Talk* also dispensed with the nattering negativism of the first LP (wherein the word "stupid" had cropped up on over half the songs' lyrics).

Nonetheless, critics and fans liked *Talk Talk Talk* even more than its predecessor. To *The Village Voice*'s John Piccarella, the Psychedelic Furs recalled "that rare Sixties pop vision, informed by Warhol and found in the best Lou Reed (or the best porn flicks) which reproduces—unadorned, unedited, and unjudged—the minute-by-minute movement of modern reality with both the clarity of photography and the transfigurative power of dream."

What's more, you could even dance to it.

(NICHOLAS SCHAFFNER)

Richard Butler
(*Columbia Records*)

U.S. Hit LPs

1980   The Psychedelic Furs (140)

Public Image, Ltd.

John Lydon
(vocals)
Keith Levene
(guitars, synthesizers)
Jah Wobble
(bass)
Martin Atkins
(drums)
Jeanette Lee
(visuals)

When the Sex Pistols misfired, John Lydon (a.k.a. Johnny Rotten) decided to start a new band that would carry out the Pistols' threat: the destruction of rock & roll. Only this time he was going to do it differently. This time he would get it right.

Lydon formed the initial version of Public Image, Ltd. (PiL, for short) with friends Jah Wobble and Jim Walker, plus original Clash guitarist Keith Levene. After a period of legal hassles, releasing Lydon from a contract with Malcolm McLaren and the other Pistols, the new band released a single ("Public Image" b/w "Cowboy Song") and played its first public performance on Christmas Day, 1978. Their debut LP, *First Edition*, was released to almost unanimous bad reviews. Lydon's a traitor to the cause, he's sold out, the Punk party line went, and the more conservative rock press went along with *Rolling Stone*'s view that *First Edition* was "industrial noise." While not perfect, the LP did have its moments, and things would improve.

PiL seldom toured, preferring to work in the studio. The sound on their new single, "Death Disco," was a revelation of compelling musical elements: Wobble's heavy dub bass, drummer Martin Atkins's disco backbeat, and Levene's guitar playing, which sounded like no other rock guitar. Instead of chord progressions and riffs, Levene relied on sheets of sound, layers of notes utilizing the guitars' natural harmonics and sustain. PiL found themselves back in critical favor.

What clinched Lydon's return was the release of *Metal Box,* a record as notable for its design as for its music. *Metal Box* comprised three twelve-inch 45s, which were placed in a film canister embossed with the PiL logo. The music inside was as hard and brittle as the box, though eminently danceable. "Dance music of the Plague," as Griel Marcus called it.

Lydon's own views on *Metal Box* were typical: "If you don't like the records in it, you can throw them away and put good ones in."

The *Metal Box* was released in America as a more conventional two-LP set titled *Second Edition*. PiL embarked on a "tour" of the States (eight gigs in eight weeks), but even this took its toll. By July 1980, both Joh Wobble and Martin Atkins had left the band, and

PiL vowed never to tour again.

In April '81, PiL proved they had more tricks up their sleeve. They released their third studio LP, *Flowers of Romance,* the name of Sid Vicious's first band. It sounded like nothing else PiL, or anyone else, had ever recorded. *Billboard* called it "the most uncommercial record ever made."

For their second American tour, PiL played two nights at the Ritz in New York, filling in for Bow Wow Wow. They didn't play a concert; instead they gave a "live video performance." The Ritz's audience was not ready for PiL's "performance," and made its dissatisfaction known, throwing bottles at the stage and rioting. Lydon still had the power to outrage, bless his heart.

(STEVE MIRKIN)

U.S. Hit LPs

1980   Second Edition (**171**)

U.K. Hit Singles

1978   Public Image (**9**)
1979   Death Disco (**20**); Memories (**60**)

Queen

If you've ever seen Queen in concert, you'd probably describe them in such terms as grandiose, theatrical, flashy, and, yes, maybe even bombastic or pretentious. But one thing's for sure: Nobody comes away bored from a Queen concert, and the same goes for the band's meticulously produced albums.

If the group's powerful blend of Brian May's hard rock guitar, drummer Roger Taylor and bassist John Deacon's complicated rhythms, and the group's soaring vocal harmonies doesn't stir you, odds are the androgynous posturings and ballet-like stage movements of hammy singer Freddie Mercury will. If that's not enough, there are Queen's famous special effects on stage—among the most spectacular in show business. Their 1977 stage show began with a 5000-pound, twenty-six-foot-high crown rising from the floor to reveal the band in an artificial fog bank.

Some people find Queen's penchant for ornate music and smoke bombs a bit overdone, but as is obvious from its sales record—by 1981, seven of its ten albums had gone gold with three going platinum as well—this band is one of the most popular in the world. It's also one of the most unusual. Brian May plays a guitar he and his father built from scratch. All four members have college degrees. And rather than work their way up the music industry ladder in the usual manner, by playing the British club circuit, they rehearsed privately for eighteen months and landed a recording contract on the basis of a demo tape.

Queen signed with EMI in the U.K. and Elektra in the U.S. in 1973. Their first LP, *Queen*, was launched with a massive promotion. Billed as a cross between the heavy metal of Led Zeppelin and the art rock of David Bowie, the group came out during the height of the "glam-rock" or "glitter" fad. Their fruity costumes, elaborate production, and Mercury's blatantly bisexual stage act contributed to this image.

The first album did not set the world on fire, but with *Queen II* in the spring of 1974 some progress was made. Still, it wasn't until the third LP, *Sheer Heart Attack*, in the fall of 1974, and the single "Killer Queen" that the band really took off. "Killer Queen" made it to number two in the U.K. and cracked the Top Ten in America.

Queen became a true international phenomenon in 1975 with the album *A Night at the Opera* and Mercury's six-minute operetta, "Bohemian Rhapsody," which topped the charts in Britain for an amazing seven weeks. Queen finally solidified its position in the upper ranks of superstardom in 1977 with the hard-rocking album *News of the World* and its double A-sided hit single "We Will Rock You" b/w "We Are the Champions."

The momentum fell of a bit in 1978 when the group's experiments on its *Jazz* album were less successful. A two-record in-concert set, *Live Killers*, filled the recording gap in 1979 before Queen knocked the music world on its ear early in 1980 with the rockabilly single "Crazy Little Thing Called Love," from their album, *The Game*. A hard-driving funk/rock "rap" number called "Another One Bites the Dust" (also culled from *The Game*) became the biggest hit of Queen's career, getting heavy crossover airplay on black-oriented radio stations. They closed out the year with the soundtrack from the science fiction film spoof *Flash Gordon* and then opened 1981 with an unprecedented tour of South America, playing to some 500,000 in Argentina and Brazil, including a record-setting crowd of 131,000 at a soccer stadium in São Paulo. Late 1981 saw Queen release a collaborative single with David Bowie entitled "Under Pressure."

(BILL KING)

U.S. Hit Singles

1975   Killer Queen (**12**)
1976   Bohemian Rhapsody (**9**);
            You're My Best Friend (**16**)
1977   Somebody to Love (**13**);
            Tie Your Mother Down (**49**)
1978   We Are the Champions/We Will Rock You (**4**);
            Bicycle Race/Fat Bottomed Girls (**24**);
            It's Late (**74**)
1979   Don't Stop Me Now (**86**);
            Crazy Little Thing Called Love (**1**)
1980   Play the Game (**42**);
            Another One Bites the Dust (**1**);
            Need Your Loving Tonight (**44**)

U.S. Hit LPs

1973   Queen (**83**)
1974   Queen II (**49**);
            Sheer Heart Attack (**17**)
1975   A Night at the Opera (**4**)
1977   A Day at the Races (**5**); News of the World (**3**)
1978   Jazz (**6**)
1979   Live Killers (**16**)
1980   The Game (**1**);
            Flash Gordon (soundtrack) (**23**)

Freddie Mercury
(vocals, keyboards)
Brian May
(guitar)
John Deacon
(bass)
Roger Taylor
(drums)

Freddie Mercury
(Perry F. Lesley)

Tom Robinson Band

Tom Robinson
(vocals, bass)
Danny Kustow
(guitar)
Mark Ambler
(keyboards)
"Dolphin" Taylor
(drums)

"If music can erase even a tiny fraction of the prejudice and intolerance in this world, then it's worth trying," declared Tom Robinson at the outset of TRB's career. In a series of heartfelt musical broadsides, Robinson decried the rise of the neo-Nazi National Front Party and enthusiastically championed the rights of women, homosexuals, and racial minorities. Though he was associated with the emerging New Wave movement, his music was, in his own words, "more mainstream . . . acceptable to the ears of the people who were frightened by the Sex Pistols." Robinson was among the first to channel the nihilistic anger of the early Punk movement toward a more positive social awareness. The uncritical adulation he instantly received may be attributed to the fact that Tom Robinson filled a desperate need, among both critics and fans, for a rock & roll singer who still cared.

Like David Bowie, he vaulted from obscurity to the front page of *Melody Maker* by uttering the two syllables: "I'm gay. . . ." Tom, however, was as down-to-earth as Bowie was not; far from being a calculated outrage, his "admission" was merely a by-product of his personal integrity and forthrightness.

The black sheep of a wealthy family, he spent much of his adolescence at a home for maladjusted boys, where he befriended Danny Kustow, an aspiring musician with whom Robinson formed a series of amateur bands. After his emergence into the real world, Robinson joined an acoustic pub trio called Café Society. A contract with the Kinks' Konk Records engendered an LP produced by Ray Davies (with whom Robinson shared a pronounced music-hall influence). When Tom decided to leave Café Society and Konk for the greener pastures of TRB and EMI, Davies belied his endearing public persona with a hardheaded refusal to release Robinson from his contract. He reportedly relented only when Tom, spotting Davies in his audience one night, launched into a version of the Kinks' "Tired of Waiting for You."

Robinson formed TRB in early 1977 after a stint on the London Gay Switchboard, in tandem with Britain's simmering racial tensions, inspired him to write more "relevant" music. Ironically, however, TRB's first hit was the out-of-character "2-4-6-8 Motorway"—an old fashioned car song in the classic rock & roll tradition.

"2-4-6" was to remain TRB's most popular song—and their best. Despite some spirited rock & roll, TRB's *Rising Free* EP and *Power in the Darkness* LP (packaged together in the U.S.) tended to bludgeon the listener with musical and verbal clichés. "Right on, sister, right on," however sincerely intended, came across as patronizing, and "better decide which side you're on . . . if left is right then right is wrong" was an insult to the audience's intelligence.

(*Harvest*)

Though the rhetoric was toned down on *TRB Two* (recorded in the wake of Ambler's and Taylor's departure), Todd Rundgren's production proved to be a dispiriting mess of organ-dominated sludge. In July 1979, Robinson conceded in *Melody Maker* that "after two and a half years, it's become a bit tame and predictable. It's time to move on and try something fresh."

After writing a few ditties with Elton John, Robinson switched from bass to rhythm guitar, and, ignoring the admonishments of EMI (thereby losing his contract), formed an entirely new band called Sector 27 with bassist Jo Burt, drummer Derek Quinton, and guitarist Stevie B. Taking their cue from avant-garde, dance-oriented groups like the Gang of Four, the Pop Group, and XTC, they issued one LP—*Sector 27*—whose breadth of musical and lyrical invention put TRB to shame. But the album sold poorly, and Robinson left in 1981 on a solo tour of Japan.

In the end Tom Robinson may be best remembered less for his words and music than for his effervescent charm and sincerity, both onstage and off, he could invariably disarm even the most hardened skeptic.

(NICHOLAS AND ELIZABETH SCHAFFNER)

Rockpile

Rockpile was a quartet with a split personality. Half the time, guitarist Dave Edmunds played front man while the other three members backed him up on songs he wrote. The rest of the time, bassist Nick Lowe was in the spotlight, and the others became Lowe's backing unit. What's more, Rockpile only existed in concert until 1980, when the group finally issued its first album under that name.

Lowe and Edmunds pulled Rockpile together in 1976, but the group's roots go back almost a decade before that. Edmunds, a Welshman, was the star of a mid-Sixties trio called Love Sculpture. They were mostly a blues band, but at the height of the classical rock craze they put out a rock version of Khatchaturian's classic "Sabre Dance" which, in late 1968, zipped to the very top of the English charts and stayed there into 1969. By 1970, Edmunds had returned to Wales, disbanded Love Sculpture, and initiated his solo career as a rock revivalist.

One of his first singles was a remake of the 1955 Smiley Lewis hit "I Hear You Knocking." Edmunds' ability to re-create the Fifties made the song a Top Ten hit even in America, and it grabbed the Number One spot in England in late 1970.

Edmunds issued more singles and, in 1972, a solo album called *Rockpile*. The records were well received in England—"Baby I Love You" and "Born to Be with You" were 1973 hits—but nothing further happened in America, which wasn't buying his Phil Spector remakes.

Nick Lowe had worked with a number of minor British pop bands in the Sixties, but it wasn't until 1970, with the formation of the group Brinsley Schwarz, that anyone began to take notice. Unfortunately, the group's music was almost smothered in an avalanche of hype. For some reason, the band's promoters decided to go all out and ballyhoo Brinsley Schwarz as—what else?—"the new Beatles." The publicists went so far as to fly influential British rock journalists from London to New York to report on the Brinsleys' American debut. America, however, had never heard of Brinsley Schwarz; the debut was poorly received; a batch of copies of their debut disc, pressed hastily for the journalists, proved defective; and the group's future was almost torpedoed right then and there.

As far as American sales went, the Brinsleys never did cross the Atlantic. They never made the Top Twenty in Britain, either, though they did develop a respectable cult following over the course of some half a dozen albums. Their sound was dubbed "pub rock." It was a clean rockabilly sound with a solidly rhythmic base. As the name implies, pub rock wasn't meant to be played in huge amphitheaters but in small halls and nightclubs; no Alice Cooper pyrotechnics, thank you. Many of the pub rockers of the Seventies—including some of the Brinsleys—have become important New Wave artists in the Eighties.

Lowe and Edmunds crossed paths in 1972, when Brinsley Schwarz cut the album *Nervous on the Road* at Edmunds' Rockfield studios in Wales. But the two didn't get together again until 1976, after the Brinsleys broke up. Finding themselves in London, Lowe and

Brinsley Schwarz: Nick Lowe (c). (*United Artists*)

Nick Lowe
(vocals, bass)
Dave Edmunds
(vocals, guitar)
Billy Bremner
(guitar)
Terry Williams
(drums)

Edmunds jammed informally with pickup bands and then decided to put together Rockpile. They enlisted drummer Terry Williams, a veteran of the Welsh group Man, and session guitarist Billy Bremner.

From the outset, Rockpile was a different kind of group. The name was appended to whoever got star billing, i.e., "Nick Lowe and Rockpile." So each time the band toured America, the quasi-band alternated lead singers. The first time, in 1976, Rockpile supported Edmunds and his album *Get It*. The second time, in early 1978, it backed Lowe and his *Jesus of Cool* (diplomatically called *Pure Pop for Now People* in the U.S.A.). And so it went.

At last, in late 1980, Rockpile toured extensively under that name alone and released the first real group effort, *Seconds of Pleasure*. Unfortunately (and surprisingly), nothing like a "group sound" emerged. Edmunds had his high voice, rubbery, twanging guitar, and great love of oldies; Lowe put out punchy Power Pop with catchy hooks. In the spring of 1981, Rockpile stunned everyone by announcing it was breaking up. Just after that news hit, Edmunds released another solo album, *Twangin' . . .*, recorded during happier days. It featured Everly Brothers-style harmonies with Lowe, solid support from Bremner and Williams, and Edmunds' strong, resonant guitar, and netted Edmunds a minor hit, a remake of John Fogerty's "Almost Saturday Night." Nick Lowe followed suit in early 1982 with *Nick the Knife*.

(HENRY McNULTY)

U.S. Hit Singles

1980	Teacher Teacher (51)

(BY DAVE EDMUNDS)

1971	I Hear You Knocking (4); I'm Comin' Home (75)
1979	Girls Talk (65)
1980	Singing the Blues (28)

(BY NICK LOWE)

1979 Cruel to Be Kind (**12**)

U.S. Hit LPs

1980 Seconds of Pleasure (**27**)

(BY DAVE EDMUNDS)

1979 Repeat When Necessary (**54**)

(BY NICK LOWE)

1978 Pure Pop for Now People (**127**)
1979 Labour of Lust (**31**)

U.K. Hit Singles

(BY DAVE EDMUNDS)

1970 I Hear You Knocking (**1**)
1973 Baby I Love You (**8**); Born to Be with You (**5**)
1977 I Knew the Bride (**26**)
1979 Girls Talk (**4**); Queen of Hearts (**11**); Crawling from the Wreckage (**59**)

(BY NICK LOWE)

1978 I Love the Sound of Breaking Glass (**7**)
1979 Crackin' Up (**34**); Cruel to Be Kind (**12**)

Roxy Music

Bryan Ferry
(vocals, keyboards)
Phil Manzanera
(guitar)
Andy Mackay
(saxophone, oboe)
Paul Thompson
(drums)
Brian Eno
(synthesizer, "tapes")

Years before anyone had heard of Blondie, the Talking Heads, or Gary Numan, *New Musical Express* was hailing Roxy Music as "one of Britain's most provocative and entertaining New Wave bands." In light of subsequent British pop history, that 1973 accolade seems uncannily apt—even if the Bryan Ferry corporation went on to outgrow its original synthesis of determined amateurism, electronic doodling, and kitsch Americana.

The son of a Newcastle coal miner, Ferry began the decade as a struggling artist, a fine arts graduate-turned-teacher of sixteen-year-old girls. Ferry, who had already worked with semipro bands and failed a King Crimson audition, found himself applying Pop Art attitudes to pop music. Rehearsing his compositions with Graham Simpson (the first in a long line of fly-by-night bassists), Ferry resolved in late 1970 to form a band called Roxy Music—after the popular Roxy chain of cinemas. First he recruited a synthesizer player, the classically trained Andy Mackay, who subsequently became enamored of the saxophone. Guitarist Phil Manzanera made the transition from "playing insane 17/8 things at ridiculous speeds" with a band called Quiet Sun to executing Ferry's Pop Art concepts in the company of one Brian George St. John le Baptiste de la Salle Eno.

Like Ferry, Eno brought a visual arts background to bear on contemporary music—a field in which both Roxyites harbored wildly eclectic tastes. In the *NME* column "Under the Influence," Eno would cite as his musical inspirations Terry Riley and Steve Reich, Buddy Holly, Jimi Hendrix ("the first to think of what he was playing in terms outside the instrument he was holding"), the third Velvet Underground LP ("my favorite album ever"), and "Early Sixties American Moody Rock" as exemplified by the Tokens' "The Lion Sleeps Tonight." Ferry's choices included the Beatles, Bob Dylan, Frank Sinatra, Lotte Lenya, Ethel Merman, and Charlie Parker.

The first *Roxy Music* LP (issued at the start of 1972), proved to be a thoroughly inspired—and discordant—melange of all the above and more. On any given selection, Ferry's still-raw vocals were apt to run the gamut from Noel Coward to Fifties doo-wop, with Mackay alternating between gritty Monster Mash sax and a lilting oboe out of some Russian ballet—and Eno supplying blips of static from another wavelength entirely.

Roxy's visual angle—largely contrived by futuristic clothes designer Anthony Price—perfectly complemented the music. The sexy lead singer's trousers, for example, were likely to sport two front zippers; *Music Scene* once reported that Eno "has been seen traveling the Underground wearing heavily applied brown eye shadow, thick mascara, lipstick, black glitter beads, pearly nail varnish, and violent purple streaks in his blond hair." Like David Bowie, Roxy Music instilled a sophisticated camp style into the glitter vogue recently instigated by Marc Bolan. And the band seemed to catapult from nowhere to standing ovations as the opener for Bowie's historic *Ziggy Stardust* concerts at the Rainbow Theatre.

The *Roxy Music* album was followed by a single "Virginia Plain," of which its author, Bryan Ferry, had this to say: "Andy Warhol and Roy Lichtenstein—the American Dream. That's what 'Virginia Plain' is all about: dreaming of going to New York and living in an attic and painting. The whole Warhol setup was fantastically attractive then." This classic seven-incher became an enormous British hit, as did the followup, "Pyjamarama." Ferry, however, insisted: "We're not a singles group really. I certainly don't want to find myself sliding down that Slade/T. Rex corridor of horror."

Roxy Music demanded attention, and got it (though not, at first, in America, where they proved a disastrous choice as Jethro Tull's opening act). Despite a suspiciously rapid ride to the top, Roxy remained the darlings of the British music press for at least the first few years. *NME* and *Melody Maker* affectionately nicknamed Roxy's tall, dark, and handsome lounge lizard "La Ferrari"; but the group's scrawny electronics wizard entranced them even more. Accompanying Roxy on a European tour, *NME* scribe Nick Kent reported mounds of mail arriving for Eno, much of it inscribed with the likes of: "Hi, I am eighteen years old and I am a good screw."

La Ferrari—who claimed Roxy was "ninety-nine percent" his trip, and who would one day fire a bassist for evidencing too much showmanship on *his* stage—was not amused. By the time the second album appeared, with another voluptuous glamour girl on the jacket, the breach between Ferry and his upstart colleague had widened to the point of public backbiting. Nonetheless, *For Your Pleasure* proved to be a stunning achievement, even surpassing Roxy

Music's landmark first album. By now Ferry had perfected his trademark croon—at once unctuous and ghoulish, while his writing grew increasingly urbane and sardonic. "In Every Dream Home a Heartache," for instance, was an ode to an inflatable mail-order sex doll.

Despite the trend towards calculated sophistication, Ferry told *NME* before entering the studios that Roxy were "using the Velvet Underground's *White Light/White Heat* as a fair example of what we want . . . we hope to make it in a single afternoon." In the words of Brian Eno, "to do things very quickly has distinct advantages—you leave all the mistakes in, and the mistakes become very interesting." If Bryan Ferry was still buying that particular conceit, he nonetheless hadn't conceived Roxy Music as a vehicle for *Eno's* mistakes. In June 1973 Eno finally announced that he was "leaving Roxy to pursue a partially defined direction—probably involving further investigations into bioelectronics, snake guitar, the human voice, and lizard girls."

"He was probably more similar to me than any other member of the band in that he wasn't a virtuoso musician at all," Ferry would tell *Sounds* two years after the split. "He was just in a very frustrating position because I was calling all the shots and there was no room for his ideas."

Charmingly titled *Here Come the Warm Jets,* Eno's first solo album featured all of Eno's former Roxy colleagues save Ferry. *Jets* was devoted to hit-or-miss experiments within the framework of the three-minute rock song. ("On Some Faraway Beach," for instance, was a transcription of something Eno claimed to have heard in a dream.) The results were by turns brilliant and tiresome.

The sequel, *Taking Tiger Mountain (by Strategy),* proved far more consistent. Allegedly inspired by a Peking Revolutionary Ballet called *Tiger Mountain*— "just a straightforward thing about the workers overcoming the tropps"—it showcased Eno's flat voice intoning vaguely Oriental non sequiturs to excruciatingly catchy melodies, accompanied by weird tape loops, clattering typewriters, everything short of the proverbial kitchen sink. This droll classic was arranged and coproduced by Phil Manzanera, who played guitar throughout.

Brian Eno returned the favor by figuring prominently on Manzanera's *Diamond Head* LP. The two also organized a band—dubbed 801 after a line from *Tiger Mountain*—for a one-shot concert; their unorthodox interpretations of the Beatles' "Tomorrow Never Knows" and the Kinks' "You Really Got Me" are preserved on the album *801 Live.* Though Eno linked up with John Cale, Nico, and Kevin Ayers for a similar event—also recorded, as *June 1, 1974*—he otherwise stuck to his decision to forswear live performances.

Having already collaborated with Robert Fripp on the avant-garde all-instrumental LP *No Pussyfooting.* Eno attempted to find a common ground between his two styles on 1975's *Another Green World.* Of the fourteen short pieces, many were instrumental, most dispensed with the solid rock core of his first two solo LPs, and nearly all were highly imaginative and melodic.

Though Eno's productions are always unique and defy classification, 1977's *Before and After Science* was somewhat more rock-oriented than *Green World,* while displaying considerably more real artistry than his earlier endeavors. Subtitled *Fourteen Pictures,* this ten-song LP was packaged with four prints by the painter Péter Schmidt, with whom Eno also "produced a boxed set of oracle cards called 'Oblique Strategies,' used extensively in the making of this record."

Leaving England for a nomadic existence, Eno established himself as a prominent figure in New York's avant-garde and New Wave circles before migrating elsewhere. During that period he found himself in great demand as a producer for such up-and-coming acts as the Talking Heads, Devo, and James Chance. He has also made several "ambient" recordings (*Music for Films, Music for Airports, Discreet Music*) and collaborated with the avant-garde composers Harold Budd and Jon Hassell, the electronic German band Cluster, and, of course, David Bowie and Robert Fripp.

In the meantime, Roxy Music's once and future helmsman, Bryan Ferry, had launched a supplementary solo career of his own. *These Foolish Things* featured wicked interpretations of Bob Dylan's apocalyptic "A Hard Rain's Gonna Fall" and Leslie Gore's teen lament "It's My Party" (in which Ferry leaves the original gender references intact). A sequel, *Another Time, Another Place,* yielded two British chart-busters, "The In Crowd" and "Smoke Gets in Your Eyes." Ferry's ultimate goal, he confessed at the time, was the silver screen. "Gatsby—now *there* was a part I always felt a great kinship towards."

Roxy Music itself remained relatively experimental, though the inspired amateurism went out with Brian Eno. The latter's replacement was Eddie Jobson, the eighteen-year-old electric violin and keyboard prodigy from Curved Air. The classically trained Jobson was as conventionally accomplished as Eno was not, and as uncharismatic as Ferry could possibly want. But any doubts concerning the viability of an Eno-less Roxy Music were removed by the *Stranded* LP; even Brian Eno conceded that it was the best thing they had ever done. Ferry was now cultivating his "European gigolo" persona; on the most stunning of Roxy's new songs—the cinematic travelogue "Song for Europe"—he even crooned the final verses in French, and onstage the camp-nostalgic trash element had been ditched in favor of a white dinner jacket and a black bow tie. *Stranded* promptly reached Number One in the U.K.

These high standards were maintained on 1974's *Country Life* (banned in some states on account of the cover girls' transparent lingerie) and 1975's *Siren* (whose "Love Is the Drug" finally established Roxy as a major attraction on both sides of the Atlantic). But Roxy Music's American breakthrough failed to keep the lid on tensions simmering within the band; and after the pop headlines blared Ferry and Mackay's unfavorable quotes about one another, it was announced that Roxy Music's members were taking an extended sabbatical to pursue individual projects. Subsequent solo albums from Ferry, Manzanera, and Mackay met with varying degrees of critical and commercial success. Bryan Ferry's efforts relied heavily on the original material that he used to reserve for the band, yet failed to do as well as either the Roxy albums or his earlier oldies collections. Ironically, Mackay's score for the popular *Rock Follies* TV serial was a British Number One.

In 1979, Ferry, Manzanera, Mackay, and Thompson confounded most observers by reuniting for an LP titled *Manifesto.* (Jobson had since joined another band, U.K., and later, Jethro Tull.) Divided into an "East Side" reminiscent of mid-Seventies Roxy and a

"West Side" devoted to sophisticated, disco-tinged pop, *Manifesto* earned the band a warm welcome back to Britain's rock hierarchy.

Flesh and Blood (1980) was all "West Side"—even to the extent of encroaching upon erstwhile Ferry solo territory with glossy readings of Wilson Pickett's "In the Midnight Hour" and the Byrds' "Eight Miles High." The departed (fired?) Thompson's tub-thumping was conspicuous in its absence, and on some tracks even Mackay and Manzanera were nowhere to be heard. Some aficionados found it difficult to recognize *Flesh and Blood* as a bona fide Roxy Music album.

One could now picture Roxy Music lasting into the next millennium, with Bryan regaling his following with favorites from the fabulous Sixties. Ferry, however, had an altogether different scenario in mind in 1974, telling *NME*'s Nick Kent: "The grand exit is a very appealing prospect. . . . The motorcycle accident and the plane crash have all been done so . . . I'm quite in favor of the pile of clothes on the beach . . . with not a note but a cassette, containing the last pained message to the world, laying on a well-pressed tuxedo carefully folded." And unfinished demos to keep the legend alive? "In my case they'd have to be finished mixes. After all, one has to keep up one's standards at all times."

(NICHOLAS SCHAFFNER)

U.S. Hit Singles

1976 Love Is the Drug (**30**)
1979 Dance Away (**44**)
1980 Over You (**80**)

(BY BRYAN FERRY)

1976 Heart on My Sleeve (**86**)

U.S. Hit LPs

1973 For Your Pleasure (**193**)
1974 Stranded (**186**)
1975 Country Life (**37**); Siren (**50**)
1976 Viva! Roxy Music (**81**)
1979 Manifesto (**23**)
1980 Flesh and Blood (**35**)

(BY BRYAN FERRY)

1976 Let's Stick Together (**168**)
1977 In Your Mind (**126**)
1978 The Bride Stripped Bare (**159**)

(BY BRIAN ENO)

1974 Here Come the Warm Jets (**151**)
1978 Before and After Science (**171**)

U.K. Hit Singles

1972 Virginia Plain (**4**)
1973 Pyjamarama (**10**); Street Life (**9**)
1974 All I Want Is You (**12**)
1975 Love Is the Drug (**2**); Both Ends Burning (**25**)
1977 Virginia Plain (**11**)
1979 Trash (**40**); Dance Away (**2**); Angel Eyes (**4**)
1980 Over You (**5**); Oh Yeah (**5**);
Same Old Scene (**12**)

(BY BRYAN FERRY)

1973 A Hard Rain's Gonna Fall (**10**)
1974 The In Crowd (**13**);
Smoke Gets in Your Eyes (**17**)
1975 You Go to My Head (**33**)
1976 Let's Stick Together (**4**); Extended Play (**7**)
1977 This Is Tomorrow (**9**); Tokyo Joe (**15**)
1978 What Goes On (**67**); Sign of the Times (**37**)

SAVOY BROWN: See Foghat

The Searchers

The Searchers are one of the most underrated of the first batch of British Invasion groups, which is surprising considering that they were the *only* Liverpool band from the mid-Sixties recording in the Eighties and that their style was the forerunner of the popular folk-rock sound exemplified by the Byrds, and later Buffalo Springfield, the Eagles, and Tom Petty.

John McNally, original drummer Chris Curtis, and Mike Pender, were schoolmates when they first performed together. In 1960 they teamed up with bassist Tony Jackson to officially become the Searchers (a name taken from a John Ford Western). Their dates often coincided with the Beatles, and they actually took the same path to stardom as the Fab Four, via a stint in Hamburg at the Star Club.

McNally remembers the early Sixties as a time when all the local Liverpool groups would observe each other's gigs, swap records, and take turns performing cover versions of the same songs—usually American hits. After the Beatles Explosion, all the Liverpool bands were under siege by record companies, and the Searchers had no trouble securing a recording contract. They signed with Pye Records, and their first single, the Drifters' "Sweets For My Sweet," was a hit.

By 1964 the teenage population of England and America was mispronouncing the word "pins," ("pin-zuh") thanks to the Searchers' rendition of the Jackie DeShannon hit "Needles and Pins" (written by the then unknown Sonny Bono and Jack Nitzsche). It was around this time that Jackson left the group, soon to be followed by the departure of Chris Curtis. They were replaced by Frank Allen and John Blunt.

Despite the fact that the group was known as "The Beatles' favorite English band," they were a throwback to the pre-Beatles musical era. With their cleancut looks and personality, they performed brilliant cover versions. That was perfectly acceptable in the early Sixties, but once the Beatles transformed the sound of music by writing their own hit songs, the public and the recording industry wanted singer/songwriters—not just performers. That dilemma, coupled with the fact that they were the only top Liverpool band *not* managed by Brian Epstein, became their major drawback vis-à-vis mass success. Still, their unique ringing guitar sound, infectious harmonies, and uncanny ability to find the *perfect* song kept the

Mike Pender
(guitar, vocals)
John McNally
(guitar, vocals)
Frank Allen
(bass, vocals)
Billy Adamson
(drums)

Searchers' music in people's minds long after the members' names and faces were forgotten.

By 1966 most of the Merseyside groups, with the exception of the Beatles, were losing their mass appeal and disbanding. The Searchers had their last hit that year, but held together, paying the rent by playing local gigs and making the rounds of the English cabaret circuit.

Ironically, the same song that brought the group worldwide recognition in 1964 was responsible for putting the Searchers back on the charts. In 1979, the Ramones recorded a cover version of "Needles and Pins," which nostalgically brought the Searchers' superior version to mind. Sire Records tracked down the band and offered them a recording contract. The Searchers were thrilled to be given four weeks of studio time to complete an album, as opposed to the few days they had been accustomed to in the mid-Sixties.

Even though the times had changed, the Searchers' new songs sounded the same—yet somehow even better this time around. "Hearts In Her Eyes" was so good that listeners were certain it had to be a hit in the golden days of the Sixties (which it wasn't!). The album was a mild success, and two years later they recorded a followup, which received rave reviews.

The Searchers may never be as big as they could have been, but just to have survived in the business for over twenty years was an achievement. Maybe they really did drink some of that "Love Potion Number Nine" after all.

(SUE WEINER)

U.S. Hit Singles

1964	Needles and Pins (13);
	Don't Throw Your Love Away (16);
	Some Day We're Gonna Love Again (34);
	When You Walk in the Room (35);
	Sugar and Spice (44);
	Ain't That Just Like Me (61)
1965	Love Potion Number Nine (3);
	Bumble Bee (21);
	What Have They Done to the Rain (29);
	Goodbye My Lover Goodbye (52);
	He's Got No Love (79)
1966	Take Me for What I'm Worth (76);
	Have You Ever Loved Somebody (94)
1971	Desdemona (94)

U.S. Hit LPs

1964	Hear! Hear! (120);
	Needles and Pins (22);
	This Is Us (97)
1965	The New Searchers L.P. (112);
	The Searchers No. 4 (149)
1980	The Searchers (191)

U.K. Hit Singles

1963	Sweets for My Sweet (1);
	Sugar and Spice (2);
	Sweet Nothins (48)
1964	Needles and Pins (1);
	Don't Throw Your Love Away (1);
	When You Walk in the Room (3);
	Someday We're Gonna Love Again (11);
	What Have They Done to the Rain (13)
1965	Goodbye My Love (4);
	He's Got No Love (12);
	Take Me for What I'm Worth (20);
	When I Get Home (35)
1966	Take It or Leave It (31);
	Have You Ever Loved Somebody (48)

SELECTER: See Two-Tone Records

The Sex Pistols

Johnny Rotten
(vocals)
Paul Cook
(drums)
Steve Jones
(guitars)
Sid Vicious
(bass)

The Pistols present a paradox: One of the most publicized and reported bands ever, and it is almost impossible to construct a coherent history. There are three versions of their story: Johnny Rotten's; manager Malcolm McLaren's three-ring publicity circus; and that of the sensationalistic British press.

The Pistols had something for everyone. To McLaren, they were a way to act out his fantasy, a slap in the face to the music industry and society in general; for Lydon, they were a band; and to the press, the Sex Pistols were the antichrists.

McLaren, a rag pusher on Kings Row in London's Chelsea district, had previously only managed one other band—the last-gasp New York Dolls. He presented them as cartoon Communists, dressed in red leather and posing the question, "What are the politics of boredom?" This did not go over well, and the Dolls broke up. McLaren returned to London, looking for a new trend. He didn't have to look far.

Working in Sex, McLaren's shop, was one Glen Matlock. Glen wanted to form a band, but he and his friends Steve Jones and Paul Cook lacked means. Malcolm took them under his wing, helped them finance the band, and gave them rehearsal space. They called themselves the Swankers, but soon changed their name to Q.T. Jones & the Sex Pistols (Malcolm's idea; it was shocking, and besides, it was free advertising for the shop). Steve Jones was found lacking as a frontman, so the band went looking for a singer. A frontman was needed. Someone suitably obnoxious and vile. . . .

Their dreams came true when John Lydon walked into Sex. He was perfect—short, orange hair, a torn T-shirt, and a perpetual sneer on his face. An impromptu audition was arranged, Lydon miming to a copy of Alice Cooper's "I'm Eighteen," and the job was his. Negotiations followed (a few pints in the pub), and John Lydon became Johnny Rotten. (He was so christened by Paul Cook, in honor of his unbrushed teeth.)

The Pistols started to play around in London, at the Nashville and the Marquee. They were soon banned from these clubs for various offenses: e.g., fights with the audience, allegedly destroying Eddie and the Hot Rods' gear, and general obnoxiousness. In the summer of '76, they gained their first residency, at a Soho strip joint. Next came a Tuesday night residency at the 100 Club, the first Punk venue. The Pistols picked up fans, nicknamed the Bromley Contingent, who included such luminaries-to-be as Sid Vicious and Siouxsie Sioux. Press coverage was mostly negative. At the end of the summer, the 100 Club held its first (and only) Punk Festival.

In October, the Pistols signed with EMI, for an undisclosed amount. Now, the fun began. On November 26, 1976, EMI released the Pistols' first single, "Anarchy in the U.K." (written by Jamie Reid, an assistant of McLaren's, not by the Pistols, as stated on the label). It garnered the expected amount of outrage in the national press, but the music press was almost unanimous in its raves.

On December 2, the Pistols were booked on Thames TV's *Today* show. Host Bill Grundy baited the Pistols, asking them to "say something outrageous." The band complied, Glen Matlock calling Grundy "a dirty fucker." The rest of the group chimed in kind. The public outcry was insane: phone calls, newspaper headlines, Parliament considering a ban on the group. One man kicked in the tube of his new color TV set. The Pistols had made the big time. Steve Jones celebrated by throwing up at Heathrow Airport. This made more headlines. Scheduled for twenty dates, the Pistols' "Anarchy in the U.K." tour played only three shows. All others were banned.

Within days, the executive minds at EMI met to consider their new stars' fate. The workers at a pressing plant were refusing to touch the Pistols' record. The papers were blaming EMI. The Pistols must go, said EMI. Fine, replied Malcolm, but not until you give us 40,000 pounds and the remaining 5000 copies of "Anarchy." They did. McLaren and his anti-Beatles had taken on the establishment and won.

But all was not well. Glen Matlock was unhappy. McLaren had taken control and "was turning the Pistols into the Monkees." Matlock opted out. His replacement was Sid Vicious, inventor of the pogo. Sid had never picked up a bass in his life—but he sure looked good onstage.

But the Pistols still needed a label. Next victim: A&M Records. A press conference was held in front of Buckingham Palace to sign the contracts (for £150,000) and announce the Pistols' next single—"God Save the Queen." "It's not a version of the national anthem," Malcolm archly announced, "but the boys' personal tribute to the Queen."

A party was held at the A&M offices, at which the Pistols were accused of everything from stuffing the toilets to raping secretaries. Protests arrived from Rick Wakeman and Karen Carpenter, among others. A&M pulled an EMI and bought off the band for £75,000. Neither the single, nor an album, tentatively titled *Spunk,* was released.

The Pistols attempted another tour, this time on the sly. They called themselves the Spots (Sex Pistols On Tour Secretly). Virgin Records, showing admirable bravery, were the third label to sign the Pistols. "God Save the Queen" was at last released, and banned immediately.

Happy that things were going so smoothly, Malcolm left for Hollywood to set up an American record deal and a movie for the band. The movie, which would take three years, four directors, and eight scriptwriters to complete, was titled *The Great Rock 'n' Roll Swindle.*

"God Save the Queen" reached number two in the charts. Everyone agreed it was outselling all other records and should have been Number One. This is the first of the many "conspiracies" that Malcolm contended were implemented to take the band away from him.

The third Pistols' single, "Pretty Vacant," was their first not to be banned. Virgin Records submitted a film of the band playing the song on *Top of the Pops*—against McLaren's wishes. He claimed Virgin was trying to turn the band into "the next Beatles" and Johnny Rotten into a conventional star.

Finally, in December 1977, the Pistols' LP, *Never Mind the Bollocks, Here's the Sex Pistols,* came out. Banned in many stores, it still went to Number One. But Rotten was unhappy—"It was madness . . . twenty guitar overdubs, and I only have one track, one take to get the vocal right . . . Depending on where you live in England, you got a different mix."

Problems arose with Sid. His girlfriend, Nancy Spungen, introduced him to heroin. In January 1978, the Pistols toured America, but not without visa trouble. Three dates were canceled, but the tour opened on schedule in Atlanta. McLaren had vetoed Warner Bros.' idea of breaking in the Pistols at Madison Square Garden, with tickets costing two or three dollars. Instead, they toured the South and Midwest, playing their last performance in San Francisco (an ironic touch—the last Beatles show was also in Frisco). They would never play New York—aside from London, the world's only other true Punk stronghold.

The band fell into disarray. Rotten and Vicious headed East. Vicious OD'ed on a plane and wound up in a hospital. Cook and Jones flew to South America to work on McLaren's next scheme—recording an album with Ronald Biggs, the Great Train Robber. Sid enjoyed some minor, morbid fame after being accused of knifing Nancy Spungen to death. He finally died himself, of a heroin overdose, in February 1979. Lydon returned to England and formed Public Image Ltd. McLaren went on to manage Adam and the Ants, eventually dismissing Adam, replacing him with fifteen-year-old Annabella Lu Win and calling the new band Bow Wow Wow.

While recording only one bona fide LP during their lifespan (McLaren and Virgin have released too many compilations to list, most notable being the soundtrack to *The Great Rock 'n' Roll Swindle*), the Sex Pistols carved a niche for themselves in music history. They were Punk pioneers, the band that died for your sins. Without the Pistols, it is almost impossible to imagine post-'77 music being the same.

(STEVE MIRKIN)

U.S. Hit LPs

1977 Never Mind the Bollocks, Here's the Sex Pistols (**106**)

U.K. Hit Singles

1976 Anarchy in the U.K. (**38**)
1977 God Save the Queen (**2**); Pretty Vacant (**6**); Holidays in the Sun (**8**)
1978 No One Is Innocent/My Way (**7**)
1980 (I'm Not Your) Stepping Stone (**21**)

Siouxsie and the Banshees

Siouxsie Sioux
(vocals)
Steven Severin
(bass)
John McGeoch
(guitar)
Budgie
(drums)

The first performance of Siouxsie and the Banshees in September 1976 was one of the exceedingly few legendary debuts in the history of rock & roll. When notorious press darling Siouxsie Sioux and her Banshees took the stage at the 100 Club Punk Festival (which headlined the Sex Pistols and the Clash), it was not only their first public outing as a unit, but the first time any of them had played his or her chosen instrument (or so the story goes): Steve Havoc on bass, Marco Pirroni (later of Adam and the Ants) on guitar, Sid Vicious on drums, and of course Siouxsie herself as The Voice, shouting out a twenty-some-minute collage of "The Lord's Prayer" and various loose threads of rock & roll's so-called rich tapestry.

Such purism could hardly last; and as their performing skills matured, the Banshees shed members as snakes shed their skins. With a lineup of Siouxsie, Steve Havoc (now called Steven Severin), John McKay (guitar), and Kenny Morris (drums), the band played its first London concert as headliners in July 1978.

Long after the other major Punk bands (and far too many of the minor leaguers) had nabbed record contracts, Siouxsie's image as swastika-emblazoned *Eismädchen* and the diamond-hard austerity of the band's music intimidated the record companies. And the band themselves held out for complete control over their product. The result was a long-term deal with Polydor and a Top Ten hit with their debut single, the surprisingly tuneful "Hong Kong Garden," in September 1978.

The album *The Scream,* which followed in October 1978, was lavishly praised by the critics. It remains one of the grimmest, coldest, most powerful statements on record (leavened only slightly in America by the inclusion of "Hong Kong Garden"). And the second album, *Join Hands,* released in fall 1979, proved that the Banshees meant business (theirs, hardly Polydor's). Turgid, morose, mesmeric, its only moment of real relief occurs as Siouxsie intones the English lyric to a music-box recording of "O Mein Papa"—a bizarre and implicitly ironic effect.

At the outset of the *Join Hands* tour, the Banshees were jolted by the sudden defection of Morris and McKay, leaving Siouxsie and Severin to cope with a series of ad hoc drummers and guitarists. With the band's future in jeopardy, Siouxsie recorded "Happy House"—arguably the Banshees' finest single—whose B-side, "Drop Dead/Celebration," bore the not so very cryptic inscription "Bye Bye Blackheads."

The A-side of that single bore an inscription, too: "Hello Budgie." Budgie, once drummer for the Slits, had become a full-time Banshee. The band had been recording with two guitarists: ex-Pistol Steve Jones and John McGeoch of Magazine (and Visage); later, McGeoch quit Magazine to join Siouxsie, Severin, and Budgie—a lineup that promised to be reasonably stable.

Perhaps because of the changing personnel, the music of the aptly-titled *Kaleidoscope,* the third Banshees album, is unusually varied; and it has a surface prettiness and allure that were new to the band's output. Siouxsie showed a new willingness to scale down her vocals and even caress a phrase or two.

Steven Severin once said—and not in jest, I'd imagine—that he'd be flattered to have the Banshees considered a singles band; and indeed, the group's 45s are consistently fine—"Playground Twist," "Christine," "Israel," "Spellbound," and "Arabian Knights," as well as those mentioned previously—all tight, kinetic, eminently danceable. Elsewhere, the band could profit from a lighter touch and a bit of self-editing. Siouxsie has rarely been seen to crack a smile; onstage, she completely lacks the ironic showmanship and self-mockery that undermine and ultimately transfigure even the doomiest efforts of her obvious one-time model, John Lydon. For all her nose thumbing and undulations, she remains poker faced: a self-proclaimed Celtic priestess in grimly earnest charge of her rites. At its best, the Banshees' music has a hypnotic, incantatory, exotic glow; at its worst, it lapses into an overblown fusion of psychedelia and borderline heavy metal—Siouxsie as Grace Slick without the pulse, the humor, and the earth-mother appeal. Siouxsie and the Banshees are an impressive, formidable band, easy to admire, less easy to love.

(PATRICK DILLON)

U.K. Hit Singles

1978 Hong Kong Garden (**7**)
1979 The Staircase (**24**); Playground Twist (**28**); Mittageisen (Metal Postcard) (**47**)
1980 Happy House (**17**); Christine (**22**)

Slade

Noddy Holder
(vocals, guitar)
Dave Hill
(lead guitar)
Jimmy Lea
(bass)
Don Powell
(drums)

Slade were a jovial foursome of noisy proletarian geezers with but one mission in life: to incite their audiences to riot and decimate the interiors of concert halls. Originally Ambrose Slade, they emerged from the grimy industrial town of Wolverhampton in 1970 with a minimum of talent and considerable roughneck enthusiasm. Right off, they attracted a rowdy working-class following who reveled in their machine-tooled three-chord splendor and goofy, gap-toothed theatri-cality. Audiences would pitch in and match the heartiness of the band, which could make a Slade concert a fearsome place to be for the uninitiated.

In the beginning, Slade had a reputation as a skinhead's band—skinheads being young toughs who shaved their heads and prowled about in gangs looking to beat up hippies and Pakistanis. Later, Slade drew a more generalized hard-rocking crowd who preferred to get their rocks off to Slade's boot-stomping anthems than to progressive-rock swill like the Moody Blues.

Slade were a motley crew. Noddy Holder would typically wear four different plaids at once, along with suspenders and a goony hat. He'd grin like some Dickensian street urchin, hacking out bar chords on his guitar and singing in a strychnine howl. Lead guitarist Dave Hill wore knee-high boots with six-inch heels and spangled his hair and clothes with what he called ''me glitter'' (this before Bowie, even).

What the hell was going on here? One rock sage got it perfectly: ''Their music is unimaginative, formulaic and monotonous, and it teaches us nothing. But does it ever sound good! Heavy beat, pounding rhythm, lyrics about drinking, dancing, or nothing at all.'' Jimmy Lea summed up Slade's angle in simpler language: ''We don't do no rock operas. We're doin' a cock opera.''

In the early Seventies, Slade ran roughshod over the British charts with an unbroken string of singles that were, in effect, football chants set to a pounding 4/4 beat. If you were looking for levels of meaning or poetry à la Cat Stevens, this was the wrong ballpark. Slade presented themselves as a case of arrested intellectual development and were proud of it. As if to underscore their dum-dum sensibility, they'd spell their song titles phonetically: e.g., ''Mama Weer All Crazee Now'' or ''Cum On Feel the Noize.''

In concert, Slade unleashed all the pent-up fury of the tromped-on British underclass. Hill would scale a speaker cabinet on the lefthand side of the stage, Lea would do likewise on the right, and with Noddy Holder sounding the charge from center stage, they'd exhort the crowd to ''Clap your hands! Stomp your feet!'' This would not abate until the floor was a pile of splintered kindling where once had been chairs. Brassieres and drained bottles added to the carnage. In their wake, Slade would leave a 2000-seat concert hall looking like a World War I battlefield.

America turned back Slade as if they were some virulent new strain of Hong Kong flu. The sight of Slade's front line bravely but futilely trying to ignite the same fire under an indifferent American audience was a pathetic one. It was unfortunate, for in fact, their best songs were irresistible slabs of hard-driving rock & roll, and Slade kicked ass with an abandon that left most American bands in the dust.

Their limited imagination, and their honoring that fact, is what made Slade great. It also proved to be their eventual downfall. Years after their reign on the charts had ended, Slade were still slogging out tunes with the same football-match bravado, but the stomp-and-swill crowd had moved on to newer heroes. A later album was called *Whatever Happened to Slade?* Pity they had to pose the question themselves.

(PARKE PUTERBAUGH)

U.S. Hit Singles

| 1972 | Take Me Back 'Ome (**97**); Mama Weer All Crazee Now (**76**) |
| 1973 | Gudbuy T' Jane (**68**); Cum On Feel the Noize (**98**) |

U.S. Hit LPs

1972	Slade Alive! (**158**)
1973	Slayed? (**69**); Sladest (**129**)
1975	Slade in Flame (**93**)

U.K. Hit Singles

1971	Get Down and Get With It (**16**); Cuz I Love You (**1**)
1972	Look Wat You Dun (**4**); Take Me Back 'Ome (**1**); Mama Weer All Crazee Now (**1**); Gudbuy T' Jane (**2**)
1973	Cum On Feel The Noize (**1**); Skweeze Me Pleeze Me (**1**); Merry Xmas Everybody (**1**); My Friend Stan (**2**)
1974	Everyday (**3**); Bangin' Man (**3**); Far Far Away (**2**)
1975	Thanks for the Memory (**7**); In for a Penny (**11**); How Does It Feel (**15**)
1976	Let's Call It Quits (**11**)
1977	My Baby Left Me—That's All Right (**32**); Gypsy Road Hog (**48**)

The Slits

Sporting hairstyles that would have done Medusa proud, appearing on stage in thrift-shop oddities, the Slits blithely refuted all the stereotypes that have been applied to female rock musicians. Anarchic musically as well as visually, the band used reggae as its starting point to create music that was at once fierce, passionate, gentle, and wryly funny. In so doing, the Slits took the Punk edict of insouciant incompetence to unimagined heights.

Formed in 1976, the Slits were soon appearing as the opening act for prominent Punk bands such as the Clash, the Sex Pistols, and the Buzzcocks. Audiences at these early Slits gigs usually found themselves confronted with complete chaos: the musicians experienced great difficulty keeping in time or in tune with one another and their gigs often came to an abrupt close when fourteen-year-old lead singer Ari Upp threw one of her frequent temper tantrums and stalked offstage. Yet those who wrote the band off as a tacky novelty were to be proven wrong.

The Slits' debut album, *Cut*, was released on Island Records in the late summer of 1979. A brilliantly simple production job allowed the inventive rhythmic drive of the Slits' music to come to the fore. While Viv Albertine and Tessa Pollitt wave various chants in and out of the melody, Ari Upp alternately growled, moaned, and warbled songs about shoplifting, modern romance, compulsive consumerism, and the horrors of the ''typical girl.''

Though the Slits have attracted an enthusiastic cult following, their inability to gain radio airplay precluded the likelihood of their becoming a household name. But the ever-rising number of women in rock clearly attests to the Slits' pioneering influence.

(ELIZABETH SCHAFFNER)

Viv Albertine (guitar)
Ari Upp (vocals)
Tessa Pollitt (bass guitar)

U.K. Hit Singles

| 1979 | Typical Girls/Heard It through the Grapevine (**60**) |

The Small Faces

Steve Marriott
(vocals, guitar)
Kenney Jones
(drums)
Ian McLagen
(organ)
Ronnie Lane
(bass)

Some groups, no matter how good they are on their own merits, are doomed to wilt in the shadow of more earth-shaking contemporaries. The Rolling Stones eventually triumphed over the Beatles through sheer longevity. Such, alas, was not to be the case with the Small Faces. Despite six English Top Ten singles during their three years together, the Small Faces are remembered today (if at all) as the "other" Mod band—after The Who.

The perspective was different fifteen years ago. Then the Small Faces were revered as *the* Mod group, whereas The Who was just another bandwagon jumper (although an obviously talented one). The Small Faces reeked of Mod: from their name—"face" being mod slang for a (self-)important person—to their impeccably tailored clothes and neat haircuts, to their musical taste for American R&B and soul.

The Small Faces had plenty to offer of their own, however. Marriott was a genuine white-soul belter, and the group's internal combustion—fueled by Jones's feverish percussion—now seems like an awesome natural resource. "Whatcha Gonna Do About It?" their first single, was fairly successful, but the Small Faces truly entered the charmed circle two singles later with "Sha La La La Lee," an insidiously appealing tune. Neither of these songs was written by the Small Faces' in-house composers, Marriott and Lane. Yet both got to display their wares on the band's first LP; one of their numbers, "You Need Loving," would later become known to millions as Led Zeppelin's "Whole Lotta Love."

Nineteen sixty-six was the Small Faces' hottest year. Besides "Sha La La La Lee," they racked up the stunningly powerful "All or Nothing" (which went to Number One) and "My Mind's Eye" as hits. But underneath the Cockney exuberance the band was shifting its style. In 1967, the Small Faces were photographed in paisley and Nehru jackets, and flirted with psychedelia in songs like "Itchycoo Park," whose sly references to getting high no doubt helped propel the band into the U.S. Top Twenty for the first and last time.

In 1968 the band moved further into gimmickry with the *Ogdens' Nut Gone Flake* album. Named after a brand of pipe tobacco, the record was packed appropriately in a round cover resembling a tin and a clear plastic pouch with a snap fastener. Their U.S. record company advertised the package as if the music were almost incidental—quite an injustice. Besides thrashing rockers (this band always knew its strength), jaunty music-hall singalongs and even a pretty instrumental, half of *Ogdens'* consisted of songs linked with an incomprehensible narrative in British doubletalk.

The concept and execution of *Ogdens' Nut Gone Flake* were flawless, but the album wasn't designed with the American audience in mind (though it went to the top of the British charts). They added a horn section for variety's sake, but they seemed destined to remain a "commercial" band whose success was confined to Britain. Marriott quit to launch Humble Pie, and the remaining Faces teamed up with Rod Stewart and Ronnie Wood.

During their glory years the Small Faces assayed several musical approaches and invariably stamped them with a joyfulness that was their trademark. It was all great fun while it lasted.

(SCOTT ISLER)

U.S. Hit Singles

1968	Itchycoo Park (**16**); Tin Soldier (**73**)

U.S. Hit LPs

1968	There Are But Four Small Faces (**178**); Ogden's Nut Gone Flake (**159**)
1970	Small Faces—First Step (**119**)
1972	Early Faces (**176**)
1973	Ogden's Nut Gone Flake (**189**)

U.K. Hit Singles

1965	Whatcha Gonna Do About It? (**14**)
1966	All or Nothing (**1**); Sha La La La Lee (**3**); My Mind's Eye (**4**); Hey Girl (**10**)
1967	Itchycoo Park (**3**); Tin Soldier (**9**); Here Comes the Nice (**12**); I Can't Make It (**26**)
1968	Lazy Sunday (**2**); Universal (**16**)
1969	Afterglow of Your Love (**36**)

Soft Machine

Michael Ratledge
(keyboards)
Robert Wyatt
(drums, vocals)
Kevin Ayers
(guitar, vocals)
Hugh Hopper
(bass)

The story of the Soft Machine is just one branch in a large family tree centered in and around Canterbury, England. The Soft Machine were simply the best known of an extended family of interlocking groups that sprouted in the mid-Sixties. Among them, there was an uncountable shuffling of members. One might justifiably liken it to the early San Francisco scene, with the same musical inbreeding and a distinctly identifiable sound.

The music of the Canterbury scene was quite unlike the gritty rock & roll and R&B of London and the cities of the industrial north. It was not so much rock song as art song. Such bands as the Soft Machine, Caravan, and Gong drew upon varied sources. They observed classical music's formalism and discipline, but like jazzmen, they'd play long, improvised solos in tricky time signatures. From rock, they took a sense of humor and forward motion. *Unlike* much rock, however, the guitar was not the main instrument: most of the bands were keyboard-based, guitars being relegated to an auxiliary function. There was nary a Chuck Berry lick in sight. And the sometimes insular humor was definitely of the dadaist school.

School is where it all began, actually: the Simon Langton School in Canterbury, where a bunch of chums in the class of '61 began congregating. Mostly, they'd assemble at Robert Wyatt's parents' mansion to read Beat Generation literature and listen to jazz records by Mingus, Monk, and Taylor, as well as avant-garde composers like Stockhausen. Precocious, for fifteen and sixteen years old.

Out of informal jam sessions evolved the Wilde Flowers, the prototype Canterbury band. Most every musician of any clout on this scene played in at least one incarnation of the Wilde Flowers. For four years ('63–'67), they played an eclectic mix of Beatles, American soul, and their own jazz-tinged tunes. More important, they split down the middle to produce the Soft Machine and Caravan, the two cornerstone bands of the Canterbury genealogy.

The first version of the Soft Machine reads like a Who's Who of British progressive rock. Daevid Allen was a psychedelic emigré from Australia. Michael Ratledge came armed with university degrees in philosophy and psychology. Kevin Ayers was a nomad who drifted to Canterbury. Robert Wyatt's restless intellect had driven him to Spain, where he studied piano, violin, trumpet, and drums.

Wyatt put together the Soft Machine in late 1966. Ratledge suggested the name (it was the title of a William Burroughs novel), and Allen phoned the author in Paris to secure his permission. At the start, Soft Machine alternated discrete songs with improvised exchanges between Ratledge's keyboards and Wyatt's drums. The original Softs released only one single, "Love Makes Sweet Music." It was produced by their manager, Chas Chandler, the former Animals bassist, and the B-side featured rhythm guitar by his newest protégé, a then-unknown Jimi Hendrix.

Through Chandler's auspices, the Soft Machine (minus Allen) supported Hendrix on his 1968 U.S. tour. At tour's end, they made their first album in New York City. Cut in four days, it has the freshness of a first take—and much of the unbridled energy of that mind-expanding period when inventive young musicians began to apprehend lysergically that they were limited only by their imagination. Ratledge played with the manic intensity of a Hendrix, and Wyatt's wispy tenor vocals and tricky drum-bashing were a joy.

Kevin Ayers, for his part, contributed some odd, obsessive material (e.g., "We Did It Again," which found him chanting those four words over and over for 3:46). Ayers, feeling the gypsy urge, soon departed the band for a small island off Spain. His replacement was Hugh Hopper, an ex-Wilde Flower. The Softs' second

album, *Volume Two*, was another wonderfully offbeat affair. Over cocktail-jazz accompaniment, Wyatt delivered whimsical, surrealist lyrics. A highlight was his recitation of the alphabet—both forward and backwards. The album reflected the band's preoccupation with "pataphysics": Wyatt's self-styled school of philosophy that married Twenties dadaism, metaphysics, and a large dose of underground humor.

In the meantime, other Canterbury pilgrims were keeping busy. Kevin Ayers cut a solo album, *Joy of a Toy*, with help from his Soft Machine mates. Daevid Allen had gone off and formed Gong, Europe's answer to the Grateful Dead. Caravan was making records that, like the Softs', mixed pop brevity with extended keyboard jaunts.

Back in the Soft Machine camp, Hopper, Wyatt and Ratledge had added several members for the album *Thirds*. A double album—one composition per side—it found the group moving in a more "serious" jazz direction, with less accent on words and vocals. It was extremely well-received; indeed, the *Village Voice* hailed it as the greatest album in pop history. Its avant-garde big-band sound did push the barriers of rock ahead still further.

Fourths took a decisive step in the direction of scholastic avant-jazz, and this shift prompted Robert Wyatt's departure. Wyatt formed a quartet, which he gave the cunning name Matching Mole (*machine molle* being French for Soft Machine). They lasted through a pair of diversionary, delightful albums that bore the unmistakable Wyatt stamp. Then, in 1975, tragedy struck when the drummer drunkenly fell three stories out a window, paralyzing himself from the waist down. While hospitalized, Wyatt composed his next album, the morbidly titled *Rock Bottom*. His drumming days over, he turned to keyboards.

As for Kevin Ayers, he remains an eccentric genius, and a walking contradiction. Ayers professes to live a life devoted to the pursuit of pleasure and sloth, yet he's faithfully written an album a year for at least a dozen years. He is an incurable romantic who celebrates the incandescent pleasures of love and passion. At the same time, he writes obsessive songs that paint the darker side of human nature. Through the years, he's taken the cream of British progressive musicians and turned them loose on some shameless pop material, making what might be called high-IQ Top Forty. He's also recorded compositions as exotic and multilevel as a Paul Klee painting. Ayers' body of solo work is among the worthiest—and most underappreciated—music of the past several decades.

The Canterbury scene remains as perplexing and involved as ever. There was a Soft Machine making records in 1980, but all four originals were long gone, having been gradually replaced by modern-jazz pros. Yet the individuals who put together the Soft Machine, Caravan, and Gong way back when have fanned out into numberless solo and group projects, all of them touched with Canterbury magic. Some things changed, but much remained the same.

(PARKE PUTERBAUGH)

Kevin Ayers

U.S. Hit LPs

1968 The Soft Machine (**160**)

(BY CARAVAN)

1975 Cunning Stunts (**124**)

SPECIALS: See Two-Tone Records

SPENCER DAVIS GROUP: See Traffic

Spooky Tooth

Gary Wright
(vocals, keyboards, synthesizer)
Luther Grosvenor
(guitar)
Mike Harrison
(vocals)
Greg Ridley
(bass)
Mike Kellie
(drums)

English Heavy. In the front ranks, Led Zeppelin, for sure. Free, with "All Right Now," and later, Bad Company. A dose of Ten Years After and some fresh Cream. And, in the vanguard of the also-rans in this category, Spooky Tooth.

No one would own up to the origins of this band's name, which suggested a regrettable dental episode. Spooky Tooth first stomped its melodic hard-rock and brontosaurus beat all over the U.K. in the late Sixties, and broke up in 1970, only to resurrect itself for a second go in 1973. Widespread popularity always just eluded them, but Spooky Tooth left behind a legacy and a lesson—that heavy rock needn't be ponderous and numbing, that it could be tuneful and invigorating too.

Spooky Tooth came together when formidable producer Jimmy Miller (Stones, Traffic) augmented the lineup of a foundering U.K. psychedelic band, Art, with a New Jersey-born keyboardist/songwriter, Gary Wright. (Art deserves a historical footnote chiefly for one hilarious single, a cover version of the Buffalo Springfield's "For What It's Worth," which they somehow mistitled "What's That Sound" and miscredited to one Stephen "Mills.") The arrival of Wright, who came to Spooky Tooth by way of graduate studies in psychology at Berlin University seemed to bring the group down to earth.

Spooky Tooth's eponymous 1968 debut album (reissued three years later in the U.S. as *Tobacco Road*) found them lending hard-edged arrangements to tunes by Janis Ian and the Band, plus pumping out some serviceable heavy-rock blueprints of their own. This record proved to be a mere warmup, however, to their leviathan second album, *Spooky Two,* which to this day remains a veritable textbook of definitive heavy-rock moves. Every song possessed a rippling power that would often explode into a hair-raising Mike Harrison growl or Luther Grosvenor guitar solo. Songs like "Waiting for the Wind" and the nine-minute "Evil Woman" had an almost classical sense of development and pacing.

Spooky Two received ecstatic reviews, and Spooky Tooth seemed poised to enter rock's upper echelon. Gary Wright must have caught a bad case of the psychedelics, though, for Spooky Tooth made a grave tactical blunder. Instead of the third album that would bring it all home for them, they made *Ceremony,* a record that remains one of the most oddball projects in all of rock history—an incomprehensible, all but unlistenable forty minutes of electronic noise performed in collaboration with French avant-gardist Pierre Henry.

Their momentum shattered, Wright left to go solo. Yet Spooky Tooth hung together, albeit briefly. The remaining three-quarters of the original Art lineup hooked up with three-quarters of Joe Cocker's Grease Band to record *The Last Puff,* which signaled the end of Spooky Tooth's first phase. While there was no original material on the LP, save one instrumental, the album held up, strangely enough, mostly due to a masterly vocal performance from Mike Harrison and admirably taut playing from the band.

During Spooky Tooth's three-year hiatus, Gary Wright released two superstar-studded albums (*Extraction* and *Footprint*); Mike Kellie drummed with Peter Frampton's Camel; and Mike Harrison cut a pair of ho-hum solo albums. The group's original bass player, Greg Ridley, had long since defected to Humble Pie, while Luther Grosvenor would eventually join Mott the Hoople under the unlikely moniker of Ariel Bender (where, incidentally, he would essay one of the worst guitar solos in all of christendom on the Hoople's "Golden Age of Rock 'n' Roll").

In 1973, Spooky Tooth was reborn, with Harrison and Wright the core of the band, which they rounded out with several members of Wright's post-solo band Wonderwheel. (One of the new additions, guitarist Mick Jones, would go on to greater fame as the founder and guiding light behind Foreigner.) The second-time-round Spooky Tooth cut *You Broke My Heart So I Busted Your Jaw* and *Witness.* Though both were well reviewed, neither exactly tore up the charts. Not surprisingly, Spooky Tooth's born-again membership soon crumbled, yet Wright found replacements and stuck it out for one dispirited-sounding LP, *The Mirror.*

Wright went back to the drawing board and reversed his fortunes in dramatic fashion with his second stab at solo success. What he came up with was a sound that was exclusively *him*—a phalanx of keyboards and his own bluesy near-falsetto. The strategy made him a platinum superstar, briefly, in 1975 with the release of *The Dream Weaver* (on which he produced every sound except for drums) and its two mega-hits, the title song and "Love Is Alive."

Subsequently, Wright found followup hits harder to come by, though he experimented even more heavily with his pop-oriented keyboard orchestra. All the while, he beamed a toothy Peter Frampton smile, exposing both rows of pearly whites—something he must have inherited when he took on Frampton's manager, Dee Anthony, as his own. Wright enjoyed a modest commercial recovery in 1981 with the single "Really Want to Know You."

(PARKE PUTERBAUGH)

U.S. Hit Singles

(BY GARY WRIGHT)

1976 Dream Weaver (**2**); Love Is Alive (**2**); Made to Love You (**79**)

| 1977 | Phantom Writer (49) |
| 1978 | Touch and Gone (73) |

U.S. Hit LPs

1969	Spooky Two (44)
1970	Ceremony (with Pierre Henry) (92); The Last Puff (84)
1971	Tobacco Road (152)

| 1973 | You Broke My Heart So I Busted Your Jaw (84); Witness (99) |
| 1974 | The Mirror (130) |

(BY GARY WRIGHT)

1975	The Dream Weaver (7)
1976	That Was Only Yesterday (172)
1977	The Light of Smiles (23); Touch and Gone (117)
1979	Headin' Home (147)

Squeeze

Glen Tilbrook
(guitar, vocals)
Chris Difford
(guitar, vocals)
Jools Holland
(keyboards)
John Bentley
(bass)
Gilson Lavis
(drums)

Squeeze was a pop band for the Eighties that lived up to its name in every way: indeed, they managed to cram more melodic hooks into three minutes than anyone should be entitled to. And though at the outset they were borne amid a tide of Punk/New Wave fandom, they managed to become quite popular without embracing either of those schools. In fact, they were far too friendly and unaffected to fall into the Punk camp, and too free of dread and pretensions to be considered card-carrying New Wavers. They weren't exactly rock, either, with all that term came to imply in the last decade. (Said Glen Tilbrook: "The connotations of rock are so bad I've never want to be associated with it.")

What, then, was Squeeze all about? Squeeze's primary asset was the songwriting team of Chris Difford (lyrics) and Glen Tilbrook (music). They were tunesmiths of the first order—indeed, they were often hailed as a latter-day Lennon and McCartney—who painted their compositions in bright hues. As a band, they brought much energy to their playing, and their arrangements were sharp, clever, and to the point. Bearing in mind that "pop" is short for "popular," Squeeze worked to reach people, and their ingenuous attempts to hook listeners implied a largeness of spirit that too often was missing on the rock scene.

Squeeze dates back to 1977 and a British EP entitled *Packet of Three*. The Difford-Tilbrook songwriting team goes back even further, though, to 1972 and '73, when Difford would work on lyrics all night long, in the morning turning them over to Tilbrook, who'd promptly begin setting them to music. This fecund partnership yielded a catalog of over a thousand songs long before they'd formed a band to play them.

From the start, Squeeze drew praise for their engaging, hummable melodies and Difford's insightful, slice-of-life vignettes. "Suburban short stories" is what one writer dubbed them, and set to Tilbrook's jauntily kaleidoscopic tunes, they compared favorably with the Beatles of "Penny Lane" et al.

Tilbrook was a boyishly ebullient singer in the Paul McCartney mold, while Difford's gritty voice operated in a lower register. Original keyboardist Jools Holland offered a bit of ragtime and vaudeville to the mix (he's since been replaced, several times). And Gilson Lavis and John Bentley made a powerhouse rhythm section.

The group was a big attraction in England, where they racked up a consistent string of hits. Touring in the U.S. behind Elvis Costello in 1980 (their tenth trek to these shores since 1977), Squeeze received a wider hearing—a trend that continued with their superb fourth album, 1981's *East Side Story*.

(PARKE PUTERBAUGH)

U.S. Hit LPs

| 1980 | Argybargy (71) |

U.K. Hit Singles

1978	Take Me I'm Yours (19); Bang Bang (49); Goodbye Girl (63)
1979	Cool for Cats (2); Up the Junction (2); Slap and Tickle (24)
1980	Another Nail in My Heart (17)

Steeleye Span

Maddy Prior
(vocals)
Tim Hart
(guitar, dulcimer, vocals)
Bob Johnson
(guitar, vocals)
Rick Kemp
(bass, vocals)
Peter Knight
(keyboards, violin, vocals)
Nigel Pegrum
(drums, woodwinds)

Steeleye Span was a contemporary rock band: bass, drums, electric guitars, a good-looking girl singer up front. Steeleye Span also germinated a fascinating concept, insofar as the songs the band performed were often hundreds of years old. Nearly all were adapted from Britain's rich folk heritage and electrically refurbished in what amounted to a fusion of centuries. *NME* (to which Tim Hart contributed a regular folk music column) dubbed Steeleye Span "ye olde English punke rocke."

The Steeleye Span story begins in 1967, when Hart and Maddy Prior left their native St. Albans to tour Britain as a folk duo, with Tim's acoustic guitar and harmonica providing a simple, traditional setting for Maddy's extraordinarily clear, ringing vocals. Their repertoire, which they painstakingly researched at London's Cecil Sharpe House library, consisted of old English songs that had long since been forgotten by all but a handful of academicians. To make ends meet, Maddy moonlighted as a lady chauffeur prior to the release of the duo's *Folk Songs of Olde England*.

In 1969, they joined forces with bassist Ashley

"Tyger" Hutchings (who had just left Fairport Convention) and another folk-singing couple, Gay and Terry Woods. Combining electric guitars with such relatively unusual folk instruments as dulcimers and autoharps, they announced that they were "not a rock band, but traditional musicians working with electric instruments." Hutchings originally christened the group Middlemarch Wait, but Hart's choice of the name Steeleye Span (from a character in the song "Horkstow Grange") ultimately prevailed. After issuing a relatively subdued LP called *Hark! The Village Wait* on RCA, the original lineup crumbled under personality clashes.

Prior, Hart, and Hutchings then recruited Martin Carthy (a celebrated folk guitarist) and Peter Knight (an unknown fiddle player), with whom they recorded a pair of 1971 albums, *Please to See the King* and *Ten Man Mop*. These featured intricate arrangements of traditional material rendered at top volume on electric guitars. In the absence of drums—for which Steeleye substituted a highly rhythmic and prominently mixed electric bass—their sound represented an unusual departure.

By 1972, Steeleye replaced Hutchings with a more rock-oriented bassist, Rick Kemp (whose portfolio included a short stint as one of David Bowie's Spiders from Mars; his receding hairline lost him the job). Kemp's arrival triggered the departure of the more folk-oriented Martin Carthy, who was replaced by guitarist Bob Johnson (who had once worked for Gary Glitter!).

On *Below the Salt* (1972) and *Parcel of Rogues* (1973), Steeleye's instrumental work assumed a more aggressive rock & roll cast, even as they developed their gorgeous four-part harmony singing—showcased to excellent advantage on "Gaudete," a Latin chant rendered a cappella, which became their first hit single.

Also during this period, they toured America for the first time. Second-billed to the likes of Procol Harum, Steeleye Span unfailingly managed to get audiences who had never heard of them up on their feet, "in delirious imitation," as one reporter put it, "of the folk dance steps Ms. Prior was performing with grace and abandon upon the stage."

A drummer, Nigel Pegrum, was finally added for 1974's *Now We Are Six*. A totally out-of-character version of Phil Spector's "To Know Him Is to Love Him" even featured the saxophone of David Bowie (perhaps he felt he owed Kemp a good turn). Wacky departures such as these purged Steeleye of any potential solemnity; on 1975's *Commoner's Crown*, amateur ukelele player Peter Sellers also made a cameo appearance. Onstage, the band supplemented its music with a madcap mummer's play in 1974. Two years later, with Britain engulfed in economic woes, they startled a London audience with a shower of bank notes from the stage during the song "Hard Times in Old England."

In 1975, Steeleye Span made a major bid for commercial acceptance with producer Mike Batt (the man behind the Wombles, a popular kiddie TV show-cum-rock group). Both artistically and commercially, *All Around My Hat* proved to be Steeleye's most successful album to date, but the followup, *Rocket Cottage,* failed to live up to its promise. The band returned to its folk roots and its 1971 lineup with *Storm-Force Ten*.

A treasured national resource in their native U.K., Steeleye Span broke up in 1978, feeling that they'd taken the concept as far as it could go. But in 1981 they were back together again, presumably because none of them fared very well on his or her own. In this rare instance, the "reunion album" proved to be cause for celebration.

Sails of Silver evinced a total mastery of the paradoxical business of implementing twentieth-century technology—electric and electronic instruments, thirty-two-track machines—to transport the listener back into a simpler and more magical era. The album featured songs about greedy giants and ghostly shipwrecks, along with the lament of a newlywed whose husband, unjustly arrested for poaching, had been packed off "to America/ to work the land that some call Virginia." Steeleye's instrumentation, like its repertoire, spanned the ages: on a rousing ditty like "Barnet Fair," an olde countrie fiddle could be heard interacting harmoniously with a space age synthesizer—even as the band rocks out more convincingly than ever before.

Most of Steeleye's ten previous LPs boasted glorious moments, but sometimes failed to strike the happy medium between ponderously heavy rock and the traditionally twee. What they often seemed to need was a first-rate rock-oriented producer. Under the aegis of Gus Dudgeon, *Sails of Silver* captured the perfect balance, and was a delight from start to finish.

(NICHOLAS SCHAFFNER)

U.S. Hit LPs

1975	All Around My Hat (**143**)
1978	Storm-Force Ten (**191**)

U.K. Hit Singles

1973	Gaudete (**14**)
1974	All Around My Hat (**5**)

Cat Stevens

Sensitive is the word most often applied to Cat Stevens, the singer/songwriter who grabbed the pop spotlight in the early Seventies.

Stephen Dmitri Georgiou's large, dark eyes and thick black beard were evidence of his Greek heritage. Born in London in 1948, he attended college there in the Sixties and, like many others, took up folk guitar. Stevens landed a recording contract in 1966 and grabbed a low rung on the British pop charts with his first single release, "I Love My Dog." His second song, the moody "Matthew and Son," established his introspective pop style and landed him squarely in the English Top Ten in early 1967.

Then, in 1968, he contracted tuberculosis, temporarily retired from performing, and spent a year recuperating. That gave him plenty of time to compose new songs, many of which turned up on his 1970 album, *Mona Bone Jakon*.

In the meantime, James Taylor and Carole King were blazing new paths as singer/songwriters, and the U.S. was responding enthusiastically to these more subdued new pop artists. When Stevens' *Tea for the Tillerman* was released in 1971, the American public found it to be just the type of music it wanted, and the single "Wild World" headed into the Top Twenty. Earnest, melodic, powerful, and yet gentle, Cat Stevens developed a large following almost immediately. "Peace Train" and "Morning Has Broken" (a reworking of a Welsh hymn) were major hits.

The years 1972 and 1973 were good to Stevens. *Teaser and the Firecat* yielded the hit "Moon Shadow," as well as "Peace Train" and "Morning Has Broken." But after 1973, the public seemed to lose interest in Cat Stevens. Perhaps his songs sounded too much alike, or perhaps his interest in Eastern religion was too deep to comprehend at the pop level.

His *Foreigner* album had an entire suite for its first side, and many found it boring. His later albums, *Buddha and the Chocolate Box* and *Numbers,* were confusing; the latter was a complicated mystical allegory that turned off former fans. Although Stevens did fairly well in 1974 with his remake of Sam Cooke's "Another Saturday Night," it was clear that his days as a major pop spokesman were over.

In early 1981, Stephen Georgiou changed his name yet again—to Yosef Islam. He proceeded to auction off all the musical instruments and gold records he had accumulated as Cat Stevens, with all proceeds going to the Companions of the Mosque, and embarked on a new career, teaching the Koran to British children. "I'm no longer seeking applause and fame," said Yosef Islam. "I've come to realize how meaningless such things are. . . . Allah be praised!"

(HENRY McNULTY)

U.S. Hit Singles

1971	Wild World (**11**); Peace Train (**7**); Moon Shadow (**30**)
1972	Morning Has Broken (**6**); Sitting (**16**)
1973	The Hurt (**31**)
1974	Another Saturday Night (**6**); Oh Very Young (**10**)
1975	Ready (**26**); Two Fine People (**33**)
1976	Banappale Gas (**41**)
1977	Old Schoolyard (**33**); Was Dog a Doughnut (**70**)

U.S. Hit LPs

1971	Tea for the Tillerman (**8**); Matthew and Son/New Masters (**173**); Mona Bone Jakon (**164**); Teaser and the Firecat (**3**)
1972	Very Young and Early Songs (**94**); Catch Bull at Four (**1**)
1973	Foreigner (**3**)
1974	Buddha and the Chocolate Box (**2**)
1975	Cat Stevens Greatest Hits (**6**); Numbers (**13**)
1977	Izitso (**7**)
1978	Back to Earth (**33**)

U.K. Hit Singles

1966	I Love My Dog (**28**)
1967	Matthew and Son (**2**); I'm Gonna Get Me a Gun (**6**); A Bad Night (**20**); Kitty (**47**)
1970	Lady d'Arbanville (**8**)
1971	Moon Shadow (**22**); Morning Has Broken (**9**)
1972	Can't Keep It In (**13**)
1974	Another Saturday Night (**19**)
1977	Old Schoolyard (**44**)

(John Rowlands)

Rod Stewart

(RDR Productions)

The first thing you notice about Rod Stewart is his remarkable voice—gravelly, rusty, raspy, sandpapery ("like a cocky costermonger," as a critic once noted). That voice has propelled Stewart through blues and soul to mainstream rock and disco. It has seen him dolled up as Rod the Mod, half-drunk onstage as the crazy, tartaned soccer player, and jet-setting to the Riviera as an international celebrity. Those strained vocal cords have felt the sting of cheap whiskey and the soothing bath of cognac.

Whatever his pose, Roderick David Stewart is unique. But his beginnings as a singer were quite ordinary. Born in North London in 1945, he was bitten by the folk bug in his early teens and bummed around the city singing in the streets. He sang folk music (accompanying himself on the banjo!) on the continent for several months before being booted out of Spain as a vagrant.

Back in England, he took a series of odd jobs (picture-frame maker, gravedigger, fence mender) before joining a band called Jimmy Powell and His Five Dimensions. Powell's group, one of countless second-string bands, did manage to play on the same bill as the Rolling Stones. But it was in 1964 that Stewart's break came. Discovered by bluesman Long

John Baldry (reportedly in a railway station), he sang second lead with Baldry's group the Hoochie Coochie Men until it disbanded the next year. Baldry formed a Rhythm & Blues outfit called Steampacket with Brian Auger and Julie Driscoll, and Stewart signed on as well. After a time he quit and joined an R&B band called Shotgun Express, which featured Mick Fleetwood on drums.

This was all small potatoes, however. In 1968, Stewart became the lead singer for the Jeff Beck Group; Beck had already made a name for himself as guitarist with the Yardbirds, and the addition of Stewart made for some memorable rock & roll. Two albums, *Truth* and *Beck-Ola,* remain as evidence of the kind of music Beck and Stewart could put out when they got together. Unfortunately, "getting together" wasn't easy for the two volatile musicians, and in 1969, after the band passed up an opportunity to perform at Woodstock ("We all wanted to go home," says Rod), Stewart quit the group along with the bass player, Ron Wood.

Enter the Small Faces, the paramount Mod R&B band. Actually, as luck would have it, the Jeff Beck Group and the Small Faces were on the same bill the first time Stewart performed with Beck. But by now—late 1969—the word "Small" had been amputated, leader Steve Marriott had left to form Humble Pie, and the Faces numbered three: Ian McLagen, Ronnie Lane, and Kenney Jones. They were looking for a guitarist and a singer. That's when Stewart and Wood appeared.

From then on, Faces became known as a hard-drinking, rollicking quintet with a boisterous (and sometimes sloppy) stage act sure to get a crowd on its feet. Stewart's gritty vocals and Wood's choppy playing mesh perfectly, and the others were a sturdy rhythm section. The Faces were always a good time onstage, but the records weren't giant sellers.

Almost as soon as he joined Faces, Stewart started a parallel career as a solo singer. He always maintained that he wasn't deserting the band. "I'll stay solo as far as records," he told an interviewer in 1970, "[but] as far as live performances, no. I'm just not responsible enough to put a band together and keep it together. I have enough of a time keeping myself together, let alone a band."

The Faces were an outlet for Stewart's rambunctious, boozy, soccer-player side, but his solo work was remarkable for its sincerity and sensitivity. His first LP, *The Rod Stewart Album* (in England, titled *An Old Raincoat Won't Ever Let You Down*), featured superb renditions of folk songs as well as his own compositions. It turned out that his hoarse, croaky voice carried a poignancy that was immediately appealing.

His first two big hits, "Maggie May" and "You Wear It Well," were uptempo rockers, but they were not the aggressive, sloppy rock & roll seen in Faces concerts; they were something more refined.

Things went smoothly for a while, with Stewart and the band each doing reasonably well, but this happy state didn't last. Ronnie Lane left in 1973 and was replaced by Tetsu Yamauchi, a Japanese bassist. In 1975, Ron Wood first began performing with the Rolling Stones—theoretically, he was on loan between Faces tours—yet later that year even Stewart evinced some dissatisfaction with the Faces and he, too, quit.

Though that pretty much signaled the end of Faces, it was far from being the end of Stewart's career. In fact, his good fortune was just beginning. Starting in 1976, he put out a series of albums that generated many big hits—"Tonight's the Night" (1976) and "You're in My Heart" ('77) being the biggest.

The disco boom held some charm for Stewart; "Da Ya Think I'm Sexy" was the disco single from his 1978 LP *Blondes Have More Fun,* which marketed Stewart as an out-and-out sex symbol, bleached tresses and all. Unfortunately, in that and later recordings, he seemed to lose the spark that made him human, opting for vacuous, trendy poses. All was forgiven in 1981, though, when Stewart released *Tonight I'm Yours,* which contained the singer's most heartfelt work since those classic early albums.

(HENRY McNULTY)

U.S. Hit Singles

1971	Maggie May (**1**); (I Know) I'm Losing You (**24**); Reason to Believe (**80**)
1972	You Wear It Well (**13**); Angel (**40**); Handbags and Gladrags (**42**)
1973	Oh! No Not My Baby (**59**); Twisting the Night Away (**59**)
1974	Mine for Me (**91**)
1975	Sailing (**58**)
1976	Tonight's the Night (Gonna Be Alright) (**1**); This Old Heart of Mine (**83**)
1977	The First Cut Is the Deepest (**21**); The Killing of Georgie (**30**)
1978	You're in My Heart (**4**); I Was Only Joking (**22**); Hot Legs (**28**)
1979	Da Ya Think I'm Sexy? (**1**); Ain't Love a Bitch (**22**); I Don't Want to Talk about It (**46**)
1980	Passion (**5**); If Loving You Is Wrong (**23**)

(BY THE FACES)

1971	(I Know) I'm Losing You (**24**)
1972	Stay with Me (**17**)
1973	Cindy Incidentally (**48**)

U.S. Hit LPs

1969	The Rod Stewart Album (**139**)
1970	Gasoline Alley (**27**)
1971	Every Picture Tells a Story (**1**); Never a Dull Moment (**2**)
1973	Sing It Again, Rod (**31**)
1974	Smiler (**13**)
1975	Atlantic Crossing (**9**)
1976	The Best of Rod Stewart (**90**); A Night on the Town (**2**)
1977	Footloose and Fancy Free (**2**)
1978	Blondes Have More Fun (**1**)
1979	Blondes Have More Fun (**1**)
1980	Foolish Behaviour (**12**)

(BY THE FACES)

1971	Long Player (**29**); A Nod Is as Good as a Wink to a Blind Horse (**6**)
1973	Ooh La La (**21**)
1974	Coast to Coast— Overture and Beginners (**63**)

U.K. Hit Singles

1971	Maggie May/Reason to Believe (**1**)
1972	You Wear It Well (**1**); Angel (**4**)
1973	Oh! No Not My Baby (**6**)
1974	Farewell/Bring It on Home to Me/You Send Me (**7**)
1975	Sailing (**1**); This Old Heart of Mine (**4**)

Stiff Records

Lene Lovich (Ron Gott)

Stiff Records was founded in August 1976 by Dave Robinson (manager of Nick Lowe and of Graham Parker and the Rumour) and Andrew Jakeman (better known as Jake Riviera) to focus the public eye on the newer Pub and Club Rock bands that might escape the attention of record industry majors. "We are dedicated to releasing three-chord songs lasting three minutes," claimed Riviera, with probable tongue in cheek. Nick Lowe's "So It Goes" (c/w "Heart of the City") was the first taste of the new label's sound.

It was Stiff that could claim the first Punk 45 to dent the British charts: the Damned's "New Rose," produced by Nick Lowe in a typical show of Stiff's generic cross-breeding. *Damned Damned Damned,* the Lowe-produced album that followed in February 1977, was both the first album of nouveau Brit Punk and Stiff's first album ever. Elvis Costello's full-length debut, *My Aim Is True* (yet another Lowe production), appeared in July, and Ian Dury's *New Boots and Panties* in September—the Dury LP remains Stiff's longest-running chart success.

In October 1977 the Stiff boat was heavily rocked by the defection of Jake Riviera, who absconded with Elvis the C. and the indispensable Mr. Lowe. He subsequently founded Radar Records, which enjoyed a distinguished but fleeting life in competition to Stiff; ultimately, the older label outlived its errant offspring.

At the same time Riviera was leaving the fold, Stiff was launching the first of its package tours featuring the cream of the new Stiffies: Dury, boisterous Pub Rocker Wreckless Eric ("If barbed wire could sing, it would sound like Wreckless Eric," remarked *Melody Maker*), Larry Wallis of the Pink Fairies and Motorhead, and, ironically, Costello and Lowe—in a splendid display of camaraderie and the-show-must-go-on-manship, the two defectors proselytized for a label they had already left.

The '77 tour never made it to the States, but the '78 model did: the Bestiff 1978 Route Tour played a sold-out run at New York's Bottom Line in late December. Sultry-voiced sixteen-year-old Rachel Sweet of Akron, Ohio, belted out the pop confections of fellow Akronite Liam Sternberg; songwriter-pianist Jona Lewie offered a quirky Pub-cum-cabaret style. Wreckless Eric, the only holdover from '77, provided a display of pop know-how and amiable boozy abandon. Mickey Jupp (frontman of the fine early Seventies band Legend and author of the endlessly covered "Switchboard Susan") didn't cross the Atlantic, but he sent his backup band along; and the Records of "Starry Eyes" fame, while not signed to Stiff, supported Sweet and played a short set of their own.

But the most striking of the Class of '78 was another transplanted American, onetime Detroiter Lene Lovich, whose brilliantly eccentric visual flair was a perfect complement to her equally idiosyncratic voice, which hiccuped its way from a throaty, smoky alto up into the soprano stratosphere, with occasional detours onto tenor sax. Lovich's *Stateless* was Stiff's splashiest debut LP since Costello's, and her "Lucky Number" became a major U.K. hit and a dance-floor classic.

Nineteen seventy-nine was the year of Britain's big ska revival, and Stiff scored a sizable coup by luring Madness away from the Two-Tone camp; the band's *One Step Beyond* emerged as the label's best-selling album since *New Boots.* Madness became enormous stars in Britain (Dury, who left the label for Polydor, proclaimed the group his successors); and their rise to fame and glory was traced in *Take It or Leave It,* Stiff's first feature film, which opened in October 1981 to surprisingly lukewarm response from the usually Madness-mad British public.

Stiff skipped a beat in its series of road tours, perhaps because 1979 belonged to Madness, who despite the switch to Stiff had been touring under the Two-Tone aegis. But the fall of 1980 brought the Son of Stiff tour, with a lineup entirely composed of freshman Stiffies: American pop trio Dirty Looks and Brit popsters Any Trouble; the Equators, with their invigoratingly uptempo reggae-got-soul; Tex-Mex sovereign Joe "King" Carrasco and his Crowns, endearing nonsense set to a wicked Farfisa beat; and medieval-garbed Tenpole Tudor, an oddly effective hybrid of the Skids and Adam and the Ants (lead singer Eddie, another Malcolm McLaren protégé, supplied the vocals on several tracks for *The Great Rock and Roll Swindle*). Of the Class of '80, only Tenpole Tudor has graduated to large-scale commercial success in the U.K.

And the parade continues: from the ashes of the Bodysnatchers, a latter-day Two-Tone outfit, rose the tackily glamorous Belle Stars; another all-girl group, the Go-Go's from California, made their vinyl debut on Stiff with the minor classic "We Got the Beat."

(PATRICK DILLON)

U.S. Hit Singles

(BY IAN GOMM)

1979 Hold On (**18**)

U.S. Hit LPs

(BY LENE LOVICH)

1979 Stateless (**137**)
1980 Flex (**94**)

(BY IAN GOMM)

1979 Gomm with the Wind (**104**)

(BY RACHEL SWEET)

1979 Fool Around (**97**)
1980 Protect the Innocent (**123**)

U.K. Hit Singles

(BY LENE LOVICH)

1979 Lucky Number (**3**);
Say When (**19**);
Bird Song (**39**) ·

(BY JONA LEWIE)

1980 You'll Always Find Me in the Kitchen at Parties (**16**); Stop the Cavalry (**3**)

The Stranglers

The Stranglers came to prominence shortly before the Punk explosion of 1976 and held the safety-pin brigade in deepest contempt. Their predilection for psychedelic drugs ("We're into acid," Cornwell told the *NME*) and Doors-like sound isolated them from the Punk mob before the fact, yet they remained vituperative.

Stranglers' founder Hugh Cornwell played bass and guitar in school rock & roll bands and later studied chemistry at Bristol University. For a time, he lived in Sweden, playing in a band with an American draft-dodger and apparently soaking up the psychedelic vibes of the late hippie era. Returning to England, he formed the Guildford Stranglers in 1974 with Burnel and Jet Black. Dave Greenfield, a veteran of obscure glam-rock outfits in the U.K. and Hamburg, answered an ad and the lineup was completed.

In 1977, United Artists released their debut LP, *IV Rattus Norvegicus,* complete with neo-Gothic graphics and a brace of forceful songs characterized by Burnel's slithering bass lines and Greenfield's fairground organ sound. "(Get a) Grip" and "Peaches," taken from that first LP, were among the first charting New Wave singles and established the group as unconventional headliners.

Despite their contempt for Punk bands, the Stranglers themselves were not above deliberate outrage and provocation. Male and female critics alike attacked the Stranglers as macho misogynists, a claim the lecherous-looking Cornwell dismissed with a leer.

Martial arts enthusiast Burnel was less glib, challenging disapproving journalists to step outside.

IV Rattus Norvegicus and its followup, *No More Heroes,* were released on A&M in the U.S. and sold steadily in the early days of New Wave's emergence. An initial American tour was met with both enthusiastic fans and feminist demonstrations. Back in England, their third LP, *Black and White,* reached the top of the charts.

Buoyed by the success of *Black and White* and their unusual cover version of Burt Bacharach's "Walk On By" as a single, Cornwell and Burnel embarked on solo LPs, *Nosferatu,* and *The Euroman Cometh,* respectively. A live LP, *X Certs,* followed by *The Raven,* enjoyed residency in the upper reaches of the U.K. charts. IRS Records compiled *Raven* tracks and various singles as *Stranglers IV,* for U.S. consumption.

Hugh Cornwell then served a highly publicized prison term for possession of drugs before the release of *Men In Black,* which was picked up in 1981 for American release by Stiff Records.

(DAVID KEEPS)

U.K. Hit Singles

1977 Peaches/Go Buddy Go (**8**); No More Heroes (**8**); Something Better Change/Straighten Out (**9**); (Get a) Grip (on Yourself) (**44**)
1978 Five Minutes (**11**); Nice 'n' Sleazy (**18**); Walk on By (**21**)
1979 Duchess (**14**); Nuclear Device (the Wizard of Aus) (**36**); Don't Bring Harry (EP) (**41**)

Hugh Cornwell
(vocals, guitar)
Jean-Jacques Burnel
(bass)
Jet Black
(drums)
Dave Greenfield
(keyboards)

Strawbs

Strawbs were less a rock band than a musical boardinghouse—a place where musicians of all types stayed for a time and then moved on. Rick Wakeman

got his start in Strawbs, and vocalist Sandy Denny also passed through before joining Fairport Convention.

The Strawberry Hill Boys first played acoustic folk

Dave Cousins
(guitar), plus fluctuating personnel

music in 1967 at the Brighton Folk Club. The band went from a trio to a quartet to a quintet and back again, more or less; shortened their name to Strawbs; recorded for five different labels; and played everything from Renaissance folk to experimental rock music. Only founding member Dave Cousins stayed with the band from beginning to end.

Electrified, yet retaining the sound of their folk roots, Stawbs joined an English folk fraternity dedicated to playing traditional folk material in a new way. Fairport Convention, Fotheringay, and Steeleye Span, along with Strawbs, were mainstays of the movement.

Throughout the band's career, personnel changes brought both new vitality and a dangerous instability. Rick Wakeman made a guest appearance on the 1969 album *Dragonfly* and was a member in good standing by the time of the live 1970 album, *Just a Collection of Antiques and Curios. From the Witchwood* (1971) is perhaps the best example of Strawbs' complex mixture of folk, classical, and rock elements.

By 1973, Wakeman had left for Yes and was replaced by Blue Weaver. That year's album, *Bursting at the Seams,* gave the group its only hit singles—Cousins' lyrical and powerful "Lay Down" and the protest song "Part of the Union." With some measure of financial success at last theirs, Strawbs moved ahead confidently. But once again, personnel changes broke up a winning combination.

Richard Hudson and John Ford, who authored "Part of the Union," left to form their own band, and immediately hit the British Top Ten with "Pick Up the Pieces." Strawbs picked up drummer Rod Coombes and bassist Chas Cronk and put out *Hero and Heroine*

and *Ghosts,* which were harder sounding than their predecessors.

By the time *Nomadness* came along in late 1975, every trace of their early folk orientation had been wiped out. The album cover showed the band in a cold ceramic-tiled chamber with a trunkful of strawberries, and the music was hard and stark. The last two Strawbs albums, *Burning for You* (1977) and *Deadlines* (1978), were confused, hastily assembled records with little in common with the Strawbs of old except the name. Cousins more or less disbanded the group in 1979. In 1980, there was some talk of a new, completely reorganized Strawbs (with Cousins at the fore, of course), but plans fell through when Cousins took a job with a radio station.

In their later years, they were basically another run-of-the-mill rock band. But in the early Seventies, the group's folk-tinged rock brought an elegant vitality and sprightly splendor to the British pop scene.

(HENRY McNULTY)

U.S. Hit LPs

1972	Grave New World (**191**)
1973	Bursting at the Seams (**121**)
1974	Hero and Heroine (**94**)
1975	Ghosts (**47**); Nomadness (**147**)
1976	Deep Cuts (**144**)
1977	Burning for You (**175**)

U.K. Hit Singles

| 1972 | Lay Down (**12**) |
| 1973 | Part of the Union (**2**); Shine on Silver Sun (**34**) |

Supertramp

Supertramp are among rock's rarest creatures, a group of multiplatinum artists who virtually no one would ever recognize on the street. Rarely interviewed and seldom photographed, they could sell over eleven million copies of a single LP and play to over 15,000 people a night, yet Supertramp remained an imageless, anonymous supergroup.

The Autobiography of a Supertramp, a 1910 novel by R. H. Davies, provided a name when Rick Davies broke up his late Sixties group, Joint, and teamed up with Roger Hodgson in 1970. Supertramp, then a quartet, released their self-titled debut to scant attention in late 1970.

By the time their second album, *Indelibly Stamped,* was released in '71, only the odd couple of Hodgson and Davies, mystic and realist respectively, remained. New recruits were brought in, then just as rapidly jettisoned after the commercial failure of the LP.

In 1973, a stable lineup was assembled. The group settled into a Somerset commune to write and rehearse the first of its concept LPs, *Crime of the Century,* which hit Number One in the U.K. charts in '74 and firmly established Supertramp among the progressive pantheon characterized by Yes and Genesis.

Confident of their appeal in the lucrative U.S. market, Supertramp relocated to Los Angeles as a permanent base. In March, 1975, while *Crime of the Century* was in its eighth month in the U.S. charts,

Supertramp played their first American gig in Milwaukee. Supertramp began a pattern of world tour/album release/world tour that saw them through the 1977 release of *Even in the Quietest Moments.*

Breakfast in America, the group's monster worldwide hit from 1978, represented a deliberate shift in Supertramp's album-making strategy. The band had become leery of its growing status as an artsy ensemble and set out to make a diverse pop LP. *Breakfast in America* earned the unusual distinction of dropping, albeit momentarily, from the Number One to the number two spot in the Billboard charts *with a bullet.* It resettled at the top spot for most of the spring of 1979. The LP went gold in nine countries and multiplatinum in nine more, and earned Supertramp three U.S. hit singles.

A concert appearance at Le Pavillon in Paris was recorded and released as the first live Supertramp LP, *Paris,* in October 1980. Some believed that Supertramp might have toured for the last time. As early as June 1979, Roger Hodgson confessed to *Melody Maker,* "Touring agrees with me less and less now. I think this is the last one for me. It's probably the last one for all of us. There's more things to life."

(DAVID KEEPS)

Rick Davies
(vocals, keyboards)
Roger Hodgson
(vocals, guitar, keyboards)
John A. Helliwell
(saxophone, woodwinds)
Bob C. Benberg
(drums)
Dougie Thompson
(bass)

U.S. Hit Singles

| 1975 | Bloody Well Right (**35**) |
| 1977 | Give a Little Bit (**15**) |

1979	The Logical Song (**6**);		1978	Supertramp (the Early Years) (**158**)
	Goodbye Stranger (**15**);		1979	Breakfast in America (**1**)
	Take the Long Way Home (**10**)		1980	Paris (**8**)
1980	Dreamer (**15**); Breakfast in America (**62**)			

U.S. Hit LPs

1974	Crime of the Century (**73**)
1975	Crisis? What Crisis? (**44**)
1977	Even in the Quietest Moments (**16**)

U.K. Hit Singles

1975	Dreamer (**13**)
1977	Give a Little Bit (**29**)
1979	The Logical Song (**7**); Breakfast in America (**9**); Goodbye Stranger (**57**)

Sweet

Like some icky confection, Sweet was devoured hungrily by a largely preteen audience and avoided by most everyone else. Early on, they were tagged a teenybopper's band, an amusing hybrid of Led Zeppelin and the Archies. Yet quite a few ears tuned in to their brand of hard-rocking bubblegum: they racked up over fifteen hit singles and sold thirty-five million records worldwide before their streak came to an end. Only a few bands can boast stats that impressive; ironically, their influence on pop music seems slighter in hindsight than those figures say it was.

Sweet came together in 1968 as a cover band, alternating Doors/Airplane psychedelia with tunes from the Tamla/Motown songbook. In 1970, they linked up with Nicky Chinn and Mike Chapman, a pair of pop songwriters who took them under their wing and provided them with an almost unbroken string of hit singles (including eleven Number One hits in Britain alone). Their first records were on a par with the 1910 Fruitgum Company—silly titles like ''Poppa Joe,'' ''Co-Co'' and ''Funny Funny.'' Sillier yet were some of the outfits they wore; early photos show them looking ill-at-ease in full American Indian drag and unbelievably tawdry in makeup and hairdos.

Though they were nothing more than a proving ground for glitter-rock at this point, some encouraging signs began to emerge. Their '72 and '73 singles—''Little Willy,'' ''Blockbuster,'' ''Hell Raiser''—mixed decibels and Double-Bubble with great success. Sweet was even penning their own tougher-sounding B-sides.

Sweet, in its middle period of ''Ballroom Blitz'' et al., compared favorably with the Marc Bolan of ''Bang a Gong'' and the David Bowie of ''All the Young Dudes.'' No less a rock heavy than Pete Townshend declared himself a Sweet fan, and one music paper, tongue barely in cheek, announced: ''It is now cool to say 'I Dig the Sweet' in mixed company.''

Despite all the accolades and gold records, Sweet was sick of the bubblegum image and intent on severing ties with their svengalis, Chinn and Chapman. For that matter, Chinn and Chapman were by then having great success cranking out hit tunes for Suzi Quatro and others. (Mike Chapman, incidentally, later found fame as a New Wave producer, pulling the strings for the Knack and Blondie, to name two.)

A less than amicable parting followed, and Sweet talked acrimoniously about their former songwriter/producers: ''Every time they heard something raw,'' said bassist Steve Priest, ''they'd sprinkle fairy dust on it.'' ''Fox on the Run,'' Sweet's first self-penned

A-side, came close on the heels of ''Ballroom Blitz'' and made both the U.S. and U.K. Top Ten. At this juncture, Sweet was indisputably on top: a European music poll from 1975 had Sweet the Number One group and Brian Connelly the Number One singer (over Robert Plant and David Bowie!).

After that pinnacle, however, Sweet did a slow fade. Having cast off the kiddie-pop associations, they subsequently proved themselves as competent a Class-A heavy band as the competition—say, Deep Purple. Their popularity waned in tandem with that of *thud-thud*, guitar-riffing hard-rock, and their neo-*Led Zep II* moves—juxtaposed with the more pristine studio confections of their later efforts—seemed dated by the late Seventies.

For a brief moment, it looked as if Sweet would break big in America; their sensibilities were akin to the sleazy glitz of the *Ziggy Stardust*-era teens and preteens who prowled Sunset Strip. But it didn't work out and Sweet simply expired, casualties of a fickle buying public. Just another fifteen-hit wonder.

(PARKE PUTERBAUGH)

Brian Connelly
(vocals)
Andy Scott
(guitar)
Steve Priest
(bass)
Mick Tucker
(drums)

U.S. Singles

1971	Co-Co (**99**)
1973	Little Willy (**3**); Blockbuster (**73**)
1975	Ballroom Blitz (**5**)
1976	Fox on the Run (**5**); Action (**20**)
1977	Funk It Up (David's Song) (**88**)
1978	Love Is Like Oxygen (**8**); California Night (**76**)

U.S. Hit LPs

1973	The Sweet (**191**)
1975	Desolation Boulevard (**25**)
1976	Give Us a Wink (**27**)
1977	Off the Record (**151**)
1978	Level Headed (**52**)
1979	Cut above the Rest (**151**)

U.K. Hit Singles

1971	Co-Co (**2**); Funny Funny (**13**); Alexander Graham Bell (**33**)
1972	Little Willy (**4**); Wig-Wam Bam (**4**); Poppa Joe (**11**)
1973	Blockbuster (**1**); Hell Raiser (**2**); Ballroom Blitz (**2**)
1974	Teenage Rampage (**2**); The Six-Teens (**9**); Turn It Down (**41**)
1975	Fox on the Run (**2**); Action (**15**)
1976	Lies in Your Eyes (**35**)
1978	Love Is Like Oxygen (**9**)

10cc

Combining art school influences with a keen ear for catchy rock riffs, 10cc was one of the Seventies' first British acts to succeed at reinterpreting for the new decade the clean, straight-ahead sounds of pop music from the mid-Sixties. The group produced compact, finely crafted tunes with a sense of wry humor that ranged from overt parody and wordplay to sly stylistic tributes.

10cc launched its recording career in 1972 on Jonathan King's UK label, scoring a British chart smash with the mock-falsetto love paean, ''Donna.'' Other hits followed, including ''Rubber Bullets'' and ''The Dean and I,'' as well as two highly acclaimed albums, *10cc* and *Sheet Music*. While ''Rubber Bullets'' and *Sheet Music* also attracted strong critical support in the States, the group did not have a big American hit until 1975, with the single ''I'm Not In Love'' and the album *The Original Soundtrack*.

The members of 10cc certainly came well prepared for their assault on the world market. During the Sixties, Graham Gouldman was a Midas-touch songwriter, penning smash hits for Herman's Hermits (''No Milk Today'' and ''Listen People''), Wayne Fontana and the Mindbenders (''Pamela, Pamela''), the Yardbirds (''For Your Love''), and the Hollies (''Bus Stop''). Later, in 1970, a band known as Hotlegs had a British Top Five novelty disc, ''Neanderthal Man.'' Hotlegs, augmented by Gouldman, became 10cc. The band practiced a democratic approach to the sharing of lead vocals and songwriting, which carried them through four years and as many albums. Nonetheless, in 1976, 10cc split in two.

Kevin Godley and Lol Creme had decided to devote their energies to actively promoting ''the gizmo,'' a musical instrument they developed during their tenure with the group. As their first solo project, they turned out the flawed but ambitious *Consequences* (''the first triple album to have been originally conceived as a 45 r.p.m. record''). In effect, the recording was meant to showcase the versatility of their invention. Subsequent Godley/Creme efforts continued to showcase the gizmo, but with more 10cc-ish hooks and packaging.

Graham Gouldman and Eric Stewart, meanwhile, continued as 10cc, producing such successes as ''The Things We Do for Love'' and ''Dreadlock Holiday.'' The duo took on several replacement members, essentially for touring purposes, and continued performing and recording with the refurbished group into the Eighties.

(WALLY PODRAZIK)

Lol Creme
(guitar, vocals)
Kevin Godley
(drums)
Graham Gouldman
(bass, vocals)
Eric Stewart
(guitar, vocals)

U.S. Hit Singles

1973	Rubber Bullets (**73**)
1975	I'm Not in Love (**2**); Art for Art's Sake (**83**)
1976	I'm Mandy Fly Me (**60**)
1977	The Things We Do for Love (**5**); People in Love (**40**); Good Morning Judge (**69**)
1978	Dreadlock Holiday (**44**)
1979	For You and I (**85**)

U.S. Hit LPs

1974	Sheet Music (**81**)
1975	The Original Soundtrack (**15**); 10cc (**161**)
1976	How Dare You! (**47**)
1977	Deceptive Bends (**31**); Live and Let Live (**146**)
1978	Bloody Tourists (**69**)
1979	Greatest Hits 1972–1978 (**188**)
1980	Look Hear? (**180**)

U.K. Hit Singles

1972	Donna (**2**)
1973	Rubber Bullets (**1**); The Dean and I (**10**)
1974	Wall Street Shuffle (**10**); Silly Love (**24**)
1975	I'm Not in Love (**1**); Art for Art's Sake (**5**); Life Is a Minestrone (**7**)
1976	I'm Mandy Fly Me (**6**); The Things We Do for Love (**6**)
1977	Good Morning Judge (**5**)
1978	Dreadlock Holiday (**1**)

Ten Years After

Ten Years After were perhaps victims of the Woodstock jinx. Their appearance in that epic film made them famous, but it also typecast them as a speed-freak boogie band. They tried to break out of the mold with limited success, but in the end audiences wanted to be strafed with TYA's amphetamine-laced rock & roll. Ten Years After boogied themselves six feet under.

The band's chief asset was Alvin Lee, or more precisely, his fingers. A lanky guitarist with Botticelli-angel blond good looks, he played a stampedingly fast guitar. His scorching leads would set a breakneck pace for the band's revved-up rock shuffles. Lee's voice was an effective instrument to boot—he almost sounded black, with the same sort of born-to-sing-the-blues voice as Steve Winwood or Joe Cocker.

Actually, Lee didn't really have the smarts or class of these two, so Ten Years After's records were usually a mixed blessing. There were no especially strong songwriters in the band, so the best moments were when Lee would take off on some frenetic solo flight.

Ten Years After were, logically enough, best experienced live, when the immediacy of being there—the sweat, volume, and excitement—would draw out the best in the band. They were, make no mistake, a killer live band—raw, unrelenting, and capable of driving an audience to frenzy. Their second album, *Undead*, recorded at a hot little club in

Alvin Lee
(vocals, guitar)
Chick Churchill
(keyboards)
Leo Lyons
(bass)
Ric Lee
(drums)

Alvin Lee (Henry McNulty Collection)

London, Klook's Kreek, holds up as among their best.

They signed to Mike Vernon's Deram label in 1967. Their first albums were enthusiastic, if flawed. *Stonedhenge* (great dope pun, huh?) was overproduced and suffered from weak material, and on *Ssssh,* some fine blues-rock stompin' was obscured by trendy electronic effects (it was, after all, 1969).

Then there was Woodstock, and Ten Years After suddenly stuck in everyone's mind. The group entered their richest musical period and several years' flirtation with superstardom. *Cricklewood Green* and *A Space in Time* fully harnessed their power: the songs had improved, the playing was crisp and tight. Touring, touring, and more touring brought home the bread.

At their best, Ten Years After were a supple, muscular band that took the blues and rocked them hard. Alvin Lee was an archetypal Seventies guitar wrangler, a groupie's dream, and a stage ham full of the axman's strutting bravado. On his own, following TYA's breakup, he's not been able to approach anything near his former stature.

But that image of him at Woodstock won't go away. Walking onstage, he ripped off a rapid-fire fusillade of notes, then led the band through a careening and barreling version of "I'm Goin' Home." At the end, the crowd cheered wildly while Lee, wearing a broad, toothy grin, muttered his thanks. Then he hoisted a watermelon (which appeared from Lord-knows-where) to his shoulders and stumbled unsteadily offstage.

(PARKE PUTERBAUGH)

U.S. Hit Singles

1970	Love Like a Man (**98**)
1971	I'd Love to Change the World (**40**)
1972	Baby Won't You Let Me Rock 'n' Roll You (**61**); Choo Choo Mama (**89**)

U.S. Hit LPs

1968	Undead (**115**)
1969	Stonedhenge (**61**); Sssh (**20**)
1970	Cricklewood Green (**14**); Watt (**21**)
1971	A Space in Time (**17**)
1972	Alvin Lee & Company (**55**); Rock & Roll Music to the World (**43**)
1973	Recorded Live (**39**)
1974	Positive Vibrations (**81**)
1975	Goin' Home! Their Greatest Hits (**174**)

U.K. Hit Singles

| 1970 | Love Like a Man (**10**) |

Them

Van Morrison
(vocals)
Billy Harrison
(guitar)
Alan Henderson
(bass)
Ronnie Millings
(drums)
Eric Wicksen
(keyboards)

"We're Them, take it or leave it,/ sweet sweat and misty mystic atmosphere," sang Van Morrison in "The Story of Them."

The story of Them was not a happy one; in the words of one of Morrison's later songs, they were "double-crossed . . . thrown in the dirt . . . used, abused, and so confused," even beyond the measure normally meted out in the early Sixties by a notoriously corrupt industry. Them's after-the-fact status as a cult legend owes as much to Morrison's later achievements as to such early Punk prototypes as "Gloria" and a few other songs on which the sheer force of his inspiration prevailed over unsympathetic producers and an unstable and intractable band.

George Ivan Morrison was born in Belfast, Northern Ireland; though working-class, his family lived in a leafy suburb off Cypress Avenue. His parents were Jehovah's Witnesses, which distanced them emotionally from Ulster's religious strife, enabling them to reserve their fanaticism for the blues and jazz on which Van was weaned. As he told his biographer, Ritchie Yorke, "I was doing what I was doing when the Rolling Stones were still in school." By the age of sixteen, he was touring England and Germany with the Monarchs, from whose ranks Morrison eventually recruited the nucleus of the straight R&B band that billed itself, simply, as Them.

Following Them's installment as house band at Belfast's Maritime Hotel, their uninhibited blues improvisations transformed them into local folk heroes. A Decca Records talent sniffer soon caught wind, and in September 1964, Them's version of Slim Harpo's "Don't Start Crying Now" appeared on a single. Their followup, "Baby Please Don't Go," was produced by an American, Bert Berns (whose songwriting credits included "Twist and Shout" and "Hang On, Sloopy"). The song was selected as the theme for TV's *Ready Steady Go,* and became a major hit on both sides of the Irish Sea.

In January 1965, Them loaded their possessions onto a boat in anticipation of London's financial and artistic rewards. Disillusionment soon followed. To a scribe from *NME,* Alan Henderson snapped: "Everybody said London was the greatest place in the world . . . load of rubbish!" *Melody Maker* reported that "Them are switched off to such an extent that it is excessively difficult to cull enough words from them to form a sentence."

This surly stance was encouraged by Them's management and record company; after all, scruffiness and rebellion had proven to be essential ingredients in the million-dollar British R&B formula as epitomized by the Animals and the Stones. Decca even titled the band's first British album *Angry Young Them.*

But if Them were angry, it was largely because they were allowed little say in the music they recorded, and the group's four instrumentalists were usually supplemented—if not supplanted altogether—by such hired hands as Jimmy Page. Their preordained role as angry young puppets was the one thing Them were *not* allowed to rebel against, unless they preferred to return to Belfast and obscurity—which is precisely what two of Them did.

Had Van been granted more control over his "product," everyone might have profited handsomely. But the Decca brass were so thoroughly out to lunch that the Morrison composition "Gloria" was simply thrown onto the B-side of "Baby Please Don't Go." It was left to a garage band from Chicago, the Shadows of Knight, to Xerox the original and collect the American gold record.

Decca followed "Baby Please Don't Go" with the Bert Berns song "Here Comes the Night" (originally recorded by Lulu), a moody, bluesy pop tune that reached number two in Britain and cracked the Top Forty Stateside. The latter feat was duplicated by the predominantly instrumental Morrison raveup "Mystic Eyes," wherein Van worked himself into a demonic frenzy on the harmonica before ululating a tale of graveyard madness.

The singer's legendary moodiness and perfectionism contributed to conflicts within the group itself. By the time of their second album and obligatory U.S. tour, only Morrison and Henderson remained from the original quintet. The new lineup included Jim Armstrong (guitar), John Wilson (drums), and Ray Elliot (keyboards), replacing the respective talents of *Angry Young Them*'s Billy Harrison, John McAuley, and Peter Bardens. In any event, half of the *Them Again* LP featured only Morrison and a cast of session musicians. Despite the limitations under which they worked, Van and friends managed some impressive forays into a jazzier idiom, and for sheer emotional catharsis Morrison's voice had no equal in the British Isles.

The American tour was largely a fiasco, though the group managed to draw an enthusiastic cult following at San Francisco's newly opened Fillmore, and Hollywood's Whisky-a-Go-Go, where the Doors served as Them's opening act. There were some celebrated jam sessions, during which the two Morrisons, Van and Jim—each of whom aspired, in his own inimitable manner, to bring a mystical and poetic bent to rock music—traded lines and ideas. In an episode more typical of the story of Them, the shows' promoter disappeared with the group's money.

Even so, Van Morrison had glimpsed the land of his dreams and resolved to return to California for good. This he eventually did, by way of New York, Cambridge, and Woodstock, after leaving Them in the summer of 1966. Henderson, Armstrong, and Elliot continued performing and recording under the old name, with Keith McDowell substituting for the irreplaceable Morrison.

In New York, Van Morrison was reunited with Bert Berns, whose new independent label, Bang Records, released Morrison's first solo works, the hit single "Brown Eyed Girl" and the LP *Blowin' Your Mind*. Following Berns' untimely death, Van was wooed to Warner Brothers with promises of artistic freedom.

Even those who recognized his prodigious talents were unprepared for the visionary song cycle *Astral Weeks*, a unique fusion of jazz, folk, and blues elements that has moved its discerning listeners more deeply than perhaps any other "rock" album. *Rolling Stone* bypassed *Tommy* and *Abbey Road* to name *Astral Weeks* 1969's Album of the Year; but wide commercial acceptance in Morrison's adopted land only came later, with *Moondance* and its sequels.

The Belfast Cowboy (as the Band's Robbie Robertson christened him) finally made good on his own terms, purely on the strength of the music. Baffled by rock's emphasis on images and theatrics, he once said of Jagger and Bowie: "I just can't figure them out. . . ." Van Morrison, however, proved that you don't need dry ice or the looks of Adonis to "let your soul and spirit fly/Into the mystic."

(NICHOLAS SCHAFFNER)

U.S. Hit Singles

1965	Here Comes the Night (**24**); Mystic Eyes (**33**)
1966	Gloria (**71**)

(BY VAN MORRISON)

1967	Brown Eyed Girl (**10**)
1970	Domino (**9**); Come Running (**39**)
1971	Blue Money (**23**); Wild Night (**28**); Call Me Up in Dreamland (**95**)
1972	Tupelo Honey (**47**); Jackie Wilson Said (I'm in Heaven When You Smile) (**61**); Redwood Tree (**98**)
1977	Moondance (**92**)
1978	Wavelength (**42**)

U.S. Hit LPs

1965	Them (**54**)
1966	Them Again (**138**)
1972	Them Featuring Van Morrison (**154**)

(BY VAN MORRISON)

1967	Blowin' Your Mind (**182**)
1970	Moondance (**29**); His Band and Street Choir (**32**)
1971	Tupelo Honey (**27**)
1972	Saint Dominic's Preview (**15**)
1973	Hard Nose the Highway (**27**)
1974	T. B. Sheets (**181**); Its Too Late to Stop Now (**53**); Veedon Fleece (**53**)
1977	A Period of Transition (**43**)
1978	Wavelength (**28**)
1979	Into the Music (**43**)
1980	Common One (**73**)

U.K. Hit Singles

1965	Baby Please Don't Go/Gloria (**10**); Here Comes the Night (**2**)

Thin Lizzy

Phil Lynott
(bass, vocals)
Brian Robertson
(guitar)
Brian Downey
(drums)
Scott Gorham
(guitar)
Gary Moore
(guitar)

Sex (if not drugs) and rock & roll neatly define the "macho cool" persona of Phillip Lynott, the black Catholic Celt who dominates Thin Lizzy, the most successful Irish group of the Seventies, which soared to "overnight" success in 1976 after forming as a more traditional folk-rock outfit in 1970.

Lynott was born in Dublin (around the corner from where poet Brendan Behan lived) in 1950, the son of a Brazilian seaman, and lived in religious poverty with his grandmother. He briefly considered a career as a boxer to rise above his circumstances, but settled on singing instead. Heavily influenced by Sly Stone, Jimi Hendrix, and Van Morrison, Lynott crooned in late Sixties West Coast-styled bands like the Black Eagles. Drummer Brian Downey, a close school chum, and guitarist Eric Bell completed the initial Lizzy lineup, releasing a Dublin "regional breakout" single "The Farmer," which preceded a long-term deal with Decca Records in November 1970.

Lizzy arrived on the London scene in 1971 and released two unnoticed LPs, *Thin Lizzy* and *Shades of a Blue Orphanage,* before scoring a hit single with a new arrangement of the Irish traditional "Whiskey in the Jar" in early 1973. But, despite a number six chart placing in the U.K., the followup single and an LP entitled *Vagabonds of the Western World* failed to ignite and Bell, citing ill health, quit the group after a New Year's concert in Belfast.

Gary Moore joined the group for a four-month stint, to be replaced by an American, Scott Gorham, and a Scot, Brian Robertson, on twin guitars. Lizzy jumped to the newly formed Vertigo label and debuted the new lineup at the prestigious Reading Festival in August 1974. That fall, Lynott's first book of poetry, *Songs for While I'm Away,* was published, preceding the release of the fourth Lizzy LP, *Nightlife.*

Extensive U.K. gigging and a preliminary stab at America in March 1975 followed, along with an LP, *Fighting* (1975), but Thin Lizzy was still considered the underdog in the pre-Punk British rock pantheon until the breakthrough of *Jailbreak* in March 1976. *Jailbreak* contained the smash hit "The Boys Are Back in Town," a Springsteen-esque slab of dynamically orchestrated macho romanticism, but Lynott's unfortunate bout with hepatitis forced the cancelation of half of their "big break" U.S. tour in June 1976. *Johnny the Fox* prefaced another stab at America in December 1976, but guitarist Robertson injured his hand, causing a postponement. Gary Moore resurfaced to replace Robertson on a support tour with Queen the following month.

Lizzy linked with producer Tony Visconti for 1977's *Bad Reputation,* which reached number four in the U.K. album charts and reestablished Lizzy's hard-rock sound after the disappointingly "mellow" *Johnny*

(written during Lynott's recuperation from hepatitis). Lizzy toured the U.S. as headliners in September. In 1978, Lynott's live reading of Bob Seger's "Rosalie" hit the U.K. charts. June saw the release of *Live and Dangerous,* which galvanized their growing Stateside following.

Again Gary Moore replaced Robertson, who went on to form Wild Horses. Lynott briefly joined forces with Paul Cook and Steve Jones (Sex Pistols) for a series of club dates under the moniker the Greedy Bastards. Intensive touring and recording occupied the group until the release of Lizzy's tenth long player, *Black Rose* in April 1979. Gary Moore exited the band once again after another extensive round of touring and recording, and he was replaced by ex-Pink Floyd stage guitarist Snowy White.

Nineteen eighty was an incredibly busy year for Lynott: Lizzy scored a hit with his lullabye to newborn daughter "Sarah"; a solo LP, *Solo in Soho,* was released, as well as Lizzy's *Chinatown;* and the press-dubbed "superstud" got hitched to Caroline Crowther (daughter of show-biz figure Leslie Crowther). As the Eighties got underway, Lynott and Thin Lizzy enjoyed the rare status of acceptance by both heavy metal and New Wave fans.

(DAVID KEEPS)

U.S. Hit Singles

| 1976 | The Boys Are Back in Town (**12**); Cowboy Song (**77**) |

U.S. Hit LPs

1976	Jailbreak (**18**); Johnny the Fox (**52**)
1977	Bad Reputation (**39**)
1978	Live and Dangerous (**84**)
1979	Black Rose (**81**)
1980	Chinatown (**120**)

U.K. Hit Singles

1973	Whiskey in the Jar (**6**)
1976	The Boys Are Back in Town (**8**); Jailbreak (**31**)
1977	Don't Believe a Word (**12**); Dancin' in the Moonlight (**14**)
1978	Rosalie (**20**)
1979	Waiting for an Alibi (**9**); Do Anything You Want To (**14**); Sarah (**24**)
1980	Killer on the Loose (**10**)

Thunderclap Newman

John "Speedy" Keen
(drums, vocals)
Jimmy McCulloch
(guitar)
Andy Newman
(piano)

In 1968, Pete Townshend of The Who wrote a letter to Andy Newman, a jazz musician whom he'd long admired, promising to make him a star. Townshend was true to his word; by July of the following year, Newman found himself entrenched in a group bearing his name whose first single, "Something in the Air," reached the Number One position in the British charts in just three weeks. Thunderclap Newman was largely Townshend's creation, and an extremely odd creation it was at that. He threw together three completely disparate characters: guitar whiz Jimmy McCulloch, who looked considerably younger than his already tender sixteen years; pianist Andy Newman, whose

portly bearing and thinning hair made him appear thoroughly out of place in a rock band; and longtime friend and protégé of Townshend's, Speedy Keen, whose previous songwriting credits included "Armenia, City in the Sky," a song The Who recorded on their *Sell Out* LP.

Unfortunately, the diversity that gave Thunderclap Newman its eclectic charm also caused its downfall. Without Townshend's guiding influence the band members, who had only met properly during the recording sessions for "Something in the Air," had difficulty communicating, despite the fact they were able to come up with one gem of an album.

"How anyone will manage to remain a nasty narrow-minded jade in the presence of this unremittingly delightful album defies the imagination" wrote John Mendelsohn of *Rolling Stone* about *Hollywood Dream,* released on Track Records in 1970. Produced by Townshend, who also served as bass player under the alias of Bijou Drains, it was a splendid pop record.

Hollywood Dream was largely ignored by record buyers, and shortly after its release the group split up. Speedy Keen and Andy Newman went on to record solo albums that for all their merits, never quite re-created the magic of Thunderclap Newman. Jimmy McCulloch moved on to an impressive career playing with John Mayall, Stone the Crows, Blue, and Wings.

Always known for taking the rock star lifestyle to excess, McCulloch was found dead in 1979.

(ELIZABETH SCHAFFNER)

U.S. Hit Singles

| 1969 | Something in the Air (**37**) |

U.S. Hit LPs

| 1970 | Hollywood Dream (**161**) |

U.K. Hit Singles

| 1969 | Something in the Air (**1**) |
| 1970 | Accidents (**46**) |

Traffic

Traffic was that rare breed of band that managed to reach a mass audience with no aesthetic compromises. Few rock groups have been so difficult to pigeonhole. Their music fell into no obvious category; it was, rather, an exotic stew of English folk, American R&B, and wide-ranging ethnocultural borrowings. A publicist's nightmare, they bent all the rules. They broke up and regrouped more times than you'd care to count, and always at ill-chosen times: upon completion of a new record, or on the eve of a tour. Yet, in typical anarchic Sixties fashion, they became one of the most popular groups in the world and demonstrated an improbable tenacity, surviving to 1974 with their core membership and artistic credentials intact.

Much of the credit must go to Stevie Winwood, Traffic's leader and a natural talent who seemingly was born with the Midas touch. His singular vision navigated Traffic through eight fitful, fruitful years, during which time they reigned on the contemporary scene as a creative force with few peers.

Even before there was Traffic, though, there was the Spencer Davis Group. It was with Davis that Winwood cut his teeth as a professional musician, earning a tag as the child genius of the British blues-rock scene. He was only sixteen years old when Davis brought him and his brother Muff into the SDG around 1964. It was a fortunate apprenticeship for Winwood. Davis, a blues scholar who also had a sharp business acumen, shrewdly allowed his protégé free reign. Early on, the Spencer Davis Group played note-for-note renditions of their fave blues and R&B tunes, slogging through seven grueling nights a week of sweaty pub dates. Soon enough, they found their footing, and when Winwood started to cut loose, the group unleashed a string of chart-topping singles.

"Little Stevie," as he was known, amazed everyone with his bluesy pipes. It was as if the soul of Ray Charles had been reborn as a scrawny British teenager. Winwood also had a commanding touch on the organ. By late 1966, it was growing obvious that Winwood was growing too fast to be contained in the Spencer Davis Group. He was looking beyond R&B to folk, classical, and rock & roll, and he began conceiving of a band that could marry many styles into an original amalgam. Already, he'd done some sessions with Eric Clapton. Playing "Superfreak" (another nickname) to

Clockwise (from top): Mason, Wood, Winwood, and Capaldi (Keystone Press Agency)

Steve Winwood
(vocals, guitar, keyboards)
Chris Wood
(flute, saxophone)
Jim Capaldi
(drums, vocals)
Dave Mason
(guitar, vocals)

Clapton's "Slowhand," they recorded three songs under the name Powerhouse for a 1966 Elektra Records sampler, *What's Shakin'*. He'd also begun jamming with local musicians at a Birmingham club called the Elbow Room. Out of those late-night jams emerged the nucleus of Traffic—Chris Wood, a reedman with a jazz background; Dave Mason, a talented guitarist who was then a Spencer Davis Group roadie; and Jim Capaldi, a rock-solid drummer.

Traffic was actually an entity several months before Winwood amicably severed ties with Spencer Davis. They played all the percussion on "I'm a Man," and Mason would occasionally plug in during the SDG's sets. But when the foursome made it official, London was buzzing with the news.

The iconography of the cottage figures prominently in the Traffic legend. It's an oft-repeated story: how they spent six months in a secluded stone cottage, forging a musical identity in the pastoral British countryside. In 1981, Winwood gave the lie to the myth, recalling the experience as "four blokes not even out of their teens, shoved together and living in squalor." Still, it's a seductive image, and the hiatus in Berkshire did give rise to their amazing first album, *Mr. Fantasy.*

Winwood made good on his promise to expand rock into other areas. Chris Wood's flutes and saxes gave the Traffic sound an enhanced textural dimension. Jim Capaldi contributed oblique, impressionistic lyrics. Dave Mason's pop leanings created an interesting tension against Winwood's more *outre* tastes. Winwood himself dispensed with conventions, melding his R&B vocal stylings to exotic folk, jazz, and Indian influences. Call it what you will, Traffic was plowing fertile new ground out in the Berkshire Downs.

Their first single, "Paper Sun," went Top Five in the U.K. To the Swinging Londoners of 1967, "Paper Sun" and the Small Faces' "Itchycoo Park," with their candy-stripe psychedelia, summed up Carnaby Street and the Summer of Love. *Mr. Fantasy,* likewise, captured that halcyon period, despite the fact it came out in radically different versions in England and America. In Britain, albums and singles have traditionally been regarded as separate entities, so "Paper Sun" was not included on the U.K. *Mr. Fantasy.* Internal conflicts within Traffic further complicated matters. By the time the LP hit these shores, Dave Mason had announced he was leaving. In the States, trio pictures of Traffic were substituted for the British cover, and the record was trimmed of some Mason compositions (replaced by Winwood-penned singles sides). Curiously, a contrived continuity was imposed on the U.S. *Mr. Fantasy,* with one-eighth level segues—a short instrumental snippet from "Paper Sun"—linking the twelve tracks together. And oddly enough, it worked, making the American release far superior to its British counterpart.

Traffic decided against replacing Mason, and consequently came over for their first American tour as a trio. In San Francisco, Jann Wenner (editor of *Rolling Stone*) and Al Kooper (who'd just put together Blood, Sweat & Tears) served as a welcoming committee. From its first issue, *Rolling Stone* had followed Traffic, and in RS 9, Wenner and Kooper, in articles on facing pages, gushed over the young genius whom they regarded as the best white blues singer they'd ever heard. All over the country it was the same story. Traffic went down splendidly in concert, and Winwood was hailed as a new pop avatar.

On their way out of the country, Traffic ran into Dave Mason in New York City. Ill feelings were repaired and Traffic, once again a foursome, flew home and headed to their upcountry retreat. Several months of woodshedding resulted in Traffic's finest hour, their eponymous second album. The vision was fully mature now, the empathy among the four musicians at its zenith. Dave Mason contributed four tunes, one of them a bona fide rock standard, "Feelin' Alright." Winwood shone on moody meditations such as "No Time to Live." *Traffic* represents the fruition of Stevie Winwood's vision of four consummate musicians embarking on a creative, collaborative odyssey across uncharted musical terrain.

None of which explains what happened next. No sooner was the new record in the shops when Traffic broke up. Winwood was odd man out this time. The other three regrouped, briefly, with organist Mick Weaver (a.k.a. Wynder K. Frog) as Mason, Capaldi, Wood, and Frog. Winwood, meanwhile, was rumored to be forming a band with Eric Clapton. The record

label assembled a farewell third album, *Last Exit,* out of leftover studio tracks and live tapes from their 1968 tour. *Best of Traffic,* released a few months later, seemed to close the files on Traffic.

Stevie Winwood spent much of 1969 involved in the Blind Faith debacle. It all started innocently enough—Winwood and Eric Clapton unpretentiously making music in the former's country home. But soon enough, the record business leeches had sunk their talons into the project and the corporate machinery was grinding out the superhype. Ominously, the press handouts read: "Robert Stigwood and Chris Blackwell in association with Ahmet Ertegun introduce Blind Faith." The principals enthused that Blind Faith's formation was a triumph of resolving insurmountable contractual difficulties (who said anything about talented musicians being motivated to play with each other?). Blind Faith was sprung on the world at a June 1969 free concert in London's Hyde Park before 120,000 fans. There was a six-week late-summer American tour (their presence trumpeted by *Time* and *Newsweek*), and then Blind Faith was *kaput,* leaving behind one modestly charming LP and a mammoth object lesson in rock ethics.

Back in England, a sadder but wiser Stevie Winwood began making a solo album with the working title *Mad Shadows.* Two songs into it, he called in Jim Capaldi to help out with lyrics, and then Chris Wood, fresh from a stint with Dr. John, was adding his horns . . . and Traffic was reborn. The project was retitled *John Barleycorn Must Die,* and it became Traffic's first gold album. Especially on the title track, the LP evidenced a return to folk roots and the communal house-in-the-country ethos.

A late-1970 American tour found Traffic accompanied by Blind Faith refugee Rick Grech. United Artists announced the imminent release of *Live— November '70,* culled from those shows. That record was never released, but the in-concert album that did come out nearly a year later was a fetching document of an extraordinary outfit. *Welcome to the Canteen* found Traffic expanded to a seven-man big band. Capaldi had relinquished his drum kit in favor of standup singing; Jim Gordon, late of Derek and the Dominoes, took over. And Dave Mason had signed on once again for a handful of gigs. The revitalized Traffic roared through their old repertoire, encoring with the Spencer Davis Group chestnut "Gimme Some Lovin'."

Traffic subsequently broke form and acted as they hadn't in all their five on-and-off years: they didn't split up, and they became a hard-working tour band. *Low Spark of High-Heeled Boys* and *Shoot Out at the Fantasy Factory* found Traffic stretching out, making music with a jazzy, stoned ambiance. By the time of *Shoot Out,* they'd taken on Roger Hawkins, David Hood and Barry Beckett; known as the Muscle Shoals Rhythm Section, that trio had backed up Aretha Franklin, Wilson Pickett, et al. *On the Road* was a two-record live memento of Traffic in the Seventies. Once off the road, Traffic pared down to a quartet for *When the Eagle Flies* (1974). It was a brooding, introspective record, and turned out to be the swan song from one of the great rock bands.

Winwood thereupon entered three years of relative seclusion, while Jim Capaldi began pursuing his solo career in earnest (he'd already made two solo albums while with Traffic).

All the while, Dave Mason had been going about his own business with mixed success. He recorded a classic Seventies album, *Alone Together*, that suggested he was one of the better guitarists around and surely among the sharpest songwriters on the scene. Pressed on multicolored tie-dyed vinyl (making it a one-of-a-kind novelty), *Alone Together* was hailed as among the first great singer/songwriter discs in that singer/songwriter-dominated decade. Its eight songs became the backbone of his live shows. Certainly, his subsequent albums didn't, as there appeared a rather drastic drop in quality. Having relocated to Los Angeles, Mason began displaying the soft-rock MOR preferences of that city's musical community. In 1981, he could be heard singing radio jingles on behalf of Miller beer.

By contrast, Winwood, having been driven to exhaustion by ceaseless touring, kept a low profile, playing the odd session but disengaging himself as best he could from the rock & roll circus. His excellent, untitled first album as a solo artist came out in 1977, causing but minor ripples. Winwood, still guarded and gun shy, refused to hit the road and once again sank back out of sight. He spent three more years in country-squire solitude, phlegmatically installing a recording studio in his home. Finally, in 1981, sixteen years after his first hit record with the Spencer Davis Group, Winwood—first Little Stevie, then Stevie, now Steve—struck paydirt one more time with *Arc of a Diver*, on which he proved himself rock music's most accomplished one-man band. The album and its hit single, "While You See a Chance," made Winwood a star all over again.

(PARKE PUTERBAUGH)

U.S. Hit Singles

1967 Paper Sun (**94**)
1970 Empty Pages (**74**)
1971 Gimme Some Lovin' Part One (**68**)
1972 Rock & Roll Stew Part One (**93**)

(BY THE SPENCER DAVIS GROUP)

1966 Keep on Running (**76**)
1967 Gimme Some Lovin' (**7**);
 I'm a Man (**10**);
 Somebody Help Me (**47**);
 Time Seller (**100**)

(BY DAVE MASON)

1970 Only You Know and I Know (**42**);
 Satin Red and Black Velvet Woman (**97**)
1977 So High (Rock Me Baby and Roll Me Away) (**89**); We Just Disagree (**12**)
1978 Let It Go, Let It Flow (**45**);
 Will You Still Love Me Tomorrow (**39**)
1980 Save Me (**71**)

U.S. Hit LPs

1968 Mr. Fantasy (**88**); Traffic (**17**)
1969 Last Exit (**19**)
1970 Best of Traffic (**48**);
 John Barleycorn Must Die (**5**)
1971 Welcome to the Canteen (**26**);
 The Low Spark of High Heeled Boys (**7**)
1973 Shoot Out at the Fantasy Factory (**6**);
 On the Road (**29**)
1974 When the Eagle Flies (**9**)
1975 Heavy Traffic (**155**); More Heavy Traffic (**193**)

(BY THE SPENCER DAVIS GROUP)

1967 Gimme Some Lovin' (**54**); I'm a Man (**83**)
1968 Greatest Hits (**195**)

(BY BLIND FAITH)

1969 Blind Faith (**1**)

(BY STEVE WINWOOD)

1977 Steve Winwood (**22**)

(BY JIM CAPALDI)

1972 Oh How We Danced (**82**)
1974 Whale Meat Again (**191**)
1976 Short Cut Draw Blood (**193**)

(BY DAVE MASON)

1970 Alone Together (**22**)
1971 Dave Mason and Cass Elliot (**49**)
1972 Headkeeper (**51**)
1973 Dave Mason Is Alive (**116**);
 It's Like You Never Left (**50**)
1974 The Best of Dave Mason (**183**);
 Dave Mason (**25**)
1975 Dave Mason at His Best (**133**);
 Split Coconut (**27**)
1976 Certified Live (**78**)
1977 Let It Flow (**37**)
1978 Mariposa De Oro (**41**);
 Very Best of Dave Mason (**179**)
1980 Old Crest on a New Wave (**74**)

U.K. Hit Singles

1967 Hole in My Shoe (**2**); Paper Sun (**5**);
 Here We Go Round the Mulberry Bush (**8**)
1968 No Face, No Name, No Number (**40**)

(BY THE SPENCER DAVIS GROUP)

1964 I Can't Stand It (**47**)
1965 Keep On Running (**1**);
 Every Little Bit Hurts (**41**); Strong Love (**44**)
1966 Somebody Help Me (**1**); Gimme Some Loving (**2**); When I Come Home (**12**)
1967 I'm a Man (**9**); Time Seller (**30**)
1968 Mr. Second Class (**35**)

The Troggs

It's no offense to the Troggs to say that, in terms of critical writing about British groups, never has so much been made over so little. The Troggs themselves would be the last people to tell you their music had any significance—and such irrelevance is precisely why rock theoreticians find the Troggs so attractive.

The band had a lovable-slob appeal from the very beginning. The unforgettable "Wild Thing" introduced the Troggs in 1966, long after the bloom was off the first harvest of British Invasion bands. With its three chords, clubfooted beat, and salacious vocal from Reg Presley (a former bricklayer), "Wild Thing"

Reg Presley
(vocals)
Chris Britton
(guitar)
Pete Staples
(bass)
Ronnie Bond
(drums)

281

beat American Punk Rock at its own game and looked forward to that music's revival ten years later. It catapulted the Troggs to Number One in the U.S. records charts (number two in England)—an auspicious beginning indeed. Their next single—the equally pounding "With a Girl Like You," didn't do as well here but hit the top in the U.K., and was followed quickly by two more British Top Ten 45s.

In the U.S., the Troggs were shaping up as one-hit wonders. The reason was obvious: this country has never had much commercial tolerance for the Troggs' brand of slambang rock. Even the so-called "golden age of punk" chronicled on collections like Lenny Kaye's *Nuggets* made only sporadic inroads on mass consciousness. "Wild Thing" was a summer novelty (an ocarina break in the middle!) but the Troggs refused to go away in the fall. Presley and company continued churning out savage, stripped-down music ("I Can't Control Myself," "Give It to Me"), with an occasional romantic ballad thrown in for relief.

One of the latter, "Love Is All Around," celebrated the hippie aesthetic and served as the Troggs' reentry to the U.S. Top Ten in early 1968. Presley, whose nasal whine was perfect for the Troggs' punky numbers, always sounded insincere on the weepers, but the song's popularity enabled the band to issue a second album. The inevitably titled *Love Is All Around* LP showed the Troggs still grappling with their favorite themes: sex ("Night of the Long Grass"), frustration ("Girl in Black"), and incest ("Cousin Jane").

After "Love Is All Around," the Troggs continued as a pop group in name only. They released more singles—including at least one stab at psychedelia, "Maybe the Madman"—but nobody was buying. As the Sixties turned into the Seventies, they looked increasingly anachronistic; the time just wasn't right for offbeat ("The Raver") or shocking ("Come Now") rock, no matter how well done.

The Troggs' resurrection undoubtedly dates from their appearance on David Bowie's *1980 Floor Show* TV special in 1973. In choosing the Troggs and Marianne Faithfull as guests, Bowie intended a Sixties homage (one can't rule out a camp factor as well), but the Troggs' spirited performance of their raunchy "Strange Movies"—then their current single!—had more zest than Bowie's ghoulish resuscitation of Sixties faves on his just-released *Pin Ups* album.

With Presley and Bond the sole remaining originals, the band had never stopped touring Britain; now critical opinion started turning back in their favor. Punk Rock (the pre-Sex Pistols variety) was seen as a refreshing antidote to the turgid craftmanship of the Genesis/Yes/ELP school, and no one could accuse the Troggs of overestimating their audience's intelligence. They even released two new albums in the mid-Seventies; now that they weren't pretending to compete in the mainstream rock sweepstakes, they could get away with smarmy sendups, like their version of the Beach Boys' "Good Vibrations."

The Troggs found acceptance, if not quite adulation, among New Wavers who saw in the band's determined grunginess a refusal to bow to societal standards. Reg Presley, an extremely affable guy, may have trouble relating to spiky haircuts and bondage trousers, but he still blows a mean ocarina. It beats bricklaying.

(SCOTT ISLER)

U.S. Hit Singles

1966	Wild Thing (**1**); With a Girl Like You (**29**); I Can't Control Myself (**43**)
1968	Love Is All Around (**7**)

U.S. Hit LPs

1966	Wild Thing (**52**)
1968	Love Is All Around (**109**)

U.K. Hit Singles

1966	Wild Thing (**2**); With a Girl Like You (**1**); I Can't Control Myself (**2**); Any Way That You Want Me (**8**)
1967	Love Is All Around (**5**); Give It to Me (**12**); Night of the Long Grass (**17**); Hi Hi Hazel (**42**)
1968	Little Girl (**37**)

TROWER, ROBIN: See Procol Harum

Two-Tone Records

1979 was emphatically the year of Two-Tone. Not since the onslaught of Punk in the summer of '76 had a movement exploded with such force on the British music scene or so captured the hearts, minds, and dancing feet of rock-loving American Anglophiles. The Specials, Madness, the Selecter, and the (English) Beat burst with irresistible energy onto the U.K. charts. Club deejays were playing ska, and record companies dusted off long-forgotten Jamaican platters from the mid-Sixties and loaded some best-selling compilation discs onto the Two-Tone bandwagon. Sharkskin suits, shades, and porkpie hats sold like never before—Two-Tone hit the fashion scene as well.

And what was the cause of all the fuss? It was ska, the lively father of rock steady and the granddaddy of reggae. Artists like the early Maytals, the Skatalites, and Roland Alphonso made some irrepressibly bouncy music that remained almost totally unknown in the States. In the U.K., however, the Jamaican community made sure that ska got its hearing and made its dent. It remained for racially mixed bands like the Specials to rediscover and resuscitate ska, in much the fashion that the Stones had embraced and proselytized for R&B. (It's a comparison that Jerry Dammers, leader of the Specials, was fond of making.)

Before the Specials, Dammers had played with a string of bands in and around Coventry, in styles ranging from reggae to soul to country & western. One of these—the Coventry Automatics, with a core of Dammers, Horace Gentleman, and Lynval Golding, and a Punky reggae sound—was the immediate predecessor of the Specials.

The early Specials recruited vocalists Terry Hall and Neville Staples, Punk guitarist Roddy Radiation, and drummer Neil (Brad) Bradbury from various Coventry-based bands.

The band recorded "Gangsters" in the spring of '79, backed with "The Selecter," a revamping of an old demo tape penned by Coventry colleague Neol Davies, who'd been playing in a band called Hard Top 22. It was released that August on the band's own label, Two-Tone, and made the Top Ten by September.

The Specials dedicated their label to a fusion of black and white musical styles and the promotion of new bands with similar ideals (soul revivalists Dexy's Midnight Runners played some early gigs as Two-Toners in the summer of '79). All-white London band Madness scored on Two-Tone with "The Prince," a tribute to Jamaican ska pioneer Prince Buster, before moving to Stiff and British superstardom with "One Step Beyond," "My Girl" (their first Number One), and the best-selling of the nouveau ska debut albums. And Neol Davies transformed the Selecter from a B-side into a band that included vocalist Pauline Black, the best of the singers to emerge from the Two-Tone brigade; "On My Radio," the first full-fledged Selecter single, was another Top Ten winner. The debut of Birmingham's the Beat—a wildly juiced-up cover of "Tears of a Clown"—followed suit in predictable fashion.

The initial impact of Two-Tone was enormous; and on a Two-Tone tour featuring the Specials, the Selecter, and Madness in October and November of 1979, most of the gigs were wild, exciting, joyous celebrations of uplifting music and dance. But problems were there from the first. Sets were periodically disrupted by rows incited by unruly skinheads and members of the British Movement and the National Front, two essentially racist right-wing organizations. Madness's solo gigs were especially prone to misplaced displays of rightist fervor, since the group's all-white lineup and skinhead look provided an easy visual hook, and the band's break with Two-Tone was certainly open to misinterpretation. But friction at Specials gigs led to cancellations and even (in conservative Cambridge) to the arrest of Dammers and Terry Hall on charges of inciting a riot.

Both the Specials and Madness released their second albums in September 1980. Madness's *Absolutely* was less ska and more music hall à la Dury. Shying away from political confrontations, the songs concentrated on working-class vignettes, laconically witty and cheerily danceable; the album and its single "Baggy Trousers" were the big winners of the second round of Two-Tone (and ex-Two Tone) action.

The Specials' round two, *More Specials*, was more equivocal; though it, too, made an initial dent in charts, it failed altogether to match the impact of its predecessor. Much of the album was a sort of homage to Muzak and movie music; as early as summer '79, Jerry Dammers had projected a Muzak-ska fusion for his band's future. (And many of the original ska hits of the Sixties had been derived from movie themes—"James Bond," "The Guns of Navarone.") Though *More Specials* was emphatically an honorable effort and full of intriguing ideas, its overall effect was a bit unsettled and diffuse—the band, somewhat ominously, seemed to be pulling in several directions at once.

As 1981 rolled round, it became ever clearer that all was far from well in the Two-Tone camp. A concert film called *Dance Craze* was delayed by production strife and failed to register when finally released, though its soundtrack did well in the charts. And the Selecter, disenchanted with the marketing of Two-Tone, split to form its own label at Chrysalis. Keyboardist Desmond Brown and bassist Charley Anderson left to create a splinter band called the People—their first single was released via Race Records, a Two-Tone offshoot founded by the Specials' Brad. The Selecter's antigun single "Celebrate the Bullet" was banned by the BBC's Radio One, who evidently took the title at face value; but neither the single nor the album of the same name managed to capture public interest. And in May 1981 Pauline Black quit the fold to pursue a solo career.

Among the Specials, too, rumors of internal strife surfaced with increasing frequency. The band had drastically curtailed its live performing, and its members busied themselves with projects of their own. The summer of '81 saw a last, somewhat grim burst of activity. The magnificently gloomy "Ghost Town" hit Number One at the height of the summer's racial and anti-Thatcher violence. The band made a few appearances in the States, but to those who remembered its first American dates only eighteen months before, an essential spark seemed to be missing. And finally, in October, vocalists Terry and Neville and guitarist Lynval confirmed the pessimists' doubts and defected to form the Fun Boy Three (and record the striking "The Lunatics Have Taken over the Asylum"). Though Jerry Dammers vowed to carry on, the future looked uncertain.

And so with the smoke all cleared from the ska explosion of '79, it's easier to say that the optimism and positive energy of Two-Tone were doomed to dissipate and sour. From the vigor and idealism of the early songs to the empty defeatism of "Ghost Town" and "Lunatics" was a short two-year ride downhill—about as long as it took the Pistols to fire their last shot. Doubtless there's some wonderful music to be made by the Two-Tone alumni, but however it turns out, it's likely to be those singles from ska-mad '79 that best show just what made Two-Tone so special and select.

(PATRICK DILLON)

U.S. LPs

(BY MADNESS)

1980 One Step Beyond (**128**); Absolutely (**146**)

(BY THE SELECTER)

1980 Too Much Pressure (**175**)

(BY THE SPECIALS)

1980 The Specials (**84**); More Specials (**98**)

U.K. Hit Singles

(BY MADNESS)

1979 The Prince (**16**); One Step Beyond (**7**)
1980 My Girl (**3**); Night Boat to Cairo (**6**);
        Baggy Trousers (**3**); Embarrassment (**4**)

(BY THE SELECTER)

1979 On My Radio (**8**)
1980 Three Minute Hero (**16**); Missing Roads (**23**)

(BY THE SPECIALS)

1979 Gangsters (**6**); Message to You
        Rudy/Nite Club (**10**)
1980 Too Much Too Young (**1**); Rat Race (**5**);
        Stereotypes (**6**); Do Nothing (**4**)

(BY THE BODYSNATCHERS)

1980 Let's Do Rock Steady (**22**)

Ultravox

Ultravox began life as a textbook example of art-school rock with a debut LP produced by no less a progressive maestro than Brian Eno. Critical reaction to the self-titled LP was less than laudatory, but U.S. New Wavers nurtured on the Bowie/Roxy Music axis warmed to the slightly pretentious lyrical posturings of tunes like "My Sex" and "The Man Who Died Every Day." Two more albums, *Ha! Ha! Ha!* and *Systems of Romance*, were in a similar mold.

Ultravox first toured the U.S. in the fall of 1979, despite the fact that they had been dropped by Island. Yet they attracted critical praise and a strong audience support, climaxing in a nine-day sellout stint at Los Angeles' Whisky-a-Go-Go. Upon their return, Foxx and guitarist Robin Simon departed, with Foxx forming his own label, Metal Beat (licensed to Virgin Records) and releasing Top 30 synth-laden singles like "No One Driving."

Currie, Cann, and Cross took solace in the good press pop's newest superstar, Gary Numan, gave them in the lengthy interviews that marked his ascendancy. Currie eventually teamed with Numan to record the *Pleasure Principle* LP and tour with him, and then entered into a studio project, Steve Strange's Visage, where he met Scotsman Midge Ure.

Ure was a veteran of the British pop scene, a centerpiece of Silk, a teenybop variation of the Bay City Rollers, while still in his teens. Ure then joined ex-Pistol Glen Matlock in the much-hyped, but short-lived Rich Kids, a move that left him in financial straits much like the surviving members of Ultravox.

Patience had its rewards, and Ure's arrival coincided with other fortuitous events—the addition of Thin Lizzy's management team and a recording deal with Chrysalis—that contributed to a remarkable career resurrection. "Sleepwalk," the initial single from the first Chrysalis LP, *Vienna*, revived Stateside interest while the moody, atmospheric title track raced to the top of the U.K. charts. While *Vienna* charted only briefly in the U.S. Top 200, the success of the single, along with the throbbing followup "All Stood Still" and the band's beautifully cinematic videos, made *Vienna* one of Britain's Top Ten best sellers of 1981.

But more important, *Vienna* marked a departure in style and status that neatly distinguished the band from the old. Fickle English critics suddenly fawned over the group, with nary a catcall at their crisp Thirties-style clothing, and even Island Records cashed in, compiling the best of their back catalogue into a single album compilation. A new LP, *Rage in Eden*, released in the fall of 1981, confirmed their amazing second-time-round ascendancy.

(DAVID KEEPS)

John Foxx
(vocals)
Chris Cross
(bass, synthesizers, vocals)
Warren Cann
(drums, vocals)
Billy Currie
(synthesizer, piano, violin, viola)
Midge Ure
(vocals, guitar, synthesizer)

U.S. Hit Singles

1980 Sleepwalk (**29**)

U.S. Hit LPs

1980 Vienna (**164**)

The Undertones

The Undertones hail from the Catholic side of Derry, the town that spawned the first of the violent encounters that have so characterized the political scene in Northern Ireland. But violence and aggression couldn't be farther from the lyrical world of the 'Tones.

The Undertones began as a true garage band in the mid-Seventies, the brainchild of drummer Billy Doherty and guitarist John O'Neill. Doherty's schoolmate Feargal Sharkey, whose distinctively throbbing, gravelly voice had won him a string of prizes in his childhood, was a natural if reluctant draftee to the band; and Mickey Bradley and O'Neill's brother Dee filled out the lineup. The newborn 'Tones played ramshackle gigs in Derry that consisted basically of old Chuck Berry tunes dished out plain and repeated on demand. And as demand heightened and their confidence increased, the 'Tones began to showcase their own material, and an ace songsmith was found in John O'Neill, whose high-powered, winningly melodic teen anthems ("Teenage Kicks," "Here Comes the Summer," "Jimmy Jimmy,") became the hallmark of the band.

An EP, *Teenage Kicks*, recorded for Belfast's tiny Good Vibrations label, was championed by BBC deejay John Peel ("We thought he felt sorry for us," the band's been known to say) and led to a contract with Sire. The Undertones' debut album was released in June 1979 to lavish critical praise and reasonable success in the unpredictable British charts. The band made its first American appearances in September 1979, supporting the Clash on tour (typically, American Sire released the album four months later). *Hypnotised*, the quintet's second album (the original, aptly descriptive title was *Fifteen Rocking Humdingers*), appeared in May 1980; while not as breathlessly "up" as the first, it showed a remarkable leap in craftsmanship and a cannily varied pace, and proved Dee O'Neill a songwriter fully able to give his brother a healthy run.

In spring of '81, the Undertones inked a deal with EMI giving them their own label, Ardeck; and a new single, "It's Going to Happen!". This gave ample proof that they'd lost none of their flair and when the third album, *Positive Touch*, reached the shops, it showed just how much had been gained: in craft, confidence, and maturity, the songs were as good as anything pop had to offer in 1981. There was a new depth and feeling in the lyrics, new delicacy in the music—far from being stagnant, the Undertones

Feargal Sharkey
(vocals)
Damian (Dee) O'Neill
(lead guitar)
John O'Neill
(rhythm guitar)
Mickey Bradley
(bass)
Billy Doherty
(drums)

songs were bubbling along delightfully in new and surprising directions.

If the Undertones lack anything of the traditional pop arsenal, it's ego—they've been all too quick to downgrade their rather remarkable talents. They're still the nice Irish boys next door, but nice boys with a secure foot in the door to rock immortality. Along with Squeeze and the (English) Beat, they're the real Top of the Pops.

(PATRICK DILLON)

WOOD, ROY: See Move

WRIGHT, GARY: See Spooky Tooth

X-Ray Spex

Lora Logic and Poly Styrene (David Keeps)

Poly Styrene
(vocals)
Lora Logic
(saxophone)
Jak Airport
(guitar)
Paul Dean
(bass)
B. P. Hurding
(drums)

The perils of Poly Styrene would have made a perfect Forties tortured torchsinger screenplay: a sensitive and flamboyant teenager rocketing from overnight obscurity to instant cult fame, suffering a mental breakdown and resurrected as something of a prophet.

After a brief stint in London's fringe theater, Poly Styrene (née Marion Elliot) assembled X-Ray Spex in March 1977 at age eighteen. Formal gigging commenced a month later at Punk's peak showcase in 1977, the Roxy. Poly's outlandish costumes (frocks made from plastic tablecloths), the band's adolescent energy, and witty sendups of consumer society in tunes entitled "My Mind Is Like a Plastic Bag" and "Artificial" garnered immediate media attention and a large, loyal following.

Two important distinctions separated X-Ray Spex from the rest of the Punk mob: the sleazy cocktail saxophone of Lora Logic, which insured that they sounded unique, more like an adrenalized Roxy Music; and the inclusion of a female musician and singer/songwriter in a commercially viable Punk combo.

Poly Styrene voiced her sentiments about women's rock & roll rights (and responsibilities) in the seminal Punk classic released in 1977 on a one-off deal with Virgin Records. "Some people think little girls should be seen and not heard," she drawls on the way to her trademark 1-2-3-4 countdown, "But I think *oh bondage up yours!*" "Oh Bondage" cracked the bottom of the Top Hundred, despite a ban on radio play and scant promotion. Shortly thereafter, saxophonist Lora Logic departed, and was eventually replaced by Steve Rudi during the year's interim between X-Ray Spex singles. Logic resurfaced as leader of the exotic Essential Logic, part-time member of Red Crayola, and a fixture of the Rough Trade recording community with a critically praised LP, *Beat Rhythm News*, to her credit.

"The Day the World Turned Dayglo," released in April 1978, was the first Punk record to be released under a band's own imprint on a major label. Around this time, strange occurrences began to plague the outwardly boisterous Ms. Styrene. She explained to the British press that the next Spex single would be pressed on vinyl the same pink color as the UFO she had recently seen. Moreover, she was abandoning her plastic fetish for natural things on the advice of the UFO's inhabitants. Prior to a sloppy but energetic gig at the London Roundhouse, Poly announced, "I'll shave me head if they try to make me a sex symbol," and during the encore of that gig removed a turban to reveal a savagely shorn skinhead coif. The single "Identity" neatly paralleled Poly's precarious psychological state.

Germ-Free Adolescent, the long-awaited debut LP, was largely comprised of previous releases, but still garnered sympathetic reviews. The title track, also released as a single, was a radical departure from the group's rough-and-tumble repertoire and X-Ray Spex's first-ever ballad. Poly had set a new course that was to meet with the disapproval of her original fans and the condescension of the U.K. press. A fifth single, "Highly Inflammable," sank without a trace, and the members of X-Ray Spex became increasingly alienated by Poly's forays into melodic acoustic music.

A final disastrous European tour followed, and just as suddenly as they had appeared, X-Ray Spex were no more.

Pretty Poly maintained a low profile until late 1980, when she released a single, "Talk in Toytown," and an LP, *Translucence*. Critics noted an almost metaphysical bent and a whimsical insularity from the commercial mainstream in the grooves and record buyers fulfilled their prophecy by ignoring the LP. But, no matter what turns she may take, Poly Styrene can rest secure that she was among the most stylish, thoughtful, and entertaining female pioneers in the whole of the New Wave.

(DAVID KEEPS)

XTC

XTC emerged as one of the more intelligent bands to ride the crest of the New Wave. Visually and musically, they offered a striking contrast to the shock appeal proffered by some of the hard-core Punk-rockers who were their contemporaries back in 1977. With their short hair, neat grooming, and unassuming dress—button-down shirts and jeans—XTC could almost pass for accountants. They may have looked average, but they sure didn't sound it: their broad imagination and progressive-minded pop sense cast them leagues ahead of their peers.

XTC's roots are in the town of Swindon, a small outpost some distance from London that guitarist/leader Andy Partridge unsentimentally described as "a gritty little concrete industry blob." Whatever rancor they carried away from their upbringing manifested itself in a brightening release of creative energy: guitars bounced off each other at odd angles; melodies were played or sung against odd meters; and quite often, the two guitars would fly into a circa-2000 Yardbirds-style raveup. And they evinced a healthy wit about them that in its wry social or personal commentary recalled the Kinks at their drollest. "Respectable Street" from *Black Sea* (their fourth album), for instance, seemed to hybridize the spirit of "A Well Respected Man" and "Dead End Street."

The group's main strength, though, was banging out crazy chords in true lunatic fashion, taking a tune to the point where you think it'd collapse into disso-nance, and then with a deft sleight of hand pulling it back into safer pop territory.

The first two albums by XTC (*White Noise* and *Go 2*) found them posing the musical question "What Is Pop?" (an actual title for what is probably their signature song) and in effect reinventing the word *pop* to suit themselves. After these, organist Barry Andrews dropped out to join Robert Fripp's short-lived League of Gentlemen and was replaced by guitarist Dave Gregory. Thus, XTC's guitar-keyboard attack became a guitar-guitar attack, and XTC began exploring the textural possibilities of this arrangement to the maximum. No complacent technicians, XTC sculpted an engrossing guitar nirvana on *Drums and Wires;* as their composing ability continued to grow by leaps and bounds with such records, XTC promised to be one of the most luminously engaging bands of the Eighties.

(PARKE PUTERBAUGH)

Andy Partridge
(guitar, vocals)
Dave Gregory
(guitar)
Colin Moulding
(bass, vocals)
Terry Chambers
(drums)

Andy Partridge

The Yardbirds

Rock & roll was never the same after the Yardbirds. It'd be no exaggeration to say that the Yardbirds elevated the electric guitar to a front-and-center starring role, and that they were in large part responsible for pioneering the sort of music that would make the "& roll" tag superfluous in rock & roll.

The Yardbirds hive was buzzing with guitar activity from the word go. Consider that some of the talent they unleashed upon the world—to wit, Eric Clapton, Jeff Beck, and Jimmy Page—would shape much of the musical direction of the Seventies and beyond. And yet most of their records have seemingly fallen into some black hole in outer space, and the Yardbirds have never really been given their due accord as a band that changed the face of rock.

The Yardbirds' success during their relatively brief tenure (1963–1968) was fairly modest—a half dozen Top Forty smashes ("For Your Love," "Heart Full of Soul," "Over, Under, Sideways, Down", etc.), but no big action with their albums. Most of their studio work was actually never even released in Britain. And their sessions were unbelievably primitive by today's standards, with a lot of songs recorded live in the studio in one take, the recording engineer setting levels and mixing tracks as the band played!

No matter. The Yardbirds rocked with an abandon—a ferocious, willful experimentalism—that made a lot of the next decade's big deals look like the doughty frauds they were. What they played was (to borrow from the lexicon of The Who) maximum R&B, wedded to a healthy dose of future shock. Such slabs of vinyl dementia as "Happenings 10 Years Time Ago" and "Shapes of Things" rank among the great full-tilt acid guitar raveups in the history of electricity. But there was also Eric Clapton's early stint with the group; "Slowhand," with his purist's approach to the electric blues, turned in some definitive performances. Any way you look at it, the Yardbirds were pretty awesome.

They got their start midway through '63 as the

Keith Relf
(vocals, harmonica)
Jeff Beck
(lead guitar)
Chris Dreja
(rhythm guitar)
Paul Samwell-Smith
(bass)
Jim McCarty
(drums)

"Most Blueswailing" Yardbirds. In their early lineup, the lead guitarist was one Tony "Top" Topham, now lost to the pages of history. Eric Clapton stepped in, and the quintet, Chicago blues fanatics to a man, began cranking out cover versions of songs by their beloved black American mentors (Bo Diddley, Willie Dixon, Muddy Waters, et al.), establishing residency at the Crawdaddy Hotel in Richmond after the Rolling Stones had vacated to become the World's Greatest Rock & Roll Band.

The Clapton era is scantily documented on record. *Five Live Yardbirds* (an in-concert set, odd for a first LP) never saw American release. On it, "Slowhand" Clapton and his bandmates whooped and rocked their way through a sweaty set of hot rock and blues, proving themselves the masters of the raveup—a Yardbirds specialty, sort of a double-time free-for-all where you blew your hottest licks.

In the studio, the Yardbirds tended to go the pop route, cutting songs by top chart tunesmith Graham Gouldman ("For Your Love") and the like. In fact, it was their steady movement in this direction that drove Clapton away in 1965. Years later, he'd wax quite rancorous about his tenure with the Yardbirds, yet his bitterness belies the excellence of his work and his seminal contributions to the vocabulary of his instrument while with the band.

Jimmy Page, then an in-demand session guitarist, was asked to join. He declined, but suggested Jeff Beck as Clapton's replacement. It was a fortuitous match; the next twenty months would prove to be a wildly productive period for the Yardbirds. Under Beck's aegis, the raveup took on an added dimension. Beck was very much the innovator, always looking to make the sound no one had heard. He was bending notes like a wild man, puncturing his speakers to get a weird, driving drone (early fuzztone), playing solos that were pure feedback, and so forth. Beck justifiably credits himself as an early pioneer of the psychedelic style, yet at his most frantic he remained true to the spirit of the Chicago bluesmen he revered.

At this time, the Yardbirds were enjoying a bout of commercial success. At least half a dozen Yardbirds singles charted in 1965 and 1966, enabling the band to tour the States, where the myopic teen mag *Hit Parader* seemed to latch onto them. One sizzling article wondered, "Are the Yardbirds Too Far Out?" Another reassured that "they're serious in their work, but love practical jokes and having a good time." As the rock & roll circus romped on, fun-loving Jeff Beck was quickly going out-of-control.

Yet there was a brief stretch back in '66 when the Yardbirds existed in a lineup that remains every guitar fan's dream. Today it hardly seems possible, but for a spell the Yardbirds could boast both Jimmy Page and Jeff Beck in the same band. The only recorded legacy of this pre-supergroup supergroup is one single, "Happenings 10 Years Time Ago," and a five-minute's worth of them playing "Stroll On" in *Blow Up*, Michelangelo Antonioni's celebrated film about Carnaby Street London.

Beck's declining mental and physical health culminated in a nervous breakdown, prompting his exit in late 1966. "I remember doing some really nice jobs with Page," Beck recollected in 1971. "It lasted about four or five months, then I had this throat thing come, inflamed tonsils, and what with inflamed brain, inflamed tonsils, and an inflamed cock and everything else. . . ."

With Page at the helm, the Yardbirds held out for another year and a half before the guitarist assembled Led Zeppelin (dubbed the New Yardbirds at their first gigs). This despite Page's contention to *Hit Parader* that if the Yardbirds ever broke up, "I'd go back to painting." Through no fault of Page's, the last-gasp Yardbirds generally recorded pop-oriented pablum under the dubious direction of their manager/producer, Mickie Most (hitmaker for Herman's Hermits and Donovan, among others). The odd galvanizing raveup was mostly relegated to the B-sides. One interesting note: once Led Zeppelin had ascended the monetary stairway to heaven, Epic Records released *Live Yardbirds Featuring Jimmy Page*. It was a horrendously recorded concert from their "farewell" tour, to which what sounds like bullfight cheers and clinking cocktail glasses were inexplicably added in the studio. Page had it lawsuited out of the stores in a week. It remains one of the most enduring (and pricey) of rock rarities.

Though the Yardbirds are generally spoken of in terms of their lead guitarists, there were four other fine musicians in the band. Rhythm guitarist Chris Dreja had the formidable task of playing sideman to three of the best axmen in all of rock music. Keith Relf had an effective, if limited voice and much enthusiasm, and drummer Jim McCarty pounded the skins fleetly and with intensity. Together, these two would later found the more delicate-sounding Renaissance. Sadly, Relf was killed in May 1976 when an ungrounded guitar electrocuted him. Bassist Paul Samwell-Smith dropped out of the Yardbirds before the Page era, and went on to oversee Cat Stevens's career.

As was stated earlier, the Yardbirds' influence on popular music has been incalculable, if not always recognized. It's a shame, for instance, that their albums were scrapped together so haphazardly and that their former record company continued to toss together unfocused "anthologies" to cash in on the belated fame of Clapton, Beck and Page. An intelligently packaged,

The only record to feature both Page and Beck

Dreja, Ralph, Samwell-Smith, Clapton, and McCarty (Peter Kanze Collection)

chronologically sequenced multialbum set of the Yard-birds' entire output would be an invaluable addition to any rock fan's archives, and damn the cost. After all, how many groups have there been that would have an ear-splitting raveup every time they plugged in?

(PARKE PUTERBAUGH)

Jon Anderson
(vocals)
Steve Howe
(guitar)
Rick Wakeman
(keyboards)
Chris Squire
(bass)
Alan White
(drums)

Yes was a band for the Seventies. They were classically trained and technically accomplished. They wrote suites, not songs, and sang in high voices about "seasons of man." Yet though Yes could at times be as guilty as the next band of art-rock's gravest offenses (ponderousness, pretension and precocity—the three *p*'s), they were often saved by a high-spiritedness and agility one did not find in, say, Emerson, Lake, and Palmer or the Moody Blues. In fact, much of their music was quite remarkable—dexterous, bracing and highly original.

The band began in 1968 when singer Jon Anderson and bassist Chris Squire struck up an acquaintance over drinks at London's La Classe club. Expounding upon their mutual concept of a band with soaring vocal harmonies and powerful instrumental backing, they went out and recruited drummer Bill Bruford, guitarist Peter Banks and organist Tony Kaye. That lineup made two albums—*Yes* (1969) and the orchestrally sodden *Time and a Word* (1970). Banks exited, forming Flash (one minor hit, "Small Beginnings"), and Steve Howe—who'd been a founding member of the seminal British flower-power band Tomorrow—was called in.

Their next project, 1971's *The Yes Album*, took real strides into new musical terrain. Howe was a more adventurous player, and the LP was a stylistic tour de force. By now, the band was adept at many types of music—folk, pop, rock, quasi-classical—and like expert jugglers, they could keep any number of balls in the air at once.

Amid all this, keyboardist Tony Kaye found himself odd man out and split, subsequently playing on Flash's first LP, forming Badger (no hits) and, much later, joining David Bowie's tour band. His replacement in Yes was a flaxen-haired, beer-guzzling virtuoso named Rick Wakeman, lately of the classical-folk Strawbs. Though Wakeman's native flamboyance had been curbed in the context of the Strawbs, it found full expression in Yes' intricate polyphony. In fact, with Yes now comprising four instrumental titans and one star-gazing singer/lyricist, they prepared to pull out all stops.

On *Fragile* and *Close to the Edge*, Yes went headlong after an orchestral-rock fusion (with the emphasis on rock). One reviewer described the music as "sound painting," and this seems accurate: it's imagistic, many-hued, and richly textured, with breathtaking dynamic shifts and an underlying chromatic restlessness. "Roundabout," in particular, impressed with its chugging melody and rapid-fire fusillades from Howe and Wakeman (certainly, along with "Stairway to Heaven," it's one of the enduring rock compositions). And though Jon Anderson's lyrics often read as gobbledygook ("My eyes convinced eclipsed with the younger moon attained with love"), one could always take him at his word that "it's not always the case that lyrics have to be heard as lyrics rather than just the sound of someone singing."

During this time, Yes was at peak power—a poll-winning, chart-topping, SRO Seventies phenomenon. But soon some cracks started to appear in their elaborate latticework. Bill Bruford left to join King Crimson and was replaced by Alan White, a veteran session drummer who'd played with the Plastic Ono Band and George Harrison, among others. *Yessongs*—a bulky, three-record live set from 1973—looked retrospectively at the Yessound, adding no new material to their repertoire.

For much of that year, the band was ensconced in the studio, working on what they intended to be their most ambitious project yet. At this juncture, it seems their ambitions got the better of them. The resulting LP, *Tales of Topographic Oceans*, a lengthy opus spread across four sides, found them close to the edge—of the abyss, that is. The first bad omen was Jon Anderson's choice of an overall theme: an expostulation of the Buddhist Four-Part Shastic Scriptures. Additionally, by its very experimentalist, open-ended nature, Yes had always run the risk of meandering, and here their luck caught up with them. *Topographic Oceans* was a sprawling, unfocused affair, their first outright failure.

The critics were merciless, the public was baffled, and Wakeman walked. His 1973 solo album, *The Six Wives of Henry the Eighth,* outsold *Topographic Oceans,* and he would continue to pursue solo projects of ever-increasing bombast. Yes found a replacement for Wakeman in Patrick Moraz, a classically trained Swiss keyboardist who'd scored more than thirty films. He made his debut on *Relayer* (1974).

There would be no new studio product from Yes for the next two and a half years. The group developed a chronic case of solo record-itis, and '75 and '76 saw individual efforts by Messrs. Anderson, Howe, Moraz, Squire, and White unloaded to mild acclaim and/or yawning. Rick Wakeman, meanwhile, set Jules Verne to music (*Journey to the Center of the Earth,* number one U.K., number three U.S.) and recycled the *Myths and Legends of King Arthur and the Knights of the Round Table.*

Just when it seemed the band had expired, Rick Wakeman rejoined in early 1977, to everyone's surprise. The rejuvenation carried them through two albums—*Going for the One* and *Tormato*—and a few more tours. Apparently, the hard lessons of *Topographic Oceans* had been learned well, because their new material was shorter and punchier.

This interlude, too, was relatively short-lived, as both Wakeman and founding member Jon Anderson left in early 1980 over the inevitable "musical differences." Undaunted, the remaining three Yesmen decided to carry on. In one of the stranger re-alignments in rock history, they hooked up with the Buggles, a pair of New Wave musician/producers. But the album *Drama* was a sad parody and the inevitable World Tour found new members Trevor Horne and Geoff Downes slipping into their new roles awkwardly at best. Not long after came *Yesshows,* a pointless live-double recorded years earlier during Wakeman's second tour of duty. Surely something had come to an end.

In general, the critics loathed Yes as much as the public loved them. You could, in a roundabout way, blame them for everything from Styx's schtick to Queen's false pomp. But that'd be unfair. Yes lit out for new territory and, at their best, made some vital, compelling music. Yes indeed.

(PARKE PUTERBAUGH)

U.S. Hit Singles

1971	Your Move (**40**)
1972	Roundabout (**13**); America (**46**); And You and I (Part Two) (**42**)

U.S. Hit LPs

1971	The Yes Album (**40**)
1972	Fragile (**4**); Close to the Edge (**3**)
1973	Yessongs (**12**)
1974	Tales from Topographic Oceans (**6**); Relayer (**5**)
1975	Yesterdays (**17**)
1977	Going for the One (**8**)
1978	Tormato (**10**)
1980	Drama (**18**); Yesshows (**43**)

(BY RICK WAKEMAN)

1973	The Six Wives of Henry VIII (**30**)
1974	Journey to the Center of the Earth (**3**)
1975	The Myths and Legends of King Arthur and the Knights of the Round Table (**21**)
1976	No Earthly Connection (**67**)
1977	White Rock (**126**); Rick Wakeman's Criminal Record (**128**)
1979	Rhapsodies (**170**)

U.K. Hit Singles

1977	Wonderous Stories (**7**); Going for the One (**24**)
1978	Don't Kill the Whale (**36**)

The Zombies

The Zombies were perhaps the most incongruously named of all the British Invasion bands. The word *zombie*, evoking the gruesome monsters of Fifties sci-fi epics, seemed to cast them in a league with the scruffy, delinquent side of British rock, the nasty R&B of the Stones and the Pretty Things. Nothing could be further from the truth. The Zombies were a well-heeled lot, five bright, bashful honor students from St. Albans of whom one American observer enthused: "They are clean-cut, quiet, well-mannered, intelligent, and all very good-looking. . . . They behave like gentlemen, and shy away from boisterous and out-of-hand affairs."

Not to mention that they happened to make some of the most distinctive, melodious pop music of any band, in any year. What gave the Zombies' sound its distinction were the ethereal, breathy vocals of Colin Blunstone. Who can forget "She's Not There," a minor-key tale of heartbreak with a near-whispered vocal? Most people who had their ears pressed to the radio will also recall "Tell Her No" and "Time of the Season." But there were other treasures as well. Rod Argent and Chris White penned a whole canon of classic choral pop, mostly released as singles from 1963 to 1967. The Zombies remain one of the most underappreciated bands of those golden years.

And one of the quirkiest. Most every aspect of their career—whether through fate or mismanagement—had an odd twist to it. They enjoyed very little commercial success in their homeland, instead making a big splash in America and countries on the continent. Their last hit single, "Time of the Season," was released as an afterthought by their record company nearly a year and two flop singles after the issue of *Odessey and Oracle,* the album from which it came. A fluke hit, it wound up selling more than two million copies in the U.S. But when hungry promoters and record-company folk went looking for the band with this monster hit, they discovered that the Zombies no longer existed. They'd broken up, with finality, upon finishing *Odessey and Oracle.* Perhaps strangest of all was the bogus Zombies tour. A shady American promoter assembled a band, dubbed them "the Zombies," and sent them out on the road. This charlatan even told *Rolling Stone* that the Zombies' original singer had been killed in a car crash and that the rest of the band were continuing to play out of respect for him and their music!

Unfortunately, the real Zombies' mid-period excellence has never been definitively captured on long players. Though they were together for four and a half years, the Zombies released only two bona fide albums. Their first LP, titled *Begin Here* in Britain and simply *The Zombies* over here, mixed striking

Colin Blunstone (vocals)
Rod Argent (vocals, keyboards)
Paul Atkinson (guitar)
Chris White (vocals, bass)
Hugh Grundy (drums)

originals with banal R&B covers. *Odessey and Oracle* came out three years later, in late 1967, and was heralded as a milestone, blending the sophisticated ideas of *Sgt. Pepper's*-era Beatles with the complex, vibrant harmonies of the Beach Boys circa *Pet Sounds*. In between, they recorded a brace of singles, which represent some of their best work.

The Zombies had two strong writers in Chris White and Rod Argent. Their specialty was adolescent angst. Most of their songs—even the driving ones—were typified by an aura of melancholy and romantic loss. Their harmonies were exquisite; Blunstone, White and Argent all shared a high timbre, and when they sang in tandem, they soared. It must have been a God-given talent: the amazing voices for "She's Not There"— lead *and* harmony—were recorded in one take, with no overdubs.

Following their breakup, Colin Blunstone retired from music, working for several years as a clerk in an insurance firm. Argent and White straightaway began assembling a new band, whose name was simply Rod Argent's surname. The quartet finalized its lineup when drummer Robert Henrit and guitarist Russ Ballard joined up with Argent and his cousin, bassist Jim Rodford. Ballard and Henrit were previously the "+2" in Unit 4+2, who'd had an international hit with "Concrete and Clay," a Ballard composition.

Argent released an encouraging first album in 1970. It retained much of the misty, spectral atmosphere of the Zombies, plus a dash more musical expertise. Around this time, Argent and White managed to coax their old cohort, Colin Blunstone, back into the studio. The singer released three singles under the pseudonym Neil MacArthur, and even had a minor British hit with a revamped, orchestrated "She's Not There."

Ditching the MacArthur moniker, and his nine-to-five job, Blunstone once again began recording in earnest. With considerable help from his friends, he spent a year making his first album, titled *One Year*. It was a gorgeous record, with loads of ballads and, on many tracks, a string quartet. *Ennismore* (1971) kept up the standard, and even found Blunstone writing most of the material. But despite much critical fanfare, his records fell on deaf ears. Blunstone continued to release albums that, if somewhat slighter than the first couple, still had their small pleasures.

Argent, meanwhile, made a rapid downward slide into realms of bad taste and bloated excess. Seemingly a Seventies malady, Argent were bitten especially hard. Each album after the first grew ever more tedious—padded out with Rod Argent's lame Keith Emerson emulations and much general meandering— and their concerts found them jamming joylessly on one chord for ten minutes at a stretch. Argent didn't so much break up as sink in quicksand. A truly perplexing turn for a once-great Zombie. Russ Ballard, the first to bail out, went solo, and Jim Rodford signed on with the Kinks.

(PARKE PUTERBAUGH)

U.S. Hit Singles

1964 She's Not There (**2**)
1965 Tell Her No (**6**); She's Coming Home (**58**); I Want You Back Again (**95**)
1969 Time of the Season (**3**)

(BY ARGENT)

1972 Hold Your Head Up (**5**)

U.S. Hit LPs

1965 The Zombies (**39**)
1969 Odessey and Oracle (**95**)

(BY ARGENT)

1972 All Together Now (**23**)
1973 In Deep (**90**)
1974 Nexus (**149**)
1975 Encore—Live in Concert (**151**); Circus (**171**)

U.K. Hit Singles

1964 She's Not There (**12**); Tell Her No (**42**)

(BY COLIN BLUNSTONE)

1972 Say You Don't Mind (**15**); I Don't Believe in Miracles (**31**)
1973 How Could We Dare Be Wrong (**45**)

(BY ARGENT)

1972 Hold Your Head Up (**5**); Tragedy (**34**)
1973 God Gave Rock 'n' Roll To You (**18**)

TRANSATLANTIC GOLD

1964-1980

PART THREE

THE BRITISH INVASION'S U.S. TOP TWENTY SINGLES, 1964-1980

NOTE: Chart positions were drawn from *Billboard;* a record's rank in the year-by-year ratings was determined first by its peak position on the weekly charts, and, second, by how long it remained on the hit parade. "Honorary" Britons who were not included in "the British Hot Hundred"—Americans like Jimi Hendrix or Australians like the Bee Gees, or U.S.-based bands with some British personnel, like Foreigner—are included here. An asterisk (*) signifies a Gold Record, certified as having sold one million copies in the U.S. by the R.I.A.A. (Record Industry Association of America).

Rank calculated from overall chart performance	Highest position reached on weekly charts	Rank calculated from overall chart performance	Highest position reached on weekly charts

1964

#	Song / Artist	Pos	#	Song / Artist	Pos
1	I Want to Hold Your Hand **Beatles***	1	35	I Saw Her Standing There **Beatles**	14
2	Can't Buy Me Love **Beatles***	1	36	Tobacco Road **Nashville Teens**	14
3	House of the Rising Sun **Animals**	1	37	Everybody Knows (I Still Love You) **Dave Clark Five**	15
4	I Feel Fine **Beatles***	1	38	Don't Throw Your Love Away **Searchers**	16
5	She Loves You **Beatles***	1	39	I Don't Want to See You Again **Peter and Gordon**	16
6	A Hard Day's Night **Beatles***	1	40	I Like It **Gerry and the Pacemakers**	17
7	Do Wah Diddy Diddy **Manfred Mann**	1	41	Matchbox **Beatles**	17
8	Love Me Do **Beatles**	1	42	Ain't She Sweet **Beatles**	19
9	World Without Love **Peter and Gordon**	1	43	I'm Crying **Animals**	19
10	Twist and Shout **Beatles**	2			
11	She's Not There **Zombies**	2		**1965**	
12	Please Please Me **Beatles**	3	1	(I Can't Get No) Satisfaction **Rolling Stones***	1
13	Because **Dave Clark Five**	3	2	Yesterday **Beatles***	1
14	Don't Let the Sun Catch You Crying **Gerry and the Pacemakers**	4	3	Help! **Beatles***	1
15	Bits and Pieces **Dave Clark Five**	4	4	Mrs. Brown You've Got a Lovely Daughter **Herman's Hermits***	1
16	Can't You See That She's Mine **Dave Clark Five**	4	5	Downtown **Petula Clark***	1
17	She's a Woman **Beatles**	4	6	Get Off of My Cloud **Rolling Stones**	1
18	Glad All Over **Dave Clark Five**	6	7	I'm Telling You Now **Freddie and the Dreamers**	1
19	Time Is on My Side **Rolling Stones**	6	8	Eight Days a Week **Beatles***	1
20	Wishin' and Hopin' **Dusty Springfield**	6	9	Over and Over **Dave Clark Five**	1
21	Little Children **Billy J. Kramer**	7	10	Ticket to Ride **Beatles**	1
22	You Really Got Me **Kinks**	7	11	Game of Love **Wayne Fontana and the Mindbenders**	1
23	A Summer Song **Chad Stuart and Jeremy Clyde**	7	12	I'm Henry VIII, I Am **Herman's Hermits**	1
24	How Do You Do It? **Gerry and the Pacemakers**	9	13	Can't You Hear My Heartbeat **Herman's Hermits**	2
25	Bad to Me **Billy J. Kramer**	9	14	Love Potion Number Nine **Searchers**	3
26	Diane **Bachelors**	10	15	I Know a Place **Petula Clark**	3
27	PS I Love You **Beatles**	10	16	I'll Never Find Another You **Seekers**	4
28	Do You Love Me **Dave Clark Five**	11	17	Catch Us If You Can **Dave Clark Five**	4
29	Sha La La **Manfred Mann**	12	18	Wonderful World **Herman's Hermits**	4
30	And I Love Her **Beatles**	12	19	Silhouettes **Herman's Hermits**	5
31	Nobody I Know **Peter and Gordon**	12	20	For Your Love **Yardbirds**	6
32	I'm Into Something Good **Herman's Hermits**	13	21	Tell Her No **Zombies**	6
33	Needles and Pins **Searchers**	13			
34	Anyway You Want It **Dave Clark Five**	14			

#	Title / Artist	Pos
22	Tired of Waiting for You **Kinks**	6
23	Ferry 'Cross the Mersey **Gerry and the Pacemakers**	6
24	All Day and All of the Night **Kinks**	7
25	You've Got Your Troubles **Fortunes**	7
26	I Like It Like That **Dave Clark Five**	7
27	Just a Little Bit Better **Herman's Hermits**	7
28	You Turn Me On **Ian Whitcomb**	8
29	Heart Full of Soul **Yardbirds**	9
30	I Go to Pieces **Peter and Gordon**	9
31	The Last Time **Rolling Stones**	9
32	Go Now **Moody Blues**	10
33	It's Not Unusual **Tom Jones**	10
34	You've Got to Hide Your Love Away **Silkie**	10
35	We Gotta Get Out of This Place **Animals**	13
36	True Love Ways **Peter and Gordon**	14
37	I'll Be There **Gerry and the Pacemakers**	14
38	Come Home **Dave Clark Five**	14
39	Willow Weep for Me **Chad and Jeremy**	15
40	Marie **Bachelors**	15
41	Don't Let Me Be Misunderstood **Animals**	15
42	Everyone's Gone to the Moon **Jonathan King**	17
43	I'm a Man **Yardbirds**	17
44	Before and After **Chad and Jeremy**	17
45	Do the Freddie **Freddie and the Dreamers**	18
46	World of Our Own **Seekers**	19
47	Heart of Stone **Rolling Stones**	19

1966

#	Title / Artist	Pos
1	Winchester Cathedral **New Vaudeville Band***	1
2	We Can Work It Out **Beatles***	1
3	My Love **Petula Clark**	1
4	Wild Thing **Troggs**	1
5	Paint It Black **Rolling Stones**	1
6	Paperback Writer **Beatles***	1
7	Sunshine Superman **Donovan**	1
8	Mellow Yellow **Donovan***	2
9	19th Nervous Breakdown **Rolling Stones**	2
10	Groovy Kind of Love **Mindbenders**	2
11	Yellow Submarine **Beatles***	2
12	Nowhere Man **Beatles***	3
13	Listen People **Herman's Hermits**	3
14	The Pied Piper **Crispian St. Peters**	4
15	Bus Stop **Hollies**	5
16	Dandy **Herman's Hermits**	5
17	Day Tripper **Beatles**	5
18	Lady Godiva **Peter and Gordon**	6
19	As Tears Go By **Rolling Stones**	6
20	Stop Stop Stop **Hollies**	7
21	Mother's Little Helper **Rolling Stones**	8
22	A Must to Avoid **Herman's Hermits**	8
23	I Couldn't Live Without Your Love **Petula Clark**	9
24	Leaning on the Lamp Post **Herman's Hermits**	9
25	Have You Seen Your Mother, Baby, Standing in the Shadow? **Rolling Stones**	9
26	See See Rider **Eric Burdon and the Animals**	10
27	Shapes of Things **Yardbirds**	11
28	Eleanor Rigby **Beatles**	11
29	A Sign of the Times **Petula Clark**	11
30	Don't Bring Me Down **Animals**	12
31	This Door Swings Both Ways **Herman's Hermits**	12
32	Try Too Hard **Dave Clark Five**	12
33	A Well Respected Man **Kinks**	13
34	Over Under Sideways Down **Yardbirds**	13
35	Woman **Peter and Gordon**	14
36	Sunny Afternoon **Kinks**	14
37	Michelle **David and Jonathan**	18
38	At the Scene **Dave Clark Five**	18
39	All I See Is You **Dusty Springfield**	20

1967

#	Title / Artist	Pos
1	To Sir with Love **Lulu***	1
2	Hello Goodbye **Beatles***	1
3	Ruby Tuesday **Rolling Stones***	1
4	All You Need Is Love **Beatles***	1
5	Penny Lane **Beatles***	1
6	Georgy Girl **Seekers***	2
7	This Is My Song **Petula Clark**	3
8	There's a Kind of Hush **Herman's Hermits***	4
9	A Whiter Shade of Pale **Procol Harum**	5
10	Don't Sleep in the Subway **Petula Clark**	5
11	Gimme Some Lovin' **Spencer Davis Group**	7
12	You Got What It Takes **Dave Clark Five**	7
13	Strawberry Fields Forever **Beatles**	8
14	Carrie Anne **Hollies**	9
15	I Can See for Miles **The Who**	9
16	San Francisco Nights **Eric Burdon and the Animals**	9
17	Brown Eyed Girl **Van Morrison**	10
18	I'm a Man **Spencer Davis Group**	10
19	Silence Is Golden **Tremeloes**	11
20	On a Carousel **Hollies**	11
21	Green Green Grass of Home **Tom Jones**	11
22	There Is a Mountain **Donovan**	11
23	(The Lights Went Out in) Massachusetts **Bee Gees**	11
24	Here Comes My Baby **Tremeloes**	13
25	Dandelion **Rolling Stones**	14
26	New York Mining Disaster 1941 **Bee Gees**	14
27	When I Was Young **Eric Burdon and the Animals**	15
28	Knight in Rusty Armour **Peter and Gordon**	15
29	Friday On My Mind **Easybeats**	16
30	Color My World **Petula Clark**	16
31	Holiday **Bee Gees**	16
32	To Love Somebody **Bee Gees**	16
33	Don't Go Out Into the Rain **Herman's Hermits**	18
34	Epistle to Dippy **Donovan**	19
35	I Was Kaiser Bill's Batman **Whistling Jack Smith**	20
36	There Goes My Everything **Engelbert Humperdinck**	20

1968

#	Title / Artist	Pos
1	Hey Jude **Beatles***	1
2	Those Were the Days **Mary Hopkin***	2
3	Fire **Crazy World of Arthur Brown***	2
4	Jumpin' Jack Flash **Rolling Stones**	3
5	Lady Madonna **Beatles***	4
6	Hush **Deep Purple**	4
7	Sunshine of Your Love **Cream***	5
8	Hurdy Gurdy Man **Donovan**	5
9	White Room **Cream**	6
10	Love Is All Around **Troggs**	7
11	Ballad of Bonnie and Clyde **Georgie Fame**	7
12	I've Gotta Get a Message to You **Bee Gees**	8
13	Mighty Quinn (Quinn the Eskimo) **Manfred Mann**	10
14	Pictures of Matchstick Men **Status Quo**	12
15	Revolution **Beatles**	12
16	Sky Pilot **Eric Burdon and the Animals**	14

17	Delilah **Tom Jones**	15	13	What Is Life **George Harrison**	10
18	Words **Bee Gees**	15	14	Wild World **Cat Stevens**	11
19	Kiss Me Goodbye **Petula Clark**	15	15	Power to the People **John Lennon**	11
20	Monterey **Eric Burdon and the Animals**	15	16	Won't Get Fooled Again **The Who**	15
21	Itchycoo Park **Small Faces**	16	17	Immigrant Song **Led Zeppelin**	16
22	Am I That Easy to Forget **Engelbert Humperdinck**	18			

1972

23	A Man Without Love **Engelbert Humperdinck**	19
24	All Along the Watchtower **Jimi Hendrix Experience**	20

1	Alone Again (Naturally) **Gilbert O'Sullivan***	1
2	Nights in White Satin **Moody Blues***	2
3	Long Cool Woman (In a Black Dress) **Hollies***	2

1969

1	Get Back **Beatles***	1
2	Honky Tonk Woman **Rolling Stones***	1
3	Come Together **Beatles***	1
4	Something **Beatles***	3
5	Time of the Season **Zombies***	3
6	I'll Never Fall in Love Again **Tom Jones***	6
7	I Started a Joke **Bee Gees**	6
8	Atlantis **Donovan**	7
9	Ballad of John and Yoko **Beatles***	8
10	Love Me Tonight **Tom Jones**	13
11	Goodbye **Mary Hopkin**	13
12	Give Peace a Chance **Plastic Ono Band**	14
13	Pinball Wizard **The Who**	19

4	Day After Day **Badfinger***	4
5	Hold Your Head Up **Argent**	5
6	Rocket Man **Elton John**	6
7	Morning Has Broken **Cat Stevens**	6
8	Rock and Roll Part Two **Gary Glitter**	7
9	I'd Like to Teach the World to Sing **New Seekers***	7
10	Tumbling Dice **Rolling Stones**	7
11	Honky Cat **Elton John**	8
12	Back off Boogaloo **Ringo Starr**	9
13	Layla **Derek and the Dominos**	10
14	Bang a Gong (Get It On) **T. Rex**	10
15	Living in the Past **Jethro Tull**	11
16	Amazing Grace **Royal Scots Dragoon Guards**	11
17	Roundabout **Yes**	13
18	You Wear It Well **Rod Stewart**	13
19	Baby Blue **Badfinger**	14
20	Black Dog **Led Zeppelin**	15
21	Conquistador **Procol Harum**	16
22	Run to Me **Bee Gees**	16
23	Sitting **Cat Stevens**	16
24	My World **Bee Gees**	16
25	Join Together **The Who**	18
26	Stay With Me **Faces**	18

1970

1	My Sweet Lord **George Harrison***	1
2	Let It Be **Beatles***	1
3	Long and Winding Road **Beatles**	1
4	Spill the Wine **Eric Burdon (with War)***	3
5	Instant Karma **John Lennon***	3
6	In the Summertime **Mungo Jerry***	3
7	All Right Now **Free**	4
8	Whole Lotta Love **Led Zeppelin***	4
9	Hitchin' a Ride **Vanity Fare***	5
10	Love Grows (Where My Rosemary Goes) **Edison Lighthouse***	5
11	Without Love (There Is Nothing) **Tom Jones***	5
12	He Ain't Heavy, He's My Brother **Hollies**	7
13	Come and Get It **Badfinger**	7
14	The Letter **Joe Cocker**	7
15	No Matter What **Badfinger**	8
16	Lola **Kinks**	9
17	Domino **Van Morrison**	9
18	Reflections of My Life **Marmalade**	10
19	Cry Me a River **Joe Cocker**	11
20	Early in the Morning **Vanity Fare**	12
21	See Me Feel Me **The Who**	12
22	Daughter of Darkness **Tom Jones**	13
23	Look What They've Done to My Song Ma **New Seekers**	14
24	I (Who Have Nothing) **Tom Jones**	14
25	Winter World of Love **Engelbert Humperdinck**	16
26	After Midnight **Eric Clapton**	18

1973

1	My Love **Paul McCartney and Wings***	1
2	Crocodile Rock **Elton John***	1
3	Photograph **Ringo Starr***	1
4	Angie **Rolling Stones***	1
5	Give Me Love (Give Me Peace on Earth) **George Harrison**	1
6	Goodbye Yellow Brick Road **Elton John***	2
7	Live and Let Die **Paul McCartney and Wings***	2
8	Daniel **Elton John**	2
9	Little Willy **Sweet***	3
10	Oh Babe, What Would You Say? **Hurricane Smith**	3
11	Smoke on the Water **Deep Purple***	4
12	Stuck in the Middle With You **Stealers Wheel**	6
13	Get Down **Gilbert O'Sullivan***	7
14	Hi Hi Hi **Paul McCartney and Wings**	10
15	Saturday Night's Alright for Fighting **Elton John**	12
16	I'm Just a Singer (In a Rock and Roll Band) **Moody Blues**	12
17	Money **Pink Floyd**	13
18	Space Oddity **David Bowie**	15
19	Out of the Question **Gilbert O'Sullivan**	17
20	Mind Games **John Lennon**	18
21	D'yer Mak'er **Led Zeppelin**	20

1971

1	Maggie May **Rod Stewart***	1
2	How Can You Mend a Broken Heart **Bee Gees***	1
3	Brown Sugar **Rolling Stones***	1
4	Uncle Albert/Admiral Halsey **Paul McCartney***	1
5	She's a Lady **Tom Jones***	2
6	Lonely Days **Bee Gees***	3
7	Imagine **John Lennon**	3
8	It Don't Come Easy **Ringo Starr***	4
9	I Hear You Knocking **Dave Edmunds**	4
10	Another Day **Paul McCartney**	5
11	Peace Train **Cat Stevens**	7
12	Your Song **Elton John**	8

1974

1	Bennie and the Jets **Elton John***	1
2	Band on the Run **Paul McCartney and Wings***	1
3	You're Sixteen **Ringo Starr***	1
4	Whatever Gets You Thru the Night **John Lennon**	1

5	I Shot the Sheriff **Eric Clapton***	1
6	Don't Let the Sun Go Down on Me **Elton John***	2
7	Junior's Farm **Paul McCartney and Wings**	3
8	The Bitch Is Back **Elton John**	4
9	Rock On **David Essex***	5
10	Can't Get Enough **Bad Company**	5
11	Oh My My **Ringo Starr**	5
12	The Air That I Breathe **Hollies***	6
13	Another Saturday Night **Cat Stevens**	6
14	Only You **Ringo Starr**	6
15	Tubular Bells **Mike Oldfield**	7
16	Jet **Paul McCartney and Wings**	7
17	Oh Very Young **Cat Stevens**	10
18	Helen Wheels **Paul McCartney and Wings**	10
19	I've Got the Music in Me **Kiki Dee Band**	12
20	Bungle in the Jungle **Jethro Tull**	12
21	Wild Thing **Fancy**	14
22	Doo Doo Doo Doo Doo (Heartbreaker) **Rolling Stones**	15
23	Dark Horse **George Harrison**	15
24	It's Only Rock 'n' Roll (but I Like It) **Rolling Stones**	16
25	Ain't Too Proud to Beg **Rolling Stones**	17
26	Touch Me **Fancy**	19

1975

1	Island Girl **Elton John***	1
2	Philadelphia Freedom **Elton John***	1
3	Fame **David Bowie***	1
4	Jive Talkin' **Bee Gees***	1
5	Lucy in the Sky with Diamonds **Elton John**	1
6	Saturday Night **Bay City Rollers***	1
7	Pick up the Pieces **Average White Band***	1
8	Listen to What the Man Said **Paul McCartney and Wings***	1
9	I'm Not in Love **10cc**	2
10	No No Song **Ringo Starr**	3
11	Someone Saved My Life Tonight **Elton John***	4
12	Ballroom Blitz **Sweet**	5
13	Magic **Pilot***	5
14	You Are So Beautiful **Joe Cocker**	5
15	Nights on Broadway **Bee Gees**	7
16	Emma **Hot Chocolate**	8
17	Can't Get It Out of My Head **Electric Light Orchestra**	9
18	Long Tall Glasses (I Can Dance) **Leo Sayer**	9
19	Number Nine Dream **John Lennon**	9
20	Feel Like Makin' Love **Bad Company**	10
21	Cut the Cake **Average White Band**	10
22	Killer Queen **Queen**	12
23	Venus and Mars/Rock Show **Paul McCartney and Wings**	12
24	Movin' On **Bad Company**	19
25	You **George Harrison**	20
26	Stand by Me **John Lennon**	20

1976

1	Tonight's the Night (Gonna Be Alright) **Rod Stewart***	1
2	Silly Love Songs **Paul McCartney and Wings***	1
3	Don't Go Breaking My Heart **Elton John and Kiki Dee***	1
4	You Should Be Dancing **Bee Gees***	1
5	Dream Weaver **Gary Wright***	2
6	Love Is Alive **Gary Wright**	2
7	Love So Right **Bee Gees***	3
8	You Sexy Thing **Hot Chocolate***	3
9	Let 'Em In **Paul McCartney and Wings***	3
10	Fox on the Run **Sweet***	5
11	Show Me the Way **Peter Frampton**	6
12	Sorry Seems to Be the Hardest Word **Elton John***	7
13	Got to Get You Into My Life **Beatles**	7
14	Love Hurts **Nazareth***	8
15	Bohemian Rhapsody **Queen***	9
16	Money Honey **Bay City Rollers**	9
17	Golden Years **David Bowie**	10
18	Do You Feel Like We Do **Peter Frampton**	10
19	Evil Woman **Electric Light Orchestra**	10
20	Fool to Cry **Rolling Stones**	10
21	Say You Love Me **Fleetwood Mac**	11
22	Rhiannon **Fleetwood Mac**	11
23	The Boys Are Back in Town **Thin Lizzy**	12
24	Baby I Love Your Way **Peter Frampton**	12
25	Fanny (Be Tender with Your Love) **Bee Gees**	12
26	I Only Want to Be with You **Bay City Rollers**	12
27	Livin' Thing **Electric Light Orchestra**	13
28	Strange Magic **Electric Light Orchestra**	14
29	Grow Some Funk of Your Own **Elton John**	14
30	You're My Best Friend **Queen**	16
31	Squeeze Box **The Who**	16
32	I Feel Like a Bullet (In the Gun of Robert Ford) **Elton John**	18
33	Slow Ride **Foghat**	20
34	Over My Head **Fleetwood Mac**	20
35	Action **Sweet**	20
36	Young Blood **Bad Company**	20

1977

1	How Deep Is Your Love **Bee Gees***	1
2	You Make Me Feel Like Dancing **Leo Sayer***	1
3	Blinded by the Light **Manfred Mann's Earth Band***	1
4	When I Need You **Leo Sayer***	1
5	Dreams **Fleetwood Mac***	1
6	I'm in You **Peter Frampton**	2
7	Boogie Nights **Heatwave***	2
8	Couldn't Get It Right **Climax Blues Band**	3
9	Don't Stop **Fleetwood Mac**	3
10	The Things We Do for Love **10cc***	5
11	Telephone Line **Electric Light Orchestra***	7
12	After the Lovin' **Engelbert Humperdinck***	8
13	Year of the Cat **Al Stewart**	8
14	You Make Loving Fun **Fleetwood Mac**	9
15	Star Wars **London Symphony Orchestra**	10
16	You Made Me Believe in Magic **Bay City Rollers**	10
17	Go Your Own Way **Fleetwood Mac**	10
18	Maybe I'm Amazed **Paul McCartney and Wings**	10
19	We Just Disagree **Dave Mason**	12
20	Boogie Child **Bee Gees**	12
21	Somebody to Love **Queen**	13
22	Give a Little Bit **Supertramp**	15
23	Say You'll Stay Until Tomorrow **Tom Jones**	15
24	How Much Love **Leo Sayer**	17
25	Signed, Sealed, Delivered **Peter Frampton**	18
26	Crackerbox Palace **George Harrison**	19

1978

1	Night Fever **Bee Gees***	1
2	Stayin' Alive **Bee Gees***	1

Rank calculated from overall chart performance	Highest position reached on weekly charts
3 With a Little Luck **Paul McCartney and Wings**	1
4 Miss You **Rolling Stones***	1
5 Double Vision **Foreigner***	2
6 Lay Down Sally **Eric Clapton***	3
7 Hot Blooded **Foreigner***	3
8 We Are the Champions/We Will Rock You **Queen***	4
9 You're in My Heart **Rod Stewart***	4
10 Time Passages **Al Stewart**	7
11 The Groove Line **Heatwave***	7
12 Love Is Like Oxygen **Sweet**	8
13 Beast of Burden **Rolling Stones**	8
14 Who Are You **The Who**	14
15 Turn to Stone **Electric Light Orchestra**	13
16 Every Kinda People **Robert Palmer**	16
17 Wonderful Tonight **Eric Clapton**	16
18 Sweet Talkin' Woman **Electric Light Orchestra**	17
19 Always and Forever **Heatwave***	18

1979

1 Da Ya Think I'm Sexy **Rod Stewart***	1
2 Too Much Heaven **Bee Gees***	1
3 Tragedy **Bee Gees***	1
4 Love You Inside Out **Bee Gees***	1
5 Don't Bring Me Down **Electric Light Orchestra***	4
6 Sultans of Swing **Dire Straits**	4
7 Goodnight Tonight **Paul McCartney and Wings***	5
8 The Logical Song **Supertramp**	6
9 Tusk **Fleetwood Mac**	8
10 Shine a Little Love **Electric Light Orchestra**	8
11 Mama Can't Buy You Love **Elton John**	9
12 Promises **Eric Clapton**	9

Rank calculated from overall chart performance	Highest position reached on weekly charts
13 Take the Long Way Home **Supertramp**	10
14 Cruel to Be Kind **Nick Lowe**	12
15 Rock 'n' Roll Fantasy **Bad Company**	13
16 Shake It **Ian Matthews**	13
17 Head Games **Foreigner**	14
18 Goodbye Stranger **Supertramp**	15
19 Blue Morning, Blue Day **Foreigner**	15
20 Blow Away **George Harrison**	16
21 Hold On **Ian Gomm**	18
22 Dancin' Shoes **Nigel Olsson**	18
23 Getting Closer **Paul McCartney and Wings**	20

1980

1 Starting Over **John Lennon***	1
2 Another Brick in the Wall **Pink Floyd***	1
3 Crazy Little Thing Called Love **Queen***	1
4 Another One Bites the Dust **Queen***	1
5 Coming Up **Paul McCartney and Wings***	1
6 More Than I Can Say **Leo Sayer***	2
7 Little Jeannie **Elton John***	3
8 Emotional Rescue **Rolling Stones**	3
9 We Don't Talk Anymore **Cliff Richard**	7
10 Sara **Fleetwood Mac**	7
11 Cars **Gary Numan**	9
12 Let My Love Open the Door **Peter Townshend**	9
13 Dreaming **Cliff Richard**	10
14 All Over the World **Electric Light Orchestra**	13
15 Brass in Pocket **Pretenders**	14
16 Misunderstanding **Genesis**	14
17 Dreamer **Supertramp**	15
18 I'm Alive **Electric Light Orchestra**	16
19 Without Your Love **Roger Daltrey**	20
20 Think About Me **Fleetwood Mac**	20

THE BRITISH ROCK DIARY
1963-1980

PART FOUR

A DAY-BY-DAY CHRONICLE

1963

January	*1*	An obscure Liverpool group called the Beatles begins a short tour of Scotland to promote its first single, "Love Me Do."
	3	The Beatles top the annual popularity poll of Liverpool's local music newspaper, *Merseybeat,* for the second time.
	5	"Love Me Do" peaks at number twenty-one on *Melody Maker*'s national British charts.
	25	A small Chicago-based R&B label, Vee-Jay Records, signs the Beatles for U.S. release.
February	*2*	As the Beatles' "Please Please Me" enters the U.K. charts, the boys from Liverpool, as supporting act for Helen Shapiro, begin their first national tour—during which Ringo Starr is thrown out of a Carlisle hotel for "extreme scruffiness."
	25	Vee-Jay issues "Please Please Me" by "the Beattles" (sic) in the U.S.
March	*2*	"Please Please Me" hits Number One on the *Melody Maker* charts.
	22	The Beatles' first LP, *Please Please Me,* is released in Britain.
April	*6*	*Melody Maker* headline announces A HAT TRICK FOR EPSTEIN as the Beatles are ousted from the Number One spot by fellow Liverpudlians and Brian Epstein clients Gerry and the Pacemakers—with a song, "How Do You Do It?" that the Beatles had turned down.
	12	"From Me to You" is released in Britain; *Melody Maker* headlines its review BELOW PAR BEATLES.
	21	The Beatles show up at South London's Crawdaddy Club to check out a local R&B sextet called the Rolling Stones.
	28	Former Epstein employee Andrew Loog Oldham attends a Crawdaddy gig by the Rolling Stones, in the company of his new boss, Eric Easton.
	29	Oldham and Easton sign on as the Rolling Stones' managers.
May	*4*	"From Me to You" hits Number One in Britain.
	18	The Beatles begin their first headlining national tour, during which they are pelted with "jelly babies"—George Harrison's favorite sweets—for the first time.
June	*3*	Del Shannon is the first American recording star to release a Lennon-McCartney composition ("From Me to You").
	7	The Rolling Stones, now a quintet, make their first TV appearance, on *Thank Your Lucky Stars,* to promote their debut single, "Come On," which is released the same day.
	15	Billy J. Kramer's version of Lennon-McCartney's "Do You Want to Know a Secret?" hits Number One on *Melody Maker*'s British charts.
July	*1*	The Beatles record "She Loves You," ignoring the suggestion of Paul McCartney's father that they maintain "British dignity" by changing the "yeah, yeah, yeah" chorus to "yes, yes, yes."
August	*3*	The Beatles register on *Billboard*'s American charts for the first time, with "From Me to You" at number one hundred twenty-five. (The single will peak at number one hundred sixteen.)
	8	The Beatles give their final performance at Liverpool's Cavern Club.
	8	The Searchers' "Sweets for My Sweet" hits Number One in Britain.
	9	The British pop TV show, *Ready Steady Go,* is aired for the first time.
	31	The Beatles' "She Loves You"—dismissed as "a nothing record" by a *Melody Maker* panel of top British disc jockeys—makes its first appearance on the U.K. charts.

September	18	George Harrison—bound for St. Louis to visit his sister—is the first Beatle to set foot in America (where he will also shake hands with President John F. Kennedy).
	29	The Rolling Stones begin their first national British tour, supporting Bo Diddley and the Everly Brothers; Diddley hires Brian Jones, Bill Wyman, and Charlie Watts as his backup band for a radio recording.
October	11	"She Loves You"—on its way to becoming the biggest-selling single ever issued in Britain—is certified as the Beatles' first gold record.
	13	The Beatles' performance on *Sunday Night at the London Palladium* is witnessed by fifteen million British TV viewers—and the word BEATLEMANIA! is splashed across the nation's front pages.
November		Brian Epstein (accompanied by Billy J. Kramer) travels to New York to lay the groundwork for the Beatles' assault on America.
	1	The Rolling Stones release their second single, the custom-made Lennon-McCartney tune "I Wanna Be Your Man."
	4	The Beatles receive British royalty's seal of approval at London's Prince of Wales Theatre.
	22	*With the Beatles*—Britain's first million-selling album—is released on the same day that President Kennedy is assassinated.
December	13	*New Musical Express* reveals that Capitol Records has signed the Beatles for U.S. release.
	18	*Variety* reports that "Liverpool beat" has boosted total British record sales by forty percent over the past year.
	26	Capitol rush-releases its first U.S. Beatles single, "I Want to Hold Your Hand."
	27	William Mann, classical music critic for *The Times* of London, anoints John Lennon and Paul McCartney as "the outstanding composers of 1963."
	29	Richard Buckle, music critic for London's *Sunday Times,* proclaims Lennon and McCartney "the greatest composers since Beethoven."

1964

January		Stickers proclaiming that THE BEATLES ARE COMING materialize on lampposts and lavatory walls across the United States.
	3	*The Jack Paar Show* presents the first film clip of the Beatles to be aired on U.S. television.
	4	A full-page ad in *Billboard* hawks THE MERSEY SOUND WITH THE LIVERPOOL BEAT . . . "Glad All Over" by the Dave Clark Five.
	6	The Rolling Stones pair off with the Ronnettes on the former's first headlining British tour.
	15	Following the first of a series of concerts in Paris, the Beatles learn that "I Want to Hold Your Hand" has hit Number One on the *Cash Box* American charts (replacing Bobby Vinton's "There! I've Said It Again"). While in France, they also hear Bob Dylan's albums for the first time, and, according to Lennon, go "potty over Dylan."
	18	The Dave Clark Five's "Glad All Over" replaces "I Want to Hold Your Hand" as Britain's Number One Hit.
February	7	The Beatles land in America.
	8	*New York Times* headline: THE BEATLES INVADE, COMPLETE WITH LONG HAIR AND SCREAMING FANS.
	9	*The Ed Sullivan Show* broadcasts the Beatles' first live U.S. performance to the largest audience ever to tune in to a TV entertainment program.
	11	The Beatles play their first U.S. concert at the Washington (D.C.) Coliseum.
		Variety headline: BRITANNIA RULES AIRWAVES.
	12	The Beatles play New York's Carnegie Hall.
	13	*New York Times* headline: WILD-EYED MOBS PURSUE BEATLES.
	15	*Meet the Beatles* hits Number One on *Billboard*'s U.S. LP charts.
	19	Banner front-page *Variety* headline: ROCKING REDCOATS ARE COMING—BEATLES LEAD MASSIVE DRIVE.
	21	The Beatles fly back to London from Miami.
March	2	The Beatles begin work on their first film.
		Tollie Records (a Vee-Jay subsidiary) is launched with a Beatles single, "Twist and Shout."
	13	*Meet the Beatles* is reported to have sold over 3,600,000 copies—more than any other LP ever released.
	14	Rolling Stones headline in *Melody Maker:* GROUP PARENTS HATE MAKES BIG HIT.
	21	Entries in *Billboard*'s U.S. Hot Hundred chart include: "We Love You Beatles" (the Carefrees); "My Boyfriend Got a Beatle Haircut" (Donna Lynn); "The Boy with the Beatle Hair" (the Swans); and "A Letter to the Beatles" (the Four Preps).
	23	John Lennon's first book, *In His Own Write,* is published in Britain to rave reviews.
	28	Beatles headline in *Billboard:* IBM COMPUTER BREAKS DOWN OVER WILD SALES FIGURES.
	30	The British press reports the first "riots" of Mods and Rockers in Clacton.
April		Bill Haley and the Comets, of "Rock Around the Clock" fame, have added "I Want to Hold Your Hand" and "From Me to You" to their repertoire.
		Pirate radio begins broadcasting off Britain's shores.

	4	Beatles singles claim the top five positions on *Billboard*'s Hot Hundred—which features seven further Beatles entries, along with seven titles by other "redcoats" such as the Dave Clark Five, the Searchers, and the Swinging Blue Jeans.
May	2	*The Beatles' Second Album* is the first LP ever to hit Number One on *Billboard*'s U.S. charts within two weeks of its release.
	30	The Dave Clark Five play Carnegie Hall.
June	2	The Rolling Stones begin their first American tour.
	23	For the first time in eighteen months, an American recording—Roy Orbison's "It's Over"—reaches Number One in Britain.
	27	With Lennon-McCartney's "World Without Love," Peter and Gordon become the first British act (after the Beatles) to hit Number One in America.
July	4	The Rolling Stones draw hundreds of complaints against their "moronic" and "insulting" behavior when they serve as panelists on the British TV show *Juke Box Jury*. Meanwhile, "It's All Over Now" gives them their first British Number One.
	6	Piccadilly Circus is closed to traffic and packed with Beatlemaniacs as Princess Margaret joins the Fab Four at the opening of their film *A Hard Day's Night*. At the subsequent celebration party, John Lennon tells Keith Richards, Brian Jones, and Bill Wyman that he only wants another year or two at the top, after which the field will be clear for the Rolling Stones.
	11	The Animals' "House of the Rising Sun" hits Number One in Britain.
	25	The Beatles' LP *A Hard Day's Night* hits Number One in the U.S.
August		*Billboard*'s U.S. Hot Hundred includes three Rolling Stones singles: "Not Fade Away," "Tell Me," and "It's All Over Now."
	18	A major British "bookie"—William Massey Ltd.—begins taking bets on which record will wind up at Number One the following week; initial odds favor Manfred Mann's "Do Wah Diddy Diddy."
	19	The Beatles' first cross-country American tour is launched in San Francisco with a ticker-tape parade and a show at the Cow Palace.
	23	*Melody Maker* headline: KINKS—READY FOR THE NEW WAVE.
	30	Marianne Faithfull makes her first impression on the British charts with the custom-made Jagger-Richards song "As Tears Go By."
September	5	The Animals' "House of the Rising Sun" hits Number One in the U.S.
	12	The Kinks' "You Really Got Me" hits Number One in Britain.
	26	Herman's Hermits' "I'm Into Something Good" hits Number One in Britain.
October	14	Charlie Watts secretly weds Shirley Ann Arnold in defiance of manager Andrew Loog Oldham's decree that no Rolling Stone marry.
	17	Manfred Mann's "Do Wah Diddy Diddy" hits Number One in the U.S.
	22	The Who are rejected by EMI Records.
	24	The Rolling Stones launch their second U.S. tour with a riotous appearance on *The Ed Sullivan Show*, following which Mr. Sullivan swears he'll never have them back.
November	7	The Beatles are off *Billboard*'s American Hot Hundred for the first time in ten months.
	21	Britain's biggest newspaper, *The Daily Mirror*, prints a letter from a reader demanding: "Is there any MP with the courage to introduce a Bill compelling boys to have their hair cut?"
	24	*The Red Skelton Show* airs the Kinks' U.S. TV debut.
December	1	Ringo Starr enters London's University College Hospital for a tonsillectomy, and rejects requests from fans eager to add his tonsils to their collections.
	5	The Beatles return to the Hot Hundred with "I Feel Fine," the first record to incorporate electric guitar feedback.
		The Rolling Stones' "Little Red Rooster" hits Number One in Britain.
	24	The Beatles' Christmas Show, costarring Freddie and the Dreamers, Sounds Incorporated, the Yardbirds, the Mike Cotton Sound, and Elkie Brooks, opens at London's Hammersmith Odeon Theater.
	26	"I Feel Fine" hits Number One in the U.S.

1965

January	2	*Billboard*'s U.S. Hot Hundred includes twenty-seven titles by British artists.
	9	*Beatles '65* hits Number One in the U.S.
	15	The Who's first single, "I Can't Explain," is released in Britain by Brunswick Records, a Decca subsidiary.
	30	The Moody Blues' "Go Now" (lead vocal by future Wings member Denny Laine) hits Number One in Britain.
February		The Dave Clark Five issue their fifth U.S. album in less than a year.
		George Harrison's dentist places LSD in George's and John Lennon's coffee.

	11	The marriage of Ringo Starr and Maureen Cox inspires predictions that female Beatlemaniacs will lose interest.
	20	The Kinks' "Tired of Waiting for You" hits Number One in Britain.
	22	The Beatles begin work on *Help!* in the Bahamas.
March	13	The Beatles' "Eight Days a Week" hits Number One in the U.S.
	18	Three Rolling Stones relieve themselves against the wall of an all-night service station.
	19	Noting that the Rolling Stones have sparked a trend among pop stars to shun ties, the magazine *Tailor and Cutter* prints an editorial imploring the group to "save tie makers" from "financial disaster." Mick Jagger responds that "the trouble with a tie is that it could dangle in the soup. . . . It is also something extra to which a fan can hang."
April	10	Freddie and the Dreamers' "I'm Telling You Now" hits Number One in the U.S., inciting the shortlived dance craze "the Freddie."
	24	Wayne Fontana and the Mindbenders' "Game of Love" hits Number One in the U.S.
May	1	Herman's Hermits' "Mrs. Brown You've Got a Lovely Daughter" hits Number One in the U.S.
	21	"Anyway Anyhow Anywhere" by The Who—who call it "the first pop art record"—is released in Britain.
	25	Dave Davies is knocked unconscious onstage by a blow from Mick Avory's cymbal, causing the Kinks to cancel the remainder of their British tour.
June	12	Queen Elizabeth II names the Beatles members of the Most Excellent Order of the British Empire.
	17	The Kinks arrive in New York for their first U.S. tour.
July	10	The Rolling Stones hit Number One in the U.S. for the first time, with "Satisfaction."
		Beatles VI hits Number One in the U.S. LP charts.
	29	The world premiere of *Help!* is attended by royalty and mob scenes in Piccadilly Circus.
August	15	At New York's Shea Stadium, the Beatles play to 56,000 fans—the largest concert audience in history.
	21	The Rolling Stones hit Number One on the U.S. album charts for the first time with *Out of Our Heads*.
	25	Allen Klein meets the Stones, who appoint him their financial manager.
September	11	The Beatles' album *Help!* hits Number One in the U.S.
	12	Paul McCartney's "Yesterday"—the first Beatles track on which outside musicians are prominently featured and three members of the group conspicuously absent—is released as an American single by Capitol.
October	26	Fans riot outside Buckingham Palace as the Beatles are formally awarded their MBE medals in the Great Throne Room.
	29	The Who release their first big British hit, "My Generation."
November	6	The Rolling Stones' "Get Off of My Cloud" hits Number One in the U.S.
December	3	Dylan-inspired "social commentary" takes a satirical turn with the Kinks' "A Well Respected Man," first issued in Britain as a throwaway on the *Kwyet Kinks* EP.
		The Beatles' *Rubber Soul* introduces pop audiences to the sitar, and other subtleties and complications.
		Keith Richards is knocked unconscious during a Rolling Stones concert ic Sacramento, California, when his guitar touches a microphone; Bill Wyman saves him from possible electrocution by immediately pulling out the main lead to break electrical contact.
	25	The Dave Clark Five hit Number One in the U.S. for the first and last time with "Over and Over."
1966		
January	8	The Beatles' *Rubber Soul* hits Number One in the U.S.
	21	George Harrison marries Patricia Ann Boyd.
	22	The Spencer Davis Group's "Keep on Runnin'" (with lead vocals by sixteen-year-old Stevie Winwood) hits Number One in Britain.
February	21	"Nowhere Man," the Beatles' first stab at social commentary, is released as a single in America.
	28	Liverpool's Cavern Club closes, £10,000 in debt; police break through barricades erected by protesting Beatlemaniacs.
March	4	London's *Evening Standard* first publishes the interview in which John Lennon notes that the Beatles' popularity has surpassed that of Jesus Christ.
April	1	David Bowie's first solo single—"Anything You Say"/"Good Morning Girl"—is released in Britain.
June	11	The Rolling Stones' "Paint It, Black" hits Number One in the U.S.
		Radio stations in France, Holland, and Germany erroneously broadcast news of Roger Daltrey's demise.
	15	The Beatles' American LP *Yesterday and Today* fails to materialize on its original release date, as Capitol Records frantically withdraws the "butcher cover" from circulation.
	16	Paul McCartney's sheepdog Martha is born, to be immortalized in the Beatles' "Martha My Dear."
	17	Paul McCartney purchases a farm in Kintyre, Scotland, to be immortalized in Wings' late-Seventies hit, "Mull of Kintyre."
	25	The Beatles' "Paperback Writer" hits Number One in the U.S.

In a *Melody Maker* poll of Beatles fans, seventy percent say the group should "continue to experiment with new sounds."

July	4	The Beatles break their Shea Stadium record by playing to a crowd of 100,000 at the Aranita Coliseum in Manila, the Philippines.
	5	The Beatles are shown out of the Philippines by vengeful mobs after they fail to attend a luncheon given in their honor by the president's wife.
	8	The Rolling Stones are accused of desecrating an American flag by dragging it across the floor of the War Memorial Hall in Syracuse, New York.
	9	The Kinks' "Sunny Afternoon" hits Number One in Britain.
	30	The Troggs' "Wild Thing" hits Number One in the U.S.
		The Beatles' butcherless *Yesterday and Today* hits Number One on the U.S. LP charts.
	31	John Lennon's remarks on Christianity belatedly spark the first Beatles bonfire, in Birmingham, Alabama.
August	6	The Troggs' "With a Girl Like You" hits Number One in Britain.
	8	*Revolver*—the Beatles' first entirely experimental LP—is released in the U.S.
	17	At a Toronto press conference, John Lennon expresses his admiration for those young Americans who have fled to Canada to avoid military service in Vietnam.
	29	The Beatles play their last concert, at San Francisco's Candlestick Park.
September	3	Donovan's "Sunshine Superman" hits Number One in the U.S.
	10	The Beatles' *Revolver* hits Number One in the U.S.
	17	The Small Faces' "All or Nothing" hits Number One in Britain.
October		John Lennon writes "Strawberry Fields Forever" on a beach in Spain, where he is playing his first straight dramatic role in Richard Lester's film *How I Won the War*.
		George Harrison is in India, studying the sitar with Ravi Shankar.
		Meanwhile, back in London, Paul McCartney composes the score for the film *The Family Way*.
	15	A little-known psychedelic group called Pink Floyd appears at a concert at London's Roundhouse to launch Britain's first "underground" newspaper, *The International Times*.
November	9	Paul McCartney's head is severed from his body in an auto accident, according to rumors that would surface three years later.
		John Lennon is introduced to Yoko Ono at London's Indica Gallery, during the opening of her show "Unfinished Paintings and Objects."
December		The four Beatles, with moustaches, regroup in EMI's Abbey Road studios to begin work on *Sgt. Pepper's Lonely Hearts Club Band*.
	3	Pink Floyd appear at "Psychodelphia vs. Ian Smith," a Roundhouse concert benefiting majority rule in Zimbabwe.

1967		
January	14	The Jimi Hendrix Experience make their first impression on the British charts with "Hey Joe."
	21	The Cream make their first impression on the British charts with "I Feel Free."
February	5	The Rolling Stones ruffle many a British feather when they refuse to join their fellow guests on the revolving stage during the finale of the TV show *Sunday Night at the London Palladium*.
	6	Mick Jagger sues *The News of the World* for libel following the scandal sheet's publication of a story insinuating he uses drugs.
	12	Responding to a tipoff from *The News of the World*, police raid Keith Richards's home, finding "dangerous drugs" on the premises and in a jacket belonging to Mick Jagger.
March	4	The Rolling Stones' "Ruby Tuesday" hits Number One in the U.S.
	18	The Beatles' "Penny Lane" hits Number One in the U.S.
	25	The Who commence their U.S. concert debut as part of Murray the K's Easter Show in New York.
April	15	*NME* ad introduces "the most significant new talent of 1967 . . . the Bee Gees."
	22	Pink Floyd make their first impression on the British charts with "Arnold Layne."
May		Paul McCartney tells a *Life* reporter that he has used LSD.
	10	Police find dangerous drugs in the home of Brian Jones, during a raid timed to coincide with Jagger and Richards's appearance at a preliminary court hearing on their own transgressions.
	12	Pink Floyd's multimedia concert "Games for May" is presented at London's Queen Elizabeth Hall.
	25	John Lennon has his Rolls Royce coated with multicolored psychedelic designs.
June	2	*Sgt. Pepper's Lonely Hearts Club Band* is unleashed in the U.S.
	10	"A Whiter Shade of Pale"—by the hitherto-unknown Procol Harum—hits Number One in Britain with godspeed.

	19	The Who and the Jimi Hendrix Experience steal the show in Monterey, California, at rock's first great outdoor festival; Brian Jones, a ghostly presence in gossamer and lace, drifts through the crowd.
	25	The Beatles—representing Britain on *Our World,* the first live TV program to be broadcast globally—reach a record viewing audience of several hundred million with their made-to-order anthem "All You Need Is Love."
	29	Mick Jagger is sentenced to three months in Brixton Prison for possession of four pep pills, and Keith Richards to one year in Wormwood Scrubs for having permitted cannabis to be smoked in his home. Charges are dismissed on July 31.
July		George Harrison has his home coated with multicolored psychedelic designs.
	1	*Sgt. Pepper* hits Number One in the U.S.
	14	The Who begin their first crosscountry U.S. tour as supporting act for Herman's Hermits.
	25	A full-page ad in *The Times* of London, signed by the four Beatles and Brian Epstein, calls for decriminalization of marijuana.
August	5	Pink Floyd's first LP, *Piper at the Gates of Dawn,* is released in Britain.
	8	An adoring train of flower children follows George Harrison down the streets of San Francisco's Haight-Ashbury as he strums a guitar singing "Baby You're a Rich Man."
	15	Tough government sanctions effectively sink British pirate radio.
	25	The Beatles and Mick Jagger join the Maharishi on a train bound for Bangor, Wales, and a seminar on TM.
	27	Brian Epstein is found dead in his home.
September	7	*Melody Maker* anoints Britain's "Magnificent Seven" guitarists: Eric Clapton, Jimi Hendrix, Jeff Beck, Jimmy Page, Pete Townshend, Stevie Winwood, and Peter Green.
	11	The Beatles' Magical Mystery Tour coach begins meandering through the English countryside.
	30	John Lennon and George Harrison preach transcendental meditation on David Frost's TV show.
October	7	The Beatles reject Sid Bernstein's offer of one million dollars to perform a single concert at Shea Stadium.
	15	*Melody Maker* headline asks WHO KILLED FLOWER POWER? as the UFO Club—a London underground mecca that helped launch the careers of Pink Floyd and Tyrannosaurus Rex—closes after seven months.
	24	Pink Floyd—with an unsteady Syd Barrett at the helm—embarks on their first American adventure.
November	21	*The Who Sell Out* is released.
December		The Rolling Stones release the year's most psychedelic album, *Their Satanic Majesties Request,* complete with 3-D cover.
	6	The Beatles' "Hello Goodbye" hits Number One in Britain.
	26	*Magical Mystery Tour*—starring, written, directed, and produced by the Beatles—is savaged by critics as the Fab Four's first flop upon its world premiere on BBC-TV.
	30	The Beatles' "Hello Goodbye" hits Number One in the U.S.

1968

January	6	The Beatles' *Magical Mystery Tour* LP hits Number One in the U.S.
	9	George Harrison flies to Bombay to record his raga-rock *Wonderwall* film score.
February	3–11	The Beatles record "Lady Madonna," "Across the Universe," "The Inner Light," "Only a Northern Song," and "Hey Bulldog."
	14	Manfred Mann's version of Bob Dylan's "The Mighty Quinn" hits Number One in Britain.
	16	The Lennons and Harrisons—followed three days later by the Starrs, Paul McCartney, and Jane Asher—travel to Rishikesh, India, for the Maharishi's advanced training course in TM.
	18	David Gilmour joins Pink Floyd, ostensibly to play second fiddle to Syd Barrett.
March	1	Ringo Starr leaves Rishikesh; the food was too spicy.
	27	The Beatles' "Lady Madonna" hits Number One in Britain.
April		The first Tyrannosaurus Rex single, "Debora," is released in Britain.
	6	Syd Barrett officially leaves Pink Floyd.
	19	John Lennon and George Harrison are the last Beatles to drop out of the Maharishi's course.
May		John Lennon and Yoko Ono spend their first evening together.
	11	Lennon and McCartney fly to New York to unveil plans for Apple Corps on a Chinese junk in the Hudson River.
	25	The release of "Jumpin' Jack Flash" indicates that the Rolling Stones have returned to their planet of origin.
June	19	"Jumpin' Jack Flash" hits Number One in Britain.
	29	London's Hyde Park gets its first taste of free rock music, courtesy of Pink Floyd.
July	17	Arriving at the world premiere of *Yellow Submarine,* the Beatles are mobbed in Piccadilly Circus for the last time.
	26	Mick Jagger turns twenty-five on the intended release date of the Rolling Stones' LP *Beggars Banquet*—which their record company refuses to distribute in its original "lavatory" cover. Meanwhile, the single "Street Fighting Man" is banned by radio stations in America on the grounds that it might incite youngsters to riot.

	30	Cashiers at the Beatles' Apple shop advise startled customers that they need not pay for their merchandise; eager mobs descend on the boutique, which is then shut down for good after seven months in business.
August	10	Cream's *Wheels of Fire* hits Number One in the U.S.
	17	"Fire," by The Crazy World of Arthur Brown, hits Number One in Britain.
	23	Cynthia Lennon sues John for divorce on grounds of adultery.
	26	Apple Corps' "First Four"—including the Beatles' all-time best-seller, "Hey Jude"/"Revolution"—are released in the U.S.
September	28	"Hey Jude" begins a long reign at Number One in the U.S. (and throughout Christendom).
October		The word "blues" is featured in three consecutive front-page *Melody Maker* headlines (e.g., THE BLUES, BRITISH STYLE; BLUES HEROES).
		John Lennon and Yoko Ono doff their underwear for the cover of their experimental LP *Two Virgins*.
	18	John Lennon and a pregnant Yoko Ono are charged with possession of cannabis following a police raid on their London pied-a-terre.
November	9	Manager John Arm brings down the curtain of the Walthamston Grenada when The Who begin smashing their instruments. "I get a bit tired of violence onstage," he says. "It's not necessary."
	21	Yoko Ono suffers a miscarriage.
	25	The Beatles' "White Album" is released in the U.S.
	26	The Cream play a farewell concert at London's Royal Albert Hall.
December	5	At a beggars' banquet celebrating the belated release of their album, the Rolling Stones ply critics and record company executives with custard pie—in the face.
	11	The Rolling Stones' *Rock 'n' Roll Circus*—costarring John Lennon, Eric Clapton, and The Who—is filmed amid great fanfare, only to languish indefinitely in the vaults.
	28	The Beatles' "White Album" hits Number One in the U.S.

1969

January	1	The Beatles plus film crew begin work at Twickenham Studios on a "back-to-the-roots" album and a documentary movie on its making, both to be called *Get Back*.
	3	Thirty thousand copies of John Lennon and Yoko Ono's nude LP cover are seized by New Jersey vice squads.
	10	Paul McCartney's plans for getting the Beatles back on the concert stage are scrapped when George Harrison stalks out of the studio in protest.
	30	In lieu of a formal concert, the Beatles cause an Apple rooftop disturbance with rousing renditions of "I've Got a Feeling," "One After 909," "I Dig a Pony," "Don't Let Me Down," and "Get Back."
February	1	Fleetwood Mac's "Albatross" hits Number One in Britain.
	3	Despite McCartney's reservations, the other three Beatles hire Allen Klein as Apple business manager.
	8	The Move's "Blackberry Way" hits Number One in Britain.
March	8	Mick Jagger becomes a "Friend of the Covent Garden Opera House."
	12	Paul McCartney marries Linda Eastman.
		That evening, following a police raid on their psychedelic bungalow, George and Pattie Harrison are arrested for possession of cannabis found in a binocular case by a Labrador retriever named "Yogi."
	20	John Lennon marries Yoko Ono in Gibraltar.
	21	The honeymooning Lennons begin their weeklong Lie-in for peace at the Amsterdam Hilton.
April	12	*Melody Maker* reports that the Rolling Stones have been offered $100,000 to play a season at the International Hotel in Las Vegas.
	23	The Beatles' "Get Back" hits Number One in Britain.
May	9	The Who give their first performance of the "rock opera" *Tommy*.
	16	Pete Townshend and Roger Daltrey spend the night in jail after roughing up a plainclothes policeman on the stage of New York's Fillmore East during *Tommy*'s live American debut.
	24	The Beatles' "Get Back" hits Number One in the U.S.
	26	John and Yoko Lennon begin a ten-day Lie-in at Montreal's Queen Elizabeth Hotel—where they record the first Plastic Ono Band single, "Give Peace a Chance," in bed.
June	4	The Beatles' "Ballad of John and Yoko" is released in America—where many radio stations ban it as "blasphemous."
	7	Instant "supergroup" Blind Faith—Eric Clapton, Stevie Winwood, Ginger Baker, and Rick Grech—play their first gig to over 100,000 at London's Hyde Park.
	8	Brian Jones announces he is "leaving" the Rolling Stones.
	11	David Bowie's "Space Oddity" is finally released in Britain, having been held back two months to coincide with the American moon landing.

		The Beatles' "Ballad of John and Yoko" hits Number One in Britain.
July	3	Brian Jones drowns in his swimming pool.
	5	The "new" Rolling Stones—with Mick Taylor replacing Brian Jones—play their first gig to over 250,000 in Hyde Park.
		"Something in the Air" by Thunderclap Newman—a Pete Townshend creation featuring Speedy Keene, Jimmy McCulloch, and Andy Newman—hits Number One in Britain.
	9	Mick Jagger is in Australia to begin work on the film *Ned Kelly,* while the other Stones attend the burial of Brian Jones in his hometown of Cheltenham.
	23	The Rolling Stones' "Honky Tonk Women" hits Number One in Britain.
August	17	During The Who's set at the Woodstock Festival, Abbie Hoffman attempts to usurp the stage with a "radical" diatribe—only to be cut short by a blow from Pete Townshend's guitar.
	18	Marianne Faithfull attempts suicide in Australia—causing her to lose her role in *Ned Kelly.*
	23	The Rolling Stones' "Honky Tonk Women" hits Number One in the U.S.
September	13	John Lennon appears with the Plastic Ono Band—Eric Clapton, Klaus Voorman, Alan White, and Yoko Ono—at the Toronto Rock 'n' Roll Revival.
	20	The *Blind Faith* LP hits Number One in the U.S.
October	1	*Abbey Road,* the Beatles' last major recorded work, is released in the U.S.
	12	A mysterious phone call prods Detroit disc jockey Russ Gibb to investigate "clues" to Paul McCartney's death said to have been planted in various Beatles recordings and LP covers.
November	7	The Rolling Stones' *Get Yer Ya-Ya's Out/Gimme Shelter* U.S. tour, their first in three years, opens in Fort Collins, Colorado.
	11	*Abbey Road* hits Number One in the U.S.
	26	John Lennon returns his MBE to Queen Elizabeth as a protest against the wars in Vietnam and Biafra—and the poor showing of the Plastic Ono Band's recent single "Cold Turkey."
December		John Lennon is named *Rolling Stone*'s first (and last) Man of the Year.
		John and Yoko Lennon advertise their slogan WAR IS OVER! IF YOU WANT IT on billboards and in newspapers in the non-Communist world's major cities.
	6	Meredith Hunter is murdered by Hell's Angels during the Rolling Stones' free concert at Altamont Speedway in northern California.
	22	Canadian Prime Minister Pierre Trudeau confers for an hour with Beatle John Lennon.
	27	*Led Zeppelin II* hits Number One in the U.S.

1970

January		John Lennon renames 1970 A.D. "Year One A.P." (for After Peace).
	3	The Beatles record their last song, "I Me Mine."
	16	Eight erotic lithographs are removed by a vice squad from John Lennon's exhibit at the London Arts Gallery.
	26	In a single day, John Lennon writes and records (with Phil Spector) his first million-selling solo single, "Instant Karma."
February	14	The readers of *Disc* vote David Bowie "Brightest Hope for 1970."
March	7	The Beatles' "Here Comes the Sun" is aired at the end of NBC's broadcast of the total eclipse.
	20	David Bowie marries Angela Barnetty.
April	3	Brinsley Schwarz's management spends $120,000 to fly a planeload of English journalists to the unknown group's third-billed debut at New York's Fillmore East.
	10	Beatles breakup headlines flash across the world's front pages upon the release of a self-interview in which Paul McCartney disavows the Beatles and announces: "My plan is to grow up."
May		John and Yoko Lennon begin primal therapy in California with Dr. Arthur Janov.
	13	The Beatles' documentary film, formerly *Get Back,* retitled *Let It Be,* premieres in New York.
	23	Mungo Jerry's "In the Summertime" (which sounds like electrified Tyrannosaurus Rex) hits Number One in Britain. (Marc Bolan takes note.)
		The *McCartney* LP hits Number One in the U.S.
June	7	The Who perform *Tommy* at New York's Metropolitan Opera House.
	13	The Beatles score their last U.S. Number One single with "The Long and Winding Road"—and simultaneously hit Number One on the LP charts with *Let It Be.*
July	7	A Beatle (Ringo Starr) turns thirty.
August	1	The film *Performance*—featuring Mick Jagger in his first major dramatic role—is shown after a year's delay.
	26	The second Isle of Wight Festival is highlighted by The Who and Jimi Hendrix, in what will prove to be the latter's final performance.

September	18	Jimi Hendrix dies in London.
October		Marc Bolan and the rechristened T. Rex soar into the British Top Ten for the first time with "Ride a White Swan."
	1	Sixty-three unruly Rolling Stones fans are arrested at Milan's Palazzo del Sport; thousands more are dispersed with tear gas.
November	21	Jimi Hendrix's "Voodoo Chile" hits Number One in Britain.
	28	Dave Edmunds' "I Hear You Knocking" hits Number One in Britain.
December	6	*Gimme Shelter,* the Maysles Brothers' documentary of the Rolling Stones' 1969 U.S. tour and Altamont debacle, premieres in New York.
	26	George Harrison's "My Sweet Lord" hits Number One in the U.S.

1971

January	1	*New York Times* headline: LAWSUIT SPELLS BREAKUP FOR BEATLES as Paul McCartney files suit against the other Beatles, seeking legal dissolution of the group partnership.
	2	George Harrison's *All Things Must Pass* hits Number One in the U.S.
March	4	*Rolling Stone* headline: THE BRITISH BOOM IS OVER.
	14	The Rolling Stones give a farewell performance at London's Roundhouse before forsaking Britain's high taxes and drug squads in favor of the sunny south of France.
	20	T. Rex's "Hot Love" hits Number One in Britain; glitter and mascara proliferate on the faces of young British males.
	26	The magazine *Tailor and Cutter* (see March 19, 1965) includes Mick Jagger in its list of Best Dressed Men.
April	13	Rolling Stones Records releases its first single, "Brown Sugar," followed a week later by the LP *Sticky Fingers*.
	17	*Melody Maker* headline: WHY DOES DAVID BOWIE LIKE DRESSING UP IN LADIES' CLOTHING?
May	12	Mick Jagger marries Bianca Perez Morena de Macias in St. Tropez; wedding guests include the other Stones, four Faces (all but Rod Stewart), two Beatles (Paul and Ringo), and Eric Clapton.
	22	The Rolling Stones' *Sticky Fingers* hits Number One in the U.S.
	29	The Rolling Stones' "Brown Sugar" hits Number One in the U.S.
June		John Lennon decides to settle in New York.
	12	The South African Broadcasting Company lifts its ban on Beatles music, imposed in 1966 after Lennon said the group had become more popular than Jesus.
July	24	T. Rex's "Get It On" hits Number One in Britain.
August	1	George Harrison's Concerts for Bangla Desh—costarring Ringo Starr, Bob Dylan, Eric Clapton, and Ravi Shankar—are held at New York's Madison Square Garden.
	7	The Bee Gees' "How Can You Mend a Broken Heart" hits Number One in the U.S.
	29	The Weeley Festival of Progressive Music climaxes with performances from the two acts that *New Musical Express* would subsequently describe as the dominant forces on the British pop scene: Rod Stewart's Faces and Marc Bolan's T. Rex.
September		Paul McCartney forms Wings.
	4	Paul McCartney's "Uncle Albert/Admiral Halsey" hits Number One in the U.S.
	18	Pink Floyd perform *Atom Heart Mother* in the first appearance by a rock group at the Classical Music Festival in Montreux, Switzerland.
		"Maggie May" is the first of five Rod Stewart singles to hit Number One in Britain.
October	2	Rod Stewart hits Number One in the U.S. on both the singles and LP charts, with "Maggie May" and *Every Picture Tells a Story*.
	30	John Lennon's *Imagine* LP hits Number One in the U.S.
November	13	"Coz I Luv You" is the first of six Slade singles to hit Number One in Britain.

1972

January		Mick Jagger and Keith Richards are ordered off the Hollywood Palladium stage after attempting to jam with Chuck Berry, who calls their sound "too busy." He later apologizes, saying he didn't know who they were.
		British front page headlines coin the words REXMANIA and T. REXTASY.
	22	David Bowie achieves instant notoriety with a *Melody Maker* interview in which he asserts he is gay.
February		Pete Townshend is on an Indian pilgrimage, viewing the shrines of Meher Baba.
	5	T. Rex's "Telegram Sam" hits Number One in Britain.
	29	John Lennon's American visa expires, precipitating a three-year struggle with the U.S. government over his application for a residency permit.
March	3	"Rock and Roll Parts One and Two" is the first of three Gary Glitter singles to hit Number One in Britain.
	9	Allen Klein presents UNICEF with a check for $1,200,000, raised by George Harrison's *Concert for Bangla Desh* album.

May	3	Stone the Crows guitarist Les Harvey is electrocuted onstage at the Top Rank Ballroom in Swansea, England.
	20	T. Rex's "Metal Guru" hits Number One in Britain.
June	3	The Rolling Stones, supported by Stevie Wonder, begin a North American tour in Vancouver.
		Jethro Tull's *Thick as a Brick* hits Number One in the U.S.
	9	David Bowie's *The Rise and Fall of Ziggy Stardust and the Spiders from Mars* is released in Britain.
	17	The Rolling Stones' *Exile on Main Street* hits Number One in the U.S.
July	15	*Honky Chateau* is the first of seven Elton John LPs to hit Number One in the U.S.
	26	The Rolling Stones' American tour concludes in New York with a concert at Madison Square Garden and a lavish birthday party for Mick Jagger at the St. Regis Hotel.
August	13	John Lennon stars at a pair of Madison Square Garden concerts benefiting retarded children.
	28	David Bowie and the Spiders from Mars make their U.S. debut at New York's Carnegie Hall.
November	18	Cat Stevens's *Catch Bull at Four* hits Number One in the U.S.
December	9	The Moody Blues' *Seventh Sojourn* hits Number One in the U.S.
	14	The Marc Bolan film *Born to Boogie,* directed by Ringo Starr, premieres in London.
	31	Mick and Bianca Jagger arrive in Nicaragua, Bianca's country of birth, bearing medical supplies for victims of the recent earthquake.

1973

January	13	Eric Clapton is roused from his heroin stupor by Pete Townshend, who organizes and participates in "Slowhand" 's celebrated "comeback" at London's Rainbow Theater.
	18	The Rolling Stones perform a benefit at the Los Angeles Forum, raising some $500,000 for Nicaragua's earthquake victims.
	27	The Sweet's "Blockbuster" hits Number One in Britain.
February	3	Elton John's "Crocodile Rock" hits Number One in the U.S.
March	8	Paul McCartney is fined £100 for growing marijuana at his Scottish farm.
	27	David Bowie, traveling in a private compartment of the Trans-Siberia Express, is detained for several hours by Soviet border officials, who confiscate Bowie's Nazi memorabilia and "subversive" literature.
	28	Pink Floyd's LP *Dark Side of the Moon* hits Number One in the U.S.
May	19	Wizzard's "See My Baby Jive" hits Number One in Britain.
June	2	Paul McCartney and Wings' single "My Love" and LP *Red Rose Speedway* hit Number One in the U.S.
	23	10cc's "Rubber Bullets" gives the group the first of three Seventies U.K. Number Ones.
		George Harrison's LP *Living in the Material World* hits Number One in the U.S.—the only Beatle solo record ever to do so within two weeks of release.
	26	Herman's Hermits, Gerry and the Pacemakers, the Searchers, Billy J. Kramer, and Wayne Fontana are dredged out of oblivion for Richard Nader's "1960s British Rock Invasion Revisited" U.S. package tour.
	30	George Harrison's "Give Me Love" hits Number One in the U.S.
July	3	David Bowie announces his "retirement" during a concert at London's Hammersmith Odeon.
September	29	*Melody Maker* 's readers vote David Bowie Britain's top male singer, and his "Jean Genie" and "Drive-In Saturday" the two best records of 1973.
October	13	The Rolling Stones' LP *Goats Head Soup* hits Number One in the U.S.
	15	Keith Richards and Anita Pallenberg are fined $1000 in France for possession of controlled substances.
	18	David Bowie films his NBC-TV *Midnight Special* at London's Marquee Club, hauling the Troggs and Marianne Faithfull out of obscurity for the occasion.
	20	The Rolling Stones' "Angie" hits Number One in the U.S.
	24	Keith Richards is fined £205 in England for possession of marijuana, heroin, Mandrax, and a gun.
	25	John Lennon files suit against the U.S., charging that authorities have indulged in phone tappings and illegal surveillance in their campaign to evict him from the Land of the Free.
November	24	Ringo Starr's "Photograph" hits Number One in the U.S.

1974

January		John Lennon and Yoko Ono undergo a trial separation with John embarking on the Sindbad's voyage of his eighteen-month "lost weekend" in Los Angeles.
	12	Lulu gears up for a comeback with "The Man Who Sold the World," a song written and produced by David Bowie, whose vocals and sax are also in evidence.
	18	Bad Company is formed by splinters of Mott the Hoople and Free.
	26	Ringo Starr's "You're Sixteen" hits Number One in the U.S.
March	12	A drunken John Lennon makes a fool of himself, donning a Kotex at Los Angeles' Troubadour Club and heckling the Smothers Brothers.

April	13	Paul McCartney and Wings' LP *Band on the Run* hits Number One in the U.S.
	22	Ken Russell's film version of The Who's *Tommy* goes into production.
May	8	Graham Bond—the organist whose Graham Bond Organization had featured Jack Bruce and Ginger Baker—leaps in front of a train in London to his instant death.
June	1	John Cale, Kevin Ayers, Nico, and Eno team up at London's Rainbow Theater.
	8	Paul McCartney and Wings' ''Band on the Run'' hits Number One in the U.S.
July	26	The first major Beatles fan convention is held in Boston under the auspices of Joe Pope's *Strawberry Fields Forever*.
August	15	Willy Russell's play *John, Paul, George, Ringo . . . and Bert* premieres on London's West End.
	17	Eric Clapton's LP *461 Ocean Boulevard* hits Number One in the U.S.
	23	Bill Nelson fires the members of Be-Bop Deluxe.
September		Steve Harley fires the members of Cockney Rebel.
	14	Eric Clapton's ''I Shot the Sheriff'' hits Number One in the U.S.
	25	Robert Fripp disbands King Crimson.
	28	The *Bad Company* LP hits Number One in the U.S.
October	25	The Incredible String Band breaks up.
November	16	John Lennon's ''Whatever Gets You Thru the Night'' and LP *Walls and Bridges* hit Number One in the U.S. David Essex's ''Gonna Make You a Star'' hits Number One in Britain.
	23	The Rolling Stones' LP *It's Only Rock 'n' Roll* hits Number One in the U.S.
December	14	Mick Taylor announces he is leaving the Rolling Stones.
	16	Mott the Hoople break up; bassist Overend Watts and drummer ''Buffin'' form a new group called, simply, Mott.

1975

February	22	Average White Band's ''Pick Up the Pieces'' hits Number One in the U.S. Steve Harley and Cockney Rebel's ''Make Me Smile'' hits Number One in Britain.
April	12	Elton John's ''Philadelphia Freedom'' hits Number One in the U.S.
	19	Ron Wood announces he will ''sit in'' with the Rolling Stones on their upcoming U.S. tour. Roger Daltrey's performance in the film *Tommy* earns him the American ABC Interstate Theater Award as Best New Star of the Year, previously conferred on the likes of Paul Newman, Steve McQueen, and Dustin Hoffman.
	23	Pete Ham of Badfinger hangs himself.
May	30	Rick Wakeman loses $60,000 of his own hard-earned cash presenting *Myths and Legends of King Arthur and the Knights of the Round Table* on ice at the Wembley Empire Pool.
June	1	The Rolling Stones inaugurate their Tour of the Americas in Baton Rouge, Louisiana.
	21	Richie Blackmore quits Deep Purple, to be replaced by Tommy Bolin.
July	7	Keith Richards is arrested in Arkansas on charges of reckless driving and possession of a dangerous weapon (a knife). Hundreds of fans besiege the jail until Richards is cleared of charges.
July	19	Paul McCartney and Wings' ''Listen to What the Man Said'' and LP *Venus and Mars* hit Number One in the U.S.
September	6	Rod Stewart's ''Sailing'' hits Number One in Britain.
	20	David Bowie's ''Fame'' hits Number One in the U.S.
October		Johnny Rotten [née John Lydon], Steve Jones, Glen Matlock, and Paul Cook form the Sex Pistols under the aegis of Malcolm McLaren at his Chelsea boutique, Sex.
	4	Pink Floyd's LP *Wish You Were Here* hits Number One in the U.S.
	7	The U.S. Court of Appeals overturns the longstanding order to deport John Ono Lennon.
	9	Sean Ono Lennon is born as John celebrates his thirty-fifth birthday. Lennon announces that he feels ''higher than the Empire State Building''—and proceeds to disappear from the Rock Biz for five years.
November	6	The Sex Pistols perform their first gig, at St. Martin's School of Art.
	8	David Bowie's reissued ''Space Oddity'' hits Number One in Britain.
	29	Queen's ''Bohemian Rhapsody'' hits Number One in Britain.
December		Rough Trade, England's leading alternative record store (and later, record label), opens shop.

1976

January	2	The Roxy Club—destined to become a London Punk mecca—opens with a performance by the Clash.
	3	The Bay City Rollers' ''Saturday Night'' hits Number One in the U.S.
	5	Former Beatles road manager Mal Evans is killed by trigger-happy officers of the Los Angeles Police Department.
February	21	*New Musical Express* accords the Sex Pistols their first review.

March	5	EMI reissues the Beatles' twenty-two U.K. singles in picture sleeves, triggering a British Beatles revival. (All twenty-two—plus a "new" single of "Yesterday"—stampede up the hit parade.)
	8	Nicolas Roeg's film *The Man Who Fell to Earth,* starring David Bowie, premieres in London.
	19	Former Free guitarist Paul Kosoff dies of drug-related complications on an airplane over the Atlantic.
April	10	Peter Frampton's LP *Frampton Comes Alive* hits Number One in the U.S.
	24	Paul McCartney and Wings' *At the Speed of Sound* LP hits Number One in the U.S.
May	15	The Rolling Stones' LP *Black and Blue* hits Number One in the U.S.
	22	Paul McCartney and Wings' "Silly Love Songs" hits Number One in the U.S.
	31	America's Beatles revival gathers momentum with Capitol's release of "Got to Get You Into My Life" as a "new" single, to be followed shortly by the *Rock 'n' Roll Music* album.
June	10	Paul McCartney's Wings establish a new record for indoor concert attendance as they serenade 67,100 fans in Seattle.
	26	The members of Roxy Music confirm that they are taking a "sabbatical."
July	27	Judge Ira Feidsteel awards John Lennon his Green Card, entitling him to permanent U.S. residency.
August	12	Stiff Records—the British New Wave's first key independent label—releases its debut single, "Between the Lines" by the Pink Fairies.
	20	Elton John and Kiki Dee's "Don't Go Breaking My Heart" hits Number One in the U.S.
	21	The Damned, Nick Lowe, and Eddie and the Hot Rods perform at the First European Punk Festival in Mont de Marsan, France.
September	4	The *Fleetwood Mac* LP hits Number One in the U.S.
	20–21	The Sex Pistols, the Damned, the Clash, and Siouxsie and the Banshees highlight the U.K.'s first Punk Rock Festival at London's 100 Club.
October	8	The Sex Pistols sign with EMI.
November	5	Britain's first Punk single, the Damned's "New Rose," is released by Stiff Records.
	14	Former Yardbirds vocalist Keith Relf is found electrocuted in his home.
	19	The Sex Pistols' recorded debut, "Anarchy in the U.K.," is unleashed by an unsuspecting EMI.
December	1	The Sex Pistols indulge in language unbecoming young gentlemen on Bill Grundy's popular British TV show *Today,* inspiring the *Daily Mirror* headline: THE FILTH AND THE FURY! TV'S GRUNDY IN ROCK OUTRAGE . . . UPROAR AS VIEWERS JAM PHONES.
	3	The Sex Pistols' "Anarchy in the U.K. tour" with the Heartbreakers and the Clash kicks off in Norwich.

1977

January	4	*The Evening Standard* reports that the Sex Pistols "shocked and revolted passengers and airline staff as they vomited and spat their way to an Amsterdam flight" at London's Heathrow Airport, where an official described them as "thoroughly unsavoury."
	10	Conservative MP Robert Adley writes EMI chairman John Read: "Your company is providing funds for a bunch of ill-mannered louts. . . . Surely a group of your size and reputation could forgo the doubtful privilege of sponsoring trash like the Sex Pistols."
	12	EMI jettisons the Sex Pistols (at the cost of £30,000 in "contract termination payoff"), and melts down all remaining copies of "Anarchy in the U.K."
February		Sex Pistols bassist Glen Matlock is fired ("because he went on about Paul McCartney," says manager McLaren), to be replaced by Sid Vicious.
	20	The Manfred Mann Earth Band's "Blinded by the Light" hits Number One in the U.S.
	27	Keith Richards is arrested in Ontario on charges of smuggling heroin into Canada.
March	5	David Bowie serves as Iggy Pop's keyboardist at London's Rainbow Theater.
	10	The Sex Pistols sign a contract with A&M on a trestle table set up outside Buckingham Palace, and announce "God Save the Queen" as their next release.
	11	Canada's First Lady Margaret Trudeau begins hobnobbing with the Rolling Stones.
	16	The Sex Pistols collect £75,000 in further contract termination payoff when A&M summarily drops the combo from its roster.
	18	The first Clash single, "White Riot," is released by British CBS.
	26	Stiff Records releases the first Elvis Costello single, "Less Than Zero."
April	2	Fleetwood Mac's LP *Rumours* hits Number One in the U.S.—to stay there for an unprecedented thirty-one weeks and sell an equally unheard-of eight million copies in America alone.
	4	*The Clash* is issued in Britain—and goes on to become the biggest-selling British import in the annals of the U.S. rock biz when American CBS deems the product unworthy of a Stateside release.
	8	The Damned's lackluster stint at New York's CBGB Club inaugurates the first U.S. tour by a British Punk act.
May	14	The Sex Pistols sign with Virgin Records.

June		Rock Against Racism, a grassroots antiracist movement, is founded in London.
	10	Joe Strummer and Nicky "Topper" Headon of the Clash are arrested for spraypainting their band's name on a London wall.
	15	Sex Pistols Svengali Malcolm McLaren is arrested when the group's Jubilee boat trip in celebration of their Virgin contract is stormed by London police.
	17	The Sex Pistols' "God Save the Queen" hits Number One on *NME*'s charts, the total absence of airplay notwithstanding.
	18	The Sex Pistols' Johnny Rotten, producer Chris Thomas, and studio manager Bill Price are attacked with razor blades by a gang of London "patriots."
	19	The Sex Pistols' Paul Cook is rushed to the hospital following a similar attack in Shepherd's Bush.
September	16	Marc Bolan is killed instantly when his car crashes into a tree in South London's Barnes Common.
December	3	Paul McCartney and Wings' "Mull of Kintyre" hits Number One in Britain—where it remains for nine weeks, to become the U.K.'s all-time best-selling record.
	28	The Sex Pistols' U.S. debut is postponed a week as the American Embassy investigates their criminal records.

1978

January	5	The Sex Pistols' U.S. tour opens in Atlanta, Georgia. Memphis police lieutenant Ronald Howell warns that his "clean city . . . will not tolerate any real, or simulated, sex on stage."
	18	Johnny Rotten quits the Sex Pistols as the band's disastrous U.S. tour peters out in California.
May	20	Paul McCartney and Wings' "With a Little Luck" hits Number One in the U.S.
July	15	The Rolling Stones' LP *Some Girls* hits Number One in the U.S.
August	5	The Rolling Stones' "Miss You" hits Number One in the U.S.
September		Stiff Little Fingers' debut LP on Rough Trade Records enters the Top Twenty without benefit of any advertising or promotion.
	7	Keith Moon dies in London of an overdose of antialcoholism pills.
October	13	Sid Vicious is accused of murdering his girlfriend Nancy Spungen at New York's Chelsea Hotel.
November	18	The Boomtown Rats' "Rat Trap" becomes the first New Wave disc to hit Number One in Britain.

1979

January	27	Ian Dury's "Hit Me with Your Rhythm Stick" hits Number One in Britain.
February	2	Sid Vicious dies in New York of a heroin overdose.
	10	Rod Stewart's "Da Ya Think I'm Sexy" and LP *Blondes Have More Fun* hit Number One in the U.S.
May	19	Three ex-Beatles (all but Lennon) play together at a wedding reception honoring Eric Clapton and his bride, the former Mrs. George Harrison.
June	30	Gary Numan and Tubeway Army's "Are 'Friends' Electric?" hits Number One in Britain.
July	28	The Boomtown Rats' "I Don't Like Mondays" hits Number One in Britain.
August		Stiff Records sets up U.S. operations in New York.
September	12	The Specials form Two-Tone Records to release their first single, "Gangsters," setting the Ska/Blue Beat revival in motion.
	21	*The New York Post* blares the front-page headline: THE BEATLES ARE BACK! EXCLUSIVE! FAB FOUR REUNITED FOR BIG UN CONCERT IN NEW YORK.
	22	Gary Numan's "Cars" hits Number One in Britain.
	24	Former LSD guru Timothy Leary comments on the rumored Beatles reunion: "I wouldn't spend a penny to see them. It's like wanting to see the 1932 Yankees. . . . They're too old. The Beatles are middle-aged musicians who need facelifts."
	29	The Police's "Message in a Bottle" hits Number One in Britain.
December	15	Pink Floyd's "Another Brick in the Wall" hits Number One in Britain.

1980

January	16	Paul McCartney is jailed in Tokyo for attempting to smuggle marijuana into the country and is set back over $1 million by the cancellation of Wings' Japanese tour.
	19	Pink Floyd's LP *The Wall* hits Number One in the U.S.
	25	Paul McCartney is released from jail.
	26	The Pretenders' "Brass in Pocket" hits Number One in Britain.
February	9	The Specials' "Too Much Too Young" hits Number One in Britain.
	23	Queen's "A Crazy Little Thing Called Love" hits Number One in the U.S.
March	15	The Jam's "Going Underground" enters the British charts at Number One.
	22	Pink Floyd's "Another Brick in the Wall" hits Number One in the U.S.
May	10	Dexy's Midnight Runners' "Gino" hits Number One in Britain.

	18	Ian Curtis of Joy Division commits suicide.
June	28	Paul McCartney's ''Coming Up'' hits Number One in the U.S.
July	26	The Rolling Stones' LP *Emotional Rescue* hits Number One in the U.S.
	29	Bernard Pomerance's play *The Elephant Man,* starring David Bowie in the title role, premieres at the Denver Center for the Performing Arts.
August	16	David Bowie's ''Ashes to Ashes'' hits Number One in Britain.
September	20	Queen's LP *The Game* hits Number One in the U.S.
	23	David Bowie, as the Elephant Man, makes his Broadway debut.
	25	Led Zeppelin drummer John Bonham dies, causing the band to call it quits.
	29	John Lennon ends his five-year-long hibernation with a *Newsweek* interview in which he announces the imminent release of a new John and Yoko LP, *Double Fantasy.*
October	4	The Police's ''Don't Stand So Close to Me'' enters the British charts at Number One.
	24	Paul McCartney receives a rhodium-plated disc from the *Guinness Book of Records* for his achievements as history's all-time best-selling songwriter and recording artist.
	25	Music publishing tycoon Paul McCartney vanquishes all lingering doubts over who won ''The Battle of the Century—the Beatles vs. the Four Seasons'' (the title of a 1964 Vee-Jay album) with the announcement that he has snapped up the rights to most of the Four Seasons' hits.
	27	T. Rex co-founder Steve ''Peregrine'' Took chokes to death on a cocktail cherry.
December	8	John Lennon is assassinated by a psychotic gunman outside his New York home, leaving much of the Western world suspended between horror and disbelief.
	14	A week of worldwide mourning culminates in hundreds of vigils, including one attended by 100,000 people in New York's Central Park opposite the Lennons' residence at the Dakota building.
	27	John Lennon's ''Starting Over'' hits Number One in the U.S. and Britain.

(© Joyce Ravid, 1980)

Selected Bibliography

(Includes books that proved helpful in researching The British Invasion *and/or are recommended for further reading.)*

THE BEATLES, Etc.

The Compleat Beatles. Delilah, 1981

Braun, Michael. *Love Me Do: The Beatles' Progress.* Penguin (U.K.), 1964

Campbell, Colin, and Murphy, Allan. *Things We Said Today: The Complete Lyrics and a Concordance to the Beatles' Songs.* Pierian Press, 1980

Carr, Roy, and Tyler, Tony. *The Beatles: An Illustrated Record.* Crown/Harmony, 1975 (rev. ed., 1978, 1980)

Castleman, Harry, and Podrazik, Walter J. *All Together Now.* Pierian Press; Ballantine, 1976

———. *The Beatles Again!?* Pierian Press, 1978

Cott, Jonathan, and Dalton, David. *The Beatles Get Back.* Apple Publishing (U.K.), 1970

Davies, Hunter. *The Beatles: The Authorized Biography.* McGraw-Hill, 1968 (rev. ed., 1978)

Davis, Edward E. (ed). *The Beatles Book.* Cowles, 1968

DiFranco, J. Phillip (ed). *The Beatles: A Hard Day's Night.* Penguin, 1977

Epstein, Brian. *A Cellarful of Noise.* Doubleday; Pyramid, 1964

Fawcett, Anthony. *John Lennon One Day at a Time.* Grove Press, 1976

Harrison, George. *I Me Mine.* Genesis (U.K.), 1980

Harry, Bill. *Mersey Beat: The Beginnings of the Beatles.* Omnibus Press, 1977

Lennon, John. *In His Own Write.* Simon and Schuster, 1964.

———. *A Spaniard in the Works.* Simon and Schuster, 1965.

Martin, George, with Jeremy Hornsby. *All You Need Is Ears.* Macmillan, 1979

McCabe, Peter and Schonfeld, Robert D. *Apple to the Core: The Unmaking of the Beatles.* Pocket Books, 1972

Norman, Philip. *Shout! The Beatles in Their Generation.* Simon & Schuster/Fireside Press, 1981

Orton, Joe. *Up Against It! A Screenplay for the Beatles.* Grove Press, 1979

Reinhart, Charles. *You Can't Do That! Beatles Bootlegs and Novelty Records 1963–1980.* Pierian Press, 1981

Schaffner, Nicholas. *The Beatles Forever.* Stackpole/Cameron House; McGraw-Hill, 1977

———. *The Boys from Liverpool.* Methuen, 1980

Schultheiss, Tom. *A Day in the Life: The Beatles Day-by-Day 1960–1970.* Pierian Press; Quick Fox, 1980

Sheff, David, with G. Barry Golson. *The Playboy Interviews with John Lennon and Yoko Ono.* Playboy Press, 1981

Stewart, Sandi. *The Beatles in Our Lives* (unpublished ms.)

Taylor, Derek. *As Time Goes By.* Straight Arrow, 1973

Weiner, Sue; Friede, Goldie; and Titone, Robin. *The Beatles A–Z.* Methuen, 1980

Wenner, Jann. *Lennon Remembers.* Straight Arrow; Pyramid, 1971

Williams, Allan, with William Marshall. *The Man Who Gave the Beatles Away.* Macmillan; Ballantine, 1975

THE ROLLING STONES, Etc.

Carr, Roy. *The Rolling Stones: An Illustrated Record.* Harmony/Crown, 1976

Charone, Barbara. *Keith Richards.* Futura (U.K.), 1979

Dalton, David (ed). *The Rolling Stones: An Unauthorized Biography in Words, Pictures, and Music.* Amsco, 1972

——— (ed). *The Rolling Stones: The First Twenty Years.* Knopf, 1981

Eisen, Jonathan (ed). *Altamont: Death of Innocence in the Woodstock Nation.* Avon, 1970

Goodman, Pete, *Our Own Story by the Rolling Stones.* Bantam, 1964

Greenfield, Robert. *Stones Touring Party.* Michael Joseph (U.K.), 1974

Sanchez, Tony. *Up and Down with the Rolling Stones.* Morrow, 1979

Scaduto, Anthony. *Mick Jagger: Everybody's Lucifer.* McKay, 1974

Watts, Charlie. *Ode to a High Flying Bird.* Beat Publications, 1964

THE WHO, Etc.

Ashley, Brian, and Monnery, Steve. *Whose Who?* New English Library (U.K.), 1979

Barnes, Richard. *Mods!* Eel Pie Publishing (U.K.), 1979

Barnes, Richard, and Townshend, Pete. *The Story of Tommy.* Eel Pie Publishing (U.K.), 1977

Butler, Dougal, with Chris Trencove and Peter Lawrence. *Full Moon.* Morrow, 1981

Dicks, Ted (ed). *A Decade of The Who.* Fabulous Music (U.K.), 1977

Herman, Gary. *The Who.* Studio Vista Rockbooks (U.K.), 1971

PINK FLOYD, Etc.

Frame, Peter (ed). *The Road to Rock.* Charisma (U.K.), 1974

Miles. *Pink Floyd.* Quick Fox, 1980

Sanders, Rick. *Pink Floyd.* Futura (U.K.), 1976

Steele, John. *Syd Barrett: A Biography.* (unpublished ms.)

T. REX, Etc.

Bolan, Marc. *The Warlock of Love.* Lupus Music (U.K.), 1969

Dicks, Ted (ed). *Marc Bolan: A Tribute.* Essex House (U.K.), 1978

Tremlett, George. *The Marc Bolan Story.* Futura (U.K.), 1975

DAVID BOWIE, Etc.

Carr, Roy, and Murray, Charles Shaar. *David Bowie: An Illustrated Record.* Avon, 1981

Fletcher, David J. *David Robert Jones Bowie: The Discography of a Generalist.* F. Fergeson Productions (PO Box 433-F, Lake Bluff, IL 60044), 1979

Tremlett, George. *The David Bowie Story.* Warner Paperbacks, 1974

THE BRITISH INVASION, NEXT WAVE, BRITISH HOT HUNDRED, Etc.

Cohn, Nik. *Rock from the Beginning.* Stein and Day, 1969

Coon, Caroline. *1988: The New Wave Punk Rock Explosion.* Hawthorn, 1977

Cross, Colin, with Paul Kendall and Mick Farren. *Encyclopedia of British Beat Groups of the Sixties.* Omnibus (U.K.), 1980

Dalton, David, and Kaye, Lenny. *Rock 100.* Grosset and Dunlap, 1977

Frame, Pete. *Rock Family Trees.* Quick Fox, 1980

Hebdige, Dick. *Subculture: The Meaning of Style.* Methuen (U.K.), 1979

Logan, Nick, and Woofinden, Bob. *The Illustrated Encyclopedia of Rock.* Harmony, 1976

May, Chris, and Phillips, Tim. *British Beat.* Socion (U.K.), 1974

Melly, George. *Revolt into Style.* Anchor, 1971

Palmer, Tony. *All You Need Is Love.* Grossman; Penguin, 1976

Parsons, Tony, and Burchill, Julie. *The Boy Looked at Johnny.* Pluto Press (U.K.), 1979

Rice, Jo and Tim, with Paul Gambaccini and Mike Read. *The Guinness Book of British Hit Singles.* Guinness (U.K.), 1979

Schaffner, Nicholas and Elizabeth. *505 Rock 'n' Roll Questions.* Walker, 1981

Whitburn, Joel. *Top Pop Artists and Singles 1955–1978.* Record Research, Inc. (P.O. Box 200, Menemonee Falls, WI 53051), 1979

———. *Top LP's 1945–1972.* Record Research Inc., 1974

[Boldface folios **(191)** indicate a section primarily devoted to the group or artist in question. Italic folios (*232*) indicate locations of photographs.]